LAWRENCE HENRY GIPSON

AUTHOR

JARED INGERSOLL: A STUDY OF AMERICAN LOYALISM IN RELATION TO BRITISH COLONIAL GOVERNMENT

STUDIES IN CONNECTICUT COLONIAL TAXATION

THE MORAVIAN INDIAN MISSION ON WHITE RIVER

LEWIS EVANS

THE COMING OF THE REVOLUTION, 1763–1775

THE BRITISH EMPIRE BEFORE THE AMERICAN REVOLUTION

VOLUME I. THE BRITISH ISLES AND THE AMERICAN COLONIES: GREAT BRITAIN AND IRELAND, 1748–1754

VOLUME II. THE BRITISH ISLES AND THE AMERICAN COLONIES: THE SOUTHERN PLANTATIONS, 1748–1754

VOLUME III. THE BRITISH ISLES AND THE AMERICAN COLONIES: THE NORTHERN PLANTATIONS, 1748–1754

VOLUME IV. ZONES OF INTERNATIONAL FRICTION: NORTH AMERICA, SOUTH OF THE GREAT LAKES REGION, 1748–1754

VOLUME V. ZONES OF INTERNATIONAL FRICTION: THE GREAT LAKES FRONTIER, CANADA, THE WEST INDIES, INDIA, 1748–1754

VOLUME VI. THE GREAT WAR FOR THE EMPIRE: THE YEARS OF DEFEAT, 1754–1757

VOLUME VII. THE GREAT WAR FOR THE EMPIRE: THE VICTORIOUS YEARS, 1758–1760

VOLUME VIII. THE GREAT WAR FOR THE EMPIRE: THE CULMINATION, 1760–1763

VOLUME IX. THE TRIUMPHANT EMPIRE: NEW RESPONSIBILITIES WITHIN THE ENLARGED EMPIRE, 1763–1766

VOLUME X. THE TRIUMPHANT EMPIRE: THUNDER–CLOUDS GATHER IN THE WEST, 1763–1766

VOLUME XI. THE TRIUMPHANT EMPIRE: BRITAIN SAILS INTO THE STORM, 1763–1775 (in preparation)

VOLUME XII. HISTORIOGRAPHY AND BIBLIOGRAPHY, 1748–1755, and GENERAL INDEX (in preparation)

"Every considerable library on American and British history will require Mr. Gipson's volumes as an indispensable work of reference, and most readers will be so captivated by the lively reports of this intelligent and humane historical surveyor as to look forward with impatience to future volumes." SAMUEL ELIOT MORISON

THE BRITISH EMPIRE

BEFORE THE AMERICAN REVOLUTION

VOLUME V

ZONES OF INTERNATIONAL FRICTION

THE GREAT LAKES FRONTIER

CANADA

THE WEST INDIES

INDIA

1748–1754

THE BRITISH EMPIRE
BEFORE THE AMERICAN REVOLUTION
VOLUME V

ZONES OF

INTERNATIONAL FRICTION

THE GREAT LAKES FRONTIER,
CANADA,
THE WEST INDIES, INDIA
1748–1754

BY

LAWRENCE HENRY GIPSON

MCMLXI
ALFRED A. KNOPF
NEW YORK

L. C. Catalog card number: 58–9670

THIS IS A BORZOI BOOK,
PUBLISHED BY ALFRED A. KNOPF, INC.

PUBLISHED SEPTEMBER 8, 1942
SECOND PRINTING, JULY 1961

*Manufactured in the United States of America
Published in Canada by McClelland & Stewart Ltd.*

THIS BOOK IS DEDICATED *to the men and women of the English-speaking world who two centuries ago proved the strength of the institutions of representative government.*

Preface

WE HAVE NOW brought to conclusion the survey of the old British Empire in the middle of the eighteenth century. The first three volumes were concerned with the provincial characteristics of the Empire as well as its tendencies in the direction of sectionalism — tendencies that would ultimately lead to its shipwreck. The last two volumes have sought to analyse in some detail the more pressing problems that confronted the Empire in its relations with the outside world. These problems involved serious issues such as disputed territorial claims, and some of them became so pressing during the period under consideration as to lead directly to the outbreak of hostilities and the final test of strength with the old French Empire.

In view of plans for subsequent volumes, which will trace the fortunes of the Empire down to the outbreak of the American Revolutionary War, it appeared undesirable to give in the volumes now concluded much stress to certain topics such as British mercantilism and the trade and navigation system that supported it, which will be considered at length, as will likewise the diverse patterns of thought that motivated the English-speaking people in the eighteenth century and that were objectified in their culture — using the latter word in its larger connotation.

The old British Empire during the last twenty-five years of its existence was something exceedingly complex. It represented the outcome of a bold experiment of permitting the establishment and development, wherever feasible throughout the dominions of the Crown, of provincial organs of self-government and of political self-expression. As a result, Boston, Providence, Hartford, New York, Philadelphia, Annapolis, Williamsburg, and Charleston became centres for the

formulation and implementation of public policy, policy which might
or might not be in accord with that of London or with that of neighbouring colonial capitals. Public opinion, which played so great a role
in the history of the old British Empire and which in the final analysis
determined policy, likewise, as a rule, was less often imperial than
provincial in its manifestations. In other words, a true view of the
Empire in its actual functioning could not but have been distorted
had I taken my seat in the office of the British minister and sought to
understand and interpret British imperial problems simply from the
outlook of that office, great as were its opportunities to receive information. In making this statement I would not deny at the same
time the possibility of presenting a fairly adequate account of the
contemporary French Empire or Spanish Empire from the angle of
observation of Paris or Cadiz. For within these two empires the authority of the Crown in each case was so great in the middle of the
eighteenth century — in contrast to that of the British Crown or of the
Parliament — that even an expressed personal preference on the part
of the monarch could have the effect of determining policy that
would influence the uttermost parts of his dominion.

It is exceedingly important to grasp the fact — something that
many students of British colonial history have not fully appreciated
and that the failure of the British ministry to comprehend before 1775
cost the British people dearly — that none of the mechanisms evolved
by the British government to keep the Empire in due subordination
were really adequate to the task with the growing maturity of the
American colonies. If subordination to London existed and was freely
accepted in the middle of the eighteenth century, it was a subordination not based upon force, as was colonial subordination within competing imperial systems, or capable under the circumstances of being
based upon force, but rather upon colonial convenience and self-
interest; if insubordination to London characterized the twelve years
between the downfall of French power in the New World and the beginning of open revolt in 1775, this was likewise based upon colonial
convenience and self-interest, expressing in each instance, whether
enlightened or otherwise, provincial public opnion. The meaning of
this to the student would seem to be that if he wishes to know intimately the Empire of the eighteenth century it is imperative that he
should leave London in the background, except when the nature of
issues projects it logically into the foreground, and, moving from
place to place, view the operation of British imperial dynamism at its

various sources of manifestation. By this means it will be possible to grasp the spirit and genius of such an Empire as the British had created, and to comprehend its major problems as seen in terms of those most immediately and acutely affected. To trace its history by thus beating its bounds may not be orthodox, it is certainly far removed from the easy, comfortable way, but to me it has presented the only practicable method of arriving at a clear understanding of something that to a degree was amorphous — an Empire that was constitutionally not an empire at all, an Empire that only with great reservations could be considered as possessing unity of pattern and unity of purpose, an Empire that was increasingly less and less the product of influence exerted by the mother country and more and more that of influences growing out of the amalgamation of various northern European streams of emigration to British North America under conditions that were destined, face to face with an unlimited frontier, to produce a civilization that was unique within the world of that day.

In this present treatise I have been impelled through the need of economy of space to pass over some topics that I had planned to comprehend and in preparation for the inclusion of which I had gathered the materials. Among these topics was that of the struggle in the middle of the eighteenth century between the Spaniards and the British in the region of Campeche Bay and involving the logwood industry. But this really fades into comparative insignificance when placed beside the struggle for the heart of the North American continent and for the control of the destinies of the subcontinent of India. Therefore it was omitted in order to give adequate treatment of Anglo-French rivalry, which looms so large in the history of the old British Empire between the years 1748 and 1754. Nor has it been possible to include in the present volume, as was hoped, an account of the tangled European diplomacy in which Great Britain was involved during the same period, to a considerable degree by reason of the fact that King George was also an elector of the Holy Roman Empire. This, however, will be considered in the volume to follow.

I am under deep obligation to those in charge of the British Public Record Office, the British Museum, the India Office, the Bibliothèque Nationale, the Library of Congress, the Canadian Archives, the Clements Library at Ann Arbor, the Burton Historical Collection of Detroit, the Chicago Historical Society, the Wisconsin Historical Society, the Nova Scotia Archives at Halifax, the Historical Society of Pennsylvania, the Pennsylvania Archives at Harrisburg, the New

York Historical Society, the Archives of the State of New York at Albany, the Massachusetts State Archives, the Massachusetts Historical Society, and the Lehigh University Library for placing at my disposal their facilities, and to the Lehigh Institute of Research for financial aid in rounding out this study. Fortunately, it was possible to gather such material as was required for my immediate purposes as was only available in Great Britain and France at a time of peace.

In closing, I may perhaps be permitted to express the hope that this volume will deserve the same appreciative reception by my fellow workers in the field of history that has been accorded the preceding volumes in this series.

" Rotha "   L. H. G.
Rydal, Pennsylvania
December 7, 1941

A GLOSSARY OF CERTAIN FRENCH WORDS
AND PHRASES USED IN THIS VOLUME

Aboiteaux — wooden type of sluiced floodgate

Arrêt — decision, decree (*arrêt royal* — royal decree)

Banalités — banalities (the old French commonplace feudal rights)

Bateaux — small boats

Canots — canoes

Castor — beaver [pelts] (*gras, sec, d'hiver, d'été, ordinaire* — worn, unworn, winter, summer, common; *castor gras d'hiver* was the prime beaver for hat-making)

Cens — quit-rents

Cens et rentes — annual charge upon lands held in *censive*

Censitaires — those obligated to pay annual quit-rents

Censive — fief or manor quit-rent

Congés — licenses or royal permits

Corvée — forced labour (obtained by *seigneurial* privilege)

Coureurs de bois — bush-ranging French fur-traders

Droit de chasse — hunting rights

Droit de justice — *seigneurial* jurisdiction, in three grades (*haute, moyenne, basse*); the *seigneurial* right to administer law and justice at some level.

Droit de pêche — fishing rights

Eau de vie — liquor (French brandy or English rum)

Écarlatine — noted English scarlet cloth, highly prized by Indians

En fief — in fee [simple] (also, *en arrière fief* — subinfeudation)

En roture — by feudal tenure (upon payment of rental)

Ferme — contract or lease (as used: the beaver export monopoly)

Habitants (*habitans*) — inhabitants of Canada

Lods et ventes — payments due when a *seigneurie* was alienated

Mémoire — memorandum or memorial report

Pirogues — dug-out canoes

Seigneuries — manors held, under feudal grants, either by the Church acting as a *seigneur* or by a lay *seigneur* who thereby gained no title of nobility

Syndic — trustee

Voyageurs — traders (especially fur-traders among the Indians); also transients (as distinguished from inhabitants)

Contents

CHAPTER I

LES HABITANTS

Various factors involved in Anglo-Saxon imperialistic rivalry	3
Geographical limits of the Province of Canada	4
Problem of careful definition	4
Conflicting claims	4
The colonization of Canada	5
Slow early growth of population to 1666	5
Subsequent increase to 1754	5
Les habitants	5
Settlement about the St. Lawrence	6
Manner of life	6
Religious influences	7
Obligations as a *censitaire*	8
The Canadian seigneuries	9
Growth of	10
Size of	10
Conditions attached to	11
The isolation of Canada in the eighteenth century	12
Restrictions upon the circulation of ideas	12
No printing press in Canada	12
The development of a distinct Canada civilization	13
The lure of the western wilderness	13
The satisfactions of life on the farm	13
The problem of marriage	14
The towns of Canada	14
Quebec	15
Population of, in 1750	15
A centre of culture	15

Extravagance of the leading people 15
Architectural adornments 16
Fortifications 17
Montreal 17
Population of, in 1754 17
America's chief fur-trading centre 17
Appearance of, in the middle of the century 17
Trois Rivières 18
The St. Maurice ironworks 18
Effect of the transfer of fur-trading to Montreal 18

Other population centres 18
Prairie de la Magdelene 18
La Chine 18
Petite Rivière 18

La Jonquière comes to New France, 1749 18
Commission and instructions 19

The defence of Canada 19
Regular soldiers 19
Militia 19
Fortified places 20
Quebec 20
Montreal 20
Fort Niagara 20
Fort Frontenac 20
Fort St. Frédéric 20
Louisbourg 20
St. Jean 20

The Indian allies 20
Groups living in a wild state 20
The annual present 20

Christianized groups at 20
Lorette 20
Becancourt 21
St. Francis 21
Sault St. Louis 21
Lake of the Two Mountains 21

The government of New France 21
Powers of the Governor General 21
Powers of the Intendant 21
The exercise of joint powers 22

Mercantilism and New France 23
  Encouragement of the producers of raw materials 23
  Limited encouragement of industry 23

Canadian commerce 23
  The exports 23
    Furs 23
    Fish oil 24
    Other food supplies 24
  The imports 24
    Cloth 25
    Arms 25
    Luxury articles 25
  Contrast between the shipping of Quebec and of Boston 25
  The adverse balance of trade 25
    Accumulating obligations 26
    Ultimate repudiation 26

New France a financial liability 26
  The royal expenditures in Canada 26
  The royal receipts in Canada 26
  Threat of repudiation in 1753 26
  The burden of Indian presents 27
  The spirit of monopoly 27
  Cupidity of royal officials 27
    Bigot and associates 27
    La Jonquière and associates 28
    The royal ironworks of St. Maurice 28

Unrest in Canada 29
  The need of regular soldiers to maintain order 29
  Mutinous attitude of the people in 1753 29

Weakness of Canada 29
  Lack of food supplies 29
    Failure of harvests 29
    The shipment of wheat to Canada 30
    The use of force by Duquesne to secure flour 31

Should France give up Canada? 31
  Arguments in favour of this step 31
  Arguments against this by Galissonière 32

The support of Galissonière's policy 33
  New France, strengthened by English supplies, prepares for the
    contest 33

CHAPTER II

THE GREAT LAKES FRONTIER

A " dependency " of Canada   35

A description of the region   35

The native possessors   36
  Trade and war   36
  Significance of the appearance of the Europeans   37

The lure of peltries   38
  The quest for the beaver   38

Indian tribes of the eighteenth century   39
  The problem of estimating tribal strength   39
  Lack of unity in face of the threat of the white man   41
  Growing sense of dependence upon European techniques   41

French efforts to Christianize the natives   41
  Activities of the Recollets and Jesuits   41
  Small measure of success   42

The fur trade   42
  Dependence of Canada upon this   42
  The Hurons as middlemen   42
  The Ottawa take the place of the Hurons   43
  The French *coureurs de bois*   43
    Efforts of the French court to discourage this group   43
    Why these efforts were ineffectual   44
  The licensing system   44
    Grave abuses of this   44
    Suppression of the *congés*   44
  The establishment of permanent posts   44
    The commandants and the fur trade   44

The problem of the price levels   45
  Albany versus Montreal   45
A combined post and licensing system established   45
  Detroit as a trading centre   45
    Cadillac's privileges   46
    Subsequent developments there   46
    Value of its peltry trade in 1741   46

The leasing system   46
  Difficulties encountered at Fort Niagara and Fort Frontenac   47

Decline of the fur trade during King George's War   47
Galissonière's opposition to this   48
  New emphasis upon the licensing system   48
  Certain posts still leased   48
  La Baye post and its exploitation   48

The trading posts   49
  Significance of their location   49
  Appearance of, in the eighteenth century   50
    Fort Detroit in 1750   50
  Distinct functions of the posts   50
    For the establishment of Crown rights 50
    For controlling the peltry trade   50
    For western explorations   50
    La Baye   51
    De la mer d'Ouest   51

The missionaries and the posts   51
  Indictments of the practices of the garrisons   51
  Relative importance of the different posts in the fur trade   52
    As to the amount of furs secured   53
    As to the quality of furs secured   54

The furs of Canada   55
  Value of different types of pelts   55
  The role of the Compagnie des Indes   56
  The relative importance of beaver skins   56

The beaver-skin monopoly   56
  Early companies   56
    The Company of " The One Hundred Associates "   56
    The Compagnie des Indes Occidentales   56
    Oudiette and Associates, 1697   57
    The Canada Company, 1701   57
    Aubert and Company, 1706   57
    The Compagnie d'Occident, 1717   58

The Compagnie des Indes, 1719–63   58
  Beaver-skin prices, 1719–37   58
  The agreement of 1737   58
  The price level in time of war, 1744–8   58
  Change in price level of 1749   58
  Efforts made to justify the lowering of prices paid   58

Profits secured from the beaver monopoly   59
  Conflicting claims   59

Position of the Compagnie des Indes   59
Position of the Canadian merchants   59

The beaver-hat industry and the beaver-skin monopoly   60
  The failure of the Compagnie des Indes to make effective its
    monopoly   61
  The importance of the illicit beaver trade   61
  Contrasting price levels at Montreal and at Albany, 1737–45   62
  The lure of British wares   62
  Inability of France to meet the needs of the Indian trade   63

CHAPTER III

THE SIX CONFEDERATED NATIONS

The importance of the Iroquoian Confederation in relation to English
  expansion   64

The strength of the Confederation   65

The location of the tribes of the Confederation   65
  The Mohawks   65
  The Oneida   65
  The Onondaga   65
  The Tuscarora   65
  The Cayuga   65
  The Seneca   65

The Iroquoian village   65
  The long house in the eighteenth century   66

Territorial claims of the Confederation   66
  The upper Ohio valley   66
    Dependence of the Mingo, Delawares, and Shawnee   66
  Northern Pennsylvania   67
  Lake Champlain region   67

Dynamic qualities of the Confederation   67
  Significance of location   68
  Significance of tradition and organized life   68

Complex organization of the Six Nations   68
  Basic features of the Confederation   69
    The " Great Binding Law "   69
    The symbolism of union   69
    Embodiment of alien groups   69

Significance of the institution of adoption 69
Dependent position of certain conquered groups 70
The brood family 70
The clan 70
The phratry 70
The tribe or nation 70

The Iroquoian matriarchate 70
Cognatic relationships 70
Female inheritance 70
Powers of the brood mother 70
The child-bearing women of the *royaneh* 70
Electors of the confederate sachems 70
Authority to correct the sachems 71
Authority of the matriarchate councils 71
Responsibility of the clan matron 71
The preservation of the clan and adoption 71
The high valuation of the life of a woman 71

Characteristics of the Iroquoian Confederation 71
Distinctions existing between the Confederated Nations 72
No peaceful secession from the union permitted 72
Divergent interests among the Six Nations 72
Absence of civil wars 72
Contrast: the Choctaw Confederation 72
A loose confederation 72
Significance of Onondaga 72
Difficulty of arriving at decisions 72
The binding force of the tradition of unity 73
The differentiation between civil and military functions 73
The sachem and the war lord 73
The principle of equality 73
Poverty of the sachems 73
Absence of slavery 73
The treatment of prisoners 73
The " gauntlet " 73
General mild treatment 73
Influence of the institution of adoption 73
Respect for women captives 73
Other characteristics 74
Attitude toward theft 74
Hospitality and fidelity 74

The search for peltries 74
Exhaustion of the local supply 74

Movement west of Lake Ontario   74
  The breaking of the Hurons   74
Movement south of Lake Erie   74
  The scattering of the Erie   74
  The Far West tribes   74

The Niagara portage   75
  La Salle's trading house, 1676   75
  Denonville re-establishes the Niagara post, 1687   75
    Anglo-French agreement of 1688   75
    The post given up   75

The Iroquois and the growing French influence   75
  The mission of Sault St. Louis   75
    The contraband trade   76
    Curious position of Albany   76
    Trade with the enemy   76
  The activity of the Jesuits   76
    Work of Father de Lamberville among the Onondaga and the
      Seneca   76
    Work of Father Milet among the Oneida   77
  Significance of the year 1701   77
    Treaty of friendship with the French   77
    The establishment of Fort Detroit   77
    The Iroquoian reaction   77
    Cession of beaver lands to the King of England   77
  The War of the Spanish Succession   78
    The Iroquoian mission to England   78
    The neutrality agreement of 1708   78
    The flourishing Albany trade   78
    The Iroquoian mission to Montreal, 1710   78
  The appearance of the French at Onondaga, 1711   78
  The vacillation of the Confederation   78
    Peter Schuyler at Onondaga   78

The Treaty of Utrecht and the Confederation   79
  The meaning of Article XV   79
    Difficulties of interpretation and application   79
  Temporary French disillusionment as to imperial expansion   80

The French and North America, 1718–20   80
  Revival of French interest in empire   80
    New Orleans   80
    Fort Louisbourg   80
  The rebuilding of the Niagara post, 1719   80

Influence of Chabert de Joncaire 81
Interest of the Albany merchants in Niagara 82
Burnet's protest at French aggression 83
The question of the violation of the Treaty of Utrecht 83
Vaudreuil's reply 83
Continued vacillation of the Five Nations 83
Pro-English and pro-French factions 84

New York and the Great Lakes trade 84
Fundamental change in policy, 1716 84
Traders sent to Irondequoit 84
French traders already established there 85
British traders in the Iroquoian villages, 1717 85
Governor Burnet and the fur trade 85
The plan of a joint-stock company 85
New York's law against the contraband trade, 1720 85
The sending of traders to mouth of the Onondaga, 1724 86
Effect of French construction of Fort Niagara, 1725 87
The building of Fort Oswego, 1727 88

Niagara against Oswego 89
The French threaten Fort Oswego 89
The fort summoned 89
Beauharnois's protest and Burnet's reply 89
Attitude of the Six Nations 89
Brighter prospects for the French fur trade 90
Significance of the presence of Englishmen at Montreal 90
The *ordonnance* of 1727 90
Ejection of the English and the decline in the fur trade 90
The sale of brandy 91
Attitude of the Church in Canada 91
The lure of English rum 91
The breakdown of restrictions on brandy 91
Oswego's growing pre-eminence in the fur trade 91
Oswego and Niagara now brought within the old "neutrality"
    policy, 1744 92
Decay of the fortifications of these posts 93
Freedom of each from attack in King George's War 93

William Johnson and the Six Nations 95
Early relations with the Indians 95
Great interest in the fur trade 95
Placed in command of the Indians and white volunteers, 1746 95
Combats the influence of Joncaire 96
The Iroquoian Mission to Quebec, 1748 97

English efforts to Christianize the Iroquois   97
    Work of the Society for the Propagation of the Gospel, 1704–48   97
    Lack of influence of the English missionaries   97

Indian relations after the Peace of Aix-la-Chapelle   98
    French strengthen their position among the Iroquois   98
        Conrad Weiser's testimony   98
        A French post above the Niagara portage   99
    The Albany conference with the Iroquois, 1750   99
        Massachusetts, Connecticut, and South Carolina represented   99
        Lack of results   99
    Oswego as a trade centre   100
        Conditions of the fur trade there   100
        Failure of the French posts to divert the trade   101
    Abbé Piquet and La Présentation   102
    Beginnings of the mission, 1748   102
        Its purpose   102
    Piquet on the Niagara, 1751   104
    The rapid growth of the mission   105
    The Abbé plans to dominate the Ohio Valley   106
        Wins support of La Jonquière and Bigot   107
        Adverse decision of the French Minister   107
    The strategic position of the Iroquoian Confederation   107
        The policy of " balance "   107
        The Seneca harass the French   108
        The Mohawks harass the English   108
    The French threat to the Ohio Valley Iroquoian hunting preserve   109
        The loss of prestige of the English   109
    The Board of Trade requests an Indian conference   111
        The circular letter of 1753   111

CHAPTER IV

"JOIN OR DIE"

The favourable response of the colonists to attend the Albany Con-
    gress   113
Virginia and New Jersey invited but not represented   113
Explanation for the appearance of the Connecticut and Rhode
    Island commissioners   113
A gathering of leading colonials   114

The powers of the commissioners analysed   114
    Anomalous situation of the New York delegation   116

De Lancey and the Congress 116
  High-handed policy of the Governor 117
    Resentment of Massachusetts Bay 117
    Suggested explanation of de Lancey's conduct 117

One clear objective of the commissioners 118
  Restoration of English influence among the Six Nations 118
    Chief grievances 118

Unwillingness of the New York authorities to have the commissioners
    deal with specific grievances 118
  The two Mohawk conferences 119

The Congress addresses the Indians 119
  As to their scattered condition 119
  As to the French penetration of their western lands 119

The reply of the Indians 119
  Charges of English encroachment and unfair treatment 120

The answer of the Congress 120
  Weiser's statement 120
  De Lancey's statement 120

Change in attitude of the Indians 121
  The Pennsylvania land purchase 121
  The Connecticut Wyoming land purchase 122

The question of intercolonial union 123
  Early efforts in that direction 123
    The New England Confederation 123
    The " quota system " in King William's War 123
    The concert of New England colonies in King George's War 123

The Committee on the Union 124

Benjamin Franklin's role 124
  Plan for a voluntary union, 1751 124
  Activities in New York 125
  The " Short Hints " 126
    Repudiation of voluntary union 126
    Parliament to settle the Constitution of the Empire 126
    Provision for a Governor General and a Grand Council 126
    Wide powers to be conferred 126
    Contemporary criticism of the plan 126

Plans presented by other commissioners 127

" A Plan for a General Union of the British Colonies in North
    America 127
Richard Peters's probable authorship 127
A voluntary union 128
To be implemented by the Privy Council 128
" A Plan of a Proposed Union of the Several Colonies " 128
Hutchinson's probable authorship 128
Two unions rather than one 129
To be effected by act of Parliament 129
Organization and powers of the union government 129

Pownall's proposals 130
Grouping of colonies for frontier defence 131

The " Short Hints " the basis for the Albany Plan of Union 131

Vote in favour of a union of the colonies 131

The " Representation on the Present State of the Colonies " 132
Hutchinson's authorship 132
Sweeping territorial claims 132
Chief recommendations 133
    An Indian superintendency 133
    The construction of frontier forts and a Great Lakes navy 133
    Limitation of the western bounds of the colonies to the Appala-
        chians 133
    The creation of western colonies 133
    A union of the continental colonies 133
    Significance of the " Representation " 133

The Albany Plan of Union, 1754 133
A fusion of ideas of the " Short Hints " and of the " Plan of a Pro-
    posed Union " 133
Not all the continental colonies to be included 134
    Position of Nova Scotia and Georgia 134
To be consummated by act of Parliament 134
    Franklin's defence of this procedure 134
No temporary, voluntary union 135
Office of President General 135
    Powers conferred 135
The Grand Council 135
    Temporary allotment of membership 135
    Permanent allotment based upon contributions 136
    Privileges of the Council as to its own sittings 136
    Philadelphia to be the temporary capital 136
Combined powers of the President and Council 136

Respecting Indian relations   136
As to western settlement   137
As to defence of the colonies   137
Limitations on law-making powers of the Council   137
  Veto power of the President General and of the Privy Council   137
Provision for a general treasury   138
Expenditure of funds   138
  Annual reports to the colonies   138

Character of the discussion preceding the adoption of the Plan   138

Was the sending of the Plan to England authorized or expected?   140

CHAPTER V

THE FATE OF THE PLAN OF UNION

The commissioners acted at Albany beyond their commissions   143
  Had underestimated the force of American colonial particularism   143

The Plan of Union and the colonial governments   144
  The Pennsylvania government   144
    Sympathetic attitude of Governor Hamilton   144
  Franklin alone of the delegates openly supports the Plan   145
    Humiliating treatment of Franklin   145
    Speaker Norris and the Assembly   145
  The Virginia government   145
    Governor Dinwiddie's critical attitude   146
    General hostility of the people   146
  The Plan all but ignored by the governments of Maryland and
      South Carolina   146
  The North Carolina government   146
    Governor Dobbs urges the Assembly to consider the Plan   146
  The New Jersey government   146
    Bitter hostility of the New Jersey Assembly   146
    Favourable attitude of the Governor's Council   147
    Governor Belcher urged to present the Plan to the ministers   147
  The New York government   147
    De Lancey submits the Plan to the General Assembly   147
    The Governor's Council favourable to the Plan   147
    The Assembly favours a union of the colonies   147
    No formal approval by the government   147
  The Rhode Island government   147
    Support of the Plan by Commissioner Hopkins   147

Opposition by " Philolethes " 148
Temporary favourable report of the Assembly 148
Critical attitude of the Governor's Council 148
Final repudiation of the Plan in 1755 148
The London agent instructed to oppose it 148
The Connecticut government 148
A committee of the Assembly considers the Plan 148
Unfavourable report 148
" The Reasons Considered and Offered " adopted 148
Basis of Connecticut opposition 148
The union too large for purely defensive purposes 148
The King's interests threatened by the proposed union government 149
Military powers as a threat 149
The large population as a threat 149
The veto power of the President General as a threat 149
Power of taxation against the rights of Englishmen 149
The alleged opposition of the Connecticut commissioners at Albany 149
Connecticut counter-proposals 149
Royal commissioners to control the Indian trade 149
The Crown to build forts and to garrison these 149
Proposed taxation of the Indian trade by the Crown 149
Proposed planting of a New England colony in the Indian country 150
Plan to hold the Indians to the English interest 150
Plan to prevent French encroachments 150
Probable influence of the Susquehanna Company in the Assembly 150
Strong endorsement of the existing constitution of the Empire 150
The Massachusetts Bay government 150
Governor Shirley's recommendations to the Assembly, October 18, 1754 151
To " ripen " the Plan for consideration of Parliament 151
A committee of the two houses on the Plan of Union 151
Agent Bollan's disturbing letter of September 19 151
Alleged design by Parliament to gain power over the colonies 151
The joint committee's report of December 4 151
The desirability of " so extensive a Union " questioned 151
Delay in consideration of the Plan by Parliament sought 152
The joint committee ordered to report some plan of union 152
The report of December 11 in favour of a union of northern colonies 152

Provisions contrasted with those of the " Plan of a Proposed
    Union "   153
Only a temporary union favoured   153
The union proposals in the House of Representatives   153
Opposition to the Albany Plan   154
Opposition to the plan for a northern union   154
Desire for a general union of the colonies   154
The union proposals in the Council   154
Apparent support of a northern union   154
Final repudiation of the Albany Plan, December 20   155
Nature of the objections to the Plan   155
A new project for a general union   155
Close adherence to the main outline of the Albany Plan   155
Divergencies from the Albany Plan   155
Temporary nature of the union   155
A weakened executive   155
Legislative supremacy of the Grand Council   156
Western bounds of colonies unchanged   156
No authority to regulate western land policy   156
Trade regulations to be enforced by the different colonies   156
Opposition to the project within and without the Assembly   156
Resolutions of January 17, 1755   157
Alone of the colonies Massachusetts Bay seriously pondered
    union   157

Governor Shirley and a union of the colonies   158
Tentative support of the Albany Plan   158
Final opposition to all suggested plans   158
Favours a Crown-appointed Grand Council   158
Favours taxation by Parliament   158

Benjamin Franklin and Shirley's proposals   158
Conditional acceptance of idea of representation in Parliament   159

Shirley's communication to the Secretary of State, December 24,
    1754   160
The Albany Plan and the royal prerogative   160
Suggested alteration of the government of the corporate colonies   161

The Board of Trade and the union of the colonies   161
Requested to prepare a plan   161
Secretary of State Robinson's letter of June 14   161
The " Project for a General Concert "   161
A union for defence by mutual consent of the colonies   162
To be submitted to the Privy Council for approval   162

To be concerned with frontier defence and Indian affairs   162
Responsibilities of colonial commissioners   162
Responsibilities of the Indian commissaries   163
Method of allocating expenses   163
Proposed appointment of a commander-in-chief and also a com-
    missary general for the colonies   163
Restraints placed upon the action of these officials   163
Anxiety of the Board to preserve "the Constitution of the Colo-
    nies"   164
The ministry and the "Project"   164
Objections raised   164
Attitude toward the "Plan of Union"   165

Were the colonies prepared in 1754 to favour any proposed union?   165

Final attainment of union   166

CHAPTER VI

LAND OF THE ACADIANS

Description of old Acadia   167

French settlement upon the peninsula   168
    Importance of tide-control   168

Activities of the Acadians   168

Population increase, 1650–1750   168
    Not aided by immigration   169

Relations with the Indians   169
    Intermarriage   169

Relations with the British after 1710   169
    Payment of quit-rent   169
        Trivial payments exacted   169
    Deputies to Annapolis Royal   169
        To present needs of communities   169
        To aid the Council with advice   169
        To report decisions arrived at   170
    Weakness of governmental control   170
        The small Annapolis garrison   170
    British indulgence of the Acadians   170
        Freedom of worship   170
        Priests from France allowed   170

Freedom of French language   170
Preservation of local custom   170

The Acadian parishes in the eighteenth century   170
  Port Royal   170
  Rivière aux Canards   170
  Grand Pré   170
  Rivière Piziquid   170
  Cobequid   170
  Beaubassin   170
  St. John River Acadians   171

The Treaty of Utrecht and Acadia   171
  Cession of the land to Great Britain   171
  The inhabitants and Article XIV of the treaty   171
    The question of immovable property   171

Desire of inhabitants to leave Acadia   171
  Action of Deputy Governor Caulfeild   171
    Refusal of passports   171
  Policy adopted by Governor Nicholson   171
    Acadians permitted to go with personal effects   171
    Requests to extend the customary year denied   171

Revival of Anglo-French rivalry in North America   172
  The building of Louisbourg fortress, 1717   172
    A threat to Nova Scotia   172
  Determination of the British government to prevent Acadian mi-
    gration   172
  Action of Lieutenant Governor Armstrong, 1725   173

The Acadians as neutrals   173
  The qualified oath of 1727   173
    Special privileges to be enjoyed by the inhabitants   173
  Growing spirit of independence of the inhabitants   173
  Spread of settlement beyond the peninsula   174
  Developing relations with Isle St. Jean and Isle Royale   174
    Inability of the Annapolis garrison to control the people 174

The Canso fisheries   175
  Protected by troops   175
  New England's interest in   175
  Cape Breton's interest in   175

King George's War and Acadia   176
  Loss of the island of Canso, 1744   176
  New England's invasion of Cape Breton   176

Attitude of the Acadians in the war   176
    Peaceful attitude of most of the people   176
The inhabitants later indicted as disloyal   176
    Powerful influence of French clergy   177
The Bishop of Quebec and the war   178
Should the Acadians be deported?   178
    Opposition of Mascarene   178
    The dilemma   179

Post-war plans for Acadia, 1748–9   179
    Shirley's proposals   179
        Relative to colonization   179
        Relative to the building of forts   180
    Survey of vacant lands   180
    Decision to colonize the eastern part of the peninsula   181

The founding of Halifax   181
    The Board of Trade and colonization from England   181
    Governor Cornwallis in charge   182
        Favourable reception by Acadians and Indians   182
    Poor quality of early settlers   182

Governor Cornwallis and the Acadians   183
    Instructions respecting the oath of allegiance   183
        Those refusing oath to be removed   183
    Aggressiveness of the authorities of New France   183
        Interference in the affairs of the peninsula   183
    British troops at Minas Basin   184
    The Acadian memorial   184
    The British reply   184
    The inhabitants decide to refuse the oath   184

The French authorities and the Acadians   185
    Design to reclaim Acadia and its inhabitants   185
    Dependence of Louisbourg upon the Acadians   186
        Cornwallis forbids all trade with any French settlement   186
    M. de la Corne sent to the borders of the peninsula   187
    Abbé Le Loutre breaks the peace   187
        Agreement with Intendant Bigot   187
        The Indians sent on the war path   188
        Cornwallis's protest   188
    The Micmac appeal to La Jonquière   189
    War supplies sent to the Indians and the Acadians   190

Acadians appeal to the French authorities   190

To Louis XV in France   190
To La Jonquière in New France   190

Developments at Halifax   191

British measures for defence of Nova Scotia   191
  At Halifax   191
  At Minas   191
  At Beaubassin   192
    Lawrence's futile expedition   193
    The burning of the village   193

La Corne's defiance at Chignecto, April 1750   193

The second expedition to Chignecto, September 1750   194
  The building of Fort Lawrence and Fort Beauséjour   194

Drift of Acadians to the isthmus   195
  No neutrality permitted by the French   195
  Settlement of Acadians upon new lands   196

Growing difficulties of the French   196
  Lack of food   196
  Dissatisfaction of the Indians   196
    The Micmac treaty with the British   197
  The Acadians weaken   197

French pressure upon the Acadians   197
  The question of supplying priests   198
    Le Loutre's policy carried out   198

Governor Hopson makes concessions   199
  Waiving of the oath for priests   199

Progress of British settlement   200
  The founding of Lunenburg   201

The Acadian exiles' petition of 1753   202
  Demand the exemptions of 1727   202

Return of Le Loutre from France   202
  Revival of Indian hostilities   203
    Effect upon the Acadians   203

Policy of Governor Lawrence   204

Impossibility of securing the loyalty of the Acadians   204
  Basis of their subsequent expulsion   205

Chapter VII

THE "NEUTRAL" ISLANDS OF THE CARIBBEANS

The "neutral" islands of Dominica, St. Lucia, St. Vincent, and Tobago 207
Present lack of economic importance 207
Their value in the eighteenth century 207
Part of a chain of possessions 207

The Carib islands 208
Dominica and St. Vincent remaining seats of Caribbean native culture 208

Dominica 208
Early description of 208
Included within the d'Esnambuc-Rossey grant of 1626 209
A part also of the Carlisle grant of 1627 209
Early French influence over the Caribs 209
Native hostility against the English 209
Aubert's treaty of friendship, 1640 209
The Anglo-French Treaty of Union and League, 1660 209
To act in concert against the Caribs 209
The role of Thomas Warner upon the island 210
Becomes English Deputy Governor 210
Sale of St. Lucia (1663) and Dominica (1668) 210
Death of Warner 210
Unoccupied by Europeans at the beginning of the eighteenth century 211
Neutralized in 1730 and its neutral status reaffirmed in 1748 211

West India Carib culture 211
The Caribs as "newcomers" 211
Theories of their origin 211
Carib method of conquest 212
Extermination of male captives 212
A distinct female language 212
Cannibalism 212
Limited to martial purposes 212
Method of waging war 213
Treachery a native characteristic 213
The blood feud 213
Lack of organized government 213
Individual leadership in warlike enterprises 213

Absolute subordination of females 214
Respect for the aged 214
Inability to endure slavery 214
Devotion to their primitive religion 214
Failure of efforts to Christianize 214
Virtues of the natives 214
Contentment and sociability 214
Hospitality 214
Honesty 214

Gradual development of barter between the Caribs and Europeans 215

French colonization of Dominica after 1730 215
Strength of the French colony in 1753 and in 1763 215
Rapid disappearance of the natives 215

St. Vincent 216
Significance of the Carib population in 1700 216
A refuge for escaped Negroes 216
The division of the island between the two groups 216
Negroes control the mountain fastnesses 216
Ill treatment of the Caribs 216
Feuquieres's expedition against the blacks, 1719 216
Plans for the disposal of them 216
The Caribs refuse assistance 217
Failure of the French 217
Peace with the Negroes 217
Numbers of male Caribs in 1763 217
French colonization of the island 217
Trade and lumbering 217
Plantations after 1748 217
Estimated numbers of Frenchmen in 1763 217
Black slavery 218

Tobago 218
Appeal of the island 218
A seventeenth-century international cockpit 218
Effort of colonization by Barbadian Puritans, 1625 218
Within the Earl of Montgomery patent of 1628 218
Coming of the Zeelanders, 1632 218
Colony of Nieu Walcheren 218
The Duke of Courland's settlement, 1642 218
The island granted to the French Company of the Islands of
America, 1642 218
The Courland-Lampsins agreement, 1654 219

The second colony of Zeelanders 219
The Duke's government repudiated, 1659 219
Courland's grant from Charles II of England, 1664 219
His inability to re-establish his authority on the island 220
The Zeelanders seek to keep control up to 1677 220
The Dutch overwhelmed by the English in 1666 and in 1672 . . . 220
Their final ejection by the French, 1677 220
The island and the Peace of Nijmegen, 1678 220
Cession of the Dutch rights to the French 220
Left deserted after the Peace 220
The Duke of Courland's unsuccessful attempts at recolonization,
1680–2 220
The John Printz Company 221
Efforts of the new Duke of Courland to gain control, 1686–99 . . . 221
The Thomas Puckle Company 221
Complaints of the French court 221
A haven for pirates, 1699–1748 221
Efforts of the Duke of Montagu to secure the island, 1729 222
A factor in Anglo-French friction, 1748 222
Agreement for its neutralization 223

St. Lucia 223
Importance in Anglo-French relations 223
Physical features of the island 223
Leigh's attempt to colonize there, 1605 224
Included within the Carlisle patent, 1627 224
Massacre of the English colony, 1640 225
French claims based upon 225
The commission of 1626 to d'Esnambuc and Rossey 225
The English abandonment of the island 225
Early French efforts at settlement 225
Continued English claims 226
Embodied within the jurisdiction of the Governor of Barbados . . 226
The " purchase " of 1663 from the Caribs 226
English repossession, 1664 226
Carew's expedition 226
Mortality of the colony 226
So-called retrocession to the French 227
Disappearance of the English, 1666 227
Rival pretensions, 1666–74 227
The French in undisturbed control, 1666–86 227
The Temple expedition, 1686 227
The Anglo-French commission, 1687 227
Neutralization of the island 227

No permanent inhabitants, 1700   227
   French resort there for lumber   227
The grant of the island to d'Estrées, 1719   228
The Montagu patent of 1722   228
   Captain Uring's colony   228
The French force the English to evacuate the island, 1723   228
   Neutralization of the island again, 1730   228
The island during King George's War   229
   Military occupation by the French   229
The Treaty of Aix-la-Chapelle   229
   For European evacuation of the island   229
   For a joint commission to determine ownership   229
   The French delay evacuation   229
Comparison of English and French claims   229
   Tacit admission by British of strength of French claims   230

Chapter VIII

EAST OF GOOD HOPE

British economic interest penetrates the Far East   231
   Foundations laid for future political control of India   231

India's geographical features   231
   Vulnerability to invasion   232

Early invaders of India   232
   No political unification   232
   No political stability   232

The Hindu Empire of Vijayanagar   232
   Control of southern India   232
   Collapse in 1565   232

The Mogul Empire   232
   Akbar the founder, 1556–1605   233
   Unification of northern India   233
   The Empire at its height under Aurangzeb, 1658–1707   233
   Slow disintegration of the Empire under Aurangzeb's successors   233
     Invasion of India by Nadir Shah, 1739   233
     Rise of the Mahratta power   233

Social structure of India   233
   Cohesiveness of Hinduism   233
   Mohammedanism   234

The coming of the Europeans   234
   Advantages enjoyed by the natives in trade   234
      Consistent favourable balance of trade   235
      The draining of Europe of its silver   235
   Rise and decline of the Portuguese trading empire   235
   The Dutch and the English competition   235

The London Company of the East Indies, 1600   235
   Characteristic activities of the Company   235
      Early trade not with India   235
   Privileges granted in perpetuity, 1609   236
   Becomes a modified joint-stock enterprise, 1612   236
      Separate and continuing joint stocks, 1612–57   236
      Cromwell's charter of October 19, 1657   236
   Surat eastern centre of the trade, 1612   237
   Rivalry with the Dutch   237
      The joint council of defence, 1619   237
      The " affair " at Amboyna, 1623   237
   The leasing of Madraspatam, 1640   237
      Building of Fort St. George   238
      Location there of the eastern presidency, 1652   238
      Drawbacks of the town   238
      Advantages of the town   238
      The Company still without political aspirations   238
   Early English rivals   238
      The Mickelborne Company, 1604   238
      The Courteen Association, 1637   238
   The patent of 1661   239
      Great extension of political power   239
   The acquisition of Bombay, 1668   239
      Held directly from the King of England   240
   St. Helena added to the Company possessions, 1673   240
   The patent of 1676   240
      Authority to suppress mutinies   240
   Vice-admiralty power conferred in 1683   241

William and Mary and the East India trade   241
   The London Company loses favour   241
   Attempts to liberalize the trade by the charters of 1693, 1694, and
      1698   242
   Creation of the General Society, 1698   243
      Exclusive right of East India trade   243
      Two rival companies within the Society   243

The creation of the United Company of Merchants of England trad-
  ing to the East Indies, 1702   243
  Terms of agreement between the two companies   243
  Possessions of the new company   244
  Loans to the government   244
  Was it to enjoy its privileges in perpetuity?   245

Attempts to tie the Company to the South Sea Company, 1720   245

The opposition of 1730   246
  Demand for a regulated company   246

Reduction of interest on government loans, 1730 and 1750   246

The East India Company as an agency of government   246
  The three presidencies   246
    Calcutta   246
    Bombay   248
    Madras   248
  Local government and the patent of 1726   249
    Incorporation of the three towns   249
    Law-making powers of the President and Council   249
    English court system established   249
    The *zemindar* courts   249
  Wide authority of the presidency government   249
    As to war and peace   249
    As to taxation and coinage   249

The East India Company in business   250
  Stockholders' meetings: the Proprietors' Courts   250
    Qualifications for participation   250
    Powers exercised   250
  The " Committees " or Court of Directors   250
    Qualifications   250
    Functions of the various committees   250
    Varied responsibilities of the directors   251
  Activities in India   251
    A business hierarchy   252
    Contacts with a native business hierarchy   252
    The " country trade "   253
  The East India merchantmen   253
    The leasing policy   253
  The outward freight   254
    Predominance of bullion   254
    Other important commodities   255
    The disposition of the cargoes   255

The return freight   256
    Difficulties encountered in filling the Company orders   256
The disposal of East India goods in England   257
    Requirement of open auctions   257
    Feeding the market   257
    Restrictions on the sale of East India fabrics   258
    Profits of the Company   259

The factories of the Company in 1750   260

Lack of interest of the Company in land possessions   260
    Great possessions of the Dutch East India Company in the Far East 260

CHAPTER IX

RIVALS FOR THE CARNATIC

Late interest of France in East India trade   261
    Activities of Breton merchants before 1660   261
    The French China Company, 1660   261

The Compagnie des Indes Orientales, 1664   261
    Île Dauphine, eastern commercial centre   261
    Transfer of the Council to Surat, 1669   261
    Acquisition of Port Louis, Brittany   262
        Construction of L'Orient   262
    Failure to make profits   262
    Unsuccessful attack upon Ceylon, 1673   262
    Failure to hold St. Thomé   262
    Occupation of Pondicherry, 1674   262
    Fall of Pondicherry to the Dutch, 1693   262
        Returned by the Treaty of Ryswick   262
    Increased importance of Pondicherry after 1699   262
    Continued failure of the Company to prosper   263
        Resort to licences to maintain the Eastern trade   263
    Consolidation with the Mississippi Company, 1719   263
        Indictment of the old company   263

The Compagnie perpetuelle des Indes, 1719   264
    Privileges secured and responsibilities assumed   264
    Speculation in its stocks   264
    Bursting of the bubble   264
    Reorganization, 1720–3   264
    Monopolies retained   264
        Far Eastern trade   264

African trade 264
Santo Domingo trade 264
Proprietorship of Louisiana 265
The export of Canadian beaver skins 265
The *ferme* of tobacco in France 265
Retrocession of Louisiana, 1731 265
Improved outlook in the Far East, 1734 265
M. le Noir Governor at Pondicherry 265
Interest of the Orry brothers in the company 265
Dupleix takes charge at Pondicherry, 1742 266
During the administration of Dupleix, 1742–54 266
The company assets 266
Distribution of shipping 266
African slaving no longer a direct interest 267
The financial report of 1752 analysed 267
The government of the company fixed by the decree of 1748 270
The stockholders' meetings 270
The *syndics* 270
The *directeurs* 270
The royal *commissaires* 270

Dupleix at Pondicherry 271
Condition of Pondicherry in 1742 271
Financial embarrassments 271
Immediate improvements 271

Anwar-ud-din 272
Nabob of Arcot, 1743 272
Supports French policy, 1744 272

War of the Austrian Succession in India 273
Commodore Barrett preys on French shipping 273
La Bourdonnais on the Coromandel Coast 273
Indecisive engagement with Peyton 273
The capture of Madras, 1746 273
The ransom treaty and its repudiation 273
Anwar-ud-din claims Madras 274
Crushing of the Nabob's army 274
French siege of Fort St. David 274
British siege of Pondicherry 274
Dupleix tries to dispose of Madras 275

Peace of Aix-la-Chapelle and the Carnatic 275
Restoration of Madras, 1749 275

Developments in the Carnatic in 1749 275

The English proceed against Tanjore   275
  The capture of Devi-Cotah   276
  The agreement with the Rajah   276
Dupleix's alliance with Chanda Sahib and Muzaffar Jang   276
  Objectives of the allies   276
  Destruction of Anwar-ud-din and his army   277
  Chanda Sahib the new Nabob   277
  The Governor and the Compagnie rewarded   277
Attitude of the two companies toward these developments   278
  The United East India Company rebukes Floyer   278
  The Compagnie des Indes rewards Dupleix   278
Dupleix and Chanda attack Tanjore and Trichinopoly   279
  The ravaging of Tanjore   280
  Terms of peace with the Rajah   280
  Muhammad Ali, Chanda's rival at Trichinopoly   280
  Attempt to besiege the stronghold   281

Nasir Jang, the Subahdar, invades the Carnatic, 1750   281
  Supported by the English   281
  His great army   281
  Retreat of the French and Chanda Sahib   281
  Capture of Muzaffar Jang   281
  Dupleix negotiates   282
  Nasir's camp attacked   282
  Withdrawal of the Subahdar's army   282
  The stronghold Jingi stormed   282
  Nasir Jang again approaches Pondicherry   282
  Again Dupleix negotiates   282
  The French attack   282
  Nasir slain by traitors   282

Muzaffar Jang becomes the Subahdar   283
  Accepted by the late Nasir's army   283
  Makes acknowledgments at Pondicherry   283
    Gifts to the Compagnie   283
    Dupleix becomes hereditary Mensebdar along the Coromandel
      Coast   283
  Plans for his rule in the Deccan   283
    Granted a French force under Bussy   284
    Revolt of the Pathans and death of Muzaffar, 1751   284

Salabat Jang the new Subahdar of the Deccan   284
  Dupleix agrees to support Salabat   284
  Bussy accompanies the Subahdar to Aurangabad   284
  The grants made by Muzaffar Jang confirmed   284

Dupleix at the height of his power   285
  Advantages of his system   285
  Its disadvantages   285
    Failure of expected revenues   285
    Effect upon commerce   285
    The need for numerous garrisons   285

The English on the Coromandel Coast   285
  Shift the burden of trade upon Fort William   285
  Strengthen their military position at Fort St. George   285
  Agree to continue support of Muhammad Ali at Trichinopoly   286
  Include rulers of Tanjore and Mysore in their understanding   286

Chanda Sahib again besieges Trichinopoly, 1751   286

The seizure of Arcot, 1751   287
  Robert Clive   287
    Earlier activities in India   287
    Commands the Arcot expedition   287
  Defence of Arcot   288
  Turning of the tide   288

Military manœuvring in the Carnatic   288
  Relief of Trichinopoly   288
  Chanda and Law besieged on Seringham   289
  Capture of d'Auteuil's relief force by Clive   289
  The fate of Chanda   289
  The surrender of Law, 1752   289

Precarious situation of Pondicherry, 1752   289
  Protected only by the sanctity of treaties   289

Dupleix's conduct in the crisis   290
  His optimistic report to the *directeurs*   290
  Refusal of offers of accommodation by Muhammad Ali   290
    Support of Mootas Ali   290
  Imposing ceremonies at Pondicherry   290
  Wins the support by the *Dalaway* of Mysore   290
  With reinforcements from home he orders his troops into action   290

Situation of the French in the Carnatic, 1752–3   290
  Destruction of the new French force, September 5, 1752   290
  Pessimistic report of the *Conseil Supérieur* of February 19, 1753 290
  Serious financial situation of the Compagnie in India   290

Campaign of 1753–4 against Trichinopoly   291
  Failure of the attempt to storm the stronghold, November 27, 1753 291
  Indecisive nature of the armed struggle to October 1754   292

Dupleix's system under fire   292
    Disillusionment of the Compagnie   292
    The Governor defends himself   292
    Attempt to come to terms with the English   293
    The futile conference at Sadras, 1754   293
        Refusal of the English to recognize Dupleix's native titles   293
        Refusal of the French to recognize Muhammad Ali   293

Conditions in India that made for an accommodation   293
    Loss of commerce on the part of the two companies   293
    The great expense of maintaining armies   293
    The danger of the growing anarchy   293

The London conference of 1754   294
    The Compagnie offers concessions   294
    The United Company demands restoration of the " ancient limits "   294

The repudiation of Dupleix   295
    His return to France, 1755   295

Godeheu's reversal of policy   295
    Demoralized condition of the French forces   295
    Appearance of Admiral Watson's fleet   296
    The provisional treaty of December 1754   296
        Native offices renounced   296
        Neutrality in all native quarrels   296
        Equality of possessions   296
        Favourable to the French   296

CHAPTER X

EFFORTS TO SAVE THE PEACE

War of the Austrian Succession   298
    Public attitude in Great Britain in 1747   298
    Effects of British naval superiority   298
        Blockade of France and Spain   298
        Capture of French and Spanish shipping   298
        Precarious situation of the French West Indies   299
        Apprehensions of the French court   299
    British financial burdens   300
        Growth of peace sentiment   300

The Congress of Aix-la-Chapelle   300

Anglo-French secret negotiations   300
Ratification of a definitive peace treaty, 1748   301
    Advantages and disadvantages to Great Britain   301
    Significance of Article IV   302

Anglo-French joint commission   302
    Allix and Hind at Saint-Malo, 1749   303
    Mildmay and Shirley in Paris, 1750–2   303
    Relations with Galissonière and de Silhouette   304

Outstanding Anglo-French issues   304
    Sea captures, 1738–48   304
    The boundaries of Nova Scotia   304
    The Caribbean " neutral " islands   306

The French demand for a settlement in one instrument of all issues   306

Mutual concessions to promote negotiation   306

The problem of the Nova Scotian boundary   306
    The terms of cession in the Treaty of Utrecht   306
    The British interpretation   307
    Was Nova Scotia Acadia?   308
    The Board of Trade and the British commissaries   309
    Shirley's draft of the Nova Scotia memorial   309
    Mildmay's critical attitude   309
    The two British memorials   310
    The French *mémoire* on Acadia   310

The problem of " neutral " St. Lucia   312
    Growing friction between the British commissaries   312
    The rival British memorials on St. Lucia   312
    The French *mémoire* on St. Lucia   312
    The British criticism of this   312

The issue over the evacuation of the neutral islands   313
    British charges of bad faith   313
    Admiral Holbourne's threat   313
    The French Minister's reassurances   314

The French reply to the British memorial on Acadia   315

The undermining of Shirley at Paris   315
    Mildmay seeks a free hand   315
    Shirley recalled to London   316
    De Cosné appointed to the commission   316

Why the joint commission was continued   317
  Mildmay's proposed solution of the diplomatic tangle   317
    Support of the Mildmay proposals   318

Heightened friction between the British and French in North
  America   318
  The French commissaries prepare to appeal their case to the world 319
    The British protest   319

The British answer to the French *mémoire* on Acadia   320

British disillusionment regarding the joint commission   320
  Mildmay's changed attitude   320
  Why the British commissaries remain in Paris   320

The French demand the use of the French language in all exchange
  of documents   321
  The British position   321
    The suspension of the joint commission's activities 322

The growing Anglo-French crisis in India   322
  The British proposals to restore harmony between the two com-
    panies   322
  The dispatch of French forces to India   323

Significant changes in the British Cabinet Council, 1754   323
  Newcastle in power   323
  Robinson in charge of the Southern Department   323

Significant changes in the French ministry   323
  Rouillé now takes over foreign affairs   323
  Albemarle's friendly interview   324

The "assassination" of Jumonville by Washington   324
  Growing tension between the two powers   324
    Robinson suggests a test of French good faith   325

Effect of the news of the surrender of Washington at Fort Necessity   325
  Rouillé minimizes the incident   325
  The British ministry orders regiments of regulars to America   326
    The French reaction to this move   326

The death of Albemarle   327

London the centre of diplomatic activity   327
  Mirepoix returns to England   328
    His instructions   328
    His interview with Robinson   329

The Robinson plan for settling Anglo-French differences in North
   America   331
  Halifax's criticism of the plan   331
The position of the French court on American issues   331
  A criticism of this position   332
    Relative to the Ohio Valley   332
    Relative to Nova Scotia   333
  The Cabinet Council plan of February 20   335
   The fairness of the plan   335
   The failure of French statesmanship   336

The two nations reconcile themselves to the waging of war   338

CHAPTER XI

SUMMARIZATION

Eighteenth-century zones of international friction   339
  Situation in the middle of the eighteenth century   339
   Quiet areas   339
   Disturbed areas   339

Patterns of statecraft in the Anglo-French rivalry   339
  Characteristics of British expansion   340
   Significance of private initiative   340
   Welcome to the oppressed Protestants of continental Europe   340
   Concentration of strength in seaboard areas   340
   Slow but steady conquest of the wilderness   340
   Movement of population unplanned   340
   Unregulated commercial expansion into forbidden areas   340
   Regulated commercial expansion remains private enterprise   340
   Small part played by the British Crown in this expansion   341
   Colonial governments under the influence of colonial ideals and
     aspirations   341
  The British Empire   341
   A business man's world   341
   A world of abundance   341
   A world of literate people devoted to freedom and opposed to
     governmental regulation   341
   A world of varied religious patterns   341
  Characteristics of French expansion   342
   Uniformity of design in the settlement of New France   342
   Concentration of authority in the Crown   342
   New World settlement a state responsibility   342

Continuation of the spirit of monopoly of the seventeenth century 342
Continuation of the paternalism of the seventeenth century 342
Over-regulation of the French settlers of the New World 342
Control of settlers by the presence of regular soldiers 342
The French Empire 343
New World centres of French court etiquette 343
Harmonious form of the ecclesiastical structure of New France 343
A world of scarcity 343
A world of officialdom 343
A world of suppressed thought 343
The French West Indies considered profitable 343
Canada and Louisiana as financial parasites 343
Failure of Canada to monopolize the fur trade 344

The strategy of French expansion in North America 344
Absence of a "frontier line" of settlement 344
Control of the continent sought by the planting of "islands" of Frenchmen 344
Gulf of St. Lawrence settlements 344
The Quebec-Montreal region 345
The Detroit settlement 345
The Illinois settlement 345
The lower Mississippi settlements 345
The Mobile Bay district 345
Other means of control 345
Garrisons of regular soldiers 345
The existence of scattered forts of strength 345
The liability of all Frenchmen to military service 345
The freedom of officials from legislative and popular checks 346
The existence of a uniform Indian policy 346
The ability of the French governors to plan in advance 346
Difficulties facing the British in meeting this strategy 346
British colonials divided in sentiment 346
Colonial assemblies refuse defence appropriations 346
Lack of British colonial military preparation 346
Lack of forts of strength 346
Lack of dependable Indian allies 346
Failure of the Six Confederated Nations to act as a buffer 346
Absorption of the people in personal affairs 346
Pacifism in Pennsylvania 346
Unwillingness of colonials to unite upon any policy 346

The lethargic British government stirred to action 346

Influence of the aggressive actions of the French in the Ohio Valley
    and elsewhere   346
A policy of limited responsibility   347
    Encouragement of the colonial governments to take united
      measures   347
    The summoning of the Albany Congress   347

The Albany Congress   347
    Its failure not to be charged to the British government   347
    High qualifications of the delegates   347
    Statesmanlike yet futile activities   347
    Bitter hostility of the colonial governments to its work   348

The halting efforts of the Board of Trade in the direction of colonial
    co-operation   348

The sending of British regulars to strengthen the colonial militia   348

The situation in the Caribbean Sea in the middle of the eighteenth
    century   348
    Comparative tranquillity   348
    The neutralization of St. Lucia, Tobago, Dominica, and St. Vin-
      cent   348
    The violation of the agreements by the French   348
    Influence of French indirection in the West Indies in determining
      British policy   348

Contrasting patterns of statecraft in Anglo-French rivalry in India   349
    The British emphasis on superior commercial contacts with the
      natives   349
    The French emphasis on superior political contacts with the na-
      tives   349
    The British concentrate their strength in the coastal regions 349
    The French concentrate their strength in the interior   349
    The British emphasize immediate objectives   349
    The French emphasize future prospects   349
    The British placed upon the defensive   349
    The French seize the initiative   349
    The British unable to take for granted government support of
      private policies   349
    The French able to take for granted government support of public
      policies   349
    The degree of success the British enjoyed depended largely on the
      financial strength of the United East India Company   349
    The degree of success the French enjoyed did not take into account
      the question of the solvency of the Compagnie des Indes   349

London disapproval of the United East India Company activities
in 1749   349
Paris support of the Compagnie des Indes activities in 1749   350
London support of the United East India Company activities in
1754   350
Paris disapproval of the Compagnie des Indes activities in 1754   350

International tension and Anglo-French relations   350
Could Anglo-French tensions (1749–54) have been liquidated
short of war?   350
The French sense of destiny in North America   351
The seventeenth-century idea of a great Franco-Indian empire   351
The eighteenth-century sense of mission   351
The English sense of destiny in North America   351
The seventeenth-century idea that the continent was to be an
English heritage   351
The eighteenth-century expression of this sense of mission   351

Diplomatic efforts to avoid war   351
The Anglo-French joint commission   351
Desire of both nations to avoid war   351
Failure of its efforts to arrive at compromise formulas   351
The failure of direct negotiation between the two courts   351
The possibility of a peaceful solution of the crisis   351
The chief responsibility of the French ministry for the war   352

Maps and Plans

I. Prospect of Quebec, 1732. (From Popple's *British Empire in America*.)   Facing page   34

II. The Indian Tribes of the Great Lakes Region. (From a section of Vander Aa's *Canada*, 1755.)   Facing page   35

III. The Country of the Six Confederated Nations, by Guy Johnson, 1771. (Emmet Collection. New York Public Library.)   Facing page   66

IV. A View of Niagara Fort, by Sir William Johnson, 1759.   Facing page   67

V. A South View of Oswego before 1755. (Emmet Collection. New York Public Library.)   Facing page   98

VI. Abbé Picquet's La Présentation Mission. (From *Mémoires sur le Canada, 1749–1760*.)   Facing page   99

VII. *Carte de l'Acadie, Isle Royale et Païs Voisins. Par M. B. Ing^r. de la Marine.* 1757.   Facing page   172

VIII. A Prospect of the City of Louisbourg after Its Conquest by Pepperrell and Warren. (Reproduced from Justin Winsor's *Narrative and Critical History of America*.)   Facing page   173

IX. *A New Map of Nova Scotia and Cape Britain, with adjacent parts of New England and Canada*, 1755. (From Jefferys's *History of French Dominion in North and South America*, 1760.)   Facing page   194

X. A Plan of the Neck of the Peninsula of Acadia showing its fortification in 1755. (From *Mémoires sur le Canada, 1749–1760*.)   Facing page   195

XI. The "Neutral" Islands of the West Indies. (From Lucas's *Historical Geography of the British Colonies. II, West Indies*.)   Facing page   210

XII. *Carte de l'Isle de Sainte Lucie. Par M. B. Ing*^r*. de la Marine,
1753.*   Facing page   211

XIII. *The Moguls Empire divided into its principal Governments.*
(From the *Gentleman's Magazine* for 1767.)
                                             Facing page   234

XIV. *Plan de Madras à la Coste de Coromandel.* (From Bellin's
Atlas Maritime.)   Facing page   235

XV. *Map to Illustrate the Wars in Coromandel, 1744–1780.* (From
Henry Beveridge's A *Comprehensive History of India,*
I.)   Facing page   274

XVI. *Plan de la Ville de Pondicheri.* (From Bellin's *Atlas Maritime.*)   Facing page   275

XVII. A *New Map of Nova Scotia and Cape Britain with Adjacent
Parts of New England and Canada, 1755. British Territorial Claims to the South of the St. Lawrence.* (From
Jefferys's *Remarks on the French Memorials . . . ,*
1756.)   Facing page   306

XVIII. *Carte d'une Partie de l'Amérique Septentrionale, 1755.
French Territorial Claims to the South of the St. Lawrence.* (From Jefferys's *Remarks on the French Memorials . . . , 1756.*)   Facing page   307

XIX. Map Showing the Iroquoian Control of the Region Between
the Cuyahoga and Sandusky Bay. (From *Amérique* Sep-
*tentrionale, par Mitchel, Paris: par Le Rouge, 1777; Cor-
rigée en 1776 par M. Hawkins.* Reproduced from Winsor's *The Mississippi Basin.*)   Facing page   330

XX. The British Proposal of 1755 for a Neutral Zone between the
Cuyahoga and the Wabash. (Reproduced from Pease's
Anglo-French Boundary Disputes in the West.)
                                             Facing page   331

CHRONOLOGY

Seventeenth-century India

The Anglo-French rivalry in India that culminated in the middle of the eighteenth century began with the granting by Queen Elizabeth I of the charter of the "Company of Merchants Trading into the East Indies" in 1600. In 1601 came the first voyage of the East India Company to the Malayan Archipelago. Between 1612 and 1640 the British East India Company factories were established at Surat, the Coromandel Coast, and the Punjab; the Armagon Factory was shifted to Madraspatam, where it was protected by Fort St. George. On April 3, 1661, with the Stuart restoration, a new charter was granted to the Company. 1664 marked the beginning of Anglo-French trade rivalry in the Far East with the establishment of two French companies. In 1668 Charles II transferred the island of Bombay to the East India Company in free and common socage. St. Helena became the second "sovereignty" of the East India Company in 1673. The following year the French gained the right to establish a factory at Pondicherry. In 1686 James II granted the Company the right to exercise "martial law." When the new charter was granted to the Company by William and Mary in 1693, the monopoly of the Company was protested by other English traders. In 1698 Parliament passed a public subscription act for a "General Society" with rights to trade to the East Indies.

1701

The French and their Indian allies conclude a treaty of friendship with the Iroquois Confederation of Nations.

July 24 Fort Detroit is established.

The beaver-hunting grounds of the Confederation northwest of Lake Ontario are ceded to the King of England.

1708

The union of the two British East India Companies is effected.

1710

The British capture Port Royal in Acadia, which becomes the capital of Nova Scotia under the new name, Annapolis Royal.

1713

April   11 The Treaty of Utrecht provides for the handing over of Acadia to the British and, in Article XIV, makes provision for the Acadians to leave.
Deputy Governor Caulfield prohibits attempts of the Acadians to leave Nova Scotia.

1714

Governor Nicholson of Nova Scotia permits some Acadians to depart.

1717

The construction of Louisbourg on Isle Royale begun by the French, who try to induce the Acadians to join them.

1719

The French establish a firm position at Niagara.

1720

Governor Burnet of New York attempts to prevent contraband trade to Canada out of Albany.

1722

The Tuscarora Indian tribe joins the Five Iroquoian Confederated Nations to make the Confederacy of Six Nations.

George I grants St. Lucia and St. Vincent in the West Indies to the Duke of Montagu, who also seeks to acquire Tobago; English settlers begin to colonize St. Lucia by December.

1725

Oswego becomes the centre of English activity on the Canadian frontier.

Baron de Longueuil secures permission from the Onondaga Council to build a new fort at Niagara.

1726

New York authorities hasten the construction of a frontier fort at Oswego.

George I grants charters of incorporation for Madras, Calcutta, and Bombay.

1727

Oct.   26 Upon the accession of George II, as King of Great Britain and Ireland, some Acadians take a qualified oath of loyalty to him.

1730

Great Britain and France agree to declare "neutral" the West India islands of Dominica, St. Vincent, and St. Lucia; St. Lucia remains a centre of contraband activities and Frenchmen reappear in some numbers.

1738

Abbé Jean Louis Le Loutre establishes an Indian mission in the heart of Nova Scotia.

1739

War of Jenkins's Ear begins.

1741

The English attempt to bring Protestant Christianity to the Indians with the establishment of a chapel at Fort Hunter, New York.

1742

Dupleix becomes superintendent of the French factory at Chandernagore.

1744

Declaration of war between the British and the French in connection with the War of the Austrian Succession.
Dupleix is made Governor of Pondicherry.
Robert Clive arrives in India.
The Six Confederated Nations block both British and French aggression.

1745

The French fortress at Louisbourg on Cape Breton Island is captured by the British under William Pepperrell.

1746

Fort St. George, and with it Madras, falls to the French under Le Bourdonnais.

Aug.　28　Sir William Johnson of New York is appointed Commissioner to, and Colonel of, the Six Nations.

1748

Apr.　24–6　Johnson at Onondaga seeks to strengthen the alliance of the Six Nations with the British; he wins their promise to meet with Governor Clinton at Albany.

Oct.　18　The Peace Treaty of Aix-la-Chapelle returns Louisbourg to the French and reaffirms the neutralization of Dominica, St. Vincent, and St. Lucia in the West Indies; Tobago is also declared neutral by diplomatic agreement between Great Britain and France.

Nov.　Eighty leaders of the Six Nations affirm their neutrality to de la Galissonière at Quebec.

1749

May	6	Edward Cornwallis is commissioned Captain General and Governor-in-Chief to lead new English colonizers to Nova Scotia.
June	22	Cornwallis arrives in Nova Scotia with 1400 colonizers.
	30	Beginning made of future 'city of Halifax.
Aug.	1	Deputies from French districts of Nova Scotia seeking religious freedom memorialize Cornwallis.
Sept.	2	The Micmac Indians send a declaration of war to Cornwallis; the French inhabitants at Annapolis Royal appeal to the Governor General of New France.
Oct.		Cornwallis forbids the Acadians to trade with the French at Louisbourg.
	26	The last day of grace for the oath of loyalty to George II to be taken by Nova Scotian inhabitants.
Nov.	16	Clive captures Arcot from the French.
		Restoration of Madras to the English.
Dec.		Two additional forts built at Halifax; Fort Edward established at Minas in the Acadian settlement; Cornwallis requests reinforcements from England.
		Temporary Governor General of New France, Comte de la Galissonière, is relieved by de la Jonquière.

1750

		The population of Quebec stands at 8,000; 44 military posts are supported by the government of New France.
		The Six Confederated Iroquois Nations number between 10,000 and 12,000 people in some 50 villages; Conrad Weiser reports on the Six Nations.
		The French build Fort Rouillé at Toronto and a fortified post, Little Niagara, above the Falls.
Jan.		Le Loutre gathers warring tribes at Chignecto, Nova Scotia, thus defeating Cornwallis's plan to occupy the Acadian settlements with troops.
April		Le Loutre burns the village of Beaubassin and the French and Canadian troops under La Corne, supported by the Acadians, occupy the region north of the Missaquash River.
	4	French and British rival armies clash west of Pondicherry.

Aug.   25   French and British "commissaries" meet in Paris under terms of the Articles of Peace to settle rival New World and Far East claims.

Sept.   The English construct Fort Lawrence on the south bank of the Missaquash.

1751

Siege of Trichinopoly by the French; Clive defends Arcot.

Abbé Piquet gets a grant for La Présentation mission on the St. Lawrence; he journeys to Great Lakes converting Indians.

May   5   La Jonquière reports the grain famine in Canada.

The French have the upper hand in the Beaubassin area with the construction of Fort Beauséjour.

July   Governor Clinton holds a conference at Albany with the Governors of other colonies and the Six Nations over French encroachments.

        5   William Johnson resigns his New York superintendency of the Indians.

1752

The French give up the siege of Trichinopoly.

Baron de Longueuil, temporary successor to La Jonquière as Governor General of New France, is replaced by the Marquis de Duquesne.

June   18   In India Jacques-François Law, commander of the French forces, surrenders the Carnatic to the British leader, Major Lawrence.

Aug.   3   Peregrine Thomas Hopson succeeds Cornwallis as Governor of Nova Scotia.

Nov.   22   Indians of eastern Nova Scotia sign a treaty of friendship with the English Governor at Halifax.

1753

May   20   The Ohio Valley Indians meet at Winchester upon the summons of Governor Dinwiddie of Virginia.

The Susquehanna Company is organized for the purpose of settling western lands claimed within the limits of the Connecticut patent of 1662.

Sept.   18 The Board of Trade addresses New York Governor Sir Danvers Osborne to call a conference between the governments of certain colonies and the Six Nations.

Oct.   12 Lieutenant Governor de Lancey takes over the government of New York upon the death of Osborne.

1754

March   6   The Duke of Newcastle succeeds to the post of First Lord of the Treasury upon the death of his brother, Henry Pelham.

June   19 The formal opening of the Albany Congress.

         24 The Congress votes unanimously in favour of a union of the colonies.

         28 Franklin's "Short Hints" become the basis of the proposed union.

July   6   The Pennsylvania Proprietors obtain at Albany a large tract of Indian land.

         9   Official negotiations are concluded between the English commissioners and the Six Nations; Thomas Hutchinson's "Representation" is presented and agreed to.

         10 The final draft of the Plan of Union by Franklin is accepted for transmission to the respective colonial Assemblies.

         11 The deed for the purchase of five million acres of Indian land is secured by the Susquehanna Company.

Aug.   Governor Dupleix leaves India, defeated and dishonoured.

Fall   The decision to send General Braddock to North America with two British regiments.

Dec.   15 The provisional treaty between the French and British Companies in India is signed at Madras.

         18 With the death of the Earl of Albemarle, British Ambassador to France, the centre of Anglo-French negotiations on territorial issues shifts to London.

1755

Feb.   20 Failure of Anglo-French diplomacy to keep the peace in India.

CORRIGENDA

PAGE 15, *line* 15, and Index, page xxiii, line 7: for "Rolland" read "Roland"

PAGES 42, 51, 53, 55 n, 101, and Index, page xxxvii: for "Michilimakinac" read "Michilimackinac"

PAGE 99, 9th *line from end of text:* for "July," read "July 1751,"

PAGE 139, *note* 80, line 7: for "William Smith, who" read "William Smith, Jr., the son of William Smith who"

PAGE 193, *line* 8: after "April" insert "1750"

PAGE 203, *line* 2: for "M" read "Abbé"

PAGE 298, *line* 14: for "Pepperell" read "Pepper-rell"

PAGE 316, *line* 2: for "January 5" read "January 5, 1752,"

PAGE 329, *line* 18: for "January" read "January 1755"

PAGE 337, 5th *line from end of text:* for "February 20" read "February 20, 1755,"

INDEX, *page viii:* for "Boishebert" and "Boishé-bert"

INDEX, *page xiii,* second column, line 3: for "1750" read "1751"

INDEX, *page xlix:* under "St. Domingue" for "267" read "268"

ZONES OF INTERNATIONAL FRICTION

CANADA

THE WEST INDIES

INDIA

1748–1754

CHAPTER I

Les Habitants

IN ATTEMPTING to analyse the factors involved in British imperial expansion in the middle of the eighteenth century we considered in the preceding volume the course of events along the northern frontier of Florida, within the lands of the Cherokee, Creeks, and Choctaw, and in Louisiana, the Illinois country, and the Ohio Valley. In continuing our study of the zones of international friction at this period in the history of the Empire we must now turn our eyes to the chief centre of French power in the New World, the Province of Canada; we must in this connection trace important developments within the region of the Great Lakes and analyse with some little care the extraordinarily delicate situation of the Six Confederated Iroquoian Nations in the face of Anglo-French rivalry and the efforts on the part of British colonials assembled at Albany in 1754 to grapple with the problem thus presented as well as with all those other factors embodied in a comprehensive plan for the defence of the western frontiers. Further, we must give our attention to the international complexities presented not only by the old-young colony of Acadia or Nova Scotia — the first French and the last British colony to be established in North America — but also by the so-called " neutral " islands of the West Indies, as well as to the position occupied respectively by the two great and rival trading companies of Great Britain and France at this juncture in the Far East — each seeking to consolidate its position — with the ultimate political and economic destiny of India and its hundreds of millions of inhabitants still to be determined. Finally, it will be necessary to turn our attention to London and Paris, to the course of diplomatic negotiation undertaken upon the conclusion of the Peace of Aix-la-Chapelle between the two crowns in a vain effort thereby to prevent the outbreak of another war, a war that statesmen in both countries felt must, were it now to come, be waged to a conclusion so decisive as to determine for all future time the great issues still awaiting settlement. In the present chapter an effort will be made to indicate the strategic importance of Canada in the contest between Great Britain and France for supremacy in North America.

The limits of the Province of Canada embodied within the governor-generalship of New France — which likewise comprised Louisiana and Isle Royale (Cape Breton) — were bewilderingly indefinite in the middle of the eighteenth century. Governor Murray in drawing up his well-known report on the previous government and actual state of that province in 1762 was obliged to confess

> " how impossible it is to ascertain exactly what part of North America the French stiled, Canada, no Chart or Map whatsoever having fallen into our hands, or public records of any kind whatsoever, to show what they understood by it." [1]

It certainly included the mouth of the St. Lawrence, but not so certainly, as will be made clear in a later chapter, the land lying southward of it; it extended northward from the St. Lawrence at least to the sources of the streams flowing into that river, but how much farther before coming into contact with the territory comprised within the patent to the Hudson's Bay Company had never been ascertained or established. Further, to the west it was understood to include the Great Lakes region, at least outside of those parts claimed and controlled by the Six Confederated Nations; still farther to the west and north of the Great Lakes its supposed boundaries again became confused with those of the Hudson's Bay Company, which claimed not only the bay but all lands drained by such river systems as those of the Nelson and the Churchill. South of the St. Lawrence and Lakes Ontario and Erie the same uncertainty existed. While there was little disposition on the part of the English to question that the Richelieu River was a part of Canada, this acquiescence did not extend to Lakes Champlain and St. Sacrement (George), which were held to lie within the territories of the Iroquoian Confederacy just as were the lands south of Lakes Erie and Ontario, although both are embraced

---

[1] This report, dated June 5, 1762, can be found in William Smith's *History of Canada*, I, Appendix, pp. 45–71.

within the St. Lawrence drainage system. Nevertheless Forts St. Frédéric, Niagara, Miami, and Ouiatenon, the last-named on the Wabash flowing southwestward, were constructed and maintained in this southern area by the Canadian authorities as symbols of possession.[2] Very naturally and properly the latter interpreted the limits of the Province in the most generous fashion and directed public policy to vindicate and uphold the same. While this was true, it may be pointed out that in a narrower sense Canada was understood by Canadians to mean more specifically that region bordering the St. Lawrence that had been the object of colonization, in contrast to the vast stretches of wilderness held as " dependencies " of the Province — using an expression employed in the royal instructions.

Waiving this difficult question of boundaries and turning to that of colonization, one may affirm that in the period under consideration Canada was beginning to present rather impressive evidence that it was emerging from much of the deep discouragement that had dogged the pathway of its founders in the seventeenth century. The painful steps in its growth may be set forth in bald figures: after over a half-century of effort there were but 3,418 white inhabitants included in the enumeration of 1666[3] — a number apparently far short of that settled within tiny Rhode Island, first colonized in 1636; by 1686, with the lapse of twenty years and as a result of the efforts of such men as the great Intendant Talon, it was credited with 12,373 whites;[4] some thirty years later, in 1719, the number had crept up to 22,530;[5] fifteen years after this it could be placed at 37,252;[6] and by 1754, according to the capitation list, at some 55,000 in round numbers,[7] as against some 40,000 occupying the reluctant soil of restricted Rhode Island, to continue our contrast.

The *habitants* — as the people were then and ever since have been called — as a rule, dwelt outside the towns.[8] Frenchmen in fact have

---

[2] While at Crown Point, Peter Kalm made the following observation: " The Englishmen insist that this fort is built on their territory and that the boundary between the French and English colonies in this locality lies between Fort St. Jean and the Prairie de la Madeleine; on the other hand, the French maintain that the boundary runs through the woods between Lake St. Sacrement and Fort Nicholson [or the great carrying-place]." *Peter Kalm's Travels in North America* (ed. A. B. Benson), II, 391–2.

[3] *Documents Relating to the Colonial History of the State of New York*, IX, 57–8.

[4] *Ibid.*, IX, 316.

[5] *Ibid.*, IX, 896–7.

[6] *Ibid.*, IX, 1047.

[7] *Ibid.*, X, 271–5.

[8] That is, of the grand total given above, 42,000 lived in the country.

always had a passionate fondness for the soil; this love of nature gripped the eighteenth-century Canadian with peculiar intensity — a love of forest, lake, and stream — in rather striking contrast to the more matter-of-fact English colonial, who thought of nature as something to be combated, subdued, and chained. But it was the great St. Lawrence, the fruition of the labour of the Great Lakes system, a river that served them so well in the summer months and was so inflexible a parent in the winter, that they loved the most. Its fertile lowlands — held within the grip of the vast Laurentian Plateau to the north and the Champlain Fault and the rocky Appalachian barrier to the south — were the source of their livelihood and here they had built their homes. Up and down the waters of the river their *canots*, *pirogues*, and *bateaux* moved to and from the market towns or from farm to farm as necessity or desire might dictate; likewise upon its lower reaches the great ships sailed upward in the late spring with goods from Europe and downward in the fall with the products of Canada before the creeping ice could lay hold upon their hulls.

Peter Kalm, moving down the St. Lawrence in 1749 from Montreal to Quebec, was impressed with the fact that the cultivation of the land, outside the environs of these two cities and of Trois Rivières, extended back from the banks only about three-quarters of an English mile.[9] " It could really be called a village, beginning at Montreal and ending at Quebec," he declared, " for the farm houses are never more than five arpents and sometimes but three apart, a few places excepted." [10] His testimony is supported by that of Captain Stoddard, who, journeying the following year from Quebec to Montreal, observed that the land within half a league on his right was full of habitations but that " from thence backward there are no inhabitants." [11] Thus along the banks of this broad and winding ribbon of silver and gold, this enchanting boulevard of nature, the *habitants* multiplied within the whitewashed stone and timber walls of their snug and picturesque dwellings. These were provided with steep, overhanging roofs and contained, as a rule, but one room and at best but three or four; the windows were covered with oiled paper, and within warmth was supplied to combat the extreme temperatures of winter by iron

---

[9] *Peter Kalm's Travels*, II, 422.

[10] *Ibid.*, II, 416. According to Governor Murray's " Report" of 1762, the arpent was ten perches, and a perch was eighteen French feet (Smith, *op. cit.*, I, Appendix, p. 46). In other words, the homes were separated as a rule by distances of between 540 and 900 French feet.

[11] *N. Y. Col. Doc.*, VI, 581.

stoves and a great fireplace where the meals were also prepared. Thus were the rude comforts provided without too much emphasis in most homes, it would appear, upon such details as scrubbing and sweeping, much to the dismay of some travellers.

The Canadians were a sturdy, hardy people, Norman in spirit if not in blood,[12] mostly inured to hardship, which, however, had not dampened the spontaneity and high spirits that characterize the French. The women, we are told, in their caps, short jackets, and skirts that were equally short, giving freedom of movement, with feet encased in sabots, sang at their work; and in their songs there was always romance. The head of the family, hat on head, his hair " behind in a cue," with pipe in mouth, prided himself upon the courtesy and dignity with which he welcomed his guests, rising as he did from his favourite chair, doffing his hat in friendly greeting, and thereupon covering his head and regaining his seat by the stove after his callers had been provided for. His position in the home was duly emphasized, especially when those of some distinction came to dine; for on such occasions he was dutifully waited upon by his good wife, who placed herself at his beck behind his chair.[13] Thus they were wont to make merry, no matter how humble their circumstances in life, with a glass or two of brandy — an article that was held to be an absolute essential not only in rendering hospitality but for the barest decency in living.

Nevertheless, our *habitant* with all his native courtesy and outward air of compliance knew how to defend his rights and interests arising within his own narrowly circumscribed world. His mind, we are repeatedly told, ran to legal subtleties and to litigation with his neighbours. But such was to be expected in any frontier community and, after all, he was, as was suggested, Norman in spirit, in general outlook on life. This meant that, as a rule, he was not only romantic in nature, high-spirited, and legally-minded, although in general quite ignorant of the law, but also deeply religious. Never was he permitted to forget the great sacrifice of our Saviour for all mankind. Every morning Kalm found both soldiers and civilians joining in the Latin

---

[12] About one-sixth of the immigrants came from Normandy, according to Abbé Freland; many other provinces, particularly Poitou, Île de France (Paris), and Pays d'Aunis with its port of La Rochelle, furnished large numbers. See A. D. DeCelles, " The Habitant, His Origin and History," *Canada and Its Provinces*, XV, 60–3.

[13] Kalm, while finding the country women submissive, notes that Canadian women in town " would willingly assume an equal if not a superior position to their husbands " (*op. cit.*, II, 417).

Kyrie Eleison.[14] Moreover, to instil in his mind an attitude of piety, here and there throughout the countryside were planted high crosses and at the foot of them were to be found all those instruments of torture that tradition declared had been used against the Son of God and of Mary the Virgin and at their top was represented the cock that crowed when St. Peter dared to deny his Master. Again, there were other reminders of the call to worship; the steeples of scores of churches, mostly substantially built of stone, could be seen as one moved along the broad waters of the river, each beckoning him to contriteness of heart and to share in the blessed miracle of the holy eucharist; and, finally, the good curé of his country parish — fifty-eight parishes there were between Quebec and Montreal [15] — a man like himself of humble circumstances, would not fail to appear at the home in times of distress and perhaps also on days of happy celebration, and always he pointed the way of salvation.

It is evident that life on the little Canadian farm, confined as it was to narrow dimensions along the waterfront but stretching far back into the deep woods, was one of extreme rustic simplicity, of simple joys and sorrows, and of only moderate cares. As a rule the *habitant* held the land *en censive*,[16] either of a lay seigneur or of the Church acting in the capacity of lord through the Bishop of Quebec or one of the various religious orders established in Canada. It is generally agreed that the required annual payments of *cens et rentes* were not especially onerous; in fact each St. Martin's Day in November when these were rendered at the seigneurie was an occasion not always of unpleasant anticipation with the gathering of all the *censitaires*. While the *cens* amounted to but a few sols, Kalm found the *rentes* in 1749 rather unequal; for a farm three arpents broad and thirty deep one might be liable — provided one's ancestor had settled early in the Province — to pay no more than from twenty to forty sols; but if the land had been taken up at a later date the annual charge might not be less than almost two *écus;* [17] the latter payment being equiva-

---

[14] *Ibid.,* II, 422.

[15] *N. Y. Col. Doc.,* VI, 581.

[16] Grants *en arrière fief* (that is, by subinfeudation) were made but were certainly not characteristic.

[17] *Op. cit.,* II, 531. Twenty *sols* were ordinarily equal to tenpence; an *écu,* to two shillings and sixpence. For an exhaustive study of French Canadian money see Adam Shortt, *Documents Relating to Canadian Currency, Exchange and Finance during the French Period.* In 1743 the sol had become depreciated in New France and it was necessary to substitute in its place a new sol, which by royal *ordonnance* was given a

lent to something over twice that ordinarily exacted in form of quit-rent in the English colonies, where two shillings on every hundred acres was rather characteristic; in fact in New England, outside of western New Hampshire, this payment was non-existent. However, just as in the English settlements, so in Canada the burden, such as it was, was lightened by the ability of those holding *en roture* to make payment as a rule in kind. As to the so-called *banalités,* for which the *habitants* were bound, these were in practice not of any significance, confined almost entirely in the eighteenth century as they were to the required use of the seigneur's grist-mill.[18] Nevertheless, one must point out that large revenues were secured by some of the seigneurs from the *censitaires,* at least by the Church, which in the eighteenth century held in mortmain much of the best land, the most favourably located, in Canada — such as much of that lying within or about the cities of Quebec, Montreal, and Trois Rivières. But one must hasten to add that the Church, it would seem, was not for this reason the object of dislike, at least on the part of the *habitant,* whose own curé shared little enough in this wealth.

The *habitants,* in other words, stood in relation to their seigneurs far differently from the peasants of France, whose numerous and just grievances were embodied in the famous *cahiers* or memorials of 1788–9. While theoretically the rights of the seigneurs were exten-sive, including, as a rule, beyond the *cens et rentes* and *banalités,* the *droit de justice,* which might be *haute, moyenne,* or *basse;* [19] while they enjoyed escheats and forfeitures of lands held in *censive* and the

value of 24 deniers (*ibid.,* II, 719). When particularly specified, *rentes* were paid in terms of the value of livres tournois; otherwise, in terms of the value of Canadian "card" money (*ibid.,* II, 730–2).

The maximum that could be charged was a sum, according to Governor Murray's General Report, "not exceeding one sol, or one halfpenny sterling, for each arpent in superficies" (Smith, *op. cit.,* I, Appendix, p. 46). Since the *arpent de Paris* was the standard arpent of Canada and equalled .84 of an acre, it meant that legally the rental on lands could be at a level quite above that prevailing in New York. In fact, Kalm in another part of his diary (*op. cit.,* II, 396) records the fact that in some parts of Canada strips of land four arpents broad and forty deep carried a rental of six French francs; this was equivalent to five shillings for 136 acres as against the New York quit-rent of two shillings per hundred acres, and of New Hampshire on the upper Connecticut of one shilling per hundred acres.

18 See W. B. Munro, "The Seigneurial System and the Colony," *Canada and Its Provinces,* II, 545–8; also by the same author, *The Seigniorial System in Canada,* Chs. VI and VII.

19 Not all seigneuries carried the right of justice. For example, between 1672 and 1675 twenty-six grants were made *sans justice* ("Remarks on the French Grants from 1672 to the Conquest," in William Smith, *History of Canada,* I, Appendix, No. VII).

corvée, providing at least a few days of labour, with the privilege of wardship and curatorship, together with ownership of treasure-trove, *droit de chasse* and *droit de pêche,* as well as the right of being consulted when the curé of the local parish was to be appointed by the bishop — yet taken all together, in practice, these, together with other rights, generally meant little more at best than a position of local pre-eminence and a fair living and at worst that the holder of them forgot his exalted position and, remembering his plebeian ancestry, took his place at the plough in the fields with the *censitaires.* For it must be pointed out that while there were, it is true, among the seigneurs those who were of noble family or who had been ennobled — some possessed of baronies — most of them were not so honoured. Further, even the nobles dwelling in Canada enjoyed no such privileged position as was provided for them in France.

Up to the year 1755 — according to an analysis of the seigneuries prepared subsequent to the fall of Canada — two hundred and twenty-eight seigneurial grants were made from the year 1674,[20] when the Crown of France took over the administration of the Province from the old West India Company. Of these, one hundred and forty came into existence before 1700; from the latter year to 1732 but seventeen grants were made; but during the period from 1732 to 1755 they amounted to seventy-one. The seigneuries varied greatly in size. Some were very small. The amount of land, however, thus comprehended in individual grants seems to have averaged about 35,000 acres or approximately 55 square miles; taken together they

---

Even those that did, brought to the seigneur little responsibility. The royal tribunals thoroughly submerged these private jurisdictions (W. B. Munro, *op. cit.,* p. 152).

[20] *Ibid.* Seigneurial grants in Canada date from 1598; under Champlain certain grants were made between 1623 and 1626; then in 1627 came the Company of One Hundred Associates which received its immense grant; on January 15, 1636 it was specifically provided that the grant in question should be held *en fief et seigneurie et justice;* the Company itself in turn made some sixty grants, many of which, however, were never exploited. In 1664 the Company of the West Indies came into existence, but it was not prepared to take up the work of its predecessor in the making of individual grants and in 1666 relinquished this right to the Crown. The year 1672 signalizes the beginning of the period of active granting of seigneuries, when the proceedings were formalized with the laying down of detailed conditions and reservations that were subsequently in the main followed but also supplemented from time to time by *édits* and *ordonnances.* For a very thorough treatment of the early seigneuries, see W. B. Munro, *The Seigniorial System in Canada,* Chs. II and III. A great source of information regarding the seigneuries in printed form is the collection of *Édits, Ordonnances Royaux, Déclarations, et Arrêts du Conseil d'État du Roi concernant le Canada* (3 vols., Quebec, 1854–6), the first volume of which is of particular importance, embodying as it does the royal ratification of concessions *en fief.*

totalled 7,985,470 acres, or about 12,498 square miles, approximately one-fourth of which total was held by the Church.[21] Thus, standing over against its neighbour, republican New England, was feudal New France.

When a seigneurial grant was made in Canada certain conditions and reservations were sure to be provided by the Crown, such as fealty and homage at the Château of St. Louis in Quebec and the presentation within forty days after receiving the grant of a plan of the seigneurie, indicating its boundaries, together with a comprehensive statement respecting it — including the total acreage and the conditions under which it was to be held. Further, the seigneur was expected to sub-grant the land or at least the greater part of it; then there was the payment of the " one-fifth " or of relief when the seigneurie was alienated; and lastly, there was at least an implied obligation of military service on the part of the seigneur — except in the case of the Church or the religious orders, largely freed of obligations to the Crown. Other conditions and reservations than the above were apt to be attached, such as the reservation of timber suitable for shipbuilding, notification of the discovery within the seigneurie of mines and minerals, and the reservation of land for highways, fortifications, and other public works and of the shore for fisheries.[22]

Here then was the seigneurie with its seigneur standing in many ways between the Crown and the *habitants* and taking his place beside the curé whose parish was generally coterminous with his domain.[23] Between him and the priest there was apt to be the fullest understanding and co-operation, especially in their relations with those placed under their control. Indeed, the curé might make his abode at the home of the seigneur. Yet neither, in the generally accepted meaning of the term, was an agent of the state. What relations

---

[21] The Church lands comprehended 2,115,178 acres; the Jesuits controlled 891,845 acres; the Bishopric and Seminary of Quebec, 693,324 acres; the Sulpicians of Montreal, 250,191 acres; the Ursulines of Quebec, 164,615 acres; other groups, such as the Ursulines of Trois Rivières, the general hospitals of Montreal and Quebec, the Hôtel Dieu of Quebec, the Sœurs Grises, and the Recollets, enjoyed smaller grants. These grants are summarized in "Lands in Canada Granted by the French Government exclusive of Islands," to be found in William Smith, op. cit., I, Appendix, No. VI; see also J. C. Taché, A Plan for the Commutation of Seigneurial Tenure (Quebec, 1854), for the Church lands calculated in terms of arpents.

[22] W. B. Munro, op. cit., p. 53, passim; see also William Smith, op. cit., I, Appendix, No. VII.

[23] In this respect the typical Canadian seigneurie and the Virginia county of the Piedmont region were alike.

the seigneur enjoyed to government were not considered to be " political." As in the case of the *habitants,* no problems of statecraft both-
ered him, for he was not permitted to concern himself with these.

The great world, in truth, was far removed from most of those who
dwelt within the Canadian seigneuries in the eighteenth century.
While it is true that elementary education was provided for the boys
and girls and that many went to the cities to continue their training,
and that the Jesuit College at Quebec was in particular a real centre
of learning and piety, where grammar, rhetoric, philosophy, and theology were effectively taught, together with physics and hydrography, yet all learning was carefully canalized. This does not imply
that books on the Index as well as others did not find their way to
New France into the libraries of the well-to-do and influential,[24] but
rather that " disturbing " works did not truly circulate. Significantly,
no printing press was permitted to exist in any portion of New France,
and books — outside of those needed for daily devotion — must have
been very scarce indeed in the homes of both seigneur and *habitant.*
Thus, undisturbed by those doubts that contemporaneously flooded
the mother country as to the justification and wisdom of the system
both secular and ecclesiastical by which society had for so long been
firmly bound, Canadians were encouraged to live in quiet and simple
faith. To most of them, in fact, *la belle France* — where many dangerous ideas were gradually being disseminated, and where also lived
the great King whom they must honour and obey and whose policies, although generally hidden from their view among the myster-
ies of state, they must support with their very lives when called upon
— was far away, for ever removed, as it were, from their sight. Even
reports of events from abroad were apt to come to them by third or
fourth hand at best. For it must be pointed out that by the middle of
the eighteenth century, with the virtual stoppage of immigration
from France that had long since taken place, even the ancestral homes
of Normandy, Poitou, and Île de France with what that frequently
implies in the way of sentimental attachment had all but faded even
from tradition among them. They had come to feel — nay, even had
been made to feel by native Frenchmen who appeared amongst them
to sojourn for greater or less periods of time — that they were, in a
sense, a distinct people. Such they had become.

---

[24] The growth of private libraries is emphasized by Richard M. Saunders in his excellent essay entitled " The Cultural Development of New France," in *Essays in Canadian History Presented to George Mackinnon Wrong,* pp. 330–3.

So our Canadian did not yearn to sail to the mother country across the broad Atlantic; he was now permanently rooted in American soil and was well persuaded, in spite of the appearance of dashing young soldiers and on rarer occasions of entrancing ladies of quality from Europe, that he himself was far happier in this great new land than he could ever be in France. No, when a yearning came over him for a view of other things, it might be, especially if he were living some distance from the city, that a trip to Quebec to see the great ships come up the river in the spring and the splendours of the churches would suffice. But if not, and particularly if he were young, the upper waters of his own broad river would be apt to beckon him. For had not his own father as a youth pushed a birch-bark canoe over the Great Lakes off to the west? Had not his uncle long since disappeared into the vast solitudes of the setting sun? Could he not satisfy that undefinable urge calling him to a life of adventure — liberated from the drudgery and monotony of tilling the land — where lost in the primeval forest he might be as free as the creatures of the wild? And should he go under the spell of this thrill, could he not realize that he would leave behind in the home an abundance of brothers and sisters to carry on — perhaps ten or a dozen or even more? They would be there, when he had left, to cultivate the kitchen garden with its peas, cabbages, pumpkins, leeks, melons, and tobacco patch, to tend the cows, horses, and chickens; yes, they would turn the field by means of the great wooden plough with its heavy wheels supporting the beam, pulled by horses working tandem or oxen in the yoke, and harvest the white Scandinavian wheat, the oats, the summer rye, and perhaps the barley.

On the other hand, if one did decide to remain at home, it was really not so hard — this life of the settled *habitant* — could one but be satisfied. There was leisure. Not all the arable land needed to be worked; for once in every two or three years that which had been cultivated could best lie fallow to take heart again, where the cattle would quietly pasture and fatten. There were also distractions — always special occasions to call one from home; there were the weekly journeys to the Friday market with the cheeses, eggs, butter, and chickens to be exchanged for imported cloth and brandy, where old friends were to be seen and perhaps new acquaintances found; there were the Sundays and the many other days of observance in the Church calendar as well as other festivals when all were very joyous and would appear in special attire and the women in every adornment. For the daughter even in the humblest family must be encouraged not to neglect her appearance, particularly when she approached the age of marriage. Indeed, in Canada a good and industrious husband was not to be had merely for the longing for a mate and a home for oneself; nor could this come to pass always by the efforts of one's parents, as was the rule in the English colonies. Even were it true that those who informed Peter Kalm that there were four women to every man in Canada were mistaken,[25] it must have seemed to many a bright-eyed girl who saw her brother and his companions with even hundreds of other young Canadians leave for the West to begin a wandering life and to end with a squaw and a family of half-breeds, that such was the case. Nevertheless, should fortune not smile upon her, she would at least have the consolation of realizing that after that secret hope and the bloom of youth had passed away there would still be a place awaiting her, perhaps in or near Quebec, or in Montreal or Trois Rivières, where behind convent walls she could be spiritually wedded, and where her remaining days could be passed in security and good works,[26] or perhaps, as a Sister of the Congregation, free in this case to live where her services were needed in instructing young girls and in charity.

But Canada of the eighteenth century, we must be reminded at this point, meant not only the smiling farms of the *habitants* along the St. Lawrence and the Richelieu — it meant Quebec, Montreal, and Trois Rivières. These all taken together with the countryside were a world by themselves, an isolated world during the long winter months when the river was frequently frozen solid or at least its waters packed with masses of ice that prohibited all intercourse with the outside world except, perchance, across the snow to Albany or to Nova Scotia. In the spring of the year — some years as early as in the month of May — the ships would at last venture up the river. With the passage of the sand bars and other obstructions on its lower course, at last the mariners and passengers would come into view of the Church of St. Anne; this was always a good omen and a signal for great rejoicing and the discharge of artillery — for the dangers of the voyage were now left behind. Then some miles farther up the river

---

[25] *Op. cit.*, II, 395.

[26] " I was told by several people here, some of which were ladies," Kalm recorded in his journal while at Quebec, "that none of the nuns went into a convent, till she had attained to an age in which she had small hopes of ever getting a husband " (*ibid.*, II, 445–6).

appeared suddenly on the horizon the outlines of the capital of New France, the centre of the gayest and most fastidious life in all the New World in the middle of the eighteenth century.

Not that Quebec was a large city. In fact, Captain Stoddard declared in 1750 that it did not contain "above half the number of houses at most" to be found within the confines of New York; [27] its population of eight thousand [28] represented indeed about one-third that of either Boston or Philadelphia. But where else in North America was there such architectural pretension, such an air of refinement, such pomp and ceremony, such a concourse of talent and wit? "I have found more learned men in Canada," declared a distinguished European traveller who had recently visited Philadelphia and New York and had lately arrived at Quebec, "than I imagined had been in all America." [29] Indeed, the somewhat insignificant-appearing hunchback Michael Rolland Barrin, Comte de la Galissonière, scholar, statesman, and gallant naval officer, who was acting in 1749 as Governor General of New France, and Jean François Gauthier, the royal physician, who both welcomed Professor Kalm, seemed to epitomize the cultivated spirit of those who had now assumed leadership in promoting enterprise and the amenities of life within the Province.[30] Not only were the King's officers from France as a rule skilled in the arts and sciences but he found that the Jesuits also excelled "in several parts of learning." Here, besides this air of learning, there was that of wealth and splendour. Even on ordinary days gentlemen ap-

[27] N. Y. Col. Doc., VI, 580.

[28] Ibid., X, 271–5.

[29] Extract of a letter from a Swedish gentleman at Quebec, August 6, 1749, Philadelphia Advices, Maryland Gazette, November 29, 1749. Peter Kalm arrived in Quebec late in the afternoon of the 5th of August, and was undoubtedly the author. Under date of July 2, 1749 Kalm records in his diary: "I found that the people of distinction, in general here [Canada], had a much greater taste for natural history and other parts of literature, than in the English colonies, where it was every body's sole care and employment to scrape a fortune together, and where the sciences were held in universal contempt" (op. cit., I, 375–6). This statement rather nettled the translator and editor, J. R. Forster, of the English edition of 1771, who took occasion to refer to the scientific activities of Cadwallader Colden, Benjamin Franklin, and John Bartram, and to those of Alexander Garden, subsequent to Kalm's observations, and to venture the opinion "that the English in America have contributed a greater share toward promoting natural history, than any nation under heaven, and certainly more than the French, though their learned men are often handsomely pensioned by their great Monarque . . ." (ibid., footnote).

[30] "He must have a mighty soul," declared the Indians after beholding de la Galissonière, "since with such a base body, our Great Father has sent him such a distance to command us" (N. Y. Col. Doc., VI, 533).

peared in lace, with swords, and the gay-hearted ladies with hair curled and powdered and ornamented with glittering bodkins and aigrettes and in shoes with such high and narrow heels that to a stranger it was "surprising how they walk on them." [31] Here even the wives and daughters of merchants presented themselves, it is recorded, each day in full dress, "and as much adorned as if they were to go to court." [32] Here people of the better class in the midst of the sparkling conversation dined with a profusion and extravagance of dishes that might well grace the table of the greatest of kings — with poultry and meats — the latter in the form of roasts, fricassees, and ragouts — with salads, fruits, sweetmeats, cheese, and a variety of wines. Other evidences of wealth were not lacking. The table service of the Governor General at the Palace was of such quantity and value that men hesitated to risk it to the hazard of transportation back to France and it became the basis of negotiation between the incumbent of that high office and his designated successor.

The city then as today consisted of the Upper and the Lower Towns, with the houses of the latter three or four stories in height, quite crowded together; there the merchants were apt to have their homes as well as their warehouses and shops; its damp streets were narrow and "very rugged." Likewise, upon the St. Charles in a second Lower Town, flanked on either side by the royal storehouse and the prison, stood the home of the Intendant, a great building — standing on the foundations of another structure, originally designed by Talon as a brewery — where the business of the Province was conducted. There at the Intendancy François Bigot, though not of the nobility, lived in almost regal manner, with a splendour even surpassing that of the Governor General. Most of the public buildings, however, were to be found in the Upper Town together with the homes of the people of quality. Here there was no crowding together of structures; spacious gardens everywhere greeted the eyes; there stood the Palace of the Governor General, there both the Cathedral and the Palace of the Bishop of Quebec, there the vast outlines of the College of the Jesuits, where young men of native talent could be educated — perhaps the largest and finest building in all North America; there the home of the Recollets, together with the *Séminaire* for the lay

---

[31] Kalm, *op. cit.*, II, 402–3. This reference to the women by Kalm was made at Montreal. But the Montreal women copied the Quebec women, who in turn sought the latest styles from Paris.

[32] *Ibid.*, II, 431.

clergy, the Convent of the Ursulines, the Hôtel Dieu for the sick, and a number of noble churches " beautifully ornamented and very rich." [33]

To protect the capital of all New France — this city of gracious and abundant living — a high wall of native limestone with bastions was by 1750 nearing completion to cover the land side; [34] this had been undertaken by the authorities after the solemn warning that came with the capture of Louisbourg in the late war.[35] As to the protection of the river front, there was the great rock rising sheer from the water, together with the bristling cannon of four powerful batteries, totalling some seventy-seven pieces, so distributed as to rake approaching ships and boats. In fact this queen of American provincial capitals now had become France's citadel of the New World.

Next to Quebec among the towns of Canada stood Montreal, with a population in 1754 one-half that of the former. With its four thousand inhabitants it was surpassed in the number of its citizens by many towns in the English colonies — by even such places as Middletown, Norwich, and New Haven, and almost equalled by Wallingford, all in Connecticut.[36] Its real importance, however, could not be properly gauged by this fact. It was the greatest fur-trading centre of all New France. There were to be found the warehouses of the Compagnie des Indes; there the places of business of the leading merchants who dealt in trading goods; there congregated each fall the *voyageurs* after half a year in the wilderness; there in the spring the deputies of the Indian tribes to meet the Governor General and to receive the King's present. The city, laid out in the form of a rectangular parallelogram with long, broad, and straight streets crossed by shorter ones at right angles, enjoyed a pleasant and advantageous location. While most of its homes were of timber and were neatly built but unpretentious, yet there was the castle reserved for the use of the Governor General, where he usually spent the winter, and churches of stone that were not without dignity, especially the great church belonging to the Order of St. Sulpice, which was declared to be " by far the finest, both in regard to its outward and inward ornaments, not only in this place but in all Canada." [37] The Seminary of this order

[33] *N. Y. Col. Doc.*, VI, 580.

[34] *Ibid.* This work was under the supervision of the naval engineer de Léry.

[35] *Ibid.*, X, 15; Arch. Nat., Col., B. 89: 172–190; for de la Galissonière's instructions, see *ibid.*, B. 86: 78.

[36] *Connecticut Colonial Records*, XIV, 483–92.

[37] *Peter Kalm's Travels*, II, 412.

likewise was able to occupy a very pretentious home since it was seigneur of the island of Montreal and from this source secured a large revenue, not a little of which incidentally found its way to France; then there were the College of the Franciscans, the Jesuit home, a nunnery, and the King's hospital for sick soldiers, together with quarters for the King's officers and troops. While the social life there was not so gay as at Quebec, Peter Kalm found the ladies of the city more beautiful than those of the former but also that they were accused of being "much wanting in French good breeding," critical of strangers, and "contaminated by the pride and conceit of the Indians," [88] as well as very jealous indeed of the women of the capital city, who were constantly brought in touch with French gentlemen and ladies sojourning there and but seldom in Montreal.

Between the two cities was Trois Rivières, little more than a village, counting but eight hundred souls, including several hundred of the workers employed at the royal smelter and forges of St. Maurice, located some distance back from the St. Lawrence and slightly to the west. Yet it was the third largest centre of population in Canada. By the middle of the eighteenth century the town had long since passed the peak of its earlier prosperous condition when much of the fur trade had centred there, and had to wait in patience for some generations before it would once again be carried forward on the wave of new enterprises. Yet here were to be found the home of the local Governor, two substantially built churches, a nunnery, and a house for the Franciscans — all of which tended to give it an appearance of importance that in actuality it did not possess. New England, in fact, was filled with towns surpassing it in both population and wealth. The other villages of the Province — such as stockaded Prairie de la Magdelene, La Chine, and Petite Rivière, and those located at Baie St. Paul and Terre d'Eboulemente — were really little more than a church, a parsonage, a school for the boys and girls, and a few homes for tradesmen.[89] Therefore it may be emphasized that within the limits of Canada there were but two places, each with a limited population, that were characterized by those activities generally associated with town life in contrast to those of the countryside. Canada really therefore meant the country of the *habitant*.

It was upon this scene that Jacques Pierre de Taffanel, the Marquis

---

[88] *Ibid.*, II, 525.
[89] *Ibid.*, II, 415.

de la Jonquière, appeared at Quebec in August 1749 to relieve de la Galissonière of his temporary appointment as Governor General. A man of great height, presenting an imposing appearance, every inch the aristocrat of old France, somewhat over sixty years of age, La Jonquière, a native of sunny Languedoc, and possessed of great wealth, had for many years served his King with distinction on the seas. In the midst of the late war he had received his appointment, but his arrival in Canada had been delayed when he and his flagship together with two other ships of the line of the squadron under his command had in 1747 fallen into the hands of the English. As a result of the sharp encounter that had taken place, he carried not only an honourable wound but also an unsullied record of bravery. Now, at last, upon the great feast-day of the Ascension of the Virgin and in the presence of the entire populace of the city, with cannon roaring and church bells pealing, he stepped ashore from his ship. Clothed in red velvet trimmed with gold lace and preceded by his bodyguard in costumes of green and followed by a great concourse of those of high and low estate, he thereupon made his way to the Upper Town. After the celebration of High Mass at the Cathedral he then proceeded to the Palace to take up the duties of the governor-generalship of New France.

In coming to Canada La Jonquière brought with him not only his royal commission but his instructions.[40] The latter made clear to him a fact that he must have known, that New France, over which he was now placed, was not only one of the earliest possessions of the King of France in America but the most extensive, stretching as it did from Isle Royale (Cape Breton) and the mouth of the St. Lawrence to the region of the Great Lakes and beyond and then southward to the mouth of the Mississippi. He was called upon to protect and further the interests of this vast empire; it should, however, be made clear that the Governors of Isle Royale and of Louisiana were also under particular instructions from the King, receiving direct orders from him, so that La Jonquière's chief responsibility after all was to watch over the welfare of Canada in time of peace and to defend it in war. To accomplish the latter end he had at his disposal twenty-eight companies of regular soldiers — eight hundred and twelve men in all, excluding the officers — and some twelve thousand militia — according

---

[40] The instructions are dated April 30, 1749; these are to be found in the Archives Nationales, Colonies, B. 89: 172–90.

to the official estimate of the entire available man-power of Canada fit for military service.[41] Further, he could rely upon places of strength. Not only was Quebec completing its new fortification, but to the west Montreal was already encased by a great bastioned wall with moat and was in possession of the Battery Royale, erected on the hill in the centre of the city and so placed as to sweep both the river and the land approaches. Farther to the west there were also Fort Niagara defending the passage to Lake Erie, and Fort Frontenac guarding the entrance to the St. Lawrence — each, however, in need of repair. On the southern confines of the Province at Crown Point upon Lake Champlain there was Fort St. Frédéric. There, perched upon a rock and surrounded by high, thick walls, loomed its lofty tower, and from bottom to top through apertures protruded the muzzles of cannon ready for any contingency.[42] Finally, protecting the mouth of the St. Lawrence and the Gulf, the great fortress of Louisbourg was once again in the hands of the French and already plans for its strengthening were taking shape. These six fortified places were also supported by such posts as that of St. Jean, a wooden structure built in 1748 to serve as a supply depot for Fort St. Frédéric at a point where the waters of Lake Champlain flow into the Richelieu, as well as those widely scattered throughout the Indian country, at each of which was to be found at least a small body of troops and at Fort Detroit a garrison of considerable size.

Finally, as a defence for Canada the Governor General was expected to depend upon the many powerful Indian tribes in alliance with the French, which could be relied upon with proper management now as in the past to raise a barrier against the hostile thrusts delivered from time to time by the English dwelling to the south. These people of the forest were under his special guardianship. Each year in the month of May, and before his return to Quebec for the summer months, he was expected to meet with their deputies at Montreal, where in solemn deliberation he would call upon them and their brethren to maintain untarnished the chain of friendship and to resist the blandishments of the English, and would distribute the King's present of arms and ammunition, as well as of less warlike articles. Small groups of them had, moreover, been Christianized, partly civilized, and colonized, as, for example, the Hurons at Lorette

---

[41] Ibid.

[42] For a recent detailed study of the region dependent upon Fort St. Frédéric, see G. O. Collidge, The French Occupation of the Champlain Valley, 1609–1759.

near Quebec; the Abenaki at Becancourt and at St. Francis near Trois Rivières; and the Iroquois at Sault St. Louis and at the Lake of the Two Mountains in the neighbourhood of Montreal.[43] While to the Jesuits had been assigned the chief task of propagating the faith among the natives — outside of the last-named mission, which had been committed to the Sulpician fathers of Montreal — these settled Indians were expected, as were their brethren living in a savage state, to look to the Governor General for guidance in all matters affecting their welfare other than in the realm of the spiritual.

Thus the safety of the Province was expected to lie in its extreme isolation, in the presence of a body of regular soldiers brought largely from France and supported by a militia trained from childhood to the use of arms, in its strategically located fortresses, forts, and posts, and finally in the Indian alliances. But the effectiveness of each of these factors to accomplish its purpose depended to a large extent upon the quality of leadership of the King's representative. In other words, to an unusual degree was the Governor General able to determine, as a rule, the immediate and future prospects of Canada in her relations with the outside world. To him the King and his ministers were compelled to turn as the chief source of information and advice with respect to edicts, declarations, and *ordonnances* that were to embody the official policy to be pursued in all matters of great public import relating to the Province. These were some of the responsibilities that now faced La Jonquière at the Château St. Louis.

However, a Governor General did not stand alone in administering the affairs of Canada. Ever since the days of Talon there had been at his side to aid him and also as frequently to check and oppose him the Intendant, who at this juncture, as has been made clear, was François Bigot, late Commissaire Ordonnateur of Isle Royale before the fall of Louisbourg. Early in 1748 he had received a commission to this high office [44] in spite of criticism levelled against his conduct of public affairs on Cape Breton. To these two great officials were issued joint instructions, with the admonition that nothing could be so opposed to the good service and tranquillity of New France as a lack of co-operation. Yet where difference of opinion might arise on any point that could not be accommodated within the Province, each was expected to present a statement to the Minister of the Marine so that with all

---

[43] There were also Algonquian and Nipissing at the Lake of the Two Mountains.

[44] His commission is dated January 1, 1748 (for this see Arch. Nat., Col., D² 3: 9); he arrived at Quebec on August 25 (N. Y. Col. Doc., X, 177).

the essential facts before him the latter could under the King's authority issue his orders. Nevertheless, when it came to any matter demanding immediate action, the views of the Governor General were always to prevail until the pleasure of His Most Christian Majesty could be known.[45]

A comparison of the joint instructions issued to the Governor General and the Intendant of New France with those sent to the Governor and Commissaire Ordonnateur of Louisiana [46] will show to what extent the two followed a common pattern. In each case the military power was vested in the hands of the Governor General or the Governor, as was the control of Indian relations. The control of food supplies, munitions of war, the royal storehouses and magazines, the provincial treasury and public finance, the hospitals, and the administration of justice and local police regulations, with the issuing of local *ordonnances* relating thereto, pertained to the office of the Intendant or of that of the Commissaire Ordonnateur, to which was attached in each case that of President of the Superior Council. Only when an extraordinary meeting of that body was to be held — when it might be called upon to consider matters other than the routine pleas, appeals, and judgments — was the Governor General or the Governor, as the case might be, requested or even expected to attend.[47] But the Council in neither instance enjoyed any share of the executive or administrative authority outside that of rendering justice and offering advice when called upon to do so.[48] Responsibility for good government and general administration, in other words, was concentrated in the hands of the two chief representatives of the Crown. What is more, they and the Superior Council were neither embarrassed nor hampered by the presence of lawyers acting as the champions of the people — those " *gens de practique et de Pallais* " (*sic*) — since " *l'expérience n'a que trop fait connaître combien ces sortes de gens sont dangereux pour les colonies. . . .*" [49]

Beyond the powers that were thus distinctly conferred upon one

---

[45] The joint instructions to La Jonquière and Bigot issued April 30, 1749 are to be found in the Arch. Nat., Col., B. 89: 191–201.

[46] For those of December 23, 1748 to the Governor and Ordonnateur of Louisiana see Arch. Nat., Col., B. 87: 288–93.

[47] Arch. Nat., Col., B. 89: 191–201. It will be noted that the old seventeenth-century struggle between Governor General, Bishop of Quebec, and Intendant to control the Council had been settled in favour of the last named.

[48] In 1754 in the enumeration there was listed beyond the President, a chief councillor and nine ordinary councillors (N. Y. Col. Doc., X, 271).

[49] Arch. Nat., Col., B. 89: 191–201.

or the other there were those to be exercised jointly by the Governor General and the Intendant, as well as by the Governor and the Commissaire Ordonnateur; these involved joint reports respecting the administration of justice and joint recommendations with reference to the filling of vacancies in the courts, the granting of land concessions, the best means of augmenting the population, and, while mentioned last, not to be considered least in importance, the extending of religion.

Not only in New France was all power concentrated in the hands of the direct representatives of the King, but this paternalistic control embodied fully the mercantilistic principles of the age. Accordingly, the *habitants* were to produce raw materials: such crops as wheat, flax, and hemp, especially the first-named, for their own needs; also horses, salt, fish, and lumber for the French West Indies, together with furs and train oil, as well as fish, to be exchanged for the merchandise of the mother country. As to industry, this was to be encouraged only in three fields: the construction of ships and the production of iron — the latter a royal enterprise carried on, as has been noted, at St. Maurice — and of naval stores, some of which, such as tar, were produced near Crown Point and at Baie St. Paul. Other manufactures were to be supplied from France. The keynote was the increase of commerce between Canada and the mother country and the other possessions of the latter, while providing the fullest protection to the interests of the French merchants and industrialists.

It will be well to examine the workings of this system. Before the disorganization that had accompanied the outbreak of the late war, Canada had been exporting — according to a report drawn up in April 1748, apparently by de la Galissonière — furs to the annual value of a million five hundred thousand livres tournois, or, in the English equivalent, £64,125; [50] of this total the beaver skins were valued at eight hundred thousand livres, or £33,336.6/6.[51] In addition, the

---

[50] The livre tournois was equal to tenpence sterling. General Murray in his famous report of 1762 gives the figures for the value of the furs exported with duties paid thereon in 1754 and 1755 as respectively 1,547,885 livres, 11 sous (£64,495.4/7 1/2) and 1,265,650 (£52,735.8/4). However, he went on to remark that intelligent traders estimated the value of this article, one year with another, to be near £140,000 sterling and thought that "a considerable quantity was run" (William Smith, *History of Canada*, I, Appendix, pp. 66–7).

[51] This report attached to the *mémoire* prepared by M. Silhouette and the Comte de la Galissonière in December 1750 for His Most Christian Majesty is among the transcripts in the Canadian Archives, the original of which is to be found in the C¹¹ A series of the Archives Nationales, Colonies. Only the main portion of this report is printed

Province was able to send away three thousand casks of fish oil, fifty thousand hundredweight of flour, twenty-five hundredweight of peas, twelve hundredweight of ship biscuits, together with some vegetables, salted beef, pork, and salmon — the total value of which was not indicated.[52] Further than this some thirty small vessels belonging to the inhabitants participated in the cod fisheries, which, however, were mainly supported by the coming each year from the various ports of France of two to three hundred ships, each of two to five hundred tons' burden. Whaling was also carried on in the St. Lawrence to some advantage, but this was by business interests of Bayonne; and, as was previously stated, iron was produced — between one hundred and fifty and two hundred tons — at St. Maurice, some of which went to Brest and some to Rochefort. But this is all that could be credited to Canada according to the report referred to above. It had no manufactures — outside of those of the home for its immediate members — except those that took place at the royal ironworks, where some cast-iron cannon and mortars of inferior quality besides iron stoves, kettles, and bar iron were produced to meet some of the pressing needs of the Province. It is true that shipbuilding for the King's account was active in 1749 at the shipyard slightly below Quebec, where, according to Kalm, "several ships" were being constructed. He declared, however, that before his departure from Canada orders had arrived forbidding the building of any further ships of war except those already on the stocks, by reason of the fact that it had been found that the American oak used in the hulls did not last as long as that of Europe.[53]

As against an exportable total of perhaps a million and three quarters livres' value at the most, the imports for the same period were estimated in the report previously mentioned at from five to six mil-

---

as one of the *Documents Relative to the Colonial History of the State of New York*, X, 220–32.

[52] In 1754 the total value of the exports of Canada, outside of articles sent to Louisbourg was £1,719,683 10s. of which total — according to figures presented in the Shelburne Papers, 64: 170–2 — furs accounted for £1,548,588 10s. In that year no flour, biscuits, vegetables, beef, or pork were exported and but 1,622 barrels of fish oil, 299 of dried cod, and 10 of salted salmon. However, 6,585 pounds of dried ginseng roots gathered in the Canadian woods, valued at £5 per pound, were sent, together with some planks, joists, small spars, and other trifles.

[53] *Peter Kalm's Travels*, II, 478. Writing to Vaudreuil and Bigot July 15, 1755, the President of the Navy Board stated that he was grieved that the results obtained in building ships in Canada were not such as to permit him to continue this activity. *Le Caribou* and *Le St. Laurent*, he declared, were of poor quality and the opinion at Brest of a third Canadian-built ship, *L'Algonkin*, was not high (Arch. Nat., Col., B. 101: 16).

lion [54] — an adverse balance of striking proportions and to be contrasted to an estimated favourable balance of 300,000 livres in 1741 during the administration of Beauharnois and Hocquart.[55] These imports consisted roughly of a thousand bales of heavy cloth manufactured at Montauban in central France, which fabric the Canadians and also the Indians preferred for their clothing, together with Siam cotton cloth, flannel, camlets, linen thread, sail-cloth, white blankets from Rouen for the Indians, firearms from Saint-Étienne, hardware, earthenware, from six to seven thousand casks of Bordeaux wine, two thousand of brandy, two hundred of vinegar, with quantities of olive oil, soap, salt, spices, and numerous other luxury articles with which each year from thirty to forty ships of from one hundred and twenty to four hundred tons' burden were laden at the French ports; in addition, there was the annual ship sent by the King which brought supplies for the garrisons and presents for the Indians.[56] As can be appreciated, only a portion of these ships — few as they were in contrast to the thousand or more that at this period sailed each year out of the waters of Massachusetts Bay — were needed for transporting the available exports of Canada either to France or to the West Indies. The remainder had to secure their cargoes from the French fisheries of the Newfoundland Banks or to return home largely in ballast. However, one item not listed that they carried to France, although insignificant in bulk, was of the highest importance: the bills of exchange drawn either by the Intendant against the royal treasury or by the representatives of the Compagnie des Indes in New France against that corporation. From 1749 to 1756 the adverse balance did not change; [57] in fact, during this period of seven years it totalled

---

[54] The imports into Canada in 1754 were valued at £5,202,461 15s. Of this total, wines and other liquors came to the astounding total of £1,418,951 7s. 6d. The adverse balance was £3,482,778 5s. — not including commodities sent from Quebec to Fort Louisbourg.

[55] For their report of October 25, 1741, see Arch. Nat., Col., C11 I. 75: 79; Shortt, Canadian Currency, Exchange and Finance, II, 690–2.

[56] In 1754 seventeen ships came to Canada from Bordeaux, nine from La Rochelle, two from Harfleur, and one from Saint-Malo, Havre, Bayonne, and Marseille respectively; in all thirty-two from France. In addition five came from St. Domingue, four from Martinique, and one from Guadeloupe (Shelburne Papers, 64: 169).

[57] In 1749 exports were valued at 1,414,900 livres, imports at 5,682,090; in 1750 they were respectively 1,337,000 and 5,154,861; in 1751, 1,515,932 and 4,439,490; in 1752, 1,554,400 and 6,047,820; in 1753, 1,706,130 and 5,195,733; in 1754, 1,576,616 and 5,147,621; and in 1755, 1,515,730 and 5,203,272. For this see " An Account of the Amount of the Value of the Imports and Exports While Canada was a Colony of France," William Smith, op. cit., Appendix No. V.

26,260,179 livres — a sum over and beyond the value of the exports. This was not absorbed — as adverse balances with respect to trade generally were within the British Empire — by many compensating so-called hidden items that tended to maintain an equilibrium, but became an accumulating dead-weight obligation, supported at best in Canada by a growing mountain of credit devices such as card money, treasury notes, and bills of exchange with the date of payment postponed, which finally, before repudiation came, amounted to some eighty million livres.[58]

That New France, even before the war that brought its downfall, was a great financial liability to the Crown, in spite of the fact that its development, such as it enjoyed, had covered a period of over one hundred and forty years, is indicated by the fact that the royal expenditures in 1749 for maintaining it amounted to 2,031,199 livres, as against which there were colonial receipts — secured from all sources, including the three per cent import and export tax on commodities provided for in 1748 — of but 233,016 livres. This meant that drafts to the amount of 1,798,974 livres had to be drawn against the royal treasury for that year by M. Bigot.[59] Indeed, the cost of maintaining Canada after peace was restored in 1748 was even more than during the period of the war and twice that of the period preceding it.[60] By the middle of 1753 outstanding drafts against the treasury had mounted to the sum of 3,495,675 livres. Thereupon the Intendant was solemnly warned by the French Minister that unless some lessening of colonial expenditures took place " *il seroit absolument impossible de les f[air]e acquittés, et il faudroit nécessairement y renoncer, quelque inconvénient qui en pût resulter.*" [61] In place of this resolute measure of repudiation, however, it was decided that the payment of the annual drafts should be spread over two or three years.[62] But nothing could put an end to the excess charges. By the late spring of 1754 the Minister informed Bigot that all available resources had been exhausted and that if it were necessary to choose between the trade of

---

[58] Adam Shortt, " The Colony in Its Economic Relations," *Canada and Its Provinces,* II, 520–3.

[59] Bigot to the Minister, October 28, 1750, Arch. Nat., Col., C11 A. 96: 82–95. Although up to the summer of 1752 the bills of exchange drawn against the treasury by the Ordonnateur of Isle Royale were promptly paid (Arch. Nat., Col., C11 I. 98: 126; Shortt, *Currency and Exchange,* II, 794), this does not seem to be true of the Canadian bills of exchange.

[60] Arch. Nat., Col., B. 97: 3.

[61] Arch. Nat., Col., B. 97: 158–63.

[62] Arch. Nat., Col., B. 97: 39.

Canada and other things it had been decided to let the trade fail at all risks;[63] he was further warned that unless expenditures could be reduced to the point where they stood some years ago, the Crown would be forced to the desperate expedient of giving up the colony.[64] But in the face of this possibility, a public loan in France was floated in an effort to meet the accumulated demands upon the colonial treasury.[65]

Perhaps no factor played a greater part in this ruinous public economy — outside of the extravagance involved in Indian presents — than that those who were taking the leadership in the development and exploitation of the resources of Canada almost without exception looked to the enjoyment of a privileged position. Such was the situation of the Compagnie des Indes, which possessed a monopoly of the beaver trade, of the Bayonne Company, with a whaling monopoly in the St. Lawrence, of that of Sieur Corva and Associates, with a salmon fishery on the same river, and of the walrus and seal monopoly of the Magdalen Islands enjoyed by the Sieur Pascund. The evil did not stop there, choking as it did free enterprise and competition. The Minister of the Marine in a letter to Bigot dated June 1, 1753 declared that excessive expenditures in maintaining Canada had come as the result of every service being turned over to some favoured individual. He asserted that

> "Sr. Bréard is quoted for all charterings for the King, the Sr. Péan for the supplies of flour and vegetables, the Sr. Claverie for all other supplies for the [King's] store at Quebec, and one Calot for those at the slaughterhouse. The same disorder is said to exist in Montreal, where Sr. Martel, store-keeper, furnishes supplies of all kinds. . . . Furthermore . . . they [that is, particular individuals] have taken possession of all trade at Detroit, and it is even stated that M. Varin is implicated in those dealings."[66]

The cupidity of Bigot, with all his talent for public administration, and other servants of the King during this critical period in the life of New France, almost staggers belief. As is well known, after the collapse of French power in North America the Intendant and some fifty other people were accused of gigantic frauds and peculations and after a momentous trial in Paris, lasting three years, were ordered to

---

[63] Arch. Nat., Col., B. 99: 26.
[64] Arch. Nat., Col., B. 99: 20.
[65] Arch. Nat., Col., B. 100: 68.
[66] Arch. Nat., Col., B. 99: 27. For Bréard's defence, see *ibid.*, C[11] A. 98: 417.

restore to the royal treasury the sum of twelve million livres.[67] Even La Jonquière, although a man of great wealth, was accused of jobbery. It was customary for the Governor General to expect two per cent of all the beaver secured by the Compagnie des Indes or its money equivalent.[68] Further, a member of the Superior Council, the Sieur de St. Sauveur, who was also La Jonquière's secretary, was accorded the exclusive trade in brandy with the Indians; as a result the Indian traders were forced to pay him " an enormous premium " to secure this article, the profits upon which were shared with the Governor General; the latter also secured the Deanery of Quebec for his nephew, the Abbé de Cabanac de Taffanel, a man of small qualifications, and for another nephew, Captain de Bonne de Miselle, a share in the exclusive trade of the Sault Ste. Marie and a patent for the lands thereabout.[69] Even the royal ironworks at St. Maurice near Trois Rivières did not escape. Peter Kalm, who examined them in 1749, was impressed with the peculiar advantages that these enjoyed; the ore lying near the surface of the ground was located conveniently to the smelters, as were limestone and wood to be transformed into charcoal; further, the two large forges and the smaller ones were likewise constructed close to the smelters; and, finally, the products produced at the former could be economically shipped by water to various parts of the Province and sold without competition from any source. Yet while the " many officers and overseers " had very good homes and appeared to Kalm in " very affluent circumstances," the King was obliged to meet annual deficits in their operation.[70] Only in 1752, after the death of the manager of these works, the Sieur Cugnet, who had pretended that they were unremunerative, was it discovered that he had accumulated a sufficient personal fortune to square all accounts with the King as well as with the other creditors.[71]

---

[67] For Bigot see Adam Shortt, *Documents Relating to Canadian Currency, Exchange and Finance*, II, 764–70, *passim*; also Shortt, " The Colony and Its Economic Relations," *Canada and Its Provinces*, II, 524–8. For example, Bigot, who had acquired the wife of Major Péan as mistress, in order perhaps to comfort the husband loaned him large sums from the public treasury with which to buy wheat for the King's account and then purchased it at a great advance in price (William Smith, *op. cit.*, I, 220–1). Péan was later fined the sum of six hundred thousand livres.

[68] Arch. Nat., Col., C^{11} A. 87: 266.

[69] Arch. Nat., Col., B. 91: 29–30; *ibid.*, B. 93: 24 1/2; Smith, *op. cit.*, I, 221–2.

[70] *Op. cit.*, II, 420–1.

[71] Arch. Nat., Col., B. 95: 46. These forges managed by the Sieurs Estébe and Martil de Bellevue between 1741 and 1747 produced iron valued at 387,653 livres with an expense about equal to the receipts. At that time iron valued at 50,432 livres was in the storehouses and represented an additional asset (*ibid.*, B. 85: 7).

In the light of this situation, with jobbing and favouritism the order of the day, it is not surprising that La Jonquière should be informed by the Minister in 1751 that in Canada many of the inhabitants "long only for independence even at the sacrifice of their own security."[72] Indeed, in 1749 the Governor General and the Intendant in asking for an increase in the number of regular troops had declared that one important reason was the necessity of controlling the people, who displayed "*une indépendance extraordinaire*" and who could be impressed only by the presence of a considerable body of soldiers.[73] When the movement to concentrate a large force upon the Ohio River and its approaches was carried into effect in 1753, we are informed that the *habitants* felt — and doubtless not without good cause — that they were greatly oppressed; for each family with three sons was compelled to provide two, and each with two, one; a sacrifice for a military adventure that seems to have fallen quite beyond the range of their personal interests.[74] This arbitrary treatment, in fact, was so deeply resented by the populace that the streets of the towns of Canada, it was declared, rang with "seditious libels" against the Governor General, the Intendant, and the Council, with the result that an *ordonnance* had to be passed severely punishing such acts.[75]

Canada, in truth, was in no position to sustain without tremendous strain any extraordinary war-time demand upon her slender resources. This is evident in what has been set forth not only with respect to commerce and finance, but also with respect to subsistence supplies. Writing on May 5, 1751 to the Minister of the Marine, La Jonquière referred to the lack of grain in the Province and the difficulty of providing bread for the people. In this connection he made clear not only that all the wheat harvested in 1749 had been consumed but that that secured in the harvest of 1750 — a very bad harvest year — was near exhaustion. What so alarmed the people, who actually threatened an uprising (*émeute*), he declared, was that there was no assurance that the harvest of 1751 would be more abundant than that of the preceding year because of the inability of the farmers as yet to sow their crops on account of the continuance of ice and snow. He therefore made clear his inability to meet the insistent

---

[72] Arch. Nat., Col., B. 93: 6.

[73] Arch. Nat., Col., C11 A. 93: 35.

[74] The testimony of Jean Silvestre, a French trader, before the Governor and Council of New York, on May 26, 1755 (New York Hist. Society, Mss. 80: 164).

[75] This is contained in a letter written to Governor Shirley by a Mr. Smith of Cape Cod who was in Canada for four years, from 1749 to 1753 (N. Y. Col. Doc., VI, 826).

demands of Louisbourg and the posts on the border of the Nova Scotian peninsula for food supplies, confessing that he did not dare to
load ships, with the slender resources still available in Canada, to
bring this relief lest the people of Quebec, perceiving that they were
being deprived of their bread, would resort to violent extremes.[76] Bigot writing on May 8 also emphasized the dangerous food shortage,
asserting:

> "The harvest the past year was so bad that I was scarcely able to
> provide for Montreal and Quebec. By the beginning of November
> [1750] the first-named was without bread — the bakers being unable
> to buy wheat in the country districts. A large number of parishes of
> the government have been so badly struck that they have not re-
> ceived any for their subsistence for four months."

He thereupon continues:

> "Disorder takes place among the people who lack bread. Having
> recourse to me, I secured as soon as possible 1,200 quintals of flour
> upon rafts [*radeaux*] and M. le Marquis de la Jonquière and I have
> by *ordonnance* forbidden the sale of wheat above five livre per
> minot. . . .
> "We do not find any other expedient for assuring bread than to
> seek wheat throughout the government of Montreal and take by
> authority what we find, paying for it 100 sols per minot."

The Intendant went on to say that he had frequently succoured the
people of Quebec; otherwise they would have revolted; and that one-
fifth of the *habitants* did not sow for lack of seed grain.[77] In fact, the
situation was so grave in 1750 that a shipload of wheat had already
been hurried to Canada from France, arriving shortly after Bigot had
written the above letter. This fresh supply, however, was totally inadequate. By September of that year the Intendant was obliged to
make clear that before the recent arrival of a ship from Bordeaux
with more wheat the *habitants* had been reduced to dire straits for
bread.[78] Nor did this condition of food shortage change greatly before
the outbreak of hostilities. When Baron de Longueuil, who took over
the administration in New France temporarily upon the death of La
Jonquière in 1752, attempted to provide food for a force of but four
hundred militia that he planned to send that same year against the

---

[76] Nat. Arch., Col., C[11] A. 97: 35.
[77] Arch. Nat., Col., C[11] A. 97: 111.
[78] Arch. Nat., Col., C[11] A. 97: 141.

revolting Miami at Pickawillany, he was unable to secure the necessary flour and gave up the project; when Marquis de Duquesne the following year finally acted to send an expedition to Lake Erie, he was obliged to use force to compel the mutinous *habitants* — actually faced by famine as the result of another poor crop — to surrender to the necessities of the state their precious wheat.[79] Unfortunately, France could herself bring little aid to Canada at this critical juncture; for the mother country, like the Province, was confronted by a food shortage also as the result of bad harvests,[80] and consequently was obliged to become a heavy importer of grain from England.[81]

Weighty reasons, it is now clear, could be advanced by Frenchmen in favour of being freed from the great liability of attempting to maintain New France under existing conditions. First of all, the immense extent of Canada and Louisiana, with the wide dispersion of the inhabitants, made difficult any co-ordination of effort in their administration even under a highly centralized system. Again, each province was placed in a state of constant peril in time of war — utterly dependent upon receiving aid by way of a single river which was liable to blockade by the enemy with the consequent interruption of all commerce and other intercourse between it and the mother country. What is more, the approaches to each could be seized and fortified — provided that the hostile power possessed adequate naval and military resources. Thus cut off, how could either survive unaided? The ever present danger of this contingency required, therefore, the maintenance at whatever cost of great stores of arms, ammunition, cloth-

---

[79] *N. Y. Col. Doc.*, X, 255. Writing to Rouillé on August 20, 1753, Duquesne refers to "the famine which met me on my arrival at Quebec, having reduced me to forwarding [to the armed forces] only 900 barrels of flour, as the whole supply" (*ibid.*, X, 257).

[80] President of the Navy Board to Raymond and Prevost at Louisbourg, July 25, 1753 (Arch. Nat., Col., B. 95: 44).

[81] "I believe it may be for the Interest of your farmers in Essex," wrote William Mildmay, one of the English Commissioners from Paris on March 8, 1752, to the Earl of Fitzwalter, "that English corn imported into Normandy, with all its charges of freight & commission, sells for about 32 shillings the English Q^r. which is two shillings cheaper than the country corn produced on the spot, which corn will yet be dearer unless the fine weather we have at present continues a long while" (Mildmay Private Correspondence, Clements Library). The dependence of France upon England for wheat in the eighteenth century is made abundantly clear in an important official report drawn up in 1752 and entitled "*Commerce général De la Nation françoise Dans les quatre parties du Monde en L'Année Mil Sept Cent Cinquante Deux.*" This report is to be found in the Library of Trinity College, Dublin; it was before 1802 the property of Frans Faget of The Hague, Treasurer to the States of Holland, and apparently came into his possession in the course of the French Revolution.

ing, and other supplies within each province, as well as an adequate force of regular soldiers. But the expense of all this vastly exceeded any revenue or other present advantage to be derived from either; in fact it was not clear but that for an indefinite period each would remain a cruel burden fastened upon the backs of Frenchmen at home already oppressively taxed. Moreover, in looking into the future it seemed impossible that Canada would ever be able to compete on equal terms in the markets of the world with the British continental colonies — except in the matter of furs, with respect to which there was also a very great problem and a very real danger that as a result of the constant destruction of the animals that yielded this resource it likewise would soon fail.

However, as against these counsels of caution and perhaps of weakness and easy discouragement such men as the Marquis de la Galissonière, late Governor General of New France, opposed arguments that seemed in the eyes of the chief ministers of the King to possess even greater validity. True Frenchman that he was, in a report prepared in December 1750 for the guidance of the latter,[82] he set forth motives of honour, glory, and religion that would forbid France for ever from renouncing voluntarily her American continental possessions. Again, he pointed out that an immense country, with a numerous people, fertile lands, forests of mulberry trees, and mines, should not be wanting some day an assured revenue. Further, assuming that this were never to be the case, how could a country be abandoned, he argued, which afforded so great an advantage over its neighbours? For Canada was the strongest possible barrier that could be opposed to the ambitions of the English; it alone was in a position to wage war upon their colonies, always so precious in their eyes, colonies which were increasing in power with such rapidity that unless some means were found to check their growth they would soon absorb not only all the neighbouring islands in the tropics but all the foreign possessions on the continent of America as well.

Why is it, he repeated, that New France in spite of its destitute condition can war against the English colonies to advantage? He then

---

[82] A transcription of the French original is in the Canadian Archives; for a translation of most of the *mémoire* see *N. Y. Col. Doc.*, X, 220–32. A marginal note on the original states that this was prepared by M. de Silhouette and Galissonière, who were acting as the French *commissaires* in the negotiations with the English at this period. Silhouette, however, in 1759 in a communication relating to the retention of Canada stated that the above *mémoire* was prepared by his colleague, with whose opinions, however, he was in complete agreement (*ibid.*, X, 941).

proceeded to supply the answer which was found not only in the success of the French in creating alliances with the many Indian nations
who had come to feel that it was to their interest that the strength of
the French and the English should remain nearly equal but also in
the fact that so many of the French Canadians lived in the woods like
Indians, which made them a most valuable asset in time of war. This
superiority over the English in America was, as it were, accidental,
he thought, and he therefore pointed out that were it not maintained
at all costs the entire destruction of the French settlements in the
New World, including the really prosperous sugar islands, would inevitably result. Should this ever happen, he warned, the effect would
be catastrophic upon France in Europe. Thereby she would lose her
old superiority over England, whose naval power, which would never
be equalled by France, had had so decisive an influence even upon
the outcome of the late war, compelling, as it did, the latter country
to surrender the fruits of its conquest of the Austrian Netherlands.
Canada, therefore, must be strengthened by every available means to
serve as a great New World rampart against English expansion and
predominant naval power, thus effectively supporting French military supremacy in Europe.

With the adoption of a policy in harmony with that advocated by
de la Galissonière we witness the progressive strengthening of Canada. It is quite certain that much of the wheat imported by France
from England during the period of peace as the result of her lack of
that article, to which reference has been made, was thereupon hurried to Canada to relieve urgent immediate needs. But this was a
costly procedure for the provisioning of the French in the New World,
dependent as they were upon outside resources. Other means had to
be found. The solution of the problem, in fact, came when it was decided to encourage the English colonial merchants to the south to
carry their food products to Cape Breton Island.[83] Thus, ironically
enough, as a result of this vital aid in the form of vast quantities of
wheat, flour, bread, and other needed articles of consumption supplied by the English colonies the authorities of New France soon
found their military forces for the first time so adequately provi-
sioned as to be able to proceed with their threatening activities along
the frontiers of these same colonies! [84]

---

[83] Arch. Nat., Col., B. 95: 44.
[84] According to Governor Robert Hunter Morris it was food supplies carried from
Boston and New York to Cape Breton that provided for the needs of the French expe-

But we must now leave the country of the settled *habitants* and bring into view in connection with this survey of zones of international friction the activities of Canadians who had turned to the life of *voyageurs* and *coureurs de bois* as well as of those Indian groups with whom they had become associated in the region of the Great Lakes and other regions geographically linked to it.

---

ditionary force to the Upper Ohio region (Morris to Thomas Penn, October 26, 1754, Penn Official Corr., Hist. Soc. of Pa.). That the menace of this commerce was fully appreciated by June 1754 at least in Massachusetts Bay is clear from a special instruction given to the delegates of that province by the General Assembly. It reads as follows (Mass. Archives, IV, 471):

"As the Trade of late carried on W^th the French at Louisbourg & Canada have prov'd of pernicious consequence . . . to His Majesty's Northern Colonies, the French (and thro them the Indian Enemy likewise) being thereby supplied W^th Provisions of all Kinds; you are therefore in Conjunction W^th ye oth^er Commis^rs. [to] consider of some proper measures to be taken by the several Governm^ts, effectually to prevent such Trade for the future."

Prospect of Quebec, 1732.

(From Popple's *British Empire in America*.)

The Indian Tribes of the Great Lakes Region.

(From a section of Vander Aa's *Canada*, 1755.)

CHAPTER II

The Great Lakes Frontier

WEST OF THE settled portion of Canada and north of the Illinois country in the middle of the eighteenth century stretched a huge " dependency " of New France covering an area of hundreds of thousands of square miles and larger by far than France herself. The waters of this region drained southward into the Mississippi or eastward into the St. Lawrence, or northeastward into Hudson Bay by way of the Nelson or the Churchill or into the Arctic Ocean by way of Slave River and the Mackenzie system. This was a land of many lakes and rivers, of great and gloomy forests.[1] In its southern well-drained portions were to be found the northern limits of the hardwoods " of prodigious girth and height," [2] with the intermingling of giant red, black, and white oak with the hickory, the wild cherry, the basswood, and the walnut; while in the damp depressions grew the birch, the balsam, the beech, and the sycamore — some of the latter, as well as other species of trees, of gigantic proportions — with the maple, the elm, and the ash, flaunting in the fall of the year an attire more gorgeous by far than ever would meet the

---

[1] M. de la Mothe Cadillac referring to this region, which he distinguishes from Canada, declared in a letter written September 25, 1702, apparently to Pontchartrain, that the trees were marvellously lofty, and, excepting the great oak, without nodes and almost without branches until near the top; here he found growing in close proximity the white and red oak, walnut, elm, white wood, mulberry, cotton, chestnut, and ash. He also refers to the wild life, the variety of birds and mammals. In his enthusiasm he continues: *Ce païs si temperé, si bon et si beau qu'on peut à juste titre appeller le paradis terrestre de l'Amérique septentrionelle . . ."* (Transcriptions, Cadillac Papers, Burton Collection, Detroit Public Library).

[2] *New York Colonial Documents* (ed. E. B. O'Callaghan), X, 203.

eye of one confined to the woods of the continent of Europe. In its northern reaches, in contrast, were massed mile upon mile the stately conifers, with the tamarack and cedar in inundated regions.

In this vast area there brooded an unbelievable quiet save when broken by cries of wild life or the forces of nature, sometimes so very terrifying. Here movement was characterized by stealth; life preyed upon life and death came swiftly to the weak, the timid, and the slow of foot — even the bravest and strongest of the denizens of the forest could only survive at times by a mastery of the stratagems of the wilds. Through the tangled woods and the clearings ranged bears, wolves, wildcats, the puma, the lynx, the wolverene, together with the red deer, the moose, the woodland caribou, the red fox, the marten, the fisher, the raccoon and the skunk; while in and about the streams and especially their upper waters swarmed the beaver, the mink, and the muskrat.

While the chief means of traversing this vast interior was by water — portaging from one navigable stream to another or moving along the chains of lakes — nevertheless, here and there on land, even where nature had erected what seemed to be impenetrable barriers of tangled wildwood — of the living, the dead, and the decaying — were to be found in the midst of an eternal gloom traces worn deep by the passing from time immemorial of beast and man. Along these one might move mile after mile until perchance out in the sunlight of some clearing close to a stream, navigable at least by a birch-bark canoe, or along the shore of a lake, a stockaded Indian village appeared with its oval or perhaps conical lodges covered with bark, characteristic dwelling of the tribes of the great Algonquian family. In the fields surrounding the palisade one might have observed the women cultivating their maize, beans, pumpkins, and tobacco or, if not so employed, sitting in front of their lodges weaving baskets or mats of reeds or dressing skins; while at the same time the men, when not at war or engaged in hunting and trapping, might be fashioning canoes from bark or the trunk of some large tree, or perhaps simply lounging about, smoking their pipes.

Indeed, for countless ages wild men had dwelt in these regions, gaining a subsistence by the chase, by fishing, by the utilization of the fruits of the forest, and by a very rudimentary type of agricultural economy. Their basic needs for food, shelter, clothing, and ornamentation were simple and under ordinary conditions could be met without inordinate effort. What could not be secured locally might be obtained by barter with other tribes. For among peoples even with the most primitive culture evidence of peaceful exchange, as a rule, is not lacking, and in the case of the North American Indians the proof that this existed long before the coming of the white man is irrefutable.[3] Doubtless among the latter a state of peace between tribes was much more characteristic than that of war.[4] Nevertheless, one is confronted with the phenomenon of migration, such as that of the Iroquoian tribes — in the case of the latter, from south to north, with evidence that it displaced an Algonquian culture in the regions where new and permanent abodes were at last established.[5] Such movements, such displacements, could hardly have taken place without friction, without, it is likely, deadly combat between groups. In other words, accepting the fact of the generally peaceable inclinations of the red men under ordinary conditions, there must have taken place, as the result of stresses — such, for example, as would develop by reason of seasons of scarcity that set men into motion — countless unrecorded struggles for favoured hunting grounds, also for favoured dwelling places; wars involving tribal prestige, for the capture or recapture of women, of reprisal and revenge for witting or unwitting insult or desecration — unless the prehistoric American Indians differed sharply from other primitive peoples, and we have no reason to believe that they did. It would therefore tax the credulity of the student to believe that the coming of the white man into the valleys of the St. Lawrence and the Hudson saw the beginning of hostilities between groups of aborigines in the region of the Great Lakes.

Nevertheless, when the Europeans in the course of time made their appearance, bringing with them their advanced civilization at least along many lines and the material evidences of this — as the result of the evolution of the Old World technology — a new and deadly source of conflict between aboriginal groups arose. In other words, the noble savage, as idealistically pictured by the *philosophes* of the seventeenth and eighteenth century, ate of the forbidden fruits of European culture and liked them, but these turned his earthly paradise into a land of discord and death. The fruits were

---

[3] T. W. E. Sowter, " Indian Trade, Travel, and Transportation," *Archæological Report* (Ontario Provincial Museum), 1916, pp. 26 et seq., *passim*.

[4] This view is stressed, and very rightly, by G. T. Hunt in his *The Wars of the Iroquois: A Study of Intertribal Trade Relations*.

[5] For a comprehensive bibliography dealing with this point see *ibid.*, pp. 15–16.

not only brandy and rum, for which the red man had a fatal weakness, but firearms, hatchets, knives, awls, fabrics, trinkets, and portable kettles, the last named not the least in importance in his crude economy. In other words, a people still living on the level of the culture of the Stone Age was suddenly elevated vicariously, as it were, into that of the Iron Age. This gave those savages who made this contact and profited by it a tremendous advantage over neighbouring and more distant groups which had not been brought in touch with the white man — an advantage that they were not slow to appreciate and sought to guard.

But that which the Europeans brought could, as a rule, be secured only as the result of barter, and what they came to desire more than all other things from the savages in exchange were the very garments from their backs — provided these were of winter beaver skin; for such well-worn garments, the prized *castor gras d'hiver*, were unsurpassed for the making of hats and commanded a high price at home.[6] So the red man was called upon to bring skins, especially those of the beaver, fresh as well as worn, if he was to secure the magic goods from across the great water, and he responded with alacrity. Not only did he lay snares in the summer and break through the beaver houses in winter and drain the ponds in spring,[7] but in his eager quest for the pelt of this shy but prolific creature — after having ruthlessly exterminated it in the region of his own hunting grounds — he thereupon turned middleman and gladly suffered great fatigues and hardships in moving up rivers and portaging many weary miles in order to come in contact with fresh supplies in the hands of distant but friendly tribes, who at first gladly disposed of their stocks for mere European trifles. So it was, we are told, that the Indians given primarily to hunting, such as the Montagnais, supported by the semi-agriculturist Iroquoian Huron and the Algonquian, soon acquired the means of driving to the south of the St. Lawrence the intruding Iroquoian tribes, later called the Five Nations,

---

[6] The name, while not used during the earlier period, became associated with this quality of beaver skin which through wear had become pliant and had lost the long hair. For the beginning of the fur trade see H. A. Innis's scholarly work *The Fur Trade in Canada*, pp. 5–20.

[7] The manner of hunting the beaver in summer, winter, and spring is described in a *mémoire* dated 1723 in the Archives Nationales, Series C11 A. 122: 307. It is among the great collection of transcripts in the Public Archives of Canada and has been printed by Innis (*op. cit.*, Appendix).

whose economy was largely based upon agriculture.[8] Be that as it may, it is certain that the latter were ultimately brought in touch with the Dutch, who also sought furs, and when the meagre supply of beaver in their own country had become exhausted, they also turned middlemen and the fierce competitors of the Huron and the Ottawa, who each in turn acted in the role of the middlemen of the French for the trade of the " Far West " Indians.[9]

It has been frequently stated that competitive trade is a form of war waged between peoples. This was literally true with respect to this seventeenth-century struggle for the control of the fur supply to the north and west of the Great Lakes. The Five Nations from the vantage-point of location and of a superior economy, if not of organization, ultimately witnessed the collapse of the Huron and the retreat of the Ottawa, without, however, attaining that control of the furs which was the eager object of their quest.

Thus, as the result of such wars, accompanied by epidemics and starvation, and the separation of groups through economic pressure or the exhaustion of hunting and trapping grounds, some tribes that early in the seventeenth century were powerful — such as the Huron or Wyandots and the Foxes — could by the middle of the eighteenth century survive only through seeking allies among their more fortunate neighbours. Others, as, for example, the Five Nations, gathering strength to themselves, as we shall note in the following chapter, ultimately became in the eyes of contemporaries so formidable that both the French and the British policies with respect to the Ohio Valley and the Great Lakes frontier, as well as that of neighbouring tribes, were profoundly influenced by their presence.

To estimate with accuracy the numerical strength of the various Indian groups dwelling in the Great Lakes dependency of New France in 1750 is quite impossible.[10] For example, the Chippewa or

---

[8] Innis, op. cit., pp. 19, 22–3. As Professor Innis himself admits, there are difficulties in fully accepting this thesis.

[9] Professor Hunt's treatment of this struggle is very excellent indeed. See in particular Chapters IV–VI of his study previously cited.

[10] See " Enumeration of the Indian Tribes Connected with the Government of Canada; the Warriors and Armorial bearings of Each Nation, 1736," Documents Relative to the Colonial History of the State of New-York, IX, 1052–8; this is summarized also in H. R. Schoolcraft's History . . . of the Indian Tribes, III, 553–8, and rather poorly in the Wisconsin Historical Collections (ed. R. G. Thwaites), XVII, 245–52. Schoolcraft calls this enumeration " the best, if not the earliest one, now in existence." Whoever was the author of it was adopted into the Oneida and belonged to the Plover

Saulteurs, living near Lakes Superior and Michigan, were credited with but 180 warriors in 1736 and with 5,000 in 1764; [11] the Cree or Cristinaux, living north and northwestward of the Great Lakes as far as the Saskatchewan, with 250 as against 3,000; [12] the Assiniboin, a branch of the Siouan family, who ranged from the upper Missouri to the Middle of Saskatchewan and were allied with the Cree, as a rule, with but 150 as against 1,500; [13] the Ottawa, north of Lakes Superior and Huron, with 380 as against 900; the Miami with their kinsmen, the Ouiatenon and the Piankashaw, all living southward of Lake Erie, with 550 as against 1,000; the Sioux of the Woods and the Lakes, with their habitats westward of Lake Michigan, with 300 as against 1,800; the Shawnee, established on the Scioto and to the southward, with 200 as against 300. There is, however, closer agreement with respect to some other tribes. For example, the Six Nations were credited with 1,100 warriors in 1736 as against 1,500 in 1764; the Potawatomi of the St. Joseph and of Detroit with 250 as against 350; the Menominee or Folles Avoines, living northward of Lake Michigan, with 160 as against 350; the Sioux of the Prairies with 2,000 as against 2,500.

The extent of the divergency in the two sets of estimates of 1736 and of 1764 may be appreciated when the total number of warriors for the northern tribes is placed at 16,323 by the first and at 73,580 by the second. The author of the latter, Captain Thomas Hutchins, considered that on the average one warrior would represent five persons as a family unit. Upon this basis the calculations of 1736 give a total of 82,015 as against a total of 367,900 for those of 1764, which only emphasizes, as was suggested, the unreliability of early calculations.[14] Were one to accept the most moderate of the estimates,

Totem. Thwaites came to the conclusion that it was Pierre Joseph Céloron, while others have favoured Joncaire; Schoolcraft gives the credit to M. de la Chauvignerie.

The figures for 1764 come from *Names of Different Indian Nations in North America, with the Numbers of Their Fighting Men. Historical Account of the Expedition against the Ohio Indians in 1764*, by Col. Henry Bouquet (London and Philadelphia, 1766). This enumeration, prepared by Captain Thomas Hutchins, who accompanied Bouquet, is summarized by Schoolcraft, *op. cit.*, III, 559.

[11] The figures for the earlier period seem to indicate only those Indians of a tribe that were settled about some trading post or who constantly resorted to it.

[12] In the calculations in 1736 only the Cree of Lake Nipigon and of the Lake of the Woods were included.

[13] Here again the figures for 1736 relate to those living in the region south of Lake Nipigon and south of Lake Superior. For the Cree and the Assiniboin see F. W. Hodge, *Handbook of American Indians North of Mexico*, I, 102–5, 359–62.

[14] According to an "Account of Indian Nations Given in the Year 1778, by a

the total is sufficiently impressive to indicate the numerical strength of the red man.

What might not this host have accomplished in combating the advance of the European and in saving the Great Lakes region for its own peculiar culture if once welded into a unity, if once skilled in the new techniques and placed under a high order of leadership! But none of these conditions for success was fulfilled. Unity even within linguistic groups could not be achieved, the new techniques were never mastered, the iron deposits remained ignored, and even the simplest repairs of the guns placed in the hands of the natives and upon which they soon became absolutely dependent not only for safety but, among the hunting Indians, for a food supply, awaited the arrival of the white trader, who usually was a Jack-of-all-trades. In fact, it is probable that few among those Indians who had fallen heir to some of the by-products, as it were, of European culture would have contemplated with equanimity at this period a sudden and total separation from them as a consequence of the disappearance of the Europeans — accepting as they did in their sober moments the devastating effects upon them of the white man's brandy and rum. But while some of the material gifts were eagerly sought after, this did not bring an equal eagerness to cast aside tribal customs and primitive beliefs, in spite of an auspicious beginning.

From the year 1611, when the Jesuit fathers Peter Biard and Enemond Masse began the conversion of the Micmac of Acadia, the French sought to bring Christianity to those tribes with whom they came in contact in North America; in 1615 the Recollet father John Dolbeau inaugurated the mission to the Montagnais near Quebec and Father Joseph le Caron that to the Hurons, and in the same year the latter began his labours among the same Indians living near Thunder Bay; by 1625 five Indian missions had been established by the Grey Friars: the Quebec, the Trois Rivières, the Tadousac, the

---

Trader who resided many years in the neighbourhood of Detroit," among the James Madison Manuscripts and presented by Schoolcraft (op. cit., III, 560-1), the Chippewa or Saulteurs were credited with 5,000 fighting men, the same figure as assigned by Hutchins in 1764; but while the latter's figures for the Menominee or Folles Avoines are 350, those for 1778 are 2,000; the estimates for the later date credit the Wyandots with 180; the Potawatomi with 450; the Miami with 300; the Shawnee with 300; the combined Piankashaw, Mascoutens, and Vermillion living about the Wabash with 800. Lieutenant Z. M. Pike in his "Indian Population of the Upper Mississippi in 1806" (ibid., III, 562-9) gives the Chippewa 2,049 warriors; the Menominee 300; the Sioux of the Lakes and the Forest 485; the Sioux of the Prairies and detached Sioux of the Forest 3,350.

Nipissing, and the Huron. In that year the Jesuits joined the Recollets in their labours in this field. But all things did not proceed smoothly toward the realization of the dream of these men of God. In the struggle for power that ensued, some of the tribes such as the Huron were broken — the latter by the might of the Iroquois in 1649 — and the missions destroyed. In 1660 the aged Father Menard laid the beginnings of the Ottawa mission on the southern shore of Lake Superior; upon his martyrdom the following year, Father Claude Allouez took up the work, and in 1665 there came into existence the mission of La Pointe du St. Esprit on Chequamegon Bay, in what is now Wisconsin; later he founded the mission of Sault Ste. Marie, that of Green Bay, and that to the Miami; during the period of his labours the Michilimakinac mission for the refugee Huron and the Ottawa also made its appearance — for he was aided by others, such as Father Marquette. However, it must be recorded that the seed fell principally upon barren ground. For in the middle of the eighteenth century, in spite of the heroic efforts of these missionaries and their successors — outside of the small groups of domiciled Indians in the settled part of Canada — the Hurons of Lake St. Clair, called a *nation perfide*, were the only fruitage, a very doubtful fruitage. Champlain's vision of a great empire of Christianized, civilized, French-speaking Indians under the steadying influence of white leaders was still a dream.

But the fur trade at least was a reality. In fact, it had gradually become a great business, one that occupied the thoughts of statesmen as well as financiers in France and that gave to Canada with its abundant wild life its principal if not its sole immediate value in the eyes of these men, as well as of the local administrators of New France. " I would have you know," declared one writer, " that Canada subsists only upon the trade of these skins and furs, three fourths of which come from the people who live around the Great Lakes." [15] Therefore all governmental as well as business arrangements seem to have been made with this fact uppermost in mind.

As has been indicated, with the exhaustion of the region surrounding the St. Lawrence, it was necessary to resort to more distant places for peltry. During the earlier period the Hurons, as was suggested, were the chief instrumentality of the French in tapping this re-

---

[15] Quoted by W. B. Munro, in *Crusaders of New France*, p. 170.

source.[16] With the breaking up of their settlements and the destruction of their power in the middle of the seventeenth century by the Iroquoian fury, aided by famine and pestilence, the Ottawa apparently took their place, according to Intendant Duchesneau, writing from Quebec in 1681.[17] They in turn were cowed and wavered under the Iroquoian blows. As a result, the Indian middlemen in the last quarter of the century gave way to Frenchmen, who in increasing numbers penetrated the wilderness. They carried arms and ammunition among other articles for barter with the distant tribes, and they finally established themselves in important Indian villages about the Great Lakes so that hitherto isolated tribes were brought directly and constantly in touch with them. Indeed, even before the disappearance of the Ottawa as the chief intermediaries in the trade, one comes to the heyday of the *coureurs de bois,* who, leaving Montreal and civilization behind them, vanished in their canoes to remain " at least two and sometimes three years and over on their voyages." [18] By 1680 it was asserted that there were " eight hundred persons or more in the bush " and that " there is not a family of any condition and quality soever [in Canada] that has not children, brothers, uncles and nephews among them." [19] Unfortunately, many of those who sought the wilds became mere barbarians, flaunting their nakedness and vices whenever they reappeared at Montreal with their furs. That this condition of affairs was by no means pleasing to the French court is not surprising. Louis XIV in that same year had called upon the Count de Frontenac

> " to excite, continually, all the inhabitants to agriculture, commerce, manufactures, fisheries, and other profitable enterprises whereby they may be confined to their work and settlements, and prevented from wandering through the woods in search of an advantage which

---

[16] *Jesuit Relations* (ed. Thwaites), XI, 143; H. A. Innis, *op. cit.*, pp. 26, 33–4; and, particularly, Hunt, *op. cit.*, Chapter V, " The Huron Trading Empire."

[17] " The Outawas Indians, who are divided into several tribes, and are nearest to us, are those of the greatest use to us, because through them we obtain Beaver . . . they go in search of it to the most distant places, and exchange it for our Merchandise which they procure at Montreal. . . . They get their peltries, in the North, from the people of the interior . . . and in the South, from the Sakis, Poutouatomis, Puants, Oumaominiees or La Folle Avoine, Outagamis or Foxes, Maskoutins, Miamis and Illinois " (N. Y. Col. Doc. (ed. O'Callaghan), IX, 160–1).

[18] M. Duchesneau to M. de Seignelay, November 13, 1681, *ibid.*, IX, 151; see W. B. Munro, *The Coureurs-de-Bois,* for a broad study of the activities of these hardy men.

[19] N. Y. Col. Doc., IX, 140, 142.

tends to the entire ruin of the Colony and of the little commerce it
may have. . . ." [20]

But this exhortation was sent in vain. Nor did various complicated
restrictions placed upon the trade solve the problem.[21] After learning " that all the families in Canada were engaged with the *coureurs
de bois*" and fearing that an absolute prohibition of the latter to resort to the Indians might lead them to take refuge among the English — something that would be " an irreparable loss to the Colony,
inasmuch as they might convey their peltries thither, they being the
first qualified to defend the country " — the King agreed in 1681 to
grant an amnesty to the disobedient and to permit twenty-five licences covering twenty-five canoes, each with three men, or a total
of seventy-five *voyageurs*, to trade in the upper country, and ordered
that an announcement at the same time should be issued to the effect
that punishment would be meted out to those attempting this without
such permission.[22] But, according to Duchesneau, the royal orders
were " despised," and with the connivance of the Governor General
some sixty thousand livres' worth of furs were carried to the English,
who paid far more than double the price for beaver — for a pound
of this peltry worth but 52 sols, 6 deniers at Montreal brought in
Albany eight livres in goods, and " Russian " beaver ten livres.[23]

The licences — *congés*, as they were called — to which reference
has been made were granted at first, as a rule, to the families of poor
officers or gentlemen as well as to others who seemed to have some
claim on the government. Unfortunately, the system of limiting
strictly the number so engaged did not meet the needs of the situation. As a result these *congés* were gradually increased so that it was
not many years before four hundred Canadians were operating in
the Indian country under the protection of the royal permits. Grave
abuses again appeared, which in 1686 led to the drastic step of suppressing *all* licences, for the purpose of concentrating the trade at
certain posts where troops were now stationed and where it might
be under proper control. By this means the commandants of these
posts became deeply involved in it. But still the lure of Albany was

---

[20] *Ibid.*, IX, 140.

[21] See L. P. Kellogg, *The French Regime in Wisconsin*, Chapters XII and XIII for
this; also Innis, *op. cit.*, pp. 41–84.

[22] *N. Y. Col. Doc.*, IX, 159.

[23] *Ibid.*, IX, 160–1. Twelve deniers equalled one sol; twenty sols equalled a livre
tournois. " Russian " or " Muscovy " beaver were selected pelts with long hair that were
exported to Russia.

so great and the facilities for sending furs there so many that M. de Callières-Bonnevue, Governor of Montreal, writing to the Marquis de Seignelay in January 1689, could not but stress the vital necessity of marching into the English territory for the purpose of seizing Albany (Orange) and New York (Manathe) and thereby preventing the total loss " of every sort of Trade " by means of the cheap bargains in goods offered by English traders to the ruin of Canada.[24] This disparity in price levels between Canada and the English province led to endless expedients in attempting to control the furs at the sources of supply. In 1716 the licensing system was restored [25] under an arrangement whereby the permissions to trade at specific places in the Indian country would be given to families of good repute that the Governor General might judge to be most needy, who in turn could sell them to the *voyageurs* in case they could not make use of them. It was the hope that by this means abundant supplies of trading goods would be carried into the Indian country, while at the same time " avoiding the frightful excesses " that accompanied the activities of the *coureurs de bois.* Also hand in hand with the granting of these licences went the continuance of the policy of maintaining supply depots at certain of the posts, the profits from which seem generally to have gone into the hands of the local commandant.

For example, some six years after the establishment in 1701 of the post at Detroit by Antoine de la Mothe, Sieur de Cadillac, the com-

---

[24] De Callières presents the matter succinctly in tabular form, showing the great disparity between the Albany and Montreal prices under the heading: " Differences in the Indian Trade between Montreal in Canada and Orange in New England, 1689 ":

The Indian Pay for	At Orange	At Montreal
8 pounds of powder	One beaver	Four
A gun	Two beavers	Five
40 pounds of lead	One beaver	Three
A Blanket of red Cloth	One beaver	Two
A White Blanket	One beaver	Two
Four Shirts	One beaver	Two
Six pairs of Stockings	One beaver	Two

" The English give six quarts of *Eau de Vie* for one beaver. It is Rum . . . distilled from Sugar Cane imported from the West Indies. The French have no fixed rate in trading Brandy: some give more, some less; but they never give as much as a quart for a beaver. . . .

" Remark. The English do not discriminate on the quality of the Beaver; they take it all at the same rate, which is more than 50 per cent higher than the French, there being, besides, more than 100 per cent difference in the price of their trade and ours " (*N. Y. Col. Doc.,* IX, 404-9).

[25] *Wis. Hist. Coll.,* XVIII, 26.

mandant was given the privilege of an exclusive trade under the arrangement that he should meet the charges of the provisions and the pay of the garrison, and the up-keep of the mission. His chief source of revenue was derived from the sale of licences to *voyageurs* and to resident traders to engage in the fur trade, which brought in some five thousand livres a year; he also sold wine and brandy, which gave him, in addition, two thousand livres, and licences to artisans who desired to ply their trade at the post — all of which provided him with a gross income of some eighty-five hundred livres. Further, he was entitled to one hundred pounds of freightage in each canoe coming from Montreal, with which merchandise he could enter directly into trade.[26] In 1726 Tonti (Tonty) junior, acting as commandant at the same post, granted an exclusive right of trade there to four of his associates,[27] forming with them, as it were, a partnership; but two years later he was released from his command, which was given to the Sieur de Boishébert, who apparently did not arrive in Detroit until 1730.[28] Again licences were freely sold upon the previous footing; in 1738 some ten or twelve were disposed of at five hundred livres per licence.[29] In 1741 M. de Noyan, in charge, declared that the value of the Detroit trade amounted to from one hundred and fifty thousand to two hundred thousand livres each year.[30]

The impression must not be left, however, that the King was by these arrangements freed from expense in connection with the Great Lakes trade. This is far from the truth. In fact, the problem of maintaining the various military posts in face of increasing financial outlay by the Crown finally led to a policy of leasing the trade at these to

---

[26] *Ibid.*, III, 167, 294; XVII, 293–7; see also Agnes C. Laut, Cadillac, pp. 125–98.

According to a report made by Noyan in 1730, " the post of Detroit brought in to the officer in command there eight or ten thousand livres' income every year; each boat pays him five or six hundred francs to obtain permission to go and trade, and the number of boats amounts to 18 or 20 a year. The voyageurs, who are obliged to lay down this sum, sell their goods — in order to recoup themselves — at very dear prices to the settlers at the place. The latter sell them again to the savages, who are the victims of this trading. Sometimes the commandant gives up the post to two or three farmers for a fixed sum, at 8,000 livres, with certain reservations; and in that case, the trade being in one hand only, the evil is still greater, settlers and savages all suffer from it . . . the officer then cannot remedy it . . . his hands are tied by an agreement which gives authority to the greed of the farmers " (Cadillac Papers, Michigan and Pioneer Historical Society Collections, XXXIV, 77).

[27] A. E. Parkins, The Historical Geography of Detroit, p. 68.

[28] Wis. Hist. Coll., XVII, 133–4, 141.

[29] Ibid., XVII, 293. A certain number, especially half-licences, were also granted without pay.

[30] Ibid., XVII, 357.

the highest bidder. Louis Denys, Sieur la Ronde, however, was granted in 1733 the rights of the post at Chequamegon Bay on Lake Superior for nine years without payment of rental under an agreement that he would proceed to discover and exploit the copper mines supposed, correctly, to be in that region.[31]

The desirability of this leasing policy, operating concurrently with the system of licences, was greatly accentuated as the result of the outbreak of hostilities in North America in connection with King George's War. Nevertheless, the war brought its troubles to those who already enjoyed leases. For example, Sieur François Chalet, a Brest merchant and a representative in Canada for the directorate of the Compagnie des Indes, held leases for the posts of Niagara and of Fort Frontenac; the commandant of each of these continued to send information during the summer of 1744 of the great numbers of canoes laden with furs and beaver skins that arrived to trade but, finding inadequate supplies of goods, and these " at such a price as to completely disgust the savages," left for Oswego. Beauharnois, now Governor General of Canada, deeply concerned at this news, brought the matter to Chalet's attention; the latter, in turn, affirmed that he had supplied his posts with everything that it was possible for him to send under prevailing conditions and that as to the prices, if he had to lower them he would prefer to cancel his leases and let the King assume the responsibility of the trade.[32]

In a letter written to the French Minister in 1745 the Governor General painted a black picture of the state of the trade — a great

---

[31] See the King's Instructions of May 12, 1733, *ibid.*, XVII, 176–7.

Trade at the Ouiatenon Post on the Wabash was controlled in 1735 by the commandant, the Sieur de Normanville, who, however, had no lease but simply a licence to trade. He transferred this that same year to two Montreal merchants under an agreement that they should pay him 2,500 livres per year as long as he should be kept in his command there; further, they were to provide him annually with 500 pounds of flour, 3 barrels of brandy, 4 barrels of wine, 50 pounds of tobacco, and presents for the Indians (Schmidt Mss. 2: 329, Chicago Historical Society). It may be noted that after 1743 Ouiatenon became a leased post. There is to be found among the Schmidt Manuscript Collection in the Chicago Historical Society (*ibid.*, 2: 327) a copy of a lease made out in 1747 for the Miami post on the Maumee in favour of Charly St. Ange. He was also given the privilege of exploiting the trade of the " Rivière Blanche " (that is, the Cuyahoga River), flowing into Lake Erie to the eastward of the Maumee, which apparently he was unable to do by reason of the Iroquoian hostility. The commandant at Maumee was not permitted to trade but was on the other hand required to protect the lessee and to cause " all the Coureurs de Bois and fugitives to leave said district." The annual value of the lease was fixed at 3,000 livres; the lease was to run for three years.

[32] Beauharnois to the French Minister, October 9, 1744, *Wis. Hist. Coll.*, XVII, 442–3.

diminution in the amount of goods taken up to the posts by reason of the small quantity in the hands of the Montreal merchants and the high prices charged for them, with the low prices offered by the merchants for pelts. In this connection Beauharnois asserted:

> "I offered licences for nothing — especially to Detroit, in order that there should be abundance of goods at that post — only ten went up this year. . . . I have not been able to find sale, either, for the usual number of licences for the post at Missilimakinac . . . which apply equally to all the other leased posts. . . ." [33]

In 1746 the situation was no better, and on October 7, 1747 de la Galissonière, who had taken the place of Beauharnois, and Intendant Hocquart wrote " that far from the Posts yielding any Revenues, they have been the cause of considerable expenditure. . . ." [34] The following year the Governor General affirmed that the expenses of maintaining the trade during the preceding two years had been so great that he doubted " whether the proceeds of the most profitable ten years of the posts " could balance the deficits. [35]

While neither the licensing system nor that of leasing the posts was free of difficulties, de la Galissonière at last came to the conclusion that experience had shown that the merits of the former far surpassed the latter. He therefore signified that he desired to follow a policy of having as few posts farmed out as possible. This recommendation was accepted by the French Minister, who in 1749 instructed La Jonquière, the new Governor General, and Intendant Bigot that only certain of the most isolated posts — those, for example, to the northward of the Great Lakes and Chequamegon at La Pointe on Lake Superior — should be leased in the future and then only with the understanding that no officer should exploit any such post and that the commandant of it should enjoy only the allowances he was entitled to receive according to his rank and the expense necessary to maintain the post in question. [36] But, as will be noted, this policy was only partially carried out and the more important fur-trading posts, with the exception of Detroit and Michilimakinac, continued in the hands of lessees.

In particular, the farming of the very lucrative post of La Baye, located at Green Bay on the western shores of Lake Michigan, had

[33] Letter of October 28, 1745, N. Y. Col. Doc., X, 21.
[34] Wis. Hist. Coll., XVII, 470.
[35] Letter of October 23, 1748, ibid., XVII, 503-4.
[36] Ibid., XVIII, 25-7.

been so long the object of such bitter criticism on the part of the Indians as well as of the local commandant that de la Galissonière determined, even before the Minister had made his decision, that this practice should be discontinued there.[37] Nevertheless, in 1747 it was again leased for a period of three years to three lessees at a yearly rental of five thousand livres in war-time — with the proviso that whenever trading supplies failed to arrive in Canada in sufficient quantity, due to hostilities, the rental should be three thousand livres — and six thousand livres in time of peace when goods were abundant.[38] Two of these lessees now proceeded to lease the post to the third, who in turn formed a company for its exploitation.[39] In 1750 La Jonquière and Bigot informed the Minister that the licence system would now be established at La Baye, and apparently this was done for a brief period. Yet in 1752 Duquesne, who was now Governor General, proposed that the post be granted to Pierre François Rigaud de Vaudreuil, the Governor of Trois Rivières, which was done — but only for a period of two years.[40] This led to renewals of the grant, as the result of the influence exerted at court by Rigaud's brother, the Marquis de Vaudreuil, who took over the position of Governor General of New France upon the retirement of Duquesne,[41] and who succeeded in 1760, in the last days of French power, in securing a life interest in it not only for Rigaud but for Madame Rigaud.[42] After this fashion was public interest sacrificed to private!

The trading posts — some of them leased and some of them free for licensed traders in the middle of the eighteenth century, as has been noted — had all been established at strategic points; some at bottlenecks in the Great Lakes system, such as Detroit, Michilimakinac, and Niagara; some at portages, as Miami and St. Joseph; some at natural places of concourse of Indians and traders, as La Baye and La Pointe. As a rule they stood near some important, or one-time important, Indian village, the scene of earlier missionary or trading activities where in the seventeenth century Frenchmen had made their appearance either to preach the Gospel or to carry on a

---

[37] See Beauharnois to the Minister, October 25, 1744, ibid., XVII, 445–6.

[38] For the agreement see ibid., XVII, 451–5.

[39] Ibid., XVIII, 7–10.

[40] Ibid., XVIII, 127–8, 132, 143.

[41] Ibid., XVIII, 164–7. In 1757 Rigaud entered into a partnership with two prominent Montreal traders, Ignace Hubert and Jacque Giasson, whereby the latter received a one-third interest in the post (ibid., XVIII, 197–9).

[42] Ibid., XVIII, 274.

legitimate trade or, perhaps, simply to be free of all the constraints of civilization. Most of them were unpretentious in appearance — "merely an inclosure made with four rows of posts from twelve to fifteen feet in height, within which are a few rough cabins constructed of logs and clay and covered with bark," according to a description of one of them left by a contemporary.[43] However, by 1750 Fort Detroit had come to possess some one hundred log and other types of houses all located within a palisade; beyond this were also cultivated lands stretching northward to Lake Huron.[44] As to Fort Niagara, it was described in that year as being an even much more substantially constructed if less well-populated post.[45] All these posts were provided with at least an officer and a few soldiers — some of course with a considerable body of troops, as was the case of the two last mentioned.

The posts of the upper Indian country served three chief purposes. First, they were the visible symbols of the formal claims of the French King, as against those of other European powers — over them waved the fleur-de-lis, thus indicating rights based not only in the first instance upon discovery and exploration but upon the old Roman law principle of *occupatio* which had been embodied in the later French system of jurisprudence; again, they were the recognized agencies not only for keeping the various tribes friendly [46] and for blocking the efforts of the Iroquoian middlemen and later of the English traders to control the Great Lakes trade but for upholding the detailed regulations of that trade. Lastly, such a post as La Baye was also designed to serve as a point of departure for expeditions seeking to

---

[43] *Jesuit Relations* (ed. R. G. Thwaites), LXVIII, 286–308.

[44] Testimony of John Patten, an English trader carried to Detroit in 1751 and subsequently sent as prisoner to France, given upon his return to America (Penn Mss., Indian Affairs, I, 65, Historical Society of Pennsylvania). In this Patten testifies that four hundred men were settled in and about the fort. However, in his so-called " Journal," among the Belknap Papers in the Massachusetts Historical Society, he states that there were two hundred.

[45] *Ibid.*

[46] In spite of the efforts on the part of the Canadian government to maintain the practice of requiring the Indians to come each year to Montreal to receive their annual present, this could not be upheld in many cases. As Duquesne made clear in 1753 (Arch. Nat., Col., C[22] A. 99: 103), the commandants of the posts could always present the urgent need of satisfying the Indians, perhaps to prevent their going to war with other tribes in alliance with the French. Indeed, to persuade the commandants to distribute presents the Indians often menaced them and in return were petted and spoiled. Nevertheless, this constant oversight over their activities doubtless frequently prevented hostile outbreaks.

uncover mines and also for that persistent but fruitless search by the servants of His Most Christian Majesty for a North American approach to the Western Sea [47] — a quest that began when Verrazano made his historic voyage in 1524 and which in the middle of the eighteenth century was being prosecuted by the Sieurs Marin, father and son, from Green Bay. The latter purpose was also involved, as the name signifies, in the establishment of the post of de la Mer d'Ouest, which in reality was a series of far-western posts in the region of Lake Winnipeg [48] and from which Le Chevalier de la Vérendrye pushed westward in his famous journey of exploration at a somewhat earlier period, hoping up to his death in 1750, to fulfil the desires of the Crown for an overland route to the Pacific.

Whether or not some of the posts in reality served any very good purpose may be open to question. At least the missionaries who sought to bring Christianity to the Indians considered them mere dens of iniquity. Their indictment of the practices of garrisons continues almost unabated from the time of their establishment in the western wilderness to the end of the French regime. For example, Father Étienne de Carheil, writing from Michilimakinac in 1702,[49] declared that the pretended service of the military posts to the King was in reality a service limited to four chief and base activities: the

[47] Fort Beauharnois, a distant outpost of La Baye among the Sioux, during its existence between 1750 and 1756 was also designed to aid in the discovery of the Western Sea.

[48] For these latter posts see Volume III, The Northern Plantations, pp. 247-8 of this series.

[49] Parkman prints most of this letter in the Appendix of his Old Régime.

Cadillac in dealing with the criticisms of the missionaries in a letter written on September 25, 1702, apparently to Pontchartrain, says: " So large a volume could be made of all that the Missionaries have said, preached and written since they have been in the lands of the Utaüois [Ottawa] against the trade in brandy, and the expeditions in the woods, that a man's life would not suffice to get through the reading of it." In continuing he observed " that the missionaries persisted so obstinately in their complaints that the court desired to put an end to them by the suppression of the congés, by prohibiting the brandy trade, by the evacuation of the posts which had been occupied there [among the Ottawa]. . . ." He argued that the proper way to stop all abuses was to concentrate all the Indian trade at Detroit, where it could be under strict supervision, particularly that of Michilimakinac. In this connection he accused the Jesuit mission there of being " the scene of all debauchery, serving as a retreat for all in rebellion against the orders of the King, and for the libertines who set out from Montreal every day taking an enormous quantity of brandy there. . . ." He declared that in presenting these facts in the presence of the Governor General and the Superior of the Jesuits the latter had replied " that the missionaries were unable to act otherwise for fear that those people would murder them as there was no one there to support them . . ." (Cadillac Papers, Transcripts, Burton Collection, Detroit Public Library).

setting up of cabarets for the debauching of the Indians, who were kept in a continual state of drunkenness; the employment of the soldiers to go from one post to another with merchandise and liquor by the commandants, who at the same time closed their eyes to the scandalous disorders of their men; the turning of the posts into mere brothels into which the Indian girls were lured; and finally the gambling and drunkenness, day and night, whenever the traders appeared. " Behold," he declared, " the four sole occupations of the garrisons here during so many years." Father Vivier, living among the Illinois Indians and writing in 1750 to his superior, shows that conditions had not changed for the better, bitterly complaining that after some six hundred of the natives had been baptized, most of them had now abandoned their religion on account of the brandy trade carried on among them, chiefly by the soldiers:

> " The Savages — and especially the Illinois, who are the gentlest and most tractable of men — become, when intoxicated, madmen and wild beasts. Then they fall upon one another, stab with their knives, and tear one another. Many have lost their ears and some a portion of their noses in these tragic encounters." [50]

Governor General Duquesne in 1753 supports this testimony, accusing Macarty, the major commandant of this region, of conducting himself infamously, having concentrated his attention upon the sale of brandy secured from Louisiana, to the demoralization of both Indians and Frenchmen.[51] Even the commandant at Niagara in 1750, according to Peter Kalm's testimony, in order to prevent the Indians from going to Oswego, was then supplying the natives with whatever quantity of brandy or rum they desired.[52]

Nevertheless, with all their disadvantages and abuses the posts continued to be regarded as essential to the preservation of the interests of New France. By the middle of the eighteenth century some forty-four of these were dependent upon that government — excluding those of Isle Royale, of the Illinois commandery, and of Louisiana — according to an undated and unsigned *mémoire*, which, however, seems to have been prepared in 1757 by Louis Antoine Bouganville, one of Montcalm's aides-de-camp.[53] Of these, twenty-

---

[50] *Jesuit Relations* (ed. R. G. Thwaites), LXIX, 201–32.

[51] Arch. Nat., Col., C¹¹ A. 99: 114.

[52] N. Y. Col. Doc., VI, 592–3.

[53] This carries the simple title " *Chaîne des Postes*," and is to be found in the Archives Nationales, Colonies, C¹⁸ E. 13: 179–215. A comparison of this with Bougan-

eight were comprehended within the Great Lakes system and the portages that led into it, while the rest were identified with the lower St. Lawrence. The *mémoire* in question gives one an insight into the comparative importance of these posts under normal conditions with respect to the yield in peltries either by direct trade with the Indians who resorted to them or as the result of the activities of the *voyageurs* who went from them to the distant and scattered villages of the natives. The most important of these was Detroit, where numerous people ordinarily were licensed to carry on the trade. " Often four hundred traders meet here at a time," declared the Englishman John Patten, who was detained there as a prisoner for some months in 1751.[54] According to the *mémoire*, it ordinarily provided from eight hundred to one thousand bundles of furs [55] and was, moreover, the entrepôt for the posts lying to the southward; just so Michilimakinac, also exploited by licences, was the entrepôt for the north-

ville's " Mémôire" printed in Pierre Margry's *Relations et mémoires inédits* (Paris, 1869), pp. 39–84, will show that much of the material of one is contained in the other and in identical language. The former was apparently prepared for Vaudreuil and the latter, dated June 30, 1757, was sent to Mme. Hérault de Sechelles. Thwaites translated and edited most of the latter for the *Wisconsin Historical Collections* (XVII, 167–95).

[54] *Wis. Hist. Coll.*, XVIII, 146.

One aspect of the supply of the western posts by Montreal with needed commodities is illustrated in the " Montreal Notarial Records," transcriptions of which are to be found in the Burton Collection at Detroit. In these are recorded the contracts entered into between Montreal merchants and those who agreed to voyage in a *canot* into the Great Lakes region. For example, on June 6, 1749 Jean Baptiste Vegia, called familiarly La Bonté Garçon, agreed to go to, and return from, Detroit within the same year in a *canot*, " en qualitté de devant ou de Derrier" (referring to the position he would occupy in the *canot*); for this he was to receive as compensation 220 livres in silver currency of the country (*ibid.*, XIII, 665–6). Sometimes the agreement provided for part payment in goods; Michil Brosseau in 1750 agreed to make the round trip the following year for " 160 livres, une chemise de cotton et une paire de mettos " (*ibid.*, XIII, 674–6); sometimes the *voyageur* agreed to go out in the *canot* but not to return, as when in 1747 Laurend Caille did so for 40 livres (*ibid.*, XII, 520–1).

It was calculated by Noyan in 1730 that it cost the *voyageur* on an average twenty livres a bundle to bring his furs from Detroit to Montreal (Cadillac Papers, Transcripts, Burton Collection, Detroit, XXXIV, 79).

[55] According to W. B. Munro (*Crusaders of New France*, p. 169), each bundle or pack weighed about fifty pounds, and forty of these normally constituted the full cargo of a large canoe. On the other hand, where portaging was not a serious problem, the bundle was much heavier. Among the transcripts in the Canadian Archives of the Hudson's Bay Company papers covering the years 1673–96 reference is made to 228 packets each weighing 80 French pounds, a total of 18,204 French pounds or 20,845 1/2 English pounds. Edward Shippen of Lancaster, Pennsylvania, who was involved in the Indian trade, declared in a letter written July 9, 1754 to his son (Shippen Collection, Edward Shippen estate, Philadelphia), that 36 bundles of skins which he had secured would weigh at least 3,600 pounds.

western posts beyond the Great Lakes. This latter post provided from six hundred to seven hundred bundles. La Baye, a leased post, at least during most of the period under consideration, as has been noted, could be counted on for from five to six hundred annually; St. Joseph, near the southeastern end of Lake Michigan at the St. Joseph–Kankakee portage, another leased post after 1745,[56] for some four hundred; Ouiatenon on the Wabash, at the point where the Indian trail led northward to the St. Joseph, leased after 1743,[57] and the leased post of de la Mer d'Ouest, for from three hundred to four hundred respectively; Miami at the Maumee-Wabash portage, leased after 1743,[58] for from two hundred and fifty to three hundred; Niagara and Chequamegon at La Pointe, the latter after 1733 a leased post,[59] for some two hundred and fifty respectively; the Lake of the Two Mountains, to the west of Montreal, with its domiciled Christian Indians, together with Carillon and Le Long Sault, for two hundred and ten; Cabitibi (Abitibbi) and Timis Kamingue (Temiscomingue), both in the direction of Hudson Bay, for one hundred and twenty each; Sault Ste. Marie, a concession to the Chevalier de Repentigny, secured in 1750,[60] for about one hundred; Nipigon, leased in 1744,[61] for from eighty to one hundred. Of less importance were Kamenistigouia (Kaministiquia), toward the northwest of Lake Superior, leased in 1743,[62] which could supply only from sixty to seventy bundles, and Michipicton, northeast of the same lake, also leased in that year, providing but from fifty to sixty. Toronto, or Fort Rouillé, in spite of the high hopes at its founding in 1750 as a means of cutting off the trade with Oswego, could furnish only from forty to fifty, and, finally, Fort Frontenac from twenty to thirty.

It should be emphasized that the value of the traffic in furs at the various posts was gauged not only by the number of bundles but particularly by the types and quality of the peltry. For example, de

---

[56] Wis. Hist. Coll., XVII, 445.

[57] Ibid., XVII, 435.

[58] Ibid., XVII, 444.

[59] Ibid., XVII, 176.

[60] Repentigny, upon securing his concession, went to the region and near the site of the old Jesuit mission proceeded to build his post. In 1751 a patent for six leagues frontage on the river and six in depth was issued to him and to Sieur de Bonne (Canadian Archives (1905), p. 154). This was designed primarily as a military and agricultural post, a refuge for voyageurs and a means of keeping the Indians from going to the English (Wis. Hist. Coll., XVIII, 99–100).

[61] Ibid., XVII, 445.

[62] Ibid., XVII, 444.

la Mer d'Ouest post was regarded as one of the most lucrative in all Canada; it was leased to the commandant, who in 1752 was the Chevalier de Niverville, for 8,000 livres; and the skins — such as the finest *castor gras d'hiver*, marten, northern fox, and others — were among the most valuable drawn from all North America.[63] But La Baye, on the western shore of Lake Michigan, was rated even higher, for its lease amounted to 9,000 livres. Unlike the last-named, which was far removed and required the use of difficult portages for the bringing of supplies and the carrying out of the furs, it was conveniently located to handle not only the lighter, more expensive pelts, but heavy and less valuable skins. It was asserted in the same *mémoire* that in three years the lessee, Sieur de Rigaud, together with Sieur Marin, the commandant, drew from it 312,000 livres; that previous to this period Marin senior, with whom was associated Governor General La Jonquière and the Intendant Bigot, drew from it in one year a clear profit of 150,000 livres. The Chequamegon post, long exploited by the de la Ronde family, was leased for 8,000 livres — the same amount as was demanded for de la Mer d'Ouest; the commandant of the former received reputedly a gratuity of 2,000 livres as well as a portion of the profits of the lease. Although but two hundred and fifty bundles of furs went annually from that place, according to the estimates given above, these furs must have been of very great value in comparison, for example, with the two hundred and fifty or three hundred bundles likewise secured at Fort Miami, the lease of which, in contrast to the above figure, amounted to but 1,200 livres; the lessee of the latter, it is clear, was limited to bartering for " southern " skins and pelts of comparatively low value.[64] The lease of the trade of Fort Ouiatenon was also rated at

[63] Governor General Duquesne, writing to the Minister in October 1753 (Arch. Nat., Col., C22 A. 99: 103), declared that the most important posts were Detroit, Michilimakinac, La Baye, de la Mer d'Ouest, and the Illinois. The rest of the posts he found provided a market for only from four to five *canots* loaded with merchandise. He was assured, however, that the Ohio River could furnish a thousand bundles of skins and expressed his intention of giving *congés* without expense to those who would develop the trade of this region.

[64] In 1749, according to the testimony of M. de Couagne, a Montreal merchant, with whom Professor Kalm lodged, the following prices prevailed in that year for skins: for elk, 10 livres; for otter, raccoon, wolverene, great and middle-sized bear, 5 livres; for wolf-lynx (*loup cervier*), 4 livres; for beaver, red fox, inferior elk and stag, 3 livres; for young bear, 50 sols; for marten, 45 sols; for wolf, 40 sols; for southern fox and catamount, 35 sols; for roebuck, 25 to 30 sols; for lynx and mink, 25 sols (Kalm, op. cit., II, 522–3).

The above figures differ from those listed in 1754 as payments made by the Compa-

1,200 livres and was concerned with such peltry as was secured at Miami.

All the furs from the upper country were supposed to be carried to Montreal by the *voyageurs*, Indians, and factors of the leased posts, where each year for weeks on end bartering with private merchants at open booths, with wild dissipation and not a little disorder and violence, was the order of the day. Ultimately the beaver skins as well as the other peltries that finally came into the hands of the Montreal and Quebec agents of the Compagnie des Indes were carried in its ships to France.

In this connection it is of interest to note that the value of the beaver exported in 1755 amounted to less than one-third of the total value of the peltries; for, while the total value of skins at Quebec before export in that year was 1,547,885 livres, 11 sols, the beaver only came to 505,319 livres. Yet it is the trade in the beaver skin that is of most significance, and it may be added that its nearest rival in value in 1754 was that of deer skin, with a value of 293,658 livres, to be followed by marten, valued at 182,324 livres, wildcat at 176,477 livres, 14 sols, and bear skin, at 130,145 livres.[65]

Throughout the history of New France, it is well to emphasize, the export of beaver skin was monopolized either by great public companies or by private individuals and their associates. Without reference to the sixteenth-century beginnings of the Canadian fur trade it may be pointed out that in the seventeenth century " The Company of One Hundred Associates " and its successor, the Compagnie des Indes Occidentales, enjoyed this monopoly; and when the latter went out of existence in 1674, the King turned it over the following

---

gnie des Indes, which are as follows: for *origineaux verts* (raw elk skin), 20 livres; for *serfs verts* (raw stag skin), 16 livres; for *renard argente* (silver fox), 12 livres; for *loup cervier* (wolf-lynx), *loutres* (otter), and *our* (bear), 10 livres; for *carajou* (wolverene) and *renard croisés* (cross fox), 6 livres; for *martre du nord* (northern marten), 5 livres, 6 sols; for *ourson* (small bear), *loup de bois* (timber wolf), *rat musqué* (muskrat), and *rat de bois* (wood rat), 5 livres; for *chat cervier* (cat-lynx), *renard rouge* (red fox), *castor sec d'hiver* (unworn winter beaver), and *castor gras d'hiver* (worn winter beaver), 4 livres; for *renard du sud* (southern fox) and *martre du sud* (southern marten), 3 livres, 10 sols; and for *chevreuil vert* (raw roebuck), 3 livres (" Quantity of Furs Exported in 1754, with the Quebec Prices of the Several Species," Shelburne Papers, 64: 161). The explanation for the difference between the two sets of figures will probably lie not only in the fact that in one case the price is that paid by the individual Montreal merchants, in the other case what the latter received from the Compagnie des Indes, but in the quality of the skins secured in one season as against that of another season and the demand of the market for particular skins.

[65] Shelburne Papers, 64: 161.

year to one Nicholas Oudiette, farmer of the royal revenues of
Canada, and his associates. To protect the interests of the Canadian
trader and merchant it seemed necessary to fix the prices that he
should pay for beaver of various qualities brought to his warehouses.
This was done by decree of the Council of State of May 16, 1677,[66]
whereby it was provided that for beaver skin that was worn by the
natives, *castor gras,* he should pay five livres and ten sols a pound,
and that for skins that had been little worn, *castor sec ordinaire,*
three livres and ten sols. He only paid for three-fourths of the beaver,
however, demanding the remainder as his right to the royal fourth
acquired with his monopoly, for which monopoly he had agreed to
pay 350,000 livres.[67] This had the effect of reducing the price actually
paid for the well-worn beaver to four livres, ten sols, and six deniers
a pound, and for the remainder but fifty-two sols and six deniers.
But Oudiette, compelled to take all beaver offered, at last found
himself faced by a glut in the market, and upon his bankruptcy in
1685 the *ferme* was transferred in turn to several individuals [68] and
in 1697 was acquired by one Louis Guigues, who, faring no better
than the rest, gave way in 1701 to the so-called Canada Company.
Some one hundred and fifty Canadian merchants were led to take
stock in this organization, which, it was hoped, might be able to
exercise a wiser control over the supply of beaver. But the temporary
acquisition of posts of the Hudson's Bay Company and with it additional sources for skins of very high quality helped to create a
problem of the first magnitude.[69] Therefore in 1706 Louis François
Aubert and Company entered into an agreement with the Canada
Company, which was approved by a decree in Council that same
year whereby the former agreed to assume the obligations of the latter, amounting to 1,475,160 livres, to take over its great stock of *castor
gras,* and to enjoy an exclusive privilege of exporting beaver for a
period of twelve years under arrangements that ultimately freed
Aubert and his associates of the necessity of purchasing any skins of

---

[66] This information and much that immediately follows relating to the purchase
price of beaver and its export is largely based upon the " *Mémoire sur le commerce des
castors* " prepared in 1751 (Arch. Nat., Col., C[11] A. 97: 262–73).

[67] Innis, *op. cit.,* p. 64.

[68] *Ibid.,* pp. 70–5.

[69] Cadillac was very bitter over the conduct of the beaver trade by the Canada
Company; in 1702 he declared in picturesque language that " *la concession du co-
merce* [sic] *que le roy a donné à la Compagnie de la Colonie exclusivement a cassé les
bras et les jambes au detroit* " (Cadillac Papers, Transcripts, Burton Collection, Detroit).

the above quality during this period; they, incidentally, on their part agreed to waive the old royal right to receive gratis one-fourth of the beaver. This agreement expiring at the end of 1717, the monopoly of the beaver trade thereupon came into the possession of John Law's Compagnie d'Occident, organized in August of that year; this privilege was to run for a period of twenty-five years beginning January 1, 1718. In 1719 the company was merged in the great Compagnie des Indes, which the following year collapsed as the result of frenzied speculation in its stocks. However, after some hesitation, as indicated by decrees issued in 1720 and 1721, on June 22, 1722 the reorganized Compagnie was confirmed in its privilege under condition that it would agree to pay for all well-worn beaver four livres a pound and for other beaver forty sols. Nevertheless, it was found impossible to continue paying at this rate. In fact the price was lowered in both 1730 [70] and 1733.[71] In 1737, after a meeting at Montreal of merchants and the local agents of the company the preceding year, it was agreed to stabilize the price at fifty-five sols a pound for winter grades and twenty a pound for other grades. These prices continued in force until the outbreak of the War of the Austrian Succession. Then, in an effort to prevent the French traders and their Indian allies from resorting to the English, the price of winter beaver was restored to four livres and that of summer beaver raised to thirty sols for the period of the war. In 1749, however, with the coming of peace, the Canadian authorities were informed that for the winter beaver secured that year the company would pay but three livres, ten sols, which would be lowered in 1750 to three livres, five sols.[72]

In justifying this step the Compagnie claimed that France alone could not consume all the beaver received from Canada and that, as a consequence, it had to sell the excess abroad wherever it could, even at a loss, in order to give this a preference over the English beaver.[73] According to a report submitted by its *directeurs* to the

---

[70] On January 1, 1730 the following prices were established: for well-worn winter beaver (*castor gras d'hiver*), 3 livres, 10 sols a pound; for thin, scraped beaver skin (*castor veule*), 2 livres, 8 sols; for winter beaver that had not been worn (*castor sec d'hiver*), 2 livres; for worn autumn beaver (*castor gras d'automne*), 1 livre, 15 sols; for summer beaver that had not been worn (*castor sec d'été*), 1 livre (Arch. Nat., Col., C¹¹ A. 97: 262–73). For a careful analysis of the various qualities of beaver skin see Innis, op. cit., p. 64.

[71] Ibid., p. 108.

[72] Arch. Nat., Col., B. 89: 139–43.

[73] Ibid.

Minister in 1748 and covering the years 1740 to 1748,[74] it had made a profit on the transactions of 1741 of 184,997 livres, with an investment in the beaver trade of 800,000 livres — the amount of its fixed capital attached to this.[75] In that year it had received from Canada 1,070 bales of beaver of all kinds, each bale weighing 120 pounds, or a total of 128,400 pounds of beaver skin. This was purchased at an average price of 55 sols per pound, which, together with the cost of freight, insurance, as well as other charges involved in transporting it to Paris, amounted to 391,788 livres and 10 sols; the interest on the invested capital — also debited against the proceeds of the sale — was 48,000 livres. The beaver was sold in Europe at an average price of 5 livres, 10 sols a pound, or for a total of 624,820 livres, 5 sols, and 3 deniers. On the other hand, according to the company's figures for the two years 1746–7, in paying the higher prices established in 1746,[76] the purchase price of the beaver secured amounted to 1,243,455 livres, 6 sols; this together with war insurance, the cost of freight, and other expenses, including the payment of interest on the invested capital, represented a total outlay of 1,884,010 livres, 19 sols. In contrast to this the sale of the beaver in Europe, it was asserted, amounted to only 1,779,522 [77] livres — or the sum of 104,488 livres short of the expenditures for the two years' operations. If the interest on the investment were placed on the credit side — amounting to 120,000 for two and one-half years — this left the company a credit of but 15,512 livres on its investment of 800,000 livres for this period of time — as against the hypothetical sum of 1,727,909 livres' profit for the same period that it was previously charged to have made by some of its critics in Canada.[78]

The company had to meet, however, a countercharge by the

---

[74] Arch. Nat., Col., C[11] A. 92: 383.

[75] In a report of the directorate of the Compagnie des Indes, dated June 11, 1752, the amount of fixed capital in the beaver trade of Canada was given as 513,582 livres as against 14,218,549 livres in the trade to the East Indies ("Réflexions et Observations sur la Compagnie des Indes," Mildmay Papers, Clements Library).

[76] For castor gras d'hiver, 4 livres per pound; for castor veule et gros cuir d'hiver, 3 livres, 15 sols; for castor d'été et automne, 30 sols. It may be noted that of the total for the two years of 339,514 pounds of beaver, 270,547 was of the veule et gros cuir d'hiver, 50,188 of castor gras d'hiver, and 18,779 was castor d'été et automne (ibid.).

[77] The gras et sec d'hiver and the gros cuir selling at 5 livres a pound, the gras et sec d'été at 2 livres, 5 sols a pound; and the refuse at one livre, 10 sols a pound.

[78] In October 1748 de la Galissonière and Bigot forwarded a mémoire from Canada which had to do with the supposed profits of the company (Arch. Nat., Col., B. 89: 143).

Canadian interests, in the form of "Observations" on its report, which, while no longer supporting claims to extravagant profits, nevertheless took the position

> "that not only has the Company experienced no real loss, as it pretends, but even that, in the two years of seventeen hundred and forty-six and seventeen hundred and forty-seven, it has realized a profit, from the Beaver trade, of four hundred and thirty thousand, seven hundred and eighty-five livres." [79]

These interests further took the position that, even supposing that the profit "proved by these observations" was insufficient, it would be better to advance the sale price of beaver in France twenty sols per pound than diminish its purchase price in Canada.[80] In this connection it was argued that this advance in France would not decrease the number of French beaver hats worn and that the maintenance of a purchase price in Canada equivalent to that paid by the English would permit the company to monopolize the American beaver trade — whereby the hat-manufacturers in France would reap the advantage of recovering markets once enjoyed in Spain, Portugal, Germany, and other countries, which the English now possessed — since the English colonies could supply but few skins.[81]

---

[79] N. Y. Col. Doc., X, 201.

[80] On the other hand Pierre André O'Hoguerty argued in his *Essai sur les Interêts du Commerce* (1754) that, were the Compagnie des Indes to limit itself to a profit of thirty per cent and let the hat-makers have their beaver at five livres a pound, the latter by diminishing to the same extent the price of their hats could ruin their English competitors. That this could be done he maintained by reason of the fact that the company paid at Quebec but 3 livres and 10 sols per pound for beaver (an understatement for beaver skins except for *castor d'été* and *rogneures de castor*, which sold for one livre and three livres respectively in 1754) and sold the same in France for 7 livres, 10 sols per pound to the hat-makers.

[81] *Ibid.* The above argument does not, of course, take into account the large supply of beaver secured from Hudson Bay by the English. However, it would appear that much of this beaver, the finest quality secured in North America, found its way to France. According to a memorial relating to the English beaver-hat industry prepared in 1764, which is among the Chatham Papers, it was not until the French came into temporary possession of Hudson Bay in 1701 that they turned to the manufacture of beaver hats. Thereupon in 1702 the King set up at Lyon at his own expense a manufactory, gave great encouragement to foreigners skilled in this branch to settle there, and prohibited the export of all beaver. As a result, the English beaver-hat industry, employing up to that time over twenty thousand people, was reduced to such extremities that many skilled hat-makers finally emigrated to France. Although Hudson Bay was restored to the English by the Treaty of Utrecht, by that time the French beaver-hat industry had become well established in Paris and other trading towns, and it so flourished, that, in the words of the memorial, it at last "monopoliz'd the whole beaver Hatt trade of Europe & the Indies, which must bring them in many Millions Sterlg. p. Annum; they serve all Spain,

Putting aside certain questions that present themselves in face of contradictory statements respecting the ability of the Compagnie des Indes to maintain the war-time price of beaver, it may be stated that for the years 1754–5 — that is, for the two years preceding the open declaration of war between Great Britain and France — the total value of the furs exported from Canada was placed at 2,813,535 livres (£117,230), or an average of 1,406,767 livres (£58,615) a year, according to calculations based upon an examination of the export duties paid.[82] However, it was estimated at the same time that the total annual value of the fur yield of the Province was not less than £140,000 sterling.[83] Assuming that this estimate was approximately correct, it meant that much less than one-half of the total yield at this period paid Canada export duties and, therefore, probably never reached France. Yet it was largely to support this trade that the latter country was being drained of its resources. The explanation of this amazing situation, of course, lies in the fact that Montreal merchants, *voyageurs, coureurs de bois*, and natives were simply seeking the most profitable avenue of disposing of their peltry and of obtaining in return merchandise that met their desires. This

Portugal, Italy, Germany, Sweden, Denmark, etc. etc. there being no Beaver Hatt manufactories in any said countries except a very small one set up in Portugal about four years ago. . . . Tis true we might have recovered a great part of this trade when the Hudson's Bay was restored to us in the year 1714 had we either prohibited the exportation of beaver as the French did in 1702 or even laid a large tax upon its export; but instead of which we only laid seven pence half penny p. skin Tax upon our imports and allowed a drawback of 4 s. upon the exports which has enabled the french to carry on that trade cheaper than we can & consequently keep continual possession of it. By reason of our allowing the export as aforesaid the price of Beaver is raised from 7 s. 6 d. p. Lb. (the price it sold at when I came from Hudson's Bay in the year 1717) to 18 shillings p. lb. . . . It appeared before a Committee of the house of Commons last Thursday sennight, that there had been near 200,000 beaver skins exported from hence to France the very last year [1763] . . ." (Chatham Manuscripts, Vols. 75–94, 1715–1763, pp. 164–7. Canadian Archives Transcripts).

[82] See General Murray's " Report," 1762, William Smith, *History of Canada*, I, Appendix, pp. 66–7. According to a detailed statement entitled " *Pelletries sorties pour france en 1754* " (Shelburne Papers, 64: 161, Clements Library), the total value of the furs (Quebec prices) sent from Canada in 1754 was 1,547,885 livres, 11 sols. Of the total, beaver skins valued at 505,319 livres were shipped, amounting to less than one-third the total, of which the *castor sec d'hiver* was valued at 428,360 livres and the *castor gras d'hiver* at but 59,772 livres. In 1755, according to another less detailed statement (ibid., 64: 165), furs were exported valued at 1,265,650 livres, 6 sols. The beaver export in this year was valued (Quebec prices) at 595,992 livres. The total value of the furs gives a figure for the two years approximately that in the Murray report.

[83] This estimate in the Murray report was made by " the most intelligent traders" (op. cit., 67).

was clearly not by way of the warehouses of the Compagnie des Indes.

For example, when the Compagnie after 1737 and before 1746 was paying fifty-five sols a pound for winter grades of beaver, and for other grades twenty sols, the English were offering four livres and twelve sols — that is, ninety-two sols a pound for skin " without distinction " and without deducting five per cent for tare as was the habit of the French company; further, " they gave bills of exchange on London payable on sight in écus valued at 48 to the mark for whatever was sent to them by the merchants and *voyageurs* of Montreal," whereas the company's agents were obliged to offer payment in bills of exchange that could not be paid on sight and were therefore subject to sharp discount if immediate payment were secured.[84] But this is only part of the explanation for the movement of a large part of the Canadian beaver and other furs to the English. The latter alone were able to provide suitable blue and scarlet cloth, so much prized by the Indians. In spite of various efforts on the part of the French, especially in 1713 to manufacture an acceptable substitute,[85] the result was failure. On October 1, 1749 La Jonquière and Bigot reported that the four bolts of French cloth sent on trial by the Compagnie des Indes were " frightful, the red cloth is brown and unpressed; the blue, of a very inferior quality to that of England." [86] In fact, the famous English écarlatine was held by all acquainted with the Indian trade to be an " indispensable necessity." This, of course, meant that at least a thousand bolts of it had to be either purchased in England, through special permission, granted to the Compagnie des Indes [87] and de-

---

[84] Arch. Nat., Col., C[11] A. 97: 262–73.

[85] Arch. Nat., Col., C[11] A. 34: 7–8.

[86] N. Y. Col. Doc., X, 200.

[87] A. M. Martin was sent by the Minister of the Marine to Canada to make a special report, especially as to the desirability of establishing there a so-called *magasin d'abondance*. In a letter written November 5, 1752 (Arch. Nat., Col., C[11] A. 98: 425) he mentioned the fact that that same year the Compagnie des Indes had sent out seven bolts of cloth manufactured in Languedoc in imitation of the English écarlatines. Upon examination by the Governor General, the Intendant, and others, it was found in comparing this with the English cloth that " *il y en avoit deux pièces parfaitement bien (unitées) et même plus belles que les écarlatines angloises.*" However, he pointed out that while the French could imitate the English product this could not be supplied for the same price for which the company purchased the latter. It therefore was suggested that the French weavers should receive a premium of three livres per bolt for cloth equal to the English product so that it could be furnished to the Canadian *voyageurs* for from seven to ten sols per *aune* (ell) with a year's credit, whereby they could offer it to the Indians at the same price as the English cloth.

nied to others by the French government, or illegally introduced into Canada from New York. Again, the English supplied the natives with a superior type of kettle; it was light and durable, made of yellow copper, and came in assorted sizes, whereas the French kettle was too heavy to be carried about by the Indians in their wanderings and could not withstand hard usage as was required.[88]

Thus it was that because of the relatively high prices paid for the furs — together with the possession of a constant supply of excellent English cloth, a favoured kind of kettle, and other desirable commodities conservatively priced — the English, while avoiding the great expense of policing the Great Lakes and the dependent parts, were able at the same time to secure perhaps the cream of the trade of those regions during the period under consideration. It is therefore no wonder that the French authorities had long sought to raise a barrier to this destructive competition. An account of their effort in this direction will be given in the following chapter, which will also attempt to analyse the strategic role of the Six Nations in the Great Lakes region.

---

[88] *Ibid.*

CHAPTER III

The Six Confederated Nations

IN THE PRECEDING chapter some of the problems involved in the exploitation of the fur resources of the Great Lakes region by the French in the eighteenth century have been surveyed. The role of the Iroquoian Confederation not only with respect to this but in relation to other phases of the history of the rivalry of the French and English in North America presents so many facets and is really of such transcendent importance for the period under consideration as to demand particular treatment. For example, from the point of view of the British colonial authorities the explanation of the penetration and occupation in force of the upper Ohio Valley by the French — described in some detail in the preceding volume of this series[1] — lay in the apparent indifference toward this movement of the Six Confederated Nations. The latter appeared to hold the key to the situation, and their manifest unwillingness to encourage English settlement and the building of forts on the Ohio and equal unwillingness to attempt to block the French pressure in that direction to a very great extent paralysed English trans-Appalachian enterprise. For, in view of the sweeping territorial claims of the Iroquois,[2] the government of Virginia and the promoters of the Ohio Company had been loath to proceed with their plans before the permission of the Onondaga Council had been secured — a permission that was, however, withheld until after the elimination of French influence in North America.

---

[1] See Volume IV: Zones of International Friction, 1748–1754, Chaps. VI–IX.
[2] Ibid., pp. 155–6.

In the middle of the eighteenth century the Six Nations and their " colonies " or detached groups living westward of the ancient sites of the Confederation seem to have numbered between ten and twelve thousand souls,[3] and their villages — some of them widely scattered — possibly as many as fifty.[4] The nearest to Albany were the Mohawk, with their chief village situated some forty miles west on the south bank of the river of that name; the Oneida, located near the sources of the Mohawk River about Lake Oneida, were some sixty miles farther west; the Onondaga were established thirty miles beyond the Oneida, with the Tuscarora villages partly in the Oneida country and partly in that of the Onondaga; thirty miles beyond the Onondaga villages came those of the Cayuga on the east shore of Lake Cayuga; finally, eighty miles west of these, in what is now Monroe and Ontario Counties, appeared those of the Seneca, " not above two hundred and forty miles from Albany." [5]

The villages of the Iroquois, according to Cadwallader Colden, writing in 1746, were of two types, the open and the " castle," the latter in the form of " a Square surrounded with Palisadoes, without

---

[3] The problem of determining the actual strength of the Six Nations in the middle of the eighteenth century is not easy. In 1736 an enumeration of Indian tribes made by some unknown Frenchmen (*N. Y. Col. Doc.*, IX, 1052–8) gives the fighting strength of the Six Nations as follows: the Onondaga 200 warriors, the Mohawks 80, the Oneida 100, the Cayuga 120, the Seneca 350, and the Tuscarora 250. In 1763 Sir William Johnson presented the following figures (*ibid.*, VII, 582), which are doubtless more accurate: the Mohawks 160 warriors, the Oneida 250, the Tuscarora 140, the Onondaga 150, the Cayuga 200, and the Seneca 1050. In 1774 Governor Tryon stated in his report to the home government (*ibid.*, VIII, 452):

" The whole Six Nations consist of about Two Thousand Fighting Men, and their number of Souls according to their latest returns at least Ten Thousand; the Seneca Nation amounting alone to one half of that Number."

In 1754 William Shirley, however, in addressing the Massachusetts Bay General Court on April 2, ascribed to them much greater power than the above accounts. He declared that, according to an account given by the Iroquois themselves in open council in 1742, they and those conquered by them and now in alliance and trade with them could place in the field between sixteen and seventeen thousand warriors. He went on to add that " one who must be a good Judge of the Strength of the Five Nations . . . being interrogated by me concerning the Number of their fighting Men, made answer that he did not know their number but well knows that they are a numerous People, a terrible Body of Men, & able to burn all the Indians of Canada " (*Mass. Archives*, XX, 199).

[4] F. W. Hodge, *Handbook of American Indians*, I, 618–19.

[5] Report of a Committee of the New York Council, November 6, 1724, Colden, *History of the Five Indian Nations* (London, 1750), Appendix, pp. 13–14. According to this report there were English settlements at that time thirty miles west of the Mohawks.

any Bastions or Out-works." [6] These in the middle of the eighteenth century were composed, as a rule, whether open or defended, no longer of long houses but of small cabins with a council house gracing the chief town of each nation. [7] Unimpressive, from every point of view, they were surrounded by fields where the women planted and harvested their maize, tobacco, and other crops. In fact, nothing about them suggested to the casual visitor that he had come in contact with an Indian group that was playing a role of first importance in the great drama that was unfolding in North America in the middle of the eighteenth century.

But the country of the Iroquois, from the viewpoint of the Onondaga Council, extended far to the west of the old settled villages and included the lands lying south of Lake Erie and west as far as the country of the Miami, the Quiatenon, and the Piankashaw, who dwelt along the Maumee and the Wabash, thus taking in most of the upper Ohio Valley and constituting a vast hunting preserve. [8] Although during the period under consideration other Indian groups — Mingo, Delawares, and Shawnee — as well as those of the Six Nations, inhabited this region, these looked to Onondaga for all great decisions,

---

[6] Ibid., Introduction, p. 9; see also L. H. Morgan, League of the Ho-dé-no-saunee or Iroquois, pp. 38–9.

[7] While it would appear that the long houses capable of accommodating some twenty families such as had characterized the Iroquois during the early history of their contact with the whites had largely disappeared by 1750 (ibid., pp. 314–15), it is nevertheless of interest to note that John Bartram sojourned in such a house in Onondaga in 1743. He refers in his Observations (London, 1751), pp. 40–1, to the fact that the town was two or three miles long, with scattered cabins, many of which held two families. The house in which he stopped was, however, " about eighty feet long and seventeen broad, the common passage six feet wide, and the apartments on each side five feet. . . ." The Reverend William Andres thus described the Mohawk villages in 1713 (letter printed in J. W. Lydekker, The Faithful Mohawks, pp. 34–8):

" Their Chief Town or Castle . . . stands by the fort, consisting of 40 or 50 Wigwams or houses, palizadoed Round. Another of their Chief Towns, between 20 & 30 houses is three or four & twenty Miles distant from this. They have several other little Towns 7 or 8 houses in a Town, and single houses up and Down pretty near their Castle. . . . Their houses are made of Mats and bark of Trees together with poles about 3 or 4 yards high."

[8] It is not without significance that Father Jacques Gravier, who travelled along the Mississippi at the beginning of the eighteenth century, should call the Ohio River country " the country of the Iroquois" (for the development of this point see C. A. Hanna, The Wilderness Trail, I, 222). The Shawnee, before their conquest by the Iroquois, were, according to Father Marquette, domiciled upon the lower Ohio in thirty-eight villages (for his " Journal" of 1873 see J. G. Shea's Discovery and Exploration of the Mississippi Valley).

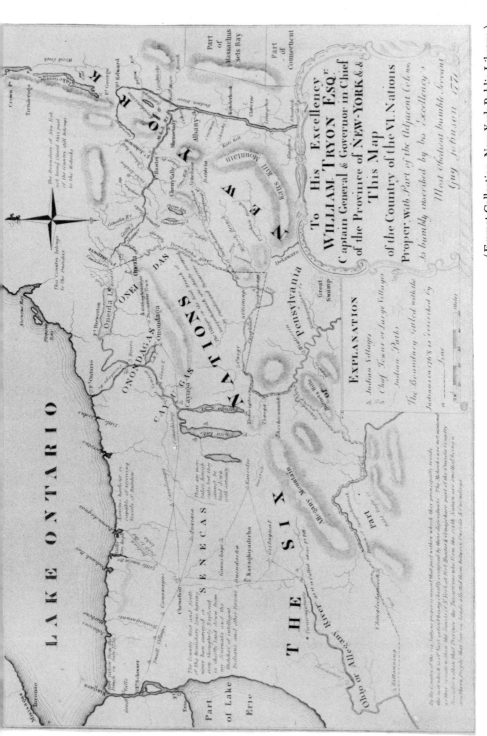

To His Excellency
WILLIAM TRYON ESQr.
Captain General & Governor in Chief
of the Province of NEW-YORK &c&c
This Map
of the Country of the VI. Nations
Proper, with Part of the Adjacent Colonies,
Is humbly inscribed by his Excellency's

Most obedient humble Servant
Guy Johnson 1771

EXPLANATION

⌂ Indian Villages
⌂🏠 Chief Towns or Large Villages
        Indian Paths

The Boundary settled with the
Indians in 1768 is described by

LAKE ONTARIO

Part of Lake Erie

THE SIX NATIONS

SENECAS

CAYUGAS

ONONDAGAS

ONEIDAS

MOHAWKS RIVER

Pensylvania

Part of Massachu sets Bay

Part of Connecticut

Ohio or Alleghany River

LAKE ONTARIO

Niagara River.

A VIEW of NIAGARA FORT,
taken by Sir William Johnson,
on the 25ᵗʰ of July 1759.
Drawn on the Spot in 1758.

particularly those having to do with the purchase of lands and the building of forts by the English.[9] Likewise, east of the Allegheny Mountains, the claims of the Iroquois to dominion were extended to cover the northern third of Pennsylvania and included not only the lands formerly possessed by the conquered Susquehannah, a people of the same blood, but those occupied by the dependent Delawares, called by the Iroquois " the Women," and the Shawnee before these two groups migrated across the mountains into the Ohio Valley — claims that were repeatedly recognized by the Pennsylvania Proprietors and the governors of their province. Finally, the Mohawks, after the breaking of the power of the Mohicans, claimed as part of their preserves all unappropriated land in the region of the upper Hudson and that about Lakes George and Champlain, which claim also was accepted by the New York authorities.[10] Here was a domain truly imperial in extent and also imperial in the sense that living within it were a number of Indian groups that were impelled by circumstances to consider themselves dependent, their security and welfare limited by the will of their Iroquoian masters.[11]

As one views the success of the Five Nations in extending their influence over a region so widespread and over the tribes inhabiting it while presenting an obstacle at times so formidable to both the English and the French in carrying forward their respective expansionist programs, one is impelled to recognize that this league represented a force that was unique at least in late seventeenth- and early eighteenth-century American history. For surely no other group

---

[9] For a treatment of this topic see Chapter VIII of Volume IV of this series.

[10] For a careful analysis of the early claims of the Mohawks to this region see G. T. Hunt's The Wars of the Iroquois, Chapter III.

[11] For a repudiation of the claims by earlier writers that the Iroquois possessed an " empire " see ibid., pp. 157 and 161. Professor Hunt, with the seventeenth century particularly in mind, is perhaps right. However, what one has in mind in using the word " empire " is important. The fourth chapter of his book bears the title: " The Huron Trading Empire." While not disposed to quarrel seriously with the term when thus employed, I would prefer to think of the Hurons as the seventeenth-century Venetians of the New World rather than the builders of an Indian commercial " empire." This the Iroquois never succeeded in becoming. On the other hand they did extend their conquests at the expense of other Indian tribes and by a process of incorporating dependent groups either by adoption or, as in the case of the Shawnee and Delawares, by accepting pledges that recognized their position of inferiority, produced an important characteristic of empire-building; this, taken together with the recognition of their control over lands far removed from their established abodes, might well entitle them to recognition in the eighteenth century as the possessors of an " empire," the decisions respecting which were dependent upon the Onondaga Council.

of North American Indians possessed dynamic qualities comparable to those of the confederated Iroquoian tribes during the period from 1649 to 1749. What is the explanation for this?

The answer not only involves the fact of a most strategic position athwart French advance toward the southwest and the English advance into the Great Lakes region by way of the Mohawk River but also, it would seem, the fact that these tribes were what they were.[12] While it has been contended that geographical environment is the chief determinant with respect to the character of the culture of the North American Indian groups,[13] this presents certain difficulties. Among these is the discovery of those factors that in the final analysis determined the geographical location of the tribes of North America before the coming of the white man. Let one assume that the Pawnee had found themselves in the above region — secured, it would appear, from the Algonquians by the Iroquois and held thereafter against all rivals. Is it likely, in the light of what knowledge we have of them, that they could have played a significant role in international affairs as did the Iroquois, could have maintained themselves against powerful enemies and conquered many of them in view of the fact that they had no martial tradition and submitted readily to slavery? Was there not, in fact, almost as much difference between North American Indian groups with respect to certain cultural traits as there was between the Negro tribes dwelling about the Gulf of Guinea, varying as they did from the fierce, head-hunting, intractable Koromantyn to the plodding, submissive Popow and the highly sensitive, rather effeminate Eboe? Further, can one lightly cast aside the significance of institutions among primitive peoples in the determination of their historic role any more than among those that are civilized?

There has in the past been general agreement among scholars that the Iroquoian Confederation or League, with all of its manifest defects, represented perhaps the most advanced forms of intertribal organization existing among the aborigines of the New World during the period under consideration.[14] This tribal nexus seems to have

---

[12] For a strong argument that the only cause for the strength of the Iroquoian position was their location see Hunt, op. cit., p. 159.

[13] For this view see Ellsworth Huntington, The Red Man's Continent, Chapter V.

[14] Professor Hunt (op. cit., pp. 8–9) rejects the significance of the confederation in Iroquoian history and places the blame for the widespread acceptance of its importance upon Lewis H. Morgan's The League of the Iroquois. However, I do not know of any eighteenth-century observer of the Six Nations who did not agree that the League's

evolved in the early part of the fifteenth century.[15] It was based upon "the Great Binding Law," or "the Great Immutable Law," given to the Iroquois, according to tradition, by their culture hero, the Mohawk Dekanawida, whose efforts were aided by Hiawatha.[16] This law embodied not only the symbolism of unity of the five arrows bound firmly together and of the "Long House" stretching from the Hudson to Niagara[17] but, what is more significant, that of the Tree of the Great Long Leaves, or the Tree of the Great Peace, planted in the heart of the Onondaga territory, under the shade of which the "Lords of the Confederation" could rest on "the soft white feathery down of the globe thistle."[18] This tree of peace was not alone for the Five Confederated Nations but its "Great White Roots" were spread out so that "any man or any nation . . . may trace the Roots to the Tree" and "be welcomed to take shelter beneath the Tree of the Long Leaves."[19] By this means universal peace, it was the hope, was ultimately to be established. This was to come by peaceful persuasion as to the advantages of accepting the Binding Law, or, if this failed, by conquest. Thus, the Confederation under the Great Binding Law had a high mission — and this mission was expressed by concrete acts — in fulfilment of which, for example, the Tuscarora were welcomed as a sixth Iroquoian nation, while the Hurons, the Petun, the Neutral, the Erie, the Conestoga — all likewise of Iroquoian stock as well as others — were broken as resisting tribes,[20] and the families of these were either scat-

---

Onondaga Council was something to be reckoned with; this is particularly true of such men as Sir William Johnson and Conrad Weiser, each of whom had lived among the Iroquois and knew the strength and the weakness of any mere confederation of Indian tribes. While most students will agree that the Confederation of the United States failed between 1781 and 1789 to achieve proper unity of action on the part of the states, yet few would assert that it was for that reason unimportant in the history of the American nation.

[15] Livingston Farrand, *Basis of American History*, p. 155; see also L. H. Morgan, *League of the Iroquois*.

[16] Arthur C. Parker, *The Constitution of the Five Nations* (New York State Museum *Bulletin*, No. 184, 1916), p. 8. "The Great Binding Law" is presented in this *Bulletin*, pp. 30–60.

[17] Farrand, *op. cit.*, p. 161. The long house is also embodied in Iroquoian cosmology. "The lodges they [that is, the beings that dwelt upon earth before man] severally possess are customarily long." This is from the Onondaga version of the story of creation, translated from the Onondaga dialect by J. N. B. Hewitt, Bureau of American Ethnology, *Report* No. 21 (1903), p. 142.

[18] Parker, *op. cit.*, p. 30.

[19] *Ibid.*

[20] For careful treatment of these wars, see Hunt, *op. cit.*

tered or received into the Confederation by adoption under the strict injunction to forget the name of their " birth nation "; still others, such as the non-Iroquoian Shawnee and Delawares, were subdued and held in a mild form of subjection under the protecting shade of the Tree of the Great Peace.

As to the polity of the Five Nations, this embraced, first of all, the primary unit, the maternal or brood family; [21] that of the clan, gens, or totem group,[22] made of a grouping of closely related families based upon a cognatic relationship that, as in the case of the brood family, forbade intermarriage between its members; that of the phratry, a grouping of clans; [23] that of the tribe or nation; and, finally, the combining of the nations into one perpetual confederation. In this complicated polity the place of women was of such importance that writers refer to the " Iroquois matriarchate."

Not only within the Confederation was the line of descent cognatic rather than agnatic, as was suggested, but all real property — that is, the lands of the clan and the houses of the brood families — belonged to the women and in a sense were entailed upon the basis of female exclusive inheritance; further, authority within the brood family was centred in the matron mother; again female suffrage took on a significance that is truly remarkable in a people distinguished for their martial spirit. For example, the child-bearing women of the lordly families (the *royaneh*) were respectively the electors of the forty-eight confederate lords or sachems as " the heirs of the Authorized Names for all time to come," [24] with the proviso that this choice made

[21] The name employed by the Iroquois to describe this was *ohwachira*. It was, according to Hewitt, "an organized body of persons tracing descent of blood from a common mother . . . forming an exogamic incest group" (Smithsonian Institution, *Report*, 1932, p. 476). See the chart presented by Goldenweiser (*Early Civilization*, p. 74) that illustrates the principle of inclusion and exclusion among the offspring of an Iroquoian woman with her daughters and daughters of the latter constituting the nexus, but with her sons likewise embodied but not their wives.

[22] In the eighteenth century the number of clans or gentes within a tribe varied. Among the Seneca, Cayuga, Onondaga, and Tuscarora, according to L. H. Morgan, there were eight respectively, among the Oneida and Mohawk but three (*Houses and Home-Life of the American Aborigines*, p. 11). Hodge, however, credits the Seneca with nine (*Handbook of American Indians*, I, 304). The Bear clan was represented in all six of the nations, the Wolf and Turtle in five — with the Tuscarora having the Gray Wolf, the Yellow Wolf, the Great Turtle, and the Little Turtle clans — the Beaver and Snipe in four, and the Deer, Hawk, and Eel in three. All members of a clan in whatever tribe were held to be related and therefore among them there was no intermarriage.

[23] There were two phratries within each tribe. See A. A. Goldenweiser, *op. cit.*, p. 75.

[24] According to Hewitt each of the chosen brood families — that is, the *ohwachira* — had an official representative in the federal council. He states that as originally instituted

by the qualified women of the clan in question was to be referred to the men of that clan and then, if accepted, to the other clans for approval.[25] Their authority did not terminate with performance of this important function; they were authorized, for example, " to correct and admonish " their lords. Again, matters of the greatest importance could not be settled by the Lords of the Confederation but had to be submitted to the decision of the qualified electors of each clan; in this connection the women had their own clan council fire at which their decisions were made.[26] Further, the matron of the clan was responsible for its preservation and she could require the men to bring into the clan by war or by other means those who could qualify to take the places of departed members.[27] It is also not without significance that the life of a woman was valued at double the life of a man, in terms of composition payment in strings of wampum.[28]

As to the original Five " Nations," these were grouped upon the

---

there were just forty-seven ohwachira and that at a later date the number was increased to forty-nine ("Status of Iroquois Woman," Smithsonian Institution, Report, 1932, p. 481). On the other hand Morgan (Houses and Home-Life of the American Aborigines, p. 29) declares there were fifty and that these were distributed as follows among the original Five Nations: the Seneca had eight, the Mohawks and Oneida nine each, the Cayuga ten, and the Onondaga fourteen. Each of the sachemships carried a hereditary title such as Handsome Lake, Man Frightened, Large Mouth, Swallowing Himself; two of these were never filled after the passing of the original holders: that held by Dekanawida and that by Hiawatha, the two founders of the Confederation; their names were, however, always called in the roll of sachems. According to the Great Binding Law as presented by Parker (op. cit., p. 42): " The Women of the Forty Eight (now fifty) Royaneh families shall be heirs of the Authorized Names for all time to come."

[25] The following clans existed within the Confederation at the time of its organization, according to the Great Binding Law: the Great Name Bearer, Ancient Name Bearer, Great Bear, Ancient Bear, Turtle, Painted Turtle, Standing Rock, Large Plover, Little Plover, Deer, Pigeon Hawk, Eel, Ball, Opposite-Side-of-the-Hand, and Wild Potatoes (ibid., p. 42).

[26] Ibid., p. 55. According to Schoolcraft, the matrons could negative a decision for war (Indian Tribes of the United States, III, 196). Hewitt emphasizes the fact (op. cit., p. 485) that the councils of the women had the right of initiative, the right of referendum, and the right of recall.

[27] Referring to this practice of adoption into the clan, Colden (History of the Five Indian Nations, London, 1750, pp. 8-9) says that the prisoners were presented to those who had lost any relative. " If the captives be accepted, there is an End to their sorrow from that moment; they are dressed as fine as they can make them; they are absolutely free (except to return to their own Country) and enjoy all the Privileges the Person had, in whose Place they are accepted; but if otherwise they die in Torments to satiate the Revenge of those that refuse them." By this means even a young boy prisoner accepted for a father who had been killed was thereafter addressed by the grown children of the latter as " father."

[28] J. N. B. Hewitt, op. cit., pp. 484-5.

basis of certain accepted distinctions: the Mohawk and Seneca were the "older brothers," the Cayuga and Oneida the "younger brothers," and the Onondaga the "fire-keepers"; the last-named and the first two were addressed by the Cayuga and the Oneida in open council respectfully as "father"; they in turn addressed the latter as "son."[29] Every five years the forty-eight Lords of the Confederation were expected to assemble for the solemn purpose of determining whether or not to maintain the Great Binding Law; for if any would not pledge continued unity this was to be dissolved;[30] and yet there was to be no peaceful secession; such an act of repudiation was to be considered treason and upon a second warning the offending nation was to be driven from its ancestral lands.[31] It is significant that in spite of serious friction within the Confederation at times[32] and the final expulsion of the Canadian expatriated Iroquois — the so-called domiciled Indians — there was never a case of the attempted secession of an entire nation. Nor was the Confederation ever involved in a terrible civil war — such as the Choctaw had to face as the result of the struggle between pro-French and pro-British factions for the control of the nation.

These facts should not, however, lead one to read into the organization and maintenance of the Confederation that which in actuality was not to be found. Matters of common concern, it would seem, were the object of deliberation as a rule at Onondaga by the Lords of the Confederation. Yet important decisions were hard to reach, especially if these involved action, as the result not only of divergent interests among the Indian tribes that composed it but of the necessity to refer

---

[29] Conrad Weiser's "Journal," 1750, Pa. Col. Rec., V, 476. The Tuscarora, after adoption, also addressed the Mohawk, Seneca, and Onondaga as father. However, according to an account of the Iroquois prepared by the Reverend J. Christopher Pyrlaeus, a Moravian missionary who lived among the Mohawk about the middle of the eighteenth century and who spoke their tongue, the Onondaga were "the head," the Mohawk "the eldest brother," the Oneida "the eldest son," the Seneca "the next youngest son," and the Tuscarora "the youngest son" (John Heckewelder, History, Manners, and Customs of the Indian Nations, pp. 96–7).

John Heckewelder, an eighteenth-century authority on the Indians, has the following to say about the term Iroquoian "nations": "The name of Five and afterwards Six Nations, was given to them by the English, whose allies they were, probably to raise their consequence, and magnify the idea of their strength; but the Indian nations never did flatter them with that high sounding appellation, and considered them merely as confederated tribes" (ibid., p. 96).

[30] Parker, op. cit., p. 45.

[31] Ibid., p. 55.

[32] G. T. Hunt, op. cit., pp. 7–8.

the tentative decisions of the council to the ratification of the local councils.

In other words, what we have is a loose " confederation." The student will therefore question the historical accuracy of the boast of the Iroquois, in calling upon the Cherokee in 1758 to support them in their hostilities against the French, when they declared:

> " Our Confederacy have always maintained their unanimity and our resolutions are to continue firm & united together. . . ." [33]

Nevertheless, there did exist various bonds of unity that were strong enough to preserve, if not to exalt, the symbols of it through the most difficult periods faced by the Six Nations in the course of the eighteenth century. Indeed, the unshaken faith of the Indians that their welfare depended upon this unity, that so long as it was maintained they would remain strong and without it they would lose all consequence, gave it the vitality to survive a series of internal crises that, as will be made clear, faced the Iroquois before 1754.

In examining further the polity of the Confederation it is of interest to note the clear distinction between civil and military authorities. A Lord of the Confederation could not go to war under this title but was temporarily divested of it and of his deer antlers should he choose to go, and then he went simply as one among the warriors. For each nation had its war lord, and the warriors of the united nations in undertaking an expedition in common were led by a specially appointed chief — all of which testifies to the advanced character of this polity. Further, so deeply were these nations committed to the principle of equality and liberty that they permitted no kind of superiority of one Indian over another; the sachems were distinguished not for their privileged position, not for the accumulation of riches, but rather for their poverty as the result of open-handed liberality; there were no slaves among the Six Nations, not even among the prisoners of war. Nor in their wars, in spite of the barbarous practices of the " gauntlet " and of the torturing of prisoners when not accepted for adoption, were their captives on the march treated otherwise than with every consideration (for they might become brothers or even fathers of the captors); moreover, according to Colden, no violence to the chastity of a woman prisoner was ever offered.[34] Their code of honour was

---

[33] *The Papers of Sir William Johnson* (ed. A. C. Flick), IX, 958.
[34] Colden, *op. cit.*, p. 8. This statement was confirmed by General Clinton in 1779,

very exacting. Among them stealing was a scandalous thing; a slant-
ing stick or pole at the door of the long house — signifying that the
occupants were absent — kept away intruders; there were no locks or
bars. Morgan, in speaking of the Iroquois, refers to his " simple integrity, his generosity, his unbounded hospitality, his love of truth, and,
above all, his unshaken fidelity. . . ." [35] Such were, it seems, among
the virtues of this fierce and redoubtable people whose greatest enemy, in fact, was the white man's strong drink.

Occupying as they did the region east, south, and southwest of
Lake Ontario for their settled abodes, the Five Nations had in the
seventeenth century so cleared it of both beaver and elk,[36] according
to Governor General de Courcelles, writing in 1671,[37] " that they experience the greatest difficulty in finding a single beaver there." As a
result, they crossed that lake in search of peltry and trapped and
hunted on the lands of the broken Hurons until the Saulteurs turned
them back. At the same time they directed their attention to regions
southward from Lake Erie where their young men went, especially
the Seneca, to hunt and to trade with the Far Western Indians. Further, some of the tribes among the latter were in the course of time led
to bring their furs to the New York traders, thus passing through the
lands of the Confederation — a situation that determined the French
authorities at Quebec, according to Governor Dongan, to bring about
a rupture between the Iroquois and these tribes,[38] which in turn led
to a prolonged period of hostilities and resulted ultimately in the destruction of the powerful and numerous Erie at the hands of their
better-armed rivals, who seem to have been adequately supplied with
guns and ammunition by the Dutch merchants at Fort Orange.[39] The
Shawnee on the lower Ohio were likewise scattered.

who declared: " Bad as these savages are, they never violate the chastity of any woman,
their prisoner " (Smithsonian Institution, Report, 1932, p. 483).

[35] League of the Iroquois, p. 111. Hewitt (op. cit., p. 487) affirms that a " dispas-
sionate survey of the underlying principles and regulations of the League of the Iroquois
. . . reveals the startling fact that the hand, the heart, and the mind of women had a
directing and molding influence in their formulation and expression, for in noteworthy
fashion they are uniformly humane — even tender, tolerant, beneficent — and prudently
designed to secure the well-being of contemporary and future generations. . . ."

[36] The student is here referred to the scholarly Introduction to Peter Wraxall's
An Abridgement of the Indian Affairs by Professor McIlwain and to an important article
by Professor Buffinton, " The Policy of Albany and the English Westward Expansion,"
Miss. Valley Hist. Rev., VIII, 327–67.

[37] Documents Relative to the Colonial History of the State of New York, IX, 80.

[38] Ibid., III, 476.

[39] G. T. Hunt, op. cit., pp. 100–2, 171.

It should be emphasized at this point that the French, in the course of their exploitation of the Western Indian trade, had come to realize the great strategic importance of the Niagara River. As early as 1676 La Salle had established a trading house and a " forge " to encourage the Five Nations to resort there to trade.[40] But in view of the hostile attitude of the Iroquois the post ultimately proved to be untenable, located as it was in the Seneca country or at least within the region claimed by the Seneca tribe.[41] For, as the result of threats by the latter in 1686, the trader La Fleur was compelled to leave and the house was reduced to ruins. The following year, however, with the outbreak of the Seneca war and the invasion of their country and the destruction of three of their villages by the Marquis de Denonville, a fort was erected on a tongue of land between the Niagara River and Lake Ontario,[42] described by Governor Dongan as " the place where all our Traders and Beaver Hunters must pass " [43] and where he had himself hoped to be able to erect an English fort. But again the expectations of the French were not realized: the place proved to be unhealthy for the troops stationed there, many of whom died; the revictualling of it, moreover, was extremely expensive, and the Illinois and other Far West Indians failed to make use of it as a place of trade and as a refuge in their war with the Five Nations as was hoped. Denonville was therefore led to give assurances to Dongan, in August 1688, that to contribute to a general peace the garrison would be withdrawn.[44] This was done.

Granting the failure of the French in their early efforts at Niagara, it would, of course, be neglecting one of the most vital aspects of the problem not to make clear at this juncture that the Iroquois, while as a rule expressing loyalty to the English interest, were by no means oblivious of the advantages of maintaining trade relations with the French. Frontenac emphasized the great importance of this in his *mémoire* to the King in 1679 when he at the same time made reference to the establishment of the mission of Sault St. Louis in the neighbourhood of Montreal (in 1676) by the ecclesiastics of the Montreal Seminary, where were congregated members of the Five

---

[40] N. Y. Col. Doc., IX, 381.

[41] Ibid., IX, 349. For the cession in 1764 of the lands about the Niagara by the Seneca to the English see the communication of Major General Burton to Sir William Johnson of April 28, 1764 (Gunther Coll., N. A. Br., Chicago Historical Society).

[42] N. Y. Col. Doc., IX, 349.

[43] Ibid., III, 476.

[44] Ibid., III, 556.

Nations who had been won over to Roman Catholicism.[45] These Christian Indians maintaining their contacts with the Confederation [46] had made the mission by 1681 the entrepôt of an important trade that involved the French *coureurs de bois* and the Montreal and Albany merchants as well as the Five Nations. Their method was to resort, as a rule, to Albany by way of Chambly with furs and return with money and merchandise — an intercourse that was illegal, depriving as it did His Most Christian Majesty's treasury of the one-fourth value of the beaver that should have gone to the " Farmers' Magazine," [47] and serving at the same time to break down the New York regulations of the fur trade, such as were embodied in the famous Albany regulations based upon its charter of 1686.[48] In fact, this multilateral trade had the effect of placing Albany in a curious and privileged position which won it exemption from the terror of Indian hostilities. For the Praying Indians — in continued league with certain Montreal and Albany merchants — not only in times of peace between the crowns of England and France, but also in war, continued freely to engage in their contraband traffic — something that outraged especially the New Englanders, who, together with the Virginians and Carolinians, from time to time were obliged to bear the brunt of the savage forays of the Canadian Indians while the people of Albany rested in peace and security and even profited by the misfortunes of their fellow colonials.[49]

Of importance equal to this contraband trade in establishing the French influence was the activity of the Jesuits within the country of the Six Nations. For example, in 1671 the Reverend Father Jean de Lamberville, a learned and devout member of the Society of Jesus, began his labours at Onondaga; in 1682 he gave assurances to Count de Frontenac that he was prepared " to second, by our very feeble power, all the good intentions you have had and still entertain toward Canada "; [50] in 1684 he used his good offices to avoid a French-Seneca war; he and his brother were active there likewise in 1686, much to

---

[45] *Ibid.*, III, 570, 722; IX, 427–8.

[46] *Ibid.*, IX, 130, 146. These " Praying Indians " or " French Mohawks " first settled at La Prairie near Montreal in 1668, and were chiefly Oneida and Mohawks. They were renounced by the Confederation in 1684 after refusing repeatedly to return to their mother towns. They also were called Caughnawaga.

[47] *Ibid.* Reference is made, of course, to the depository of the King's revenue, the collection of which was farmed out in Canada as well as in France.

[48] See C. H. McIlwain's *Wraxall's New York Indian Records*, pp. lvii, lxi.

[49] *Ibid.*, pp. li–lii.

[50] *N. Y. Col. Doc.*, IX, 193, 252–6.

the embarrassment of Governor Dongan, a fellow Roman Catholic [51] — for they energetically supported Governor General Denonville's efforts to checkmate the New York Governor, who was aiming at winning over to the English the Ottawa and the Hurons and launching a united Iroquoian-Ottawa attack against Canada.[52] In fact, Denonville credits him, as the result of his care and shrewdness, with averting the storm, " which was the more dangerous as we were unprepared to protect ourselves against their incursions." [53] However, with the outbreak of the Seneca war the following year Lamberville withdrew from Onondaga; but his influence remained there. Of equal aid to the French cause was the Reverend Pierre Milet, who in 1668 appeared at Onondaga and in 1671 — the year that Lamberville began his labours — established a mission among the Oneida; he subsequently was at both Niagara and Frontenac. While at the latter place he was captured by the Iroquois and, although theoretically held as a prisoner among the Oneida, became an adopted member of the tribe and enjoyed an authority equal to that of any of the sachems.[54] Thus were the foundations laid for the influence exercised by the French over the Iroquois in the eighteenth century.

Passing over the period of the first colonial war, it may be pointed out that the year 1701 is of great significance in the history of the relations of the Five Nations with their white neighbours. It witnesses the conclusion of a treaty of friendship between the French and their Indian allies and the Confederation, with the Iroquois taking the initiative. It also witnesses the establishment of Fort Detroit, a place of strategic importance equal to that of Niagara (much, however, to the surprise and uneasiness of the Iroquois, who claimed that it was erected in the midst of their beaver grounds and without their consent), with the bland assurance by the French Governor General that its chief purpose was benevolent, as it was designed to " prevent all inconveniences of the Waganhaes " (Ottawa) and to supply the Confederation with necessaries such as powder and lead while they were hunting.[55] Finally, it witnesses the formal cession to the King of England — as a reply to this encroachment on the part of the French — of all of the beaver hunting grounds of the Confederation northwest of Lake Ontario and between Lakes Huron and Erie and

[51] Ibid., III, 454–7, 488–90.
[52] Ibid., IX, 297.
[53] Ibid., IX, 358.
[54] Ibid., IV, 47; IX, 665.
[55] Ibid., IV, 891–2.

extending to the head of Lake Michigan and to the country of the Twightwee (Miami) — in length some eight hundred miles and in breadth some four hundred miles and including specifically " Tieugsachrondio, alias Fort de Tret " (Detroit) [56] — which indicated that the Indians were hoping that by this means their claims to this vast stretch of wilderness won by " a fierce and bloody warr with seaven nations of Indians called the Aragaritkas " (Hurons) would be made secure and the lands preserved from intrusion by the French and the Canadian Indians — a hope that was not fulfilled.

When the War of the Spanish Succession broke out, the services of the Confederation were enlisted by the English, but little was accomplished by the Indians in spite of the fact that to give them a proper impression of English prowess a delegation was sent to England.[57] In fact, in 1708 the Five Nations in conjunction with the Praying Indians of Canada, with the concurrence of the government of New York, " procured a kind of tacit Neutrality between the Colony of New York & Canada . . . by which means Peace was enjoyed in this Colony & all the designs of the Govr of Canada were bent upon New England, who were greatly harrassed & suffered much. . . ." During the hostilities the merchants of New York appear to have had a " flourishing Trade at Albany as well from Canada as the Westward. . . ." [58] Furthermore, in 1711 Charles le Moyne, Baron de Longueuil, with a company of Frenchmen, including the famous Joncaire, constructed a log house at Onondaga after showering the Indians with presents of an estimated value of six hundred pounds.[59] This occurred after a visit made the preceding year to Canada by a number of their sachems, on which occasion they had promised the Governor General that they would live in peace with the French. But their vacillation, or perhaps rather their lack of unity of policy, was emphasized by the fact that upon the arrival at Onondaga of Colonel Peter Schuyler from Albany they permitted him to tear down the blockhouse and also to destroy

---

[56] For the deed of cession see *ibid.*, IV, 908–11.

[57] For relations during this period see W. T. Morgan, " The Five Nations and Queen Anne," *Miss. Valley Hist. Rev.*, XIII, 169–90.

[58] *Wraxall's New York Indian Records*, p. 58. *N. Y. Col. Doc.*, IX, 842; Cadwallader Colden, " History of the Five Indian Nations: Continuation, 1707–1720," *Colden Papers*, IX, 366. This portion of Colden's *History of the Five Indian Nations*, published in Volume LXVIII of the *Collections* of the New York Historical Society (1937) had never appeared before in print. The revised edition of the *History* appearing in 1747 carried the account down to 1697. The " Continuation " covers the years 1707–20; there is thus left a gap in the *History*.

[59] *Wraxall's Indian Records*, p. 83; *N. Y. Col. Doc.*, V, 243–4.

the materials collected by the French for a chapel, and to " set up the Queens Arms in all ye Indian Castles through wch he went. . . ." [60]

At the termination of hostilities between the British and the French in the framing of the treaty of peace at Utrecht, the following article (Article XV) was embodied:

> " That the Subjects of France inhabiting Canada, and others shall hereafter give no hindrance or molestation to the five Nations or Cantons of Indians subject to the Dominion of Great Britain, nor to the other natives of America who are friends to the same. In like manner, the Subjects of Great Britain shall behave themselves peaceably toward the Americans who are subjects or friends to France, and on both sides they shall enjoy full liberty of going or coming on Account of Trade. As also the Natives of those Countrys shall with the same liberty resort as they please to the British or French Colonies, for promoting Trade on one side and the other, without any molestation or hindrance either on the part of the British Subjects or of the French. But it is to be exactly and distinctly settled by Commissarys who are and who ought to be accounted the Subjects & friends of Britain or of France." [61]

The meaning of this article led to endless disputes. It is quite apparent, however, that the intention of the British negotiators was to bring about a recognition on the part of the French authorities that the Five Nations were dependent upon the British Crown, with the understanding that certain other Indian groups not specified were likewise dependent upon the French Crown. Equally apparent was the intention of granting to all groups of Indians freedom of trade with both the British and the French colonies and the same freedom of trade on the part of the British and French in the Indian country. But did the freedom of trade thus allowed imply the right of the English to erect trading posts among the French Indians, or the French among the Five Nations? Was not such an act as the erection of a post accepted by both nations as a sign of territorial possession? Yet, if this were so, the question still remained: What lands belonged to the Five Nations and what lands to the French Indians? These were questions, among others, " to be exactly and distinctly settled " by commissioners to be

---

[60] *Colden Papers*, IX, 402; *N. Y. Col. Doc.*, V, 248.

[61] For the text of this treaty see George Chalmers, *A Collection of Treaties between Great Britain and Other Powers* (1790), I, 340–86; for excerpts see William MacDonald, *Select Charters and Other Documents Illustrative of American History, 1606–1775,* pp. 229–32.

appointed by the two Crowns — something that was not seriously attempted until after the Peace of Aix-la-Chapelle in 1749.

The Treaty of Utrecht was entered into by France when thoroughly exhausted as the result of a prolonged period of hostility against a powerful alliance. Its terms with respect to the European settlement — including the disposition of the crown of Spain — were far from disadvantageous to her, while admittedly falling short of her earlier expectations. Yet those relating to North America represented not only a sharp decline in her prestige in this portion of the New World, but also perhaps a temporary disillusionment as to the value to her of her overseas empire — including as they did a recognition of the British claims to Hudson Bay and to Newfoundland, the relinquishment of Acadia, and the formal acknowledgment that the Five Nations were "subject to the Dominion of Great Britain." However, her recuperative powers were great and among her statesmen were men of imagination who looked into the future and who were brought to realize the enormous strategic importance of the asset that she still enjoyed in the control and possession of the two great rivers of North America which in each case gave an entrance into the very heart of that continent. It is therefore not surprising that after a very brief breathing-spell she should set about to consolidate her position with increasing aggressiveness and confidence: in 1718 she laid the foundations of New Orleans on the Mississippi as the new capital of Louisiana; she made much more secure the entrance to the St. Lawrence by proceeding between 1717 and 1720 to lay the foundations for the great fortress of Louisbourg at old Hâvre à l'Anglois on Cape Breton Island, thus offsetting in a measure her loss of the Acadian peninsula; [62] further, she turned her attention to the strengthening of her position in the Great Lakes region by rebuilding the fort on the Niagara River.

In the movement to reoccupy the Niagara River the French enjoyed two advantages in securing the toleration if not the permission of the Five Nations to this end. Jesuit priests had continued to labour in the villages of the Confederation throughout most of the war, and

---

[62] The relation of Cape Breton to the fisheries was also a motive in the building of Louisbourg. "You will also have the goodness to direct that Île Royale [Cape Breton] be fortified," wrote Governor de Vaudreuil in 1716. "Were it to fall under the domination of the English, in addition to the loss of the Cod, it would also be attended by that of the Canada trade" (N. Y. Col. Doc., IX, 871). Its fortification was apparently begun in 1717.

their influence was very great over some of the Indians.[63] At the same time the Sieur Chabert de Joncaire, not only a representative of the French interest in trade — an interest, as has been noted in the preceding chapter, that had bitterly clashed at times with the program of the French missionaries — but also an adopted son of the Seneca, one who had so won the confidence of these Indians that they had appointed him in 1700 " Plenipotentiary of the affairs of our Seneca village " in all negotiations with the French and who was held to possess in 1708 " all possible influence among the Senecas, and a great deal at Onontague " (Onondaga), according to Governor de Vaudreuil, was employed to maintain an attitude of neutrality on the part of the Indians with respect to the hostilities then going on.

Joncaire's activities seem to have centred on the Niagara, where French traders congregated without molestation.[64] In 1708 he sought in vain to persuade the French authorities to rebuild the fort at Niagara; [65] two years later, in 1710, he and Baron de Longueuil, who had been adopted by the Onondaga, appeared in the chief Onondaga town with a small party of Frenchmen and warned the Iroquois that if they joined the English on an intended expedition to Canada, as was rumoured they were about to do, the French would not only come themselves but set the Far West Indians upon them to destroy them " Root & Branch." As a result of this threat the " French faction " prevailed in the Confederation Council.[66] The following year the two Frenchmen reappeared, after escorting a party of pro-French Iroquois to Montreal, and proceeded to build a house of planks at Onondaga, as was previously stated, and also a blockhouse in the chief Seneca town and, according to reports, made plans also to erect a fort at the latter place.[67] Yet it is true that Peter Schuyler of Albany was also at the same time equally active among the Iroquois to undo the work of French priests and traders; in 1712 he persuaded all but the Seneca to fit out an expedition against Canada, and some twelve hundred warriors assembled for that purpose and constructed canoes. The Seneca, on the other hand, sent their leaders to the number of

---

[63] The Reverend Jacques d'Heu, for example, was busy at Onondaga during the war in checkmating the English. See his letter to the Marquis de Vaudreuil of May 24, 1708, ibid., IX, 815–16.

[64] Ibid., IX, 814.

[65] H. L. Osgood, The American Colonies in the Eighteenth Century, I, 479.

[66] N. Y. Col. Doc., V, 218, 225.

[67] Ibid., V, 243, 253; Wraxall's Indian Records, p. 81; Colden Papers, IX, 399.

forty-five to Montreal to reaffirm their fidelity — with Joncaire acting as their intermediary and interpreter.[68] This intimacy of both Joncaire and Longueuil with the Iroquois was to continue after the war.

In 1716 Longueuil, returning from the country of the Five Nations, recommended to the Quebec authorities the construction of " a small post north of Niagara, on Lake Ontario " at Irondequoit Bay, which would have the effect of deterring " the Mississagué and Amicoué Indians from going to the Iroquois to trade, when passing from hunting in the neighbourhood of Lake Earié " — the trade of which post was to be carried on for the account of the King.[69] Joncaire already had established a small trading place there as well as at Niagara. No steps were taken, however, to erect a fort at Irondequoit. Nevertheless, at this juncture Joncaire introduced to the Seneca his little son and asked them to receive him and to care for him in the same friendly manner as he himself had ever been treated by them.[70] This son, Philip Thomas, was to exercise in his day a great influence over the Seneca and the Indians of the Ohio Valley.[71]

Meanwhile the French trade of the upper Great Lakes region continued to pass along the Niagara. To avoid the great falls a road had been constructed round the cataracts, over which rolled " two or three times a year " carts loaded with supplies or furs. Moreover, the Indians dwelling in the Seneca village near by were frequently employed by the French to carry over the portage the goods of those going to the upper country or returning therefrom.[72] The control of the Niagara was indeed almost indispensable to the French in the course of trade. It is therefore not surprising that in 1719, when a report reached Quebec that the Albany merchants were seeking to establish a settlement there, Joncaire, by order of the French Governor, prevailed upon the Indians to construct — or at least to permit the construction of — a picketed trading post on the river.[73] This post,

---

[68] N. Y. Col. Doc., IX, 864.

[69] Ibid., IX, 874. The Missisauga were a division of the Chippewa or Saulteurs and lived in the eighteenth century between Lakes Erie and Huron; the Amikwa, another Algonquian tribe, also lived in the region of Lake Huron.

[70] Wraxall's Indian Records, p. 117.

[71] For an account of his activities see Volume IV of this series, pp. 192, et seq., passim.

[72] N. Y. Col. Rec., IX, 885.

[73] The reports that reached the Albany Indian Commissioners indicated that the post was constructed without the leave of the Indians and that the French planned to keep horses and carts there for the transportation of goods and to prevent the " Foreeign Nations from Tradeing to Albany " (ibid., V, 528; Wraxall's Indian Records, p. 128).

some forty feet in length and thirty in breadth, was located just below the falls on the east bank at the beginning of the portage.[74]

Immediately the question arose as to the violation of the Treaty of Utrecht on the part of the French. William Burnet, who now took over the governorship of New York, felt impelled to launch a strong protest with Vaudreuil over this act, which he felt represented hostile encroachment, in defiance of the articles of peace.[75] The latter replied that " you are the first English Governor-General who has questioned the right of the French, from time immemorial, to the post of Niagara, to which the English have, up to the present time, laid no claim," [76] which if not quite accurate, in light of Governor Dongan's protests at the existence of a French post there, at least was indicative of the determination of the Governor General of New France to hold his ground.

The Indians themselves were bluntly reminded by agents sent by the New York Indian Commissioners to a gathering of Seneca, Cayuga, and Oneida sachems in 1720 at one of the Seneca castles that almost twenty years earlier, in order to make secure their western lands and hunting places, they had deeded these to the Crown of Great Britain to be held in trust for them, but that now they were permitting their country to be violated not only by the existence of Detroit but also by the new post at Niagara. To this they replied rather feebly that

> " we must Joyne our Opinion with yours that if wee suffer the french to settle at onjagera . . . wee will be altogether shut up and Debarred, of means for our lively hood. . . ." [77]

They therefore requested that an Englishman be sent with a delegation to bid Joncaire tear down what had been erected. In harmony with this decision, the interpreter, Lawrence Claus (Claasse), with three Seneca sachems, appeared at Niagara and protested the construction of the post; later at a gathering of the Seneca not only was dissatisfaction voiced by the Indians themselves in the presence of

The French dispatches indicate that the Indians themselves built the post, doubtless for pay, as the result of the influence exerted over them by Joncaire (N. Y. Col. Doc., IX, 897).

[74] Ibid., IX, 897; Wraxall's Indian Records, p. 127; Colden Papers, IX, 433. This point is carefully treated by F. M. Severance, An Old Frontier of France, pp. 183–93.

[75] N. Y. Col. Rec., IX, 899.

[76] Ibid., IX, 901.

[77] Ibid., V, 545.

Joncaire but they requested the Governor of New York to use his influence to have the house destroyed " that they may . . . preserve their Land & Hunting." [78]

But Joncaire was left there at his fort undisturbed. To what extent the Seneca were in earnest in their opposition to the French establishment at Niagara is difficult to judge. On the surface they seem to have been swayed first by one side and then by the other. While there continued to exist pro-French and pro-English factions within the tribe, it is not to be doubted that Joncaire's influence was, in spite of all obstacles, so great among these Indians as one of their council that he was even able to bring about the degradation of a pro-English chief sachem, Blewbek (Blawbeck), and secure his place for one that he favoured.[79] Yet behind all this vacillation was the desire of the Iroquois to live at peace with both English and French and to profit by the intercourse with them. They doubtless disliked the building of the post and, further, were impressed with the fact that the goods available to be sold in it were largely English goods conveyed to the Montreal merchants from Albany. They were convinced, and with reason, that their own traffic with the Far West Indians in these same goods would be seriously prejudiced by this situation and were therefore anxious to see an end to the Albany-Montreal contraband intercourse.[80]

The intensification of the French interest in the region about the Niagara subsequent to the Treaty of Utrecht now led to a fundamental change in the Albany Indian trade policy.[81] In 1716 six traders were given licences by the Indian Commissioners to trade beyond the limits of the city at Irondequoit, which was at the mouth of the Genesee, a point half-way on the southern shore of Lake Ontario between the mouth of the Niagara River and the Onondaga where

---

[78] Wraxall's Indian Records, p. 128. At this meeting Joncaire declared to Claus " you only indeavor to have that house Demolished for fear that the French should stop the Trade to Albany." To which the latter replied " that the French had built that house in order to have the Command of that Pass by which the 5 Nations passed to the Country where all their Bever hunting lay & to command their Trade & to force them to buy at such extravagant rates the french should please to put upon their goods. . . . That now they sold a Stroud Blanket for 8 Bevers or a white blanket for 6 Bevers whereas they could buy them at Albany for half that price which the said Indians affirmed was true " (Colden Papers, IX, 433–4).

[79] Wraxall's Indian Records, p. 127; Colden Papers, IX, 432.

[80] Wraxall's Indian Records, p. 130.

[81] A. H. Buffinton, " Albany Policy and Westward Expansion," Miss. Valley Hist. Rev., VIII, 357.

Fort Oswego was soon to be built.[82] However, upon their arrival at this place they found Joncaire's trading house, referred to previously, inhabited by five French traders and a smith — the latter sent by the Governor General of Canada without any expense to the Indians to keep their guns in repair. When the English traders thereupon requested the privilege of erecting a post there, the Seneca readily gave their consent; they also asked for an English smith.[83] But a policy of joint Anglo-French occupation of a place in the Iroquois country was not to be contemplated by the New York authorities, who, nevertheless, were not prepared to eject the Frenchmen. As a result, to offset the activities of the latter, five persons, including a smith, were sent into the villages of the Confederation late that same year, to remain there until the following fall " to watch the motions & defeat the Intrigues of the French." [84] But this did not check the activity of the French. After their establishment at Niagara in 1719, as we have noted, news was brought to Albany in the fall of the following year by friendly Seneca that Frenchmen were also occupying four other places in the Iroquois country, including the trading house at Irondequoit.[85] It was further reported that two of the leading Seneca sachems had actually taken their families to Canada, that others were to follow, and that at one of the Seneca castles the French colours had been hoisted. Again Albany traders, accompanied by a smith, were dispatched into the Iroquoian country to watch developments and to oppose the designs of their rivals.[86] Governor Burnet, in fact, from this time on did everything within his power to encourage the movement of traders into the Indian country, which meant breaking down the old regulations and the Albany monopoly. He now even supported the idea of a joint-stock company among traders who would settle at Irondequoit and thereby eliminate the French by underselling them; in 1720 he prevailed upon the Assembly to pass a law to prevent the contraband trade to Canada out of Albany whereby the French had flooded their posts with English merchandise. But neither the joint-stock company nor the stoppage of European trading goods to Montreal could be realized. The western trade became and remained an open trade. As for that to Canada,

---

[82] This is called on Evans's map of 1755 " Niederundaguat."

[83] Wraxall's Indian Records, pp. 113–17.

[84] Ibid., p. 117.

[85] Ibid., p. 131. McIlwain seeks to identify the other places as Oswego, Cayuga village, and Cayonhage on the Salmon River.

[86] Ibid., pp. 131–2.

Wraxall declared that " the greatest Fortunes have been got . . . by the Canada Trade " on the part of Albany merchants.[87] Nevertheless, some among the latter interested in direct trade with the Iroquois and with the Far West Indians — among which number was included a majority of the Indian Commissioners — continued to work for its elimination.[88]

In tracing the more significant developments within the Confederation, it should be pointed out that in 1722 the League received an important increase in strength and numbers when the warlike Tuscarora, also an Iroquoian tribe, removed from North Carolina and settled down between the Oneida and Onondaga and were formally received as a sixth nation the following year.[89] Thus the importance of maintaining control over the Confederation and its trade was heightened. Therefore in 1724 Burnet requested permission for traders to go to the mouth of the Onondaga and erect a blockhouse. Although the Indians preferred to have the English build the intended post on Lake Oneida, they nevertheless finally agreed to the proposal, but requested that goods be sold as cheaply there as at Albany, which was so manifestly unreasonable, in light of the additional carrying charges, that they also gave way on that point. By the following year the trade at Oswego had become permanently settled and a temporary trading house established, in spite of the

[87] *Ibid.*, p. 141.

[88] In November 1720 the New York Assembly passed an act forbidding the sale of Indian goods to the French. In 1724 twenty London merchants presented a petition to the Privy Council in opposition to this law, which they felt was disadvantageously affecting the sale of English trading goods. This on April 30 of that year was referred to the Board of Trade. On July 7 several New York merchants appeared before the Board and supported the contentions of the London merchants that the act was hindering the exportation of British goods. In this connection it was asserted that not one-half as much goods were exported to New York as previous to the act and that the price of furs to the British manufacturers as a consequence had risen from twenty-five to thirty per cent. After considering all the facts, including Governor Burnet's report on the favourable results of the law, the Lords Commissioners recommended that no directions should be sent to New York. When the petition in question reached New York, a committee of the Governor's Council was appointed to consider it and to frame an answer. Its report made clear that, according to the custom-house books, more furs were being exported from New York than before the passage of the act and that the price of strouds that sold for £10 apiece in Albany had advanced at Montreal from £13 2s. 6d. to £25 and upward. For the petition of the London merchants, the action of the Lords Commissioners, and the report of the committee of the New York Council, see the Appendix to the London edition of 1750 of Colden's *History of the Five Nations*, pp. 3–25.

[89] *N. Y. Col. Doc.*, V, 672; *Wraxall's Indian Records*, p. 144. The Five Nations, as early as 1713, apparently began sheltering some of the Tuscarora (*N. Y. Col. Doc.*, V, 371).

threats of the French to prevent this.[90] In that year, with all barriers down, about one hundred persons went westward to trade with the Indians and in the course of the spring and summer brought back to Albany over 788 bundles of skins, in contrast to 200 bundles brought by the Far West Indians directly to this city and to Schenectady and 176 bundles coming from Canada by way of Chambly — according to a report of the Indian Commissioners.[91] There is little doubt that the English traders enjoyed such decisive advantages on Lake Ontario over their rivals that it permitted them, where competition was possible, to secure the cream of the business. As Cadwallader Colden pointed out in 1724 in his memorial on the fur trade:

> " But as our Indian Traders not only have a double Price for their Indian Goods but likewise buy the Goods they sell to the Indians at half the Price the French Indian traders do — The French Traders must be ruined by carrying on this trade in competition with the English of New York and the French Indian Traders had been ruined before now if they had not found means to carry their Beaver to Albany where they get double the Price they must have sold for in Canada." [92]

By the time that Oswego became a centre of English activity the French trading post at Niagara, but hastily constructed, was apparently in a ruinous condition. At least in 1725 Longueuil, an adopted Onondaga, as has been made clear, secured the consent of the sachems of that tribe — although the post was not on their tribal lands, but on that of the Seneca, who at least appeared to oppose the plan — to build a new one some three leagues below the cataracts, urging that the present house " was grown old and rotten & spoiled his Goods." [93] The site finally agreed upon was the point of land between the east bank of the river and the lake — a place that not only dominated the vital Niagara Passage but which seemed to be well

---

[90] The Indian Commissioners on August 12, 1725 referred to a report that the Indians were about to sell to the French "the Land . . . on Onondaga River where our People trade with the far Indians" (*Wraxall's Indian Records*, p. 159). According to Burnet, writing to the Marquis de Beauharnois in 1727, the English had "carried on a trade there regularly for more than five years running without opposition . . ." (*N. Y. Col. Doc.*, V, 830).

[91] *Wraxall's Indian Records*, pp. 159–60.

[92] He makes clear in his memorial that they paid the Indians twice as much for their furs as did the French. For this important document see *N. Y. Col. Doc.*, V, 726–33.

[93] *Wraxall's Indian Records*, pp. 164–5; *N. Y. Col. Doc.*, V, 787.

situated to help control the trade of the southwestern shores of Lake Ontario. There the following year was constructed a substantial square stone fort,[94] within which a small body of regular troops was stationed.[95] In addition to this, two sloops were built on Lake Ontario to carry supplies and to patrol the waters thereof. However, Governor General Beauharnois and Intendant Dupuy, who were now in charge of affairs in New France, felt that this was not enough; they therefore proposed not only to rebuild the trading house near the portage at the cost of over twenty thousand livres, but to convert it into a second fort; [96] likewise, in order to cut off the communication of the English with Lake Ontario, they proposed to erect a third fort at the mouth of the Onondaga, or, as the French called it, the Choueguen,[97] where the English were now established. These proposals, however, were not carried out. It is true that the King in 1727 authorized the immediate rebuilding of the ruined post at the portage, but this authorization was soon after countermanded.[98] In fact, in 1726 some three hundred English traders spent the summer on the lower Onondaga engaged in trade, and the following year the New York authorities hastened to construct a real frontier fort there, of equal strength with that of Niagara, as the result of an appropriation for that purpose by the Assembly. Writing to the Board of Trade in August, Burnet with an evident feeling of pride gives the following description of it:

> " But this new house at Oswego will make a stand that will Embolden our five nations, and will not easily be taken without great Cannon, the wall being four foot thick of large good stone, and it is represented to me that the French cannot bring large cannon against it, since they have no way but to come up from Montreal to the Lake against a Violent Stream . . . and if they had cannon to carry, it is thought they could not set them along, and by land it is all over precipices and Mountains, and rivers to cross on both sides of the great River, so that it is not believed practicable for them to bring battering cannon any way." [99]

---

[94] Ibid., VI, 126, 183; IX, 976, 977. It had been planned that the fort would be upon the site of that erected by Denonville. But the engineer de Léry decided otherwise.

[95] Ibid., VI, 227.

[96] The cost of Fort Niagara was placed at 29,295 livres.

[97] N. Y. Col. Doc., IX, 977.

[98] Ibid., IX, 979, 1003-4.

[99] Ibid., V, 826. For a map of Oswego in 1727 drawn by M. de Léry see ibid., IX, 996.

He also informed the Board that the fort was provided with a double garrison, provisions for six months, and an adequate supply of ammunition for its defence.

When the news arrived in Canada that the fort was under construction, Beauharnois summoned in haste a meeting of the " estates " of Montreal at his quarters in that city to take into consideration whether the best means of preventing this was not to dispatch to the place immediately a detachment of regulars, militia, and Canadian Indians. He declared in writing to the Minister that there was but one opinion on that point,[100] with the result that he determined to send a summons to its commander, Captain Bancker,

> " to draw out at furthest within a fortnight the Garrison of this place with arms, munitions and other Effects belonging to the people of Albany or other places, to cast down the block house and all pieces of work you raised up contrary to Righteousness. . . ." [101]

He also directed a vigorous protest to Burnet, who in turn wrote an extended and exceedingly able reply that dealt not only with Oswego but with Niagara and the status of the Five Nations under the terms of the Treaty of Utrecht.[102] The English Governor in this connection made perfectly clear that Oswego would be defended against any attack.

In view of this resolute attitude and the support that the Six Nations had given in establishing the post, Beauharnois now decided to forgo the plan of dislodging the English by force — not only because of his uncertainty of success but also " out of deference to the dispositions of the Iroquois on that subject." [103] He realized, however, that French prestige was at stake, especially in view of information that he had received that English " underground Belts " were being carried to divers Indian nations, among these the Foxes, who had killed a number of Frenchmen, with the result that he determined to use the forces gathered for the Oswego expedition against that nation.[104] In addition to this, he strongly recommended to the Minister that, since the English were now established at Oswego, a fort should be built, at an estimated expense of 38,047 livres, some eight

---

[100] *Ibid.*, IX, 1085.

[101] *Ibid.*, V, 828; IX, 973–4.

[102] *Ibid.*, IX, 970–3; V, 829–32.

[103] *Ibid.*, IX, 1003, 1085. This resolution was supported by the King, who decided " that no public movement be made at present against that establishment."

[104] *Ibid.*, IX, 1086.

or nine leagues west of that place on Cayuga Bay,[105] which he felt not only would bring about such a decline of activity at the former post that it ultimately would be abandoned but also would place the French in such a position that when war broke out again, they could drive the English out of the Lake Ontario region. But the proposal was disapproved. One reason for this, besides the question of the expense, was that the Minister was able in his report to the King to make clear that the pressure of Oswego had not proved so disadvantageous to the French after all, since the trade carried on for His Majesty at Frontenac and Niagara was two-thirds more in 1728 than in either 1726 or 1727.[106] To what extent " the large number of English artizans, merchants, and others established at Montreal " at this juncture [107] was responsible for this increase in the business at those two posts, by providing the French with trading goods at a low price, can only be conjectured. But it is not without significance that — in harmony with Intendant Dupuy's fears that this gathering of foreigners indicated some design against the city and his recommendations to the Minister that the families of these be removed to Quebec — not only was a royal *ordonnance* issued late in 1727 forbidding strangers to engage in trade and even to remain in Canada unless settled as cultivators on the land or working at some handicraft,[108] but under this law the somewhat dubious character John Henry Lydius, who had resided in Montreal since 1725 and who was married to a half-breed, was in 1730 placed under arrest, fined three thousand livres,[109] and banished from the colony for ever for carrying on an unlawful English trade.[110] Certainly, soon after these measures were taken against the English intruders the trade of the two French posts gradually declined; in 1736 Beauharnois and the new Intendant

---

[105] That is, at Sodus Bay.

[106] N. Y. Col. Doc., IX, 1010–11.

[107] Ibid., IX, 985.

[108] Ibid.

[109] It is of interest to note that Lydius, in default of the payment of his fine, was sent to Rochefort, France. As he claimed to have goods valued at 12,000 livres in Montreal, which he apparently agreed to turn over to the authorities, he was thereupon released from prison and permitted to go to Holland, but under no conditions was he to return to Canada (Maurepas to Beauharnois and Hocquart, April 10, 1731, Cadillac Papers, Burton Collection).

[110] N. Y. Col. Doc., IX, 1019–20. That Lydius was not eliminated from the contraband trade between Albany and Montreal is indicated by the fact that he subsequently established his place of residence above Saratoga, along the leading contraband path. His home became a landmark and is indicated on Lewis Evans's map of the Middle British Colonies of 1755. For references to his settlement in 1744 see *ibid.*, IX, 1101–2.

Hocquart jointly declared that the posts, although they had together "produced some years ago, as much as 52,000 lb. of peltries, have these four years past returned only 25 to 35,000 lb." They themselves placed the entire blame, whether correctly or not, " to the discontinuance of the distribution of Brandy to the Indians whereof it is the King's pleasure that Messrs de Beauharnois and Hocquart be very sparing." [111] Not that brandy by a special royal relaxation could not be sold at the two posts in question as the " sole allurement " to keep the Indians from going to the English, but that the keepers of the stores at those places — in light of a pastoral letter of the Bishop of Quebec against the debauching of the Indians — were so fearful of committing an offence in the category of " reserved cases " [112] that they were reluctant to avail themselves of the special permission to dispense these liquors.[113] As a result, the Governor General and the Intendant declared that on account of the abuandance of rum at Oswego the Indians from all the posts of the upper country repaired to it without any means of stopping them at Niagara — all of which represented the official version of the cause of the dropping off of the peltry receipts at Niagara and Frontenac at this period.

Whatever scruples the keepers of the French trading goods may have had against dispensing rum soon passed away [114] and yet the Indians continued to resort to Oswego. The Iroquois likened this post, in 1737, to " a trap which when you Intend to Catch a prey you lay a bait in it and so when the Creature comes to Eat the bait he is Catched," [115] and, in 1740, to " a Silver mine " for the white people who came there to trade.[116] To Governor Clarke, writing to the Board of Trade in 1742, it was " a place of vast Importance to the British Trade and Interest." [117] In the month of August 1749, according to the return made by John Lindsay, commissary at the post, 1,385 packs of peltry were brought there by the Indians of ten Western tribes and eight French *coureurs de bois,* having a total value of £21,406. As against this, Niagara could depend upon receiving but from two hundred and fifty to three hundred packs and Frontenac from twenty to thirty, according to a report of a somewhat later

---

[111] *Ibid.,* IX, 1049.
[112] That is, cases reserved for the decision of the Bishop.
[113] *N. Y. Col. Doc.,* IX, 1024, 1049.
[114] *Ibid.,* IX, 1112.
[115] *Ibid.,* VI, 105.
[116] *Ibid.,* VI, 177.
[117] *Ibid.,* VI, 221.

date.[118] Indeed, in spite of the enormous advantage in location of Detroit over Oswego, the latter could count upon securing twice as many packs in the ordinary course of trade as a result of the lower price levels of European goods.[119] In 1743, according to Lewis Evans, who visited it in that year, it was rather

> " a Collection of trading huts, built for the residence of the Indian Traders during the mart, or trading season, than a fix't habitation of settlers. It consists of about seventy logg-houses, in two rows, forming a street, on the west shore of the river at its mouth. The Fort stands at the point next the Lake." [120]

Needless to say, it was of the utmost importance to the French to bring about the abandonment of Oswego with its destructive competition for the peltries — Canada's one great staple export — especially since the Far West Indians otherwise would be inclined to sell at one of their outer posts or to go to Montreal. But in peace and war the Six Nations stood as a barrier to the realization of this. Moreover, the post, largely dominated by the Albany mercantile interests, was also, it seems, brought within the scope of the old " neutrality " policy practised by these interests. For example, in 1734 Colonel Jeremiah van Rensselaer, proprietor of the great manor of Rensselaerswyck, visited Canada with a passport issued by the Governor of New York, under pretence of making a tour. While there he and the other men from Albany who accompanied him sought out the Marquis de Beauharnois and privately informed him of something that the latter already knew: that the Marquis de Vaudreuil during the last war had always spared New York and had counselled the Indians not to make incursions into it, and that a secret correspondence had been maintained between the French Governor and Albany. Van Rensselaer went on to declare that the Dutch were more intimate with the Indians than were the English, and that the Dutch would now make no move against the French and had acted with fidelity to the neutrality agreement for twenty years. In his turn Beauharnois put their minds at rest by assuring them that he was inclined to adopt Vaudreuil's policy.[121] In submitting the matter to the Minister of the Marine, then the Count de Maurepas, the latter gave the French Governor freedom of action in the matter while at

---

[118] *Ibid.*, VI, 538.

[119] *Ibid.*

[120] For this see Thomas Pownall's *Topographical Description*, Appendix No. I.

[121] *N. Y. Col. Doc.*, IX, 1039–40.

the same time pointing out " that the Lord of Orange [Van Rens-
selaer] had not responded, as he ought, to the regard that was had for
him, there having been several English parties at Orange and in the
vicinity [during the last war], of which he gave no notice." [122]

In the light of the vast importance of Oswego to the English and
Niagara to the French it is very surprising that they both were allowed to fall into a ruinous condition. In 1742 Lieutenant Governor
Clarke reported to the Lords Commissioners of Trade the defenceless
condition of the former, manned by only twenty men without ammunition.[123] Although it was in somewhat better state of defence
when King George's War broke out two years later, it was very vulnerable. As for Niagara, before 1744 it relied upon the protection of
only thirty-four soldiers and received in that year but thirty additional men. Its chief defence consisted of five antique pedreros and
four two-pounders.[124] In the course of that war neither post was
seriously threatened, although the Governor General in the spring
of 1744 had received the most positive orders relative to Oswego to
the effect that in case of hostilities " his first care will be to destroy
this post and from this time forward he should work with a view
to prompt action ";[125] and in the following year, after the war had
begun, the importance of its destruction was again emphasized.[126]
Beauharnois, in apologizing to the Minister for his inaction with respect to the post, declared in 1744 that the Six Nations remained
the chief impediment, for they persisted " in their usual sentiments,
that the traps at Choueghen and at Niagara should remain undisturbed . . . and that they will, moreover, remain neuter in our differences with the English." For Beauharnois visualized nothing less
than the destruction of Niagara, the life-line for the Great Lakes and
interior system of Canadian posts, by a combined attack of the English and the infuriated Six Nations, should he threaten Oswego.[127] He

---

122 Ibid., IX, 1048.
123 Ibid., VI, 215. Late in 1743 Governor Clinton called upon the Indian Commissioners to reinforce the garrison with a corporal and nine men and to send out " a
sufficient quantity of powder and ball with the utmost expedition." In 1744, with the
outbreak of the war, he ordered six pieces of cannon and an additional reinforcement
of troops (ibid., VI, 249, 264).
124 Ibid., IX, 1104.
125 " Orders of the King," Canadian Archives, Report (1905), I, 26, 30.
126 Ibid., I, 43.
127 N. Y. Col. Doc., IX, 1105–6. While Oswego was underselling Niagara and
Frontenac and thus attracted the Far West Indians, the Iroquois in 1744 did complain
to Clinton that, whereas goods were sold there " very cheap " the first two years of its

was assured at the same time by the Indians that the English had "promised to undertake nothing unless constrained thereunto, nor unless a commencement be made at this side." [128] In fact, the only threat to Niagara came from the Tionontati Hurons (Chanunda-dies) [129] and the Ottawa, who in 1747 took the warpath against the French in the upper Great Lakes region and who, according to Colonel William Johnson, offered to destroy Niagara if the English would provide them with ammunition and the Six Nations would give them liberty to carry out their design.[130] In that same year Clinton and his Council, it is true, formulated a plan for an immediate attack upon Niagara, as well as upon Crown Point; but as the necessary supplies had to be secured from the Assembly, which was dominated by Albany, and as that body demanded information respecting the plan, this had to be put aside, since Clinton was rightly convinced that information of any intended attacks would inevitably be carried to the enemy! [131]

As for Oswego, the President of the French Navy Board early in 1748 impressed upon M. de la Galissonière that the most important operation that he could undertake would be the capture of Oswego and that it should be possible to accomplish this without stripping the colony of its defences, especially if the troops that were being

---

existence, these were now so dear that the trade there was no longer advantageous. They asked that these be sold at the earlier rate (ibid., VI, 265). It may be surmised that both Niagara and Oswego at the beginning, in keen competition for the Indian trade, sold goods at rates that were unprofitable. Thomas Butler, writing from Oswego on September 16, 1744, declared, " I don't now in the least suspeckt that this place will be atacked, as the Five Nations seem to have it at Heart " (Sir William Johnson Papers, ed. James Sullivan, I, 22).

[128] N. Y. Col. Doc., IX, 1106. Doubtless a promise made by the Albany Indian Commissioners.

[129] These Indians, a blend of the Tionontati or Tobacco Indians and refugee Hurons, were living at this period in the region of Lakes Erie and Huron in the neighbourhood of Detroit.

[130] N. Y. Col. Doc., VI, 386, 387, 389; Sir William Johnson Papers (ed. James Sullivan), I, 106. It is true that Captain de Raymond, commanding at Niagara, in 1748 wrote most pessimistically regarding the fort, located in the midst of Indians who had killed Frenchmen, a place maintained at the greatest expense and yet least designed to bring aid: " It is the gateway for all the different tribes who inhabit the upper country, throughout the extent of Canada, to go to Oswego, to Albany, to Boston, and to all the English and who do nothing but go and return to the English " (Arch. Nat., Col., C¹¹ A. 92: 338).

[131] N. Y. Col. Doc., VI, 402; Johnson Papers, I, 87, 113.

sent from France should arrive without accident.[132] Writing in reply, Galissonière declared on October 8 of that year:

> "I have been so persuaded of the necessity of taking possession of Oswego that I have been upon the point of undertaking it with a half hope of success and with every appearance of bringing upon ourselves as a result war with the Five Nations; the chief reason that has held me back is that their deputies agreed to come in the spring and I was hoping either to persuade them of the desirability of this for their own sakes or to intimidate them at least for a sufficiently long period to strike the blow." [133]

His plans, with the news of the preliminaries of a peace, were put aside. Thus the Iroquois continued to stand as a barrier to aggression on the part of either side so far as Oswego and Niagara were concerned.

In considering the problem of the relations of the Confederation to the struggle between the English and the French, it should be pointed out that in the course of the war the figure of William Johnson began to loom large in Indian affairs in combating the powerful influence not only of Joncaire but of the Abbé Piquet (Picquet) of the Lake of the Two Mountains. About the year 1739 this remarkable man purchased land on the Mohawk about forty miles from Albany along the great artery of commerce between that city and the Iroquois country. Mount Johnson, his residence, located on the north bank of that river, soon became a gathering place of the Indians, whom he treated not only with fairness but with infinite tact. He was received into the Mohawk tribe with the name *Warraghiyagee* (Waraghiyaghey), became one of the sachems, and upon the death of his common-law wife, an indentured German servant, established, among other Indian women who had won his favour, a niece of Chief Hendrick as the mistress of his home and, with her passing away, Molly Brant. He was interested not only in land but in the Indian trade, and in the course of time he became, according to Cadwallader Colden, "the most considerable trader with the Western Indians," sending more goods to Oswego than any other, which goods were disposed of by his factors.[134] In 1746, when the contractors who had heretofore supplied the Oswego garrison were unwilling to continue without extraordinary inducements on account of the dangers,

---

[132] "Orders of the King," *Canadian Archives, Report* (1905), I, 100.

[133] Arch. Nat., Col., C11 A. 90: 140.

[134] N. Y. *Col. Doc.*, VI, 740.

Johnson was selected to carry on this work. That same year even a greater responsibility was placed upon his shoulders by reason of the loss of influence of the Indian Commissioners among the Six Nations; for he not only was authorized to organize, among the latter, war parties to raid the French, but was commissioned by Governor Clinton colonel of the warriors of the Confederation and of white volunteers and also commissary of stores.[135] Clinton, of course, greatly desired to bring the Indians actively into the war. In line with this policy, small parties of Mohawks were sent out in 1747 which returned with scalps,[136] but, significantly enough, these hostilities were all in the direction of Canada by way of Crown Point and the great carrying place and were not directed against the Lake Ontario region or Niagara. It is also significant that young Chabert de Joncaire dwelt in security among the Seneca as a member of that tribe, just as his father, who passed away in 1740, had. In fact, his influence over the Seneca was so great that Clinton urged Johnson to use whatever tactics might be necessary either to win him over to the English or to bring him captive to Albany.[137] But Johnson was unable to find means to accomplish either objective. However, late in August 1747 he himself headed an expedition of Indians toward Crown Point without much result. He attributed the lack of success of this to the fact that while some of the Iroquois Indians were anxious to strike the French, others were apparently just as anxious for any accommodation with the latter and actually went to Canada that same year under guise of making peace and sought unsuccessfully to persuade the Caughnawaga Iroquois of Sault St. Louis to return home, all of which, as he later impressed upon the Indians, had tied his hands.[138] Early the following year he received the appointment of colonel of fourteen companies of New York militia and in the spring he journeyed to Onondaga to persuade the faltering Six Nations to be firm in their English alliance and not to go again to Canada as they desired to do in order to try to persuade the Governor General to free some of their brethren held prisoners of war. On this occasion Johnson exercised all the eloquence at his command and brought the Indians to agree not only to go to Albany to meet Governor Clinton rather than go to Canada but to call back to their

---

[135] *Johnson Papers*, I, 49, 59–62.

[136] *Ibid.*, I, 93–6.

[137] *Ibid.*, I, 78. In 1747, on account of ill health, Chabert retired from the Seneca country and was relieved by his brother Clauzonne Joncaire. *N. Y. Col. Doc.*, X, 163.

[138] *Johnson Papers*, I, 160, 163.

castles their scattered members and to permit the English to erect forts in their midst for their protection — something, however, that with the approach of peace was not done.[139] On the other hand, and in spite of all promises, in November of the same year some eighty of them, representing all of the nations but the Mohawks, made their appearance at Quebec at the Castle of St. Louis under the guidance of Lieutenant de Joncaire and, in reply to the questioning of Comte de la Galissonière, repudiated the assertion of the English that they were subjects of the King of Great Britain. Many of them also, it would appear, asked to be instructed in Christianity and reaffirmed the neutrality of the Confederation, while admitting that some of their young men had sent war belts to the Far West Indians without the consent of the Council. Joncaire declared that these deputies were the principal chiefs of the Seneca, Onondaga, Oneida, and Cayuga.[140]

The demand of the Iroquois to be instructed in Christianity naturally raises the question what the English had done, if anything, to make the higher appeals to the Indian and to draw him to them in the name of religion. The record is not particularly impressive in spite of the conscientious labours of a number of Anglican missionaries.

The chief agency for promoting this activity was the Society for the Propagation of the Gospel in Foreign Parts,[141] whose work was initiated by the sending of the Reverend Thoroughgood Moore to New York in 1704. But the good missionary was faced with disheartening difficulties: the Indians themselves were not receptive; he found them in fact hostile to the Englishman's religion, not only by reason of their aversion to the New Englanders, but of the bad example set by the Albany garrison, and the misrepresentations made by the Dutch.[142] After a year he became convinced that before the Iroquois would ever be converted the barbarous white colonials would have to be. However, in 1711 the Reverend Thomas Barclay, minister of the Albany church, had some success, but he soon affirmed that un-

---

139 *Ibid.*, I, 164; *N. Y. Col. Doc.*, VI, 425.

140 *Ibid.*, X, 186–8; Galissonière to the Minister, November 8, 1748, Arch. Nat., Col., C11 A. 90: 248–54.

141 See F. J. Klingberg's "The Noble Savage as Seen by the Missionary of the Society for the Propagation of the Gospel in Colonial New York, 1702–1750," *Historical Magazine of the Protestant Episcopal Church*, VIII, 128–65, and his "Sir William Johnson and the Society for the Propagation of the Gospel (1749–1774)," *ibid.*, VIII, 4–37.

142 For a communication from him see *ibid.*, VIII, 132.

less the Indians were kept from liquor no permanent good would be accomplished.[143] Nevertheless, by the following year a chapel in the Mohawk country had been built and the Reverend William Andrews took up his work there with zeal; by 1715 some one hundred baptized Indians were attendant upon his preaching. But this represented the high point in his success, for by 1719 because of the hostility of the Dutch Albany traders he had become thoroughly discouraged with his own efforts and so had the Society.[144] In fact, it was not until 1735 that work among them again showed promise, when Henry Barclay, the son of Thomas, was appointed missionary to the Mohawks. Under him a stone chapel was built by subscription at Fort Hunter in 1741 and he remained at his post until, in the midst of King George's War, he accepted an appointment as rector of Trinity Church in New York. His efforts and those of his successor, the Reverend John Ogilvie, were encouraged by William Johnson; [145] but these, as well as those of the early missionaries, were largely confined to the lower Mohawk Castle. In other words, the influence of this missionary activity did not extend much beyond the group of Indians that already were through economic reasons closely attached to the English.

With the Peace of Aix-la-Chapelle everything relative to the relations of the Six Nations with the English and French tended to take on the pattern that had characterized the period preceding the war. Nevertheless, while representatives of these continued to go both to Albany and to Montreal, there was manifested a rather marked pro-French leaning. Onondaga, Cayuga, and Oneida appeared at the latter place protesting their friendship, and the Seneca sent word of their continued fidelity.[146] Conrad Weiser, who had been raised among them and was an adopted son and a sachem, on going to Onondaga from his home in Pennsylvania in 1750 was struck by the change. He reported that the Onondaga, the Cayuga, and the Seneca had " turned Frenchmen," and that the Oneida tended that way. In fact, he found Onondaga " thick with French praying Indians." [147] William Johnson's effective influence with the Confederation seemed

---

[143] For his letter see *ibid.*, VIII, 140.

[144] For letters written by Andrews to the Society see J. L. Lydekker, *The Faithful Mohawks*, pp. 43–50.

[145] *Ibid.*, pp. 53–60, 64–76. A number of letters written by Barclay and Ogilvie covering the period from 1744 to 1752 are here presented.

[146] Arch. Nat., Col., C[11] A. 93: 205.

[147] Pa. Col. Rec., V, 471, 480.

A South View of OSWEGO, on Lake Ontario, in North America.

Explanation
1 The River Onondago
2 Lake Ontario

(Emmet Collection. New York Public Library.)

Abbé Picquet's La Présentation Mission.

(From *Mémoires sur le Canada, 1749-1760.*)

to be limited to the Mohawks, although he remained personally popular with the other nations. After the close of the war his position gradually became so uncomfortable — because of the hostility of his Albany enemies who sought to undermine him and of the withdrawal of the liberal financial support that the Crown had provided for his activities among the Confederation — that he was finally led to resign his superintendency in 1751. He maintained himself at Mount Johnson, however, when not in New York in attendance at the Governor's Council, to which he was admitted early in 1750; his interest in the Western Indian trade, especially at Oswego, did not diminish, nor, it may be added, that in lands in what is now central New York. His retirement from his post brought about the restoration of the power of the Albany Indian Commissioners, much to the disgust of the Indians, and renewed activity in the contraband trade between Albany and Montreal.[148]

As to the French, their aggressiveness was indicated in 1750 when they built a fortified post above the falls on the Niagara at the head of the portage while at the same time laying plans to strengthen the post below the falls. Clauzonne de Joncaire was installed at the new post, known as Little Niagara,[149] while his brother was busily engaged in combating English influence on the Ohio. When this development was brought to Governor Clinton's attention, together with the seizure of English traders among the Far West Indians, he thereupon dispatched a special messenger to the Governor General of Canada with a letter of complaint; he also invited the governors of other colonies to join him in a conference with the Six Nations at Albany to defeat the designs of the French to withdraw the affections of these Indians from the English. In July, with commissioners from Massachusetts Bay, Connecticut, and South Carolina present, he called upon the Iroquois to maintain their traditional alliance and to prevent the French from encroaching on their lands.[150] They were profuse in their promises, but that was all the satisfaction that the English got. As to the complaint addressed to the Marquis de la Jonquière, the latter put on a very bold front and sent to Clinton a reply which, even if bad history and ignoring the terms of the Treaty of Utrecht, was at least firm. With respect to the Iroquois he declared:

---

[148] *N. Y. Col Doc.*, VI, 720, 870.
[149] *Ibid.*, VI, 706; X, 240; F. H. Severance, *op. cit.*, pp. 374–5.
[150] *N. Y. Col. Doc.*, VI, 717–26.

"If the Five Nations were to subject themselves to any Crown, they could not help acknowledging the dominion of the King, my Master, and their natural Inclination would lead them to do so.

"In fact, Sir, you are not ignorant, and ancient and modern history bear testimony, that the French are the first white men that appeared on the territory of the Five Nations. It is with them that they first formed an alliance of friendship.[151] It is from that that they received their first assistance; accordingly from that very moment did they call the French their Father. It is unquestionable, then, that the French were the first to penetrate into the territories of the Iroquois; from that very moment they have taken possession of it, and this possession has been uninterrupted." [152]

Significantly, La Jonquière did not, in spite of his sweeping claims with respect to the Six Nations and their lands in the above communication, raise the issue of the right of the English to maintain themselves at Oswego. As to the trade of this post at the close of the war, it took two rather distinct forms: barter with the Indians and wholesale trade with Canada. Benjamin Stoddard, commander at Schenectady under Johnson, who early in 1749 decided "to make one trip to Oswego and try whether fortune will be more favorable to me in trade than she has been in the life of a soldier" [153] and who subsequently was appointed to the command there, complained of the great quantity of goods carried there by the traders and of the fierce competition among the latter. To dispose of their wares he affirmed that they "will be Obliged to live by the Loss and not the Profit of their Summers Work." [154] He himself, it is of interest to note, felt impelled, in the face of a glutted market, to write to Montreal offering his goods in job lots; as a result, his correspondent there apparently sent canoes which returned with a great part of his wares.[155] Again, at this juncture, the idea of establishing a trading company at Oswego with a monopoly of trade was revived. Stoddard affirmed:

"I am certain that if some such Scheme does not go on that the Trade of this Place will soon be ruined, for their [sic] is such a Number of Traders here and such Vile Steps taken to undermine each other in his trade that it consequently can't hold long; and the little low

---

151 La Jonquière was apparently correct in this statement. See G. T. Hunt, op. cit., pp. 27 et seq., passim.
152 N. Y. Col. Doc., VI, 732.
153 Johnson Papers, I, 217.
154 Ibid., I, 236.
155 Ibid.

means used in the Trade to hurt each other must give even the Savages a Damn'd mean Opinion of us; especially our Honesty." [156]

Nevertheless, there came to Oswego in that year, among other Far West Indians, one hundred and sixty Potawatomi with one hundred and forty packs of fur, eighty-eight Twightwee with seventy-seven, two hundred Missisauga with one hundred and seventy-five, eighty Menominee with seventy, seventy-two Michilimakinac with sixty-three, and two hundred and fifty-six Chippewa with two hundred and twenty-four; in addition to these, three hundred and forty-four Christian Indians came from the Lake of the Two Mountains and the Sault St. Louis with three hundred and one packs sent undoubtedly by Montreal merchants, and thirty-six French traders with thirty-five packs.[157]

As has already been emphasized, the magnet that drew these sixteen hundred Indians to the post, causing them to avoid Detroit and Niagara, and the agents of the French "Beaver Company" and the merchants at Montreal, was the high price paid for beaver. This was taken, irrespective of quality, at the uniform rate of four livres and four sous per pound weight as against three livres and ten sous at the French posts for only the best quality of beaver, according to the rate fixed by the Compagnie des Indes at the end of the war, which in 1750 was dropped to three livres, five sous, making a wide differential for all furs in favour of Oswego — not to take into account the much lower price level of the trading goods furnished there.[158] In fact, the disparity of the trade at Fort Niagara with that of Oswego in that year amounted to a ratio roughly of one to ten with respect to the canoes bringing furs to market by way of the Niagara portage, according to the admission of the Sieur de Beaujeu, commandant at the former post. This disparity would have been even greater, he declared, had he not distributed brandy to the savages at the low price of thirty sous for a pot, to hold them there.[159]

In vain the French built the trading post above the Niagara rapids, as has been indicated, and also Fort Rouillé at Toronto in 1750 to help

---

[156] Ibid.

[157] N. Y. Col. Doc., VI, 538.

[158] Ibid., X, 200. This question of price disparity has been treated rather fully in the preceding chapter.

[159] He secured one hundred and fifty packs of furs. The average number of packs carried in an Indian canoe was seven (Ibid., V, 538), which meant that about twenty-one canoes were held at Niagara, while according to his statement two hundred and twenty went on to Oswego (Arch. Nat., Col., C¹¹ A. 95: 257).

head off this stream of traffic when Forts Frontenac and Niagara had failed to do so — in the light of the practice of the Indians of crossing Lake Ontario from the northwest shore to go to Oswego. In vain Bigot hoped to deflect them from going to this post by setting a low price on goods at the competing French posts.[160] Men, civilized and uncivilized, do not ignore the lure of profit when they sally forth to find a market for what they have to sell.

Nevertheless, the French had something to offer to the Iroquoian Confederation that the English were not in a position to challenge, something that went far to attach these Indians to them with bonds of fellowship stronger than those of the mart. Indeed, at this period a new and powerful influence made itself felt within the Confederation, especially among the Onondaga, with the erection of the near-by mission of La Présentation by the Abbé Piquet (Picquet). This capable and patriotic, even if extremely egotistical Frenchman, who had for some years represented the St. Sulpician community at the Lake of the Two Mountains mission,[161] decided in 1747, in the midst of the war, to send a delegation of his Christian Iroquois to the Six Nations with peace belts. It was planned that they were to go as if at their own initiative. The idea was to sound out the disposition of the Confederation and to gain information as to what was going on within it, especially in the light of alarming reports of its plans to strike at Canada. When the Indians, however, arrived at Fort Frontenac they determined to abandon the project, doubtless realizing the hazards involved in it, and surrendered their belts to the commandant of that post.[162] However, the following year, having been impressed with the fact that many of the Indians were inclined to accept Christianity, Piquet determined, with the hearty encouragement of de la Galissonière, to establish a mission close to the Iroquois country and in the neighbourhood of Fort Frontenac.[163] For this purpose he received a

---

[160] By the establishment of these two new posts La Jonquière had optimistically anticipated an annihilation of the traffic of Oswego, whereby "all the peltry of the North and South, an enormous quantity, would remain in the colony" (Arch. Nat., Col., C^{11} A. 93: 207.)

[161] Canadian Archives, Report (1905), I, 27, 43, 46, 87.

[162] N. Y. Col. Doc., X, 154.

[163] Galissonière, writing to the Minister on October 5, 1748, declared that in the preceding year upon his arrival in Canada he had found a goodly number of the Iroquois who had expressed a desire to embrace Christianity and that some of them during the past winter, in spite of the war and manœuvres of the English, had also testified the same to M. Piquet. While he confessed that he did not have the same faith as had the missionary as to the possibility of converting the savages, he felt that it was a matter

money grant and three leagues of land from the Canadian authorities.[164] Late in September he left to select a site and finally decided to locate at the mouth of the Oswegatchie, which flows into the St. Lawrence where the town of Ogdensburg is now standing. The river was called by the French La Présentation and the mission was thus given the same name. The land thereabout was described as the finest in Canada, "with oak timber, and trees of a prodigious girth and height." There the Abbé with twenty-five Frenchmen and four of his Iroquois erected a storehouse and a small stockaded fort — all of which was done with the consent of representatives of the Six Nations who were present to encourage him and who agreed to follow his advice and to establish a village there.[165]

The Abbé Piquet's plan embodied the excellent idea of persuading the Indians to settle down to a life of husbandry, especially to undertake the raising of cattle, swine, and poultry on the beautiful prairies that adjoined the primeval forest. The forest in turn was to be exploited to furnish lumber and, in anticipation of this, provision was made for a sawmill. To support this undertaking La Jonquière and Bigot sent five two-pound-calibre cannon for the fort, which inspired the Indians who came to settle there with confidence in their safety.

To the Canadian authorities and the French Minister the significance of the establishment lay not only in the blocking of the English advance in that direction — since otherwise it would be possible for the latter, once in possession of the Oswegatchie, to cut off communication between Montreal and the upper posts — but also in the possibility that drawing a goodly proportion of the Iroquois to the mission and placing there an experienced and disinterested officer with a strong detachment would do away with the contraband trade of this region and would also contribute to the fall of Oswego.[166] Although late in October 1748, during the absence of Piquet with most of his Indians at Montreal, a party of Indians, supposed to have been Mohawks, attacked the mission — it was charged at the instigation of Colonel William Johnson — and burned the stockades and two ves-

---

of the highest importance to undertake the proposed mission for the purpose of dividing the Confederation and maintaining its neutrality and independence (Arch. Nat., Col., C¹¹ A. 90: 140).

[164] The land concession was actually made in October 1751, and was ratified by the Crown on July 3, 1752 (Arch. Nat., Col., B. 95: 130–2).

[165] N. Y. Col. Doc., X, 203.

[166] La Jonquière and Bigot to the Minister, October 31, 1749, Arch. Nat., Col., C¹¹ A. 93: 51; Canadian Archives, Report (1905), I, 115.

sels, the Abbé was not discouraged. For La Jonquière now sent a detachment of soldiers to La Présentation for its security, and the work of rebuilding the defences was soon completed.[167] The degree of confidence that the Governor General reposed in the missionary at this period is indicated by the fact that the latter agreed to go early in the spring into the region of Lake Erie to search out suitable places for the location of new trading posts to be established at the charge of the King and to report to him.[168] Apparently Piquet was unable to leave at this juncture. However, in 1751, in the month of June, he set forth by canoe to Lake Ontario and moved up the Niagara to Lake Erie, but now primarily for the purpose of drawing more of the Six Nations to the mission.[169]

This trip is worthy of more than passing notice since it throws much light on the situation under consideration. At Fort Niagara the Abbé encountered no Indians with whom he could speak and therefore confined his observations to the ruinous condition of foundations of the fort as the result of the washing away of the earthworks by the heavy rains.[170] Pushing on beyond the portage, he came to Clauzonne de Joncaire's new trading post, where he was received, he reported, with much joy by the Seneca there. He found this place very badly supplied with trading goods. Many of the Indians, who had come there in great numbers that year on account of the popularity of Joncaire, were impelled, he declared, when they could not get what they wanted, to go on to Oswego. He counted fifty-one canoes that had left Niagara for that place. As to the post itself, he found that one house had to provide for the needs of the commandant and the trader and that the stockade, in the form of a triangle, was badly made, " *le toute contre les règles de la fortification.*" As all the Indians there,

---

[167] N. Y. Col. Doc., X, 205.

[168] Arch. Nat., Col., C¹¹ A. 93: 207.

[169] For his " Journal " covering this trip see *ibid.*, C¹¹ E. 13: 229–58.

[170] Galissonière, writing to the Minister on October 5, 1748, refers to a report that the river is gradually undermining the earthworks of the fort. He, however, thought that it could await repairs for a time (Arch. Nat., Col., C¹¹ A. 90: 140). John Patten, a Pennsylvania trader who was brought as a prisoner to Niagara at this period, affirmed that the fort was " built of hewed Loggs framed and fastened together in many Places with Iron Pins, and is about eighty Yards in Length and fifty in breadth, and has five Stone Barracks for the Soldiers, and mounts five Carriage and five Swivel Guns, besides some Chamber Pieces, the Carriage Guns he supposes to be Six and Four Pounders, that the Walls of the Fort are about one Foot thick, and those of the Barracks two feet and a half, that there was during the time he stayd there, a Captain, Lieutenant, Ensign and forty Men, besides a Smith and Cooper who work for the Indians . . ." (Penn Mss., Indian Affairs, I, 65, Hist. Soc. of Pa.).

both men and women, were drunk, in order to appeal to them he was obliged to tarry until they were sober. Nevertheless, with the co-operation of Joncaire, he secured thirty recruits, and on the return trip for the first time these Seneca rendered homage to God in prayer in the chapel of Fort Niagara. Passing by Oswego, he observed the fort, which reminded him of a very low-decked ship, with the upper story provided with a machicolation; the structure, he noted, although surrounded by a stone wall flanked with two bastions, was very vulnerable: " two batteries, each of three twelve-pounders, would be more than sufficient to reduce this establishment to ashes." Upon returning to La Présentation late in July, he drew up a statement regarding the progress of the mission which he attached to the " Journal " covering his trip and forwarded to La Jonquière. According to this, he had begun his work two years previous with but six Iroquois; the next year there were eighty-seven settled at the mission; at the time of writing the number had increased to three hundred and ninety-six " without counting perhaps more than one hundred and fifty that Monsieur Chabert de Joncaire should bring this autumn." What was even more important than the mere numbers of recruits in his eyes was the fact that the settlement was composed of families " the most ancient and considerable among the Iroquois " and was already sufficiently powerful to bind the Five Nations. Here now, he declared, in a burst of irony, was " the establishment which officers, interpreters, merchants looked upon as a chimera, an extravagance . . . a post dangerous to the state, which the jealousy, the antipathy, the disposition of a thousand rash commentators would undoubtedly have destroyed had it not been for the judicial and enlightened firmness of those who govern the country." All this, he assured La Jonquière, he had done for the glory of God and the King his master.

In its maturity La Présentation must have presented a rather impressive appearance, in contrast to the ruinous condition of some of the French posts, such as that of Miami. There was not only the palisaded rectangular fort, at each corner of which was a bastion or, perhaps more accurately, a blockhouse,[171] but also a chapel, a storehouse, a sawmill at the rapids, a barn, a stable, and other conveniences, together with the three Indian villages and the cultivated fields. All this Piquet had brought to pass and more too. For, understanding the

---

[171] For a contemporary plan of La Présentation see *Mémoires sur le Canada, 1749–1760* (1873), p. 13; this plan is reproduced in Winsor's *Narrative and Critical History of America*, V, 3.

weakness of the Indians for finery, he had on one occasion garbed about a hundred of his Onondaga converts " all in very fine Cloathes, laced with Silver and Gold," and had taken them down and presented them to the French Governor at Montreal.[172]

Piquet was a fighting priest. Not satisfied with his remarkable achievement at La Présentation and in full confidence of his ability to command the Iroquois Confederation, early in February of the following year, 1752, he unfolded to La Jonquière and Bigot a bold project: that of going into the valley of the Ohio at the head of five hundred domiciled Indians and seven hundred Iroquois — to the exclusion of the Mohawks. As these would be joined not only by six hundred other Iroquois living about the Ohio, as well as other Indian groups dwelling there, but by two thousand Choctaws — to whom he would bring Christianity — making a total of thirty-eight hundred warriors, he not only would be able, he asserted, to drive the English traders from their establishments in the valley, but would also fall upon the rebellious Miami as well as the " Nation du Chien," apparently the Cherokee,[173] who were charged with destroying in their wanderings two years earlier some of the domiciled Iroquois.[174] In a mood of great exaltation of spirit he declared:

> " *Je me trouve donc, messieurs, dans l'occasion de pouvoir étendre l'empire de Jésus Christ et du Roy mes bons maîtres jusqu'aus extrémités de ce nouveau monde et de plus faire avec quelques secours que vous me procurerés, que la France et l'Angleterre ne pourraient faire avec plusieurs millions et toutes leurs troupes.*" [175]

---

[172] For the other side of the picture see Conrad Weiser's " Journal " covering his trip to Onondaga in 1750 (Pa. Col. Rec., V, 475). Weiser declared that several of the converts returned to Onondaga and " drank away their fine Cloathes and reported that the French Priest at Swegatsy was not good and endeavored to make Slaves of the Indians, notwithstanding his Fine Speeches he makes to the Indians. . . ." The interpreter, after hearing the Indians mocking one another, telling one another: " Go and get baptized again," came to the conclusion that the Indians would not pay any respect to religion " if they do not get by it."

[173] For the alliance of the " Dog Tribe " with the English in 1757 see N. Y. Col. Doc., X, 587. In September 1751 the Cherokee were accused of killing the domiciled Indians, and La Jonquière thereupon encouraged the Iroquois at La Présentation to attack them (ibid., X, 237). According to Hodge, the only tribe called the " Chiens " were the Cheyennes. He does not associate this name with the Cherokee. Parkman, however (Montcalm and Wolfe, II, Appendix A), gives them this identification.

[174] Piquet to La Jonquière and Bigot, February 8, 1752, Arch. Nat., Col., C¹¹ A. 98: 96.

[175] Ibid. Before sending his proposal to the Governor General and the Intendant he unfolded it to the Indians at La Présentation in a general assembly. On this occasion a leading Indian named Carassakaua, to further the plan, offered to go early in the spring

This daring enterprise both La Jonquière and Bigot approved, as well as Longueuil, who temporarily took over the responsibilities of the governor-generalship upon the death of La Jonquière. Bigot also agreed to supply the Indians with munitions, with the understanding, however, that Piquet would not take with him any Frenchmen, so that the nations that were struck could not charge that the latter had killed them.[176] But the French Minister, when the proposal was laid before him, not only considered it " *chimérique* "[177] but came out flatly against a contemplated Indian war and in favour of employing only Frenchmen in solving the problem of the control of the Ohio Valley, combined with a policy of reconciliation with the alienated tribes. As a result, the militant Abbé was obliged to content himself with the less exciting adventure of a trip to France to see the King, accompanied by two of his Iroquois and an Algonquian on board the ship *Algonkin,* which had been constructed at Quebec. He also received an extra gratuity of three thousand livres from his royal master as a token of satisfaction with his zeal.[178]

The events just narrated would leave the impression that the Confederation, outside of the Mohawks, had quite repudiated the old English alliance in favour of the French. This impression is reinforced by a letter from Richard Peters, Secretary of Pennsylvania, to Thomas Penn in the summer of 1753. Peters writes:

> "The great misfortune is that since the death of Canassatego, Toganunty, Schaioady & Schicklalamy, the chiefs of the Six Nations, not being bred up in the tender sense these persons had of the English affection for them have acquired a perfect Indifference & give way to those who sollicit best, & in this respect the French, by their situation, frequent Journeys & address, infinitely surpass the English."[179]

Nevertheless, the degree to which Piquet, Joncaire, and others could control the actions of the Confederation is problematical. For example, the domiciled Iroquois at Sault St. Louis and the Lake of

---

to the Flat Heads, whose language he spoke and who esteemed him, to call upon them to drive out the English among them, to gather supplies, and to come under the French flag.

[176] Bigot to the Minister, May 6, 1752, Arch Nat., Col., C11 A. 98: 86.

[177] Arch. Nat., Col., B. 99: 158 (a)–61; *Canadian Archives, Report* (1905), I, 168.

[178] *Ibid.,* I, 194; Arch. Nat., Col., C11 A. 99: 74. It is uncertain whether the Indians were received at Versailles. The presence of the Indians in France was not welcomed by the court (*Canadian Archives, Report* [1905], I, 199).

[179] Penn Official Correspondence, Hist. Soc. of Pa., VI, 73.

the Two Mountains were convinced that La Présentation was "filled with spies." [180] It is certain that some of the converts went to Albany and received English medals and just as certain that some of them upon returning sent these medals to Governor General Duquesne and even expelled from the mission one who was suspected of having " an English heart." [181] All this would seem to point to the fact that the Indians were, in the main, stark realists; they were fully aware that both the French and the English were competing for their goodwill, each offering something that the other could not give in the same measure, each playing their own game, each striving for certain objectives that boded the aborigines no good, each able to direct against them an overwhelming power if not checked by the other. However, as between the two, the English — including the Dutch and Germans of New York and Pennsylvania, who were, of course, subjects of the King of England — presented a much more serious threat, arising out of their utter lack of appreciation of the red man as an individual possessed of a highly developed culture of his own, their overwhelming numerical preponderance, their insatiable appetite for good arable land, and the ever westward and northward pressing of their settlements into his country. Yet the English could offer greater material rewards to him for his exertions in the chase, and, after all, he was inclined to live for the moment, to seek the satisfaction of immediate desires, whatever they might be, which, as a rule, were unhappily of the grosser type.

It is therefore not surprising that the policy of the tribes within the Confederation became one of " balance." For example, many of the Seneca, over whom the brothers Joncaire exercised so great an influence, gave support, nevertheless, to the rebellious Hurons in the Sandusky region. On the other hand, the Mohawks, in spite of the equally great influence exerted over them by William Johnson, notified Governor Clinton in 1753 that they were determined to drive away from their country certain Englishmen who kept encroaching on their lands — ever claiming more and more land — and they left the conference in a rebellious frame of mind.[182] The year following this incident the Oswego traders were led to complain loudly that in passing through the Mohawk country the discontented Indians "board our Battoes, with axes, knives, ettc. and by force take what

---

[180] N. Y. Col. Doc., X, 263.
[181] Ibid.
[182] Ibid., VI, 783–8.

Rum they think proper, hooping and yelping as if they Gloried in their depredations, and threatening Murder to any that oppose them. . . ." [183]

Yet, granted that individual Englishmen had ignored and were still ignoring the rights of the Indians in their encroachments upon Iroquois land, the French authorities went far beyond this in taking away or at least ignoring the rights of the Confederation to much of the soil that it claimed as its own. For, as the result of the royal instructions to Governor Duquesne, they had reversed their earlier position which admitted that the Ohio Valley belonged to the Confederation and now denied it, setting forth a sweeping claim in the name of the King to the exclusion of the Indians. This appropriation of their hunting grounds might well have aroused the bitter hostility of the Six Nations. However, as they watched the manœuvres of the English and the French, especially in relation to the control of the trans-Appalachian region, they became convinced, after the French had appeared in force on Lake Erie in 1753 without any interference, that the latter were invincible, and some of their chief sachems in conferring with Johnson were led to

> "confess the Truth [that they were] quite afraid of them, & therefore sitting quite neuter & hanging their Heads, but [affirmed that] if once they should see the English rise up & make Resistance, they

---

[183] *Ibid.*, VI, 858. At a meeting of the New York Provincial Council on June 18, 1754 ("New York Council Minutes Etc., 1684–1754," New York Public Library) de Lancey laid before the board a minute from the Indian Commissioners' Proceedings setting forth "divers Complaints made to them: that the Connojahary Indians forceably take away from the Oswego Traders and that the Oneida Indians oblige the traders to let them carry their goods over the Carrying Place and to pay double and sometimes more than double the customary rates which the Germans are willing to take. . . ."

At this juncture the Indian Commissioners submitted to the Governor certain recommendations which they felt would, if carried into effect, re-establish the English influence among the Six Nations: that the Indians should be exhorted to dwell together in their respective castles and particularly that the Mohawks, Onondaga and Seneca should each live in one general castle; that a fort should be built in the Onondaga country and another in the Seneca country at each of which a missionary should reside; that the selling of rum in the castles of the Indians should be restrained; and that no Frenchman should be permitted to reside among them and trade with them.

Conrad Weiser, the Pennsylvania interpreter, an adopted son of the Iroquois who had exercised at times great influence over the Confederation, was led in 1754 to confess in his discouragement at the turn of affairs: "I am quite Perplexed in my Mind, and do not know how to act in Indian Affairs any more, they are apostates as to their old Natural principal of Honesty, and become Drunkards, Rogues, Thieves and Liars" (letter to Richard Peters, March 15, 1754, Weiser Correspondence, Hist. Soc. of Pa., I, 44).

could be sure all the Nations chearfully would Join them, & doubt-less frustrate the designs of the French, being much more inclined to live under the Protection of the English then [than] the French, as they must [much] more fear then [than] love them." [184]

The Iroquois, it must be confessed, had had good reason to lose some of the old respect that they had at one time displayed toward the English. They were fully aware of the rivalry that existed between the people of the different colonies over questions relating to the fur trade and Western land pretensions, of the efforts of the Pennsylvania traders before 1753 to draw to themselves the peltries of the Lake Erie region at the expense of Oswego and the Albany merchants, of the jealousy that these same traders displayed toward the Ohio Company factors when the latter entered into competition with them on the upper Ohio. They were also fully aware of the sharp divergence in point of view of the people of New England and of the citizens of Albany with respect to relations with Canada, in times not only of peace but of war, and of the clash of competing interests within the Province of New York, as evidenced " by the violent antagonism of groups growing out of the management of Indian affairs." [185] They therefore saw no evidence of a unified English policy as they did in the case of New France, but each interested colonial government, especially at the conclusion of the late war, inclined to pursue its own line of action without regard to the objectives or even the objections of its neighbours. Thus, working at cross-purposes, there was confusion and weakness and faltering among the English in the eyes of the Indians when the impending crisis called for union and strength and decisiveness.

Under these circumstances the great defects of the singular merits of the British colonial system were laid bare, not only to the Six Nations but also to the authorities in Great Britain. As disturbing reports flooded in from America describing the unimpeded movements of the French into the Ohio Valley and the growing alienation of the Iroquoian Confederation and tribes in friendship with them, the conviction came home that steps must be taken without delay to remedy the situation. As to the nature of these steps there was uncertainty; but at least the Six Nations must be reconciled and must be impressed with the fact that the English could speak with one voice.

---

[184] Dan Claus to Governor Hamilton, January 18, 1754, Pa. Provincial Papers, XII, 54; Conrad Weiser's " Journal," N. Y. Col. Doc., VI, 797.
[185] Ibid., VI, 805.

On September 18, 1753 the Board of Trade, which was permitted at this juncture to exercise a great deal of initiative in colonial affairs, addressed a letter to the new Governor of New York, Sir Danvers Osborne, expressing its displeasure and surprise that the provincial authorities had permitted a serious misunderstanding to develop between themselves and the Mohawks and calling upon him to take immediate steps to restore the former friendship by means of a conference with the whole Confederation, to which the governments of Virginia, Maryland, Pennsylvania, New Jersey, New Hampshire, and Massachusetts Bay were to be invited to send commissioners and presents and for the furtherance of which presents from England were also to be sent in the name of His Majesty.[186] The proposed meeting of the colonial commissioners had a limited but important objective as expressed by the Lords Commissioners, which was " to take care that all the Provinces be (if practicable) comprised in one general Treaty " with the Six Nations, " to be made in his Majesty's name "; since it appeared " that the practice of each Province making a separate Treaty for itself in its own name is very improper and may be attended with great inconveniency to His Majesty's service." With this letter went a circular letter addressed to the Governor of each of the above-named colonies.[187] Upon the arrival of the packet in New York, it came into the hands of Lieutenant Governor de Lancey, who had taken over the duties of Osborne upon the death of the latter on October 12 and who set energetically to work on the plans for the conference.

It should be pointed out that in the late spring of 1753 the New York authorities, realizing that the Albany Indian commissioners were completely lacking in influence among the Six Nations, determined to send Johnson to them to do his utmost to bring them into a better frame of mind. At a meeting in Onondaga the latter part of July he appeared before them and, while sturdily rebuking them for their misconduct and lack of co-operation, did much to straighten " the fine shady Tree which was planted," as he declared to them, " by your forefathers for your ease and shelter . . . [but which was] almost blown down by Northerly winds." [188] Yet, the Indians made clear to him their dilemma:

---

[186] *Ibid.*, VI, 800–1.
[187] *Ibid.*, VI, 802.
[188] *Ibid.*, VI, 810.

"we dont know what you Christians, English and French together intend; we are so hemmed in by both, that we have hardly a hunting place left. In a little while if we find a bear in a tree there will immediately appear an owner of the land to challenge the property, and hinder us from killing it, which is our livelihood. We are so perplexed between both that we hardly know what to say or think." [189]

The date fixed for the conference was June 14, 1754 and the place Albany rather than Onondaga, as had been suggested by the Lords Commissioners.[190] These arrangements, however, precluded representation on the part of Virginia, since Dinwiddie had already summoned the Ohio Valley Indians to meet at Winchester on May 20 with all that this seemed to imply.[191]

As will be noted in the chapter to follow, the Albany treaty conference proper actually became subordinate to that on intercolonial relations. Had Dinwiddie and his council anticipated this development, doubtless the Old Dominion, in spite of her preoccupation with the crisis in the Ohio Valley, would have found means to be represented.

---

[189] *Ibid.*, VI, 813.

[190] *Ibid.*, VI, 800, 817.

[191] Governor Dinwiddie, in replying on January 29, 1754 to de Lancey's invitation to send commissioners to Albany, declared: "The conference . . . interferes with the meeting I have proposed with the Six Nations & the S[thern] Ind[s] on the 20th of May next." He went on to say that he was convinced that the Assembly would be very backward in sending commissioners to Albany, as the charge of the intended meeting at Winchester and the raising of men to defeat the designs of the French would be considerable (Dinwiddie Private Papers, Sparks Transcripts, II, 69, Virginia State Library). In writing to the Board of Trade on March 12, Dinwiddie in excusing his failure to carry out his instruction, stressed the importance of the Winchester meeting as against that at Albany. For at the former place he expected to meet "many Chiefs of different Nations . . . and think the Southern Indians are more to be counted [on] than the Five Nations, being ten times their number" (C. O. 5: 1328, pp. 193–4). The conference, however, as it turned out was of slight significance.

CHAPTER IV

"Join or Die"

I N SPITE OF the unwillingness of Virginia to undertake any responsibilities in connection with the Albany Indian conference, the
other colonies particularly specified by the Board of Trade and
invited by Lieutenant Governor de Lancey, with the exception of
New Jersey, responded favourably; [1] and, in addition to these, Connecticut with particular objectives in mind sent three of her most influential men and Rhode Island two of hers.[2] All in all, it was a gath-

---

[1] On April 25, 1754 Governor Belcher addressed the New Jersey Assembly respecting the proposed Albany conference, and laid before it letters from the Earl of
Holderness and the Board of Trade (New Jersey Archives, XVI, 455–8). On the 27th
the Assembly made its reply. While agreeing "that there should be a strict Union among
all his Majesty's Colonies on this important Affair" of the Indian policy, it nevertheless
declined to be involved in the conference since the colony had never been a party to
any Iroquoian treaty, did not carry on any trade with those Indians that were concerned,
and was already involved financially. Belcher thereupon rebuked the members, but
rather mildly, for their apparent indifference (ibid., XIX, 361–7).

[2] The presence of representatives from Connecticut and Rhode Island at Albany
requires additional explanation. Although the Board of Trade had not suggested the
calling of those from either to the conference, it appears that Governor Shirley was
mainly responsible for this step. Writing to him on March 5, 1754, de Lancey says: " I
thank you for what you say as to Connecticut & Rhode Island; I had discoursed with
some gentlemen here upon the expediency of acquainting the Government of Connecticut with the intended interview who all agreed in Opinion with your Excellency
as being persuaded of their readiness to join in so public a measure — of Rhode Island
we desponded as they are secured by being covered with other colonies. I shall write
to them both on this subject" ("Massachusetts Archives," IV, 442–4, Mass. State
Archives). It is clear that Shirley had in mind the welding of a union of the old continental colonies and saw the importance, therefore, of the representation of the two
at Albany.

ering of men of high distinction,[3] and was held, very rightly, to be one of great significance, one that would perhaps go far beyond the expressed intentions of the Board of Trade. Apparently all the delegates except Thomas Hutchinson of Massachusetts Bay were present when on the morning of June 19, five days after the date set in the formal summons, twenty-three commissioners appeared in the Albany City Hall and, in the presence of de Lancey, produced their powers and instructions.[4]

As to the powers vested in the commissioners, they varied greatly. Those given to the Massachusetts Bay delegation permitted it not only to make a treaty with the Indians but to enter " into articles of Union and Confederation with the aforesaid Governments for the general defence of his Majesty's subjects and interests in North America, as well in time of peace as of war." [5] The New Hampshire dele-

---

[3] New Hampshire commissioned Chief Justice Theodore Atkinson, Meshech Weare, Speaker of the Assembly and later Governor, Richard Wibird, and Henry Sherburne, Jr.; Massachusetts Bay, Thomas Hutchinson, who had been repeatedly selected as Speaker of the General Court and was now a member of the provincial council, Colonel John Chandler, Judge of the Worcester County Court, Colonel Oliver Partridge, perhaps the leading man in western Massachusetts and later to be a member of the Stamp Act Congress, Samuel Welles, and John Worthington; Rhode Island, Chief Justice Stephen Hopkins, who in 1755 became Governor and later signed the Declaration of Independence, and Martin Howard, Jr.; Connecticut, Deputy Governor William Pitkin, Roger Wolcott, Jr., a Justice of the Superior Court, and Colonel Elisha Williams, at one time president of Yale College and also later London Agent; New York, sent but did not commission Lieutenant Governor de Lancey, who presided, Attorney General William Smith, the future historian, Colonel William Johnson, also of the council and the most deeply versed of all the commissioners in Indian relations and soon to become a baronet, Joseph Murray, and John Chambers; Pennsylvania commissioned John Penn, son of Richard Penn, one of the Proprietors and later to become Governor, Richard Peters, Secretary of the Province, Isaac Norris, Speaker of the Assembly, and Benjamin Franklin, one of the greatest among the men of the eighteenth century; Maryland, Benjamin Tasker, Jr., President of the Council and in 1753 Acting Governor, and Major Abraham Barnes. See *Massachusetts Historical Society Collections* (third series), V, 10–17.

[4] *New York Colonial Documents,* VI, 853.

[5] *Mass. Hist. Coll.* (third series), V, 9–10. In the case of the Massachusetts Bay delegation at least, the formal commission granted to it must be distinguished from the elaborate instructions and additional instructions that were furnished by the Assembly for its guidance. The instructions are grouped under eight headings and the additional instructions under four. The first called for " a general, firm & perpetual union & confederacy, for mutual assistance by men or money or both, in peace & in war. . . ." The second, for an agreement as to the proportion of the required men and money that each government should provide " for the Comn safety." The third, for concerted measures for the immediate removal of the encroachments made by the French on His Majesty's territories. The fourth, for authorizing a gift to the Six Nations to be contributed by the Province. The fifth, for the erection of forts in the Iroquoian country as places of

gates were authorized simply " to agree upon, consult and conclude what may be necessary for establishing a sincere and lasting friendship and good harmony with the said Six Nations of Indians ";[6] those of Connecticut were to join " in concerting proper measures for the general defence and safety of his Majesty's subjects in said Governments and the Indians in alliance with them, against the French and their Indians ";[7] while those of Rhode Island were to join " in consulting what methods are proper " to preserve the friendship of the Six Nations and to prohibit the French and Indian allies from encroaching on the lands within the dominions of His Majesty, " and in general, as far as the abilities of this Government will permit, to act in conjunction with the said Commissioners in everything necessary for the good of his Majesty's subjects in those parts, and to answer, as far as we can, the designs of his Majesty's instructions to this Colony communicated to us by the Earl of Holderness."[8] As to the Pennsylvania commissioners, they were in conjunction with the others authorized " to renew, ratify, and confirm the leagues of amity subsisting between us and the said nations of Indians," to give them presents, and conclude everything necessary " for the engaging them heartily in our interest and for frustrating any attempts which have

refuge for the Indian women and children. The sixth, for obligating the commissioners to remind the others of " the vast expence & burden of this province for more than fifty years past, in opposing the french & their Indians . . . which amounts to an immense sum beyond our just proportions, & will entitules [sic] us to some Reimbursement or at least to a more favourable future quota." The seventh, for concerting " some method of carrying the design of this union into execution on any Sudden emergency. . . ." The eighth, for making clear that the Assembly leaves the commissioners to act on their " discretion & best thots on the spot & in these present exigencies " (Mass. Archives, IV, 471). Besides these instructions approved by the two chambers on April 18 and 19, on June 6 certain additional instructions were provided. The first of these called for the building of a " fortress " close to and dominating the French Fort St. Frédérick at Crown Point; the second, for the consideration of proper measures for stopping the colonial trade with " Louisbourg & Canada . . . the French (and thrô them the Indian enemy likewise) being thereby supplied wth provisions of all kinds," which " have prov'd of pernicious consequence to His Majesty's northern Colonies . . ."; the third, for the regulation of the Indian trade in such a manner as may best secure the advantages of it to his Majesty's subjects; the fourth, for the attaining of important ends of the " proposed Confederacy," by holding " stated Interviews (either annually or otherwise as the present Commiss[rs.] shall judge to be necessary) and that ye place or places as well as the time for such Interviews be agreed on & Ascertained " (ibid., IV, 471). Thus, as will be noted, the Massachusetts Bay commissioners were given full powers not only to consummate a colonial confederacy but to implement it.

[6] Mass. Hist. Soc. Coll., V, 11.

[7] Ibid., V, 12.

[8] Ibid., V, 13.

been made to withdraw them from it." [9] Finally, those from Maryland were empowered to " enter into a league of amity with the said Indian nations " and to deliver them a present; further, as it had been intimated that the commissioners of several of the neighbouring colonies would be instructed to concert measures for better securing the alliance of the Indians and for the more easy defence of His Majesty's dominions on this continent, they were " to observe well what propositions shall or may be made concerning such general scheme," but were not authorized " to stipulate . . . that the Province will advance any sum of money or number of men toward erecting forts or garrisoning them, or to any such purposes " but were merely to report upon the same that the Governor " may not be ignorant after what manner we can best contribute to the success of any such scheme as shall be proposed . . . for the defence or utility of his Majesty's American dominions and subjects." [10]

It will be noted that nothing is said above respecting the powers and instructions of the New York delegation. Its position was peculiar. In the words of the report of the Massachusetts Bay commissioners:

> " His Honour the Lieutenant Governor of New York was also present, as were four of the Council of that Province, but the said Council did not appear as Commissioners, or show any special powers to act in behalf of that Government." [11]

Nevertheless, those members of that body gathered at Albany insisted on participating in all the activities of the Congress as though fully qualified to do so. Their chief and immediate concern was an intercolonial agreement for the erection of posts at the common expense in the Indian country and not the establishment of any form of permanent union. Had this been otherwise, it is quite clear that representatives of the elected branch of the Assembly would have been present and that the group would have been provided with the usual type of credentials. This leads to the query: Why was this not done? The answer doubtless lies in the fact that Lieutenant Governor de Lancey had determined to control the deliberations of the Congress. Had the New York delegation been furnished with commissions which he himself would have been obliged to sign, it is quite unlikely

9 *Ibid.*, V, 14–15.
10 *Ibid.*, V, 15–17.
11 Mass. Arch., IV, 459–64.

that he would have been actively identified with the conference. As it was, he was the only chief official of a colony in attendance. It will be noted that he had been empowered by the Board of Trade to *call* the Congress, but that is as far as his authorization went.

It is important in this connection to observe that the Albany Congress was not permitted to organize as such bodies representing co-equal governments had by long usage been accustomed to do. There was apparently no committee on credentials, none either on organization or on nominations. De Lancey, in other words, supported by his own group, insisted on organizing the conference and, in so far as was possible, controlling its proceedings as the presiding officer. That this rather high-handed conduct was resented, at least by the delegation from Massachusetts Bay, which, as has been noted, came carefully prepared and empowered to carry through an ambitious program, is quite clear. In fact, the House of Representatives, after the delegates had returned to the Province, took note on November 13:

> "That at the late Congress at Albany, certain Indignities were by some persons in Power offered the Commissioners of that Congress, as also such Treatment relative to the Business, which by his Majesty's special Direction they met to do, as may seem inconsistent with the General Design & Business of this Meeting, and the Respect due to their Commissions."

It was thereupon voted that a committee consisting of the members from the House and one from the Council should "enquire into the Affair, with Power to take Affidavits, And to report as soon as may be."[12] The growing menace of the French doubtless helps to explain why the issue was permitted to die in committee — after all, it was in the nature of a post-mortem examination.

Before dismissing the point at issue it may be suggested that two motives may have impelled de Lancey to take the course that he did in violation of all parliamentary procedure. He may, on the one hand, have decided that by this means he could keep under cover certain unsavoury facts relative to the relations of the Province with the Indians and, on the other, may have felt that his guidance was essential if the conference was to agree to do the things that the government of New York felt must be done to meet the crisis along its own borders.

---

[12] Mass. Arch., General Court Records, XX, 314.

But to return to the conference itself. All the colonies there represented had at least one object in common in sending commissioners
to Albany: the re-establishment of friendly relations between the
Iroquoian Confederacy and the British, with the correction of whatever abuses had been permitted to develop; as to these, the commissioners, with the opening of the Congress, were made fully aware of
the danger that the Six Nations might be wholly lost to their enemy.
This was evident not only by the small number of Indians that put in
an appearance, in spite of the fact that it had been widely adver-
tised among them that a very large present had been prepared for
them, but also by their rather calculated coldness and even scarcely
veiled air of hostility.[13] The French influence over them was very
evident, as was the fact that they had very definite grievances. Although de Lancey made it quite plain to the commissioners from the
other colonies that he did not want them to take cognizance " of the
details " of the past relations of New York authorities and people
with the Iroquois,[14] the two chief grievances — having to do with the
fur trade and the disposal of their land — could not be hidden. As to
the first, the commissioners

> " found upon enquiry, that, on the payment of twelve pence per gal-
> lon duty to the Government by the English trader, the Indians may
> be supplied with unlimited quantities of Rum at Oswego & other
> licensed places on the said frontiers; that by this means they are
> almost continually drunk and, at least, imagine that in their drink
> they have been abused & imposed upon in their trading." [15]

The Albany interests, it goes without saying, were not at all favourably disposed to the idea that their activities be the subject of intercolonial scrutiny and regulation.

As to the second grievance, that over land, this carried implications
most delicate in nature, in light of the fact that Philip Livingston, one
of the most influential men in the Province, was charged with appropriating the very land upon which one of the Mohawk towns was
standing;[16] while another party was likewise charged with having
secured a patent for some seven hundred thousand acres " without
any Conveyance from the Indians of their Title." [17]

---

[13] Mass. Arch., IV, 459–64.
[14] Ibid.
[15] Ibid.
[16] Ibid., General Court Records, XX, 332.
[17] Ibid.

Therefore, it is not surprising that at the first two conferences with the Mohawks alone the representatives of other governments than those of New York were excluded. On June 27 the Lower Castle in the presence of the Lieutenant Governor and members of his council complained:

> "We understand that there are writings for all our lands, so that we shall have none left but the very spot we live upon and hardly that." [18]

De Lancey thereupon promised them that if this were true, justice would be done them and that in this connection the records would be carefully examined. The next day the Upper Castle was likewise received and was found to be in a truculent mood, complaining that the late governors of the Province had turned their backs upon the Six Nations "as if they were no more." [19] The minutes of the two meetings are very defective but there is every evidence that great efforts were made to appease the Mohawks. On the 29th the first of the general conferences took place, at which an address previously agreed upon by the Congress was delivered. Having condoled with the Indians on the death of some of their leaders — always a customary procedure as a preliminary at all Indian treaties — they not only were called upon, and in particular the Onondaga, to return to live in their ancient abodes, but were very pointedly questioned as to whether the French were taking possession of their western lands with their permission. [20]

Not until July 2 were the Indians prepared to make reply; then it was that Chief Hendrick of the Mohawks, speaking for the Confederation, sought to make clear why the Indians were living in a scattered manner. It was, he asserted, because of "your neglecting us for these three years past." [21] Taking a stick and throwing it behind his back, he proceeded:

> "You have thus thrown us behind your back, and disregarded us, whereas the French are a subtle and vigilant people, ever using their utmost endeavours to seduce and bring our people over to them." [22]

---

[18] N. Y. Col. Doc., VI, 865-6.

[19] Ibid.

[20] For the prepared speech see ibid., VI, 861-3.

[21] Reference is here made to the retirement of Colonel William Johnson from Indian affairs three years previous, much to the discontent of the Indians, who now asked for his reinstatement, "for we all lived happy, whilst . . . under his management, for we love him, and he us, and he has always been our good, and trusty friend" (ibid., VI, 870-1).

[22] Ibid.

Turning now to the encroachments of the French upon their land, the speaker affirmed that the French had gone upon it without the consent of the Confederation and he also added that the governors of Virginia and Canada were quarrelling over the land, while the Governor of Virginia and that of Pennsylvania had made paths through it to carry on trade and had built houses without acquainting the Indians with their action. In other words, it was contended that there were three groups of encroachers and not just one in the Ohio Valley. This was not all. While the English sought to keep the Indians from resorting to the French, Hendrick charged that they themselves were supplying the French not only with goods but with arms:

> ". . . the Indians of Canada come frequently and smoak here [in Albany], which is for the sake of their Beaver. . . . Look about you and see all of these houses full of Beaver, and the money is all gone to Canada, likewise powder, lead and guns, which the French now make use of at Ohio. . . . The goods which go from hence to Oswego, go from thence to Ohio which further enables the French to carry on their designs at the Ohio." [23]

In answering these grievances the following day, the commissioners pointed out that the French had no right to encroach since the Indians themselves had put their hunting lands under the King's government with the understanding that " the property or power of selling it to any of his Maj$^{ty's}$ subjects having authority from him, we always consider vested in you." And as to the activities of the Pennsylvania and Virginia traders, the Congress permitted Conrad Weiser, who had accompanied the Pennsylvania delegation, to speak. The latter, an adopted son of the Iroquois, thereupon made clear that the road between Pennsylvania and Ohio was an old road, that the Delawares and Shawnee who had gone there thirty years ago had invited the traders; further, that Governor Dinwiddie had sent belts to the Six Nations to get them to come and treat but they had not responded and that only with the appearance of the French, at the request of the Ohio Indians, had the Virginians erected a house. As to the further charges that the Albany merchants had supplied the French with arms, de Lancey, whose own family had been deeply involved in the Canada trade, felt impelled to declare that he had made inquiry and could assure the Indians that they had been misinformed.

---

[23] *Ibid.*

The Indians at the conference displayed on July 5 a marked change in attitude. They now admitted that the road to the Ohio from Pennsylvania was an old road; they now thanked the Governor of Virginia for assisting the Ohio Indians, "who are our Brethren and Allies"; nevertheless, they stressed, as they had in their previous talk, the defenceless state of the frontiers " and of the Country of the Five Nations. . . . We beg you will resolve," they pleaded, " upon something speedily. You are not safe from danger one day." [24] Further, they requested that rum might no longer be sold in their castles and that a church with a bell in it be built at Conajohary, which " will tend to make us Religious and lead better lives than we do now." [25]

At this gathering John Penn announced that the Pennsylvania commissioners were about to purchase land from the Indians " below the lattitude 42° ".[26] and the Indians also made declaration that they were about to sell it, with the result that on July 6 a deed was signed

---

[24] Ibid., VI, 872–7.

[25] Conajoharie was the Upper Mohawk Castle. There in 1734 Jacob Eblig carried on a Christian mission, under the auspices of the S.P.G.; there likewise in the middle of the century an Indian convert, Abraham, laboured (Historical Magazine of the Protestant Episcopal Church, VIII, 153, 159).

[26] In view of " the rashness of the New England People to propose to settle on Wyomink," early in 1754 the Pennsylvania authorities came to the conclusion to endeavour to persuade the Six Nations to sell the remaining lands to which they had claims that lay within the boundaries of the Province. Conrad Weiser, the Pennsylvania Indian interpreter, was requested to hurry to Onondaga for the purpose of persuading the Indians to come to Philadelphia to make a treaty. On March 15 he wrote to Richard Peters, the Provincial Secretary, declaring that it was impossible for him to walk from " Shomockin to Onondago " and that to go on horseback was equally impossible " because of the many Branches of the Susquehanna River." While admitting that he did travel there on foot early in the spring of 1736, he declared that he almost perished " by miserys and Famine . . . suffered." He therefore gave it as his opinion that his suggested trip be postponed, at least until after the Albany Congress, especially since some of the Iroquois chiefs took the position that all their treaties should be made in Albany — a position also held by Colonel Johnson. His letter is illuminating on more than one point. In recommending that the Pennsylvania commissioners to Albany lay before the chief of the Six Nations the proceedings at Carlisle the preceding fall with the Ohio Indians, with the later purported release of Pennsylvania lands to the Proprietors, he added: " let them take with them the string or rather Belt of Wampum sent from Shanapin on Ohio to the Governors of Philadelphia and Williamsburg, and let . . . the said Chief know what the message was, tho forged. It would incline them to treat with us for the Land rather than to leave us to deal with the Ohio Indians for it, and I may perhaps fall in with some greedy fellows for money, that will undertake to bring things about to our wishes." Again, as to Colonel Johnson, Weiser felt that he, Johnson, was " in our way as to Land Affairs " and still retained " our large Belt . . . sent to Onondago in . . . 1749, for obtaining the Lands on Juniata etc. . . ." (Weiser Correspondence, Hist. Soc. of Pa., I, 44).

by which for a consideration of four hundred pounds New York currency a vast expanse of land from the west bank of the Susquehanna to the western boundary of the Province lying southward of 41° 31′ was released to the Pennsylvania Proprietors.[27]

Meanwhile, the Connecticut commissioners, who were also members of the so-called Susquehanna Company organized in Connecticut in 1753 for the purpose of settling on western lands that were now claimed to be within the limits of the Connecticut patent of 1662, were likewise busy with the Indians. For the Company had its eyes on the fertile lands of the upper Susquehanna, a region long held to be embraced within the boundaries of Pennsylvania, and now seized this favourable opportunity – aided by the Indian trader John Henry Lydius and the Indian missionary the Reverend Timothy Woodbridge, and in face of the protests of the Pennsylvania commissioners – to secure for the consideration of two thousand pounds current money of New York a deed from the Six Nations for some five million acres of land. This deed, procured under circumstances of unusual secrecy, was signed on July 11 at the termination of the Congress and became the basis of a prolonged and bitter contest between the two colonies.[28]

Although there were still problems to be worked out, especially those involving the Mohawk lands, by July 9 the official negotiations between the commissioners and the Six Nations had been concluded. The latter were now apparently in a happy frame of mind – no longer clouded – protesting the strength of their fidelity to the English cause; they left for their homes, soon after concluding the Connecticut business, so loaded down with presents that thirty wagons were required and were furnished by de Lancey to transport these gifts to the Indian country.[29]

---

[27] For this deed and the negotiations leading up to it see the *Pennsylvania Colonial Records*, VI, 111–29. At first the Indians offered to sell their lands only as far west as the " Allegheny Hills "; the Pennsylvania commissioners, however, refused to consider this, letting the Indians understand that they suspected " some underhand Dealings between the Six Nations and the Governor of Canada." To free themselves from this imputation, the Indians were led to grant all the lands to the western extremity of the Province, provided commissioners would " consent to make the Creek Kayarondiaragh the northern Boundary of the Deed to be executed by Us on Susquehanna." This was agreed to. It is of interest that although the Pennsylvania Commissioners desired that this land treaty be embodied in the minutes of the Albany Congress, their request was refused (*ibid.*, VI, 114).

[28] See *The Susquehanna Company Papers* (ed. J. P. Boyd), I, 101–23; L. H. Gipson, *Jared Ingersoll*, Chap. XI.

[29] It may be noted in passing that among the presents provided by the King were

But to return to the proceedings of the Congress. On June 24 the question was raised as to " whether a Union of all the Colonies is not at present absolutely necessary for their security and defence." The idea itself was not a new one. In the seventeenth century the New England Confederation had maintained itself from 1643 to the withdrawal of the Massachusetts Bay charter in 1684; during the Leisler regime in New York measures for defence were concerted in 1690 with Connecticut and Massachusetts Bay; in the midst of King William's War a plan suggested by Governor Fletcher and modified by the Board of Trade was worked out providing quotas of troops from the various neighbouring colonies down to and including Virginia to assist in the defence of the New York frontier; [30] and during Queen Anne's War in 1709 the plan of quotas was revived by the Crown for an expedition to be launched against Canada by way of New York; [31] in the course of King George's War not only was there " the concert " of the New England colonies against Cape Breton, but Governor Clinton of New York in January 1745 informed Governor Thomas of Pennsylvania " that the Assembly had requested him to appoint Commissioners to Treat, in conjunction with such Commissioners as should be appointed by the Neighboring Governments, for concerting measures for the mutual Security, Defence, and Conduct of the Northern Colonies during the present war. . . ." [32]

In the light of past experience with intercolonial co-operation, therefore, it is not surprising that when at Albany this question of a union to meet the emergency was raised it was passed by the assembled commissioners " in the affirmative unanimously." [33] As a re-

---

guns. A Mr. Milliquet, appointed agent to send over to New York His Majesty's present, appeared before the Board of Trade late in the spring of 1754 to inform the Lords Commissioners " that some part of the guns furnished by the Ordnance for this service was not yet shipped " (Board of Trade Journal, 1754–1758, p. 3).

[30] In the Instructions to Sir Danvers Osborne the quotas recommended by William III to the colonies under the royal sign manual are set forth: Massachusetts Bay was to furnish 350 men, New Hampshire 40, Rhode Island 48, Connecticut 120, New York 200, East New Jersey 60, West New Jersey 60, Pennsylvania 80, Maryland 160, and Virginia 240. Governor Shirley, in commenting upon these quotas in his letter of January 6, 1754, shows that they no longer represented the relative strength of the colonies (C. O. 5: 14, pp. 105–8).

[31] H. L. Osgood, American Colonies in the Eighteenth Century, I, 81, 98, 429.

[32] Pa. Arch. (first series), V, 80. For various plans of union preceding this see Justin Winsor, Narrative and Critical History, V, 611–14, and especially " Plans for the Union of the British Colonies of North America, 1642–1776," compiled by F. D. Stone and printed in H. L. Carson's Constitution of the United States, II, 429–503.

[33] N. Y. Col. Doc., VI, 839–60. The above vote would indicate that many thought-

sult, each delegation was called upon to choose one of its number to act on a committee to prepare and receive plans of union. Those appointed were in each instance among the most politically experienced, if not the most learned, men of the colony in question: Thomas Hutchinson for Massachusetts Bay, Theodore Atkinson for New Hampshire, William Pitkin for Connecticut, Stephen Hopkins for Rhode Island, William Smith for New York, Benjamin Tasker for Maryland, and Benjamin Franklin for Pennsylvania.[34] At this session the proposal was also made to construct two forts in the Indian country, but it was agreed that it would be best to lay this aside until a method of effecting a colonial union was considered.

Among those just mentioned who were chosen to draw up a plan none was more deeply convinced of the necessity of adopting some scheme than was Franklin. On account of the importance of his contribution it would be well to indicate to what extent his ideas on this subject had been matured before his arrival at Albany. As early as March 1751 he had laid down a rough outline for a colonial union which, it is of interest to note, embodied most of the ideas to be found in his later plan. " A voluntary union entered into by the Colonies themselves," he then declared, " would be preferable to one imposed by Parliament; for it would be perhaps not much more difficult to procure, and more easy to alter and improve as circumstances should require and Experience direct." [35] With the developing crisis in North America in 1754 his thoughts turned again to the necessity of some sort of union of the colonies. In his *Pennsylvania Gazette* on May 9 there appeared certain reflections upon the disadvantages that the colonies laboured under in facing the French who had taken possession of the Forks of the Ohio. These apparently were penned by him and certainly expressed his sentiments:

---

ful colonials fully sympathized with Governor Shirley's point of view as to the vital necessity of an immediate union of the colonies. Addressing the Massachusetts Bay Assembly on April 2 of that year he said: " In forming this general Union, Gentlemen, there is no time to be lost; the French seem to have advanced further toward making themselves Masters of this Continent within these last five or six Years than they have done ever since the first beginning of the Settlements upon it " (Mass. Arch., Court Records, XX, 198–201).

[34] *N. Y. Col. Doc.*, VI, 860.

[35] Franklin to James Parker, March 20, 1750/1, *Writings of Benjamin Franklin* (ed. A. H. Smyth), III, 42. This plan of union was appended to Archibald Kennedy's pamphlet on Indian affairs that Parker printed the same year and to which reference will be made.

" The confidence of the French in this undertaking seems well grounded in the present disunited state of the British colonies, and the extreme difficulty of bringing so many different governments and assemblies to agree to any speedy and effectual measures for our common defence and security; while our enemies have the great advantage of being under one direction, with one council, and one purse."

The article was illustrated by a woodcut of a snake separated into parts, representing the colonies, with the motto beneath it: " Join or Die " — a device that was also employed at the beginning of the Revolutionary War. In going to Albany, Franklin was, therefore, strongly committed to the general idea of establishing a concert of colonies. Arriving in the city of New York on June 5, he busied himself in conferences, over this project as well as Indian affairs, with leading New Yorkers,[36] especially with James Alexander and Archibald Kennedy.[37] He also consulted with Thomas Pownall, who had recently come to America with the late Governor Osborne, as his secretary, and who in 1755 was to secure a commission as Lieutenant Governor of New Jersey and in 1757 one as Governor of Massachusetts Bay. On June 9 Alexander, in writing to Cadwallader Colden, declared that after some discussion with Franklin and Richard Peters as to the difficulties of establishing a union that might affect " our

[36] *Pa. Arch.* (first series), II, 145.

[37] Franklin records in his *Autobiography*: " In our way thither, I projected and drew a plan for the Union of all the colonies under one government. . . . As we pass'd thro' New York, I had there shown my project to Mr. James Alexander and Mr. Kennedy, two gentlemen of great knowledge on public affairs, and, being fortified by their approbation, I ventur'd to lay it before the Congress " (*Writings of Franklin*, ed. Smyth, I, 387).

Kennedy was Receiver General of New York and a member of the Governor's Council. In 1751 he drew up a paper embodying certain ideas relating to Indian affairs; his friends advised " the publishing of them with Franklin's remarks, to which he . . . agreed *absque nomine* " (*Colden Papers*, IV, 264). This appeared in that year under the title of *The Importance of Gaining and Preserving the Friendship of the Indians to the British Interest Considered* and embodied the idea that commissioners from all the colonies would meet yearly at either New York or Albany to fix their quotas of the general expense and to provide for erecting forts and blockhouses as might be deemed necessary. To this was appended, as was made clear in an earlier footnote, Franklin's first plan of union. James Alexander, a descendant of the Earls of Sterling and heir to the title, a former Jacobite, was at this period a member of the Governor's Council of both New York and New Jersey and Surveyor General of the latter. He was one of the most distinguished lawyers in America during this period, and he and William Smith defended Zenger during the early stages of the famous libel suit; he was also a founder of the American Philosophical Society. His son was the Earl of Sterling of Revolutionary War fame.

liberties on the one hand, or [be] ineffectual on the other," Franklin had agreed "to set down some hints of a scheme that he thought might do." [38]

This plan, called "Short Hints toward a Scheme for Uniting the Northern Colonies," is of great interest to the student.[39] While it includes most of the features of his earlier plan of 1751, as was suggested, it discards one — a very essential feature — that of a voluntary union, which in 1751 he thought could be brought about if " half a Dozen men of good Understanding and Address " furnished " with a reasonable Scheme and proper Instructions " were sent as " Ambassadors to the other Colonies, where they might apply particularly to all the leading Men, and by proper Management get them to engage in promoting the Scheme. . . ." [40] Now he had come to favour the idea that after the project of union had been " first well considered corrected & improved by the Commissioners at Albany," it was " to be sent home, and an Act of Parliament obtain'd for establishing it " — thus ignoring the constitutional claims of the colonies by imposing the union upon them.

The " Short Hints " called for the appointment by the King of a " Governor General " who would be paid by the Crown and who would be empowered to negative all of the acts of the Grand Council. The members of the latter were to be chosen by the respective colonial assemblies, with each colony enjoying at least one representative and the larger colonies " in proportion to the Sums they pay Yearly into the General Treasury," raised by excises as well as by duties on liquors and tea and licences on public houses. The Governor General and the Grand Council were to take over Indian treaties, and land purchases not within proprietary grants, make new settlements, maintain soldiers, build forts, equip war vessels, " and every thing that shall be found necessary for the defence & support of the Colonies in General, & encreasing & extending their settlements, etc." The meetings of the Council under ordinary circumstances would be " at the capital of each Colony in Course."

Although Alexander upon receiving the " Short Hints " agreed that this scheme of union " seems extreamly well digested, & at first sight avoids many difficulties that had occur'd to me," he found it, nevertheless, defective in that no provision was made for a Council of

---

[38] *Colden Papers*, IV, 442.
[39] For this see *ibid.*, IV, 443–4; *Franklin's Writings* (ed. Sparks), III, 26–7.
[40] *Writings of Franklin* (ed. Smyth), III, 41.

State to be chosen by the Grand Council and to assist the Governor General in making specific plans under general grants of power by the Grand Council.[41] To Colden, to whom Alexander appealed for advice, the Franklin draft raised many serious questions. Among these was that of the desirability of attempting to achieve union by way of an act of Parliament rather than by agreement of the colonial assemblies; again, the likelihood that the Crown would oppose giving to the Grand Council executive power in conjunction with the Governor General in view of its elective character; further, that the Grand Council if elected for a short period would not pursue steady measures, and if elected for a long time and not removable by the Crown would become dangerous; again, that the attempt to fix certain times and plans for its meetings would be granting to it a privilege that neither the Parliament nor the Privy Council possessed — one that might be destructive to the Constitution of the Empire; and, finally, that it was not clear that the commissioners could speak the sense of their constituents. "What authority have they to do this? I know of none from either the Council or Assembly of New York." [42] Colden, in forwarding his queries to Franklin at Albany on June 20, wrote that he had made them with that freedom

> "which I believe you expect from me that in case you find any weight in any of them you may make your scheme more perfect by avoiding reasonable exceptions to it & have the pleasure of adding this to many other well received schemes which you have formed for the benefite of your country." [43]

His last query, relative to the competence of the commissioners to speak for their constituents, was certainly most apropos in view of the fact that only three of the delegations were selected by their respective colonial assemblies — those of Massachusetts Bay, Connecticut, and Rhode Island — and that only one had been specifically authorized to enter into articles of union with those from the other colonies, that of Massachusetts Bay as a result of the recommendations of her popular Governor, William Shirley.[44]

But Franklin's "Short Hints" was not the only plan submitted for consideration of the Congress. Apparently his colleague Richard Peters prepared "A Plan for a General Union of the British Colonies of

---

[41] *Colden Papers*, IV, 442.
[42] *Ibid.*, IV, 449–51.
[43] *Ibid.*, IV, 451.
[44] *Correspondence of William Shirley*, II, 59, 112.

North America "[45] which did less violence to the existing constitutional arrangements of the Empire than did Franklin's. This provided for " a Committe of Union " to be appointed by each colonial assembly to correspond with the other committees. The colonies, according to this, were to be grouped into four divisions: one for New England, another for New York and New Jersey; a third for Virginia, Maryland, and Pennsylvania; a fourth for Georgia, South Carolina, and North Carolina. Each division was to hold an annual meeting of the committees within it which would recommend to the governments represented proper measures to be taken as occasion arose; each colony was to raise a company of one hundred men to be supported by excises on rum, shoes, leather, etc., and the regiment of thirteen companies, to be known as " the Union regiment," was to be commanded by officers appointed by the Crown. This " little standing Army " was to resist the French encroachments, assist in making roads and building forts, and so on. There was to be a " Union Fund " to be raised by the issue of paper money and through participation in the Indian trade by the committees, and a " Fort Fund " to be devoted particularly to the building of eight forts to protect the frontiers. As to the adoption of this plan, it was to be submitted not to Parliament but to His Majesty and " such reasonable alterations to, or additions made, as he in council shall direct."

It also is clear that a third plan was formulated, perhaps at the Congress itself, by one of the Massachusetts Bay commissioners — apparently by Thomas Hutchinson [46] — a plan which, like the one

---

[45] A manuscript in the handwriting of Peters is in the Pennsylvania Archives at Harrisburg, No. 677. This was printed in Carson's *The Constitution of the United States*, II, 472–4.

[46] *Mass. Hist. Soc. Coll.*, VII, 202–7. We are confronted with a problem the solution of which presents difficulties. Hutchinson does not mention in his writings, so far as I have been able to ascertain, that he either brought or formulated a plan. In referring to his own activities at the Congress and to those of Franklin, he records at the end of the fifth volume of his Diary (*Diary and Letters of Thomas Hutchinson*, ed. P. O. Hutchinson, p. 35): " The same famous Dr. Franklin was one of the Commissioners from Pensilvania. He, with Mr. Hutchinson, were the Committee who drew up the plan of Union, and the representation of the state of the Colonies. The former was the projection of Dr. F., and prepared in part before he had any consultation with Mr. H., probably brought with him from Philadelphia; the latter [that is, the ' Representation of the Present State of the Colonies '] was the draught of Mr. H." In his *History of the Province of Massachusetts Bay from the Year 1750, until June, 1774* (p. 21), he also says: " The plan for a general union was projected by Benjamin Franklin, Esq., one of the commissioners from the province of Pennsylvania, the heads whereof he brought with him." By the above statements Hutchinson dissociates himself from the authorship of any project of union, although he does state that he and Franklin were the committee to draw up the

just considered, adhered much more closely to established constitutional arrangements than did Franklin's. This was designed to group the colonies into two unions, rather than one, a northern and a southern, which would be brought into existence by an act of Parliament. The northern union was to include all the colonies embraced within the old Dominion of New England as it was constituted in 1688 and

plan. This assertion is hardly accurate unless by it he implies that the general committee on a plain of union designated the two to act as a subcommittee to bring before them a matured draft — something that is quite likely to have happened under the circumstances. Yet we are confronted by the "Plan of a Proposed Union of the Several Colonies of Massachusetts-Bay, New-Hampshire, Connecticut, Rhode-Island, New-York, and New-Jersey" which was "recommended by commissioners from several colonies, met in Congress at Albany" (*Mass. Hist. Soc. Coll.*, VII, 203–7) — a plan that Franklin could not have presented to the Committee on the Union and would not have favoured for particular reasons.

The following quotation from the formal report of the Massachusetts Bay commissioners to the Assembly of the Province throws additional light upon the "Plan of a Proposed Union" ("Mass. Arch.," IV, 459–64): ". . . your commissioners were in some doubt, whether it might not be convenient that the colonies should be divided into at least two Districts, as the great distance of the two extream parts of his Majesty's Governments from each other, must render it always very burthensome to some or other of the Members to give their attendance, be the place of meeting where it will and in a Government of so large an extent there will be danger of some parts being neglected or unequally considered; but as the designs of the French may probably require the united strength & councils of the whole British Continent and as it seemed to be of the last importance that all affairs which relate to the Indians should be under but one direction, and considered without any special regard to any particular government we were induced to prefer the present plan."

This plan was, as is clear, discussed at Albany and apparently excited the particular hostility of de Lancey since it sought to combine the office of President General and that of the governorship of Massachusetts Bay (William Smith, *History of New-York*, in *New York Hist. Soc. Coll.*, V, 185, note). Much of it conforms to the phraseology of the final "Plan of Union" word for word, as will be made clear. In fact, circumstantial evidence points most strongly to Hutchinson as the author of it, especially as it, in common with the "Representation of the Present State of the Colonies," of which he was the acknowledged author, calls for the limiting of the western boundaries of some of the colonies. Hutchinson is silent on these points, as has been indicated — even the plan in his own handwriting that was later submitted to the Massachusetts General Court he ignores — perhaps preferring to place the full responsibility for the "Plan of Union" upon the shoulders of Franklin, who himself declared that, when he laid his "Short Hints" before the Congress, "It then appeared that several of the Commissioners had form'd plans of the same kind" (*The Writings of Benjamin Franklin*, ed. A. H. Smyth, I, 387). It well may be that Hutchinson, whatever may have been his part, was later very glad to let Franklin have the full credit of the authorship of a plan which was bitterly denounced in the colonies, especially in Connecticut, Rhode Island, and New Jersey and even in Boston town meetings — he had his own troubles. Nevertheless, his influence in the shaping of the famous "Plan" must have been very great, especially in eliminating certain basic features of the "Short Hints" in favour of others embodied in the plan for two unions rather than one.

thus comprehended all the colonies from New Hampshire to Pennsylvania, but not including the latter. As in the former Dominion government the seat of the government of the northern union, "for the time being," at least, was to be in Massachusetts Bay, whose Governor was also to be the President General. The similarity of the plans, however, ceases at this point. For the President General was to receive a salary not from the Crown but from the Grand Council of the Union and was to enjoy very limited powers in legislation, having simply "a casting voice, whenever an equi-vote shall happen in the Grand Council" — a mere echo of the authority enjoyed by Sir Edmund Andros. He and the Grand Council were to control all Indian relations involving the colonies within the union and were to be responsible for the safety and interests of the colonies embraced within it "against all their common enemies." In harmony with the principles underlying the New England Confederation of 1643, the Grand Council was to raise men and funds only by making requisitions upon the assemblies within the union, the colonies themselves choosing those measures to meet the requisition "in such manner and form, as to them appears equal and right." Moreover, the popular chamber in each assembly was to choose the representatives to the Grand Council for a term of three years. Out of a total of twenty-three representatives for the northern union, Massachusetts Bay was to enjoy seven, Connecticut and New York four each, New Hampshire and New Jersey three each, and Rhode Island two. While the President General, under this scheme, was to command the forces of the union, the Grand Council was to nominate all general officers and the colonial assemblies the other commissioned officers. Finally, it was laid down: "That the particular military, as well as civil, establishments and constitutions of each colony, remain firm and entire without any other change or alteration than is herein before mentioned, this general union notwithstanding."

A fourth plan was submitted late in the deliberation of the commissioners by Thomas Pownall, who was not a delegate to the Congress but was in Albany and closely associated with Franklin and the other members of the Pennsylvania delegation, especially in the Indian conferences. This was not concerned so much with constitutional arrangements as with measures that should be taken by the colonies in concert to defeat the designs of the French. It could be done with the least exertion and greatest hope of success, argued Pownall, by the building of forts and fleets to dominate the disputed waters of the adjoining lakes. "New Hampshire, Massachusetts and Rhode Island might be alloted to . . . Lake Champlain — Connecticut, New York and New Jersey to Lake Ontario — Pennsylvania, Maryland[,] Virginia and perhaps the Carolinas too to Lakes Erie, Illinois ettc." To him the possession of naval superiority on these lakes would be much more decisive in retaining control of the Indians than the attempt to repel the French by land operations and would also cut Louisiana off from Canada.[47]

As the Albany Congress was busy during the first days preparing an address to the representatives of the Six Nations, to which reference has been made, it was not until the afternoon of June 28 that the special committee on plans of union was able to secure a hearing. It, however, had come to the decision to make Franklin's " Short Hints " — probably by this time expanded in committee — the basis for the proposed union, and so reported at this session. As a result, copies of it were taken by the commissioners for study, after which the meeting adjourned.[48] On the following day and the day after, the plan was debated; and on July 2 the question was put, " whether the Board should proceed to form a plan of Union of the Colonies by Act of Parliam^t," and passed in the affirmative.[49]

The significance of this decision of the Albany Congress seems to have escaped most students of the constitutional history of the old

---

[47] N. Y. Col. Doc., VI. The author of A Review of Military Operations in North America (Mass. Hist. Soc. Coll., first series, VII, 87), who is supposed to be William Livingston, taunts Pownall with " shining in a borrowed dress." He writes: " The scheme of a naval armament on Lake Ontario, projected by Lieut. Governor Clarke, before the late war, submitted to the ministry, and now strongly recommended by the Commissioners of the Massachusetts-Bay, by some means or other happened to be hinted without doors. Mr. Pownall, intent upon rising into significance among the colonies, chose not to slip so favourable an opportunity of distinguishing himself, as he could now lay hold of, from these whispered intelligences. He accordingly drew up some loose, indigested proposals with respect to American affairs." In 1760, three years after the publication of the pamphlet, those who had been the Massachusetts Bay commissioners signed a statement that the Pownall proposals were presented to the Congress by de Lancey and that these were considered to be of sufficient importance to justify a vote of thanks and that no one at the Congress nor since it considered that these were borrowed. (Savage Papers, II, 137, Mass. Hist. Soc.)

Colonel William Johnson also offered certain suggestions " for defeating the designs of the French." These did not go beyond the building of a more powerful fort at Oswego and the construction of another at Onondaga and making these general marts. He also would place young men of learning among the Onondaga, Seneca, and Mohawks to become interpreters and perhaps " schoolmasters or Catechists " to the Indians (N. Y. Col. Doc., VI, 897-9).

[48] Ibid., VI, 863.

[49] Ibid., VI, 868.

British Empire. Granting that the commissioners had no power to bind the colonies, outside, possibly, Massachusetts Bay, and also that the project for the union failed to be approved when later submitted to the colonial assemblies, the vote, nevertheless, represents the consensus of opinion of the most representative and, all in all, the most capable and politically experienced body of colonials from a majority of the thirteen colonies that ever met in conference prior to the Stamp Act Congress. It is evident that most of them believed not only that Parliament possessed the authority to alter the basic constitutional arrangements within the Empire — something that was later sweepingly denied here in America — but that it was natural and proper that Parliament should do so when circumstances so required.

On July 4 and 5 the plan of union was again debated; the Indian negotiations thereupon demanded the chief attention of the commissioners until on the 9th the committee on plans submitted its " Representation on the Present State of the Colonies." This, drawn up by Thomas Hutchinson, was " considered paragraph by paragraph, some amendments made, and the whole was agreed to. . . ." [50] The " Representation " laid down the claim that the coast " from Georgia on the South to the River St. Lawrence on the North except the Island of Cape Breton and Islands in the Bay of St. Lawrence, remains plain and indisputable " English territory, as was all land between the Atlantic Ocean and the South Sea between 34° and 48° north latitude.[51] It included a specific denial of the right of the French to any part of the disputed region to the west and north of the Nova Scotia peninsula and claimed Lakes Champlain, Ontario, and Erie, " and all the Countries adjacent," as territory belonging to the Six Nations. The encroachments of the French upon this territory were denounced and these were pointed out in detail. It also made clear that the British colonies " in a divided disunited state " had never made any joint exertion to defeat the measures of the French and that " particular Colonies are unable and unwilling to maintain the cause of the whole." After referring to the neglect of the affairs of the Iroquoian confederation and the appropriation of the Indian lands " by private persons for trifling consideration," certain broad recommendations were thereupon presented, which were as follows:

---

[50] Mass. Hist. Soc. Coll. (third series), V, 64; Diaries and Letters of Thomas Hutchinson, p. 55; New York Mercury, July 29, 1754.

[51] The sea-to-sea claims of North Carolina, South Carolina, and Georgia were ignored.

That the French encroachments be removed; that the Indians in alliance be placed under some wise superintendency; that forts be built within each of the nations; that warlike vessels be provided to patrol the Lakes; that the sale of Indian lands be properly regulated; that " the bounds of these Colonies which extend to the South sea, be contracted and limited by the Alleghenny or Apalachian mountains,[52] and that measures be taken for settling from time to time Colonies of His Maj[tys] protestant subjects, westward of said Mountains in convenient Cantons to be assigned for that purpose; and, finally, that there be a Union of His Maj[tys] several Governt[s] on the Continent, that so their Councils, Treasure and strength may be employed in due proportion ag[st] their common enemy." [53]

The " Representation " — one of the most strongly imperialistic documents of the eighteenth century — which could only have been addressed, on account of the nature of its contents, to His Majesty in Council, was forwarded by de Lancey to the Board of Trade, together with the other papers relating to the Congress. One can see in it certain basic features that underlay not only the subsequent establishment of the Indian superintendencies [54] and the Proclamation Line of 1763 — which latter bore especially heavily on Virginia — but also the idea of the creation of trans-Appalachian colonies, and even commonwealths as embodied in the famous Northwest Ordinance of 1787. This document should, therefore, not be ignored in any analysis of the evolution of British colonial policy.

On July 10 the entire day was spent considering the final draft of the " Plan of Union." This as now matured was a fusion of ideas embodied in Franklin's " Short Hints," apparently after it had assumed literary form, and the " Plan of a Proposed Union," formulated, it would seem, by Hutchinson.[55] It proposed a union of all the conti-

---

[52] It can be appreciated how little this would arouse the enthusiasm of the Virginians with their great plans for trans-Appalachian expansion. Yet the idea became embodied in the Proclamation of 1763, at least with respect to immediate settlement.

[53] *Mass. Hist. Soc. Coll.,* V, 63–9; *N. Y. Col. Doc.,* VI, 885–9.

[54] See John R. Alden, " The Albany Congress and the Creation of the Indian Superintendencies," *Miss. Valley Hist. Rev.,* XXVII, 193–210.

[55] Jared Sparks, the editor of *Franklin's Writings,* in comparing the " Plan of Union " with the " Plan of a Proposed Union," which he seems to have accepted as the work of Franklin, says that the latter " is a rough draft of the above Plan, with certain unimportant variations " (*ibid.,* III, 36, note). The " variations," as will be noted, were most important. Frothingham (*Rise of the Republic,* pp. 140–1), in referring to the work of the committee on a plan of union, says that " two political schools were about equally represented in the committee. . . . In Hutchinson it was the vision of a clear

nental colonies with the exception of the buffer colonies of Nova Scotia and Georgia, and the Lower Counties on the Delaware.[56] This union was to be attained in the following manner:

> "That humble application be made for an Act of Parliament of Great Britain, by virtue of which, one General Govern^t may be formed in America, including all the said Colonies, within, and under which Govern^t each Colony may retain its present constitution, except in the particulars wherein a change may be directed by the said Act, as hereafter follows." [57]

Franklin later explains the reasons for the decision to proceed by act of Parliament:

> "Where it was considered, that the colonies were seldom all in equal danger at the same time, or equally near the danger, or equally sensible of it; that some of them had particular interests to manage, with which a union might interfere; and that they were extremely jealous of each other; it was thought impracticable to obtain a joint agreement of all the colonies to a union, in which the expense and burthen of defending any of them should be divided among them all; and if ever Acts of Assembly in all the colonies could be obtained for that purpose, yet as any colony, on the least dissatisfaction, might repeal its own act, and thereby withdraw itself from the union, it would not be a stable one, or such as could be depended on. . . . Therefore the commissioners came to another previous resolution,

---

intellect distrusting the capacity and intelligence of the people. In Franklin it was the insight of a philosopher . . . determined to labor for the liberties of his Country." This is sheer nonsense with reference to the positions assumed by these men in 1754. As will be noted, Franklin's " Short Hints " showed much more distrust of the people of the colonies than did the " Plan of a Proposed Union." No one at Albany was prepared to go farther than Franklin in imposing the work of the Congress on the American people by act of Parliament. Certainly Hutchinson's later plan, to be discussed in the following chapter, showed much more faith in the colonial governments and the colonials to act for the common good than did Franklin's " Short Hints."

[56] As for these omissions, Nova Scotia was already protected by a considerable concentration of British regular troops and by fortified places erected at the expense of the Crown; Georgia had also been the object, ever since its establishment, of special solicitude on the part of the Crown and Parliament, and it may have been felt also that the colony would eventually be absorbed by South Carolina; the Lower Counties were doubtless regarded as a mere appanage of the Province of Pennsylvania.

[57] This clause follows very closely the language of the " Plan of a Proposed Union." For the " Plan of Union " see N. Y. Col. Doc., VI, 889-91 and the Mass. Hist. Soc. Coll. (third series), V, 70-4; Franklin's Writings (ed. Jared Sparks), III, 36-55. The last-named reference is especially valuable as it presents the " Reasons and Motives " for each of the articles.

That it was necessary the Union should be established by act of Parliament." [58]

A careful analysis of this remarkable statement seems to indicate that Franklin, if not all the other commissioners, had come to feel that an American union by agreement of the colonies themselves was simply beyond the range of practical statesmanship at this period. To begin with, he reasoned that it could not be brought about since some colonies "had particular interests to manage, with which a union might interfere" — for example, Virginia and Connecticut; further, if this difficulty would be surmounted, a voluntary union "would not be a stable one, or such as could be depended on" — colonies, if dissatisfied, would withdraw; therefore, only a union imposed by Parliament could meet the demands of the crisis that now confronted the British colonials in North America. His own experience with the Quaker Assembly of Pennsylvania and his knowledge of the lack of co-operation of other colonies in defence measures during the recent war must have led him to feel the folly of trying to work out a plan of voluntary intercolonial integration.

Under the "Plan of Union" provision was made for a President General to be appointed and supported by the Crown,[59] and a Grand Council, the members of which were to be chosen by the respective houses of representatives [60] upon the basis of the following allotment for the first three years: Massachusetts and Virginia seven representatives each, Pennsylvania six, Connecticut five, New York, Maryland, North Carolina, and South Carolina four each, the New Jerseys three, and New Hampshire and Rhode Island two each.[61]

---

[58] *The Works of Benjamin Franklin* (ed. John Bigelow), II, 352. Frothingham (*Rise of the Republic*, p. 150) in stating that Franklin's original draft did not contemplate the change in the local constitutions by act of Parliament was in error.

[59] Franklin in his "Short Hints" gives him the title of Governor General; the "Plan of a Proposed Union" gives him the above title but provides that he shall be paid by the Grand Council, another indication of the liberal point of view of the author of this project.

[60] The question as to the election of members of the Grand Council by the House of Representatives in each colony led to a heated debate. The New York delegation — representing the Council and not the lower house — made an effort to give the Governor and Council a share in this. This was opposed since seven out of eleven of the governors and their councils were appointed by the Crown, "And so the people in all the colonies would in effect be taxed by their governors" (*Writings of Franklin*, ed. Smyth, III, 209).

[61] The "Plan of Union" is closely in accord with the "Plan of a Proposed Union"; the latter, however, allotted to New Hampshire three members and to Connecticut four; the latter also was interested primarily in a northern union and so does not mention the more southern colonies.

These representatives were to be elected for a three-year period and paid for their services.[62] A ratio between the number of representatives and the amount of contributions to the general treasury was ultimately to be maintained,[63] with the provision that each colony should have at least two members on the Grand Council,[64] which should " neither be dissolved, prorogued, nor continue sitting longer than six weeks at one time without their consent, or the special command of the Crown." [65] It was to meet " once in every year, and oftener, if occasion require, at such time and place as they shall adjourn to, at their last preceding meeting; or as they shall be called to meet at by the President General, on any emergency, he having first obtained in writing the consent of Seven Members to such call, and sent due and timely notice to the whole." [66] The place of meeting was to be " for the present time at the City of Philadelphia." [67] A quorum to do business was placed at twenty-five, " with one or more from a majority of the colonies." [68]

As to other features of the " Plan of Union," the President General, with the advice of the Grand Council, was to hold or direct all Indian treaties in which the general interest or welfare of the colonies was concerned; he was also to make peace or declare war with the Indian nations, as well as provide laws for regulating the Indian

[62] Here again the " Plan of a Proposed Union " is in harmony with the above, employing the identical language.

[63] The " Plan of a Proposed Union " states that the colonies were " to pay their proportion of money, according to the proportion herein before settled for members to be chosen for the Grand Council from each colony "; the " Short Hints " stipulates that representation shall be " in proportion to the Sums they pay yearly into the General Treasury." Hutchinson's later plan follows the idea expressed in the " Plan of a Proposed Union."

[64] The minimum representation accorded to each colony in the Grand Council by the " Plan of a Proposed Union " was two; the " Short Hints " provides for at least one.

[65] This is also the language of the " Plan of a Proposed Union."

[66] This again is similar to the language of the " Plan of a Proposed Union " with some modifications. The latter states: " That the Grand Council shall meet once in every year, and oftener, if occasion require, at such time and place as they shall adjourn to, at their last preceding meeting; or as they shall be called to meet at, by the President-General, on any emergency, he having first obtained, in writing, the consent of five of the members to such call; or, on application made to the President-General by ten of the Grand Council, in writing under their hands, to have a meeting called, he shall send due and timely notice to the whole."

[67] Here the " Plan of Union " differs from the " Plan of a Proposed Union," which provides that the Grand Council " shall meet, for the first time, at the town of Boston, in New-England."

[68] In the " Plan of a Proposed Union " the quorum was to be twelve members, " with one or more from a majority of the colonies."

trade, and to " make all purchases for the Crown, of lands not now within the bounds of particular Colonies, or that shall not be within their bounds when some of them are reduced to more convenient dimensions." [69] Further, the union government, as thus constituted, was to make settlements on such purchases, granting the lands in the King's name and reserving a quit-rent for the use of the general treasury; [70] these settlements were to be governed and regulated by laws provided by it " till the Crown shall think fit to form them into particular Govern[ts]." [71]

To defend the colonies, the President General and the Grand Council were to be further empowered to raise and support soldiers and to build forts and equip war vessels. For these purposes they were to lay and levy such duties, imports, or taxes as to them should appear equal and just,[72] with the provision not only that the assent of the President General to all acts of the Grand Council was necessary [73] but also, it should be noted, that these acts were to be sent home for the approval of the Privy Council, which was to disallow the same within a period of three years.[74]

---

[69] This is also the language of the " Plan of a Proposed Union," except that the latter in the last clause reads: " or that shall not be within their bounds, when the extension of some of them are rendered more certain." The " Short Hints " also provides for these powers, but not in the same language, although nothing is said in it about reducing the western claims of the colonies. Hutchinson, who drafted the " Representation on the Present State of the Colonies," recommended the Appalachian Mountains as the western boundary for the colonies then in existence with claims westward. Franklin took over the idea in the " Plan of Union " with an important modification. The expression that he uses: " when some of the colonies shall be reduced to more convenient dimensions," was not later clear to Hutchinson, who remarks (History of Massachusetts Bay, p. 22, note): " I am not now able to ascertain the colonies to which Mr. Franklin had a special reference. Probably Connecticut was one, and perhaps Virginia another. This reduction could be made only by authority of parliament." It is clear that Franklin did not propose to limit Pennsylvania to the region east of the Appalachians, as he was busy negotiating with the Indians and, with the other Pennsylvania commissioners, refused to consider their offer to release their lands up to these mountains, insisting on a release of lands up to the boundary fixed by the patent of 1681.

[70] This provision is almost identical with a corresponding provision in the " Plan of a Proposed Union."

[71] This again is to be found in the " Plan of a Proposed Union." Here one has the basic idea first put forth by an American assembly that organized territories were destined to become commonwealths.

[72] Here the " Short Hints " are followed. The " Plan of a Proposed Union " provides that requisitions of men and money were to be made upon the colonial governments.

[73] The " Short Hints " declares that he was to have " a negation on all Acts of the Grand Council, and carry in execution whatever is agreed on by him and that Council "; the " Plan of a Proposed Union " gives him simply a " casting voice " in case of a tie.

[74] Nothing corresponding to this is to be found in either the " Short Hints " or

Finally, a general treasurer and a particular treasurer for each government should be appointed by joint action of the President General and the Grand Council, who together might order sums in particular treasuries to be placed in the general treasury; the money in which was to be issued only by joint orders of the two. All accounts were to be settled yearly and reported to the general assemblies of the colonies.[75]

The plan as outlined above — whatever may have been its defects and whoever in actuality may have been its chief architect — is a glowing tribute to the capacity of the commissioners who assembled at Albany to rise, at least temporarily, above local and selfish interests, to think in terms of the general welfare of the British colonies.[76] For in many respects it goes beyond the provincialism of the Articles of Confederation of 1781 and, if it could have been carried into execution, would have doubtless served as an effective agency for grappling successfully with many of the most serious problems that soon faced the colonies in their relations both with the French and the Indians in the course of the Seven Years' War and with the mother country at its termination.[77] One brief description has survived of the deliberations of the Congress, doubtless furnished by Attorney General Smith of New York:

---

the "Plan of a Proposed Union." Franklin defends this feature of the Plan in the following language: "This was thought necessary for the satisfaction of the Crown, to preserve the connection of the parts of the British empire with the whole, of the members with the head, and to induce greater care and circumspection in making of the laws, that they be good in themselves and for the general benefit" (Writings of Franklin, III, 224). Franklin's defence of the practice of submitting colonial legislation to the approval of the Crown may be contrasted with the fiery denunciations of this by Patrick Henry in the Parson's Cause at a later period.

[75] These provisions are also to be found in the same language in the "Plan of a Proposed Union."

[76] The difference between Franklin's "Short Hints" and the "Plan of Union," according to one writer who calls it "an essential difference," is that Franklin's original and decided preference was for an executive officer who would possess actual executive powers. The Congress in several instances curtailed and hedged in this power (W. H. Foster, Stephen Hopkins [Rhode Island Historical Tracts, No. 19], pp. 181-2). If this were true, Franklin was much more active in supporting the prerogatives of the King, who would appoint the "governor general" provided for in the "Short Hints," than met the approval of the majority of the commissioners.

[77] As Franklin put it in his Autobiography: "I am still of the opinion it would have been happy for both sides the water if it had been adopted. The colonies, so united, would have been sufficiently strong to have defended themselves; there would then have been no need of troops from England; of course, the subsequent pretence for taxing America, and the bloody contest it occasioned, would have been avoided" (Writings of Franklin, ed. Smyth, I, 388-9).

"The speakers . . . were not many; but of those who spoke, some delivered themselves with singular energy and eloquence. All were inflamed with a patriot spirit, and the debates were nervous and pathetic. This assembly . . . might very properly be compared to one of the ancient Greek conventions, for supporting their expiring liberty against the power of the Persian empire, or that *Lewis* [78] of Greece, Philip of Macedon." [79]

After the acceptance of the plan for transmission to their respective assemblies,[80] Franklin in self-defence doubtless felt it wise, with the prospect of facing the Pennsylvania Assembly, to append to each

[78] Indirect reference is here made to Louis XV of France.

[79] *Review of Military Operations in North-America* (Mass. Hist. Soc. Coll., Vol. VII), p. 77.

[80] As to the acceptance of the "Plan of Union" by the commissioners, Hutchinson in later years declared: "Some of the delegates had very full powers, while others were limited, and held to make report to their constituents. This plan, therefore, though unanimously voted, was to be of no force until confirmed by the several Assemblies" (*History of Massachusetts Bay*, pp. 22-3) — something that Franklin, as has already been noted, thought was impossible to realize in connection with any conceivable project of union. William Smith, who represented New York on the committee to bring in a plan, wrote that "except Mr. Delancey," toward whom Smith was bitter, "every member consented to this plan and . . . he [de Lancey] made no great opposition. Besides, he had objections not to be started [stated?] before auditors of too much sagacity not to discern the motives which excited them. . . . But a single member could be influenced . . . Mr. Murray," another New York commissioner, "a man of pride without ambition, or a single talent for intrigue — cold, distant, formal, and disgusting." He also recorded: "The Eastern colonies were most ardent for the union, excepting Connecticut, who was too jealous of the power of the President," and further that de Lancey hinted "that Massachusetts acted with an aim to procure the President's chair for their Governor, and predicted, as he well might, that it would not be much encouraged by New-York" (see his *The History of the Late Province of New-York*, II, 183-5, N. Y. Hist. Soc. Coll., 1830, Vol. V). In "The Reasons Considered and Offered, by the Assembly of the Colony of Connecticut, Concerning the Plan of Union," approved October 2, 1754, it is stated that the Connecticut commissioners "objected to the proposed plan . . . and therefore never came into or gave any consent to the same" (*Mass. Hist. Soc. Coll.*, first series, VII, 213). But, one can question, as has been asserted, "that there was a very vigorous opposition, particularly on the part of the Connecticut delegates," during the sessions of the Congress (William E. Foster, *Stephen Hopkins* [Rhode Island Hist. Tracts, No. 19], p. 182, note). A *Review of Military Operations in North America*, written in 1756 apparently by William Livingston, asserted that the "Plan of Union" was "approved at the time by every member of the Congress except Mr. De Lancey" (*Mass. Hist. Soc. Coll.*, VII, 77); Franklin, in later years, affirmed that "after many Days' thorough Discussion of all its Parts in Congress it was unanimously agreed to" (*Writings of Franklin*, III, 227); while de Lancey, writing to the Board of Trade on July 22, in referring to his proposal to the commissioners that they agree to build certain forts, says: "but the Commissioners would hear of nothing but the plan they have drawn up" — indicating with the above statements a good deal of enthusiasm at the time for the project (*N. Y. Col. Doc.*, VI, 852).

article the reasons that led to its inclusion, as well as other observations, all of which were framed with great skill.[81] For example, to disarm opposition, he made it clear that the union was for very limited
but essential purposes. In other words, the power granted to the President General and the Grand Council to make laws and to levy duties
and taxes was restricted to making provision for the establishment
and government of new settlements, to providing for the defence of
the colonies, and, above all, to regulating Indian affairs.

While the impression is left that Philadelphia, by reason of its convenient location, was to be the meeting place under ordinary circumstances of the Grand Council, yet provision was made for its gathering in any colony which might be particularly in need of assistance.
Nothing was said as to the seat of residence of the President General
and, under the articles of union, it would not have been impossible
for him at the same time to have exercised the duties of governor of
a royal province if it had seemed wise so to commission him — for example, to combine the office of Governor of the Province of Virginia
or of New York and that of President General of the British Colonies
in North America. Nevertheless, serious objections to this procedure
would doubtless have arisen had the plan been adopted.

It will be noted that no mention was made in the resolutions
adopted relative to the transmission of " the Plan of Union " to Parliament or to the ministers. In the " Reasons and Motives on which the
Plan of Union was Formed," prepared in 1754 after the Congress and
referred to above, Franklin states:

> " This [the ' Plan of Union '] was respectfully sent to the Assemblies
> of the several colonies for their consideration, and to receiving such
> alterations and improvements as they should think fit and necessary;
> after which it was proposed to be transmitted to England to be per-
> fected, and the establishment of it there humbly solicited. This was
> as much as the commissioners could do." [82]

---

[81] " My plan, with my reasons in support of it, is to be found among my personal
papers that are printed," wrote Franklin in his Autobiography (Writings of Franklin,
ed. Symth, I, 388). Franklin's continued faith in the soundness of this project seems
to be proved by a statement printed on April 9, 1789, in connection with the plan. " On
Reflection, it now seems probable, that, if the foregoing Plan, or something like it,
had been adopted and carried into Execution, the subsequent Separation of the Colonies
from the Mother Country might not so soon have happened, nor the Mischiefs suffered
on both sides have occurred, perhaps, during another Century " (ibid., IV, 226–7).

[82] Works of Franklin (ed. John Bigelow), II, 352–3. Yet Franklin's " Short Hints "
indicate that upon arriving in New York he favoured a direct appeal from the commissioners to Parliament. Stephen Hopkins, one of the Rhode Island commissioners,

The Plan, however, was forwarded directly to the Board of Trade by de Lancey, together with other papers relating to the Congress, as is made clear in his letter of July 22, 1754.[83] Whether this step was in some informal manner authorized by the commissioners or was anticipated by them is by no means clear.[84] It is quite evident, however, that the Lieutenant Governor of New York was under obligation to report fully the proceedings of the Congress, especially as it had been called at the request of the Lords Commissioners. Doubtless to such ardent advocates of a union as Franklin there was the hope that it might be favourably received at home and be enacted into law by Parliament without waiting for the dilatory reactions of the various colonial assemblies. The latter — under the theory that guided Franklin at this juncture — did not necessarily have to be consulted before Parliament acted and, furthermore, could not be depended upon to make the necessary sacrifice to establish a union.

It is not without significance that at least one writer who at this time submitted the Plan to careful but critical analysis, in observing the phrase: " That humble application be made for an Act of Parliament," arrived at the above conclusion:

"Now, How was this Application to be made? It is not said, that humble Application be made by the several Governments, if they acceded to said Plan; nor was the President of said Congress at Albany, ordered (by any Thing that appears) to wait any fix'd Time,

smarting under attacks for his part in the Congress, declared in A True Representation of the Plan Formed in Albany (1755; Rhode Island Hist. Tracts, No. 9), with respect to the Plan, that the Commissioners " did not, as is falsely asserted, order it to be sent home." He also went on to state: " They did not establish it as an Act or Ordinance of the Board of Commissioners, as they might have done, by the Authorities given them " — an assertion that led an opponent, one " Philolethes " in his A Short Reply to Mr. Hopkins's Vindication (1755; ibid., No. 9), to reply that this was false, pointing as proof to the limited powers of the Maryland commissioners.

[83] N. Y. Col. Doc., VI, 851. In communicating the plan de Lancey shows no sign of opposition to it, although William Smith later stressed the fact of his opposition in the Albany Congress.

[84] Governor Sharpe of Maryland was seemingly greatly surprised to learn that de Lancey had sent the " Plan of Union " home before the colonies had had an opportunity to express themselves upon it. Writing to Lord Baltimore on August 8, 1754, he enclosed a copy of it, " which Scheme is to be laid before the Legislature of the several Provinces at their next meeting for their Amendment or Approbation; but it has been intimated to me that the Govᴿ of New York has already without tarrying for the Opinion of Assemblies transmitted a copy thereof to the Board of Trade for their Honours' Consideration " (Archives of Maryland, VI, 79). It will be noted in this connection that the Maryland commissioners were not permitted by their instructions to enter into any plans but were simply to observe and report.

to receive the Assent or Dissent of the several Governments; nor have the Governments been informed by that Congress that they ever designed to wait their Consent to said Plan; And how improbable is it, that they ever designed to wait for the Governments Resolve, when neither Time, Place, nor Person was pointed out to receive the Governments Answer; notwithstanding, the Plan is at Home, and by our [that is, the Rhode Island] Agent's Letter, before the Parliament for Confirmation." [85]

According to the report made to Shirley by the Massachusetts Bay commissioners, those attending the Congress were " very near unanimous " on three points: First, that a general union of the " Forces and Councils " of the colonies was necessary at this juncture to save them from the French encroachments; second, that an effectual scheme for such a union could only be placed into execution by Parliament; third, that the proportion of the general expense that each colony should bear should be estimated by the number of members allotted to each on the Grand Council.[86] A fourth point, not here mentioned, upon which the commissioners would have been as unanimous was that taxation of colonials for their common welfare should be by measures adopted, not by Parliament — except through its approval of the " Plan of Union " — but by the Grand Council. Thus this hope of a union such as they had agreed upon seemed to rest entirely upon the action of home government.

---

[85] A Short Reply to Mr. Hopkins's Vindication by Philolethes (Rhode Island Hist. Tracts, No. 9, pp. 53–4).

[86] N. Y. Col. Doc., VI, 931. According to advices sent from Boston on July 22 and printed in the New York Mercury of July 29, 1754, "the Commissioners from the several Governments were unanimously of Opinion, That a Union of Colonies was absolutely necessary in order to defeat the Schemes of the French."

CHAPTER V

The Fate of the Plan of Union

I N THE PRECEDING chapter the chief events relating to the Albany Congress have been considered. The commissioners sent from the colonies there represented, having completed their work, thereupon returned home to give an accounting. In this connection it is important to re-emphasize the fact that, outside of the Massachusetts Bay delegation, adequately endowed with discretion to act in all ways needful to meet the exigencies of the situation, they had come to this important meeting quite unprepared through any express delegation of authority to do the one thing that seemed of paramount importance once the Congress had seriously settled down to business.[1] To aid in re-establishing friendly relations between the Six Nations and the English was clearly within the scope of their commissions but, in so far as they had given their endeavours to the formulation of a plan for the setting up of a colonial confederacy endowed with powers of government that would affect those exercised by the respective colonial governments, they had clearly acted *ultra vires.* This may be one reason why evidence is lacking that they as a group upon their return took little more than a passive attitude toward their achievement in the field of statesmanship, of vast potential importance as it was to all colonials. Doubtless many of them were quite taken aback when they were again made aware of some-

---

[1] In the words of the Massachusetts Bay commissioners in their report to the Assembly: " The Commissions from the other Governments were also produced but the powers from divers of them appeared to be very insufficient for the purpose which your Commissioners conceived to be mainly intended by their meeting " (" Massachusetts Archives," IV, 459–64).

thing that in those days of constructive enthusiasm at Albany they had perhaps momentarily lost sight of — the intense particularism of most British colonials. But they did not have long to wait to witness the rise of so resolute an opposition to their united, if not unanimous, recommendations that doubtless most of them, whatever may have been their personal feelings and ambitions, were driven either into silence or to an open repudiation of the Plan of Union.

Since the Pennsylvania delegation was responsible for offering the plan which became the basis for that finally evolved and recommended to the consideration of all the continental colonies outside of Nova Scotia and Georgia, it would be well to consider first of all the fate of the Plan of Union at the hands of the Pennsylvania Assembly. Governor James Hamilton lost no time in recommending it to the sympathetic consideration of that body. On August 7 in addressing the two chambers he referred to the Representation of the Present State of the Colonies drawn up at Albany as well as the Plan of Union:

> " And as both those Papers appear to me to contain Matters of the utmost Consequence to the Welfare of the Colonies in general, and to have been digested and drawn up with great Clearness and Strength of Judgment, I cannot but express my Approbation of them, and do, therefore, recommend them to you as well worthy of your closest and most serious Attention." [2]

But Hamilton was about to bring to a close his administration. To his successor, Robert Hunter Morris, Governor Shirley of Massachusetts Bay, in spite of objections to certain features of the Plan, which he felt would be corrected by Parliament, wrote on October 21 urging him to support it:

> " The best advice I can give you, is to lose no time for promoting the Plan of an Union of the Colonies for their mutual defence to be concerted at home, and establish'd by Act of Parliamᵗ, as soon as it is possible. . . . I am labouring this point, *totis viribus*. It would ease you of a great part of the burthen, your Governmt. may probably bring upon you otherwise, in the Management of Military and Indian Affairs." [3]

But the government of Pennsylvania was in no mood to look kindly on the Plan. For reasons that are not clear, Governor Morris did not

---

[2] *Pennsylvania Colonial Records*, VI, 135.
[3] *Correspondence of William Shirley*, II, 96.

follow the advice of Shirley. There is no evidence that he made a single gesture in support of it. What may have been the attitude of the Penns toward it has not come to light in the correspondence between the Proprietors and the Governor although both John, the son of Richard, and Richard Peters, the proprietarial secretary, were members of the Pennsylvania delegation at Albany and presumably looked favourably upon the accomplishments of the Congress. It seems that Isaac Norris, the Speaker of the Assembly and a man of great influence in all governmental affairs, who was also at Albany, was either indifferent toward the Plan or quietly hostile to it. In fact, Benjamin Franklin appears to have been its only outspoken advocate. However, and in spite of the fact that he was a member of the lower house, he was — doubtless with the connivance of Speaker Norris — treated most shabbily by that body. As he himself records:

> " The House . . . by the Management of a certain member, took it [the Plan] up when I happen'd to be absent, which I thought not very fair, and reprobated it without paying any attention to it at all, to my no small mortification." [4]

The Pennsylvania House of Representatives, it should be made clear in this connection, was dominated by the Quakers, who had no sympathy whatsoever with any of those preparations for military defence of the colonies implied in the Plan.

As for Virginia, in light of the fact that the position assumed by the Albany Congress relative to the trans-Appalachian claims of the colonies was in fundamental opposition to the whole program of the extension of the political authority of the Province into the valley of the Ohio, it is quite easy to understand why Governor Robert Dinwiddie took no steps to urge a favourable consideration of the Plan of Union upon the Council or the Assembly. Indeed, some features of it apparently took him by surprise when he had had an oppor-

---

[4] Writings of Franklin (ed. Smyth), I, 389. The record of the Assembly respecting the plan is very brief; it reads as follows: " The part of the Governor's Speech, relating to the Plan of Union among the several British Colonies on this Continent was read; and, after a considerable debate whether the said Plan should be either recommended or referred to the Consideration of the succeeding Assembly, the Question was put, upon Motion made, that the said Plan of Union be referred to the Consideration of the next succeeding Assembly? Past in the Negative." This vote was apparently carried on August 15, 1754 (Votes of the Assembly, Pa. Arch., eighth series, V, 2732-3). It well may be that Franklin received the implied rebuke by reason of his willingness to ignore the colonial assemblies in consummating a union of the American colonies. This fact must have been known in Philadelphia.

tunity to examine it after it had been forwarded to him by Peter Wraxall, secretary for the Congress. Writing to Governor Hamilton of Pennsylvania on July 31, he observes:

> "As it's an extraordinary Piece, and some new positions in it not before ventur'd on, I do not care to give any opinion on it till I hear how it is rec'd at Home." [5]

But in a later letter addressed to the Earl of Halifax he made clear that the Plan was "by no means agreeable to our People." [6] While it seems to have been all but ignored by the governments of both Maryland [7] and South Carolina, the irrepressible Governor of North Carolina, Arthur Dobbs, presented it to the Assembly on December 12, which gave him the occasion to sing the praises of the mother country for its benevolent attitude toward the colonies. He declared that while the people of Great Britain were

> "loaded with Debts and enormous, tho' necessary Taxes, [the government] hath not only protected these colonies but indulged them in . . . the easiest taxes (spent for their own Support), of any civilized Nation on the Globe . . . whilst Britain is struling under these Difficulties, altho' the Parliament hath a Power of taxing the Colonies for their own Support . . . yet His Majesty, in Regard to his faithful Colonies, is only desirous that they should unite and form a society amongst themselves, to raise a proper and adequate Quota or Fund for their mutual Support and Defence, that the United Force of the Colonies may act together and leave it to the Colonies to consider of the most equitable and proper Method of raising the Taxes which are necessary for the Support of his government, their own Peace and Safety." [8]

But the above sentiments were not aroused in other quarters by the Plan. The assembly of New Jersey saw in it something that would strike at the very vitals of the constitution of that province and

---

[5] *Dinwiddie Papers*, I, 254–5, 257. Dinwiddie in a letter to James Abercrombie in London dated August 15 is more specific in his criticism. To him there were "some Articles in it of an extraordinary nature, the Presid$^{t.}$ of the Grand Council is to be invested with large powers of indeed very near to y$^{t.}$ of a viceroy" (Dinwiddie Transcripts, II, 1645, Mass. Hist. Soc.).

[6] *Ibid.*, IV, 25.

[7] It is true that Governor Sharpe of Maryland wrote to Lord Baltimore on August 8 expressing his surprise that de Lancey should have sent the Plan to the Board of Trade before the colonial assemblies had had an opportunity to consider it (*Archives of Maryland*, VI, 79).

[8] Dobbs Papers, Public Record Office, Northern Ireland.

trusted that it would never be given countenance by " a British Legislature." [9] On the other hand the Governor's Council, while showing
a preference for James Alexander's idea of a legislature of three
branches rather than of two branches (that is, the President General
and the Grand Council), nevertheless prayed Belcher "to Lay the
Same before His Majesty's Ministers." [10]

As to New York, on August 20 de Lancey appeared before the General Assembly and, without making any recommendations, stated:

> " When I was at Albany, I proposed to the Commissioners of the
> several Governments met there, the building of Forts in Proper
> Places . . . but without any Effect; they seemed fully persuaded of
> the Backwardness of the several Assemblies, to come to joint and
> vigorous Measures, that they were unwilling to enter upon the Con-
> sideration of these Matters, and formed a Plan for a general Union
> of the Colonies, to be enforced by Act of Parliament, which together
> with a Representation they prepared of the State of the Colonies,
> I shall order to be laid before you." [11]

The New York Council, it would seem, was favourably disposed
toward the Plan in view of the fact that they were well represented
at Albany even if not in the role of formal commissioners. Moreover,
the Assembly, after receiving a copy of it from de Lancey, declared
in their address to him of August 22:

> " We are of opinion with your Honor, that nothing is more natural
> and salutary than a union of the colonies for their own defence." [12]

Manifestly, New York had much to gain by the Plan of Union, but no
steps were taken beyond the broad approval of some sort of colonial
union.

With respect to the corporate colonies, both the Rhode Island and
the Connecticut Assembly were unfavourable to it. Within the former [13] the question of the adoption of the Plan became a heated issue. Stephen Hopkins, one of the commissioners, pointed out the
" absolute necessity " of some such proposal in the eyes of the Congress in a pamphlet entitled: *A True Representation of the Plan
Formed at Albany* — a rather halting defence of the conduct of the

---

[9] *New Jersey Archives*, XVI, 492.
[10] *Ibid.*, XVI, 488.
[11] *New York Mercury*, August 26, 1754.
[12] Justin Winsor, *Narrative and Critical History*, V, 205.
[13] See *Rhode Island Colonial Records*, V, 393, for the report of the commissioners.

Commissioners — which impelled one signing himself " Philolethes " to publish *A Short Reply to Mr. Stephen Hopkins's Vindication, and False Reflections against the Governor and Council of the Colony of Rhode-Island*.[14] The latter asserted, in referring to the Plan of Union, that it would

> " the Instant it was established . . . revoke all His Majesty's Governors Commissions in North-America, and destroy every Charter, by erecting a Power above Law, over the several Legislatures." [15]

Nevertheless, it seems to be true that Hopkins succeeded in getting a favourable report in the General Assembly in August by having it included, according to his critic, with a number of other matters, " and the Plan of Union artfully tack'd to the rest, which being read in the Lower House, the Report was received, and in consequence all their [the Commissioners'] Doings, etc. [approved]." The Governor and Council, " who perceived the Fraud, of the Plan's being included with their other Proceedings acquainted the Lower House." [16] However, the latter could not be prevailed upon to take hostile action against the Plan until in March 1755 it voted, on the recommendation of Governor Greene, that the London agent of the colony should exert himself against the adoption of the project, " if any thing shall be moved in Parliament . . . which may have a tendency to infringe on our charter privileges." [17]

In Connecticut when the Plan was submitted to the Assembly a committee was appointed to bring in recommendations regarding it.[18] These were unfavourable and led to the adoption on October 2, 1754 of " The Reasons Considered and Offered, by the Assembly of the Colony of Connecticut, Concerning the Plan of Union." [19] The proposed union was objected to upon the following grounds: that the suggested territory to be embodied in it was too large for purely defensive purposes; that the proposal to authorize the President General and the Grand Council to nominate and commission all military

---

[14] For these see *Rhode Island Historical Tracts*, No. 9.

[15] *Ibid.*, p. 51.

[16] *Ibid.*, p. 58; *Rhode Island Col. Rec.*, V, 394. In accepting the report of the commissioners in August, the Assembly had reserved the Plan for further consideration.

[17] *Ibid.*, V, 424.

[18] The chairman of this committee was William Pitkin, one of the Albany commissioners who was on the Albany committee to prepare a plan. That there were any differences in point of view developed within the Connecticut delegation regarding the Plan is not apparent.

[19] For these see the *Massachusetts Historical Society Collections*, VII, 207–9.

officers would be " highly detrimental to his Majesty's interest "; that
the growing population " brought into one point, all to move under
the direction of such President-General and Council, might in time
be of dangerous consequence to his Majesty's interest, and the good
of his loyal subjects here "; that the negative voice of the President
General over the acts of the Council might " bring his Majesty's interest into danger," since this officer might not pursue proper methods for the country's good and since the hope of enjoying liberty had
encouraged the settlement of the colonies and encroachments upon
this would discourage the people; that the proposal to authorize the
President General and Grand Council to levy taxes " throughout this
extensive government," was " a very extraordinary thing, and against
the rights and privileges of Englishmen," which were " highly prized
by the people of these colonies, who . . . delight in obedience to,
and admire the protection and privileges of, the laws of England ";
lastly, that, by reason of the shortage of money among the inhabitants of the northern colonies, " to bring on themselves large and
heavy taxes, more than they are well able to pay, must occasion
grievous complaints." The document made clear that it was for

> " these reasons, more largely insisted on, and discussed at the con-
> gress of the commissioners in Albany in June last — the gentlemen,
> who were commissioners from the colony of Connecticut, objected
> to the proposed plan; and thought they were never answered and
> obviated, and therefore never came into, or gave any consent to
> the same." [20]

The Assembly, while thus making clear that the Plan of Union was
not acceptable, nevertheless took the rather surprising position in
view of its implications that the regulation of the Indian trade should
be left to commissioners " of his Majesty's appointment." Power was
to be vested in the latter not only to build forts needful for the defence of the Indians but to keep those forts sufficiently garrisoned —
presumably with regular soldiers and without regard to peculiar interests of particular colonies — the expense of maintaining which
could be largely defrayed from the " profits " of the Indian trade, a
trade, therefore, that would be taxed for that purpose by authority of
the home government! Finally — at this point the influence of the
Susquehanna Company in the shaping of the report becomes very

---

[20] William Smith of New York, who attended the Congress, admits that Connecticut
" was too jealous of the power of the President " (The History of the Late Province of
New York, II, 183-5).

evident — it was argued that should His Majesty be pleased to encourage his subjects " to plant a government or colony " on lands in the Indian country " to be formed and conducted as the New-England Colonies have been, nothing would tend more to secure those Indians to his Majesty's interest . . . and prevent the encroachments of the French; and so the great ends proposed effectually answered, without any discouragement to the people of these colonies, and without the least prejudice or injury to their privileges." [21]

It will be noted that no mention is made in " The Reasons " to the proposal embodied in the Plan of Union for the reduction of the bounds of some of the colonies " to more convenient dimensions " — which Hutchinson later suggested probably had in mind the western claims of Connecticut and Virginia. To what extent the inclusion of this clause may have led to opposition, whether latent or open, of the Connecticut commissioners to the Plan while at the Congress cannot be stated; although in the light of the activities of the Susquehanna Company in Albany during the sessions of the Congress and the vested interest of the three commissioners in it,[22] one may guess that after the land purchase was consummated by it, if not before, a determination was reached to block any endorsement of the projected union in the Assembly. In view of the fact that Connecticut was one of the first of the thirteen states to adhere to the Constitution of the United States — which went much farther than did the Plan of Union in encroaching upon the individual rights of the American commonwealths — it may be surmised that in 1754 there were special reasons for the peculiar strength of the opposition to the proposal. However, it may be pointed out that as a document, if taken at its face value, " The Reasons " is an almost unprecedented American endorsement of the then present Constitution of the British Empire and of the laws governing it and shows a degree of solicitude for " his Majesty's interest " that almost startles one in view of the traditional, if latent, republicanism that had characterized the attitude of the colony down to that time.

In Massachusetts Bay, which alone had given full powers to its commissioners to conclude a union of the colonies, there was less opposition to the Albany Plan. Yet it failed of approval in the Assembly, in spite of the fact that on October 18 Shirley in addressing the two

---

[21] *Mass. Hist. Soc. Coll.*, VII, 210–14.

[22] Colonel Williams and Roger Wolcott, Jr., were members of the Company and so was Pitkin's son, William (*Susquehannah Company Papers*, I, 88).

houses urged that the proposal " projected and agreed upon " by the commissioners required " the Speediest Dispatch, to ripen it for the Consideration of the British Parliament, whose Authority is judged requisite for effecting, and consolidating so desirable an Union." [23] On the following day the House of Representatives appointed a committee of seven including the speaker to join with a committee of the Council to prepare an answer.[24] On October 22 a joint committee was selected to study the Plan of Union [25] and on the 25th the delegates to Albany presented to the Council a formal report.[26] Although the subject continued under consideration in committee, it was not until December that it came before the General Court for action. Early in that month a disturbing letter addressed to the Speaker of the House by the London agent, William Bollan, on September 19 [27] was laid before the representatives and thereupon referred to the Committee on the Plan of Union.[28] This communication made clear the fears of the agent that — under guise of a plan for " raising, collecting and uniting the Forces of all the Colonies " — members of Parliament had in mind " a Design of gaining power over the Colonies." On December 4 the committee reported:

> " That although they apprehend that an Union & such an one as may probably require a parliamentary Interposition is necessary for the Safety of his Majesty's Provinces on the Continent, and for the Relief of this Province on whom the expence & burthen of the War has hitherto chiefly lain, yet the Committee humbly apprehend that so extensive an Union as is proposed would be attended with such manifest inconveniencies as would very much impede if not totally prevent the main design aimed at.
>
> " And as the said plan may be sent home & endeavours used to effect it; [29] the Committee are of opinion that the Agent be instructed

---

[23] Massachusetts General Court Records (State Archives), XX, 1753–1755, p. 279.

[24] Journal of the House of Representatives, October 19, 1754, p. 55.

[25] On November 13 Colonel Hall and Mr. Allen were substituted on the committee by the House of Representatives for Judge Russell and Colonel Otis, who were absent ("Mass. Arch.," VI, 166, A). The original committee of the House was the Speaker, Judge Russell, Colonel Brattle, Colonel Choate, and Colonel Otis; that for the Council was Samuel Watts, Ezekiel Cheeves, Andrew Oliver, and Stephen Sewall (ibid., IV, 473).

[26] Ibid., IV, 459–64.

[27] The letter is in the Massachusetts Court Records, XXI, 195–7.

[28] Journal of the House of Representatives, December 3, 1754, p. 137.

[29] Apparently the committee was not aware that the Plan had been sent to England by Governor de Lancey.

to use his endeavours to prevent any procedure upon it until he shall have further Instructions from this Court." [30]

This report was on the same day read in the Council and " so far accepted as that the Comm[ee] be directed forthwith to sit again & consider, & report such Plan of an Union as to them appears the most salutary." Further, Thomas Hutchinson and Benjamin Lynde were added to the committee.[31] The House, however, decided to be more deliberate and voted that the report should be taken up the following day, with the result that Hutchinson was deputed by the Council to present a message which urged the House to pass upon it

> " as soon as may be; because they apprehend it a matter of great Importance to the Province: That there was a Vessel near ready to sail to *England;* and unless something be done thereon, so as to be sent over by this Opportunity, they are apprehensive the Province may be in Danger of greatly suffering in its most important Interests." [32]

But the House could not be rushed into action. On December 5 there was " a large Debate " that carried over into the afternoon; and on the 6th the discussion of the issue assumed the proportions of " a very large Debate," which was finally terminated in the afternoon when it was agreed to support the action of the Council.[33]

On December 11 the joint committee, apparently divided in its sentiments, nevertheless now submitted to the General Court, as a substitute for the Albany Plan of Union, a project of union simply for the more northern colonies,[34] with a recommendation that the London agent be instructed to take the proper steps for obtaining an act of Parliament " whereby the union prepared in this plan may be carried into execution." It also recommended that the agent use his endeavours that the southern colonies might also be united in a " Confederacy for the further Defense & Security of his Majesty's Territories on the Continent." [35] The new plan was somewhat in line

---

[30] " Mass. Arch.," December 4, 1754, VI, 169.

[31] *Ibid.,* VI, 169, A.

[32] *Journal,* December 4, 1754, p. 141.

It may be noted that Hutchinson was selected to present this urgent message from the Council. If the rule in this instance was followed that the mover of motions for purely routine actions is called upon by the chair to carry them into effect, this may throw additional light upon his attitude at this period respecting the extension of the authority of the British government over the colonies.

[33] *Ibid.,* pp. 142–3.

[34] This plan is to be found in the " Massachusetts Archives," VI, 171–5.

[35] *Ibid.,* VI, 176.

with the proposed plan for a northern confederation offered at Albany apparently by Hutchinson, but with certain important differences, all in the direction of providing not only the Crown with more effective control but also the new central government, to be set up, with adequate power to levy, if need be, on the colonies and to raise and maintain a union army and warships and build forts for the attainment of somewhat more limited objectives than were expressed in the former. The union now proposed, however, was to terminate at the end of six years or at the end of the anticipated war between Great Britain and France.[36]

On December 12 the report of the joint committee was placed before the House of Representatives,[37] and the next day this was re-read

---

[36] The "Plan of a Proposed Union" presented at Albany, as has been made clear, provided for a union through act of Parliament of all the colonies from New Hampshire down to but not including Pennsylvania; the plan now presented, likewise to be brought into existence through Parliament, was to include only New England and New York. Again, the former provided for a "President General, who should be the Governor of the province of Massachusetts-Bay for the time being" and who was to receive a salary from the Grand Council; the latter gave to Massachusetts Bay no such preference but simply made provision for a "President to be appointed and supported by the Crown." In case of his death, according to the former, the Lieutenant Governor of Massachusetts Bay was to exercise his powers "till the arrival of a new Governor for said colony"; according to the latter, the Speaker of the Council should take over his office and was "to continue till the King's pleasure be known." In the former he was to have a "casting voice, whenever an equi-vote shall happen in the Grand Council"; in the latter his assent was "requisite to the validity of all Acts of the Council." As to the place of meeting in the first instance, in the former Boston was selected, in the latter Providence. Further, in the former the Grand Council was empowered to make all purchases from the Indians of lands "not now within the bounds of particular colonies, or that shall not be within their bounds, when the extension of some of them are rendered more certain" and to erect new settlements and provide for the levy of quit-rents; in the latter — doubtless mindful of Connecticut's sensibilities — no authority was specifically granted to these ends. Each of the plans provided for making requisitions upon the colonies concerned for funds; the earlier plan, however, is silent as to the course of action of the Grand Council should a colony neglect or refuse to contribute its just proportion; the later plan stated that the "Grand Court shall have power to levy the same in such manner as they shall judge reasonable, and least prejudicial to the Colony or Colonies so refusing or neglecting as aforesaid." Again, the earlier plan depended upon the particular colonies to furnish their respective contingents of troops; the latter authorized the Grand Court to "raise & pay Soldiers, & build Forts for the defence of any of the s^d. Colonies, and equip Vessels of force to guard the coasts & protect the Trade" — with the proviso that it "shall not impress Men in any Colony without the Consent of its Legislature." Finally, the earlier plan had in view a permanent union of the northern colonies, while the later proposed that the union should be but for six years, unless a war should then be in progress; in this case it should continue until peace should be concluded, "and no longer" — clearly an emergency union.

[37] *Journal*, December 12, 1754, p. 150.

as was the "proposed Plan accompanying the same." Again there took place "a large Debate," which was continued to the 14th, when the question was put "Whether the House accept of the General Plan of Union, as Reported by the Commissioners convened at Albany in June last?" This was voted upon negatively without so much as a roll-call. Thereupon the question was put "Whether it be the mind of the House, that there be a General Union of his Majesty's Colonies on this Continent, except those of Nova-Scotia and Georgia?" By a very close vote of forty-one to thirty-seven it was agreed to repudiate any partial plan of union in favour of a general plan.[38] Thereupon a committee of seven was appointed to join with a committee of the Board to report on a general plan of union other than the Albany Plan.[39] As to the reactions of the Council respecting this vote, one can only surmise that it was not entirely favourable, that a majority of the members, including Hutchinson, favoured a partial union. For in place of some speedy action relative to the decision of the House, it was not until the 20th that the Board was prepared to co-operate with the representatives in formulating a new general plan of union.[40] However, by the 26th the joint committee was able to send to the lower house a new plan.[41] On the 28th an effort was made to have it printed for the purpose, doubtless, of dissemination among the voters. This was defeated — doubtless by the supporters of the plan. That same day a communication from the Council was received calling upon the House to join with it in preparing an answer to London Agent Bollan's letter of September 19, already referred to, and to direct him "to use his utmost Endeavours to prevent the Union of the Colonies upon the Plan proposed by the Commissioners at *Albany*, it having been disapproved by both Houses." This was approved with the amendment that Bollan was at

[38] *Ibid.*, December 13 and 14, 1754, pp. 151–3. The votes of thirty-two members were not recorded. This may indicate that many members could not arrive at a decided opinion (*Commonwealth History of Massachusetts*, II, 460).

[39] The membership of this committee from the House now included five members favouring a general plan — James Bowdoin, James Otis, Judge Chambers Russell, John Tasker, and Robert Hall — and two who favoured a partial union — John Choate and William Brattle. The Board members were not only the four originally appointed but also Benjamin Lynde and Thomas Hutchinson (*Journal*, December 14, 1754, p. 153).

[40] On December 17 the House became anxious as to the fate of its vote and sent Colonel Brattle to wait upon the Board to inquire whether that body had passed upon it and if not to urge that they do so "as soon as may be." Brattle returned to report that the Board "had not so far considered the same as to come to a Vote thereon as yet" (*ibid.*, December 17, 1754, p. 158).

[41] *Ibid.*, December 26, 1754, p. 181.

the same time to be informed " that this court have the affair of the Union of the Colonies now under Consideration. . . ." [42]

The final position of the General Court with reference to the Albany Plan was embodied in a communication addressed to Bollan on December 31 by Secretary Willard. It made clear that this Plan had been " almost unanimously disapproved by both Houses. . . ." The chief objections were to the

> " perpetuity of the proposed Union; the great sway which the Southern Colonies (the Inhabitants whereof are but little disposed to and less acquainted with affairs of war) would have in all the determinations of the Grand Council, etc. But the great and prevailing reason urged against it was, that in its Operation, it would be subversive of the most valuable rights & Liberties of the several Colonies included in it; as a new Civil Government is hereby proposed to be establish'd over them with great & extraordinary power to be exercis'd in time of Peace, as well as War; such as those of making Laws to be of force in all the Colonies; building Forts and Ships of War, and purchasing Lands at discretion; and for these purposes raising monies from the several Colonies in such Sums and in such Manner as the President and Council shall think fit. These powers are in the Judgment of the two Houses inconsistent with the fundamental rights of these Colonies, and would be destructive of our happy Constitution." [43]

In turning now to this new general project of union,[44] the question arises to what extent it departed from the rejected Albany Plan. Its devotion to the main outlines of this is clear, yet the divergencies are sufficiently striking and designed to obviate objections. To begin with, the union was to be temporary in nature — to be limited to a period of but six years " unless at the expiration of said six years there should be war between Great Britain and France, in which case the said powers shall continue until the end of said war and then expire "; [45] again, the chief executive officer was to be a President, not a President General; [46] further, no member of the Grand Council was

---

[42] Journal, December 26 and 28, 1754, pp. 181, 184, 185: " Mass. Arch.," VI, 181.

[43] For this letter see the Commonwealth History of Massachusetts, II, 461.

[44] This is to be found in the " Mass. Arch.," VI, 171–5, and is in Hutchinson's handwriting. It was reproduced with some inaccuracies — without reference to capitalization and punctuation — by Frothingham in his Rise of the Republic, pp. 613–6. H. L. Carson in his One Hundredth Anniversary of the Framing of the Constitution (II, 474–8), reprints Frothingham's defective version.

[45] Here the language of the partial plan of union considered December 11 is followed.

[46] Again the partial plan of union is followed.

to be chosen or appointed to any office, civil or military, by the President or Council.[47] Moreover, nothing was said as to the reference of the acts of the President and Council to the mother country for approval or disapproval; [48] nothing likewise was said respecting the limiting of the western bounds of colonies or the purchase of western lands from the Indians or the collection of quit-rents from these lands or making new settlements thereon or their control by the union government until erected into colonies.[49] Further, the laws passed by the Council for the regulation of the Indian trade were not to extend to life and limb and were to be enforced not by the union but by the colony within which the offence was committed or, if outside of the bounds of any colony, by the colony into which the offender should be taken. However, provision was made for the appointment of collectors of the union revenue which should be secured by " some general duty on wines and spirituous liquors or other luxurious consumption " and for laws not only for enforcing the collection of this revenue [50] but " for restraining supplies to and communication with any of His Majesty's enemies, whether by flags of truce or in any other manner."

One might have thought that, in the light of the great emergency facing the country, so innocuous a union, temporary in nature as it was, would have found favour; but it failed of acceptance in the House of Representatives. Particularism was again triumphant. Nevertheless, it may be noted that on December 27 by a vote of forty-eight to thirty-one the deputies agreed, rather than reject the proposal outright, to suspend further consideration of it until they could consult their constituents of the towns.[51]

---

[47] This diverges from all the previous plans, including the partial plan presented at Albany — that is, the " Plan of a Proposed Union."

[48] In this respect it follows the partial plan.

[49] Again this follows the partial plan.

[50] The substance of this last clause is also in the partial plan.

[51] Frothingham, *Rise of the Republic*, p. 174; *Commonwealth History of Massachusetts*, II, 462.

On January 1, 1755, the Council, apparently favourably disposed toward the new project for a general union, sent to the House the following communication urging speedy action ("Mass. Arch.," VI, 183):

" It appearing to the Board to be of very great Importance that a speedy Determination should be had by this Court upon some Method of uniting the Forces of the Colonies; And this Affair having been under the Consideration of a Committee of both Houses, Whose Report now lies before the honble House of Representatives; the Board therefore think themselves obliged earnestly to recommend to the House to come into some Resolution upon said Report as soon as may be, that so the Board may likewise

That there was much deep hostility in Boston to any such project of union as that evolved by the joint committee is indicated by the reception that it received in a large town meeting on January 17, 1755 [52] when after full debate it was resolved:

" That the Gentlemen the Representatives of the Town by and hereby are Instructed to Use their utmost Endeavours to prevent the Plan now under Consideration of the General Court for an Union of the several Governments on the Continent taking effect — and they also Oppose any other Plan for an Union that may come under the consideration of the said General Court, whereby they shall Apprehend the Liberties and Priviledges of the People are endangered." [53]

Boston having thus spoken " her mind," one can appreciate the fact that the rural and more isolated towns of the commonwealth would be little inclined to oppose her on an issue demanding a comprehensive view of public affairs. They were doubtless even more strongly opposed to the idea.

The cause of political union, even a union of a temporary nature, for the North American British colonies, thus failed in the chief stronghold of sentiment favourable to it — the Commonwealth of Massachusetts Bay. In fact, the forces supporting the traditional order of things within the eleven colonies concerned were too powerful to overcome even in the face of the most deadly menace from without. Yet it is to the credit of the Massachusetts Bay General Court that it alone gave to the problem prolonged and sympathetic attention; that, unlike the assemblies of the other colonies, where the Albany Plan was either treated contemptuously or placidly ignored after either a half-hearted defence of the work of the commissioners or the expression of vague sentiments in favour of some sort of union, it alone sought earnestly to find a solution through the modifications of the project so as to secure the anticipated benefits, while at the same time meeting the objections of those British colonials who feared for the loss of their old liberties and other privileges. Indeed, taking into consideration the fact that Benjamin Franklin was born

have an Opportunity of considering & determining thereon, and doing their Part to prevent the Ill Consequences that may attend a delay in so interesting a Concern."

In reply to this message the House informed the Council that it had not passed on the report of the joint committee. Nor is it clear that this was ever considered. The members at last had heard from the people.

52 *Mass. Hist. Soc. Coll.* (first series), IV, 85.

53 This resolution is printed in the *Commonwealth History of Massachusetts*, II, 463.

and reared within the Province, it may be affirmed that the men who had sprung from the soil of Massachusetts Bay alone in 1754 arose to any commanding height of statesmanship, alone had a vision of a new and better political order for English-speaking people in North America. In view of this fact it is somewhat remarkable that the contribution of the commonwealth to the establishment of the later Confederation and the federal union under the Constitution of 1787 was slight in comparison to that made by some of the colonies to the southward.

As for Governor Shirley, the foremost advocate in Massachusetts Bay of a colonial union, it is clear that he was not at all favourably impressed with some features of the Albany Plan. At the same time he seems at first to have felt that this, modified at home in certain important respects, would open the way to union. He apparently became convinced, however, that neither it nor any of the substitute plans presented by the joint committees of the General Court would meet the needs of the situation. Further, by December he had become persuaded, and rightly, that there was no prospect of a voluntary union on the part of the colonies. While adhering to the Albany proposal for a President General appointed by the Crown, he had now come to favour likewise the appointment of the Grand Council by the same authority, as against selection of its members by the colonial assemblies; finally, he had come to favour a system of taxation of the colonies by act of Parliament as the only method that would really guarantee a fund for general defence. These ideas were submitted to Benjamin Franklin, who was in Boston at the time. Franklin, while admitting " that this general government might be as well and faithfully administered without the people, as with them," nevertheless argued, in a letter addressed to the Governor on December 17, that " where heavy burthens are laid upon them, it has been found useful to make it as much as possible their own act." [54] The next day he amplified his ideas in a lengthy communication which carefully traversed the ground with respect to the taxation of the colonies and is one of the ablest papers of this period relating to government. It is well summarized in the statement:

> " That to propose taxing them by Parliament, and refuse them the liberty of choosing a representative council to meet in the colonies, and consider and judge of the necessity of any general tax and the

---

[54] Letter of December 17, 1754, *Works of Benjamin Franklin* (ed. John Bigelow), II, 376, 377.

quantum, shows a suspicion of their loyalty to the crown, or of their regard for their country, or of their common sense and understanding, which they have not deserved." [55]

Franklin at the same time argued strongly for the Albany Plan, stressing especially the point that it would not give to the representatives of the people — as Shirley had come to fear — excessive power, declaring:

> "That the powers, proposed by the Albany Plan of Union to be vested in a grand council representative of the people, even with regard to military matters, are not so great as those which the colonies of Rhode Island and Connecticut are intrusted with by their charters, and have never abused. . . ."

Further, should the alterations proposed by Shirley be made in the Plan, he saw danger ahead:

> "Then the administration of the board of governors and council so appointed, not having the representative body of the people to approve and unite in its measures . . . will probably become suspected and odious, dangerous animosities and feuds will arise between governor and governed, and every thing go into confusion."

The views here expressed, it may be pointed out, were not inconsistent with his view that the only way to secure a union of the colonies within the British Empire was by appealing directly to Parliament. Any scheme for bringing the colonies to act together that could satisfy the colonials, he realized, must provide a large measure of local or at least popular control over the government set up and the measures pursued by it. According to his view, taxation by Parliament would therefore not meet their objections, no matter how just were the measures.

Shirley now countered with a suggestion that to meet anticipated colonial criticism of taxation by Parliament the colonies should be allowed representation in that body. Franklin in reply to this on December 22 affirmed that he was of the opinion

> "that such a union would be very acceptable to the colonies, provided they had a reasonable number of representatives allowed them; and that all the old acts of Parliament restraining the trade or cramping the manufactures of the colonies be at the same time repealed, and the British subjects *on this side the Water* put, in those respects,

---

[55] *Ibid.*, II, 377–83.

on the same footing with those in Great Britain, till the new Parliament, representing the whole, shall think it for the interest of
the whole to re-enact some or all of them. . . . I think, too, that the
government of the colonies by a Parliament in which they are fairly
represented, would be vastly more agreeable to the people than the
method lately attempted to be introduced by royal instructions, as
well as more agreeable to the nature of an English Constitution and
to English liberty. . . ." [56]

' Two days after receiving this communication Shirley wrote to Secretary of State Robinson. He declared that the Albany commissioners "must be considered as the most intelligent persons of their respective Governm[ts] on the general state of the Colonies" and

"that their determination of these points ought to be look'd upon
as the declared sense of all the Colonies; and this [Plan] together
with their representation of the state of the Colonies seems to have
laid a good foundation for immediately proceeding at home to the
forming of a proper plan in all points for a General Union of the
Colonies, settling the quotas of men & money for each Colony . . .
to be establish'd by authority of Parliam[t] and carry'd into execution
in the Colonies without further consulting them upon any points
whatever." [57]

In this he said nothing about colonial representation in Parliament.
On the other hand he pointed out that the method of electing the
representatives to the Grand Council by the assemblies, as envi-
sioned by the Albany Plan, was on account of the power given to the
Council to raise taxes. Nevertheless, this body, representative of all
the people of the colonies, would, he feared, enjoy certain powers —
such as making peace and war with the Indians, disposing of military
commissions, raising troops, and erecting forts — that would be " a

---

[56] Ibid., II, 384-7. Thomas Hutchinson in commenting upon this statement at a
later period (History of Massachusetts Bay, 1748-1774, p. 24) declared that Franklin
" looked upon the colonies as so many counties gained to Great Britain, and all included
in the British Empire, which had only extended itself by their means." He then went
on to say: " It will be difficult if this principle be admitted, to justify the revolt of the
colonies, in which Mr. Franklin was very instrumental. He departed from his principles,
and declared, fifteen years after the date of those letters, that he was of opinion, Britain
and the colonies were under separate legislatures, and stood related as England and
Scotland stood before the union " — a notion which would have been considered most
revolutionary if not preposterous by Franklin and doubtless by the other men who
gathered at Albany and who agreed that only Parliament possessed the necessary authority to alter the constitutions of the colonies.

[57] N. Y. Col. Doc., VI, 931; Correspondence of Shirley, II, 113-14.

great strain upon the prerogative of the Crown and contrary to the English Constitution "; for, as he pointed out, these powers had up to the present been vested solely in the respective governors of the colonies, except in the case of Connecticut and Rhode Island. As to the two last-named, he declared that he was persuaded it would be best to give them the type of government under a royal governor such as Massachusetts Bay possessed. He then raised the question: If it were desirable to discourage " the old Charter form of government " in the colonies, would it be proper to pattern the union upon this " charter " type? Finally, he observed " that the prerogative is so much relaxed in the Albany Plan, that it doth not appear well calculated to strengthen the dependency of the Colonies upon the Crown, which seems a very important article in the consideration of this affair." Although Shirley admitted in this communication that he had drawn up " a rough sketch " of a project of union, he went on to say that he did not think it proper to transmit this, especially in light of the fact that the Lords Commissioners for Trade and Plantations were, he understood, themselves forming a plan.

The above half-hearted endorsement of the Albany Plan did not tend to promote its acceptance by the government of Great Britain, irrespective of the positive hostility shown toward it by the various colonies. But let us now turn our attention to the developments in England as these related to a colonial union.

The project for a union set forth by the Lords Commissioners for Trade and Plantations came as a result of orders of His Majesty transmitted by Sir Thomas Robinson, Secretary of State for the Southern Department, who requested the Board on June 14 to prepare a " Plan of General Concert " of the North American colonies " for their mutual and common defence." [58] On August 9 they forwarded to him

[58] Board of Trade Journal, 1754–1758, pp. 49, 50, 65; N. Y. Col. Doc., VI, 901. On April 30 Halifax had sent to Robinson a proposal for a series of forts on the frontiers from Nova Scotia to Florida to be constructed by the governors of those colonies in which they would be located, and to be placed in such a manner as to cut the French forts off from the French settlements. These were to be garrisoned in part at least by the independent companies in the New World and were to serve as centres for the Indian trade. To control more effectively Indian relations, two districts were to be erected, each under a general Indian commissioner, who would appoint deputies, hold conferences, and make presents to the Indians. This would be financed by placing the colonial revenues in a fund through act of Parliament (Brit. Mus. Add. Mss. 33029, folio 109). The expense of such undertakings, however, had to be considered. This seemed especially to concern the Duke of Newcastle, who on June 15 wrote to Horace Walpole, Auditor General for the British Plantations, asking for suggestions as to the best method of securing the necessary funds for supporting resistance to the French. The latter reply-

their " Draught of a Plan or Project for a General Concert " together with a representation embodying their observations upon it. The institution of this general concert visualized certain steps that fully took into account the sensibilities of the colonial governments — something that both Franklin's " Short Hints " and Shirley's suggestions ignored or at least disregarded. Unlike the two last-named it was to be brought about " by the mutual consent and agreement of the Colonies themselves " — and not simply by act of Parliament. In fact, Parliament was to have no hand in the matter. The colonial governments upon receiving copies of the " Draught or Project " were to appoint commissioners, as they had done for the general treaty at Albany with the Iroquois; these were to take into consideration the recommendations embodied in the same and thereupon prepare a " Project or draught of a General Convention," which in turn should be laid before the assemblies for alterations and additions. Within two months the commissioners were again to meet to take into consideration these suggested changes and thereupon, "having finally settled the whole, the Convention shall be fairly drawn up and signed by each Commissioner and transmitted hither " for His Majesty's approbation, after which it would be binding upon all the colonies — even those that might neglect to appoint a commissioner to aid in its formulation. The main outlines of the " Project " are as follows:

Circular letters were to be sent to all the governors setting forth the dangers confronting the colonies and the necessity not only of providing and maintaining for defence a proper number of forts upon the frontiers, as well as troops for " the general security service

---

ing on the 18th emphasized the fact that the mother country was " loaded with immense debts contracted for ye good of all His Majesty's Dominions " and " at a great annuall expense in shipping for ye protection of them by sea." In this connection, he made clear that if the expense of defending well-settled and flourishing colonies were to fall upon Parliament, " ye Landed Gentlemen of this Country will be terribly alarmed with a notion that might prevayl, that they are to be taxed on all occasions to defend our American Borders . . . as this Nation is at present at so great a charge in ye settlement of Nova Scotia, for the security of these very Colonys." If other sources of revenue for American defence could not be found, he recommended a lottery in England (Add. Mss. 32735, folios 485–9). On the 22nd he again addressed Newcastle with the suggestion that paper money might be issued by Virginia and secured by establishing a liquidation fund and that Pennsylvania and Maryland should act in concert with her in meeting the encroachments of the French. He also recommended " a plan of union " of all the colonies " under the protection & with ye approbation of ye Crown of Gr. Brittain, for their mutual security & defence . . . by a convention for settling ye respective proportions of assistance to be furnish [sic] by them . . ." (Add. Mss. 32535, folios 539–41).

and defence of the whole," but also of placing Indian affairs under one general direction and making provision for presents and other contingent charges for that service. These matters were to be submitted to the serious consideration of all the assemblies, each of which was to be requested to appoint a commissioner to meet with those of the other colonies to deliberate on the best way of providing the desired defences and also Indian presents and support for Indian commissaries to be stationed at the forts to regularize the trade. The allocation of the general expense of these undertakings was, according to the " Project," to be made by the commissioners thus appointed. To this end they were to be furnished with authenticated accounts of the expense that each colony had faced during the past twenty years. However, the quotas finally agreed upon were to take into consideration not only the number of inhabitants, but likewise the trade, wealth, and revenue of each colony. As to exceptional charges, as in case of invasion, these were to be in like manner allocated.

The Lords Commissioners at the same time recommended that, to co-ordinate defence measures in the colonies, a commander-in-chief as well as a commissary general for Indian affairs should be appointed by the Crown, to be supported out of the funds thus voluntarily raised; further, that these two officials should be empowered to draw upon the treasury in each colony for the necessary and ordinary charges " in proportion to the quantum settled for each Colony; taking care to transmit annually to each colony a particular estimate, expressing the particular service for which such draughts are made "; finally, that they should submit annually to each colony a statement on oath involving all disbursements. As a safeguard against extravagance in frontier defence the Lords Commissioners suggested that in case a colony were invaded its governor, council, and assembly should estimate the amount of the extraordinary expenses required for protection, which estimate should be forwarded to the other colonies and the sums required of each should be finally agreed upon at a general meeting of commissioners — a majority of whom, with five constituting a quorum, having the power to bind the colonies. These quotas for the common defences — to the amounts respectively agreed upon — should thereupon become a first charge on each colonial treasury, and in case the treasurer of a colony did not have at hand a sufficient sum to cover them he should be empowered to borrow the amount due, for repayment of which provision should be made by the assembly. Further, to guard against mismanagement, a commissioner from each colony should be expected from time to time to inspect the state of the colonial defences and to report to his assembly, which in turn should also from time to time represent to the commander-in-chief the state of the colony and such measures as were necessary for the general good.

This plan of union contained much that is commendable – unequal as it was to meet the exigencies of the colonial situation – and is a tribute to the desire of the Board of Trade to evolve one in harmony with " the Constitution of the Colonies." [59] It was the object of serious deliberation on the part of the King's ministers. On August 25 the Lord Chancellor presented observations on the plan that made clear some of its defects; [60] on September 13 Charles Townshend, who, transferred in April from the Board of Trade, had become a Lord of the Admiralty, presented even more serious objections to it. He declared:

> " It is my opinion that the Plan begins a great work in a wrong manner; whatever is done, can only be done by an Act of Parliament, concerted with great prudence & knowledge; & I am sure . . . from past experience in like cases that the Provinces are more likely to accept such a candid & just plan sent from hence in an act of Parliament than to form one in any meeting by their deputies or in their assemblies. I shall endeavour to prepare such a plan . . . with a fund which all the Provinces will, I am certain, approve & chearfully pay." [61]

Late in October the Lords Commissioners, doubtless having been made to realize that their own plan was not acceptable to the leading

---

[59] Halifax to [Newcastle], August 15, 1754, Add. Mss. 32736, folio 243.

[60] Hardwicke thought that the method of calling into existence such a union would involve " Great Obstructions, & Delays." He favoured a plan whereby the commissioners who were chosen to draw up the project would send it directly to England to be approved by the King, who would then transmit it, if so approved, to each governor with instructions to lay it before his council and assembly. He also thought that the method laid down whereby the other colonies would come to the support of the one attacked was " too much entangled," involved " too many Steps to be taken." The Duke of Newcastle agreed with him (Add. Mss. 32736, folios 344-5).

[61] Ibid., folio 508. Townshend pointed out that " it is impossible to imagine that so many different Representatives of so many different Provinces, divided in Interest & Alienated by Jealousy, & inveterate prejudice, should even be able to resolve upon a plan of mutual security & Reciprocal expence, which shall be consistent with their Instructions and agreeable to the whole."

It will be noted that Townshend, who as Chancellor of the Exchequer in 1767 was convinced that he had a plan for raising an American fund that would be acceptable to the colonies, was thus confident in 1754 that he could devise such a plan.

ministers, sent a representation to His Majesty in Council enclosing the proceedings of the Albany commissioners, who "having agreed upon a plan of Union, which, as far as their sense and opinion of it goes, is complete in itself, we shall not presume to make any observations upon it, but transmit it simply for Your Majesty's Consideration." [62] It should not be assumed, as it has been by some writers, that by this action the Board dismissed the plan contemptuously. Doubtless the members felt somewhat chastened as the result of criticism of their own plan and, with the arrival of the news of the disastrous outcome of Washington's campaign, had come to realize that time was lacking to place in motion the machinery for any methodical plan of union. Nevertheless, as to the Board's real desire to see the colonies evolve their own plan of union rather than have one formulated for them in England, there can be little doubt in view of a letter addressed by the Lords Commissioners to Governor Shirley, which was dated July 5, 1754. It reads as follows:

"We sincearly wish that every Colony had shown the Same obediance to his Majesty's orders and the Same Spirit and Inclination to oppose the Design of the French as have been shewn by the Province of Massachusetts Bay — If that had been the Case & if Each Colony had sent Commissioners to the meeting . . . at Albany some general Plan might have been Concerted Which in the Separate and divided State of the Colonies is impossible to be done without some such general Congress, but we are sorry to say very little regard has been had by other Colonies to his Majesty's orders for their own security: — It seems to be the opinion and is the Language of Every Colony that an Union of Interest for their Common Defence is absolutely Necessary, & yet no one Step is taken to Effect such an Union. . . ." [63]

In fact, the difficulties facing any attempt to consult the wishes of the colonies in the matter of the union were clearly set forth by Governor Shirley in his letter of January 24, 1755 to the Secretary of State for the Southern Department:

"There is no Appearance of the several Assemblies agreeing among themselves upon any one Plan of an Union, either General or Partial. By what I can learn of the Sentiments of them all, the only three points they can agree in are: that there is a Necessity for an Union; that it must be establish'd by Act of Parliament, whatever it is, & that they don't like the plan concerted by the Commissioners at

62 N. Y. Col. Doc., VI, 917.
63 Israel Williams Papers, I, 71, Mass. Hist. Soc.; see also ibid., I, 70.

Albany wch. all of 'em conceive to infringe upon their Colony-liberties, & privileges. Now, Sir, when it is consider'd that the Albany Commissioners were of the Assemblies's choosing, & in reality a Sett of Gentlemen of the best Abilities that perhaps could be found among 'em, & all zealously attach'd to the Interests of their respective Gov^ts; That the Plan they concluded on is particularly guarded against breaking in upon the Privileges of any one particular Gov^t. within the Colonies; That the Power of raising the Forces & erecting the Forts necessary for the defence of the propos'd General Gov^t., the Appointment of Officers Military as well as Civil within it, & the raising & disposition of the Money for the Support of it, are by that Plan vested in the People, or which is near the same thing: the Grand Council chosen by the several Assemblies, leaving to his Majesty the mere Shadow of a Power in the Negative Allow'd to his Governor General, when all this, I say, Sir, is consider'd, & the Assemblies still think this Plan not popular enough, it seems to take away all Expectation that any plan will ever be concerted, in the Colonies. . . ." [64]

Thus the union of the American colonies was obliged to wait.[65] And when it came, twenty-one years later, it was directed, not against the encroachments of a foreign power — for France, after tremendous exertions and sacrifices on the part of the mother country, had for ever been eliminated from North America — but against Parliament over that which was regarded as its encroachments upon the constitutional rights of the colonial governments. Nevertheless, it is of interest to record that — while under the cloud of a great menace — leading colonials had in 1754 recognized this ancient body as possessing final authority in all matters involving the Constitution of the British Empire, granting that by 1775 not only this conception had passed into the limbo of outworn doctrines and theories but also the recognition of its right to formulate and maintain any imperial regulation not in accord with colonial desires. America at length came of age.

---

[64] Parkman Transcripts, XL, 147–9, Mass. Hist. Society.

[65] It appears, however, that the ministry seriously contemplated sending over to America a lord commissioner and that they had gone so far as to designate tentatively Lord Willoughby for the position, who had declined the appointment, with the result that it was agreed to offer it to Colonel Cornwallis, the founder of Halifax (H. L. Osgood, *The American Colonies in the Eighteenth Century*, IV, 323).

CHAPTER VI

Land of the Acadians

N ow that we have passed in review political developments in
Canada, the Great Lakes wilderness and its geographical dependencies, including the country of the Iroquoian Confederation as well as the regions southward and west of the English settlements of the Atlantic seaboard, it is necessary before taking our
temporary leave of North America to turn our attention to the home
of the Acadians, where international friction of the most intensified
type made its appearance during the period under consideration.

Old French Acadia was a land of rivers, of deep bays and other in-
dentations as the result of submergence of the coastal plain, a land of
innumerable lakes, of low-lying hills covered mile after mile with a
dense growth of spruce, fir, and pine, with which were interspersed
the deciduous birch, oak, and maple, and, along the upper reaches of
la Baye Françoise — called by the English the Bay of Fundy — of vast
salt marshes washed by the high tides when not protected by dikes.
There is even today, in spite of three centuries of colonization and
the spread of settlement and civilization throughout this region, a
quality of wildness, of sombreness in the landscape that must have
characterized it in the seventeenth and eighteenth centuries. Let one,
indeed, but stand in the late afternoon on the low ridge of Beauséjour rising from the narrow Isthmus of Chignecto and look eastward
over the marshes of the valley of the Missaquash, then southwestward toward the distant Cumberland Basin, and then westward in
the direction of the great Tantramar marsh to encompass a pano-
rama perhaps not to be surpassed in solemn impressiveness by any
in North America. Here the greys and mauves of low-lying clouds

seem finally to settle upon and embrace the greys and mauves of the interminable marsh, dotted here and there with grazing cattle and hay barns, the latter severe in line and uniform in appearance. For all nature tends to be subdued in form and tone within the reaches of the Bay of Fundy; only here and there at rare intervals does some object appear in a certain majesty of line, such as the rocky ledge of Cape Blomidon looming across Minas Bay from Grand Pré. The high tide with its murky waters is succeeded by low tide with its mud flats; while the hills and highlands, outside the clearings for farms and habitations, offer but an unchanging aspect of somewhat forbidding mystery.

Here, in this region of marsh and forest, the Acadians settled in the course of the seventeenth century. French peasantry they were; a simple people instilled with no sense of a high calling, such as possessed their early leaders — de Monts, Champlain, Poutrincourt, Lescarbot, La Tour, and de Charnisay. First having established themselves firmly at Port Royal, now Annapolis Royal, having there gained possession of the tide-swept flats by applying the knowledge of diking familiar to those who had dwelt along the lower reaches of the Loire River in France, having thus turned those dreary, muddy stretches into meadows where horses and cattle could at last graze belly-deep in the lush marsh grass, they or their children appeared in Minas Basin, then along Cobequid Bay, and finally upon Chignecto Bay, repeating in each instance the conquest of the mud flats by means of dikes furnished with *aboiteaux* — a simple wooden device for keeping out the tide and permitting a continuous drainage of the land.

Thus, here and there upon elevations commanding the diked marshes, settlements appeared about the great bay with the building of churches and rude hand-edged clapboard dwellings, barns, and granaries, and the planting of apple trees. Not only did the people turn to tillage and the grazing of flocks but they built boats and the men fished with line and net, and some turned to trade with the near-by tribes of Indians; not only did they find it possible in this isolated region of North America to survive, but they were able to live in rude comfort. From a few hundreds in the middle of the seventeenth century, by the middle of the eighteenth these Acadians had grown to number perhaps ten thousand.[1] This substantial increase, it should

---

[1] In 1671 the population was but 441; in 1714 it was only 1,773 (J. B. Brebner, *New England's Outpost: Acadia before the Conquest of Canada*, p. 46). By 1748, ac-

be pointed out, was not to any appreciable extent brought about through accession of numbers from France but rather by natural increase. Indeed, when Acadia was ceded to Great Britain in 1713 by the Treaty of Utrecht, its population was not more than eighteen hunded; most of these people were apparently descended from settlers who had arrived a generation or two before. After the cession not only were Frenchmen not encouraged to enter the Province but inducements were extended by the authorities of New France to draw away the old settled inhabitants. However, the latter did not leave, but, remaining, interbred and multiplied and doubtless felt that the blessing of the Lord was upon them and that, even under an alien master, the land they possessed and had come to love would always belong to them and to their children.

The Acadians were, in truth, peaceable, sober, fairly industrious, pious, and intensely home-loving. Not the least of their achievements was that they had succeeded in adjusting harmoniously their relations with the Micmac, Abenaki, and other less important Indian groups living about their settlements without at the same time debauching them — thanks to a certain amount of intermarriage with these natives, who had been converted by the French missionaries into ardent — nay, fanatical — adherents of the Church of Rome. Further, their relations with the British authorities at Annapolis Royal after 1710 and up to 1750, even if very casual, to say the least, were not on the whole particularly unfriendly. It is true that as a visible sign of obedience, if not of goodwill, they were expected to make some payment in kind by way of quit-rent for the lands they occupied — in place of the old seigneurial dues for which under the French regime they had been liable. But this levy was so trifling — a mere bushel of wheat and a couple of capons from each farm — that, according to Acting Governor Paul Mascarene, it scarcely totalled ten pounds a year for the whole province! [2] They were also expected to elect from time to time deputies to appear at the fort at Annapolis Royal for the purpose of making recommendations as to what was needful to be done for the welfare of their respective communities, of advising with the members of the Provincial Council on matters of

cording to Lieutenant Colonel Mascarene, there were between four and five thousand capable of bearing arms (Nova Scotia State Papers, Public Record Office, A. 32: 232; these papers will be referred to subsequently by the following abbreviation: P.R.O., N.S., with the proper reference to series, volume, and page). Governor Cornwallis the following year estimated the population at ten thousand (P.R.O., N.S., A. 35: 4).

[2] P.R.O., N.S., A. 50: 162.

common interest, and of reporting the decisions of the latter upon returning home. These relations might imply the existence of effective control of their lives on the part of the British Crown. Government, however, did not under ordinary circumstances carry with it much authority in Nova Scotia, as it was supported in peace-times by only a small garrison that seldom left the precincts of the English fort. An Acadian, indeed, might conceivably have lived to maturity and died in the settlements somewhat remote from Annapolis Royal without ever having had any personal contact with a British official. In other words, there was no attempt before the period under consideration at Anglicization, no interference with the religion of the people, no effort to exact from them more than a mere lip-service type of allegiance to the King of England. They were permitted to retain their language for all purposes, their French Catholic priests, their seventeenth-century local customs in the utmost freedom from restraint; they dwelt in peace and plenty, gathering for worship at their chapels, marrying off their sons and daughters, tilling their fields, and pasturing their cattle in the salt marshes, fishing the near-by waters, and bartering for furs — a striking and happy contrast to the restricted conditions of existence of most of the peasantry living contemporaneously in France, the land of nativity of their forefathers!

As has been stated, in the middle of the eighteenth century most of the inhabitants were living in the region of the Baye Françoise. For example, in the parish of Port Royal, extending about a dozen leagues inland from Annapolis Royal on either bank of the river flowing into the harbour, dwelt some two thousand communicants who assembled to worship in the church located in the lower town. About twenty leagues distant by a road cut through the woods was the Minas Basin, as it was known, divided at this period into four parishes, one on the Rivière aux Canards, where dwelt some six hundred communicants, another at Grand Pré with a thousand communicants, the third the Church of the Assumption, and the fourth the Church of the Holy Trinity, both on the Rivière Piziquid and under the care of the same curé, with a total of some eighteen hundred communicants. A fifth parish, that of Cobequid, to the east of the Minas Basin, possessed about eight hundred communicants, while a sixth, that of Beaubassin or Chignecto, taking in people dwelling on some eight streams flowing into Chignecto Bay, could boast of approximately twenty-five hundred communicants, although during most of the period of recent hostilities between England and France there had been no curé to care for their spiritual needs. Besides these organized parishes there were numerous small detached settlements, too small to justify the presence of a resident priest, as, for example, that on the St. John, where, however, a missionary to the Abenaki Indians resided.[3]

By the Treaty of Utrecht, as was pointed out, Acadia had been handed over to the English, who in 1710 had succeeded in capturing Port Royal. There is every reason to believe that the *Grand Monarque* was indeed happy to bring the War of the Spanish Succession to a termination, whereby, in exchange for this somewhat dreary region, as it was held to be, and the inhabitants who chose to remain within it — insignificant in number at best — together with other considerations, he was able to secure one of the great objectives of the war: the right of succession of a member of his own family to the Crown of Spain which brought with it possession of the vast Spanish Empire. As to the fate of the Acadians, Article XIV of the treaty provided the customary saving clause in the transfer of a people from one allegiance to another: that those dwelling within the limits of the Province should have the liberty during the period of a year to retire to other parts with their movables should they not choose to become subjects of the Crown of Great Britain. It further appears that, after the conclusion of the treaty, the King of France secured the consent of Queen Anne that such as desired to depart should be given the opportunity to dispose of their immovable property.[4] When informed of the terms of the treaty, many if not most of the inhabitants of the parishes of Port Royal, Minas, and Beaubassin resolved to leave but were refused passports for this purpose by Deputy Governor Caulfeild, who was at this juncture in control in the absence of Governor Nicholson. The latter, upon taking up his duties in 1714, went so far in conforming to the agreement between the two crowns as to permit a gathering of the inhabitants in the presence of representatives of the French government who had come from Isle Royale (Cape Breton) for the purpose of securing the names of those desiring to depart as well as those who had determined to remain. Nicholson even permitted a certain number to leave with their personal effects, including their cattle and sheep,

---

[3] See " Description de l'Acadie avec le nom des paroisses et le nombre des habitants," Arch. Nat., Col., C11 A. 82: 363.

[4] L'Hermitte to Governor Nicholson, July 21, 1714, P.R.O., N.S., A. 5: 14; also B. Murdoch, A History of Nova Scotia, I, 333, for Anne's letter to Nicholson of June 23, 1713.

on ships sent from Louisbourg by the commandant of that place, which was soon to become heavily fortified and a symbol of French determination to contest British influence in North America.[5] However, when it came to requests made by the French officials that the inhabitants desiring to place themselves under the protection of the King of France be allowed still another year to remain upon their lands without molestation; that, further, they be permitted to transport all their effects, including their dismantled dwellings, and for that purpose to build vessels and to receive for these French equipment; and that, finally, they be given an opportunity freely to sell their lands to Englishmen with an unlimited time accorded for that purpose, Nicholson was impelled to declare that he had no authority to designate the time when the year of grace should either commence or end but must refer this matter as well as the other requests to Her Majesty's decision.[6]

The death of Queen Anne at this juncture, with the coming of the Hanoverians to the throne, the stiffening of the diplomatic relations between England and France as a result of the efforts of the Old Pretender, with French support, to stir up rebellion, the feverish activity of the French on Isle Royale from 1717 onward in the building of a great stronghold at Louisbourg, which was viewed by their rivals not only as a defensive measure to protect French interests in Canada and about the Gulf of St. Lawrence but also as an ominous sign that France had repented of her decision at Utrecht, at least respecting Acadia: all these events combined to persuade the government of Great Britain to employ every means to prevent so great an accession of strength to the French living near the borders of that province as would have come in the wholesale migration of the Acadians to Isle Royale, or Cape Breton as it is now and was then called by the British.[7] Therefore, as a result of various obstacles raised against a migration under conditions that would appeal to the thrifty inhabitants, and also of a policy of indulgence and what one may call, to employ a somewhat hackneyed phrase, one " of salutary neglect," the great body of Acadians, in spite of their avowed loyalty to the King of France, continued to dwell in their accustomed and beloved abodes. Gradually the thought of departure apparently receded into the background. It is true, however, that in 1725, in face

---

[5] See, for example, the list for August 18, 1714, P.R.O., N.S., A. 5: 33–4.
[6] P.R.O., N.S., A. 5: 35–8.
[7] See J. B. Brebner, New England's Outpost, pp. 66–7.

Carte de l'Acadie, Isle Royale et Païs Voisins. Par M. B. Ingr. de la Marine. 1757.

A Prospect of the City of Louisbourg after Its Conquest by Pepperrel and Warren.

(Reproduced from Justin Winsor's *Narrative and Critical History of America*.)

of a temporary revival of this movement, Lieutenant Governor Armstrong was impelled to forbid the making of a road from Annapolis Royal to Minas, which he felt would have facilitated it, and, indeed, any shifting of the inhabitants from place to place without his express permission.

In 1727, the year of the accession of George II, the question of the relations of the Acadians to the British Crown was again brought to the forefront when, in the presence of a military force, most of the adult males of the various parishes to the north of Annapolis Royal were led to take the following oath in the presence of Ensign Robert Wroth:

> "*Je . . . promets et jure sincèrement que je serai fidèle à Sa Majesté le Roy George Second et à ses successeurs. Dieu me soit en aide.*" [8]

However, attached to this oath were certain stipulations that the inhabitants insisted upon: that they should be permitted to enjoy the continued possession of their lands, that they be exempt from all necessity of bearing arms, that French priests should continue to be supplied to them by the Bishop of Quebec, and, finally, that should they see fit at a later time to leave the Province, they be freed of their obligation of allegiance to the King of England. In agreeing to some of these stipulations Ensign Wroth, unfortunately, quite exceeded the authority conferred upon him by his commission. However, Governor Philipps claimed to have secured in 1729 unconditional oaths of the Acadians, but the veracity of this claim has been questioned.[9] Indeed, the whole issue of the oath was soon allowed to rest in view of the weakness of the British in Acadia. The officials of New France, on their part, must also have realized that the Acadians under the agreement of 1727 could now never be employed against them and might on the other hand well be a source of strength to the French Empire at some future time. For, could they not, by means of priests sent to them from France, be continuously kept in mind of their national origin and buoyed in maintaining not only loyalty to the Catholic Church but even to His Most Christian Majesty, who stood in a special sense as the champion in North America of that culture

---

[8] In a petition signed by the French inhabitants in September 1753, it was stated that this was the oath administered by Ensign Robert Wroth (P.R.O., N.S., B. 6: 235). See J. B. Brebner's *New England's Outpost*, pp. 86–98 for a careful treatment of the oath.

[9] *Ibid.*, pp. 93–9.

which they had inherited and which they cherished even in their simple ways of life?

By 1740 the population of Acadia, according to Major Mascarene, had doubled if not tripled in comparison with the period of the cession of the Province, and the number of French priests permitted to minister to them had also doubled. As to the influence of the presence of the latter, he affirmed that they would always be a hindrance to the inhabitants becoming good subjects.[10] With their steady growth in number in the eighteenth century the Acadians were constantly presented with the problem of obtaining fresh lands, for such as were in possession of the earlier settlers had been gradually divided and subdivided among their descendants. However, upon application to the Governor for additional allotments they were at last told by Mascarene that by his instructions he was permitted to grant unappropriated lands only to Protestant subjects. As a result, there gradually took place a movement of population to the outskirts of the peninsula, especially west of the Bay of Chignecto, where at Shepody, Petitcodiac, Memramcook, and elsewhere — in spite of proclamations and orders — from time to time groups proceeded to squat and dike and build settlements. Indeed, the growing recalcitrance manifested on the part of the Acadians in the '40s of the eighteenth century had its centre among those dwelling beyond the range of any type of political control that could be exerted from Annapolis Royal, those made resentful of the restrictions on landholding, those, incidentally, brought most constantly in touch with the French dwelling on Isle St. Jean and especially on Isle Royale, to which islands they continually resorted to sell the fruits of their labour. In all this they were encouraged by the habitual inertia of the government of the Province. For so difficult and dangerous was it considered to attempt to enforce orders upon the Acadians, because of the weakness of the garrison at Annapolis Royal and the ruinous condition of the fort there, that no effort was made to do so, especially since no effective naval support, so necessary under the circumstances, was at hand.[11] In vain went Mascarene's warnings to the Duke of Newcastle that the people of Minas and especially of

---

[10] P. Mascarene to the Duke of Newcastle, November 15, 1740, P.R.O., N.S., A. 25: 75.

[11] *Ibid.* Orders, however, were issued from time to time covering the settlements beyond the peninsula (see J. C. Webster, *The Forts of Chignecto*, p. 22).

Chignecto were " contentious, intractable & will not conform themselves to the good order established for their own peace and Tranquility." [12]

While it is true that Acadia made no appeal before 1749 to permanent English settlers, it possessed one asset that soon after the
Treaty of Utrecht began to attract attention. This was the fisheries
about the region of the Strait of Canso, that narrow body of water
separating Cape Breton Island from the peninsula, and the small
island bearing the same name. By the beginning of the third decade
this activity had assumed such great importance that for its protection four companies of regular troops were stationed on the island [13]
and by 1732 over a hundred ships, colonial and British, were visiting
these waters. As to the fisheries, these were almost completely absorbed by New England men. In their schooners and sloops of from
thirty to forty-five tons, manned by from four to seven sailors, they
procured during the year last named something over twenty-five
thousand quintals of cod. This fish caught off banks lying between
fifteen and thirty leagues distant from Canso was thereupon brought
to shore to be properly cured, after which it was disposed of chiefly to
traders who came in their sackships from Great Britain.[14] The War
of Jenkins's Ear, which broke out in 1739, however, had an unfortunate effect upon this enterprise; for it cut off the Iberian Peninsula
and Mediterranean markets where most of the cod had been sold.
As a result, the importance of Canso had so declined by 1741 that
only thirteen ships came to fish — all from New England — and but
little more than five thousand quintals of cod were cured.[15] Nevertheless, the Canso fishery had given the people of New England,
and especially of Massachusetts Bay, a stake of great importance in
Acadia by reason of which they could by no means be indifferent
to the progress of events there. One thing deeply concerned them:
the growing importance of the French interest in the same fisheries
with the development of Louisbourg as not only a military but a
trading centre. By 1732 over two hundred ships belonging to Cape
Breton were concerned, it was asserted, in the catching of cod, in

[12] P.R.O., N.S., A. 25: 75.
[13] For the condition of Canso in 1721, its value and defences, see P.R.O., N.S., A. 14.
[14] Robert Ffytche to the Board of Trade, November 4, 1732, P.R.O., N.S., A.
21: 41. For New England and the cod fisheries see H. A. Innis, The Cod Fisheries,
pp. 160–7.
[15] P.R.O., N.S., A. 25: 8.

addition to some seven hundred shallops engaged in off-shore fishing.[16] Friction between the two groups could hardly be avoided. In this connection there developed among the New England men, who, of course, returned to their homes at the end of the season, an apprehension that the French as the result of the advantage of location would eventually drive them from their favoured banks and take possession of the island of Canso in spite of the presence of the garrison. As a result of this growing concern, repeated requests were lodged with His Majesty's government to construct suitable fortifications there as a counter-stroke, as it were, to those imposing ones surrounding Louisbourg. This was not without good reason. In fact, war had hardly been declared between England and France in 1744 when a sufficiently powerful French force was launched against Canso to overpower the weak garrison. Unless something of a heroic nature were now done, it seemed apparent that these fisheries had been lost to the enemy. It is therefore not surprising that Governor Shirley of Massachusetts Bay should find no difficulty in enlisting the enthusiastic support of New England to put an end to the encroachments of the French at Louisbourg and that he should be able to depend upon the masters and crews of sloops and schooners accustomed to resort to the strait to play their part in the successful campaign against that stronghold.

When the news spread among the Acadians that war had been declared, there was a searching of hearts. The authorities at Annapolis Royal had for many years sought to make the people " sensible of the difference there is between the Brittish and French Governments by Administering impartial justice to them and in all other respects treating them with lenity and humanity "; further, with the outbreak of hostilities they took measures to remove from the midst of the latter priests who were suspected of stirring up a spirit of rebellion; for example, the curé of Beaubassin Parish, charged with openly promoting the French interest, was ordered to leave the country.[17] To the credit of the inhabitants it may be said that the great majority remained passive, if not loyal. Nevertheless, in drawing up the final indictment against them in 1755, it was asserted that when the fighting missionary Le Loutre had moved in 1744 through

---

[16] P.R.O., N.S., A. 22: 7. For the Cape Breton fisheries in 1745 see H. A. Innis, op. cit., p. 168. In that year 500 Cape Breton shallops produced a total of 150,000 quintals of cod.

[17] Colonel Mascarene to the Board of Trade, October 17, 1748, P.R.O., N.S., A. 32: 240.

the settled districts with a band of some three hundred of his hostile Indians bent on attacking the English at Annapolis Royal and had camped within a quarter of a mile of the fort, not a single inhabitant gave intelligence of this, with the result that the Indians were able to fall upon and destroy the unwary English found outside the fort; it was also charged that not more than one inhabitant gave warning that same year of the approach of French forces under du Vivier by way of Minas for the purpose of surprising the fort, and that during the summer of 1746 the Acadians not only voluntarily supported some seventeen hundred Canadian soldiers within their districts but that many actually joined in the investment of the fort, making fascines and even carrying arms; finally, it was charged that when the New England troops, about five hundred in number, were camped at Grand Pré the following winter, the French, through information furnished by inhabitants of that place and led by some of them, were able to fall upon this force without warning and to kill or capture most of it.[18]

Mascarene, writing to the Board of Trade in 1748 at the end of hostilities, while conceding that most of the Acadians had been kept from joining the enemy in arms, nevertheless warned that they could not be relied upon and that should it so happen that the French forces succeeded in overrunning this region, it would certainly mean an accession to their armed strength of between four and five thousand men. To him the crux of the problem of winning their loyalty was, as was previously suggested, the presence of French priests, and he strongly recommended to His Majesty's government the sending of both French Protestant ministers and Catholic priests of non-French origin. He went on to declare:

> "I would be happy could this province be rid of these Inhabitants, especially [those] who have openly declared themselves for the Interest of the Enemy; but as this cannot be done at present without sending so many Inhabitants to the French settlements of the Islands of Cape Breton and St. Johns, now going to form themselves again around us, it is a perplexing Dilemma which requires speedy Instructions."[19]

---

[18] These charges were made by Chief Justice Belcher on July 25, 1755 before the Governor and Council of Nova Scotia (P.R.O., N.S., A. 58: 38–48). See, however, for the defence of the inhabitants before the Council, Nova Scotia Archives, I, 134–9; also A. G. Doughty, The Acadian Exiles, pp. 114–17, and J. B. Brebner, New England's Outpost, pp. 111–18, 224.

[19] Letter of October 17, 1748, P.R.O., N.S., A. 32: 231–43. On August 22 of

It must be recognized that after the Peace of Utrecht there gradu‑ally developed, especially in New France, a powerful irredentist movement for the purpose of redeeming Acadia. This had the sup‑port of clergy as well as laity. For example, the Bishop of Quebec, within whose diocese Acadia lay, wrote to the French Minister in 1747 in the midst of the war:

> "Je suis sur le point de m'adresser au gouvernement anglois pour obtenir permission d'envoyer des missionnaires à L'acadie, le bien de la religion, celuy du Service de la Majesté l'exigent."

In the same letter, in referring to the French victory at Grand Pré, he declared:

> "Je suis persuadé, Monsieur, que Messrs le général et intendant, vous rendront un Compte exact, et que pour animer de plus en plus les officiers vous récompenseres Messrs de Ramesay, Coulon et la Corne." [20]

In other words, here is a patriotic Frenchman — who happens also to be a servant of the Church — seeking to do his bit in the realiza‑tion of hopes of his fellow countrymen with respect to Acadia. It may be added that such an attitude on the part of the spiritual su‑perior of this people, in the light of all the influence that was exerted by him over their lives, did not make it any easier for them to live up to the spirit of even the modified oath of allegiance they had given to King George II.

It is of interest to note that in the course of the war the report was industriously circulated among the inhabitants that the English had determined either to destroy them or to remove them to other parts of His Majesty's dominions. While the question of their forcible re‑moval had certainly been agitated from time to time, the difficulties involved had been so effectively presented by Lieutenant Colonel Mascarene to Governor Shirley in 1745 that the latter had seen fit to issue the following year a circular letter which was buttressed by a royal proclamation setting at rest all these rumours and quieting

---

that year Mascarene received a communication from the Bishop of Quebec "desiring leave to send two or three Romish priests amongst the inhabitants, and signifying his intentions of coming into that province (with his leave) to confirm . . ." (Board of Trade Journal, 1741–9, pp. 368–9). As a result, the Governor, in great perplexity, not only wrote to the Bishop discouraging the plan for a visit but placed this delicate situa‑tion before the Board of Trade.

[20] The Bishop of Quebec to the Minister, July 10, 1747, Arch. Nat., Col., C^11 A. 89: 255.

the minds of the people. This drastic expedient in fact had to await the passing of another decade and the appearance of an even greater crisis in Anglo-French affairs in North America. In truth, these simple folk who chose to style themselves "neutrals," whose only desire was to live in obscurity, isolated from the trends of the age, were fated to be used by both England and France as pawns in the tremendous game of empire-building in North America, a game that continued to be played from the early part of the seventeenth century for over a hundred and fifty years. Nevertheless, when thinking in terms of the value of Acadia to the British Empire in the middle of the eighteenth century, it must be confessed that the presence there of these inhabitants was held to be much more of a liability than an asset. But to lose them to New France was not to be lightly contemplated, in face of the potential military threat that this accession of strength might bring — a threat especially to the preservation of sovereignty over the region itself. This was the perplexing situation confronting the government of Great Britain when in 1748 by the Treaty of Aix-la-Chapelle it was agreed, in the balancing of considerations, that Louisbourg should be returned to the French.

If, as suggested, it were unwise, especially on account of the restoration of near-by Louisbourg, to permit the departure of the Acadians to French territory, British statesmen reasoned that it now was imperative to take steps without delay to break up the racial and religious homogeneity of the Province by adding British and foreign Protestants in such numbers as ultimately would submerge these French-speaking Catholic neutrals. To such men as Governor Shirley of Massachusetts Bay and Captain Charles Morris, employed by him in Nova Scotia, it was a matter of vital importance that in bringing in loyal Protestants these should be planted in juxtaposition to the French settlements, so that there would take place

> "Consequently an Intercourse of Trade and Intermarriages, whereby in Time they will come to have one common Interest & mutually send out Colonies to settle the Inland Country." [21]

A happy outcome Shirley thought might be promoted by compelling the inhabitants to hold their lands by knight service, if not prohibited by the terms of the capitulation, "for the sake of drawing with it to

---

[21] These words are from Captain Morris's "Observations upon His Survey of the Upper Part of the Bay of Fundy and Plan for English Settlers," February 18, 1749 (P.R.O., N.S., A. 33: 160–71).

the King, the marriage of their sons and Daughters which might go far toward promoting their Intermarrying with Protestants and re-forming their families to that Religion." [22] Further, not only was it felt that a real stronghold must at last be built on the eastern coast of the peninsula powerful enough to neutralize the influence that Louisbourg had exerted upon Acadian affairs in both peace and war, but Shirley thought that it was of vital importance that another, capable of holding twelve hundred soldiers, should be constructed upon the Isthmus of Chignecto, to be "the Key to the whole Penin-sula," which, "by lying on the back of all the settlements, would countenance & promote the growth of the Protestant ones & Keep those of the French in due subjection." [23]

The necessity for the immediate construction of a fort upon the isthmus, in fact, was daily impressed upon those guiding the affairs of the Province — in the light especially of the attitude of the au-thorities in Quebec with respect to the boundaries between New France and Acadia. For it was clear that Governor General de la Galissonière took the position that not only the inhabitants of the St. John River region and those living about Beaubassin were under the protection of the King of France but even those in the very heart of the old Acadian settlements to the southward of Minas Basin. Early in the year 1749 he protested vigorously against the claims of the commander at Annapolis Royal to receive the submission of the Abenaki Indians on the St. John and his efforts to bring back the inhabitants of Beaubassin to loyalty to the Crown as well as against his expulsion of a French missionary from the district of Minas and the burning of the homes of two of the inhabitants living in this region who had vigorously supported the French cause. [24]

In preparation for the new order of things, Shirley, who played a dominating role in Acadian affairs at this juncture, [25] arranged for a survey of vacant lands located in the neighbourhood of the Acadian settlements. It was found that abundant suitable uplands existed as yet unappropriated, but that the salt marshes, considered to be so

---

[22] Shirley to the Duke of Bedford, March 3, 1748/9, P.R.O., N.S., A. 33: 198–9.

[23] Governor Shirley to the Duke of Bedford, February 18, 1748/9, P.R.O., N.S., A. 33: 148–9.

[24] Galissonière to Mascarene, January 15, 1749, P.R.O., N.S., A. 33: 18–19.

[25] This role is very carefully developed in J. B. Brebner's Now England's Outpost in his chapter on "The Puritan Crusade"; see also my own essay: "Acadia and the Be-ginnings of Modern British Imperialism," in Essays in Modern English History in Honor of Wilbur Cortez Abbott (1941), particularly from p. 179 to p. 186.

vital for the success of those engaged in raising cattle and in general farming, had already been appropriated and diked off by the French inhabitants. Only by bringing about a division of these marshes between the old and new settlers could the latter succeed in establishing themselves successfully in these regions, it was felt. But could this be done without serious difficulties? Shirley thought that the solution of the problem lay in a rigid examination of land titles. Acting Governor Mascarene, doubtless fully aware of the hazards involved in seeking to scatter Protestants among the French inhabitants, does not seem to have been enthusiastic over this plan but, to "counterbalance the Deadweight of these French inhabitants," preferred to recommend planting, at least at first, British families about the eastern coast where few Acadians lived; and this was the policy finally adopted by His Majesty's government.

In setting the new colonization enterprise in motion and watching over it during the period of its infancy, the Board of Trade, under the presidency of the Earl of Halifax, was indefatigable. It also moved rapidly. By the spring of 1749 it had received the applications of some three thousand British subjects to go to Acadia; transports had also been arranged for; [26] and by the middle of May about fourteen hundred set sail for America.[27] To lead them the Honourable

---

[26] Board of Trade to the Duke of Bedford, April 20, 1749, P.R.O., N.S., A. 34: 28–9.

[27] It may be of interest to follow briefly the steps taken by the Board of Trade to ensure the success of this enterprise. Early in March 1749 it was proposed to send three thousand Protestants to the Province. On March 22 a contract was entered into with Chauncey Townshend, a London merchant, to provide subsistence for this number. Thereupon it was agreed that the contractor should furnish to each settler for the passage and for one year thereafter each week five pounds of bread or flour, three pounds of beef, one-fourth pound of butter, one pint of peas, one-fourth pint of vinegar, one-fourth pint of oatmeal, one-half pint of rum, and one-half pint of molasses, for which he would be entitled to receive fourpence for each settler for each day's subsistence plus three and one-half pence a week per person for the rum and molasses. Somewhat later — in view of the uneasiness of those who had agreed to go lest they be put on short rations — it was ordered that for the first three months an allowance of provisions equal to ninepence a day should be made for each settler.

The health of the prospective colonists during the voyage was also given due attention. The Board arrived at the opinion that each ship to be chartered for the purpose should be furnished with "Sutton's Air Pipes." On April 5, however, it was recommended that of the twelve ships hired for the voyage but eight should be furnished with the pipes, and the others with ventilators. A conference was also held with the Surgeon General as to other means of keeping the people in good physical condition; in this connection it was finally recommended that medicines such as were used in the hospitals of Flanders should be sent out with them. As to their spiritual welfare, the Society for the Propagation of the Gospel in Foreign Parts came forward with an offer to pay to six missionary clergymen who would accompany them seventy pounds a year,

Edward Cornwallis was commissioned Captain General and Governor in Chief of Nova Scotia, a man in most respects admirably fitted to assume so great a responsibility. The new Governor upon his arrival on the eastern coast on June 22 of that year was happy to find the French inhabitants at Merligueche Bay far from hostile. They even declared that "they always lookt upon themselves as English subjects . . . and shewed me unfeigned joy to hear of the new settlement." [28] He was also able to report that the Indians were likewise very peaceable and that many had come to the new settlement with their chiefs — to all of whom he had given tokens of goodwill with promises of friendship and protection, as well as presents, as soon as they had agreed in their tribes to enter into a treaty and to exchange their French commissions for those in His Majesty's name. [29] Those factors for the success of the great enterprise involved in the attitude of the French inhabitants and the Indians toward the new settlement seemed, therefore, to be favourable.

Steps were immediately taken to select a site for the new town and stronghold. This was done with great care [30] and thereupon the work of clearing the land and erecting habitations and defences was speeded to the extent that conditions would permit. Unfortunately, the number of industrious, active men proper to establish a new settlement was very small — not more than three hundred out of the total. The rest Cornwallis described as " poor, idle, worthless vagabonds that embraced the opportunity to get provisions for one year without labour, & sailors that only wanted a passage to New England." " Many," he lamented, " have come as into a hospital to be cured "; numbers he found were quite destitute, without shoes, stockings, or shirts. [31] All these unfortunates and incompetents were a serious liability and a brake on enterprising action. The Governor,

---

"the highest salary allowed to any missionary employed by the Society," and fifteen pounds a year to each of six schoolmasters (Board of Trade *Journal*, 1741–9, pp. 390–449).

As to the numbers sent to Nova Scotia after 1749 and before 1753: in 1750 there were sent some 514 British subjects and 322 foreign Protestants; in 1751, 1,004 foreign Protestants; in 1752, 1,135 British subjects. These with the 1,400 sent in 1749 total 4,375. Up to January 1, 1753 the cost of the enterprise totalled £336,707 2s. 10d. These figures were laid before the French ministry and are to be found in Affaires Étrangères, Mémoires et Documents, 10: 48–58.

[28] Cornwallis to Board of Trade, June 22, 1749, P.R.O., N.S., A. 34: 110.

[29] Cornwallis to the Duke of Bedford, July 23, 1749, P.R.O., N.S., A. 34: 195.

[30] A shift was made in the site selected by the engineer Durel (P.R.O., N.S., A. 34: 193–4).

[31] Cornwallis to the Board of Trade, July 24, 1749, P.R.O., N.S., A. 34: 202.

nevertheless, by utilizing the labour of all present, soldiers as well as civilians, soon had the satisfaction of seeing the substantial beginnings of the future city of Halifax.

In framing Cornwallis's instructions the government clearly indicated that the time had at last arrived when the uncertainty regarding the status of the French Acadians must be removed for all time. By the Forty-first Instruction he was called upon,

> "as soon as seemed proper after his arrival, to issue a declaration in his Majesty's name setting forth that although sensible that many indulgences had been shown to them by the King's predecessors in allowing them the free exercise of their religion and the quiet possession of their lands, these had not met with a dutiful return but on the contrary many of them had openly abetted or privately assisted the enemy with quarters, provisions, and intelligence and by concealing its designs from the commander of the province; yet, in hopes of inducing them to become true and loyal subjects, his Majesty was pleased to declare that they should continue the free exercise of their religion, as far as the laws of Great Britain shall permit, and the peaceable possession of their lands, provided, that within three months from the date of said declaration, or at such time as the Governor should think proper, they would take the oaths of allegiance provided by the laws of the Kingdom and likewise behave themselves as good subjects, giving all possible assistance to such persons as his Majesty shall think proper to settle within the province."

Further, in anticipation that difficulties might be encountered in securing oaths from all the Acadians, the Forty-second Instruction provided that

> "if any of the said French Inhabitants should, notwithstanding the Encouragement given them to become good subjects to us, be desirous of removing out of Our Government, you are to take particular care as on you lies that they do no Damage, before such their Removal, to their respective Houses and Plantations." [32]

In this connection the Governor was called upon to observe that the time allowed to the inhabitants by the Treaty of Utrecht for removing their effects to any part of the French possessions in America had long since lapsed.

In view of the extreme aggressiveness of the authorities of New France with respect to what the British felt were purely Acadian af-

---

[32] For these instructions see P.R.O., N.S., E. 34: 29.

fairs, and especially their disposition to interest themselves in the concerns of the inhabitants as though the latter were in reality French subjects, Cornwallis determined not only to summon to Chibuctou Bay at the earliest practicable moment all their deputies to make clear His Majesty's pleasure, but also to send two companies of soldiers to Minas, where the latter were to construct barracks, as well as a sloop to patrol the Basin. It was hoped thereby that all correspondence with the French of Canada would be terminated on the part of the Acadians and further that should any of the latter, in spite of these precautions, " be decoyed " to the St. Lawrence, to Louisbourg, or to Isle St. Jean, it would be possible to prevent their carrying off their effects. " I think 'tis necessary," he declared, " to shew them that 'tis in our power to master them or to protect them." [33]

In response to this determined attitude on the part of the British authorities, on August 1 deputies from the French districts arrived at Halifax and presented to Cornwallis a memorial which they avowed represented the sentiments of all. In this they requested the free and public exercise of their religion, with missionaries as usual sent from France, and an entire exemption from bearing arms. As to the last request, they affirmed that should they take the oaths of fidelity without reservation, the Indians would massacre them all.

The Governor, in reply, readily agreed to the free exercise of their religion, provided that they would be faithful subjects of the King and that no priest would attempt to officiate without having first obtained permission and taken the oath of fidelity to the King. As to the request for exemption from bearing arms, however, he declared that by order of the King no subject enjoying the privileges of his government and possessed of a dwelling and land within the Province could be released from an entire fidelity to him nor from the natural obligation of defending himself, his home, his lands, and his government. Forthwith, he proclaimed in the name of His Majesty, George II, that before October 26 every inhabitant was expected to take the oath of fidelity.[34]

Upon returning to the settlements the deputies laid the royal declaration before the inhabitants. The latter, after adequate deliberation, came to the decision not to take the new oath. Again they united in a petition to Cornwallis, which emphasized not only the

---

[33] Cornwallis to the Duke of Bedford, July 23, 1749, and also the same to the Board of Trade, July 24, 1749, P.R.O., N.S., A. 34: 189–227.

[34] See P.R.O., N.S., A. 34: 228–31.

unhappy consequences that they would have to face on the part of the Indians should they do so but also that it would be contrary to the earlier oath that they had taken, thus annulling the privileges that they enjoyed by that oath; further, they affirmed that if, notwithstanding their humble representations, His Excellency was still determined to exact this oath from them, they would prefer to leave the country rather than submit, and therefore requested that they be allowed the period of a year within which to depart with their movable effects, conformable to the Treaty of Utrecht.[35]

Early in September Cornwallis replied to this. Among other things he charged that they evidently thought themselves independent of all government; and then proceeded to remind them that since the end of the year stipulated by the Treaty of Utrecht for the evacuation of the country those who had chosen to remain from that time on became subjects of the King of Great Britain as that treaty had stipulated and as the King of France had agreed. Further, he made clear that if General Philipps had permitted them to make a reservation in the oath, he had not done his duty and even so this oath had in no wise diminished their obligations to act always under all circumstances as a subject should act according to the laws of his God and King.[36]

It is possible that had the hope of seeing Acadia once again reunited to the French Empire been quite dissipated from the thoughts of loyal Frenchmen, the inhabitants left to themselves, especially after the lapse of so long a period of time since the loss of their French nationality, which few of the some ten thousand in 1749 had ever enjoyed, would never have seen fit now to have made a fundamental issue of the oath — so contented were they in most, if not all, respects with their general situation. But it is important not to lose sight of the fact, previously stressed, that the regaining of the Province had long been a major policy of the French monarchy and, in spite of the tentative oath of loyalty earlier taken to King George, the inhabitants were fully expected to do their part in supporting a program with this definite objective in mind now launched on the borders of the peninsula. That this project was a motivating force in Canada is made abundantly clear. Governor General de la Galissonière, in writing from Quebec to the French Minister the latter part of July of the year under consideration, declared, when referring to the British

---

[35] For this petition see Arch. Nat., Col., C[11] A. 87: 369.
[36] Arch. Nat., Col., C[11] A. 87: 371.

claims to lands from the St. Lawrence to Beaubassin and from Canso to Gaspé, that if this territory were abandoned to England it would be necessary to renounce all communication by land from Canada to Isle Royale and to Acadia and " every means of support‹ ing the one and retaking the other." [37] He declared further that it would deprive almost all the Acadians of every hope of taking refuge upon French lands and by this abandonment would drive them to despair. In stressing the contribution that these people had been making in supporting the interests of the French King, he asserted that Louisbourg was absolutely dependent upon them for subsistence.[38]

In truth, from the time of the erection of the fortifications at Louisbourg and the arrival of a French garrison, that stronghold had been largely sustained with the meat, grain, and other supplies that came in an endless stream from the region of Minas Basin and the Bay of Chignecto. British authorities were not unaware of it and quite naturally were determined at last to put an end to an intercourse that boded no possible good for the Empire. It seemed moreover essential now to reserve all available food produced within the Province for the support of the thousands of new settlers coming to Nova Scotia, who would not be in a position for some time to come to provide for their own needs. Cornwallis was, therefore, directed by his original instructions to issue a proclamation forbidding all persons, under a severe penalty, to export out of the Province to any French settlement whatsoever any corn, cattle, or other kind of provisions without express permission from his own hand.[39] This he now proceeded to do. There was, of course, no design to destroy by this measure the market of the Acadians, but to transfer it from Louisbourg to Chibuctou Bay.

As soon as the design on the part of the British to cut off all intercourse between the Acadians and the Canadians became apparent, the authorities of New France, not only because the labour of these inhabitants was most vital to the maintenance of Louisbourg, but for many other reasons that are easily understood, now determined to employ every possible means that would place the Acadians be-

---

[37] The French is " et à tout Moïen de secourir l'une et de reprendre l'autre " (Arch. Nat., Col., C¹¹ A. 93: 133).

[38] His words are: " enfin ils empêcheront la communication de l'Acadie avec Louisbourg dont la subsistance dependra absolument d'eux" (ibid.).

[39] This was Instruction No. 46 (P.R.O., N.S., E. 34: 32).

yond British control while arousing in them at the same time a spirit of resistance. Not only were those who had settled outside the peninsula about Chignecto Bay forbidden to recognize the authority of the Governor at Halifax, but a force under an experienced officer, M. de la Corne, was sent into this region. Further, steps were taken to bring about a migration of those settled in the interior of the peninsula.[40] In this connection one of the most effective of all instrumentalities employed by the French for the moulding of the Acadian will to their desires was the Indian tribes living in and about Acadia who could easily be turned loose upon the inhabitants at any moment should the latter seem disposed to turn their backs upon their French brethren and fellow Catholics.[41] Closely related to this was the position assumed by some of the missionary priests, especially Abbé Jean Louis Le Loutre. He, in the enjoyment of a pension of eight hundred livres from the Crown of France, had in 1738 established an Indian mission at Shubenacadie in the very heart of Acadia; there he came to exercise an unlimited influence over the Micmac and their allies, whom he gathered together to the number of three or four hundred twice a year to celebrate Mass.[42] His zeal not only for his Church but for the French Crown knew no bounds and his great dream was to bring about the restoration of Acadia.[43]

The Abbé had been exceedingly active in the late war and in this connection was accused by the English at Annapolis Royal, as was previously stated, of conducting his savages against them. However, in the midst of hostilities he had sailed to France to report to his superiors and to seek additional aid for the reconquest of Acadia; after two unsuccessful attempts he had returned to the Province by way of Louisbourg during the summer of 1749. There, it is to be noted, he met M. Bigot, the newly appointed Intendant of New France, who had been sent to Isle Royale, where he had previously acted as the Commissaire Ordonnateur, to aid in re-establishing the

---

[40] This is well illustrated from one angle by the financial support which the Quebec authorities gave to M. Gautier for the purpose of engaging his fellow Acadians to retire to either Isle St. Jean or Isle Royale. See M. Bigot to the Minister, September 30 and October 11, 1749, Arch. Nat., Col., C11 A. 93: 253, 283.

[41] The writer of the " Description de l'Acadie avec le nom des paroisses et le nombre des habitants " in the year 1746 estimated the number of Acadian Indians at one thousand (Arch. Nat., Col., C11 A. 87: 363).

[42] Ibid. See also the letter of the Minister to Count Raymond of July 21, 1752, Arch. Nat., Col., B. 95: 265–8.

[43] For example, see the restraining letters to Le Loutre from Versailles of March 24, 1749 and of August 27, 1751 (Arch. Nat., Col., B. 90: 291–2; 93: 224–5).

French regime with the departure of the English. The two, after hearing reports to the effect that both the Indians and the Acadians were freely resorting to the new settlement of Chibuctou to receive presents and to establish friendly relations with the English, now came to the determination that, whatever be the cost, they would break this alliance.[44] Bigot thereupon promised the priest arms, munitions, food, and clothing — all to be sent from Quebec with this specific purpose in mind. These particular military supplies were, therefore, consigned directly to him and not to any of the French commandants along the Acadian border-lands. He assumed the fullest responsibility not only for the incitement of the Indians and subsequently of the Acadians against the English in time of peace, but for placing in their hands these weapons for the waging of war.[45] In the light of this fact, it is in no way surprising that his reappearance in the Province — without, of course, securing the consent of Governor Cornwallis — coincided with the beginning of hostilities on the part of the hitherto friendly natives.

Well knowing Le Loutre's record of hostility, Cornwallis, as soon as he was apprised of his movements, protested to Desherbiers, commandant at Louisbourg, against his activity within Acadia, but was most politely informed by that estimable gentleman that he himself was in no way responsible for the conduct of the priest and could not even order him to return to Isle Royale since Le Loutre was under the authority of the Governor of New France and had been sent to his mission by the King of France himself, who would not, he was very sure, have given him any orders to do that which he had been accused of doing.[46] Nevertheless, the Micmac of Le Loutre's own

---

[44] In a letter to the Minister dated October 18, 1750, Bigot makes clear this understanding with Abbé Le Loutre. He writes:

"*Lorsque J'y arrivay l'après que les Sauvages et L'accadie avoient esté recevoir des présents à Chibouctou et qu'ils estoient amis des Anglais, nous convainmes, M. Le Loutre et moy qu'il faloit a quelque prix que ce fut, rompre cette alliance. Et je pris sur moy de lui promettre armes, munitions, virres et étoffes de Quebec*" (Arch. Nat., Col., C¹¹ A. 95: 51).

[45] For an invoice of one of the consignments to Le Loutre from Bigot sent on the French ship *London* see Mémoires et Documents, Amérique, 9. I: 245–9.

[46] Desherbiers to Cornwallis, October 15, 1749, P.R.O., N.S., A. 35: 79–84. There is ample proof of the very great influence of Le Loutre in France. Writing in May 1754, the Minister of the Marine declared: "*L'abbé Le Loutre a rendu constamment les services les plus importants à religion et à l'état*"; in June he writes: "*Je ne saurois trop vous representer combien il seroit important de pouvoir donner satisfaction à ce missionnaire indépendamment des services considérables qu'il rend depuis plusieurs années à l'État et à la Religion*" (Arch. Nat., Col., B. 100: 56, 83).

mission were the first placed in motion to proceed against the English settlements and also, ominously enough, to hover about the Acadians breathing out dire threats as to their fate should they dare to depart from their neutrality and submit to the demands of the Halifax authorities. Before beginning actual hostilities, however, these Indians sent to Governor Cornwallis a declaration of war in faultless French and employing the familiar form of address, classic in eloquence. Translated into English, it is as follows:

> " Sire, the place where thou art, the place where thou lodgest, the place where thou art making a fortification . . . this place belongeth to me. I am come from this ground, as the grass; a native, I was born here, from father to son; this place is my land, I swear; it is God who hath given me it to be my country for ever.
>
> " I am going to lay bare first, all that my heart thinketh toward thee, because the works that thou art carrying on at Chebuctoak cannot but give me strongly matter for reflection. My King and thy King hath distributed the lands between them. . . . But for myself I can make no alliance or peace with thee. Show thou me where I, native to this land, can retire! Thou driveth me, thou! Show me therefore where thou wilt that I should seek refuge! . . . I am coming to see thee incessantly, yea, surely, I shall see thee and I hope that this that I will hear from thee will move a little the heart! " [47]

The Micmac thereupon carried the war belt first to the St. John River Indians, who had previously sent a delegation to Halifax for the purpose of establishing peace and had even accepted English commissions and barrets,[48] and then to Canada to engage not only the Canadian Indians but the French government to aid them in blotting out the English settlement at Chibuctou Bay.

While Governor La Jonquière, successor to Galissonière, upon receiving the war delegation, was obliged to declare to the Indians

---

[47] The Micmac Indians to Cornwallis, September 23, 1749, P.R.O., N.S., A. 35: 69–71.

[48] It should be noted in this connection that M. Germain, the French missionary to the St. John Indians, with a show of real solicitousness wrote to Captain How at Annapolis, with whom he was acquainted, warning him that the Micmac warriors had come with the war belt and he feared that his Indians could not be kept from supporting their brothers (letter of November 18, 1749, P.R.O., N.S., A. 35: 147). Germain, it may be added, had previously acted as curé at Annapolis before taking up his work with the Abnaki. When the latter threw in their lot with the Micmac they were given every encouragement by their priest, who thereupon became one of Le Loutre's aides in driving the Acadians into resistance to the English.

that France was at peace with England and therefore could not join in a military enterprise against that power, nevertheless Bigot, to fulfil his part of the secret agreement with Le Loutre, promptly sent to Shediac on the frontier of the Acadian peninsula — where a French detachment had now been posted — guns and other military supplies not only for the Indians but for those Acadians who could be persuaded to take up arms against the English. As the step taken by the Intendant was one fraught with great danger, one that easily might lead to open hostilities between Great Britain and France, he took care to inform the French Minister that this war material had been sent " under pretext of engaging in the fur trade." [49] Further, food supplies for those Indians who had taken the war path were secured by Le Loutre from M. Bonaventure, commandant of the French garrison on Isle St. Jean.[50] " The French," complained Corn-wallis with good reason on September 11, " are certainly doing everything in their power to excite the Indians to molest us. I heard t'other day from an officer (a settler) at Minas, that they are all at Cobequid with Leutre who is sent with French presents." [51]

Everything indeed now pointed to the development of a new and very grave crisis in the affairs of Acadia. Many of the inhabitants themselves, encouraged by most of their priests — who had no thought as good Frenchmen of taking an oath of fidelity to the King of Great Britain and of ignoring the claims of their superior, the Bishop of Quebec, as Cornwallis had insisted they should do — now proceeded to appeal to Louis XV of France to interpose in their behalf that they might be allowed to remain in the enjoyment of their special exemptions and, if this were impossible, to grant to them concessions of lands along the borders of Acadia.[52] In appealing to the Governor General of New France some one hundred and twenty-five settlers of Annapolis Royal went even farther in laying bare their true sentiments in a memorial to him. They declared that they had taken the resolution to approach the French since the Lord had not permitted their compatriots to come to them, and then affirmed:

---

[49] His words were: " *J'envoie . . . fusils et autres munitions tant pour eux* [that is, the Indians] *que pour les Acadiens qui voudraient prendre les armes avec eux et le tout n'est envoyé que sous prétexte de traiter avec les sauvages leurs pelleteries* " (letter of September 30, 1749, Arch. Nat., Col., C¹¹ A. 93: 253).

[50] Bigot to the Minister, October 11, 1749, Arch. Nat., Col., C¹¹ A. 93: 283.

[51] Cornwallis to the Board of Trade, P.R.O., N. S., A. 35: 47.

[52] This appeal was dated October 12, 1749 (Arch. Nat., Col., C¹¹ A. 87: 367).

"It is well known how long we maintained ourselves here without aid before submitting ourselves to their domination, few in numbers as we are. One need only read the history of Father Charlevoix to know how we have resisted the instances and even the violence to compel us to take the oath and that we took it only after the Governor of Louisbourg had told us that it was necessary to seek to accommodate ourselves with these people . . . and only then when there had been separated from it the obligation to take up arms against our dear French brethren, from whom we no longer desire to be separated." [53]

They thereupon sought the privilege of a retreat on some stream below the St. Lawrence suitable for husbandmen and fishermen where they could live " as good Catholics and faithful and obedient subjects of our King of France."

Their attitude was not unknown to the English. " You have a secret, I fear, an inveterate Enemy preying upon your Bowels, masked, but rotten at bottom whom no lenity can please nor anything but severity or greater power can bring . . . to Duty and Allegiance," wrote Cornwallis pessimistically in October to the Board of Trade in emphasizing the strange conduct of the Acadians.[54]

The occupation of frontier Acadian settlements by French troops, the beginning of the Indian raiding, and the stubborn resistance of the French inhabitants to taking an unqualified oath of loyalty to the Crown, all combined, therefore, to speed the preparations for the defence of the Province. By the middle of October some three hundred houses had been completed at Halifax together with two picketed forts and a barricade that encircled the town; by December the number of houses ready for occupancy had increased to four hundred, and two additional forts had been built. Further, the land about the town, at least that within musket range of the road, had been cleared and a company of rangers employed to scour the woods in search of hostile red men. The settlers at Halifax, therefore, by the beginning of winter were fairly comfortable and secure.[55] A military post, Fort Edward, likewise was established at Minas in the heart of the Acadian settlements to support that of Annapolis Royal, and two armed sloops were dispatched to the Bay of Fundy for the purpose of cutting off communication between the Acadians and the French. Finally, a road twenty feet in width was cut through

[53] *Requête des habitans du Port Royal à M. Jonquière*, Arch. Nat., Col., C¹¹ A. 87: 373.
[54] Letter of October 17, 1749, P.R.O., N.S., A. 35: 111–12.
[55] For a description of Halifax at this period see P.R.O., N.S., A. 36: 5–8.

the woods from Halifax to Minas Bay, and bridges over the streams erected so as to facilitate communication between the two otherwise detached regions. All these precautions, however, did not prevent occasional deadly forays on the part of the Micmac, who were joined by the Abnaki of St. John River as well as by groups from the Canadian tribes such as the Hurons. These Indians, moreover, under the leadership of the redoubtable Le Loutre, in the beginning of the winter served notice upon the inhabitants of Minas and of Piziquid that upon pain of death for refusal they were to take their arms and march to Grand Pré to give them assistance. " Sire, it is to your own interest and that of God that brings us to drive the English from these parts. You see your missionaries driven out, your churches abandoned, your religion snuffed out, it is God that sends you help," ran the summons.[56]

Anticipating a general movement of the Indians as soon as the ground was covered with snow, and feeling under necessity to take measures to prevent the inhabitants about the Bay of Fundy from going over in a body to the side of " the enemy," Cornwallis early in January determined to make an unexpected descent upon the Acadian settlement of Chignecto, where Le Loutre had gathered the warring tribes. This movement, according to instructions given to Captain Cobb, was largely for the purpose of seizing this fighting priest, described as " the Author and Adviser of all the Disturbances the Indians have made in the Province." [57] He was also to secure as many as possible of the hostile Indians as well as of those inhabitants who through Le Loutre's instigation had been guilty of harbouring and assisting the savages. However, as the result of undue publicity given to the enterprise in Boston, where Cobb had gone to recruit men, it seemed inadvisable to prosecute it. Nevertheless, Cornwallis was not mistaken as to the tremendous influence exerted by Le Loutre in Acadian affairs, the weight of which was also fully recognized at Quebec. " One thing is sure," declared Bigot in a letter to the French Minister, " without this missionary who has made the Acadians believe whatever he would and has promised them much, they would be very tranquil and so would the English be at Chibouctou and on very good terms with the Indians." [58]

<hr/>

[56] " Orders by the Savages to the French Inhabitants," December 12, 1749. P.R.O., N.S., A. 35: 183–4.

[57] For these instructions see P.R.O., N.S., A. 36: 15–16.

[58] " *Il est sûr que sans ce missionâire qui a fait croire aux accadiens ce qu'il a voulu et qui leur a promis beaucoup, ils seroient très tranquiles et que les Anglois feroient de même*

The alarming state of affairs demanded most prompt and decisive action on the part of the English unless they were willing to resign to their rivals all the Province outside of the neighbourhood of Halifax. As early as December 1749 Cornwallis had urgently requested reinforcements from England. Later, upon receiving notification of his appointment as colonel of a regiment stationed in Newfoundland, he ordered two of its companies to join him in Nova Scotia. In April, without waiting for aid to arrive from England, in the hope of being able to put an end to the constant interference of the French with the Acadians, he sent Major Lawrence with a force of four hundred men, a third of whom were regular soldiers, to Minas with orders to sail thence to the village of Beaubassin, which was to be occupied and fortified with a blockhouse. However, upon approaching the village, consisting of some one hundred and forty dwellings on the south bank of the Missaquash, it was given to the flames by Le Loutre's Indians, the priest himself, it was asserted, applying the torch to the parish church.[59]

Although Lawrence succeeded in making a landing not far from the ruins of Beaubassin, he now found himself confronted not only by a large body of Indians protected behind the dikes, but by a greatly superior force of French and Canadian troops occupying a strategic position under the command of La Corne, supported by not less than a thousand hostile Acadians who had been led by Le Loutre to desert their homes. With these decisive advantages the Frenchman coolly informed the British officer that all the region to the north of the Missaquash River belonged to France and that he would defend it from invasion. The situation portended nothing but disaster should the British troops attempt to advance. Lawrence, therefore, after demanding why it was that the town had been burnt although acknowledged to be on English soil even by La Corne himself, and also the whereabouts of "the villain Le Loutre," was obliged to content himself with an evasive reply and thereupon withdrew his soldiers to the waiting ships.[60]

Cornwallis in reporting on the dangerous situation at Chignecto to the home government declared that La Corne's strength was not less than twenty-five hundred armed men including regular troops,

à Chibouctou et très amis des sauvages. . . ." This letter is dated October 18, 1750 (Arch. Nat., Col., C[11] A. 96: 51).

[59] Canada and Its Provinces, XIII, 91–2.

[60] For Major Lawrence's "Journal of Proceedings," see P.R.O., N.S., A. 36: 250–75.

Canadians, Acadians, and Indians. He further stated that the French commandant and Le Loutre had brought over many of the inhabitants as the result of numberless messages and threats. Of those still remaining in Acadia, he affirmed that "not one of them would sow the land; they make no scruple to declare that this proceeding is entirely against their inclination but that La Corne and Loutre threaten them with a general massacre by the savages if they remain in the Province." [61] It can be well understood that the Governor was very much relieved when he received word in June that a regiment from Ireland was proceeding to Nova Scotia. In the same letter he was specifically instructed to occupy Chignecto or some other suitable place in the region of Beaubassin.

By September preparations for the second movement up the Bay of Fundy were complete. It was then decided for strategic purposes to occupy only that region conceded to the English by the French commandant. On the 17th a fleet of seventeen sail appeared off Beaubassin, where a body of Indians and Acadians, protected behind an entrenchment which Le Loutre — according to the French officer, Sieur de la Vallière — had had them make, offered rather feeble resistance before retreating, in spite of the efforts of the French priests Germain and Laterue to urge them to hold their ground. [62] The French troops, although in evidence, were careful not to become engaged in the fighting.

Lawrence, having gained a foothold, chose a permanent site for the fort on the south bank of the Missaquash, not far from the present city of Amherst, [63] and, in spite of continual harassment on the part of the hostile Indians, the Acadians, and also disguised Canadians, was able to occupy it by the beginning of October. Previous to this the enemy had set fire to all the houses and barns in the region round about, which made the garrison absolutely dependent upon supplies coming by water. The French encamped on the elevation of Beauséjour to the north of the Missaquash had already begun the construction of a strong fort of five bastions. Thus the rivals now faced one another at Beaubassin. [64]

---

[61] Letter of May 1, 1750, P.R.O., N.S., A. 37: 5–7.

[62] See de la Vallière's "Journal de ce qui s'est passé à Chienetou" (Chignecto) (Arch. Nat., Col., C¹¹ A. 87: 376).

[63] The site of Fort Lawrence is marked by a monument.

[64] In this connection the student should consult The Forts of Chignecto by Dr. John C. Webster.

*A New Map of Nova Scotia and Cape Britain, with adjacent parts of New England
and Canada,* 1755.

(From Jefferys's *History of French Dominion in North and South America,* 1760.)

The Plan of the Neck of the Peninsula of Acadia showing its
fortifications in 1755. (From *Mémoires sur le Canada, 1749-1760.*)

With respect to these hostilities carried on in time of peace it may be pointed out that upon receipt of the news that the English had secured a footing in the region of Chignecto, Governor General La Jonquière sent orders to de St. Ours, commanding at the French fort, to arm all the inhabitants and to co-operate with Le Loutre in engaging the Indians to harass the English continuously and to do everything possible under the circumstances to compel them to abandon their position.[65] In connection with this activity, Governor Cornwallis asserted that he possessed the information that La Jonquière, acting through Le Loutre, gave to the Indians a reward for every prisoner or for every head or scalp secured within Acadia.[66]

As for the inhabitants themselves, who, as the result of the various pressures brought to bear upon them, had been led, many of them doubtless most reluctantly, to leave their habitations and to retire to the north and west of the bay, their lack of almost every comfort and some of the necessities of life soon brought about in many of them a determination to voice their discontent. La Corne, writing at this juncture to La Jonquière, declared that those from three of the Acadian settlements begged him to permit them to return to their homes and that they were joined by those from three others, including even the inhabitants from Beaubassin, in representing their sad situation and dilemma. To encourage them the Governor General sent word from Quebec that he would not abandon them and that — supposing it should happen, contrary to the rights of the King of France, that their lands were declared to be under the dominion of the King of Great Britain — they would be well received upon other lands of his and their King.[67] However, there was to be no such thing as "neutrality" permitted on the part of any person dwelling on French soil, much as this had been previously encouraged among the Acadians by the authorities of New France. Therefore when La Jonquière was informed by Le Loutre that a refugee inhabitant had refused the oath of fidelity to His Most Christian Majesty, he immediately issued an *ordonnance* to the effect that all who within eight days after its publication had not taken the oath and had not been

---

[65] La Jonquière to the Minister, October 3, 1750, Arch. Nat., Col., C[11] A. 95: 267.

[66] Cornwallis to the Duke of Bedford, June 24, 1751, P.R.O., N.S., A. 42: 199.

[67] La Jonquière to the Minister, October 3, 1750, Arch. Nat., Col., C[11] A. 95: 267. This, of course, indicates that La Jonquière took the position that France had claims on lands lying well within the peninsula in counter-distinction to the position assumed by de la Galissonière in 1749 that France had only ceded the peninsula to Great Britain.

embodied in the militia companies would be branded as rebels and as such chased from the lands they were occupying.[68]

During the fall of 1750 and the following spring the British garrison within the fort south of the Missaquash, which had received the name Fort Lawrence, had to face repeated attempts to dislodge it. One incident that especially embittered the English was the treacherous killing of Captain How from ambush by Indians and Acadians when he came from the fort to the river to meet a French officer sent by La Corne with a flag of truce. How, who had an intimate acquaintance with many of the Acadians now in arms, had made himself especially obnoxious to those who were irreconcilable enemies of the English by reason of his constant efforts to persuade the inhabitants to return to their old homes.[69]

Up to the end of June 1751, it may be said, the French had the upper hand in the region of Beaubassin, keeping the British within their fort and on the defensive. This was true in spite of the fact that French regular troops were not employed, although many Canadians disguised as Indians assisted in the sporadic raiding of the fort. However, the problem of providing food for so many concentrated about Fort Beauséjour became so serious as the result of a great shortage of grain in Canada and also because of the constant watchfulness of the British armed sloops in the Bay of Fundy and even in the Gulf of St. Lawrence — preventing as they did the flow of provisions to the French from the interior of the peninsula and even from Canada — that it at last seemed imperative to scatter these forces. Many of the refugee inhabitants were thereupon either settled upon lands well to the north and west of the bay or sent to Isle St. Jean; the Canadian Indians, having become extremely restless, were now permitted to return to their homes, but they did not do so before expressing their dissatisfaction with the food shortage by killing the cows, sheep, and pigs of their allies, the Acadians, settled in this region, much to the bitter chagrin of the latter; a large band of Micmac likewise were led away to St. Michel near Quebec by Le Loutre, a host in himself, who thereupon proceeded to the last-named place to make clear to La Jonquière and Bigot the growing difficulties of the situation. Indeed, the French influence within the Acadian peninsula and the region thereabout had now passed its

[68] La Jonquière to the Minister, May 1, 1751, Arch. Nat., Col., C¹¹ A. 97: 16.

[69] For Captain de la Vallière's account of the killing of How see his " *Journal de ce qui s'est passé à Chienetou*," previously cited.

high point and from this time on slowly gave way to that of the British.

As an indication of the gradually changing situation, some of the Micmac left within the Province, and therefore temporarily freed from the influence of Le Loutre, now showed a disposition to come to an arrangement with the English. The reports of this change in attitude so disturbed Count Raymond, Governor at Louisbourg, that he summoned those Indians of that tribe living on Cape Breton Island to engage them to go into Acadia to break the peace which their brothers were about to cement with a treaty.[70] In spite of this, those living especially in eastern Acadia, about a hundred in number — called "bad subjects" by Prévost, the Commissaire Ordonnateur at Louisbourg — at length under their leader, Jean Baptiste Cope, entered into a treaty of friendship with the Governor at Halifax in the autumn of 1752.[71]

Further, as to the French-speaking inhabitants who still remained within the Province, the news that came to them of the manifold difficulties faced by those who had become refugees had the effect of lessening greatly their desire to leave their warm homes, fertile fields, and well-filled granaries. Those of the Rivière aux Canards, instead of preparing to depart, now begged Governor Cornwallis to send them a priest, whom he proceeded to arrange to secure through negotiation with Count Raymond at Louisbourg. Peregrine Thomas Hopson, who at this juncture of affairs succeeded Cornwallis, was able to report in the latter part of 1752 that the Acadians "appear to be much better disposed than they have been." [72] In fact Abbé Gérard, in charge of the Acadian parish at Cobequid, now informed the Governor General of New France that his people had testified that they were prepared to submit themselves to the English and, indeed, without his knowledge had actually written to Chibuctou Bay to this effect. The good Abbé went on to say that even had he been informed of

---

[70] Count Raymond to the Minister, September 18, 1751. Arch. Nat., Col., C¹¹ A. 31: 62. "Les Anglais, fâchés des insults que les sauvages leur ont faites jusqu'au départ de l'abbé Le Loutre pour Québec, ont peine à se persuader qu'elles n'aient été concertées avec le commandant françois," wrote M. Franquet from Isle Royale to the French Minister, December 12, 1751 (ibid., 31: 132).

[71] For a copy of the treaty signed November 22, 1752 see P.R.O., N.S., A. 50: 1–8. When the Abbé d'Isle-Dieu, Vicar General of the French colonies and in charge of the missionary activities, heard of the treaty, he described it as "un événement assés fâcheux" (Arch. Nat., Col., C¹¹ A. 99: 152–206).

[72] Governor Hopson to the Board of Trade, December 10, 1752, P.R.O., N.S., A. 50: 44.

this step he could have done little to divert them from it in view of the fact that he himself had taken an oath of fidelity to the English King and had given his word of honour at Halifax not to leave the Province without permission. His scruples, in fact, had kept him in Acadia long after he had received orders from his superior, the Bishop of Quebec, to go to Isle St. Jean, for he had not secured permission from the British Governor to leave. To Acting Governor General Longueuil, deeply concerned with the unfavourable turn of affairs in Acadia, this sensitiveness of the missionary about keeping his word seemed very much out of place; and he therefore proceeded to advise him that, without attempting to mix in casuistry, he would have little to answer to his conscience by making use of his authority over the inhabitants of Cobequid to divert them from the English. As to the oath he had taken, Longueuil argued that there had been little legitimate reason for demanding this and that nothing required him to keep it. Whether this line of reasoning now satisfied the conscience of the priest or other factors operated to influence him, Gérard soon afterwards left Acadia to join the Isle St. Jean refugees.[73]

At this juncture a difference of opinion as to proper strategy to be employed with respect to the Acadians became manifest. Count Raymond of Louisbourg, as previously pointed out, had agreed to secure a French missionary for the Acadians of the Rivière aux Canards parish and likewise Longueuil, writing to the French minister, stressed, in harmony with this, the necessity of providing priests as usual for the French-speaking inhabitants still remaining in Acadia:

> " It is certain, Sir, that not being able at present to bring these people over to the territory of the King we should at least seek to maintain in them their sentiments of religion and loyalty to the King." [74]

The Abbé Le Loutre, however, went on record as strongly opposed to supplying any more priests to those still under the jurisdiction of the British government. Therefore, when two of the priests labouring within Nova Scotia, M. Deseuslaves of Annapolis Royal and M. Chauvreux of Piziquid — both of whom seem to have been rather favourably disposed toward the English, especially the former, according to Colonel Mascarene — appealed for additional missionaries to assist them, Le Loutre was able to present so convincing a case in favour of a refusal of the request as the surest way of drawing

---

[73] M. de Longueuil to the Minister, April 27, 1752, Arch. Nat., Col., C¹¹ A. 98: 338.
[74] *Ibid.*

all faithful Catholics away from Acadia that his views were accepted both by the Abbé d'Isle-Dieu, Vicar General of New France, and the French minister.[75]

It is interesting to note in this connection that the Vicar General thought it unwise to present to the two priests the true reason for his refusal to aid them for fear that the intelligence would come to the knowledge of either the English government, which might draw some advantage from it, or the Acadians, who might judge by the refusal that they were being abandoned to the English. "So it will suffice," he informed the Minister, "to apprise these two good missionaries that it may not be possible this year and under the present circumstances to send them the help they request."[76] Every effort, however, was made to supply Le Loutre with the five additional priests that he desired for the refugee Acadians. Therefore, when in July two priests from the Seminary of Saint Esprit were sent out, the Vicar General assured the French Minister that every precaution had been taken that these recruits to the mission field would report directly to Le Loutre at Beauséjour and would not be detained by the Acadian priests who had so insistently requested aid

> "in spite of the fact that this may be against the best interest and against the views of the court, since so long as priests are furnished, this would serve to retain the Acadians under the domination of the English, being further solicited by their own greed and desire to retain their small possessions within the peninsula."[77]

The English at Halifax were not unaware that the French authorities, spiritual as well as lay, had fixed upon the policy referred to above for the purpose of drawing all the French-speaking inhabitants from the peninsula. Therefore, when in February 1753 the Governor received a petition from one of the villages praying that a priest who had refused to take the oath, a M. Lemaire, might still be permitted to serve them, it was decided to grant this concession for a period of six months on the grounds that the priest had refused the oath on account of instructions he had received, "there appearing no other way for the present to counter the schemes the French so daily

---

[75] The Vicar General described the two Acadian priests as "two good and virtuous missionaries who have good, sound views but are not sufficiently enlightened [assés éclairés]" (M. l'Abbé d'Isle-Dieu to the Minister, March 28, 1752, Arch. Nat., Col., C¹¹ A. 98: 376).

[76] Ibid.

[77] Abbé d'Isle-Dieu to the Minister, July 24, 1752, Arch. Nat., Col., C¹¹ A. 98: 382.

practice on said Inhabitants." [78] A similar petition was granted to the inhabitants of Minas in September. In this instance the inhabitants stated that a deputation had been sent to the Bishop of Quebec praying to be supplied with priests, but that the Bishop had refused them, saying, apparently rather abruptly, that he had not the slightest intention of doing so on account of the oath exacted from the missionaries.[79] As to the priest promised by Count Raymond at Louisbourg, it may be added that in the light of this commitment the Vicar General, in consultation with Le Loutre, who arrived in France the latter part of the year 1752, decided to make the concession and found in the Seminary of Saint Esprit one whom they considered fit for the delicate post in the interior of Acadia, M. de Vern. It was agreed, however, that he should sail to the New World in the same vessel as Le Loutre so that the latter might instruct him on his way over.[80] It would appear, however, that at the last moment a M. Daudin was substituted for M. de Vern,[81] and also that he was so well instructed by the redoubtable Le Loutre that upon his arrival he succeeded in fanning every little discontent of his peaceably inclined parishioners into a white heat of resistance to the government before his expulsion from the Province as a public enemy was threatened.

In turning our attention now to the English settlement at Halifax, it may be pointed out that throughout the administration of Governor Cornwallis, which lasted until August 1752, when, as was stated, Colonel Hopson took over the administration of affairs, little progress was made in the planting of outlying settlements by reason of the hostile activities of the Indians kept in motion by Le Loutre. The settlers, composed not only of English but likewise of Germans and Swiss, were accommodated in some fashion or other within the palisaded town and largely subsisted at the government's expense, which was so very great as to cause the deepest concern on the part of Cornwallis and also of the Board of Trade lest Parliament grow weary of paying the large annual deficits. While there was much criticism of the type of English settlers sent over, there was even greater objection to many of the Germans secured by a government agent. Among the latter, complained Governor Hopson, there were "many,

---

[78] Minutes of the Governor's Council, February 26, 1753, P.R.O., N.S., B. 6: 88-9.

[79] Minutes of the Council for September 12, 1753, P.R.O., N.S., B. 6: 225-30.

[80] Abbé d'Isle-Dieu to the Minister, March 21, 1753, Arch. Nat., Col., C[11] A. 99: 152-206.

[81] See Minutes of the Council for August 15, 1753, P.R.O., N.S., B. 6: 212.

very many poor, old, decrepit creatures both men and women who were objects fitter to have been kept in alms houses than to be sent over here as settlers to work for their bread." [82] Indeed, some of these who were Catholics, but who had been accepted as Protestant immigrants, became so restless that they finally deserted to the French Isle St. Jean. Not until the fall of 1753 did it seem safe to lay out a definite settlement for these foreigners at an old fishing post Merligueche, some sixty-five miles south of Halifax on the eastern coast. To give the settlers adequate protection while houses and palisades were being built, a detachment of regular troops accompanied them. For a time everything ran along with great smoothness, but late in December of the year of their arrival they were thrown into so mutinous a spirit by certain ringleaders, especially one by the name of Hoffman, that it was necessary to disarm them. [83] After this incident the settlement, known as Lunenburg, became quiet and the hardworking elements among the Germans proceeded to devote themselves with great zeal to the improvement of their individual land grants. Therefore, by the beginning of the year 1754, besides Halifax and the outlying town of Dartmouth in Chibuctou Bay, only Lunenburg had been settled by the British along the eastern coast, although it is true that preliminary steps were taken to plant the Musquodoboit Valley, and in that year some twenty thousand acres of land were granted about the present site of Lawrencetown, east of the Bay of Fundy. [84]

In turning again to consider the condition of the Acadians it may be affirmed that during the absence of Le Loutre, who was again in France at this period, the fortitude of the refugee inhabitants greatly weakened. They found themselves faced with innumerable difficulties in re-establishing themselves to the west of the Missaquash and they longed to return to their old abodes. The commander at Fort Lawrence in Chignecto, well aware of their situation — as the result of secret information supplied him from Fort Beauséjour by Thomas Pichon, the commissaire, who had become a British agent [85] — made

---

[82] Governor Hopson to the Board of Trade, October 16, 1752, P.R.O., N.S., A. 49: 67.

[83] Colonel Lawrence to the Board of Trade, December 5 and 29, 1753, P.R.O., N.S., A. 54: 254-9.

[84] It may be pointed out that at the head of Bedford Basin Fort Sackville, an outlying post, had also been established by 1754. Its name was later changed to Bedford.

[85] The career of Pichon will be given somewhat detailed consideration in Volume VI of this series.

frequent overtures to them at the request of Governor Hopson, who was especially concerned to win them back. As a result, late in the summer of 1753 some eighty of them joined in a humble petition which was sent to Halifax and thereupon communicated to the Council. In this they made clear their desire to return to their possessions, all but ruined during three years of abandonment. However, they stipulated that they must be given definite assurance that they would enjoy every concession granted to their predecessors in the year 1727 and be permitted to take the identical oath used at that time. The Council, after deliberation — apparently convinced that the old oath was meaningless in the eyes at least of those who, in spite of having taken it, had gone over to the enemy so precipitously and had taken the oath of fidelity to the French King — determined to make an addition to the earlier oath for purposes of clarification. Instead of the words: " I sincerely promise and swear to be faithful to His Majesty King George II and his successors. So help me God," there was substituted: " I sincerely promise and swear to be faithful and maintain a perfect loyalty to His Majesty King George II. So help me God! " [86] It was agreed that should the inhabitants take the substitute oath before the 20th of November in the presence of Commander Scott at Fort Lawrence they would be admitted to a peaceable and quiet possession of their lands, would have the free exercise of their religion and a sufficient number of priests allowed them, and would also enjoy all of the privileges granted them by the Treaty of Utrecht.[87]

Unhappily an accord was not reached in view of the fact that the refugees demanded without the slightest alteration all the special exemptions permitted to them in 1727. Colonel Lawrence, who had now taken over the administration of Acadia, was, therefore, obliged to inform the home government in December that, in spite of all happy anticipations the petitioners had not as yet accepted the offer.[88] The truth of the matter is that Le Loutre had meanwhile returned from France to the scene of his chief activities — and with redoubled zeal. The presence of this remarkable man brought an immediate stiffening of resistance to British influence in Acadia from every quarter. His first concern seems to have been to get control of the Indian

---

[86] " *Je promets et jure sincèrement que je serai fidèle et que je porterai une loyauté parfaite vers Sa Majesté le Roy George le Second.*"

[87] Minutes of the Council, September 27, 1753, P.R.O., N.S., B. 6: 235–41.

[88] Lawrence to the Board of Trade, December 5, 1753, P.R.O., N.S., A. 54: 221–3.

situation and he thereupon took steps to recall those Micmac, Mari-chite, and Abnaki who had gone over to the English. In fact M. Maillard, another French missionary, later known as the Apostle to the Micmac, as soon as he had received information on Isle Royale that a portion of that tribe living in Acadia had, in the absence of Le Loutre, signed a treaty, entered the Province for the purpose of bringing back these "false brothers."[89] The two missionaries, soon after Le Loutre's arrival in Acadia, betook themselves to Louisbourg to perfect plans for again breaking the peace within the Province.[90] By the middle of August the Commissaire Ordonnateur at that place, M. Prévost, was able to advise the French Minister that the natives were again disturbing "our neighbours" without respite. They had recently, he declared, carried to Fort Beauséjour eighteen scalps taken from the English in the different raids they had made against their settlements and that M. Le Loutre had been obliged, as a re-sult, to pay them eighteen hundred livres silver of Acadia, and that he himself had reimbursed him.[91] It is of interest to note that he there-upon informed the Minister that since he himself did not have funds for such scalp payments and since these were ultimately paid from those set aside for the extraordinary expenditures of the colony, he would pray M. Bigot to confide to the missionary an advance in form of letters of credit to be paid in Louisbourg to the Indians, "who were not fond of paper."[92]

The terror now spread by Le Loutre's Indians did not fail to have its effect upon the Acadians. It is therefore not surprising that in the month of June 1754 a delegation representing the former inhabit-ants of Chignecto should appear before Captain Scott at Fort Law-rence and, while expressing their longing to return to their old abodes, should insist, nevertheless, that they must have guarantees of permission to remain neutral and exempt from bearing arms — privileges they did not of course enjoy on French territory — other-wise it would be impossible for them to think of returning, much as they desired to do so, since "they would every day run the risque of having their throats cut and their cattle destroyed."[93] As it was not possible for Scott to give them the guarantees sought, they returned

[89] Abbé d'Isle-Dieu to the Minister, July 29, 1753 and September 7, 1753, Arch. Nat., Col., C11 A. 99: 152–206.

[90] Ibid.

[91] M. Prévost to the Minister, August 16, 1753, Arch. Nat., Col., C11 (IV), 33: 197.

[92] Ibid.

[93] See the Minutes of the Council, June 21, 1754, P.R.O., N.S., B. 7: 47.

to Beauséjour, where, according to private information supplied by M. Pichon and conveyed to Colonel Lawrence at Halifax, they appeared

> "in a very ill humour with Le Loutre, the missionary, and with the French Commandant, and . . . represented to them the Hardships they labored under, in not being suffered to accept the proposals of the English, in a Remonstrance that was little short of a Mutiny." [94]

But the Indians, in face of this spirit of disaffection within the ranks of the Acadians, proceeded to inform the refugees, as the latter left Mass held in the chapel Le Loutre had built at Beauséjour, that if any should have the temerity to return to their habitations under English domination, they would be regarded as enemies and treated as such.[95]

In other words, the influences that continued to sway the Acadians were those centred at Quebec and not at Halifax. Therefore, we need not wonder that at this juncture, especially in view of the renewed Indian terror, whatever desire may have existed to seek an accommodation with the authorities at the latter place, it was not allowed to find expression. On the contrary, the inhabitants of Annapolis Royal, Minas, and Piziquid, to the number of three or four hundred, in spite of the refusal of the Governor of Nova Scotia to permit them to leave the Province, were led to go to the neighbourhood of the French fort at Beauséjour to assist in building dikes. This was done in face of an offer of gainful work within the Province in the building of a road between Halifax and Shubenacadie, a place where Le Loutre had previously had a mission and where it was proposed now to establish an additional military post to hold in check the Indian raiders. In fact, Lieutenant Governor Lawrence felt impelled to issue a proclamation ordering all Acadians to return to their homes or refuse to do so at their peril. Moreover, the latter now ceased the practice of bringing their provisions to Halifax for sale and, in spite of the most rigid prohibitions, carried these to the French and Indians, who could not otherwise have subsisted on the borders of Acadia. Further, the inhabitants of Piziquid, who previously had apparently willingly provided firewood for Fort Edward, located there, refused longer to furnish this necessity and in general showed a very hostile

---

[94] Colonel Lawrence to the Board of Trade, August 1, 1754, P.R.O., N.S., A. 55: 198.

[95] Le Loutre to Colonel Lawrence, August 27, 1754, P.R.O., N.S., B. 7: 63-74.

attitude. It is not without significance that this took place as soon as
M. Daudin, the priest sent the previous year to Acadia by the Abbé
d'Isle-Dieu in company with Le Loutre, came into their midst. So
serious became the situation, in fact, that it seemed necessary to order the priest out of the Province as a public enemy and to threaten
the inhabitants with summary military punishment.[96] Ultimately
Daudin was permitted to remain when his parishioners promised to
mend their ways.

In concluding this account of the land of the Acadians, it may be
said that by the late summer of 1754 Lieutenant Governor Lawrence
had come to the conviction that it was impossible under given conditions to make of the inhabitants a body of loyal subjects. In a letter
to the Board of Trade dated August 1 he laid bare his sentiments,
declaring that

> "as it has been generally imagined here, that the mildness of an
> English Government would by Degrees have fixed them in our in-
> terest, no violent measures have ever been taken with them. But I
> must observe to your Lordships that this Lenity has not had the least
> good effect; on the contrary, I believe that they have at present laid
> aside all thoughts of taking the oaths voluntarily . . . and, indeed,
> while they remain without taking the oaths to His Majesty . . . and
> have Incendiary French Priests among them there are no Hopes of
> their Amendment."

He then went on to say, significantly:

> "As they possess the best and largest Tracts of land in this province,
> it cannot be settled with any effect while they remain in this situa-
> tion, and tho I would be very far from attempting such a step with-
> out your Lordships approbation, yet I cannot help being of the opin-
> ion that it would be much better, if they refuse the oaths, that they
> were away.
> "The only ill consequence that can attend their going would be
> their taking arms and joining with the Indians to distress our settle-
> ments, as they are numerous and our troops much divided. . . ."[97]

Thus was the ground laid, after much temporizing and shifting of
policy still to come, for the ultimate scattering of the Acadians along
the Atlantic seaboard the following year, with the outbreak of hostili-

[96] See Minutes of the Council for September 24, October 1 and 2, 1754, P.R.O.,
N.S., B. 7: 92–4.
[97] P.R.O., N.S., A. 55: 192–4.

ties and the collapse of the French defence at Beauséjour — unhappy victims of the Anglo-French struggle for empire in North America! The position that they occupied in 1754 was anomalous, to say the least. Most of them, in fact all but perhaps a very few elderly survivors from the French period of control, had been born on British soil and were therefore, by the very rule of international law that the King of France himself recognized and enforced — that is, the rule of *jus solis* — subjects of the King of England, owing to him loyalty and obedience. But this they were never permitted, by those leaders spiritual and lay to whom they looked for guidance, to render, as the Dutch in New Netherlands after the conquest and cession of this province had not scrupled to do. On the other hand the slowly expiring hope was sedulously fanned in the breasts of the new generation of Acadians as the decades passed after 1713 that some day France could not fail with all its military might once again to repossess Acadia — their land.

CHAPTER VII

The "Neutral" Islands of the Caribbeans

N OT ONLY WERE the disposition of the trans-Appalachian region and the determination of the limits of Nova Scotia matters of bitter dispute between the British and the French in the eighteenth century but likewise the issue involving the so-called "neutral" West India Islands of Dominica, St. Lucia, St. Vincent, and Tobago.[1] With the exception of the last-named, they are scarcely more than a series of mountain peaks and valleys dotting the sea. Dominica, the largest, is but twenty-nine miles in length and sixteen in breadth at its maximum width, with an area of two hundred and ninety-one square miles. Thus insignificant in size and now unimpressive, at least in economic importance, although their mountain slopes are still densely covered with locust, yellow sandalwood, bastard mahogany, ironwood, cedar, and many other varieties of trees and shrubs, it may be a matter of surprise to some living in the twentieth century that any great stir could ever have arisen over their ownership; and that their fate, particularly that of St. Lucia, should have assumed great magnitude in international diplomacy.

However, the two rival empire-builders, it may be emphasized, considered the four islands most vital links in a chain of possessions that each had been slowly but actively welding for a century and a quarter in the region of the eastern Caribbean Sea. For Dominica was

---

[1] These islands were classified by the Spaniards as among the Windwards; Dominica was held by the English to be the most southern of the Leewards and Tobago, to lie south of the Windwards (C. P. Lucas, A Historical Geography of the British Colonies, II, The West Indies, pp. 32–3).

held by the French to be a life-line between Guadeloupe and Martinique, lying as it does midway between the two; St. Lucia, south and therefore to the windward of their last-named possession and yet very close to it, was, to the advantage of the English, to the leeward of densely populated Barbados and thus as easily approached from the latter in the days of the sailing vessel as it was difficult to approach from Martinique by reason of the adverse trade wind. As to St. Vincent, although lying not far south of St. Lucia, it is to the windward of Barbados and was, as a result, much less accessible to the English than was St. Lucia. The fourth island, Tobago, is far to the southward of St. Lucia; in fact, between the two lie not only the Grenadines but Grenada, where the French had established themselves in undisputed control after exterminating the native population. All that need be said here is that it was fertile and easy to exploit under peaceful conditions and gave to the power that controlled it, if that power were unfriendly to France, the ability to threaten Grenada.

Of the four islands under consideration, two were at this period uninhabited by Caribs — St. Lucia and Tobago; as to Dominica and St. Vincent, these for over a century had been the chief centres of Carib culture and in the eighteenth century were the only Caribbean islands inhabited by the natives, who had been either driven out of the rest or exterminated. Only in Dominica, indeed, were the Caribs able to live without much interference from others during the first half of the century. The island was quaintly, if rather inaccurately, described by a writer in the latter part of the seventeenth century in none too flattering terms:

> "It is very mountainous in the midst, which encompasses an inaccessable bottom, where, from the tops of certain Rocks, may be seen an infinite number of Dragons, Vipers, and other most venomous and dreadful creatures, whom none dares come near, yet there are many Fertile Villages, producing several Commodities, but chiefly Tobacco, which is planted by the English, but the Natives, which are Canibals, and very barbarous, doth much hinder the coming of the English to settle there, for the Canribbeans [sic] are very populous in it. . . ." [2]

With respect to the first efforts at political control on the part of Europeans, Dominica, together with St. Lucia and St. Vincent, was

---

[2] R. Blome, The Present State of His Majesty's Isles and Territories in America (London 1687), p. 73.

apparently included within a rather general commission given by Richelieu in 1626 to Pierre d'Esnambuc and Urbain de Roissey (Rossey), authorizing French settlement, within certain geographical limits, of all islands in the West Indies not already inhabited by Europeans.[3] The following year the island was likewise given in the same free-handed manner — with many others in the West Indies, including the two above mentioned — to the Earl of Carlisle by Charles I of England. Yet neither of the rival grantees took any steps to colonize it, perhaps regarding it as a rather forbidding place. Nevertheless, the French resorted to it very early to engage in trade with the Caribs and established friendly relations with them.[4] On the other hand, the treacherous conduct of a shipmaster in 1639 added to the hostility that the Caribs had begun to display toward the English. Arriving at Dominica, by displaying a French flag he enticed some of them aboard his vessel to engage in trade; whereupon he weighed anchor with the idea of taking them away in order to sell them into slavery. Not only was the attempt unsuccessful, but this led to savage reprisals against the English settlements on the other islands.

As to the French, their influence on the island was further extended by the Governor of Guadeloupe, M. Aubert, who concluded a treaty of friendship with the Caribs in 1640. Twenty years later not only was an agreement entered into between the French and English in the West Indies in the offensive and defensive so-called Treaty of Union and League signed in St. Christopher in January 1660, providing that the two peoples should act in concert against the Caribs in case of attack and that the latter should be permitted to enjoy without disturbance the possession of Dominica and St. Vincent, but in March of that year the Governor of Guadeloupe, Sieur Houel, brought fifteen of the leading natives of these islands to agree that were the two islands confirmed to them, they in turn would renounce pretensions to all others in the Caribbeans.[5]

Soon after these negotiations the English secured a powerful, even

---

[3] The text of this is given by J. B. du Tertre (*Histoire Générale des Antilles habitées par les Français* [Paris, 1667–71], I, 8–11). The only islands specifically mentioned were St. Christopher and Barbados.

[4] R. Blome, op cit., p. 74.

[5] While the French and English documents are in substantial agreement as to the above facts, there is sharp disagreement as to other points; for these divergencies see *All the Memorials of Great Britain and France since the Peace of Aix la Chapelle . . .* Part II, Memorials concerning St. Lucia (The Hague, 1756), pp. 14–15, 68–9. This will be referred to subsequently under the title of *Memorials concerning St. Lucia.*

if uncertain, ally in Dominica in the person of Thomas Warner, reputed to be the natural son of Sir Thomas Warner, late Governor of the English Leeward Islands,[6] and of a Carib woman called Madame Ouvernard. Warner, together with his mother, after the death of Sir Thomas, came to live among the savages. He was given not only a captain's commission by Francis Lord Willoughby but one granting him authority as Deputy Governor of Dominica. Taking advantage of his position among his own people — for he considered himself a Carib both in religious belief and in manner of life, going naked among them — he seems to have engineered some sort of sale in favour of the English not only of St. Lucia in 1663, to which reference will be made, but of Dominica as well in a treaty concluded in 1668.[7] But this growing understanding was not to last. Warner's Caribs were accused of making incursions against Antigua, from which many of them had been driven and to which they desired to return, and Warner himself was implicated. As a result, his own half-brother, Captain Philip Warner, who was pure English and had no love for him, led a force from Antigua first against the Windward Caribs, which was given support by Warner's natives, and then, stopping at Dominica, invited Warner and some sixty of his fellow Caribs to a feast, at which he and the other natives were put to death after they had become intoxicated.[8] This act not only enraged the other Dominica Caribs but doubtless made Warner's mother, whose influence among her people was very great, a bitter enemy of the English, whom she had once so greatly favoured. It may be added that she lived to a great age and in 1700, although she was said to be well over

---

[6] William Lord Willoughby, writing to M. De la Barre on January 3, 1668, in referring to Warner says that he was the " deputed son of Sir Thomas Warner and educated with him till 30 years of age, he took the oath of allegiance to his Majesty and received a Commission from Lord Willoughby's predecessor [Francis Lord Willoughby] to be Deputy Governor of Dominica " (Calendar of State Papers, America and West Indies, 1661–8, pp. 535–6). Warner was recommissioned by William Lord Willoughby (ibid., p. 587). In this commission he was characterized as " a Musteech, whose father was Governor of St. Kitts and his mother an Indian and who has suffered exceedingly by the French for his loyalty to the English."

[7] For the so-called conveyance of Dominica to William Lord Willoughby in 1668 as a composition for injuries done to the English by the natives see ibid., 1700, pp. 155, 334.

[8] The Calendar of State Papers, America and West Indies series, contains many references to this episode. Philip Warner was placed under arrest; the case was carried to England and then later transferred to Barbados. In this connection efforts were made by depositions to prove that Thomas was not related to Philip. Ultimately the latter was acquitted of the charge of murder.

The "Neutral" Islands of the West Indies.

(From Lucas's *Historical Geography of the British Colonies. II, West Indies.*)

Carte de l'Isle de Sainte Lucie. Par M. B. Ing. de la Marine, 1753.

a hundred years old, was still possessed of her faculties and some of her old high spirit.[9]

Although an effort was made on the part of the English after the Peace of Ryswick in 1697 — with the re-establishment of friendly relations with the natives — to build a fort on the Dominica seashore for the protection of those who went there for lumber, this was foiled by the French Governor of Martinique.[10] Consequently, at the beginning of the eighteenth century the island contained no Europeans outside of one or two Frenchmen who had fled there for safety; nor did it offer an easy place of refuge for Negroes, as did St. Vincent. Here, in other words, was the one remaining centre, outside of northern South America, where the Carib culture, once spread throughout the Lesser Antilles, was still dominant during the period under consideration. In 1730 the island, together with St. Vincent and St. Lucia, was by agreement between the crowns of Great Britain and France declared " neutral " and was therefore not to be colonized by the subjects of either pending a settlement of rival claims; this neutralization was re-affirmed in 1748 at Aix-la-Chapelle.

In the light of the fact that with the Peace of Paris of 1763 Dominica was confirmed to Great Britain and thereupon was opened to settlement, which brought with it the ultimate disappearance of most of the natives and the dilution of their mores, it would be well at this point to make some reference to the Carib culture before considering the situation of St. Vincent, Tobago, and St. Lucia.

The Caribs were, it would appear, and speaking of course in comparative terms, newcomers to those islands where they were found by Columbus and the Spanish discoverers. Some of those who early laboured to Christianize them were persuaded that they originally came from the North American continent in the region of Florida and that in migrating they avoided the larger, well-populated Antilles in moving southward in their large *canots* propelled by paddles and sails through the eastern Caribbean Sea. The movement continued, it was surmised, until they not only had occupied all the lesser islands, but had secured a footing on the shores of South America in the region of what is now Venezuela and the Guianas.[11] This theory

---

9 Father Labat (Labbat) lodged in her *carbot* during his visit to Dominica in 1700. See his *Nouveau Voyage aux Isles de l'Amérique* (Paris, 1722), IV, 300. This work is not signed by the author; his name will therefore be given in brackets.

10 *Ibid.*, IV, 312–13.

11 " *Les Auteurs qui ont parlé de leur origine, croyent qu'ils viennent de la Floride. . . . Cette pensée est fondée sur ce que certain Indiens de la Floride parlent à peu de*

of their origin, however, is not generally held. For it is now considered likely that they originated in the northwestern part of South America.[12]

The Carib method of conquest seemed to have involved the extermination of all male enemies, with the careful preservation of the females. The latter, it may be noted, even centuries after this conquest had taken place, always employed, except when addressing the men, a language very different from that used by the Caribs and closely akin to that spoken by the natives of the Greater Antilles.[13] The word " Carib " means, significantly, " stranger ";[14] this was used interchangeably with the word " Banare," meaning " those from the sea." These people were not by nature or by acquired appetite, we are told, man-eaters. Father Labat, who associated with them and with Frenchmen who had long lived among them, while admitting that some Europeans had been killed, roasted, and eaten by them, called this lapse into cannibalism

> " une action toute extraordinaire chez ces Peuples: c'étoit la rage qui leur fasoit commettre cet excès. . . ."[15]

---

chose près le même langage que nos Caraïbes, & ont les même coûtumes, ce qu'on ne trouve point dans aucuns des Indiens des grandes Isles, & de quelques endroits de la Terre ferme dont le langage n'approche en aucune façon de celui nos Caraïbes, quoi qu'il approche beaucoup de celui que parlent les femmes (ibid., IV, 332–3). Father du Tertre in his Histoire Générale des Isles de S. Christophe, de la Guadeloape . . . et Autres dans l'Amérique (Paris, 1654, p. 401), says that they themselves believe they are descended from the " Kalibis qui demeurent à la terre ferme. . . ." But the Caribs of South America were themselves considered newcomers in those places that they inhabited.

[12] The Carib stock, from the viewpoint of present-day scholarship, was at one time widespread. Gregory Mason in his recent thoughtful study South of Yesterday, in treating the Tairona, who once dwelt on the north coast of Colombia, relates them to this stock; it is also surmised that the once powerful Caras and Chibehas of Ecuador and central Colombia were likewise branches of it. However, the Carib is but imperfectly understood as yet, according to P. A. Means, a leading authority on prehistoric culture groups of Central and South America (New York Times Book Review, October 27, 1940).

[13] [Labat], op cit., IV, 333; du Tertre, op. cit., p. 462.

[14] For a study of Carib dialects see L. Adam, Matériaux pour servir a l'établissement d'une grammaire comparée des dialectes de la Famille Caribe (Paris, 1893).

[15] Op. cit., IV, 321–3. Blome (op. cit., p. 75), writing also in the seventeenth century, says of the Caribs: " They can't endure to be called Cannibals: they do eat the flesh of their enemies, which they say is to gratify their revenge, and not out of any delicacy they find in the meat." Du Tertre (op. cit., pp. 449–51) affirmed that their hatred of their native enemies was so insatiable that when they had married one of their female prisoners they even would kill and eat the male children that she might bear her Carib husband. The same author offers an explanation for the fact that they gave up the practice of eating Europeans. It seems that after they had consumed a Spanish priest so many of them died as a result of this feast that they decided never again to run the risk of partaking of a white man (ibid., p. 452).

It is true that when they killed an enemy, provided he were not a fellow Carib, they would roast his body and fill their calabashes with the drippings, which were later consumed. But this repulsive practice, it was argued, was not for the purpose of sating an appetite for human food, but to possess trophies of victory which were found useful when the warriors sought to whip themselves into a fury before again attacking their enemies — a practice that might be compared to that of the North American Indians in preserving the scalps of their enemies. However, in waging war they never exposed themselves willingly, always employing stratagem and stealth. Clothing themselves with the leaves of trees, if it were daylight, they would approach their enemy until close enough to their unsuspecting quarry to let fly their poisoned arrows with amazing speed and deadly accuracy. In attacking a village, they preferred to approach at night and, setting fire to the huts with blazing arrows, would thereupon in the light of the flames pick off those who attempted to escape the conflagration. Never did they forget an insult even by a fellow Carib, yet they never openly challenged another to combat; biding their time, they would then kill from the rear.[16]

Among most primitive peoples there have existed such devices as composition payments for the life of an individual; for example, the *wergild* of the early Germans. But the Caribs had not advanced to a point to enjoy either a tribal government or a tribal law except in the most rudimentary form. Therefore no means were at hand when a member of one household had been wronged by a member of another to prevent the gradual extermination of either as a result of the blood feud, a practice that, according to Father Labat, kept the population down to a tenth of what it otherwise would have been.[17] Possessing no chiefs or headmen by reason of a fierce spirit of independence and equality — something that precluded the control of any of the adult males in the family *carbot* even by their father — if action were to be taken involving a common interest it was necessary for the person who had it at heart to summon his fellows to his *carbot* for a feast, always a drunken orgy induced by fermented cassava. In the midst of this he made his proposal and appeal. Whether it was acted upon depended solely upon the attitude of each individual, who remained perfectly free to co-operate or to refuse to do so. But this spirit of independence was absent in one respect; for the Carib

---

[16] [Labat], *op. cit.*, IV, 340–2.
[17] *Ibid.*, IV, 316.

possessed absolute authority over his wives. Their obedience to him was implicit since he held over them the power of life and death; a careless, disrespectful word, a seeming neglect of his honour or of his personal convenience, was enough to justify the destruction of the offender. It may be added, however, that advanced age brought with it not only great respect but a certain authority, whether such persons were male or female; " the younger sort," according to Blome, " complying in all things with their sentiments and wills." [18]

Accustomed to do only what pleased his fancy and only at such times as were most convenient to him, living a life of ease, waited upon by his wives, who never ceased labouring from morning to night, the Carib could not adjust himself to the compulsions and severities of slavery; in fact it was abundantly proved in attempting to enslave him that he would die of pure grief.[19] Nor could he be Christianized, at least under conditions existing in Dominica and St. Vincent. Priests laboured long and faithfully among this people, but Father Labat testified that all was in vain. A Carib separated from his fellows might act as a true convert for a long period of time, going through all the motions of devotion; but let him but for a day rejoin his group and immediately he lapsed back into his paganism, becoming, as a rule, even more attached to his old devil-worship than before and in other respects more dangerous to Europeans.[20] As a result, in the latter part of the seventeenth century all missionary enterprises were abandoned on Dominica as quite useless.[21]

But one must not think that the Caribs were lacking in all virtues. Father du Tertre, who perhaps saw them under circumstances that tended to favour them unduly, declared that he found them to be the most contented, the happiest, the least vicious, the most sociable, the least affected, and also the least tormented with maladies of any people in the world. Neither were there rich nor poor among them, all limiting their desires to that which seemed to them immediately useful, despising a superfluity as something unworthy of possession.[22] Blome, also writing in the seventeenth century, stresses their fundamental honesty as " great enemies of thieving " and as living without

---

[18] Op. cit., p. 77. This seems to contradict the statement relative to the lack of authority of a father over his son. Reference is here made to people of great age.

[19] Ibid., p. 75.

[20] Op. cit., IV, 371.

[21] Ibid., IV, 373. Du Tertre, writing in 1654, still hoped that the Caribs would be won to Christianity although he recognized the formidable obstacles in the way (op. cit., pp. 460–6).   [22] Ibid., p. 397.

distrust of one another.[23] Moreover, they delighted in hospitality and among themselves freely supplied one another's wants. Thus living this life generally of quiet contentment, many of them, it is said, attained the age of a hundred or even a hundred and twenty years.[24]

With all this simplicity and distrust of riches that characterized the natives of Dominica, one might have thought that they would have shunned the grasping Europeans. But this was not the case. They came to desire greatly the white man's axes, knives, needles, and sail-cloth, his crystal beads, mirrors, and other things, some of slight value, as well as his brandy or rum.[25] They had at first believed that all these would come as gifts, but found that they had to give in return. This developing trade and the lure of the natural resources of the island ultimately led to its settlement by the French.

As was previously indicated, Dominica was in 1730 neutralized with the understanding that neither the British nor the French would colonize it. Nevertheless, the latter coming from near-by Guadeloupe and Martinique, and apparently with the consent of the natives, gradually established a foothold upon its fertile rim, where they laid out their plantations. It was charged in 1753 by the Earl of Holderness, upon the basis of letters received from Captain Pye, " Commodore on the Barbadoes station," and from his first lieutenant, that Dominica, " so far from being evacuated according to agreement and the repeated orders said to have been sent to the West Indies for the faithful execution of it," was actually inhabited by some four thousand Frenchmen, who had placed large quantities of land under cultivation with the laying out of sugar plantations, had established a regular form of government, and had formed themselves into a militia commanded by an officer receiving orders from the Governor of Martinique, M. Bompar.[26] While this was denied in a most peremp-

---

[23] Op. cit., p. 77. Blome, of course, does not take into account the existence among them of the blood feud.

[24] Du Tertre, op. cit., p. 398.

[25] Ibid.

[26] Holderness to Albemarle, August 24, 1753, British Diplomatic Instructions, 1689–1789, VII, France, Part IV, 1745–89 (Camden, Third Series, Vol. XLIX), p. 39. On February 7, 1748 in an address to the King, the Governor and Assembly of Barbados stated that from very small beginnings the French had made themselves masters of Dominica; " they have driven them [the natives] to a small corner of the Island, taken Possession of the rest for themselves, & set up in Defiance of your Majesty's Right & Sovereignty over the same, & of their own express agreement with your Majesty in 1730, a regular form of government there, all the powers whereof . . . are now strictly & publicly exerted . . ." (Mildmay Book of Memorials, Clements Library).

tory manner by the French Minister,[27] it is, nevertheless, a fact that at the close of the Seven Years' War it was found that over six thousand acres were under cultivation upon which were living close to two thousand Frenchmen, who possessed nearly six thousand black slaves busily occupied in producing coffee, cocoa, and cotton. The Caribs themselves, who could have been counted in terms of thousands in the seventeenth century, by 1763 had so dwindled that in the enumeration of that year they were credited with but "about sixty families."[28] The day of their mastery of the little island was thus already a thing of the past.

As to the other Carib island, the oval-shaped St. Vincent, little need be said, for its history followed closely that of Dominica in most respects. By 1700 it still possessed a far larger number of natives than did the latter[29] and was called by Labat "*le centre de la République Caraïbe*."[30] However, besides the natives, there had gradually congregated upon it large numbers of escaped Negroes, many of them from Barbados,[31] who by the above date not only had firmly established themselves in their independence but had increased to the point that they had become much more powerful than the Caribs. As a result, the island was divided between the two peoples, the Negroes taking possession of the inaccessible mountainous interior, thus holding the Caribs along the coasts at their mercy and — much to the futile chagrin of the latter — frequently appropriating their wives and daughters.[32] The natives having complained to Frenchmen who frequented the island to trade of constant ill treatment on the part of the blacks, a project at last was formed by the Chevalier de Feuquieres, Governor General of the French Caribbee Islands, to capture the Negroes and thereupon sell them for a handsome profit to the Spaniards on the mainland for work in the mines. The Caribs

---

[27] *Diplomatic Instructions, 1689–1789*, VII, France, Part IV.

[28] *Acts of the Privy Council, Colonial, 1745–1766*, p. 587.

[29] [Father Labat], *op. cit.*, IV, 442–3.

[30] *Ibid.*

[31] Colonel Philip Warner of Antigua, in an account of this Caribbee island prepared in 1676, affirmed that " St. Vincent is possessed by the French, where are about 3,000 Negro inhabitants, and in no other island is so many Indians " (*Calendar of State Papers, Col.*, 1675–1676, p. 367). Labat, who visited the island in 1700 and there met and conversed with the Jesuit Father le Breton, a missionary to the natives, emphasizes the fact that at an earlier period the Caribs would often return the escaped slaves to their masters or sell them to the French or to the Spaniards, but that they had given up the practice (*op. cit.*, IV, 442–3).

[32] *Ibid.*, IV, 443–4.

having readily agreed to assist in subduing them, a force of five hundred men left Martinique and landed on St. Vincent in 1719. But now the natives, perhaps cowed by the blacks and also perhaps fearing for their women living with the latter, refused the aid they had promised and the Negroes, entrenching themselves securely in the mountain fastnesses, made devastating nightly raids upon the French, killing many of them. In vain the leaders of the expedition called upon Martinique for additional assistance, and when it was not to be had, they were obliged to give up the enterprise and to make peace with those they had expected to conquer.[33] Thus in the middle of the eighteenth century the St. Vincent natives were divided into two groups, the red and the black Caribs; the latter, with flat heads, were considered "most Robust and most Numerous," while the former were more diminutive in appearance.[34] These people at the time that the island came into the possession of Great Britain with the Peace of 1763 could boast of but six hundred to eight hundred males capable of bearing arms.[35]

Colonization of St. Vincent by the French during the first half of the eighteenth century followed much the same pattern as did that of Dominica. With peace established between them and the dominant blacks, the way was opened to the development of trade, which led to lumbering, and lumbering to the laying out of plantations after 1748 in the southern portion of the island.[36] At the same time the Caribs gradually concentrated in the northeastern part, in the neighbourhood of the then quiescent volcano Soufrière. Indeed, at the time that St. Vincent was relinquished to the British, there were possibly between a thousand and fifteen hundred Frenchmen dwelling upon it, who were successfully engaged in raising crops and also

---

[33] Ibid., IV, 447–8; C. P. Lucas, op. cit., p. 210.

[34] "State of the Island of St. Vincent, 1765," Shelburne Papers, 77: 113–19. In his An Historical Account of the Island of Saint Vincent (London, 1831) Charles Shephard, seeking to account for the flat heads among the black Caribs, states (p. 22) that when the French from Martinique appeared on the island with slaves, the former "retired to the thickest part of the woods and to create a distinction proceeded to flatten the foreheads of all their new born infants as a token of independence."

[35] "État présent de l'Isle St. Vincent," 1763, Shelburne Papers, 74: 119–21. In that year the total Carib population on the island was, however, calculated to be four or five thousand (Acts of the Privy Council, Col., 1745–1766, p. 586).

[36] In 1748 the Governor and Assembly of Barbados stated in their memorial that the Caribs were still too powerful to permit the French to make the same progress in settlement as they had made on Dominica and St. Lucia. However, those who would were encouraged to plant there under the protection of the Governor of Martinique (Mildmay Book of Memorials).

sheep, horned cattle, and "beasts of labour." They were aided in these enterprises by almost thirty-five hundred Negro slaves.[37]

Little Tobago — roughly shaped like a great fish swimming with open mouth and headed in a northeasterly direction through the Caribbean Sea — was the third among the so-called "Neutral Islands." In contrast to the others — with their mountainous formations as the result of submergence of the lower coastal plains — it presents, except in its north and north central portions, the most inviting prospect to the agriculturist by reason of the absence of forbidding peaks and declivities. That, together with its proximity to the coast of South America, may well account for the fact that in the seventeenth century its fertile lands became a veritable international cockpit where Dutchmen, Courlanders, Englishmen, and Frenchmen fought for control. It was discovered by Columbus in 1498; in 1580 the English flag is said to have been raised there, but on doubtful authority.[38] However, it appears that an effort was made in 1625 to colonize it from Barbados by a group of Puritans, but the settlers were soon dispersed by the natives.[39] Although it was included in a grant made to the Earl of Montgomery in 1628,[40] it fell to the Dutch four years later to make the first serious effort at possession when two hundred Zeelanders appeared and proceeded to settle. They gave it the name Nieu Walcheren. Unhappily, they met the same fate at the hands of the Caribs the following year as had the Barbadians. Not until 1642 was another effort made, this time by the Duke of Courland, who sent two ships from the Baltic loaded with prospective planters; these succeeded not only in building a fort but in putting some of the fertile land under cultivation. That same year the French King seems to have included it in the commission granted to the Compagnie François des Isles de l'Amérique, which, according to the French contention, established the Sieurs de Vueüil and Remy as

---

[37] Acts of the Privy Council, Col., 1745–1766, p. 586. According to the "État présent de l'Isle St. Vincent," referred to in footnote 35, there were 696 Frenchmen and 340 slaves.

[38] C. P. Lucas, op. cit., p. 357, note.

[39] Ibid. The Sieur de Rochefort, who published in 1666 his Relation de l'Isle de Tabogo ou de la Nouvelle Oualcre, says (p. 58) that the Caribs had not for a century inhabited the island; for they abandoned their beautiful and large villages to seek shelter from the attacks of their traditional enemy, the Aroüagues of the mainland, on St. Vincent, where they joined other Caribs and from which island they launched expeditions against the foe.

[40] Montgomery's grant included Trinidad, Tobago, Barbuda, and Fonseca (Calendar of State Papers, Col., 1574–1660, pp. 87–8).

governors of it about the year 1648.[41] This, at best, seems to have been a very feeble effort to assert control. The Duke of Courland, however, may have sensed danger to his infant colony from the direction of France and may therefore, according to the English authorities, have been led to enter into the agreement with the Lampsins brothers of Flushing, Holland, in 1654, whereby they were permitted to send a second group of Zeelanders to the island on condition that they make a certain annual payment to the Duke.[42] This harmonious arrangement, however, was not to last; in 1658 the Duke was made a prisoner by the Swedes and, when the news of this reached Tobago, the garrison of Courlanders was persuaded by one of the Lampsins partners to repudiate the authority of the Duke's Governor and to turn over the fort to the Dutch. There were now established on the island not only Courlanders and Zeelanders but also a small body of French who had come from the mainland of South America. Complicating the problem, Louis XIV, in 1662, created Cornelius Lampsins Baron of Tobago, while acknowledging in the patent that Tobago was dependent upon the States General of Holland.[43] Meanwhile, the Duke of Courland, having obtained his freedom, now turned to Charles II of England and in 1664 secured a grant of the island on condition that he suffer only his own subjects

---

[41] The Duke de Maurepas's reply to Yorke's *Mémoire* on Tobago, 1749, Mildmay Book of Memorials, Clements Library.

[42] J. Yorke's "*Mémoire au sujet de Tobage*," 1749, Mildmay Book of Memorials. Right at this point there occurs a discrepancy in the accounts of the attempts at settlement of Tobago. César de Rochefort in 1665 published at Leyden his *Tableau de l'Isle de Tobago* and the following year it appeared in Paris under the title of *Relation de l'Isle de Tabago ou de la Nouvelle Oualcre*. He says (pp. 58–71) that for twenty years after the first Flemish attempt at settlement the island was deserted and that in 1654 Adrien and Corneille Lampsins, who were well acquainted with the West Indies in connection with the provision trade, decided to colonize it. Adrien was a director of the Dutch West India Company of the Middelburg Chamber and Corneille was at one time Burgomaster and Senator from Flushing and perpetual deputy from the Province of Zeeland in the States General. The island, embraced within the grant to the Dutch West India Company, was granted to the two under condition that the governor of it should be approved by the States General. In 1655 Hubert de Beucren was approved as Governor and proceeded to settle men on the island. Soon after this the Duke of Courland sent a great warship to America, to discover and plant an island, which appeared at Tobago and disembarked a hundred people, who, without opposition from the Zeelanders, located in an attractive part of the island. However, after four years the Germans, not being reinforced, were obliged to retire, leaving Tobago to the peaceable possession of those to whom it pertained. De Rochefort, it should be pointed out, was strongly committed to the interest of the Lampsins family.

[43] Lucas, *op. cit.*, pp. 258–9.

and those of England to settle upon it.[44] But he was unable to re-establish himself there by reason of the presence of the hostile Zee-landers, who, however, were themselves ejected in 1666 by two Eng-lish privateers sailing from Jamaica.[45]

At this time it was reported from Barbados that the island was pretty well stocked with Negroes, cattle, and horses and that there were eighteen sugar works.[46] A band of Frenchmen soon drove out the small English garrison but afterwards departed, whereupon the Dutch put in a reappearance; in 1672, with the outbreak of the Third Anglo-Dutch War, the Dutch were overwhelmed by the Barbadians under Sir Tobias Bridges. The English, however, were not prepared to remain, but destroyed the fort and the dwellings before departing. Again the persistent Dutch returned, now under the direct sponsor-ship of the Dutch West India Company, only to be driven out in 1677 by a French fleet under Count d'Estrées, but not until after two se-vere battles. This continual hard fortune seems at last to have dis-couraged the Dutch, for they made no further efforts to colonize Tobago, and apparently in the Peace of Nijmegen, signed between the French Crown and the States General the following year, the is-land was conceded to the French[47] — at least, that was the French contention.[48] In support of this, it may be said that never again did Holland put forth pretensions to it. By the year of the peace just referred to, the island was deserted by both the Dutch and the French.[49]

The withdrawal of the Dutch government, however, brought the Duke of Courland again into the picture. In 1680 he sought to equip some vessels in Dutch ports to prosecute his colonization enterprise,

[44] Cal. State Papers, Col., 1661–1668, pp. 255–6.

[45] De Rochefort (op. cit., pp. 67–71), writing in 1666, the year of the ejection of the Zeelanders, reported that there were about twelve hundred people in Tobago engaged in sugar, tobacco, cotton, indigo, and ginger culture; that the Governor's Council was com-posed of a burgomaster, five escheuins, a secretary, and the officers of militia; and that there were both Fleming and Walloon churches. In Chapter VII of his account of Tobago he traverses the island with the reader, pointing out the location by name of each important settlement and plantation.

[46] Cal. State Papers, Col., 1661–1668, pp. 343–5, 363.

[47] Lucas (op. cit., p. 260) takes the position that it was restored to the Dutch. Arti-cle 8 of the treaty, upon which the French based their claims, reads as follows:

"Chacun demeurera saisé et jouira affectivement des païs, villes, et places, terres, isles, et seigneuries, tant au dedans que dehors l'Europe qu'il tient et possède à present, sans être troublé ni inquiété directement ni indirectement de quelque façon que ce sort."

[48] Maurepas's reply to Yorke's Mémoire on Tobago, 1749, Mildmay Papers.

[49] Cal. State Papers, Col., 1677–1680, p. 290.

although manifestly in disregard of his English patent of 1664. Failing in this, he turned to England and in 1681 entered into an agreement with a Captain John Pointz and Company whereby the latter, under conditions, was given a grant to a hundred and twenty thousand acres of land — although the island can boast of less than seventy-five thousand acres — and the privilege of remaining neutral in case of hostilities between the Duke and the King of England! [50] The following year to form the proposed colony a hundred more men left England under a Governor appointed by the Duke. But the colony did not take root.[51] In spite of the illness and final death of Duke Jacobus, the House of Courland carried on. In 1686, doubtless feeling that their title was under a cloud, the new Duke, now through his London agent, Baron Blomberg (Bloomberg, Blumberg), petitioned James II to encourage the settlement of the island under the patent of 1664. However, the opinion of the Attorney General was adverse to the continued validity of the claim on the ground that Duke Jacobus had not fulfilled any part of the conditions attached to the grant, which, as a result, had now reverted to the Crown. Further, he pointed out that were the island settled by foreigners it would not be lawful for them to trade with the English plantations or the English plantations with them.[52]

The young Duke of Courland — not to be discouraged, and ignoring the contract entered into with Pointz and Company, as well as the adverse decision of the Attorney General — after waiting some twelve years, in the month of March 1698 offered to Sir William Waller, together with Thomas Puckle and Company, another English partnership, a fifty-thousand-acre tract on Tobago provided that they could give him three thousand pounds in cash and pay a quitrent of twopence an acre on the land. Then, in a surprising turn, the following year he approached the Dutch with an offer to cede his rights — whatever they were — to the States General. But the French government, getting wind of this, instructed its Ambassador to The Hague to interpose objections; as the result of which the Grand Pensionary Heinsius gave assurance "that one had not forgotten the cession made by the Treaty of Nijmegen, that there would be no question of any establishment of the Dutch in Tobago."[53]

---

[50] *Cal. State Papers, Col., 1681–1685*, p. 181, and 1700, pp. 140–1.
[51] *Cal. State Papers, Col., 1681–1685*, p. 406.
[52] For this opinion see *Cal. State Papers, Col., 1699*, pp. 234–5.
[53] Contained in Maurepas's reply to Yorke's *Mémoire*, Mildmay Papers.

Meanwhile, the new English Company, apparently quite unaware of the Duke's manœuvre, in May 1699 petitioned the Crown to aid its settlement of the island lest it should fall " into the hands of the French or Dutch who both Court it." [54] The Board of Trade the previous December had taken the position that the enterprise would be prejudicial to Barbados; to meet the objections of the Barbadians the Company now agreed not to engage in the production of sugar in Tobago. However, Pointz and Company had revived its rival claims; what is more, the French Ambassador, the Comte de Tallard, was ordered to complain of these activities in the direction of colonization of the island, which in turn led the Privy Council not only to review the history of the Courland claims, but to set forth England's rights and to forbid any Englishman from embarking upon the intended enterprise.[55]

As to fair Tobago itself, it was now the haunt of pirates and privateers — an island where once the homes and plantations of peaceable and industrious agriculturists had dotted the coastline! Thus it was to remain until the vexed question of its ownership had been settled. It is true that in 1729 the Duke of Montagu, who had received a grant of St. Lucia and of St. Vincent in 1722 from George I, sought to secure Tobago as compensation for fruitless expenditures in attempting the colonization of St. Lucia and in this connection concerted an arrangement with the heirs of John Pointz. But when the Duke of Broglie, the French Ambassador, getting wind of this, sought out Townshend, he was informed that Montagu's application would not be honoured. Indeed, outside the fact that at certain times of the year a vessel would cast anchor in one of the roadways of the island for the purpose of securing wood or engaging in turtle-fishing, no Europeans for fifty years appeared there in any peaceful pursuit.

With the termination of hostilities between Great Britain and France in 1748, however, Tobago took on new significance. For immediately two French ships of the line were sent there and, finding the British armed ship *Boston* at anchor off the coast, ordered its commander, Captain Wheeler, to leave under threat of attack; the latter was informed at the same time that French troops and others had been sent to settle the island.[56] A shore battery was erected and

---

[54] *Cal. State Papers, Col.,* 1699, p. 203.

[55] *Cal. State Papers, Col.,* 1700, pp. 140–1.

[56] The Governor and Assembly of Barbados to the King, February 7, 1748/9, Mildmay Book of Memorials.

a proclamation bearing the name of the Marquis de Caylus, the French Governor of Martinique, was issued in which was asserted "in high haughty terms the incontestable right of the French King thereto and that his Property therein has been authentically acknowledged by Treaties, & that no [other] Prince or Sovereign State had ever form'd any pretensions to the Dominion or sovereignty of the said Island." [57]

Nevertheless, as the result of the exchange of a series of diplomatic notes in which the respective rights to Tobago by the crowns of France and Great Britain were set forth and defended, it was at last agreed that the island should be declared neutral together with the two Caribbee islands and St. Lucia; that each power should evacuate any nationals living upon it; and that it, together with the other three, should be a subject for consideration by a joint Anglo-French commission to meet in Paris.

Important as were Dominica, St. Vincent, and Tobago in the eyes of British and French statesmen in the middle of the eighteenth century, none of these began to compare with St. Lucia. It is hard to realize that this tiny speck in the ocean — but forty-two miles long and only twelve at the widest point, with a total area of two hundred and thirty-eight miles — was ever coupled with the great Hudson Bay region on equal terms as the subject of dispute and negotiation, in 1687, when an Anglo-French commission was set up to consider the rival claims of each of these powers in the New World. It is equally hard to realize that the disposition of the island in 1750 was held by the French to be a matter of equal moment to the settlement of the boundaries of Nova Scotia when once again a board of commissioners was created to arrive at an agreement on various New World issues, which ended by all but ignoring the other so-called Neutral Islands.

St. Lucia is one of the most beautiful among the beautiful small islands of the Caribbean Sea — a mass of mountains arising abruptly from the water with their summits bathed in perpetual mist. Lafcadio Hearn wrote in approaching it:

> " A beautiful fantastic shape floats to us through the morning light; first cloudy gold like the horizon, then pearly gray, then varying blue, with growing warm green lights . . . everywhere mountains sharp as broken crystals." [58]

---

[57] Ibid.
[58] Two Years in the French West Indies, p. 92.

Breen, who lived upon it for thirteen years, declared that " it is second to none in the number and capaciousness of its harbours and the richness and resources of its soil."[59] In one of its deep inlets, the Carénage, subsequently renamed Castries, Rodney sheltered his great fleet before the historic battle with de Grasse in 1782 off Dominica. In fact, its superb harbour facilities as well as other advantages in strategic location led France in the days of Napoleon to consider making it, according to Governor Noguès, " the capital of the Antilles, the general market of the Windward Islands, and the Gibraltar of the Gulf of Mexico ";[60] and in our own day it has been chosen by the United States, in its agreement with Great Britain, as the naval and airplane base in the region of the Windward Islands. Although named after a saint, for a century and a half it was associated with violence as was perhaps no other West India island, large or small, with the exception of Tobago. Seeking solace within its outstretched mountainous arms, men only too often found themselves embraced with the kiss of death — death wafted from the fever-infected shores and mountain valleys,[61] from the deadly and aggressive fer-de-lance — unknown to either Dominica or St. Vincent — from the poisoned arrows of the wild Caribs, and from mortal combat between the forces of Great Britain and France. Thirteen British regiments during the long period of struggle over its possession gained the right to inscribe the name of little St. Lucia upon their colours!

St. Lucia was discovered in 1502 by Columbus, who bestowed upon the island its name; it was rediscovered by the Earl of Cumberland in 1593, but apparently not until 1605 did any European take an interest in it. In that year Captain Nicholas St. John, serving under Sir Oliph Leigh (Leagh), while on his way to Guiana landed there to trade with the Caribs. A settlement was projected, but the prospective settlers were soon driven off by the natives.[62] Reference is also made to a second attempt at colonization upon it by Leigh in 1606.[63] In 1627 it was included among the West India Islands patented to the first Earl of Carlisle by Charles I of England. But in

---

[59] Henry H. Breen, St. Lucia: Historical, Statistical, and Descriptive, p. vii.

[60] Ibid.

[61] The island is no longer considered to be an unhealthful place of residence, but earned that reputation in the seventeenth and eighteenth centuries.

[62] A. P. Newton, The European Nations in the West Indies, 1493–1688, p. 135; J. A. Williamson, The Caribbee Islands under the Proprietary Patents, p. 13.

[63] Memorials concerning St. Lucia, p. 47.

efforts to colonize it neither he nor his heir, the second Earl, was successful. Although it was asserted on rather doubtful authority that between 1635 and 1640 four groups of prospective settlers attempted in vain, each in turn, to get a footing upon it, at least it is reasonably certain that a group appearing in 1640 was mostly massacred by the natives.[64] With the English for the next two decades involved in serious domestic difficulties, energies that might have gone into colonization were diverted. As a result the French, now settled on the near-by island of Martinique, were given the opportunity of establishing themselves on St. Lucia.[65]

The legality of the French occupation was based not only upon the commission given in 1626 by Richelieu to d'Esnambuc, the colonizer of the French portion of St. Christopher of the Leewards, and also to the adventurer de Rossey, to plant all the islands between the 11th and 18th degrees north latitude not occupied by Christians, to which reference has already been made, but also upon the premise that the English had abandoned the island. As to this abandonment, it was later asserted by the British that the Carlisle interests did continue, in spite of the presence of the French, to make at least feeble efforts — specifically in 1644, 1645, and 1647 — to exploit the resources of St. Lucia before surrendering to the restored Stuarts their patent covering their claims in the Caribbeans.[66] Be that as it may, there is little doubt that during the period of French control up to 1664 some definite progress, in spite of great difficulties, was made

---

[64] *Ibid.*, p. 48; J. A. Williamson, op. cit., pp. 152–3.

[65] The British Commissaries in Paris in 1751 charged that the Frenchman, Sieur du Parquet, "contrary to the Law of Nations & to the Amity then subsisting between the two Crowns, taking Advantage of the Distress of the English possessed himself of the Island within about two months of the Massacre" (C. O. 323: 13. O. 90). In reply the French Commissaries stated that it was not until 1643 that St. Lucia was given by du Parquet to Sieur Rousselan, who in that year built a fort upon its shores and cultivated an estate (*ibid.*). Later, in 1754, they corrected the date of the first French settlement to read 1650 a decade after the disappearance of the English (C. O. 323: 13. O. 127). According to this version, in that year du Parquet, the Governor of Martinique, purchased the claims of the bankrupt French Compagnie des Isles de l'Amérique to the islands of Martinique, St. Lucia, and Granada, and thereupon proceeded to settle St. Lucia. However, it appears that two years earlier a small colony was placed upon the island for the purpose of establishing French claims (S. L. Mims, *Colbert's West India Policy*, p. 44).

[66] *Memorials concerning St. Lucia*, p. 56. It may be well to point out that in 1643 Francis Lord Willoughby secured a lease of the Carlisle proprietary rights for twenty-one years, to begin in 1646. For a discussion of the confused relations between the various English groups interested in the West Indies see C. M. Andrews, *The Colonial Period of American History*, II, 250, 272.

in the settlement of the island with the laying out of plantations.[67] Nevertheless, the English interest in it did not disappear. Especially after the establishment of sugar plantations on Barbados, it was regarded as a desirable and logical place for settling the surplus English population of the latter.[68] In this connection, the island continued to appear in the commission of the Governor of Barbados as one of the possessions of England under his supervision. Moreover, in 1663 it was "purchased" from a small group of Caribs under the influence of the mestizo Warner, whose activities in relation to Dominica have already been considered;[69] and the following year Francis Lord Willoughby, who had been invested with the governorship of the "Caribbee Islands" and a moiety of the revenues from the same for seven years, sent a regiment of soldiers from Barbados under Colonel Carew to repossess it. According to one authority, the latter suddenly appeared with some fourteen hundred troops on five warships, accompanied by six hundred natives, in their *canots*, led by Warner; the French settlement of St. Alonzie and Fort de Coque (Coc), defended by the Sieur Bonnard with only forty soldiers, were obliged to capitulate.[70]

The English hold upon St. Lucia after the French capitulation appeared at first to be firm; on the contrary it was most precarious. The soldiers were soon faced not only with a scarcity of food but with great mortality as the result of tropical fevers — in three months some six hundred are said to have died of the bloody flux. Even the Caribs, who had, as is noted, supported the English reoccupation, now turned upon them, attacking them mercilessly. According to the French version of what took place, the English settlers — with their numbers at length reduced to but eighty-nine and labouring

---

[67] Rousselan, who was the first Governor, died in 1655, and two years later du Parquet, with proprietarial claims to the island, also passed away. After the death of the former, who had married a Carib woman and was well liked by the natives, St. Lucia had a succession of governors: La Rivière, Haquet, Le Breton, de Coutis, d'Aigremont, Lalande, and Bonnard. Of these, three were killed by the natives, one was forced to flee from his enraged soldiers, one was recalled, and one fell victim to the climate (Breen, *op. cit.*, pp. 47–8). Du Tertre stresses the fact that the settlement was a costly one in lives and wealth (*op. cit.*, I, 433).

[68] A. P. Newton, *op. cit.*, p. 244.

[69] The French claimed in 1754 that the purchase was made by Warner for the English government from four drunken Caribs who had no authority to represent their nation (C. O. 323: 13. O. 127, and *Memorials concerning St. Lucia*, p. 19.

[70] Du Tertre, *op. cit.*, III, 86–9; [Labat], *op. cit.*, IV, 458–9. The French *Mémoire* of 1751 says that Bonnard had eighty soldiers (C. O. 323: 13. O. 90).

under the conviction that their misfortunes were a judgment of God for having deprived their rivals of this fair possession — deputed five of their number to appear before the Governor of Martinique to make a restitution of it.[71] Although Robert Cooke, the Governor of St. Lucia, apparently disavowed this action of the deputies, nevertheless in January 1666, with the outbreak of war between England and France, the surviving English, after some eighteen months' occupation of the island, proceeded to set fire to their untenable fort and disappeared, to be replaced once again by the French.

During this period the English pretensions to St. Lucia were maintained by William, brother of Francis Lord Willoughby, up to the date of his death in 1673, and those of the French by the new Company of the West Indies, created in 1664, which surrendered its rights to the Crown, however, in 1674.

Although it is frequently stated that St. Lucia was restored to France by the Peace of Breda of 1667, this was denied by the English, who, to the contrary, affirmed that their rights to it were confirmed since it was in their possession in 1665 — a determining date laid down in the treaty. Nevertheless, it can hardly be questioned that for twenty years after their voluntary desertion of the island the returning French were left in undisturbed control; then in 1686 Captain Temple was sent by the Governor of Barbados to drive out their rivals and did succeed in demoralizing their settlement. This led to the appointment the following year of an Anglo-French commission to come to an agreement, as was previously mentioned, on the respective rights of the two nations to St. Lucia and Hudson Bay. Although no agreement was reached other than that neither party should use violence to assert its rights and that the island should be "neutralized," it continued to be exploited, at least to some extent, by the French. In 1700 Father Labat visited it. Although he found no permanent settlers, he did encounter some Frenchmen from Martinique who were engaged in making boats and in securing mahogany boards and planks and who for this purpose had constructed a building on one of the rivers.[72] In fact, in June of that year reports of these activities came to the attention of Governor Ralph Grey of Barbados, who thereupon protested to the Marquis d'Ambli-

---

[71] For the purported words of the deputies see Memorials concerning St. Lucia, p. 22.

[72] [Labat], op. cit., IV, 450. Labat says that as a result of the long wars, lasting from 1671 to 1688, all the settlers of St. Lucia departed for Martinique, Guadeloupe, or other French islands (ibid., IV, 460).

mont, Governor General of the French Islands and demanded the complete evacuation of the island.[73] Grey, however, failed to secure the support of the English Crown, which was adverse at this time to taking any hostile measures against the French.

With the outbreak the following year of the War of the Spanish Succession, interest in St. Lucia drops into the background. In fact it was not until 1718 that the island came again to the forefront when Marshal d'Estrées received it as a gift from the French Crown and proceeded the following year to send there an *état major* and a number of families. This brought such sharp protests from the English court that the French Regent, the Duke of Orléans, agreed that everything should be left in the condition it was in before the grant until conflicting rights had been ascertained. On the other hand, King George I in 1722, upon the petition of John Duke of Montagu for St. Lucia, as well as for St. Vincent, acceded to the request, with the result that that very year the latter sent out Captain Nathaniel Uring to take possession of them.[74] In December, Uring disembarked on the first-named some five hundred settlers and their families who had been transported in seven ships. After the colonizers had fortified themselves Uring published on the 30th of the month a declaration commanding " all strangers having homes to submit to the English government or go elsewhere under penalty of trouble." In turn the Chevalier de Feuguieres (Fouguieres), Governor General of the French Islands, ordered Uring to retire from St. Lucia within a period of fifteen days; when he did not comply Feuguieres sent against him " some two or three thousand men." Faced by overwhelming odds, in January of the following year, the English Governor agreed to evacuate the island with his cannon and other supplies in seven days — with the understanding that neither the French nor the English should inhabit it until a decision had been reached by the two crowns, but that the ships of either might freely anchor in its coves to secure wood and water. Under cover of this arrangement, the French charged that Englishmen began to settle there, setting up lumber yards and engaging in a contraband trade with the near-by French islands.

Finally in 1730, as the result of continued complaints, both courts

---

[73] *Calendar of State Papers, Col.*, 1700, p. 429.

[74] See the *Relation of the Late Intended Settlement of the Islands of St. Lucia and St. Vincent in America in the Right of the Duke of Montague, and under His Grace's Direction and Orders in* 1722 (London, 1725).

agreed not only on a mutual evacuation but that the island, together with St. Vincent and Dominica, should remain "neutral." St. Lucia, however, still continued to be a centre of contraband activities, and Frenchmen likewise reappeared in some numbers.[75] With the outbreak of King George's War, a French garrison was installed there likewise and remained in control until the Treaty of Aix-la-Chapelle, when Louis XV agreed to an entire evacuation in order "to make known to the King of Great Britain by means of commissaries . . . the legitimacy of the rights of France upon this Island."[76] But the French evacuation was delayed in spite of this understanding. Among other excuses for this delay were urged complications arising over St. Martin of the Leeward group of islands, the northern portion of which had been possessed by the French and the southern by the Dutch — an arrangement that still subsists to our own day. In the course of the war, it seems that the Dutch, in the face of a solemn agreement entered into in 1734 for reciprocal co-operation in case the island were attacked by a third power, permitted the English free passage through their portion of it; thereupon the latter fell upon the French, drove them out, and confiscated their possessions. His Most Christian Majesty's Minister, therefore, made clear the determination of his government to continue in St. Lucia until the English had left St. Martin, as they were expected to do under the terms of the treaty of peace.[77] But even after the English complied, the French continued to abide on the disputed island.

Here, then, was the background of the dispute over St. Lucia, a dispute which it was hoped might at long last be terminated by the Joint Commission of 1750. In favour of the English one could urge prior interest in the colonization of the island and, in spite of the failure of attempts to achieve this, a consistent maintenance of claims as indicated by the commissions issued to the Governor of Barbados. On the other hand, in favour of the French one could urge not only the inclusion of St. Lucia by inference in the commission issued to d'Esnambuc and de Rossey in 1626, but that the French, rather than the English, made the real advances after 1650 in the direction of exploiting its resources and also were most consistently active in this

---

[75] In a report on St. Lucia drawn up in 1751 by an unnamed Frenchman for Mildmay, one of the English Commissaries, it was asserted that before 1744 the only Frenchmen on the island were boatmen, mulattoes, and vagabonds (*Lettre à M. Mildmay sur les Moyens de Conciliation*, Mildmay Papers).

[76] C. O. 323: 13. O. 90.

[77] C. O. 323: 13. O. 89.

direction. It is not without significance that the only maps that dealt intimately with the physical features of the island were made by Frenchmen and that the English map-makers of the eighteenth century were obliged to rely upon these and copy the French names attached to promontories, coves, mountains, and rivers. In fact, it may be said that the British ministry was not at all clear that the English claims were superior to those of the French and indeed was quite prepared to permit the Commissaries to agree that if his British Majesty " shall have & enjoy the quiet & peaceable possession of the Island of Tobago . . . His most X^{tian} Majesty shall have & enjoy the quiet & peaceable possession of the Island of Lucia " — with St. Vincent and Dominica still to remain, as in the past, neutral, " with Liberty to the subjects of either Crown to Trade or settle thereon." [78] But this arrangement was also to go hand in hand with the acceptance by the French of the British claims respecting the scope of " ancient " Acadia, and therefore, with the breakdown of diplomacy relative to issues in North America, it failed of realization.

With the outbreak of hostilities in 1756 the island was in the firm control of the French, and only in 1762 were they driven out by Rodney and Monckton. However, by the Treaty of Peace of 1763 it was specifically agreed that the French claim should be respected with the acceptance at the same time of the British claims to St. Vincent, Dominica, and Tobago.

One might have thought that little St. Lucia would now be permitted to drop from the history of international conflict, but in the course of the Revolutionary War Rodney again conquered it, and between 1782 and 1803 it passed back and forth six times, now to England and again to France, until in 1814 it came with its French-speaking, Roman Catholic population to abide permanently within the British Empire. A final chapter in the turbulent history of the Caribbean region now opens up in our own day with the extension of the American system of defences to the island.

---

[78] P.R.O., Nova Scotia, A. 39: 276-9.

CHAPTER VIII

East of Good Hope

U P TO THIS POINT the series of which the present volume is a part has been concerned with regions that either look out upon the Atlantic or border upon rivers and lakes that empty their waters into it. But by the middle of the eighteenth century Great Britain, whether consciously or unconsciously, had already committed herself to the task of laying at least the economic foundations of her future control over the great subcontinent bordering the Indian Ocean. This control, however, was not to be realized except in the face of the most serious challenge on the part of her great rival, France, which, in fact, anticipated her in the application here of certain principles of statecraft which ultimately were to form the superstructure of the British raj in India. However, before bringing into view the activities of agencies employed by the two nations in this struggle for power during the period under consideration, it is important to consider the milieu within which these operated and this struggle took place.

India, stretching almost two thousand miles from the Himalayas to Cape Comorin and almost the same distance from east to west at the greatest width, seems to the casual observer to have been especially set apart by nature for the peaceful evolution of an indigenous civilization, protected as the peninsula is from outside interference by formidable barriers. Upon its northern flank towers the mightiest mountain chain in the world; upon the eastern roll the waters of the Bay of Bengal and upon the western those of the Arabian Sea, both of which are very dangerous during the monsoons; likewise both the eastern and western shores lead up to twin mountain chains, the Eastern Ghats and the Western Ghats, presenting, especially the latter, serious obstacles to any approach to the great plateau of the Deccan.

Strange as it may seem, with all this protection no region in any part of the world has been more subject to invasion and harassment for thousands of years than has India and, stranger still, not by what would seem to be the easiest approaches — by water — but by what is in appearance, at least, the most difficult, that by way of the passes of the Himalayas and their offshoots and thence into the great valley of the Indus and then eastward to the Ganges or southward through the barrier of the jumbled Vindhyas and into the Deccan and the southern coasts.

Who were the first intruders in India may never be known, but it is unlikely that the Negroid aborigines who faced them were capable of effective resistance and yielded the more favourable areas in retreating into the central tropical fastnesses. Wave after wave they came — Dravidian, Indo-Aryan, Persian, Greek, Scythian, Parthian, Hun, Mogul, and Afghan, as well as others — sweeping into the great northern plains, some to retreat after a time, but others to remain; some, such as the Indo-Aryan, as a result of repeated waves of migration, finally inundating the Deccan, each adding its contribution, great or small, whatever it was, to the cultural pattern as well as to the blood streams. Kingdoms and tribal republics without number waxed strong but to disappear, cities innumerable reared their walls, their palaces and temples against the sky, many to leave hardly a trace. But never, so far as the records indicate, was the country politically united and at peace before the establishment of the British raj. For never could any of these some six hundred native states that ultimately appeared maintain themselves permanently against hostile thrusts either from without or from within.

It is true that between the fourteenth and sixteenth centuries to the south of the Vindhya Mountains and the Nerbudda River the great Hindu Empire of Vijayanagar maintained an undisputed sway, uniting the peninsula proper for the first time apparently in its long history; but its rajah was hopelessly defeated in 1565 by the Mohammedans, who thereupon, with an unbelievable ferocity, proceeded systematically to destroy the great imperial capital — from all accounts one of the most beautiful and impressive cities of the world of that age — and to massacre its population. It is also true that later the Moguls made a great effort to unify India in its entirety,

politically. Timur in the fourteenth century captured from the Turk-
ish Tughlaks old Delhi in the Punjab, which likewise was given
over to massacre; but the conquerors receded; then Baber in the early
sixteenth century, appearing with his hordes in the plains of Hindustan, overthrew the Afghan Lodi dynasty, and his grandson Akbar
(1556–1605), after seven years of fighting, succeeded in founding
his Mogul Empire, which, like that of Vijayanagar in the Deccan,
survived some two centuries. But even this Empire, which at its
height brought the greater part of India under one sway, and was
certainly by far the most ambitious and statesmanlike attempt at
unification up to that time, fell short of gathering within its folds the
southern part of the peninsula. Under Aurangzeb, who died in 1707
after a reign of almost fifty years — much of the latter portion of
which was spent in camp in a fruitless effort to conquer the Deccan
— the Mogul raj suffered serious reverses. Aurangzeb's successors —
no longer brought to the imperial throne by the earlier chaotic yet
stern and efficient method of the Moguls of trial by battle among the
armies of contending aspirants — found themselves helpless either
to hold back the invading horsemen of the Persian Nadir Shah, which
swept like a devastating torrent through Hindustan in 1739 before
disappearing, or to assert their authority over either the *viziers* in
their own palaces or the *subahdars* and *nabobs* (*nawabs*), who governed their provinces. Again, therefore, India — especially in view
of the rise in the Western Ghats of the Mahrattas with the plundering proclivities of their formidable and swift-moving mounted armies
— sank into a limbo, not so much of neglect or oblivion as of violence
and political anarchy.

Yet this is but a part of the history. If the annals of India indicate
kaleidoscopic changes in political arrangements, if there is revealed
in these an absence of the sort of genius among the leaders for maintaining governmental stability such as gave the rulers of the Roman
Empire their chief claim to greatness, these at the same time indicate
how great a culture can evolve and maintain itself among a gifted
people in spite of indescribable political disorders. In fact, the social
structure of India, in contrast to the political, long before the dawn
of recorded history in the modern sense, hardened to a granite-like
cohesiveness that since has defied and mocked the turbulent shifting sands of political change. Much, if not all, that is comprehended
in Hinduism — the inexpressibly complicated social institutions, such
as the caste systems, the religious systems, and the symbolism of art

— in spite of minor variations introduced, was as much a fact in the eighteenth century, and is today for that matter, as it was two, perhaps even three, thousand years earlier. This social structure, in the form of a pyramid, presented at its apex during the period under consideration the most extravagant display not only of riches but of unlimited authority, temporal and spiritual, over the lives of countless millions less fortunate; and, at its base, a picture of unbelievable human degradation and submissiveness.

Side by side with Hinduism, in northern India Mohammedanism had taken lodgment with equal firmness; after battering in vain for centuries to shatter the unshatterable imperturbability of its rival, it had at last reconciled itself to the impossibility of the task.

Upon this scene of more recent conquerors jostling more ancient conquerors, the Portuguese appeared in the closing days of the fifteenth century — not with any hope of themselves becoming in turn conquerors of the long line of conquerors, but with that of tapping the trade of one of the world's greatest centres of population and wealth. Yet India for centuries before this event had had commerce with the outside world: the Arabs by ship in the Arabian Sea and by caravan across the wastes of their own deserts to the Mediterranean ports, and the Chinese in their massive junks, both had carried away the products of the land in exchange for others that it lacked. There were not only pepper and other spices, precious stones, among these the diamonds from the mines of Golconda, raw silk, fabrics of silk and cotton, some of wonderful fineness of quality, with many other objects of luxury exhibiting great artistry in handicraft but also crude salpetre, so essential to the manufacture of gunpowder. While the Hindus seem to have played little part in the transportation to other lands of the largess of their own, as merchants and traders operating at home they needed little instruction in the driving of a bargain. What gave them and other non-Europeans settled among them in business an initial advantage over the Europeans — which advantage they continued to hold — was the extreme eagerness of the latter — the Portuguese, the Dutch, the English, the French, and others from northern Europe — to acquire some of the bounty at hand — a bounty in excess of the needs of the privileged classes and beyond the dreams of the exploited masses — with an equal inability to offer in exchange articles from Europe that could either accentuate the ostentation of those already surfeited in luxury or mitigate the wretchedness of the oppressed groups.

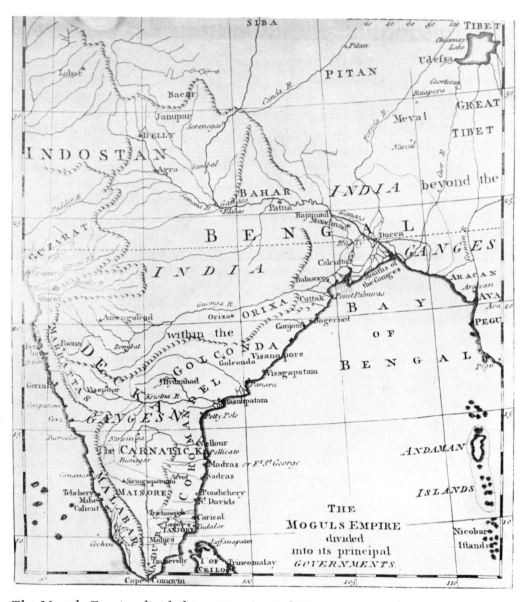

The Moguls Empire divided into its principal Governments.

(From the *Gentleman's Magazine* for 1767)

(From Bellin's *Atlas Maritime*.)

Consequently out of a consistently unfavourable balance of trade appeared a remarkable phenomenon: the slow movement for centuries of a stream of precious metal from west to east; from the mines of the viceroyalties of New Spain and Peru to Europe and thence, in spite of the futile efforts of Spain to retain it, on to India where by subterranean channels, some very dark indeed, it was destined to be finally sucked into the vast buried hoards of the Indian potentates.[1]

For a century the Portuguese, although faced by accumulating difficulties — as the result of inefficiency, corruption, religious bigotry, and the practice of violence — were able, after the destruction of Arab sea-power, to enjoy their monopoly of ocean-borne commerce between India and Europe; then in the latter part of the sixteenth century the Dutch, followed by the English, put in an appearance, which led in the course of the next half-century to their practical elimination as an important factor in the trade of the Indian Ocean and their complete disappearance from the area of the Spice Islands. This was accompanied by sharp rivalry between the latter powers to determine which should fall heir to this vast commercial empire, and the seventeenth century was on the wane before anything like an accommodation could be reached.

It was in the forty-third year of the reign of Queen Elizabeth that English trade to the Far East was first publicly sanctioned when " the Governor and Company of Merchants of London trading into the East Indies" were granted a charter which gave them an exclusive right against all other Englishmen to traffic for a period of fifteen years in that vast area between the Cape of Good Hope and the Strait of Magellan. The activities of the Company, numbering some two hundred and fifteen subscribers at two hundred pounds a share, were under the terms of the patent to be determined by a governor and committee of twenty-four elected annually. As a result of this grant, early in the year 1601 five ships, the largest of six hundred tons, left the Thames with goods to the value of £6,860 and silver to that of £28,742.[2] But it was not India itself that was sought, in spite of an address sent by Elizabeth to Akbar, the Great Mogul,

---

[1] In 1726 it was estimated that from 1602 to that year silver valued at £150,000,000 sterling had been exported to India " never to return " (Anderson's *Origin of Commerce*, III, 386).

[2] *Ibid.*, I, 22; Sir William Foster (*England's Quest of Eastern Trade*, p. 153) gives the value of the silver as £21,742.

but the Malayan Archipelago, where at Sumatra and Java pepper was secured and where in the Strait of Malacca a large Portuguese vessel was captured and looted of its burden of Indian cloth and spices. Such was the beginning of the activities of the first English East India Company.

Other succeeding voyages were likewise directed to this more distant region, and the ships returned home loaded with raw silk, calicoes, indigo, cloves, and mace.[3] The year 1609 saw not only the beginnings of direct contacts with Arabia and India — which were by no means promising in view of the hostility of the Turks at Aden and Mocha and of the Portuguese along the northwestern coast of India — but also the granting in perpetuity by James I of the privileges that the Company had earlier received. Up to the year 1612 its affairs were conducted upon the basis of a regulated rather than a joint-stock company, each separate adventure representing the contribution of a specified number of individuals who upon the return of the fleet would appropriate the profits. In that year it was agreed that the business should be managed upon the basis of a joint-stock company only[4] and the capital, amounting to £429,000, was hopefully set up as a permanent fund. But apparently not until in the days of Oliver Cromwell, with the granting of his "letters patent under the broad seal of England dated 19 October 1657,"[5] did the old prac-

---

[3] For the history of the early voyages in behalf of the Company see ibid.; also Purchas His Pilgrimes (ed. 1905), Volumes II–V, viii, and xiv; Hakluyt's Principall Navigations; Calendar of State Papers, East Indies, 1513–1616; and the publications of the Hakluyt Society, for many original sources.

[4] John Bruce, Annals of the Honourable East India Company (1810), I, 165.

[5] James Mill (History of India, I, 79), with reference to the patent of 1657, says: "Whether the expected charter had been actually received is not ascertained"; while Henry Beveridge in his Comprehensive History of India (I, 279) says that the only evidence of the charter's existence is derived from a reference made to it in a petition which the Company presented to Cromwell in 1658 and a letter of the same year from Fort St. George to the factory of Surat to the effect that the Lord Protector had signed the Company's charter. However, the very day that the charter was issued, the Company drew up its so-called "Preamble," embodying the statement given in the text. This, also, in reciting the terms of the charter, declared: That subscriptions to the joint-stock of not less than £100 would be received and that at the end of seven years from the date of payment the undivided stock would be valued by a committee, whereupon any adventurer who so chose would be paid his share according to the same valuation; it likewise made clear that those with £500 invested were entitled to a vote in the Company meetings, while committee men were to be possessed of £1,000. It is of interest to note, in this connection, the statement that the Company would endeavour to unite the trade of Guinea to that of India for the procuring of gold and elephants' "teeth." The Preamble, bearing the date October 19, 1657, and subscribed to by all adventuring "in the general joint stock," is presented in John Dunning's "An Account of the Charters Granted to the

tice of separate adventures really come to an end; although it is true that with the acquisition of property, separate and continuing joint stocks are a feature of the Company's activities from 1612 to 1657.

Meanwhile, in spite of continued open hostilities with the Portuguese, the Company succeeded in establishing in 1612 a principal factory at Surat and minor ones in three other towns on the Gulf of Cambay, all under the favour of the court of the Mogul. To this court was also sent Sir Thomas Roe as a royal Ambassador, who spent four years in India and who, after becoming fully acquainted with conditions, strongly advised the Company to confine itself to trade, avoiding the building of forts and any military action upon the mainland, which policies, he insisted, had been the undoing of both the Portuguese and the Dutch. In 1614 permission was given to establish a factory on the Coromandel coast at Masulipatam; in 1616 came the re-establishment of one at Agra in the Punjab. By 1618 the Company embraced almost one thousand stockholders and the subscription in that year amounted to £1,600,000. Its chief establishments were now at Surat in India and at Bantam in Java. But rivalry with the Dutch beyond the Strait of Malacca was moving toward a decision and not even the adoption by treaty in 1619 of the so-called Anglo-Dutch joint "Council of Defence," with power to compose all differences and to divide the trade of that region between the two, was able to prevent friction between the English Company and the great Dutch United East India Company, culminating as it did in the arrest and execution in 1623 of the English traders at Amboyna on charges of conspiracy to destroy the Dutch. This rivalry was also a potent factor in its affairs along the east coast of India, as was that of the Portuguese, especially along the Malabar. Even at Surat the Dutch attempted unsuccessfully to drive out the English by underselling.

In 1626 the Company was permitted to establish a factory — subordinate to that at Masulipatam, at Armagon, likewise on the Coromandel — for the purchase of chintzes; in 1640 this latter station was shifted still farther south to the small village of Madraspatam when the local ruler agreed to lease it and to permit its fortification — a concession not to be obtained at Masulipatam — with the result that

East India Company" (pp. 12–14), which brings the history of the activities of the Company down to the reign of George III. The manuscript, covering one hundred and fifty-two pages, is among the Shelburne Papers (Volume LXXXIX) in the Clements Library.

upon the erection of Fort St. George Madras rather than Masuli-patam became the Company headquarters for the coast and about the year 1652 the so-called "Eastern Presidency" was established there.

Madras had many striking drawbacks: lacking a proper harbour, the Company ships were obliged to ride at anchor off the shore and to be serviced by native boats that could ride the surf; these ships were also compelled to leave in the fall of the year to seek refuge elsewhere with the coming of the monsoons;[6] further, the purchases of the Company had in the main to be made some distance inland in the more populous centres of the Carnatic; lastly, the town was by no means a natural stronghold and was always vulnerable to at-tack. Nevertheless, it was felt, although without foundation, to be removed from the main scenes of violent internal conflict that were slowly engulfing India, and, rightly, to be possessed of the strategic merit of location to guard the English interests along the Coromandel from hostile ships of war. But with its fortification the East India Company, whether wisely or unwisely, departed from the advice of Sir Thomas Roe.[7]

In spite of this development, the directors still conceived the corporation to be without political aspirations, except in so far as these would provide the necessary stability to ensure a peaceable prosecution of its business. Nor were threats to this stability all from warring armies in India or from the Dutch or even the Portuguese. In 1604 the Company was obliged to witness the violation of its privileges by a company headed by Sir Charles Mickelborne, one of its own charter members, with a licence from James I to trade to China, Japan, and other places in the Far East, and in 1637 came a

[6] For example, Rear Admiral Charles Watson was instructed under date of March 2, 1754 that it would not be safe for his ships to remain on the Coromandel Coast later than the first week in October. He was therefore ordered to proceed thereafter to Bombay, where he would receive advice from the Company's officers as to the most advantageous employment of his squadron during the monsoon (India Office, Home Series, Miscellaneous, 93: 165–6). Even before the period of the monsoon the situation of vessels on the coast in the presence of a gale was extremely precarious. On April 13, 1749, forty-five ships were driven ashore, while others were dashed to pieces (India Office, Abstracts of Letters, Coast and Bay, 5: 167–8).

[7] It should be made clear that the building of a fort at Madras was neither ordered by the Company nor even approved by the directors when the news arrived that the agents had undertaken its construction (Annals of the East India Company, I, 377, 393; James Mill, op. cit., I, 66). However, it is equally clear that the agents were not over-ruled, in spite of the strong preference of the directors for a continuation of trade without the financial and political commitments implicit in the building and maintenance of forts.

still more serious violation when Charles I granted to Sir William Courteen's Association a permission to traffic in those parts of the Far East where the Company had no settled factories. While the Association, operating upon the basis of a regulated company, did not survive for much more than a decade before being joined to the Company in a "united joint-stock," the affairs of the latter appeared in so unfavourable a light that even after the granting of the Cromwellian patent of 1657 investors could not easily be attracted, especially since various groups, the owners of particular joint stocks, continued to quarrel with one another over many matters of policy. But by that year the Company had factories scattered about in the territories of no less than fourteen different native states.

The restoration of the Stuarts saw the Company under the necessity of securing a new charter. This bears the date of April 3, 1661 and represents a great advance over earlier patents with respect to the powers that it was permitted to enjoy. For the first time those of a political nature are more emphasized than those relating to trade, although in connection with the trading privileges the directors were permitted to export out of the realm as much as £50,000 in silver for each voyage.

The Company was now authorized to empower the local governor and council of a factory to exercise authority in both civil and criminal causes over all living under the Company's protection and to seize anyone who should presume to appear in the East Indies without leave or licence, provided that he was one of the King's subjects, and send him back to England, "there to receive such condign Punishment as the merits of his Case shall require & the Laws of the Nation allow." But this was not all. The corporation could, on its own authority, send out ships of war and men under arms for the defence of its property; it could build such "castles" as it might see fit at St. Helena — the island as yet was not in its possession — and elsewhere to the east of the Cape of Good Hope, and, under its common seal, could even make peace and war with or against any non-Christian people dwelling in those places where it was privileged to trade.[8] Thus a business corporation began to take on the characteristics of a subordinate government.

The next event of significance in the life of the Company was the acquisition in 1668 of the island of Bombay, somewhat earlier secured by Charles II as a part of the dowry brought to him by the In-

---

[8] Shelburne Papers, 89: 17–21; Bruce, op. cit., I, 557.

fanta Catherine of Portugal. For over half a century the English had cast covetous eyes upon this, one of a group of closely connected islands possessed in turn by the Hindus and by the Mohammedans before these had fallen to the Portuguese in 1534. Nevertheless, the town upon it had as yet obtained little of the wealth, population, and distinction as a great commercial centre that were to be its share in the years to come. Under the terms of the charter of March 27 of the above year the island was put in a distinct category with respect to places where were located factories of the corporation; for it was provided that the King's subjects there dwelling, together with their posterity, were to enjoy every liberty of natural subjects " as if they had been abiding & born in England." [9] In contrast to the annual rental of twelve hundred pagodas payable for Madras to the native overlord, the Company was able to hold Bombay in free and common socage directly from the King of England by an annual payment of ten pounds. Five years later St. Helena became the second so-called " sovereignty " of the Company when it was granted in full proprietorship together with adequate powers of government.[10] In 1676 another sovereign attribute was conferred upon the Company when it was permitted to coin money at Bombay, which money was to be current within the limits of its charters " so as it is not called by the name of any coin in England." [11]

With growing political powers it is not surprising that these should be used to the fullest extent by the East India Company — and perhaps even overstepped when the occasion demanded it. There must have been the feeling that the Company had overstepped its powers when it made the successful application to have embodied in the charter granted in 1676 a pardon in advance for " all treasons, misprisons, murders, etc.," that might later be charged against its officers and agents in suppressing, through the exercise of martial law, mutinies that broke out in both Bombay and St. Helena.[12] As a re-

---

[9] Shelburne Papers, 89: 25–8; Bruce, op. cit., I, 104, passim; Mill, op. cit., I, 84–6.

[10] For the charter of 1673 see ibid., II, 232–4, and Shelburne Papers, 89: 31–3. The Company had been permitted to fortify and colonize St. Helena under terms of the charter of 1661, as is indicated in the text, which it proceeded to do. However, it was captured by the Dutch in 1673, but retaken the same year by the royal navy. Thereupon the King was led to make an outright grant of it to the Company.

[11] Shelburne Papers, 89: 29–30.

[12] The charter provided for pardon for all acts committed on or before September 16, 1676, apparently the day that application was made for the new patent, which issued from the seals and was signed on October 5 of that year.

sult, the authority to employ military law was likewise expressly conferred upon it in 1683; at the same time provision was also made for the exercise of vice-admiralty jurisdiction, by the permission granted to erect courts of judicature, to consist of one person learned in the civil law and two merchants, which should determine, "according to equity & the laws & customs of merchants," all cases involving seizure and forfeiture of ships and merchandise appearing within the region of the Company's monopoly, contrary to its rights.[13]

One might have thought that with all this support from government, which brought with it a great accumulation of power, the East India Company would have possessed the instrumentalities and resources to have overcome every obstacle that confronted it. But this was not the case. It had to witness not only the loss of its agency at Bantam in Java as the result of the hostility of the Dutch, but likewise the closing of its factories in Bengal when its agents entered into conflict with the local Nabob. Even the Mogul Emperor, Aurangzeb, turned upon its factories and seized that at Surat. Its expenditures in building forts and fitting out ships of war moreover now laid it under a heavy debt, and as a climax to its discouragements it found itself face to face with a horde of interlopers who bade defiance to its authority, which they claimed extended only to the factories and not to the high seas. Once again, therefore, it was able to secure an extension of its authority over the lives of English subjects when in 1686 James II granted to it the right to exercise "martial law" in time of hostilities within the area of its monopoly — that is, not only within the presidencies but in the waters of the Indian Ocean.[14]

With the coming of William and Mary to the throne, however, a new and a more serious threat to the continued existence of the East India Company than any of the above appeared in the determination of the House of Commons to bring about its dissolution in favour of a new company. Doubtless one source of the strong disfavour into which it had fallen was the feeling that it had mismanaged Indian affairs, with the emphasis that it placed at this period upon the acquisition of dominion in India and the revenues attendant thereupon as against the increase of trade. For, in the words of the directors in 1689:

---

[13] This is embodied in the charter of August 3, 1683 (Shelburne Papers, 89: 34–7).
[14] Shelburne Papers, 89: 39–41.

"The increase of our revenue is the subject of our care, as much as our trade: — 'tis that must maintain our force, when twenty accidents may interrupt our trade; 'tis that must make us a nation in India."[15]

Moreover, its continued monopoly of the lucrative India trade created a host of enemies without Parliament, who now proceeded to close in upon it. Not even the charter of 1693 secured from the new rulers, together with those of 1694 and 1698 — all of which sought to meet some of the criticisms by making the advantages enjoyed by the stockholders much less exclusive — were able to appease its opponents or meet the constitutional objections of the majority of the House of Commons, which now took the position that no royal patent but only an act of Parliament could keep Englishmen from trading to the East Indies.[16]

---

[15] Bruce, op. cit., III, 78; Mill, op. cit., I, 108.

[16] Shelburne Papers, 89: 44–53. By the charter of December 15, 1693, which continued the life of the Company for twenty-one years, it was declared that the King and Queen desired to make the East Indian trade "more national, general and extensive than hitherto" by adding new subscribers. It was therein provided that for every vote in the general court a member must have £1,000 invested in the funds and that no one should have more than ten votes; further, that all the imports of the Company were to be sold "openly and publickly by Inch of Candle at their public sales" (that is, the goods that were offered for sale must be disposed of to the highest bidder before the inch of candle had burnt itself out); that the exports of goods out of the Kingdom to the East Indies must have an annual value each year of at least £100,000, and that on the return there must be delivered to the officers of the ordnance five hundred tons of saltpetre at a specified price; finally, that the books of the Company must remain open for all Englishmen to enter "new subscriptions for a succeeding new general joint stock."

The charter of September 28, 1694 sought to democratize, as it were, the Company management. It provided that oaths were to be required of those voting in the general court and of the officers with respect to their qualifications; that no governor or deputy governor should continue in office longer than two years or be eligible to be re-elected to office until after two years had elapsed; and that, of the twenty-four "committees" or directors, at least eight must not have held office the preceding year; further, the governor or his deputy was required to summon a general court within eight days after being requested to do so by six or more members duly qualified to vote; and, finally, elaborate provision was made governing the funds of the Company to prevent any group within it securing an unfair benefit by, or control over, them.

This liberalization of the Company was also the chief objective of the charter issued on April 13, 1698, the tenth year of the reign of William III, especially in view of the fact that "the greatest number of adventurers are excluded from the Genl Courts and a majority of votes lie in a few hands." The amount to be invested in the funds of the Company to entitle one to vote was therefore again fixed at £500, instead of at £1,000 as provided for in the charter of 1693, and in place of a maximum of ten votes permitted to each investor, according to the amount of his investment, it was now provided that this should be limited to five votes, to enjoy which at least £4,000 had to be in the joint stock. To prevent the Dutch from acquiring a monopoly of the importation of diamonds and

The outcome of the opposition to the Company — doubtless supported by many of its stockholders as the result of its great losses of ships and cargoes in connection with the war being waged with France, which had prevented the payment of dividends for some years [17] — was the passing of an act by Parliament in 1698 for raising a public subscription of two million pounds. Under the terms of the act [18] this fund was to be loaned to the government with an interest of eight per cent; the subscribers to this were to be thereupon embodied in a so-called " General Society," with an exclusive right to trade to the East Indies. According to regulations laid down, the members, whether corporations or individuals, were privileged to trade only to the amount of the subscriptions respectively paid in, and to this end as many as saw fit could establish a new joint-stock company or trade outside the same.[19] As a result, " the English Company trading to the East Indies " made its appearance under the Great Seal — in spite of the fact that the old London Company was still privileged to trade until Michaelmas 1707. The latter, however, not only shrewdly bought shares in the new company to the extent of £315,000, but proceeded with superior facilities and its long experience to offer such severe competition to its rival in India that soon a demand arose that the two coalesce. With the passing of William III in March 1702 and the declaration of war by Queen Anne in May, this demand became so insistent, in view of the vital necessity of presenting a united front to France, even in the Indies, that a tripartite indenture was entered into between the Queen, the old company and the new company on July 22 of that year; under its terms the old company agreed to take over a sufficient portion of the subscription to the General Society to make its investment in the two million pounds' loan equal to that of the new company; the latter in turn agreed to pay to the old company a sum sufficient to give each an equal investment in the forts, factories, and other permanent assets of the old company in the East Indies. The two companies, therefore, although maintaining separate existence — the old one at its Leadenhall Street quarters and the new one at Skinner's Hall

---

other jewels into Europe and this branch of trade " being utterly lost to the Kingdom," the Company, which manifestly was not meeting this challenge, was also now given leave to issue special licences to those desiring to export precious stones from the East Indies to use the Company ships for this purpose.

[17] Anderson's *Origin of Commerce*, III, 183-4.

[18] 9 and 10 William III, c. 44.

[19] Shelburne Papers, 89: 56-71: Anderson, op. cit., III, 187-91.

on Dowgate Hill — were committed to carry on the trade with the East Indies in a joint account for a period of seven years, with each exercising an equal authority in the management of the trade, at the end of which the old company was to surrender its charter and the whole trade was to be "forever" conducted by the new company, which should take the name: "The United Company of Merchants of England trading to the East Indies."[20]

It may be well at this point to indicate the nature of the interest that the old company had acquired in the East Indies at the time of the agreement.[21] This interest included not only the outright possession of the islands of St. Helena and Bombay, but factories at Surat, Agra, Lucknow, and at three other towns in northern India; on the Malabar coast three forts, one of which was at Tellicherry, together with a factory at Calicut; along the coast of Persia three factories; upon the Coromandel and eastern coast extending up to Bengal not only Fort St. George and Fort St. David but its fort at Vizagapatam, together with factories at seven other towns; in Bengal Fort William at Calcutta and factories at Patna and in six other places; finally, on Sumatra, York Fort at Bencoolen and three main factories together with other "out-factories depending on Bencoolen." In addition it still retained certain "rights" in Bantam in the island of Java and in the "South Seas," which, however, were very vague since the factories once possessed to the east of Sumatra had now been closed as a result of the all too successful competition of the East India Company of the United Netherlands. These assets, as well as others of perhaps not less value, were now at the services of the United Company when, as the result of the award of the Lord High Treasurer, the Earl of Goldophin, acting as arbitrator, the complicated affairs of the two companies were arranged in September 1708, and the old company thereupon surrendered to the Queen its corporation and all its charters.[22]

Before the final union was effected, it should be pointed out, the nation, now involved in the War of the Spanish Succession, urgently required funds. Therefore, Parliament early in the above year exacted a loan of £1,200,000 from the General Society without in-

---

[20] Anderson, op. cit., III, 218–20; Shelburne Papers, 89: 71–97. In this connection the cession of Bombay and St. Helena was provided for by the old company to the new.

[21] This is set forth in the so-called "Quinque Partite Indenture" of July 1, 1702 (Shelburne Papers, 89: 103–9).

[22] Shelburne Papers, 89: 109–16.

terest,[23] which, added to the original £2,000,000 that had been previously furnished to the government at eight per cent, made a total
loan of £3,200,000, upon which total it was agreed that five per
cent should thereafter be paid; it was also agreed that to secure the
above amount and to provide adequate working capital the United
Company should be permitted to borrow £1,500,000 or to call upon
the stockholders by assessment for this amount. As a compensation
for this aid, the government in turn agreed that the Company, instead of facing the possibility of termination with three years' notice
after September 1711, should be guaranteed an existence for a period
three years after March 1726, and until its capital had been repaid.
Since this seemed to imply a lack of permanence in the position of
the United Company such as would discourage the forming of "lasting settlements for the support and maintenance thereof for the
benefit of the British nation," Parliament was prevailed upon in 1712
to pass an act [24] which by title appeared to imply that even should
the loan to the government be redeemed, upon three years' notice —
now after Lady Day 1733 — the Company would continue to enjoy
in perpetuity its exclusive trade.[25] Although this purpose could not
actually be drawn from enacting clauses of the statute, there undoubtedly now existed within and without Parliament a conviction
that it was against the national interest to paralyse the corporation
with respect to future plans for the development of Far Eastern
trade by permitting too great uncertainty as to its status.

It may be mentioned in passing that in the course of the South
Sea Company's speculative orgy, when the frailty of the whole ambitious scheme was becoming apparent and the investors in its stock
saw their paper profits evaporating with the steady decline in its
value, a plan was devised whereby both the Bank of England and the
United Company were to take over nine millions of its stock.[26] This

---

[23] 6 Anne, c. 17.

[24] 10 Anne, c. 28.

[25] In the Company's reply to those who sought in 1730 to strip it of its privileges is
the following clause (VII):

"That although the company have a claim to a perpetuity in this trade, by the act of
the tenth of Queen Anne, cap. xxviii, yet some doubts arising . . . because that act
. . . does not explicitly enact a perpetuity of this trade to the company . . . as the act
of that same session expressly does in favour of the South Sea Company," etc.

For this reply see Anderson, op. cit., III, 410–11.

[26] Ibid., III, 353. It is true that four millions of South Sea Company stock was en-
grafted into the capital stock of the Bank of England; the remaining thirty-two millions
was in 1723 almost equally divided into South Sea annuities and South Sea stock.

proposal not only was after heated debate approved by the Company in a general court but was even confirmed by an act of Parliament in 1720; nevertheless, it was not carried into execution. As a result the corporation was permitted to move along on even keel until early in 1730, when a powerful opposition was raised to the continuance of its monopoly on the part of certain mercantile and financial groups who in February offered to redeem by 1733 its loans to the government and after that day to permit a sum equal to the total amount — that is, £3,200,000 — to be enjoyed by the government at only two per cent interest instead of five. The plan had in mind the erection of a regulated company which was to enjoy a monopoly of eastern trade for thirty-one years. This was to be limited to those who secured licences for their private adventures from the new company and paid into its treasury one per cent of the value of their exports to India; it also sought the privilege of levying a five per cent duty on all commodities imported from India by company members,[27] for the purpose of creating a fund to support the forts and settlements. Although the effort failed, in order to secure a renewal of its privileges to run to Lady Day 1769, a period of thirty-three years, the United Company was obliged to accept a reduction of one per cent in interest of the above loan to the government, making its receipts from that source but £128,000 instead of £160,000.[28] Having surmounted this crisis, it again moved along without much interference from government for the next twenty years; then it was compelled, in 1750, very much against its desire, to agree to another reduction of one per cent after 1755 in the interest upon its loan.[29]

The United East India Company, in view of the developments just described and covering a century and a half of its history, must in the eighteenth century be considered from two closely related but yet distinct points of view: first, as an agency of government, endowed with power to legislate for as well as to administer the affairs of those localities where it had acquired an interest more or less permanent in nature, and also to control the activities of all peo-

---

[27] Ibid., III, 406–10.

[28] 3 George III, c. 14. The Company, incidentally, paid £200,000 for this renewal.

[29] In 1745 it loaned another million pounds to the government at three per cent. Between 1750 and 1755 it received 3½ per cent interest on the main loan of £3,200,000; after the latter date, three per cent on the whole loan (Minute Book, 68: 549–72; 650–1).

ple of British nationality who came within the sphere of its monopoly; secondly, as a trading corporation.

Regarding the first aspect, it is not without significance that with the growing anarchy in India, within and without the borders of the great Mogul Empire, especially after the death of Aurangzeb in 1707, the three towns which now became the so-called Company "presidencies" — Madras, Bombay, and Calcutta — experienced an extraordinary growth. This was not only on account of the facilities that each offered for trade but seems to have come particularly by reason of the fact that they all may be described as places of refuge for those natives with wealth and others living in India who sought security. Each, it may be noted, had come under the control of the old company by peaceful means and not through conquest.

As to Calcutta, its beginnings are identified with the activities of a resourceful agent of the Company, Job Charnock, who was placed in charge of a factory first at the inland town of Patna; then, as a result of the interference with the trade, he and his associates retreated in 1686 first to Hugli, on the river of that name, and then later as the result of continued interference that same year still farther down the river to Sutanati; and finally they were compelled to transfer their activities to the very mouth of the river. After further discouragements and an attempt to open up again at Sutanati in 1687 and the failure of Captain Heath to bring effective naval aid, it was at last determined by the Company to withdraw from Bengal. Thereupon the Nabob, by no means happy over this decision and in order to bring about a resumption of English trade, which, he realized, had greatly helped to enrich his province, agreed to remit all customs and, in view of the same, to accept the lump sum of three thousand rupees annually. As a result Charnock returned to Sutanati. Then in 1696 came the building, with the consent of the local Governor, of Fort William for the protection of the agents and in 1698 the purchase of the village of Sutanati and also of Kalikata as well as a second neighbouring village, out of which cluster grew the city of Calcutta, in spite of the presence of fever-breeding swamps and tide inundations. By 1710 the population was placed at 12,000 and by 1752 it had jumped to 117,000; with steady and corresponding increases it finally became the metropolis of India and one of the world's largest cities. Nor was this all, for as the centre of vast wealth concentrated in native hands, it was one day to be hailed, perhaps over-enthusiastically, by Macaulay as "the city of palaces."

The rise of Bombay to greatness is almost as striking. Although the Portuguese had held it for over a century before its transfer to the English crown in 1661, their misgovernment, their shortsighted business methods, which impoverished rather than enriched, their social and moral disintegration, their religious intolerance and persecutions, all combined to make the island a place to be avoided. In contrast to Surat, the chief seaport of the Mogul Empire, with perhaps three-quarters of a million inhabitants, it could boast of but some ten thousand. But with its acquisition by the Company in 1668 and the substitution of a mild form of government in place of one that had been harsh, of toleration for all forms of religious belief in place of a policy repressive of all but the Roman Catholic; with the increased security now also afforded the natives and others from the looting Mahratta horsemen and piratical fleets, it at last began its remarkable development so that in the course of time, with its superb harbour facilities, its improved sanitation, together with other advantages, it took away from Surat the long unchallenged commercial supremacy on the Arabian Sea and became the second city of India, and, more truly than even Calcutta, a " city of palaces." In contrast, Portuguese Goa, another great rival, exposed to hostile interference and poorly administered, declined as rapidly as Bombay expanded. At the height of its glory in the sixteenth century it was one of the greatest cities of India; in 1695 it could lay claim to a population of only twenty thousand; by 1775 this had sunk to sixteen hundred.

As to Madras — located " on one of the most incommodious spots imaginable " — while its growth was slow during the first decades of its possession by the English, the increasing political disturbances in eastern India starting about the year 1685 led to " a prodigious resort of Indian merchants to this place," apparently from more exposed places, such as the once great city of Masulipatam. As a result, in addition to Fort St. George and the so-called " White Town " to the north, there came into existence the very populous so-called " Black Town " adjoining the latter. By the middle of the eighteenth century Madras could boast some eighty thousand people, and eventually took its place as the third largest city in India. Including the outlying territory — stretching some five miles along the coast and a mile inland — its population in 1746 numbered about two hundred and fifty thousand of which only about three hundred were English, counting two hundred soldiers.[30]

---

[30] Mill, op. cit., III, 46-7.

It was perfectly natural that with the concentration of Europeans as well as natives within these presidencies the demand should arise for setting up a form of local government in harmony with English practice. The permission for the Company to accomplish this end, in the exercise of powers that it had previously received by patent, was granted in 1726 in a charter issued by George I on September 24.[31] Thereby the towns of Madras, Bombay, and Calcutta were incorporated and provided with a mayor and aldermen and a mayor's court of record competent to handle both civil and criminal cases which were disposed of upon the basis of English law; the post of sheriff was also given legal sanction. The Governor and Council of each presidency were authorized not only to fill these offices but to make by-laws, rules, and ordinances " agreeable to reason & not contrary to the laws of England," which, however, should not have force until approved and confirmed in London by a Court of Directors of the United Company; further, the five senior members of each council, together with the governor, were commissioned justices of the peace and as such not only could hold courts of quarter sessions with power of oyer and terminer and jail delivery but could in their individual capacity act in certain matters. In the case of the Presidency of Madras, for example, one member of the council was expected to exercise this office at Madras, another at Fort St. George, another at Fort St. David, farther down the coast, another at the factory in Vizagapatam farther up, and finally another at Bencoolen on Sumatra. Besides the mayor's court and that of the quarter sessions for Europeans just described, provision was also made for so-called *zemindar* courts, in which Indian law was applied to the natives living within the jurisdictional limits of the three presidencies. Finally, the new charter provided that ships of war sent from England might be subject to the authority of the local governor, who was also the commander-in-chief of the land forces of his presidency — forces consisting not only of Europeans but also of native troops known as sepoys. Therefore, after 1726 not only could the governor and council of each presidency make war and peace upon native rulers, not only could they coin money, raise a revenue, and do many other things associated with the exercise of plenary power under terms of earlier grants, but they could now establish a perfectly regularized form of English local government within their jurisdiction

[31] For a copy of this see Shelburne Papers, 89: 116–28.

for Europeans, and for those natives enjoying their protection an even-handed justice based upon local law and custom.

But, after all, the United East India Company was not primarily interested in the exercise of political authority to the east of the Cape of Good Hope — at least down to the outbreak of the Seven Years' War — but in trade, in spite of the efforts of Sir Josiah (Josia) Child, the Company's powerful governor, in the direction of territorial acquisitions during the latter part of the preceding century. The most elaborate machinery, in fact, had been evolved both in London and in India in the light of experience to further that end. The stockholders, who under the new patent were now limited, in contrast to the seventeenth-century practice, to but one vote,[32] and that only provided that at least £500 had been invested in stock, were at their Proprietors' Courts, among other privileges enjoyed, able to vote on large questions of policy and to elect annually, among the holders of at least £2,000 in stock, the so-called twenty-four "Committees" or directors, who themselves formed a court which had full responsibility for the making of most decisions necessary to the proper conduct of a great and complex business. However, the actual day by day administration of the affairs of the United Company by the directors was carried out through the appointment of some ten or more committees from their membership, the most important of which by far was that of Correspondence. This committee was charged with policy-framing, as well as policy-execution in the broader aspects. As the name implies, it was in charge of the all-important correspondence with India and much of its work was highly confidential; the Committee on Secrecy was also faced with great responsibilities, especially in the middle of the eighteenth century in its negotiations with the French East India Company;

---

[32] The number of votes cast at the Proprietors' Court varied greatly. On April 6, 1748 but 178 votes were cast; on April 5, 1749 the number was 222; but on January 4 of the following year, when a very real issue was presented having to do with the reduction of interest paid by the government on the £2,200,000 loan, the number was 505 (Minute Book, 1748-50, 63: 3, 298, 571-2). The last number accounts for but £252,500 in stock. This would indicate that most of it was held either by those who possessed large blocks of it but were entitled to but one vote or by those who possessed stock valued at less than £500. In 1708 one individual owned as much as £28,000 in stock, and there were trust accounts for some families which ran even higher. Clive at a later period attempted to circumvent the rule by purchasing stock to the value of £100,000, which he divided into two hundred voting blocks and distributed among his relatives and other supporters; unfortunately for him, the City in opposition to him rallied its forces and outbid him (R. M. Mottram, Traders' Dream: The Romance of the East India Company, pp. 139, 191).

then there were the Committees on Accounts, on Buying, on the India House, the last-named not too important, on Law Suits, on Private Trade, on Preventing Private Trade, on Shipping, on the Treasury, and, finally, on Warehouses.[33]

There was plenty of work for the directors: the purchase of manufactured articles and silver for export to the East; the securing of government licence for sending the latter out of the country;[34] the leasing of the proper amount of ship tonnage and the manning of these ships with the proper complement of officers and sailors; the placing of these officers under proper bond; the instruction of the company agents in India upon a multitude of matters, among others the quantity, variety, and quality of various commodities to be obtained under market conditions in England and elsewhere; the raising and dispatch of armed forces and ships of war to strengthen the forts, especially in time of peril; the protection of the corporation from litigation and from hostile attacks within Parliament and without; the advantageous disposal of the great imports from India and farther eastward, in harmony with charter and statutory restrictions; and the satisfaction of the claims of stockholders and other creditors — together with many other activities inseparably connected with the politico-economic basis of the Company's activities in the eighteenth century. All these, so far as England was concerned, were centred at the old East India House on Leadenhall Street — purchased in 1710 after a long period of leasing from the owner, reconstructed and enlarged in 1726[35] — and at the East India docks on the Thames.

In India the governors and councils of the three presidencies received the goods and precious metals consigned to them and thereupon proceeded to dispose of both in the most advantageous way — the first by auction and the second by minting. They also busied themselves in filling orders from Leadenhall for the purchase or manufacture of certain goods and in this connection set into motion the very complicated machinery devised to obtain such goods from the native producers. Members of the council of a presidency were also likely to be at the head of some factory located within the juris-

---

[33] Minute Book, 1748–50, 63: 6–8. James Mill, op. cit., III, 6–9, in the enumeration of the committees does not mention the Committee on Secrecy, which really appears to represent a division of labour between it and the older Committee on Correspondence.

[34] For example, see Minute Book, 1748–50, 63: 72.

[35] For the history of the East India Company headquarters see Sir William Foster's Old East India House.

diction of the presidency, which position occupied most of their attention. They were assisted in their activities by their fellow senior merchants, and also by junior merchants, by factors, and by writers — groups so classified by the directors according to whether one was an eleven-year man or better in point of view of service, an eight-year man, a five-year man, or, finally, a man without that length of experience or better,[36] with the responsibilities and rewards, as a rule, bearing close relation to the period of service. This hierarchy of British employees in turn usually dealt with a native industrial hierarchy, especially in drawing upon the cloth supplies of India: the calicoes, muslins, chintzes, and ginghams, together with a wide variety of other fabrics, many of them taking their names from localities.[37] Contact was made through a permanent native employee of the Company, a *banyan*, who would contract for the services of certain big native brokers called *gomastahes* with headquarters in towns that produced the particular fabrics that were desired; these brokers would thereupon summon to their so-called *cutcheries* intermediate brokers, who upon agreement entered into contract with the weavers, which generally involved certain advance payments of the little brokers, who in their turn made the detailed contracts with money and supplies of raw materials. While the weavers were liable to extortionate treatment and exploitation, on occasion at least, through the functioning of this system,[38] two factors operated to mitigate the evil: one was that the native ruler of the region in question had a most direct and positive interest in protecting the weavers' gains, which, if generous, in turn buttressed his own financial position; the other was the existence of competition among various European and non-European groups at Surat, on the Malabar and Coromandel Coasts, and in the Gangetic basin for the products of the India looms throughout the period under consideration. In other words, it would be as difficult to prove that this class of skilled artisans — impoverished as it was as the result of conditions deeply

---

[36] Mill, *op. cit.*, III, 20.

[37] For example, in 1750 the following goods were ordered from Bengal: allibannies, addaties, allibatties, bastoes, bandannoes (bandannas), ballasores, chilloes, chowtars, coopies, chints, cullannies, cossaes, chuckloes, cushtaes, dooreos, emmerties, gurrahs, ginghams, together with raw silk (Letter Book, 1748–50, 28: 87–112). Sometimes light is shed upon the appearance of these articles. For example, there was ordered from the Coromandel Coast in the same year bright red allejars, very best Pullicut bettellees, green and purple Moorish chintzes, small white, blue striped, and red striped ginghams (*ibid.*, 28: 8–12).

[38] Mill, *op. cit.*, III, 14.

embedded in the social structure of India — did not benefit financially from the appearance of the European traders as it would be to prove that the trading ability of the American Indians in the Great Lakes region was not greatly improved as the result of French and English rivalry for the furs that they brought to market.

The filling of the orders of the London directorate of the Company for particular commodities was not, of course, limited by the process described above. For while its officials rigidly guarded its monopoly of trade between Great Britain and India, much of the goods intended for the home market was secured in India by means of the so-called " country trade "; in this individual members of the Company and others — even " Moors, Armenians, and Hindus " — might be licensed to engage in private business for the ultimate benefit of the corporation; they in turn disposed of their purchases to its agents for export.[39] This country trade might be inland or by sea, even to China, and if by sea, it might be in ships not chartered by the Company but licensed to trade under its authority. Further, there was, of course, nothing to prevent a native merchant securing upon his own initiative, particularly in the inland towns outside of its jurisdiction, commodities which might be profitably disposed of to its agents.

In turning to a more detailed analysis of the activities of the Company it may be said that during the early part of the eighteenth century an average of some fifteen ships were taken into the service and sent to the East Indies each year; [40] in 1748 twenty-one ships were taken and in 1749 twenty-three. These were not ships of great tonnage — all, in fact, were stated to be under five hundred tons' burden.[41] The terms of the agreement with the owners were based upon

---

[39] From time to time private individuals were given permission to go to India as "free merchants." For example, in 1749 Samuel de Castro and David Lopez Fernandes each gave security to the amount of £2,000, which was approved under condition that in going out they would abide by the Company's regulations (Minute Book, 1748–50, 63: 207–8).

[40] For example, in 1700 fourteen ships were sent out; in 1706 but nine; in 1719 the number reached twenty-two; in 1726 it dropped to eleven; and in 1730 it was thirteen ("Account of Ships and Goods Exported to the East Indies," C. O. 390: 6. 183).

[41] A ship of standard specifications was constructed for this trade by those interested in placing it in this service. For example, according to data furnished, all but one of the twenty-one ships accepted in 1748 had a burden of 499 tons, and seventeen of the twenty-three accepted in 1749; four of the remainder were of 498 tons' burden, one of 400, and one of 350 (Minute Book, 1748–50, 63: 117, 120). But one must bear in mind that ships of 500 tons and over were required by law to provide the services of a chaplain, an expense that owners sought to avoid, and therefore they would understate the ship's tonnage.

the payment of freight at a specified rate, which varied — according to destination and the character of the articles to be transported — from £26 to £32 a ton in the middle of the eighteenth century.[42]

As has been previously suggested, in the outward freight the most important item was bullion — from the point of view of value. As a rule, during the early part of the eighteenth century this was from five to seven times the value of all other commodities sent to India. For example, in 1729, the year that a serious attempt was made by a rival group to overthrow the Company, the total value of the exports was £756,074,[43] of which total £630,264 was in bullion.[44] In 1730,

---

The tonnage of the East India vessels, as the text indicates, was not "displacement tonnage" but capacity for the conveyance of goods plus kentledge — that is, the pig-iron ballast. This ballast, which was permitted to remain in the hold of the ship, accounted, as a rule, for 80 tons out of the 499, which left 419 for goods ("Fifth Report from the Committee of Secrecy on the State of the East India Company," Reports from the Committee of the House of Commons, 1772–1773, IV [1804], 279). However, it was stated in 1750 that some of the ships sent to Bengal carried only one-half of this kentledge (ibid).

All those who owned ships in the service of the East India Company, at least in the middle of the eighteenth century, were owners of stock in the Company. They numbered thirty-one in 1751 and in that year pledged to maintain forty-eight ships available for the service. A larger number had apparently been built, with the result that there was complaint on the part of these owners that some of their vessels had not been employed for two years or upwards (ibid., p. 278). In order to determine which ships to accept the directors of the Company resorted on August 18, 1749 to balloting, as the result of which thirteen ships were taken into the service (Minute Book, 63: 430–1). These ships were assigned to a particular service: four were engaged for China, four for the Coromandel Coast and the Bay of Bengal, two for Bombay, one for Persia and Bombay, one for St. Helena and Bencoolen, and one for Benjar, Borneo. The previous year in September the Directors ordered a "Publication" to be affixed to East India House and at the Royal Exchange inviting proposals from persons willing to let their ships to the Company for the ensuing year (ibid., 63: 111). Whether this practice as well as that of balloting was customary the Minute Book does not indicate. Certainly on August 31, 1748, when the Salisbury and Boscawen were taken into service, the formalities were not observed (ibid., 63: 96–7).

42 The freight to Bombay in 1748 was from £28 to £31 a ton; that to the Coromandel Coast and to the Bay of Bengal from £26 to £29; that to China "in proportion," with proper demurrage (Minute Book, 1748–50, 63: 117). In the case of one "China Ship" returning with 11 tons of chinaware, 393 tons of tea and silk, and 15 tons of "private trade" — with chinaware carried for £29 per ton and tea and silk, as well as the private trade, at £32 — the total freight charge was £14,148 6s. 8d. (Reports from the Committee of the House of Commons, 1772–1773, IV [1804], 279).

43 "Account of the Ships and Goods Exported for the East Indies," C. O. 390: 6. 183. This survey covers the years 1698 to 1731. In this connection it may be noted that in the course of the War of the Spanish Succession the India trade did not suffer greatly, it would appear. In 1702 the outward freight was valued at £220,000 in round numbers; in 1707, after some sharp variation, it reached a level of over £500,000, which was maintained until 1712, when there was a slight drop. This, of course, indicates the degree to which the royal navy made navigation on the high seas safe for shipping.

1,923,083 ounces of silver valued at £535,067 11s. were sent. The
next most important item that year was broadcloth valued at £71,-
685 11s. 6d.; then followed perpetuanas, a very durable woollen fabric, valued at £17,589 15s.; then lead valued at £8,799 18s. 5d.; iron
at £5,350, and other commodities of less value, together with factory, naval, and garrison stores, totalling in all, with the bullion,
£661,603 15s. 9d.[45] During the period from 1749 to 1754 the value
of goods and stores for India increased in relation to the value of bullion; in 1749 this reached £272,877 as against £900,000 in bullion,
and in 1753 was £369,283 as against £944,256 in bullion.[46]

Upon reaching India the silver ordinarily was minted into rupees
— two of which were usually rated at the value of a crown — and
then placed in circulation.[47] The goods, on the other hand, were

[44] It should be pointed out that, according to the report referred to in the preceding
footnote, from 1698 to 1708 the expression " gold & silver " is used; in 1708 it was " silver "; in 1709 it was " bullion." In 1712 silver to the value of £107,403 was exported; the
value of this export gradually increased until in 1716 it had reached £485,412. The following year, on account of the scarcity of silver coin in England, the gold coin, it was
felt, was rated too high; as a result, and upon the advice of Sir Isaac Newton, the guineas
were reduced in value from twenty-one shillings and sixpence to twenty-one shillings. It
was hoped thereby to keep the silver at home. But what actually happened was that the
supply of gold in England was increased by reason of the profit involved in bringing it
from India and China (Anderson, op. cit., III, 299). Commenting upon this, one author
declared: " For silver ever has, and probably ever will hold the prerogative of being the
fixed standard; gold being always valued by silver, but not silver by gold " (ibid.). In this
connection it may be noted that between August 1715 and the following August, 1,542,-
155 pounds in gold was coined in the Tower of London and but 7,000 pounds in silver
(ibid., III, 293).
    As a rule the silver for export to India was secured in the course of trade, in connec-
tion with which favourable balances were paid for in this metal particularly by Spain
(J. O. McLachlan, Trade and Peace with Old Spain, 1667–1750, pp. 13 et seq., passim).
But frequently it was necessary to meet the vast demands of India by its purchase. The
business of furnishing this to the Company seems to have been in the hands of merchant
brokers. To illustrate. Among the Rodney Papers in the Public Record Office (G.D. 20:
6) is a letter from Rodney to Captain Montague of the Mermaid; in this the latter was
ordered to take on board at Lisbon a considerable sum " in specie " which several British
merchants desired to remit to Cadiz " for the purchase of silver bought up there for the
service of the United Company of Merchants trading from Great Britain to the East
Indies."
[45] C. O. 390: 16. 199. This may be taken as fairly typical although in 1711 the value
of the bullion was but £372,264 11s. out of a total of £556,342 19s., with broadcloth valued at £130,824 15s., perpetuanas at £14,730 14s., and tin at £10,859 13s. to mention
only the more important items (ibid., 390: 16. 189).
[46] Reports from the Committee of the House of Commons, 1772–1773, Vol. IV
(1804), p. 75.
[47] Some conception of the standard of living of the people of India can be drawn
from the fact that at Bombay and along the Malabar Coast the budgrook was a common

disposed of at auction at the various Company factories, which at the same time were furnished with supplies of rupees for the purchase or the manufacture on contract of return cargoes. For example, in 1730 these consisted of such articles as cotton and silk piece goods, cotton yarn, raw silk, saltpetre, pepper, redwood, shellac, and stick-lac, as well as tea from China.[48]

Sometimes there were difficulties encountered in filling the orders of the directors for particular products. In 1750 they complained of the "extravagant price" asked for raw silk in Bengal and hinted that they suspected that this was due to the buying up of the greatest part of the silk crop by those who thereupon held it for a high price.[49] That same year they likewise protested the equally "extravagant price" of pepper purchased on the Malabar Coast, as the result of high prices paid by both the Dutch and the French for it, in spite of the fact that it was "a falling commodity in Europe."[50] Although the finest quality was from this coast — the Carwar — it may be noted that increased attention was thereupon given to developing a supply in Sumatra.[51] The purchase of cloth in the Carnatic likewise at times

---

coin in circulation with a value of 27/800 of a penny, two of which were equal to a re, five rez equalled a pice, sixteen pices equalled a larce, twenty pices equalled a quarter, 240 rez equalled a xeraphim, four quarters equalled a silver rupee, fourteen quarters equalled a pagoda, and sixty quarters equalled a gold rupee, which was valued at £1 15s. In other words, it took over 5,332 budgrooks to equal the value of a pound sterling. This data is contained in an elaborate merchant's chart of foreign coins current in the eighteenth century, a copy of which is in the Virginia State Library.

[48] There was brought from the Coromandel Coast and the Bay of Bengal in that year in three ships 371,000 piece goods, 73,000 pounds of raw silk, 682,000 of saltpetre, 93,000 of pepper, 192,000 of redwood, 2,200 of cotton yarn, 18,800 of shellac, 9,000 of stick-lac; in addition three China ships returned that year with 1,707,000 pounds of tea (Anderson, op. cit., III, 417–18).

[49] Letter Book, 1750, 28: 86. The directors asserted (ibid.) that some years previous the Company servants at their factory at Cazembazar bought up the greatest part of "the Pultan among themselves . . . selling the silk to the Company under Fictitious Names. . . ." While they did not feel that any of their present servants were concerned in this instance in their own private accounts, yet the President and Council of Bengal were ordered to suspend from the service any that might be found so concerned.

[50] Letter Book, 28: 132–3. The President and Council of the Bombay Presidency were advised on March 8 that in order to get sufficient pepper to fill up the homeward-bound ships they might secure a supply at Anjengo on the Malabar Coast, if no other means could be found, by furnishing the King with arms (ibid.).

[51] India Office, Coast and Bay Letters, 1755, 6: 18–20, 25–8. In this connection a survey of the pepper plantations of the island was undertaken and inducements put forth to encourage the cultivation of this crop by the natives. On January 10, 1755 the Company servants at Fort Marlborough near Bencoolen wrote that in five years they hoped to provide exports of this in excess of a thousand tons; they warned, however, that it took four years for a pepper garden to come into bearing.

presented difficulties. At Vizagapatam, in 1745, the market was disturbed when the Dutch offered " great prices for a bad manufacture intended for some market in India being too bad for Europe ";[52] it was also disturbed the same season at Madras when the delivery of " fine goods at an abatement " was hindered by reason of the plundering activities of the Mahrattas who seized and set fire to a thousand ox-loads of cotton and thread.[53]

With the return of the loaded ships the Company was then confronted with its greatest responsibility — the profitable disposal of the cargoes. All its imports, with the exception of the saltpetre brought for the government, had, under the terms of the charter, to be sold at open auction " by inch of candle " to the highest bidder. But the proper time for the sale of the different commodities was within the discretion of the directors as well as the amounts to be offered of each of these.[54] Care had to be taken not to depress the market by offering at one time too large a quantity of goods.[55] As to

[52] Coast and Bay Letters, 1745, 5: 42–3.

[53] Ibid.

[54] To illustrate, on March 16, 1748 the directors ordered that on April 14 the " Prohibited Goods [that is, the cotton and silk fabrics that could not be sold for use in Great Britain] and Lacquer'd Ware in Private Trade " be put up for sale; that on April 19 there should be an auction of tea, and that on April 21 one for the drugs with notice thereof given as usual (Minute Book, 1746–8, 62: 510).

As to the so-called " private trade " referred to in the preceding paragraph, this was permitted to a limited degree to the captains of the East India ships as a part of their compensation, with the right of fifty tons of freight on the outward voyage and twenty on the return, so that in the course of the two-year adventure a captain might earn as much as £12,000 (R. H. Mottram, Traders' Dream, p. 127). On September 7, 1748, for example, Captains Lascelles, Baker, Haldane, Wilson, and Kent requested the directors that their "Lacquer'd Ware, Drugs, Arrack, and Rattans etc. lately brought home by them may be put up to sale." The directors thereupon on the 21st of the same month ordered that " the Arrack and Rattans in Private trade by the ships Dragon, Grantham, Onslow, Lynn, Norfolk, Stafford, York, Prince Edward, Portfield, and Ilchester be put up to sale on Wednesday the 19th October next " (Minute Book, 1748–54, 63: 101, 111).

[55] This may be illustrated by the sale of tea in the year 1730. Both in 1728 and in 1729 over a million pounds of tea were disposed of at auction; the average price in 1728 was seven shillings ninepence and a fraction a pound; while in 1729 the average price dropped to five shillings eightpence and a fraction. As a result, although 1,707,000 pounds of tea were received in 1730, only 48,884 pounds were put up at auction, which brought on an average almost twelve shillings a pound; the following year 1,021,690 pounds were sold, with the result that the average price dropped to six shillings eightpence and a fraction; and when in 1734, 1,417,431 pounds were auctioned off, the average price dropped to three shillings twopence and a fraction (Public Record Office, T. 64: 273).

The following interesting memorial under date of May 11, 1748 is found in the Minute Book of the Directors (Vol. 63: 27–8): "The Memorial of Several Traders in Tea whose names are herewith subscribed being read, setting forth they apprehend the putting up Lotts of Tea in small quantatys will greatly conduce to advance the Price, and the sale of East India cloth, this after 1700 was under severe restrictions as the result of parliamentary enactments in behalf of the products of British looms. In fact, it could only be imported to be sold for export.[56]

While the United Company was faced by many serious business problems and forced to make heavy financial commitments in order to support and protect its factory system in India,[57] it nevertheless

thereby offer Great Encouragement to renew the late Pernicious Practice of Smuggling, they therefore hope the Court will use all possible means to support the late Salutary Law made for the benefit of the Consumption of Tea in this Kingdom and not suffer so small a quantity as is consumed in America to influence the Price of the Whole Sale."

By a statute passed in 1748 (21 George II, c. 14) tea exported to Ireland and America was freed of inland duties, which doubtless encouraged the Company to secure a higher price for it at the auction, by feeding it to the market in small allotments. The directors, therefore, after considering the above memorial, voted to " abide by the manner of the Intended Allotment."

[56] The laws placing restrictions upon East India goods began with 11 and 12 William III, c. 10; then follow 12 William III, c. 11; 2 Anne, c. 9; 3 Anne, c. 4, f. 8; 10 Anne, c. 29; 7 George I, c. 7 and 21; 10 George I, c. 11; 9 George II, c. 4; and 15 George II, c. 31. The last of these laws, passed in 1742, provided that under certain restrictions and by the giving of heavy bonds it would be possible to take these goods from the warehouses where they were stored for the purpose of reconditioning them so that they might be sold to advantage " in the foreign markets."

While the silk industry had its beginnings in England in the Middle Ages, the cotton industry seems to date from the beginning of the seventeenth century. Fustians were apparently the first English cotton fabric, although possessing a linen warp (E. Lipson, The Economic History of England, II, 94–7). By 1701 almost two million pounds of cotton were imported for manufacture and by 1751 almost three million pounds. By the middle of this century the finer types of fabrics were being made. In 1754, for example, the Princess of Wales was given a " Piece of English Chints, of exquisite Workmanship, printed on a British cotton," which she declared was preferable to any India chintz, and to encourage such enterprise she signified her intention of having it made into a garment for her own use (New York Mercury, July 15, 1754. London Advices, March 23).

[57] In 1730 the Company alleged that the maintenance of its forts and factories cost £300,000 yearly; that, in addition, it paid £300,000 in customs to the government (Anderson, op. cit., III, 410). In a more detailed statement covering the years 1729–33 the cost of civil administration of the Calcutta Presidency was given as £159,905, the military £95,084; and buildings £8,218, totalling £263,207; civil administration of the Madras Presidency £50,680, the military £38,760, and buildings £1,508, totalling £90,948; the civil administration of the Bombay Presidency, £197,177, the military £223,294, and buildings £11,950, totalling £432,421; the civil administration at Bencoolen in Sumatra, £23,976, the military £18,816, buildings £436, totalling £43,228; and the civil administration of St. Helena, £6,282, the military £13,636, totalling £19,918 — making a grand total for the period of £859,822. During the period from 1750 to 1755 the cost of civil administration of the Calcutta Presidency was given as £241,016, the military £97,393, totalling £338,409; the civil administration of the Madras Presidency, £192,646, the military £369,931, totalling £562,577; the civil administration of the Bombay Presidency, £267,117, the military £258,462, totalling £520,579; the civil administration of Bencoolen, £70,138, the military £36,087, totalling £106,225; the civil administration of St.

made very substantial profits. In fact, outside of the Hudson's Bay Company stock — stock that was never quoted on the market — its stock represented, all in all, perhaps the best English investment during the first half of the eighteenth century.[58] From 1708 to 1756 the Company paid out in dividends a total of £12,457,476, or an average of £262,262 for each of the forty-seven years; this meant that the dividends averaged £8 4s. on each £100 of its working capital of £3,194,080. In 1750 the amount to divide was £255,526 8s., which allowed an eight per cent dividend; in 1755, however, it dropped to £127,763 4s.,[59] and in that year the dividend dropped to six per cent, although the value of the cargoes received that year was well over two millions sterling.[60]

Helena, £6,845, the military £42,597, totalling £49,442 — making a grand total of £1,577,232 (Reports from the Committee of the House of Commons, 1772–1773, IV [1804], pp. 80–3).

[58] In November 1711 it was quoted at £124 1s. 4d., Bank of England stock at £111 1s. 4d., the new South Sea Company stock (before the acquisition of the asiento) at £77 1s. 2d., and the Royal African Company stock at £4 1s. 2d. (Anderson, op. cit., III, 262); in October 1749 it stood at £190, the Bank of England stock at £140 1s. 2d., the South Sea Company stock at £115 3s. 4d., with the Royal African Company stock now worthless; in November of that year it reached £191 1s. 2d., the Bank of England stock had dropped to £137, and the South Sea Company stock to £114 3s. 4d. (Glasgow Courant, October 9 and November 20).

[59] Reports from the Committee of the House of Commons, 1772–1773, IV (1804), 73–5. In this connection it should be pointed out that in 1730 the interest on the funds loaned to the government was reduced to four from five per cent; in 1745 the Company, in addition to the advance of £3,200,000 already made to the government, now made another of £1,000,000 at three per cent; in 1750 it was compelled to accept another reduction in interest on the larger sum, under an agreement that from 1750 to 1755 this would be at the rate of three and one-half per cent, and after that year of three per cent.

The strong financial position of the Company from 1745 to 1754 is indicated by the fact that in 1745 it possessed a balance of £801,413 out of which to pay dividends and to provide betterments; in 1746 it reached £908,823, in spite of the continuance of the war with France begun in 1744; in 1747 it was £598,224, and in 1748, £606,625; in 1749, however, it dropped to £206,069 and in 1750 was £245,302; in 1751 it mounted to £451,774, in 1752 it was £411,074, and in 1753, £562,592; in 1754 it again dropped to £303,260, and in 1755 was but £134,236 (ibid., pp. 73–5).

In contrast to the above dividends, it was estimated in 1728 that the Dutch United East India Company from 1605 to that year, by reason of its virtual monopoly of the finer spices, paid an average annual dividend of something over twenty-four per cent. These dividends ranged from seventy-five per cent to twelve and a half per cent. The working capital of this company was £650,000 sterling (Anderson, op. cit., III, 396).

[60] Ibid., III, 594. From March 1749 to March 1750 the value of the goods and bullion exported was £1,172,946, and of bills of exchange honoured, £111,901; the sales for this year totalled in value £2,697,699; from March 1753 to March 1754 the value of goods and bullion exported was £1,313,540, and of bills of exchange honoured, £182,910; the sales for that year totalled £2,255,760 (Reports from the Committee of the House of Commons, 1772–1773, IV [1804], 75).

In bringing to a conclusion this survey of the activities of the United East India Company it may be pointed out that by the middle of the eighteenth century the great corporation possessed the following establishments: St. Helena; factories at Bassora and Gomroon, both on the Persian Gulf, where the Dutch also were established; factories at Surat, Agra, Amadabat, and Lahore, in northern India; Bombay, with factories at Carwar, Calicut, Tellicherry, and Dabul on the Malabar Coast; Fort St. George, Madras, Fort St. David, with a fort and factory at Vizagapatam, and a factory at Ganjam on the Coromandel Coast; Fort William at Calcutta, together with factories at Ballalore, Cazembazar, Decca, and Patna in the Gangetic basin; a factory at Bencoolen and Fort Marlborough in Sumatra; and, finally, the factory at Benjar in Borneo. Yet it did not seek empire. In fact, and in spite of British naval superiority, the Dutch had established many more forts and factories to the eastward of their possession of Good Hope, holding in sovereignty Ceylon, Malacca and surrounding territory, the Spice Islands, western and northeastern Java — all of the island soon to fall under their domination — and numerous ports on the Malabar Coast taken from the Portuguese, among these the strong fort at Cochin, with others on the Coromandel Coast and still others in Bengal, in particular the factory of Chinsura, together with several factories on Sumatra, two in Siam, six on Borneo.[61]

It was no longer the Dutch, however, that the English had to fear in the region of the Indian Ocean, but the rising power of France. The consideration of this rivalry is so important as to demand distinct treatment in the chapter that follows.

---

[61] Anderson (op. cit., III, 534–5) gives a list of Dutch posts as of the year 1747; it would appear that not all of them had real significance in that year as a result of a retrenchment policy on the part of the Dutch United East India Company.

CHAPTER IX

Rivals for the Carnatic

THE SEVENTEENTH CENTURY saw the beginnings and the culmination of the struggle between the old London East India Company and the Portuguese and the Dutch in the area of the Indian Ocean and to the eastward thereof; it signalized the destruction of the Portuguese empire of the east, if not the complete withdrawal of Portugal from that region, the building up of a great Dutch East India empire upon the ruins of the former, and the firm entrenchment of the English at three strategic ports along the littoral of the subcontinent of India, with the establishment of numerous dependent factories.

It was not until 1660, curiously enough, that France, in spite of the expansion of empire in the New World and a growing interest of Breton merchants in the Far East, attempted to capitalize this latter interest. In that year a company was organized to trade with China, but soon after its establishment it languished; then in 1664, the year that saw the creation of the Compagnie des Indes Occidentales, to which reference has already been made in an earlier chapter, there was also established Colbert's Compagnie des Indes Orientales, which received a monopoly of trade eastward of the Cape of Good Hope for a period of fifty years, together with other privileges and immunities granted the following year. Its directorate of twenty-four proceeded thereupon to set up on Île Dauphine (Madagascar) a superior council to have general charge of the commercial activities; which centre was shifted to Surat, however, apparently in 1669, although not until 1671 was this transfer fully legalized by letters patent.[1] Soon after its creation the company likewise received the harbour of Port Louis in Brittany for the use of its ships. Near this in the course of time appeared its new port, L'Orient, where were concentrated its ships, warehouses, and offices outside of the Paris headquarters. Although it had agreed to pay to the King three million livres for the enjoyment of its monopoly, this sum, because of discouragements, was remitted and, as an additional inducement to persevere in its undertaking, an exemption of import duties on its commodities was secured.[2]

But prosperity did not come, in spite of the flourishing condition of both the Dutch and the English companies. In fact, the French were in competition with capable and also highly experienced rivals. In an attempt to get control of the cinnamon trade of Ceylon, monopolized by the Dutch, an unsuccessful attack was made upon that island in 1673 by French ships of war; nor was the fleet more successful in retaining hold of St. Thomé on the Coromandel Coast, which was occupied only to be recovered by the Dutch, who had taken it previously from the Portuguese, but had themselves given way to a native force. Nevertheless in 1674, as the result of the energy of a M. Delton, a merchant of Lyon, permission was granted to the company by the deputy of the Nabob of the Carnatic, Ram Raja, to erect a factory at Pondicherry — a small village inhabited by poor, native fishermen lower down the Coromandel Coast — under conditions that customs duties be paid. Under François Martin, Delton's successor, a fort was erected there in 1687 and prospects for a developing trade seemed good, when in 1693 the aggressive Dutch with their superior sea-power in the Indian Ocean descended upon the town and after taking possession of it succeeded in retaining it until by the Treaty of Ryswick it was handed back. That the Dutch East India Company anticipated its permanent possession after its capture is indicated by the fact that the territory immediately dependent upon it was greatly enlarged through the purchase of surrounding lands, with the result that the French were obliged to reimburse it for these expenditures.

With Martin again installed in 1699 as the Governor and Commandant General, Pondicherry took on new importance with the establishment there of a superior council, to which the factory at Masu-

---

[1] Bibliothèque Nationale, Anciens Fonds Français (referred to subsequently as Bib. Nat., A. F. F.), 8971: 1; Anderson's *Origin of Commerce*, II, 9.
[2] *Ibid.*

lipatam, also on the Coromandel Coast, and that at Chandernagore on the Hugli in Bengal were now made dependent. But still the affairs of the company did not prosper. In the early part of the eighteenth century, in order to be able to maintain the appearance of fulfilling its original purpose, its directors, faced by great indebtedness, were obliged to grant licences to individual merchants to undertake voyages to the Indies. One need not be surprised, therefore, that the company lost favour. In 1719 — in a royal edict, issued by the French Regent, that consolidated it with John Law's Mississippi Company — it was indicted in the following terms:

> "That notwithstanding the sums of money, ships, etc., bestowed on the East India Company from time to time, and its many privileges and immunities since its first erection, in the year 1664, yet instead of increasing its commerce, it had totally abandoned its navigation, and was about to sell its exclusive privileges to some private persons for certain allowances; although they [the *directeurs*] might as well have made their commerce profitable to their proprietors and to the Kingdom, as the East India Companies of other nations have done. — That although the original fund was not large enough, yet they injudiciously lavished it away; borrowing money afterwards at ten per cent interest. Nay, they even paid five pounds per cent per month for the interest of the bullion they procured for their eastward cargoes, which swallowed up all the profits of the voyage. — That King Louis the Fourteenth still continued his kindness to that company; but the East Indians complaining that the company did not pay either principal or interest of their just debts, and that they had not sent one ship to Surat in sixteen years' time, they being greatly in debt there, from whence cottons and almost all the spices and drugs of India and Arabia are brought, the subjects of France, to their immense loss, are compelled to buy of strangers those and other Indian wares, not only for home consumption, but also for carrying on the trades of Senegal and Guinea; though at treble the prices they would otherwise have cost. Neither is their trade to China better conducted than that of India. For retrieving therefore the commerce and honour of France in India, by paying the company's debts (of many millions) there, the King hereby nullifies the privileges of that company, and unites them to this Western or Mississippi Company, which will thereby be strengthened. Thus, having before joined the Senegal Company to the western one, this newly-consolidated company will have the four quarters of the globe to trade in." [8]

---

[8] For the English translation of the original French see Anderson, *op. cit.*, III, 311–12.

Thus under name of the Compagnie Perpetuelle des Indes this corporation, mighty in appearance but in reality a house of cards, began its career. In August of the same year all the revenues of the Kingdom were farmed out to it and its monopoly was extended to the year 1770, in consideration of which it agreed not only to loan the King twelve hundred million livres for the payment of the national debt, but to pay fifty-two million annually, and another fifty millions for the sole privilege of coining all money. Thus, by a mere *arrêt* of the King, which made the company stock a legal tender, the debts of France were liquidated, with the same stock reaching the speculative value of twelve hundred per cent and beyond in 1719. This gave a nominal value to the three hundred million livres of stock of three hundred and sixty thousand million livres or eighteen thousand million sterling — estimated to be about one hundred and eighty times as much as the entire specie of all Europe.[4] In 1720 Law's Bank, now the Bank of France, which had itself issued notes to the amount of one thousand million livres — more paper than all the banks of Europe were able to circulate — was joined to the Compagnie des Indes for a period of fifty years. In this year the stock of the company towered at two thousand and fifty per cent and then in a frenzy of speculation in May the famous bubble burst.

In the great confusion that now arose, with royal *arrêts* following one another in quick succession, it was impossible at first for the *directeurs* to determine what privileges the Compagnie des Indes would retain. However, on September 27, 1720 the company received in perpetuity an exclusive privilege to carry on trade with the African coast; in 1723 its capital was fixed by an *arrêt* at one hundred and twenty million livres, the annual interest on which — placed at eight millions — was guaranteed out of the profits of the *ferme* of tobacco and of the beaver monopoly. In 1725, however, the capital was increased to 143,640,987 livres and in 1740 was given as 161,900,000 livres.[5] At the same time the commerce of the East Indies was assigned to it " as a collateral security for the present, to be employed for enlarging the funds and for discharging the incumbrances thereon." [6] Hence it retained its monopoly of all trade to the Far East, to the coast of Africa, and to Santo Domingo, the proprietorship of

---

[4] *Ibid.*, III, 313. France was supposed at the time to have about £18,000,000 in specie out of a total estimated one hundred millions sterling for all of Europe.

[5] Wilbert H. Dalgliesh, *The Company of the Indies in the Days of Dupleix*, p. 61.

[6] Anderson, *op. cit.*, III, 381; Pierre Margry, *Découvertes et Établissements des Français de L'Amérique Septentrional*, V, 589–90.

the Province of Louisiana, together with the exclusive right not only to export all beaver skins from Canada to France but to the *ferme* of tobacco. But even so all was not well. The Province of Louisiana, instead of being a great asset, showed itself to be a greater liability by reason of the necessity on the part of the Compagnie to assume the entire cost of its administration. As a result, after laying out some fifteen million livres in its improvement, there came in 1731 the retrocession to the Crown of all rights to it, which then included the Illinois country.[7]

The great company — which owed " *son origine et son établissement à la ruine d'une infinité d'autres, qui ont toutes faillé et échoué dans leur entreprises malgré les grands fonds qu'on leur avoit avancé* "[8] — did not, however, even after being freed of the encumbrance of Louisiana, free itself from the entanglements of debt and great expense involved in the building of new ships, in the rebuilding of its factories in India, and in the construction of the superb harbour facilities at Port L'Orient. However, under the governorship of the enterprising M. le Noir, stationed at Pondicherry between 1726 and 1735, its affairs, at least in the Far East, began to display great improvement.[9] Whereas previous to this period it was not uncommon for but " one ship from India once in every two years " to arrive at L'Orient, in 1730 four ships returned — which perhaps was not too impressive a showing in view of the fact that in that year seventeen ships leased by the English United East India Company docked at London.[10] However, by 1734 fourteen of its ships were reported to be in the Far East and by August of that year twelve of them had returned.[11] M. le Noir in India was succeeded in 1735 by M. Dumas, another enterprising, if self-advertising official.[12] Even more important, perhaps, was the impetus given to the affairs of the Compagnie by Philibert Orry, who in 1737 became the King's Comptroller General of Finance, and by his brother, Orry de Fulvy, who represented him in the deliberations of the Directorate as his commissioner. Be-

---

[7] Ibid.

[8] " *Mémoire sur le commerce de France,*" p. 25, Mildmay Papers, Clements Library.

[9] Bib. Nat., A. F. F. 8971: 3. M. le Noir was Governor from 1721 to 1723 and then again from 1726 to 1735.

[10] Anderson, op. cit., III, 413.

[11] Anderson (op. cit., III, 474) presents a table indicating the cargo of the returned ships. Coffee, tea, drugs, etc., amounted to over five million pounds weight; 387,800 pieces of calico were likewise included, together with many miscellaneous articles such as fans, mother-of-pearl counters for card-playing, painted paper, and painted handkerchiefs.

[12] M. Dumas was in control in India from September 1735 to October 1741.

tween that year and 1742 an average of seven ships sailed from L'Orient to India.[13] In 1742 the sale of Eastern commodities at L'Orient reached the sum of twenty-four million livres,[14] which served to indicate to the British and Dutch East India companies that they were likely to be face to face with a serious rival for the Far Eastern trade. That year also was significant in that Joseph François Dupleix was transferred from the superintendency of the factory at Chandernagore, where during the preceding twelve years he had shown great energy, to the post of *gouverneur* and *commandant général* of all the company's factories in India, taking the place of M. le Gou, who had succeeded Dumas in 1741.

Before entering upon a consideration of Dupleix's momentous administration of French affairs in India between 1742 and 1754, it would be well to bring under further scrutiny the great Compagnie Perpetuelle Française des Indes, particularly with regard to its functioning during the period that he was in office. The first observation is that the corporation was, as was made clear, heavily financed; it was in possession not only of vast concessions in Asia, Africa, and the New World, but of an excellent seaport in France itself, provided with impressive wharves, quays, warehouses, and other buildings; in 1754 its ships in the India service numbered at least twenty-six; [15] those in the Canadian service, in connection with its monopoly of the beaver trade, eight; nine were reserved for the African coast, but not for slaving; while fifteen more were utilized in French coastal waters.[16]

The company's marine earlier in the century, it may be pointed out, had been divided into two distinct classes: the so-called *première navigation* and the *seconde navigation*; the first was to the re-

---

[13] Arch. Nat., Col., C² 27: 106; 28: 4, 258; 29: 5, 189.

[14] Anderson, *op. cit.*, III, 381. The above amount was almost equal to a million pounds sterling. In 1667 the livre tournois was made the only legal livre in France; its value in the eighteenth century was generally tenpence, but in 1795 at the time of its replacement by the franc, it was equivalent to about 9⅖ pence.

[15] "State of the French Shipping in . . . 1754," Shelburne Papers, Clements Library, 36: 104. According to the "*État des Vaisseaux de la Compagnie des Indes*" — the author of which is unknown — which is appended to a letter written by the British Ambassador to the French court, the Earl of Albemarle, dated December 18, 1754, besides the possession of seven frigates, the company had twenty-two merchantmen; the names of all these vessels are given (*ibid.*, 36: 108). Still another writer in 1754 says that of about thirty vessels used in the East Indies, only fourteen or fifteen sail each year, of which four are always destined for China ("*Relation touchant la Navigation de la Compagnie Français des Indes, ibid.*, 36: 112).

[16] "*État des Vaisseaux de la Compagnie des Indes*," Shelburne Papers, 3 : 108.

gion east of the Cape of Good Hope, the second to Africa and the New World; the first involved ships carrying an armament of from fifty to seventy guns, all in all the finest ships; the second, ships of forty guns or less.[17] But the *seconde navigation*, with a particular responsibility of providing the French American colonies with Negroes, had not proved at all successful — "*soit par l'infidélité des Commis de la Compagnie, soit par le défaut de Payment des habitants des Colonies, soit Enfins par mauvaise régie*" — with the result that this was discontinued as a direct activity of the company and once again the practice was adopted of granting special permits to captains of ships, who, as a rule, agreed to pay ten livres for each Negro transported and sold in the French possessions; this, according to one writer, was supposed to bring in the annual sum of about 100,000 livres.[18] The vessels, therefore, which had been devoted to slaving were now distributed to the other services, that of the East Indies taking over those that were best adapted to its needs.

But the effective utilization of its marine was dependent upon its financial resources. In analysing the financial report of the Compagnie des Indes rendered June 11, 1752, at the highest point in its activities, one finds that its capital was given as 39,614,398 livres.[19] This was separated into three distinct funds: active capital, capital not employed directly in trade, and inactive capital. As to the first, amounting to 16,346,309 livres: 14,818,549 livres of this active capital were involved in the trade with the East Indies; 2,014,178 livres in the Spanish galleon trade, for the purpose of providing the company with piastres for its Far East business; and 513,582 livres in the Canada beaver trade. With respect to the second category — that is, of capital employed, but not in trade — which totalled 5,486,322 livres: 2,306,719 livres were in tobacco, apparently still to be disposed of, with 109,448 livres in addition in the Havre manufacture of this

---

[17] "Relation touchant la Navigation de la Compagnie Français des Indes," Shelburne Papers, 86: 112.

[18] *Ibid.* Another Frenchman complained that, whereas all the subjects of England and Holland could engage in the slave trade in taking out permits, it was different in France, where, under terms of letters patent granted in 1727, the company even five years after one had encroached upon its monopoly of this trade could bring an action against an interloper, who, if convicted, was thereupon consigned to the galleys and his property confiscated with one-third of it going to the informer ("*Mémoire sur le commerce de France et sur l'État présent de ses colonies*," Mildmay Papers, Clements Library).

[19] This apparently does not take into account the 100,000,000 livres paid in 1717 into the royal treasury in return for which it enjoyed the tobacco *ferme* (W. H. Dalgliesh, *op. cit.*, pp. 60–1).

article; 2,029,032 livres were debited against the King; 109,288 livres appear as "*fonds payés pour l'ancienne Comp^e· des Indes*"; 525,000 livres were invested in "*immeubles, forts et habitations*"; 300,000 in the "*hôtel de la Compagnie*"; and 25,835 in furnishings. Finally, in the third category, inactive capital, totalling 16,981,767 livres, 3,248,487 livres were in ships at L'Orient that for one reason or another were laid up; 7,129,014 livres were involved in bad debts incurred by West India planters in the purchase of slaves from the company; [20] another 3,917,119 livres in bad debts owed by those in Louisiana; 2,073,556 livres were tied up in Senegal, and 603,691 livres in Barbary. The report [21] likewise credits the company with 800,000 livres owed by the French Marine for supplying it with hemp and with 4,000,000 livres due from the King for food supplies and "*arrearages de contratre*" (*sic*) which item was not included in the tabulated statement. Thus, less than one-half the company's capital was available for trade.

Reference has been made in the preceding paragraph to debts due the company in Louisiana. This should not be passed by without a word of comment. Curiously enough, in spite of the surrender of its proprietorship of that province in 1731 the Compagnie was apparently in the middle of the century putting about a million livres into the promotion of local enterprise there.[22] This investment seems to have been a dead weight upon it. A M. de Kernsoret asserted in 1753 that about eleven or twelve million livres' worth of Negroes, food supplies, tools, etc., had been sent to the Mississippi for which there had not been returned to Europe commodities worth more than a hundred thousand écus.[23] With respect to the profits coming from the Canadian beaver monopoly, it was stated by the company directorate in 1748, as has been made clear in an earlier chapter, that —

---

[20] With respect to this item there is the following explanation: "*Il est dû depuis longtems à la Compagnie des Indes par les habitans de St. Domingue et de la Martinique et de la St. Louis, pour la fourniture des negres, 7,139,014#.*" This credit was extended "*pour leurs faciliter l'amélioration de leurs habitations*" (*Réflexions et Observations sur la Compagnie des Indes*," Mildmay Papers, Clements Library).

[21] The report of June 11, 1752 is summarized in the document cited in the preceding footnote.

[22] The author of "*Réflexions et Observations sur la Compagnie des Indes*," previously cited, writes: "*Comme la Compagnie dit dans son balan que dans trois ans, elle ne sera plus obligé de fournir un million par année à la Louisiana, ce sera encore une augmentation de fonds de 1,000,000#.*"

[23] Bib. Nat., Amérique, 10, I, pp. 3-14; see also Volume IV, pages 113-16 of the present series for this letter.

with 800,000 livres invested as fixed capital in this commerce — during the preceding two years the cost of carrying on the business was 104,488 livres more than the sum realized in the sale of the beaver skins in Europe and that in 1741, under more favourable conditions, a profit of only 185,032 livres was secured.[24] While critics of the company insisted that in reality an annual profit on the beaver trade amounted in 1746 and 1747 to some 215,393 livres,[25] even this showing, assuming it were correct, is far from impressive. On the other hand, in 1752 the value of the East India commodities brought to L'Orient is said to have totalled 7,376,473 livres upon sale, from which a net profit of 2,633,148 livres was secured after deducting about a million livres for the cost of maintaining the posts in India and in Senegal.[26] However, this phantom profit, as it proved to be, was small in contrast to that secured from its tobacco monopoly. This monopoly after 1730 seems to have been turned over to the *Ferme Générale* and yet in that year it brought to the company a revenue of over 7,500,000 livres.[27]

It is quite evident that the Compagnie des Indes was, behind all the trappings of a great private enterprise, in reality largely a projection of the state itself into business — a part of the machinery of government obediently acting upon the orders of the King's ministers and continually supported by royal authority, to which its stockholders were accustomed to look for payments of dividends which the Crown itself had guaranteed. As one French writer puts the matter, in contrasting it with the East India companies of Great Britain and Holland:

> " *La notre est Royale, et les directeurs ni entreprennent et n'operent rien que sous le bon plaisir du Roy, qui y governe en maître. . . .*" [28]

In fact, it was charged that a majority of the company's *directeurs* were themselves not personally interested in its prosperity, having in reality in their possession none of its stock, but borrowing the latter from others upon occasion whenever the question arose as to whether they were holders of it.[29] This may account for the fact that in the

---

[24] For the *directeurs'* report to the French Minister see Arch. Nat., Col., C¹¹ A. 92: 383. It will be noted that in 1752 but 513,582 livres were invested in the beaver trade.
[25] *New York Colonial Documents*, X, 201.
[26] " *Réflexions et Observations sur la Compagnie des Indes*," Mildmay Papers.
[27] W. H. Dalgliesh, *op. cit.*, pp. 61–2.
[28] " *Mémoire sur le Commerce de France*," Mildmay Papers.
[29] " *Réflexions et Observations sur la Compagnie des Indes*," Mildmay Papers.

eyes of one of its French critics in the middle of the eighteenth century

> " sa conduite est si pitoyable, que malgré tous . . . avantages, elle
> ne peut parvenir à gagner la confiance du public, qu'on ne peut
> empêcher de faire des réflexions sur tout ce qui lui arrive journelle-
> ment." [30]

The true situation of the Compagnie Française des Indes in relation to the French Crown may be appreciated by the fact that in the
middle of the eighteenth century almost one-fifth of the then outstanding fifty-six thousand shares was owned by the King himself,
while a substantial portion of the remainder was in the hands of those
high in the royal favour and therefore enjoying his protection. Under
a decree issued in 1748,[31] giving a much more definite character to
the frame of government of the corporation than heretofore, it was
provided that there should be held an annual meeting of those stockholders possessed of at least twenty-five shares. At this meeting the
Minister of Finance was expected to preside. Its business consisted
in the reading and more or less perfunctory discussion of the annual
report of the directorate, the raising of questions relative to the dividend payments — of particular interest at all times to the stockholders — and the election of one of the six *syndics*, who each enjoyed a
six-year term on the directorate. But this election was by no means
free, for the directorate — dominated by the eight *directeurs* appointed for life by the Crown — was privileged under the above decree to submit to the stockholders' meeting the names of four individuals; the stockholders then were privileged to reduce the list to
two names, from which the King made the final selection.

The real decisions of the company were made, of course, by the
syndics and *directeurs* meeting in council, at which two royal *commissaires* — also provided for in the decree — were likely to be present, who could speak for the Minister. These same *syndics* and *directeurs* were likewise in charge of the many bureaus and committees
in which the actual business of the company was conducted and
were, incidentally, well compensated.[32] However, impressive as was
the *Compagnie* thus organized, its activities lacked the substantial

---

[30] " Mémoire sur le Commerce de France," Mildmay Papers.

[31] For a summary of this decree as well as others see Henry Weber, La Compagnie
Française des Indes, 1604–1875; W. A. Dalgliesh, op. cit., Chapter I.

[32] For a detailed survey of the business activities of the company see ibid.

qualities that characterized those of the rival Dutch and British companies. In the words of Lally de Tollendal:

"... la Compagnie des Indes française, ainsi que l'a dit Voltaire, n'a jamais su faire ni la guerre, ni la paix, ni le commerce; parce qu'il y avait opposition direct d'abord entre messieurs de Paris et messieurs de Pondichéry . . . ; puis entre Paris et Versailles, c'est-à-dire entre la Compagnie et le ministre; entre une moitié de la Compagnie et l'autre; entre les deux commissaires du roi, qui, établis pour réunir, ne faisaient que diviser." [33]

It was this body, composed of royal commissaires, directeurs, syndics, and stockholders, and by no means dependent upon profits made in trade, to whom Dupleix was responsible when he took upon himself not only the governorship of the chief French centre of activity in the Far East but likewise that of commandant général des comptoirs français dans l'Inde. As in the case of the English United East India Company, the Compagnie des Indes was interested, so far as its relations with India were concerned, primarily and fundamentally in the conduct of profitable overseas business enterprises. But Dupleix, soon after assuming his new post, projected himself into the labyrinth of Indian politics — something that he seems to have avoided in Bengal during the eleven years in which he had acted as local directeur of the Chandernagore factory and during which he not only had rebuilt and greatly enlarged the town but had amassed a private fortune of some million livres in the course of business.

The Pondicherry factory at the time that he took over affairs was in financial difficulties. For it was in arrears more than five million livres, apparently to those in India that had made advances to it. Dupleix came to its rescue, supplying out of his own funds the wherewithal by means of which vessels were equipped, warehouses refilled, and even fortifications for the town constructed.[34] But he also seems to have become convinced that the Compagnie would never be able to rival the prosperity of that of the English in India unless it became a territorial power. This, thereupon, became his aim. In contrast, a careful reading of the dispatches to London from Madras by the President and Council of Fort St. George fails to disclose any move-

---

[33] Article "Dupleix" in Michaud, Biographie Universelle, XII, 15.
[34] Ibid.

ment in the direction of territorial expansion at this time on the part of the English.[35] Letters written before 1746 were concerned with details of business transactions and, incidentally, with news of the harassments that the Mahrattas were inflicting upon the inhabitants of the Deccan and the more distant parts of the Carnatic. Outside of these latter incidents, which indicate the growing anarchy in the affairs of India, it may be said that those Europeans dwelling along the Coromandel Coast were fairly undisturbed and peacefully occupied. War, however, broke out in 1744 between Great Britain and France, and this gave to Dupleix an opportunity to project a new era in the history of the coast, and also of India, by laying the foundations of a new system.[36]

Opportunity came also with the contest that had developed over the nabobship of Arcot, which position brought with it control of the Coromandel Coast. The family that had held this office for thirty years under the old Nizam, the Subahdar of the Deccan, was displaced in 1743 when the latter named as the Nabob Anwar-ud-din (in the French, Anaverdikan), one of his own officials, as against the claims of the son-in-law of the late Dost Ali, Chanda Sahib, who had been carried into captivity from the Carnatic by the Mahrattas in 1741. At first Dupleix accepted the new Nabob; and when the news arrived of the opening of hostilities between Great Britain and France the Governor naturally sought his aid, in view of predominant British sea-power, in protecting the French interests in India. As a result, Anwar-ud-din was persuaded to send letters to Madras notifying the officers of the post that the Mogul's protection had been granted in the waters of India to the ships of both natives and foreigners. In other words, the Nabob sought, and very properly, to maintain peace between the two powers in so far as the Coro-

---

[35] For a survey of English activities along the Coromandel Coast and in Bengal see "Coast and Bay, Abstracts of Letters," Volume V, September 5, 1744 to April 13, 1751, India Office. This will be cited hereafter as "Coast and Bay Letters."

[36] Under title of "Suitte du Précis" there is to be found among the papers of the Compagnie des Indes a detailed indictment of the conduct of Dupleix, who was charged with projecting a revolution in India. This apparently was drawn up in 1754. The author in bringing it to conclusion writes: "Les suites de cette revolution ont une Complication et des Circonstances qui sont presumer que le premier sistèm [système] etoit peu de chose dans son origins, mais que de degré il s'en est formé vu, que les differentes positions, ont encore fait variés à mesure que l'on s'y trouvoit (Bib. Nat., A.F.F., 8971: 74-5).

Tibulle Hamount in his Dupleix (p. 7) goes so far as to claim: "On ne se doute guère que, pour arriver à la domination de l'Inde, il [Dupleix] inventa et met en application un système politique vast et sûr, que les Anglis ont copié servilement. . . ."

mandel Coast was concerned. Dupleix himself also proposed a neutrality both on land and on sea.[37] However, Commodore Barnett's squadron, under a royal commission, had appeared early in the year 1745 in the Indian Ocean and had proceeded to capture a number of French ships.[38] When the Nabob thereupon expressly forbade any hostilities on land, the Madras council agreed to this but made clear that it could not be accountable for the conduct of the King's warships, which were not under its control.[39]

Unhappily for the British, the hard-pressed Dupleix was able to summon to his aid La Bourdonnais from Mauritius. This gallant officer, appearing the following spring with a fleet of eight vessels, all but one of which were converted merchantmen, gave battle to Peyton, the successor to Barnett upon the latter's death.[40] After indecisive action the British commander, leaving the coast to its fate, sailed to Calcutta to refit. This gave an opportunity for La Bourdonnais without interference to invest Madras. The President and the Council of the fort had been relying too greatly upon the ability of the Nabob to prevent hostilities on land, which he had forbidden, as was stated, and especially upon his goodwill toward the English in view of the fact that his own family had been residing at Madras for some time as the guests of the Company.[41] However, Dupleix, it would appear, won his neutrality at this juncture by agreeing to turn Madras over to him should it be captured. Poorly fortified, poorly prepared for a siege, the town held out for a month and then in September 1746 capitulated. The following month a ransom treaty was signed whereby the President and Council agreed that the United East India Company would provide the sum of 1,100,000

---

[37] Clive Papers, India Office, Home Series, Miscellaneous, 806: 24.

[38] Barnett left England in April of the preceding year with three ships of the line and one frigate. The squadron was sent as a result of an appeal made to the admiralty for the protection of the United East India Company's shipping.

[39] India Office, Coast and Bay Letters, 5: 43.

[40] In this engagement the British navy made a very poor showing. La Bourdonnais had one ship of the line of seventy guns, but the largest of these were eighteen-pounders, whereas Peyton had three ships of the line and the lower tiers of each were furnished with twenty-four-pounders. Peyton's own ship, the most powerful, stayed so far away from the action that no one on board was killed, although the action lasted for two hours. Peyton himself claimed that the weight of the metal, in firing the guns of the flagship, was so great as to threaten to shake the ship to pieces (India House, Minutes, 63: 633–44).

[41] In a letter written from Madras by the President and Council on January 23, 1746 the following item appears: " Expenses of *Nabobs* Family's residence lessen'd a good deal last year and reduced still more this. Old lady loth to Trust her Person or Money in a Moors government " (India Office, Coast and Bay Letters, 5: 49–57).

pagodas, in successive payments, for the return of the town.[42] But the most serious friction now developed between Dupleix and La Bourdonnais, each claiming jurisdiction over the town and its inhabitants. La Bourdonnais claimed to be under instructions not to make any permanent conquests and had therefore agreed upon the basis of the treaty to restore the town to the English in three months after arrangements had been made for the gradual payment of the ransom; Dupleix, determined to keep Madras and therefore to repudiate the ransom treaty, claimed instructions — doubtless general in nature — that would permit him to do so. With the approach of the monsoon La Bourdonnais was compelled to leave the Coromandel Coast, and Dupleix, now in undisputed control of the situation and supported by the *Conseil Supérieur* of Pondicherry, not only carried out his plan with respect to the treaty but as a token of his determination to eliminate the British from this region proceeded to turn upon their remaining fort, St. David, to the south of his own post. Before this took place, however, Anwar-ud-din, who had been promised Madras, upon hearing of its capture proceeded to send a large army there, doubtless with the feeling that the presence of this force would remind Dupleix of this agreement. To the amazement of the natives, this great but really undisciplined and poorly led force was scattered to the winds by a handful of highly disciplined and competently commanded Frenchmen and sepoys trained in the European fashion. It was this victory, as James Mill points out, that "first broke the spell which held the Europeans in subjection to the native powers."[43]

It is needless to dwell upon the unsuccessful attempts of the French thereupon made to capture Fort St. David or those, equally unsuccessful, on the part of the English, at last assisted by a fleet under Boscawen, to capture Pondicherry. Dupleix, while strengthening the fortifications of Madras, at the same time bent his efforts toward persuading the rich native merchants dwelling there to remove to Pondicherry, so that the latter place should fall heir to the great commerce of the former. But not even threats of confiscation of their property would induce them to do so, since, we are told, they "feared that the French might forcibly convert them to the Christian faith

---

[42] India Office, Minutes, 63: 363–80. The pagoda of the Coromandel Coast was at this period valued at eight shillings and ninepence, whereas the pagoda of the Malabar Coast had a value of but eight shillings.

[43] *The History of British India*, III, 65.

"Map to illustrate the Wars in Coromandel, 1744–1780."

(From Henry Beveridge's *A Comprehensive History of India*)

PLAN DE LA VILLE DE PONDICHERI

RENVOY

A . Le Fort
B . Ouvrage a Corne
C . Bastion de St Laurent
D . Bastion de St Louis
E . Bastion d'Anjou
F . Bastion d'Orleans
G . Bastion de la Porte de Madras
H . Bastion du Nord Ouest
I . Bastion de St Joseph
K . Porte de Valledaur
L . Bastion Valledaur
M . Bastion sans peur
N . Porte Villenour
O . Bastion de Villenour

P . Bastion de la Reine
Q . Bastion de l'Hopital
R . Bastion Goudelour
8 . Petite Batterie
1 . l'Eglise des Capucins
2 . l'Eglise des Jesuites
3 . Jardins de la Compagnie
4 . Jardins des Jesuites
5 . Jardins des Capucins
6 . l'Hopital
7 . Ancien Jardin de la Compag.
8 . l'Hotel de la Compagnie
9 . Maison du Gouverneur
10 . l'Hotel de la Monnoye

11 . Cimetiere des Malabares
12 . Cimetiere des François
13 . Grand Marché
14 . Prison des Malabares
15 . Ouvrages neufs faits en
   1740 et 1741
16 . Ouvrages de 1740
17 . Marché de St Laurent
18 . Batterie des Toilles
19 . Place du Mas
20 . Les Missionaires
21 . La grande Pagode

Echelle de Cinq Cent Toises.

100   200   300   400   500

LA MER DES INDES

(From Bellin's *Atlas Maritime*.)

and would not allow them any civil liberty such as they had enjoyed at Madras."[44] Then, without waiting for orders from France, Dupleix apparently made an offer to Nasir Jang, son of the Nizam of the Deccan who died in 1748, and the reigning Subahdar, to exchange Madras for two regions in the Carnatic: Villenore and Valudavor.[45] However, the Treaty of Aix-la-Chapelle, which in 1748 brought hostilities between the British and the French to an end, provided for its retrocession to the former, and in the summer of 1749 Boscawen took it over.[46]

It is not without significance that the year 1749, following that of the peace, was one of great activity on the part of the British and the French in consolidating their positions both in North America and in India. This witnessed, on the one hand, the founding of Halifax by the British with the purpose of getting a firm control over the Nova Scotian peninsula; and, on the other, the sending of French troops to seize the land approach to the same peninsula; in Virginia, feverish activity in allotting to groups of individuals great blocks of choice land in the disputed Ohio Valley; and in Canada, the sending of Céloron de Blainville into that same valley with a force of French and Indians to take formal possession of it in the name of the King of France.

In India during the same year there took place the British enterprise against the Rajah of Tanjore and that of the French against the Nabob of the Carnatic.[47] As to the former episode, the local representatives of the United East India Company were led to espouse the cause of a claimant to the throne of Tanjore. Since the troops had not yet been withdrawn that had been sent to defend the British interests in India after the loss of Madras, it was possible to agree to give him military aid to establish himself. The first expedition that went from Fort St. David by land failed of its objective; however, another

---

[44] See the "Private Diary of Ananda Ranga Pillai, 1736–1761," *Journal of Indian History*, VIII, 30–1.

[45] *Ibid.*, VIII, 32.

[46] It is of interest to note that, while the treaty of peace does not specify that Madras should be exchanged for Louisbourg, in February 1747 the *Conseil Supérieur* of Pondicherry wrote to the Compagnie des Indes suggesting three ways of dealing with Madras: first, keeping it to exchange for Louisbourg; second, selling it to the United East India Company; third, exchanging it for territory nearer to Pondicherry (*ibid*).

[47] The Carnatic, it should be pointed out, was to Europeans that region between the Eastern Ghats and the sea, bounded on the north by the Kistna and on the south by the Coleroon; beyond the latter river were the Mahratta Kingdom of Tanjore and the Hindu Kingdom of Trichinopoly, in the so-called southern Carnatic.

sent by water succeeded in capturing the Fort of Devi-Cotah on the Coleroon River. Meanwhile, both President Charles Floyer and Admiral Boscawen, in command of the British fleet in Indian waters, had come to distrust the claimant to the throne,[48] with the result that they decided to give up his cause and entered into an agreement with the reigning Rajah in the following terms:

> "That the Fort of Devi-Cotah with as much land as would produce 9000 [pagodas] per annum should be ceded to the English East India Company for ever; that the King of Tanjore defray all expenses of the expedition against him and allow the pretender an annual income and the English would be accountable for his person." [49]

The only possible excuse, consistent with the English emphasis in India on trade, that could be offered for this adventure and its outcome was that in 1739 Tanjore had conceded the port of Karikal with the surrounding territory to the French company and had made no corresponding concession to the English company, as its importance would warrant.

The French enterprise of the same year was based upon an understanding between Dupleix and two natives; one was Chanda Sahib, claimant of the nabobship of the Carnatic, who, as previously stated, had been made prisoner by the Mahrattas in 1741 upon their incursion into this region, but who, thanks largely to Dupleix's intervention and promises, had been released; [50] the other was Muzaffar Jang (in the French dispatches, Mousafirsingue), claimant of the subahdarship of the Deccan, which brought with it the overlordship of the Carnatic. This triumvirate had as objectives the overthrow of both the ruling Deccan Subahdar, Nasir Jang, who had succeeded his father, the Nizam, and the ruling Carnatic Nabob, Anwar-ud-din.[51] It

---

[48] India Office, Orme Manuscripts, India, I, 219–25.

[49] Ibid. The amount of the expenses was placed at 100,000 rupees, or one lac. The pretender was allowed three hundred rupees per month (India Office, Coast and Bay Letters, 5: 231–40).

[50] The French were already deeply obligated to Chanda Sahib, who had shown his friendship in securing for them Karikal in 1739 (Bib. Nat., A.F.F., 8971: 105).

[51] The details of this alliance between Dupleix and Chanda Sahib and Muzaffar Jang are preserved in a series of letters which the two latter wrote to the former. These made clear that if Muzaffar should get into power in the Deccan, as overlord of the Carnatic he would make Chanda Sahib not only the Nabob of Arcot but Subahdar of all the Carnatic. In these letters, translated into French, each expresses an absolute dependence for success upon French military aid (Bib. Nat., A.F.F., 8971: 117–23). Muzaffar's claims to be the Subahdar of the Deccan were based upon the fact that he was the grandson of the Nizam, was the only legitimate heir, and had secured a patent to this office from the Mo-

was agreed that the latter should first of all be disposed of.[52] To accomplish this end, Dupleix sent eight hundred Frenchmen, a thousand well-disciplined sepoys, or native troops, and a train of artillery, under the command of his brother-in-law, d'Auteuil. This contingent, joining the forces of Chanda and Muzaffar, fell upon those led by the centenarian but still vigorous Nabob. In the action that took place the Nabob was slain and his army was scattered by the intrepidity of the French attack. Dupleix had not long to wait for his reward. Chanda Sahib, soon after the victory, appeared at Pondicherry and now in his capacity of Nabob of the Carnatic proceeded to grant *paravana* to the Compagnie des Indes for forty-two *aldees,* or villages, in the Villenore country, lying in the neighbourhood of Pondicherry; to Dupleix personally he presented Covelong; to Madame Dupleix, Porto Nova; to d'Auteuil, Allumhana; and to a relative of Madame Dupleix, the Padre de la Purification, St. Thomé, the last-named lying close to Madras.[53] Muzaffar Jang, not to be outdone, although his rival was still on the throne, granted *paravana* for other towns and districts, including the then very important weaving and commercial centre Masulipatam, some distance to the north of Madras. By means of all of these grants Dupleix was able to report that the Compagnie des Indes would come into possession of eighty *aldees.*[54]

Such were the activities of the British and French in the Carnatic in 1749. The servants of both the British and the French companies without authorization involved themselves in the turbulent politics of India — each with the purpose of securing some addition to the holdings of their respective companies; each interfered in a disputed succession; each previously had recognized the legitimacy of the rule of the individual whose domains were invaded by their troops,

gul (*ibid.,* 8971: 105). According to Ananda Ranga Pillai, who had assisted the French and was at the time of writing in their service, Dupleix had previously recognized Nasir Jang in applying to him, as was stated earlier in the text, to agree to give to the French company two districts conveniently located with respect to Pondicherry, in exchange for Madras (*Journal of Indian History,* VIII, 31).

[52] Anwar-ud-din was quite unaware of the project, and when news came to Arcot of the movement into the Carnatic of Muzaffar Jang, he wrote unsuspectingly to Dupleix requesting aid. " Vous m'avez regardé jusqu'a présent comme votre Père, et Moi de mon côté je vous ai toujours reconnu pour mon fils," began the appeal (Bib. Nat., A.F.F., 8971: 124). However, as has been emphasized, the two had previously clashed over the control of Madras.

[53] India Office, Coast and Bay Letters, 5: 168–9.

[54] Bib. Nat., Nouvelles Acquisitions Françaises, 9145: 2. (This series will be referred to subsequently as Bib. Nat., N.A.F.)

and each thereupon sought to justify their conduct to their superiors at home in flagrantly violating their instructions.

In London the news of the Devi-Cotah enterprise was received with anger and dismay. " You seem to look upon yourselves as a military colony than the Factors and Agents of a Body of Merchants," wrote, caustically, the directors of the East India Company in January 1750 to the President and Council, still holding forth at Fort St. David, who were accused of embarking upon " an unjust and rash Enterprise and concerted and carried on without Authority and contrary to the True Interest of the Company." In particular, President Charles Floyer and Richard Prince, also a member of the Council, and Major Stringer Lawrence, who had charge of the expedition, were singled out for special rebuke. Nevertheless, in view of the fact that the enterprise had been carried out at great cost to the Company, the Council was instructed to keep the port, which should be made as useful as possible, " but more particularly in a comercial way which is our True interest." [55]

As to the reactions of the Compagnie des Indes — in view of the fact that Dupleix had reported in March that the troops he had agreed to supply to Chanda Sahib were to be supported without cost to the company, and in July, the nature of the agreement that he had made with Chanda Sahib for the transfer of Vellenore and its forty-four dependent *aldees*,[56] with anticipated annual revenues from these of twenty thousand pagodas — upon receipt of news of the victory over Anwar-ud-din the *directeurs* wrote approvingly to Dupleix of " *la glorieuse action de nos troupes* " and further that

> " *cette victoire nous paraissoit honorable à la nation et utile à la compagnie, puisqu'elle devoit assurer la jouissance paisible des aldées dont vous aviés avec habileté negocié la cession de la part du nouveau Nabob. Nous vous disions . . . que nous ne manquerieres pas de demander au Roy des marques d'honneur pour les officiers qui s'étoient distingués dans cette action.* " [57]

In other words, the United East India Company sharply rebuked those servants who had engaged in the Tanjore enterprise while, in contrast, the Compagnie des Indes acclaimed those of its own involved in the overthrow of the Nabob. It is therefore not surprising that Dupleix and the *Conseil Supérieur* at Pondicherry should con-

---

[55] Letters of January 23, 1750, India Office, Letter Book, 28: 52–4.

[56] At one time Dupleix speaks of the gift of forty-two aldees, and at another of forty-four.   [57] Letter of July 15, 1750, Bib. Nat., N.A.F., 9145: 24.

tinue with confidence to promote a system which bade fair to bring to their nation immense benefits; nor is it more surprising that Thomas Saunders, who had taken Floyer's place as representative of the United East India Company, and the Madras Council should feel constrained to limit their activities to checking those of their rivals. In fact, in October, Boscawen sailed with the fleet for Europe, taking with him most of the English soldiers. The assumption was that again peaceful activity would take the place of warlike along the Coromandel. But there was to be no peace.

The next adventure upon which Dupleix embarked — with the natives of India now almost terrified at the mere thought of opposing French soldiers [58] — was against the same Rajah of Tanjore [59] who

---

[58] Chanda Sahib, writing to Dupleix for aid in the capture of the fortress of Gingy, admitted that he himself would have twenty thousand horsemen but that the fortress would be abandoned without fail by his enemies without a struggle as soon as they would learn that he was supported by French troops (Bib. Nat., A.F.F., 8971: 120).

[59] James Mill (op. cit., III, 92, note) declared that the directeurs of the Compagnie des Indes "accused Dupleix again falsely of being the author of the ill-timed invasion of Tanjore." He bases his judgment upon the Orme manuscripts in the India Office and a Memoire pour Dupleix. However, there has survived a detailed account of events in the Carnatic and along the Coromandel Coast from July 1748 to October 17, 1752 prepared by one who was in Pondicherry during this period and who left on the date last mentioned to return to France upon the Centaure. This account is detached and generally sympathetic with what Dupleix was seeking to accomplish. With respect to Tanjore, the author of it writes: "Mousafersinque [Muzaffar Jang] resta quelques mois a Arcatte; pendant ce tems, M. Dupleix donna ordre a nos troupes de marcher vers le Royaume de Tanjour, dans lequel est le fort de Karical. Nous avons plusieurs sujets de plainte contre le roi de ce pays, qui deux ans auparavant, nous avoit fait la guerre injustement et nous avoit obligé de lui payer tous les ans un certain tribut. Sandesaeb [Chanda Sahib] avec 12 mil Cavaliers s'etant joint a nos troupes on brule tout les environs de la ville de Tanjore, et l'on en forma le sieze pendent 15 jours que le roi se trouvant presée, se determina non seulement a lever le tribut qu'il avoit exigé cedevant, mais encor a ajouter 80 Aldees a celle de Karical, et a payer 3 lacs de roupées pour les frais de la guerre" (Arch. Nat., A.F.F., 8971: 105). Obviously, by the very nature of the demands made upon the Rajah the enterprise was in the interest of the French. It is true that a very different version of the incident, which supports Mill, is given by the President and Council writing from Fort St. David. It states that Muzaffar Jang and Chanda Sahib, "assisted by the French with fourteen Europeans, a great number of Seapoys and Peons, & some artillery," set out from Pondicherry with the plan of capturing Trichinopoly, but hearing that the garrison of the fortress had been reinforced by English troops from Devi-Cotah, turned their course to Tanjore. Having almost ruined the country and having laid siege to the capital, they obliged the Rajah to agree to pay them "60 Laach Rupees" (India Office, Coast and Bay Letters, 5: 231–2). It seems possible to reconcile the two amounts — outside of the presence of Muzaffar Jang — by assuming that when Chanda Sahib left Pondicherry with his army and a few Europeans he had agreed with Dupleix to go directly against Trichinopoly, and that hearing of the presence of the English at that place, he decided to join the French force that had proceeded against Tanjore and then, after dealing with the

felt the impact of the British. The Rajah, it seems, was still demanding tribute for the use of Karikal and it was charged that two years previously he had engaged in hostile acts against the French. Chanda Sahib at the same time had his eyes on Trichinopoly, a populous city with half a million souls and an almost impregnable stronghold, located close to the Tanjore territory. He therefore joined the French and together they compelled the Rajah to sue for peace. But this native prince was given no such comparatively modest terms as the English gave him in connection with their demand for Devi-Cotah. Not only was he obliged to forgo the payments that he had been entitled to receive for the lease of the Karikal region but to agree to add eighty more *aldees,* or villages, to those already within the bounds of Karikal, and, finally, to contribute to the French three lacs of rupees, to cover the expense of the campaign.[60] According to the English account, the unhappy Rajah was compelled further, in order to save his Kingdom from Chanda Sahib, to agree to pay to the latter sixty lacs.[61] Well may Dupleix have felt that all native India was in a fair way to fall into his control!

But there were still complications. When Chanda Sahib had set forth for Trichinopoly he went in search of his rival for the nabobship of Arcot, Muhammad Ali, the son of the late Anwar-ud-din. Muhammad, after the disastrous battle that cost his father his life, had fled southward and been received in the fortress city. From there he appealed to the English at Fort St. David for aid and, to show his goodwill, presented to the Company in his capacity of Nabob the two towns of Bahur and St. Thomé, both of which, incidentally, Chanda had also given to the French. As a result, the President and Council proceeded to take possession of the places by ejecting the French, and sent from Devi-Cotah a contingent of troops with artillery that joined Muhammad at Trichinopoly.

Rajah of Tanjore, to secure the aid of the French in investing the fortress. It is certain that when the news arrived of the movement of Nasir Jang into the Carnatic, there was a considerable French force in the region of Trichinopoly in addition to Chanda's army. It is also certain that Muzaffar Jang was not in contact with these French troops, because we are told that he retired with his army in the face of Nasir Jang until he could join them as they marched back to protect Pondicherry. Dupleix's long letter to Governor Saunders, dated February 18, 1750, refers to the march of the French army to Trichinopoly, of the demand made upon the Rajah for contribution, and of the siege of the capital (India Office, Home Miscellaneous, India, 93: 82–106; for this see also *Records of Fort St. George, French Correspondence, 1752,* pp. 1–41).

60 Bib. Nat., A.F.F., 8971: 105. The lac was valued at 100,000 rupees.

61 India Office, Coast and Bay Letters, 5: 232.

After Chanda and the French had dealt to their satisfaction with Tanjore, it would appear that the combined force started to besiege the fortress. Little did Chanda realize, little did Dupleix, that the high rock dominating the city would at long last be to each an Achilles' heel; that the repeated efforts to secure it would ultimately take from one his life and from the other all his dream of power and glory! In the midst of the siege the news arrived that the reigning Subahdar of the Deccan, Nasir Jang — apparently stirred to action by the English [62] — was moving eastward through the Carnatic directly upon Pondicherry with a great army of six hundred war elephants, one hundred and thirty thousand horsemen, and an equal number of foot soldiers, supported by a train of two hundred cannon. Immediately the siege of Trichinopoly was suspended, the French and Chanda pressed northward to throw themselves between the invading army and the French post. As for Muzaffar Jang, nephew and rival of Nasir Jang, faced by this overwhelming force, he withdrew from the neighbourhood of Arcot until he was able to make contact with the French marching northward. Some distance to the west of Pondicherry on April 4, 1750 the rival armies came into contact. By this time the English force that had been defending Trichinopoly, together with other troops from Fort St. David, had joined the ranks of Nasir Jang; Muhammad Ali with a contingent was also there. But no decisive action resulted. According to Dupleix, Nasir Jang's cannon operated by the English opened fire on the French and the fighting — such as it was — continued until darkness.[63] For once the French officers — whether already dissatisfied with the campaign or fearing the great odds against them with the English supporting Nasir Jang — decided to retreat. With great difficulty and only after a forced march of eight hours, continuously harassed by the Mahratta horsemen commanded, it is stated, by English officers, were the French forces and those of Chanda able to reach the protection of the batteries of the town.[64] As for Muzaffar Jang, this proud young man felt that it was not the part of a great ruler to retreat. In spite, therefore, of the flight of most of his own army he held his ground until he was taken prisoner. All this was a sad blow to French prestige. But Dupleix in the hour of crisis proved to be a host in himself.

[62] The President and Council sent to Nasir Jang a present of 20,518 pagodas early in 1749 (India Office, Coast and Bay Letters, 5: 158–64).

[63] Dupleix to Saunders, February 18, 1752, India Office, Home Series Miscellaneous, India, 93: 82–106.

[64] Bib. Nat., A.F.F., 8971: 105.

After Nasir Jang had advanced within two leagues of Pondicherry his army halted. Thereupon Dupleix proceeded to get in contact with him, indicating that their mutual interests might be served in cooperating with each other. With the capture of Muzaffar Jang, the latter's cause seemed hopeless, but Dupleix sought to secure a recognition of the claim of Chanda Sahib to the Carnatic. Although these negotiations were fruitless, they at least gave the French Governor the opportunity to gather valuable information, especially with reference to the slackness of discipline in Nasir's army. It was discovered that the troops were accustomed to drug themselves with opium before retiring for the night. As a result of this information a small body of Frenchmen entered the camp one night in a surprise attack and slaughtered, with only the loss of three men, over a thousand of the enemy. The importance of the episode lies in the fact that thereafter the tide turned against the Subahdar. He retreated to the fortress of Jingi (Gingi in the French), and the English, with the coming of the rainy season, returned to Fort St. David.

But the French now took the initiative. A force stormed Jingi. Nasir, who had left this stronghold, determined to drive the enemy from the Coromandel Coast; he again gathered an army — for the first army had disappeared with the return of the contingents to their abodes — and again approached Pondicherry to besiege it. But no action took place; the rains were especially heavy; food and forage were scarce; cattle, horses, and elephants attached to the army died by the thousands; the soldiers cursed Nasir for having brought them such a distance for so pitiable a war; and the native princes were anxious to return home. Under these circumstances Dupleix found confederates within the great army, particularly the Pathans. These agreed to support Muzaffar Jang and the French in case the latter should attack. Infirm of purpose, Nasir Jang had permitted himself once again to open negotiations with Dupleix. Indeed, his envoy had actually reached an accord with the Governor when de la Touche with some eight hundred Frenchmen, some four thousand natives, and a train of only twenty pieces of cannon — not realizing that the Subahdar had ratified the projected treaty — launched an attack on the morning of December 16, 1750 against the great army of the Deccan, composed of forty thousand infantry, forty-five thousand cavalry, seven hundred war elephants, and an artillery train of three hundred and sixty cannon. In the midst of the fighting, Nasir — first giving orders to have the head of Muzaffar, a prisoner in his camp, brought to him — mounted his war elephant, but was soon shot by the Nabob of Karnul, one of the confederates. Displaying his head upon a lance, the conspirators now presented Muzaffar Jang, greeted him as their lawful ruler, and placed him upon the late Subahdar's elephant. The army was quick to recognize him and the battle ceased at his order.[65]

No longer now was Muzaffar Jang a needy adventurer held in confinement, but a great ruler. Yet he realized that he owed this change of fortune almost entirely to Dupleix and the French army and therefore proceeded to Pondicherry to make due acknowledgment. Met by Dupleix outside the town gate, he left his elephant and, seating himself familiarly beside the French Governor, the two were carried into the town in the same palanquin. Under a great awning a throne had been erected. Even upon this symbol of power he insisted that Dupleix should sit beside him. He was again proclaimed by Dupleix Subahdar and ruler of Golconda; all made their submissions to him and Dupleix. With this ceremony over, he proceeded to shower Dupleix and his family and the chief French officers with gifts; he gave to the Compagnie des Indes the stronghold of Jingi and its dependencies and the island of Divi, confirmed the previous gift of Masulipatam and its dependencies, added to these places Narsapoor, Nizampatam, near Madras, and even other possessions, with such a lavish hand that in the words of one who was a witness of it: ". . . *les anglais se trouvoient reserres de tout cotes par nos terres qui de voient donner a la Compagnie au moins 15 lacs par an."* [66] Finally, Dupleix was recognized as hereditary *Mensebdar* of all the eastern part of the Carnatic from the Krishna to Cape Comorin.[67] This really represents the high point in the developing of his system. Under it the pagodas struck at the Pondicherry mint were to be accepted not only within the jurisdiction assigned to him but throughout all the domains of the Subahdar of the Deccan. Dupleix was now one of the great princes of India.

Muzaffar Jang still had work to do before he could consolidate his position in Golconda and the rest of the Deccan. He must, among

---

[65] See "*Relation de la dernière Affaire de l'Inde qui a mis fin à tous les Troubles de l'Inde,"* Bib. Nat., A.F.F., 12087: 153–5; this is also to be found in the India Office, Home Series, Misc., 93: 151–8; for another contemporary account see Bib. Nat., A.F.F., 8971: 105–7.

[66] *Ibid.* Fifteen lacs amounted to 1,500,000 rupees.

[67] Bib. Nat., A.F.F., 8971: 70.

other things, go to Aurangabad, long the capital of this great domain, to receive the recognition of those nabobs and rajahs and other princes who were not with his army; he must moreover on his way visit the city of Golconda. But he felt that he could not sufficiently rely upon his own army to accomplish his ends and consequently asked Dupleix for a French detachment. This was granted and in the middle of January 1751 the Subahdar with his army left for Golconda accompanied by six hundred picked French troops [68] under the command of the most capable and resourceful of French soldiers in India, the Marquis de Bussy-Castelnau.[69]

But all did not go well. There soon developed deep discontent within the ranks of Muzaffar's own army. The Pathans, who had conspired to destroy Nasir Jang, harboured a deep sense of resentment that they had not been more liberally rewarded out of the great treasure that had belonged to the late Subahdar, most of which apparently was left at Pondicherry. This flamed into open revolt after the army had proceeded some sixty leagues from Pondicherry; and in the midst of the fighting that ensued Muzaffar Jang was killed by a well-directed arrow. But there was in the camp Salabat Jang, the eldest surviving son of the old Nizam and brother, therefore, of the late Nasir Jang. Bussy thereupon, after getting Dupleix's advice by courier, elevated him to the subahdarship — through agreement with the principal leaders of the army — escorted him now, in place of his predecessor, and became his chief adviser at Aurangabad in the Deccan during a period of some seven stormy years. But while Bussy himself profited immensely by his presence there and his officers and even his common soldiers reaped great rewards, they were not available to help shape the course of events in the Carnatic and in Bengal, where, after all, the great decisions were reached affecting the destinies of India.

Salabat Jang, upon assuming power, confirmed everything that Muzaffar Jang had done in behalf of Dupleix and the Compagnie des Indes. This meant that the profits from administering the *aldees* would be more important than those from commerce; that combining the two — governmental administration and commerce — would bring a period of unrivalled prosperity to the French in India. On the surface, therefore, the outlook appeared most glowing. Indeed,

---

[68] One account gives the number as four hundred (Bib. Nat., A.F.F., 8971: 106).

[69] " *Précis des affaires l'Inde depuis le départ de M. Bussi avec l'armée maure jusqu'a la suspension d'armes* " (Bib. Nat.. A.F.F., 12087: 126).

Bussy, after he overcame one obstacle after another in the Deccan, wrote to Dupleix enthusiastically:

> "*Mettez-nous en force, avant un an l'empereur* [that is, the Mogul] *tremblera au nom de Dupleix.*" [70]

And, pray tell, what was there to stop Dupleix from becoming master of India? The English were hemmed in; the pretensions of Muhammad Ali to be the Nabob of Arcot had been repudiated by the late Subahdar in favour of those of Chanda Sahib; in fact, Muhammad himself had at one time agreed to give up Trichinopoly if Muzaffar Jang would accord him a stronghold in Golconda — something that would remove his disturbing presence from the Carnatic.

But Dupleix's system involved the maintenance of the Subahdar on his throne in the Deccan, and the Nabob, the latter's viceroy, in the Carnatic, and that meant fighting and the straining of resources in each instance. Under the disturbed conditions which continued to exist, moreover, the anticipated great revenues from the grants received at the hands of both the Subahdar and the Nabob were not forthcoming. Commerce, likewise, was gradually stifled. Further, to maintain control in the Carnatic it was necessary to garrison not only such important centres of wealth and population as Arcot and Jingi, but a number of other strategic places. [71]

While this was going on, the English were not exactly idle. Since normal trade at Madras and at Fort St. David with the inland countries, under the circumstances, was out of the question, [72] Fort William in Bengal, therefore, became the chief centre of commercial activity of the Company along the bay and coast. To promote this, late in October 1750 there was sent from Fort St. David over three and a quarter millions of Arcot rupees and twenty chests of unminted silver. At the same time, significantly, on the advice of Major Lawrence,

---

[70] Michaud, *op. cit.*, XII, 17.

[71] *Ibid.*

[72] In a petition to the Lords Justices by the directors of the East India Company under date of August 19, 1752 — after the news had arrived in London of the sweeping concessions made to the French by the Subahdar — it was stated that "your Petitioners' settlements on the Coast of Coromandel are surrounded by the French and your petitioners' trade and commerce with the inland parts of the country is rendered precarious, in such manner that the French can prevent provisions coming to your petitioners' settlements and can impose what duties or customs they think fit upon any goods or commodities that are to pass through the places or countries the French are in possession of, and, whenever they please can cut off and totally prevent your petitioners' settlements . . ." (India Office, Home Series, Misc., 93: 78–80).

five thousand bags of saltpetre were ordered by the President from Bengal and seven thousand barrels of it from Bombay.[73] Reinforcements were requested the following spring and sent to Fort St. George from Bengal. Moreover, Muhammad Ali was persuaded not to turn Trichinopoly over to his rival.[74] Should Chanda Sahib and the French attempt again to take it, he was assured that he could expect assistance. While the President and Council, now again installed at Madras, were thus preparing to resist Dupleix's system, and had cut off all communication with the French as though in a state of open war, they nevertheless were anxious for an accommodation with the latter that would restore the old tranquillity and prosperity along the coast. On July 5, 1751 they wrote to the directors in this vein:

> " Peace on a firm foundation is greatly to be desired [in view of] the Calamitous Expensive situation with a Stagnated Trade considered, added to the Treachery and Infidelity of these people [the natives] and the annoyance they may be of by having learnt so much of War & by the warlike stores scattered in the Country." [75]

Yet the only acceptable peace must now include, they felt, not only the recognition of the claims of Muhammad to rule as the Nabob throughout the Carnatic, and the inclusion in the peace of the rulers of Tanjore and Mysore, but also the relinquishment by the French of those new possessions that now blocked the former activities of the English, in favour of other possessions to be granted by the Nabob that would not do so.[76]

Chanda Sahib had set his heart upon Trichinopoly. There he himself had dwelt for some years in security — after seizing it through guile — before it had been taken by the Mahrattas in 1741, which led to his late captivity. With the possible exception of Jingi, it was the strongest place in all the Carnatic. As a result, early in April 1751 he left his capital, Arcot, supported by a French contingent determined to capture the great city on the Cauvery. A force sent from Fort St. David to aid Muhammad Ali fell back before Chanda until under the walls of the stronghold. Thereupon the place was besieged while

---

[73] India Office, Coast and Bay Letters, 5: 240–50.

[74] In fact, President Saunders claimed that Muhammad had in July 1750 mortgaged it to the East India Company for a loan (India Office, Home Series, Misc., 93: 82–106).

[75] India Office, Coast and Bay Letters, 5: 347–8.

[76] Ibid. Earlier, it is true, the English would have been satisfied to have had Trichinopoly secured to Muhammad and upon that basis were prepared to recognize Chanda Sahib.

at the same time the resourceful Dupleix sought with his customary dexterity to bring Muhammad Ali into an agreement to deliver it up peacefully.

At this juncture Robert Clive attracts attention and forecasts the great role that he was to play in India. In 1742, the same year in which Dupleix was made Governor of Pondicherry, he had been appointed a writer by the Court of Directors of the United East India Company.[77] Upon his arrival in India in the spring of 1744 he was, at the age of eighteen,[78] placed in the office of the secretary of the presidency with an allowance of five pounds a year. After the capture of Madras — escaping to Fort St. David by blacking his face and in the habit of a native — Clive, being " of a martial disposition," put aside his pen and temporarily acted as a volunteer with the rank of ensign in the defence of that place and in the later siege of Pondicherry; in 1749 he also engaged in the capture of Devi-Cotah, in which he led a desperate assault. It was noted that he always sought a post of danger and in such posts presented remarkable presence of mind and coolness of judgment;[79] yet he again returned to his civil employment until the crisis in the affairs of the Company along the Coromandel projected him again into action.

In order to draw Chanda Sahib from the siege of Trichinopoly, Clive, with the rank of captain in the commissary, proposed to President Saunders that he be permitted to lead a force to capture Arcot. By stripping the defences of both Madras and Fort St. David, he was furnished with two hundred Europeans and three hundred sepoys and, in all, five field pieces. Marching rapidly upon the place,

---

[77] Although his post was the least important at the gift of the Company, he was obliged to furnish security to the amount of £600 (India Office, Home Series, Misc., 806: 2).

[78] Clive was born on September 29, 1725. He seems, however, to have advanced his age upon entering the service of the Company. From the " Madras Public Proceedings," under date of December 3, 1745, is the following notation: " Robert Clive. Time of arrival, May 31, 1744. . . . Present employment — under the Secretary. Present salary — £5. Age 24 (India Office, Home Series, Misc., 806: 3).

[79] The Orme Manuscripts in the India Office furnish interesting details of his early career in India. Also occasional reference is made to his activities in the letters from Fort St. David and from Madras. For example, in 1749 the complaint was lodged against him by the Reverend Francis Fordyce, chaplain, for an assault. Upon inquiry it was found that the latter possessed " an insolent & medling disposition," while Clive was esteemed to be " a very quiet person & no ways guilty of disturbances." As a result the Reverend Robert Polk was appointed chaplain in place of Fordyce (India Office, Coast and Bay Letters, 5: 173–83). For this and other early episodes in the life of Clive see A. M. Davies, Clive of Plassey and H. H. Dodwell, The Nabobs of Madras.

which was weakly defended by only eight hundred of Chanda's troops, he was able on August 26 without the slightest difficulty to occupy it and take possession of the fort, which was in a ruinous condition.[80] Upon news of this event, Chanda — while remaining in front of Trichinopoly — in order to recapture his capital detached part of his army, which was soon joined by his son the Rajah, Sahib, and three hundred troops from Pondicherry.[81] For over fifty days Clive and his little garrison were constrained to put forth the most heroic efforts to hold the fort, with the town itself in the hands of the enemy. One force ordered to relieve him was driven back. However, the Mahrattas, who were hostile to Chanda, hovered about the city, and Captain Kilpatrick with reinforcements pressed forward in November. After a terrific assault on the night of November 16 the enemy, doubtless apprehensive of the near approach of the relieving column, suddenly left the city.[82] The capture of Arcot was described by one Frenchman who was at Pondicherry as "*le commencement de nos désastres.*"

It is impossible to set forth in detail the manœuvring of the conflicting parties that followed in the Carnatic. Chanda Sahib, supported by the French under d'Auteuil, continued doggedly with his army to invest Trichinopoly; not so effectively, however, that Muhammad Ali could not be reinforced by the new allies that he had won by great promises — the native rulers of Mysore and Tanjore. Major Lawrence with Captain Clive also appeared on the scene to aid him, supported by four hundred Europeans and over twice the

---

[80] An account of the defence of Arcot written by one of Clive's sergeants describes the little army marching "without opposition through the town amidst a million spectators whose looks betrayed them . . . notwithstanding their pretended friendship and dirty presents" (India Office, Orme Mss., India, II, 277–92); another account of the defence by an eyewitness, Dr. Wilson, has also been preserved (*ibid.*, II, 292–6). Orme's *History of the Military Transactions in Hindustan* goes into great detail regarding the events at this period in the Carnatic.

[81] Orme gives the number as one hundred and fifty; but I am relying upon a statement by one serving in the French army in India at the time. He says that Dupleix "détache . . . un corps de 300. hommes; 10 pièces de canon, et 2. mortiers a grenader, pour les ordres de M. Véry; il enjoint à cet officier de prendre sa route vers Arcate, déscalader cette place et de passer, disoit-il, au fil de l'épée, tous les coquins qui feroient quelque resistance" (Bib. Nat., A.F.F., 12087: 126). Dupleix in writing to the *directeurs* asserts: "nous y avons environs 60 blancs, et une trentaine de Topasses" (*ibid.*, N.A.F., 9146: 266). But Dupleix's testimony cannot be relied upon.

[82] While the English defending the fort testified to the reckless bravery of the natives, especially in connection with the great assault, Dupleix refers contemptuously to them, who, he asserts, on this occasion, "*se comporterent au plus mal*" (Bib. Nat., N.A.F., 9146: 266).

number of sepoys. There were marchings and counter-marchings each side seeking to gain an easy victory over the other. D'Auteuil, at the head of the French force, asking to be relieved, was superseded by Law, who, together with Chanda Sahib — both now forced to act on the defensive — was impelled to take a position on Seringham, an island of the Cauvery, close to Trichinopoly. The besiegers were thereupon besieged. A relief force sent by Dupleix under d'Auteuil was obliged to fall back and was finally captured by Clive; the flower of Chanda's army meanwhile scattered in the face of a hopeless situation, some of the troops actually taking service with the English; the Nabob himself was advised by Law to make his escape, to keep from falling into the hands of his deadly enemy, Muhammad Ali, but he delayed too long; at length in desperation he decided to place himself at the mercy of Monacjee, commander of the Tanjore troops, who had not forgotten how his own country had recently been ravaged by Chanda; and when the Rajah ordered the Nabob's execution, this was carried out with the full approval of Muhammad Ali, in spite of the efforts of Major Lawrence to send him to Madras for safe custody.[83] As to Law, that unhappy commander was obliged to surrender on June 18, 1752. Thus the French were faced with the loss of most of their active and effective troops in the Carnatic. In fact, even Pondicherry at this critical juncture might have been captured with ease. According to one of the French officers then serving under Dupleix, "*Pondichery même n'etoit gardé que par la foi des traites*";[84] according to a naval officer who arrived shortly after Law's surrender, there were only thirty French soldiers to defend the town and Major Lawrence, well aware of its weakness, had determined to get possession of it and also of Dupleix, but was forbidden on the peril of his life to do so by President Saunders, who was not anxious by such an overt act to shoulder the responsibility for the outbreak of open war between Great Britain and France.[85]

But Dupleix, who was not only the French Governor of Pondicherry but likewise the *Mensebdar* of the Coromandel Coast, was a man of unlimited determination and also of endless devices. To re-

---

[83] Dupleix charged the English with the assassination of Chanda Sahib. He declared that this was " *medité et decidé dans un conseil de leur adherens, où le commandant de leur troupes a presidé . . .*" (Bib. Nat., N.A.F., 9146: 298).

[84] Bib. Nat., A.F.F, 12087: 127–8.

[85] Bib. Nat., A.F.F., 8971: 108–9. Lawrence, it was declared, had developed an intense hatred of Dupleix on account of the treatment he had received at the latter's hands while a prisoner at Pondicherry during the recent war.

assure the *directeurs*, he wrote optimistically on the 30th of the same fateful month of June that the Compagnie des Indes "*toutes ses dépenses payées, elle avoit dans l'Inde un fonds d'avance de 24,110,418 livres. . . .*" [86] With equal optimism he brushed aside the offers of accommodation on the part of the triumphant Muhammad Ali — now without a serious rival for the nabobship of the Carnatic, in spite of the setting up of one Mootas Ali for that high honour — and determined to insist on an arrangement which would take fully into account his own theoretical authority, such as would have only been possible had the new Nabob been in his power. Even with the raiding Mahrattas coming up to the very bounds of Pondicherry to carry away cattle, so helpless was he, nevertheless, upon the appearance of an envoy, said to have come from the court of Delhi bringing with him *paravana* confirming the grants by the late Muzaffar Jang to the Compagnie and also to him, under the resounding title of "*Dupleixcan, Bahadours, Yafersingue,*" [87] that he now sought to impress those natives of the region gathered at Pondicherry with his power and pre-eminence by placing nine bedecked elephants in line in a grand procession, each bearing the different marks of the dignities that had been conferred upon him.[88] He soon succeeded in attaching to the French cause the *Dalaway*, or regent, of Mysore, who had been promised the possession of Trichinopoly by the tricky Muhammad Ali for his aid, and when the promise was not fulfilled turned against him; Dupleix also secured money and reinforcements of French troops from home, and again sent an army into the field, still determined to lay his hands on the coveted fortress. Unhappily, this new force was surprised and cut to pieces on September 6 only three leagues from Pondicherry.[89]

But no defeat apparently could now dismay the infatuated Dupleix, who, however, was careful to maintain an attitude of great reticence in communicating with the directorate. Nevertheless, the true state of affairs in India at last began to dawn upon that body. For on February 19, 1753 the *Conseil Supérieur* at Pondicherry wrote that, far from having great funds in advance, as Dupleix had assured the *directeurs* the preceding June was the case, the Compagnie actually owed in India two million; that its resources were quite exhausted,

---

[86] Quoted in Michaud, *op. cit.,* XII, 18.

[87] Bib. Nat., A.F.F., 8971: 113.

[88] *Ibid.* There has been much controversy as to whether these patents were really from the Mogul.

[89] Bib. Nat., A.F.F., 12087: 128.

with nothing for current expenses; and that, in order to borrow three hundred thousand rupees to freight two ships with pepper from the Malabar Coast, it was necessary to pay interest at the rate of twenty per cent to those who would advance the funds.[90]

Passing over his attempt to have his troops attack the English factory of Fort St. David at Cuddalore and to burn its gardens, which they refused to do,[91] and over other incidents, in the month of June 1753 Dupleix felt that with the arrival of additional reinforcements from France he could now guarantee the success of the *Dalaway* of Mysore in front of Trichinopoly, and with a combined force no larger than the defending force sought vainly to capture it; again after some skirmishing Lawrence forced his way into the place with a great convoy. In the latter part of September in the midst of the skirmishing that took place, the English, with six hundred Europeans, four thousand sepoys, and two pieces of cannon, attacked at night the enemy army of fourteen hundred whites, eight thousand sepoys, eighteen thousand cavalry, and twenty-five cannon and drove the latter forces into wild retreat.[92] Dupleix, however, with additional reinforcements, on the night of November 27 attempted to storm Trichinopoly, and again there was failure with loss of over

---

[90] Quoted in Michaud, *op. cit.*, XII, 18. Yet the same ship that carried this dispatch of the *Conseil* likewise carried Dupleix's long letter of February 16 to the company. This was chiefly a defence of himself and others who had been given special consideration by Chanda Sahib and by Muzaffar Jang and his successor. The Compagnie had, it seems, secured an *arrêt* of the King to unite with its holdings in India the *aldees* granted to individual Frenchmen, as violating a law that forbade any French subject becoming a pensioner of any foreign prince. Dupleix contended that this law did not have in mind a situation such as had arisen in India. He called the attention of the *directeurs* to the great sacrifices of those in India, who had now provided the nation with " *revenus immenses*," and emphasized the undying loyalty of these men to the Crown. He also did not hesitate to point out what an unfortunate impression would be spread in France if those who had served the company so well should by its despotic action be reduced to misery. Further on in this communication, in again referring to the vast revenues upon which the company could now rely, he declared that the English company — the only true enemy the French had in India — not having any such resources, would inevitably be ruined unless it sent orders to its agents in India to cease acting against the French (Bib. Nat., N.A.F., 9145: 92).

[91] One of Dupleix's own officers, unfriendly to him, writes of this incident: " Une démarche aussi hardie pour un particulier que celle de faire attaquer les établissmens de la Compagnie d'angleterre qu'un traité récent et solennel devoit naturellement mettre à l'abri de toute entreprise, semble dénoter clairement que le projet de M. Dupleix étoit de ralumer la guerre entre la france et l'angleterre, et de justifier par ce moyen l'irregularité du plan qu'il s'étoit formé: il vouloit conquérir ou pour mieux dire infester toute la presqu'île de l'inde . . ." (Bib. Nat., A.F.F., 12087: 129).

[92] Bib. Nat., A.F.F., 12087: 131.

four hundred Frenchmen either killed or taken prisoner.[93] In fact, until the following October the history of the Carnatic is in a sense the history of the determination of the Presidency of Madras to preserve the stronghold from the grasp of Dupleix — and, incidentally, from that of the ruler of Mysore, with whom he was allied — and the equal determination of the latter to acquire it at all costs, with now the French and again the English gaining some momentary success.

But Dupleix found himself, meanwhile, enveloped in other worries. The Compagnie des Indes, with a growing sense of disillusionment regarding the soundness of his policies, late in December of 1752 and early in January 1753 addressed to him three letters, each now filled with strong rebukes, blaming him for disturbing the peace of the Carnatic and placing it in an uproar through antagonizing the English and the Dutch at Masulipatam and elsewhere and through his support of one group of native princes against another, with the consequent decline of commerce. As a result in September of the latter year in a long communication he sought not only to clear himself of the imputation of having became a political adventurer with objectives out of harmony with those legitimately embodied in his office, but to point out why the French cause had suffered serious reverses. He himself placed the blame for the unfortunate turn of affairs upon the incapacity of those officers who had served under him; he justified the repeated efforts to capture Trichinopoly since, he claimed, "*qui y gouverne, reçoit les pouvoirs du Gouverneur d'Arcatte*"; he even turned upon the *directeurs* to warn them in turn that they were being misguided by the English version of what was happening in India:

"*Ainsi, Messieurs, les idées que vous voulés prêter aux Anglois ne sont nullement celles qu'ils ont eû, et qu'ils ont encore. . . .*"

In fact he went so far as to assert that "*en toutes occasions ils sont été les aggresseurs . . .*" and that he had avoided giving "*la moindre atteinte aux traites, ainsi le bon droit sera toûjours de nôtre côté. . . .*" Then, after promising the reimbursement of all expenses incurred in connection with the hostilities, he proceeded to ask for five thousand additional French troops and a yearly complement thereafter of three hundred, and for two or three officers of high rank worthy to command them.[94]

But the tide was turning irresistibly against Dupleix and his sys-

---

[93] Bib. Nat., A.F.F., 12087: 133.   [94] Bib. Nat., N.A.F., 9146: 250–71.

tem. The *directeurs,* seeing nothing but ruin and disaster in the wake
of this system, were now thinking only of a restoration of peaceful,
non-political, commercial activity in India and made clear to the
French Governor that he must try to seek an accommodation with
the President and Council of Madras. Under this pressure Dupleix
proposed to Saunders a conference and the President agreed. As a
result, representatives of the two companies met at the Dutch post of
Sadras, between Pondicherry and Madras, early in 1754; but this
served only to sharpen the antagonism between them, especially in
view of the fact that the French deputies were ordered to insist, as a
preliminary, that Dupleix should be recognized as "*Nabob pro-
tecteur de la côté Coromandel*"[95] — something that the English
would not do, implying as it did that they must thereafter acknowledge his superior authority even in Madras and at Fort St. David;
nor would they recognize the still higher authority of the Subahdar
of the Deccan, Salabat Jang, supported and maintained as he was by
Bussy's army. In turn, the French would not for one moment agree
to accept Muhammad Ali as the Nabob of Arcot and all of the Carnatic. Neither side was at all impressed by the patents and other
proofs displayed by the other in support of its pretensions. Clearly
Dupleix could make no peace that would not sacrifice his system and
he was not prepared to do this.

At home both of the rival companies were searching for means to
remedy the situation in India on the Coromandel Coast, a situation
that was regarded as deplorable. Madras — as was the case with Pondicherry — no longer had significance as a great emporium of trade.
Indeed, the whole weight of providing tonnage for the English company's ships arriving in the Indian Ocean had now, as has been
suggested, fallen upon Calcutta;[96] further, the maintenance of the
English troops along the Coromandel Coast — the cost of which,
amounting to some one hundred thousand rupees a month, Muhammad Ali had agreed to bear — had fallen upon the Company itself by
reason of the fact that the Nabob could not collect his revenues because of the widespread anarchy within the Carnatic.[97] This anarchy
was present likewise in the Deccan. Not only was the Mahratta army
plundering the possessions of the weaker rajahs, but a rival to Salabat
Jang, one Firuz Jang, with a commission from Delhi as Subahdar and

[95] Bib. Nat., A.F.F., 12087: 133.
[96] India Office, Coast and Bay Letters, 6: 1-4.
[97] India Office, Coast and Bay Letters, 6: 36-9.

an army to support it, put in his appearance. Conditions were no better in northern India. Ahmad Shah, the Grand Mogul, could hardly tell which were his greater enemies: his own powerful feudatories or the Afghan Ahmad Shah Afdali, who in 1752 invaded the Punjab and secured the cession of that province; in fact on June 2, 1754 he himself was deposed by the very man to whom he had so recently granted the Deccan, but who found it easier to get rid of an emperor than to contend against Bussy's veterans. This anarchy pointed to the vital importance of Anglo-French co-operation to stabilize conditions, if possible.

It is therefore not surprising that early in 1754 one of the *directeurs* of the French company appeared in London with a plan which was designed to put an end to the troubles — at least along the Coromandel Coast. This called for an alliance between the two companies for the purpose of a mutual support of the commercial privileges of each; it also called for the giving up of Masulipatam on the part of the French and the island of Divi on the part of the British, both of which possessions should be turned over to the Subahdar of the Deccan; the claims of Dupleix to the overlordship of the Coromandel Coast it also placed in the discard. However, the Compagnie des Indes, in consideration of these concessions, such as they were, expected the recognition of its claims to a great region surrounding Masulipatam, almost thirteen thousand square miles in extent. The British, as might have been expected, were not at all enthusiastic about an agreement that ignored the claims of Muhammad Ali in the Carnatic and that would leave the French entrenched not only in the Deccan but in the coastal region of the so-called Northern Circars.[98] In fact, the directors of United East India Company took the position that unless the French would agree to bring themselves within their "ancient limits," it would be better to go on in the present manner in India, making alliances with the local princes, with the expectation that gradually the natives would become more warlike and thus "better able to keep the French in order." In this connection they made an interesting observation that shows how little they anticipated future developments in India:

> "It may be said They [the natives] will do the same to us [that is, keep the English in order]; let it be so; it is far better that the Natives should be masters of that Country, and give the law to both the

---

[98] For an extended analysis of the French plan see India Office, Home Series, Misc., 93: 146–60.

French and us than that we should remain there in a mean, declining way, receiving laws from the French. The credit of the English as merchants is superior in India to that of the French, & they will always have the Preference in all India Governments who are their own masters, so long as they preserve their mercantile reputation." [99]

Although the above effort to bring about an understanding between the French and British in India failed, the Compagnie des Indes had already determined to sacrifice Dupleix and sent to take his place one of the directorate, M. Godeheu, who arrived at Pondicherry in the month of August 1754 bearing detailed instructions,[100] not only as *commandant général* of the French establishments but as royal *commissaire* — instructions designed to restore tranquillity once again to the Coromandel Coast. He was authorized, among other things, should Dupleix seek to retain his power as a prince of India, to place him and Madame Dupleix under arrest. But the former Governor now only sought to vindicate his conduct at home and departed peacefully. Stripped of his honours [101] and of his great personal fortune, which had been drained off in supporting his vast enterprise, he returned to France hoping that at least he would secure financial reimbursement for what he had spent in the public cause. But even this was denied him. Scorned as the author of those evils that had beset the Compagnie des Indes, he was permitted to plead his cause in vain and to die, if not in obscurity, at least in want.

Godeheu, soon after his arrival, sent one of his staff officers to Madras to sound out President Saunders. Upon his return he reported that Saunders's intentions toward the French were friendly.[102] Although the French had received a reinforcement of twelve hundred men, half of whom were German mercenaries, their situation in India was still none too favourable. The European troops, Godeheu found, were in a mutinous condition, their pay was four months in arrears, their rations were uncertain, and their want of clothing had reduced them almost to nakedness; [103] the sepoys in the service, for

---

[99] *Ibid.*

[100] Bib. Nat., N.A.F., 9145: 197–208.

[101] Dupleix, however, was permitted to enjoy the revenues of the *aldee* granted to him. But, unfortunately, he could not secure these, because of hostilities.

[102] Bib. Nat., A.F.F., 12087: 135. This officer, who had served under Dupleix, pays a high compliment to Saunders. Referring at a later date to the report that he made to Godeheu, he writes: " *Sur le compte que je lui rendir* [sic] *des bonnes intentions de M. Sanders, il commença à entretenir avec lui une correspondance qui eut bientôt tout le fruit que l'on devoit attendre de deux esprits aussi justes et aussi bien disposés* (ibid.).

[103] *Ibid.*

lack of pay, likewise were revolting; even the Rajah of Mysore, who had become an ally, was threatening to desert them and refused to render the promised financial aid. With the news of the appearance off the Coromandel Coast of Admiral Watson's fleet with almost a thousand British troops, Godeheu, therefore, was led to agree on October 11 to a three months' suspension of arms as proposed by Saunders.[104] However, the further proposal by the latter that each company should retire " to their Ancient Districts with a Moderate Addition " did not, at first, appeal to the French, who sought to reserve their grants to the northward of Madras, which, it was contended, could not be detrimental to the English. A spirit of mutual give and take, nevertheless, took the place of the late struggle for exclusive power and on December 15 a provisional treaty was signed at Madras that held out the promise of better days for India.[105]

By this treaty it was agreed that each company would renounce for ever all native offices and dignities and should never interfere in any differences arising between the native princes; that all places except those stipulated in the definitive treaty should be delivered up to the natives by both parties; that the English should retain Madras, Fort St. David, and Devi-Cotah, and the French Pondicherry and Karikal; that the French should be permitted to establish another limited settlement on the Coromandel Coast to make up for their inequality; that both Masulipatam and the island of Devi should be neutral ground, with an equality of interest — together with other provisions designed to give each an opportunity to follow its legitimate commercial interests without interference on the one hand or monopoly on the other, as, for example, the right of the English to enjoy the same privileges in the Northern Circars as the French.

In view of the actual rather than the theoretical position of the two companies, the agreement was probably more favourable to the French than to the English.[106] Bussy's strategic position in the Deccan, in control as it were of the court of the Subahdar, was not af-

---

104 India Office, Coast and Bay Letters, 6: 36–9. This was formally ratified on November 15, 1754 (India Office, Home Series, Misc., 93: 223–7).

105 For the treaty in both English and French see India Office, Home Series, Misc., 93: 244–50, 254–8.

106 Most historians are apt to emphasize the great sacrifices of the French in giving up so gracefully vast revenues secured from the grants made to the Compagnie des Indes. The truth is that these revenues were non-existent and that there remained in the treasury at Pondicherry when a suspension of arms took place only 120,000 rupees, less than enough to provide the expenses of the troops for one month (Bib. Nat., A.F.F., 12087: 136).

fected, with all that this might imply for the Carnatic as well as the Deccan in the maintenance of French influence. By it Godeheu felt that he would be able to purchase for his nation, at worst, a breathing-spell along the Coromandel Coast — and that breathing-spell was a matter of the most vital importance if hostilities were to be resumed — and, at best, an opportunity to concentrate, as before 1744, upon the peaceful acquisitions of wealth with the growth of commerce. But forces were at last let loose in India that denied this happy outcome and that no desire for peace on the part of the two companies could dissipate.

CHAPTER X

Efforts to Save the Peace

HE WAR OF THE AUSTRIAN SUCCESSION had brought in its course little sense of buoyancy to the people of Great Britain. "For God's sake," wrote Bishop Trevor during the dark days of July in 1747, "when shall we have done fighting for a desperate game, with Flanders gone, Zeeland going, and the K. of Sardinia retired to defend his frontier? and we are amusing ourselves with, I know not what Imaginary advantages."[1] His correspondent, Bishop Sherlock, agreed that "our affairs abroad seem almost Desperate: Some of the Fr. officers here on paroll say the Dutch have been neither good friends to France nor good allies to England."[2] Beyond the continent of Europe in the course of the war developments did not appear in any too rosy a light in spite of the capture in 1745 of the French fortress of Louisbourg on Cape Breton Island by the New England troops under William Pepperell aided by a fleet under Commodore Peter Warren; for in 1746 Fort St. George at Madras fell to La Bourdonnais.

Yet there was another side to the picture. British superior sea-power bore heavily upon the enemy and wound about France and Spain a relentless blockade of their shores, besides sweeping the seas of their shipping. According to one estimate, up to June 1745, 695 French and Spanish ships had been captured; from that date to April 1746, 521 more had been accounted for; from April 1746 to May 1747, 521 more had been added; and from May 1747 to April 1748, 720 — making a grand total of 2,457 captures in the course of the

---

[1] "Weston Papers," *Historical Manuscripts Commission, Tenth Report*, p. 297.
[2] *Ibid.*

war.[3] With French overseas commerce paralysed, with industry dis-
rupted through the loss of markets, with the French West Indies
faced by economic collapse and even by famine — a fate only warded
off, ironically enough, by the succour brought from the English colonies in English so-called " flags of truce "[4] in the course of the exchange of prisoners — with these ominous facts in mind the conviction had come home to the court of France with increasing force that
the victories in the Low Countries, spectacular as these had been,
were really Pyrrhic in nature. Not that Frederick of Prussia, its ally,
had not firmly entrenched himself in Silesia; not that Maria Theresa,
in spite of her determination to prosecute the war, had shown any
capacity to strike back effectively at France as well as at Prussia and
her other opponents; not that the Russian army of thirty thousand
under Repnin, subsidized by Great Britain and Holland, had been
either ready for action in the region of the Rhine after its long march
or greatly feared, but rather that naval superiority seemed destined
to determine in the long run the outcome of the war, by determining
the fate of the French Empire. In truth, by 1747 there was sensed the
great danger that the prized sugar islands might not be able to hold
out much longer against blockade, that even the winning of Madras
might not be a matter of much moment were that city and Pondicherry to be cut off from the outside world by British sea superiority,
and that even Canada, now isolated, might be lost, lacking proper
defences as it did, especially after the capitulation of the great fortress of Louisbourg, a place much more powerfully fortified than was
either Quebec or Montreal.

Thus a deeply apprehensive France had found herself faced by an
England that was becoming increasingly anxious to be extricated

---

[3] For these figures see the *Pennsylvania Journal and Weekly Advertiser*, February 21,
1748/9. According to the *Maryland Gazette* of June 21, 1749 the total was 2,804 enemy
and neutral vessels captured. It will be of interest to group these captures geographically
and by nation. As to the French merchant ships, 140 were captured in the Mediterranean,
804 in the Atlantic going to or from their possessions or to Spanish American ports, 487
in the region of the English Channel, 157 about Newfoundland and Cape Breton, and
41 in the waters of the East Indies or those off China; in addition, 348 French privateers
were captured, and 34 French men-of-war. The Spaniards suffered the loss of 385 small
vessels that were carrying stores in the Mediterranean for the French and Spanish armies
in Italy, 71 ordinary merchant ships gathered up in American waters, 91 along the Atlantic coast of Spain and Portugal, 34 registered ships, sailing to or from America, and 96
privateers. As to neutral ships acting in violation of the rules of war, 110 were taken and
their cargoes condemned.

[4] For the " flag of truce " trade, see Richard Pares, *War and Trade in the West Indies, 1739–1763*, pp. 446–55.

from the implications of a continuation of the war. It was affirmed in 1747 that in the House of Commons "there was a manifest dejection on many faces, when eleven millions (now considered as an annual charge during the War) was proposed."[5] It was likewise affirmed in that year that both inside and outside the ministry, Horatio Walpole's plan — that of "procuring such a peace, as may leave Europe in quiet for some years," by the process of detaching Frederick from his French connections by supporting him in his determination to retain Silesia and thereby bringing him into a strong alliance with the maritime powers — "prevails very much. . . ."[6] With the appearance of Saxe's army before Maestricht and yet with Holland's treasury empty and her troops fighting but half-heartedly, and the Russians, the Bavarians, and other states of the Empire with troops in the pay of the Republic loudly insisting upon the payment of subsidies, some of which at least Great Britain in addition to her own had been obliged to underwrite, additional reasons for a prompt peace could be advanced.

In March 1748, therefore, a congress assembled at Aix-la-Chapelle. It was hoped by many that, like the Congress of Westphalia held a century earlier, it would undertake the great task of including in a general settlement the multitudinous problems of contemporary Europe. But this was not to be. On April 30 not only were open preliminary articles of peace signed by the representatives of Great Britain, France, and Holland[7] and, in addition, a secret article which pledged the three powers to seek peace among themselves were it delayed by the other powers, but on the same day another secret article agreeing to an *immediate* cessation of hostilities.[8] In truth, the city of Aix-la-Chapelle during the making of the peace bore little resemblance to those of Münster and Osnabrück in Westphalia during the years between July 1643 and October 1648, where the Thirty Years' War was brought to conclusion and where plenipotentiaries vied with one another in sumptuous entertainment while interminable delays were permitted as the result of quarrels over precedence and other matters hardly more fundamental. In contrast, in 1748 during a period of five months negotiations steadily proceeded in the midst

---

[5] *Hist. Mss. Com., Tenth Report*, p. 299.

[6] *Ibid.*

[7] Duc de Broglie, *La Paix d'Aix la Chapelle*, p. 312.

[8] This secret article, signed after the preliminary articles and the first secret article, is to be found in the volume of "Memoirs" among the Mildmay Papers in the Clements Library at Ann Arbor.

of great secrecy until on October 18 ratification of a definitive treaty was concluded.

Englishmen could as a result of the peace boast that the principal objects of the war, at least as far as these related to the Continent and Great Britain, had been accomplished: the defeat of the design of the Bourbon powers to aggrandize themselves in such a way "as might be dangerous to the Liberties of Europe," with the preservation of the balance in western Europe; [9] the repudiation by France of the Jacobite Pretender as the rightful heir to the throne of Great Britain; and the renewal in the most positive terms of the guarantee of the Pragmatic Sanction, except with respect to Silesia and the County of Glatz, which went to Frederick, and Parma and Piacenza, left to Don Philip.[10] By this treaty France agreed not only to retreat from the Low Countries and to destroy the fortifications at Dunkirk but to hand back Madras, while Great Britain, manifestly with great reluctance, in turn agreed to restore Cape Breton Island and, to make good this pledge, sent to Paris as hostages two of her leading peers, the Earl of Sussex and Baron Cathcart, who, arriving there in November and after experiencing many courtesies at the hands of the King and his entourage at Versailles, were permitted to depart in October of the following year upon receipt of the news of the punctual fulfilment of the agreement on the part of His Britannic Majesty's government.[11] Two days after this peace was confirmed Spain also adhered to it.

---

[9] "If there was a Principle which our Forefathers adopted as the *Paladium* of their Liberty; if there was a Blessing which they courted at the Price of their Ease, and pursued with the Loss of their Blood, it was to preserve the Balance of Power," declared the author of *The Conduct of the Government with Regard to Peace and War* (Dublin, 1748, p. 9). Continuing, he says: "By the *Balance of Power* he [a Briton] understands that happy temper of Interests abroad by which the Trade, the Peace, the Liberty, and the Religion of his Country is secured."

[10] *Considerations on the Definitive Treaty signed at Aix-la-Chapelle October 7/18, 1748* (London, 1748), pp. 24–8. The guarantee to Frederick is contained in Article XXII. Article XXXIII bound Frederick, in case he accepted the advantages of Article XXII, to guarantee the execution of the whole treaty.

[11] It should be pointed out that Article V of the treaty in general terms states that all conquests made either in Europe or in the East or West Indies shall be restored, while Article IX, which specifically referred to Cape Breton, only includes Madras by inference. See George Chalmers, *Collection of Treaties between Great Britain and Other Powers before 1790*, I, 424–42; also *A Collection of All the Treaties of Peace, Alliance and Commerce between Great-Britain and Other Powers from the Revolution of 1688 to the Present Time* (London, 1772), pp. 68–107; portions of the text are printed in *European Treaties Bearing on the History of the United States and Its Dependencies* (ed. C. O. Paullin), IV, 73–5.

But all Englishmen had not favoured the war nor did they acclaim the peace. " Thus ends the war that ill-timed brat of the Granville policy, fostered by hags who had just so much art as to lay their spell upon the parent but not the power to raise the half-begotten off-spring to any growth and stature," wrote Westmorland to Lady Den-bigh upon hearing of the terms of the preliminary articles of settle-ment.[12] To a writer in the *Gentleman's Magazine* the maritime powers showed

> " so prompt and unfeigned a Disposition toward Peace, that they join'd in a *separate article* with the Common Enemy, to compel their common Friends into his terms or relinquish their Alliance and leave them to his *Most* Christian Discretion."

Further, in the issue of May 9, 1749 of the *Caledonian Mercury* it was pointed out that the war begun in 1739 with Spain, involving the issue of " a free navigation without *Search* (or cutting People's Ears off) to the West Indies," soon involved the British nation in another with France,

> " who contrary to treaty had open'd and fortified the Harbour of Dunkirk. Be it then, I say, remember'd, that *Great Britain,* after a vast *Profusion* of Blood, and running in Debt full *Thirty Millions,* when it had reduced the Royal Fleets of France and Spain to so wretched a condition that they durst not appear at Sea, and had by the brave *New-Englanders* taken the important Isle of *Cape-Breton* did by that very memorable Peace . . . not only generously restore *Cape-Breton* to the Crown of *France* . . . but . . . concluded a most gracious and honourable Peace with that Nation [Spain]; leav-ing the Grand Affair of the *Search* and the Barbarities us'd toward her gallant sailors just where she found them."

Nevertheless, most of the people of both Great Britain and France welcomed the coming of peace with joy and fervently prayed that this might be lasting, with the amicable settlement of whatever issues still subsisted between them which might imperil it. The efforts to save the peace, entered into with high hopes in an atmosphere of friendliness and finally discontinued in the midst of one of disillu-sionment and mutual resentment, must be now considered in some detail.

The fourth article of the Preliminary Articles of Peace provided for the appointment of " commissaries " by the courts of France and Great Britain for the purpose of dealing with the question of prizes

---

[12] *Hist. Mss. Com., Eighth Report,* Part I, sec. iii, p. 570.

taken at sea after the close of hostilities. The commissaries were also, it was agreed, to arrive at an understanding relative to the ransom and exchange of prisoners and likewise to undertake the vitally important tasks of determining not only the respective rights of the two nations to each of the so-called Neutral Islands of the West Indies but the proper boundaries to be assigned to British Nova Scotia. In this connection, the final treaty provided that, prior to this settlement of outstanding difficulties, all things in both the West and the East Indies were to be put on the same footing " they were actually or ought to have been in before the commencement of the last war." As a mark of good faith each Crown pledged itself to send orders for the immediate evacuation of the Caribbean " Neutral " Islands by those of its nationals who had established themselves upon them.

Little need be said regarding the fruitless efforts of the first British commissaries, Messrs. Allix and Hinds, who met with M. Guillot, appointed by His Most Christian Majesty at Saint-Malo in 1749, to come to an understanding over the specific question of prizes taken at sea.[13] The two sets of instructions were too far apart to make possible the slightest progress since those of the British limited consideration, in accordance with Article IV of the treaty, to prizes taken subsequent to the time when hostilities were to cease, while the French provided for the consideration of all ships captured whether before the war or subsequent thereto. As a result up until May 1750 negotiations were largely confined to the ordinary diplomatic channels,[14] when William Mildmay, kinsman of the Earl of Fitzwalter, one of the Lords Commissioners of the Treasury, made his appearance in Paris with a special commission for settling all accounts relating to the ransom and exchange of prisoners.[15] He had also in April, before his coming, been joined with Governor William Shirley of Massachusetts Bay in a new and enlarged commission " for settling several Points in dispute betwixt the Crowns of Great Britain and France." [16]

---

[13] For a brief discussion of this see Max Savelle, *The Diplomatic History of the Canadian Boundary*, pp. 21–2.

[14] *British Diplomatic Instructions, 1689–1789*, VII, France, Part IV, 1745–1789 (ed. L. G. W. Legg), pp. 1–9. From February 1749 to July of that year Colonel Joseph Yorke represented Great Britain in France as secretary of the Embassy, whereupon William Anne Keppel, Earl of Albemarle, who arrived in Paris on July 25, took over affairs and remained in charge until his death on December 22, 1754.

[15] Mildmay " Letter Book," Clements Library. His instructions are to be found in *Diplomatic Instructions*, VII, France, p. 307.

[16] The commission, dated April 14, 1750, is set forth in Latin and is among the Colonial Office Papers, Class 323, lettered O. 49. 4.

Upon the arrival of the latter in Paris in August the two, after being presented to the King and Queen, and " to Madame La Marquise at Her Toillette," were thereupon introduced to the Comte de la Galissonière, late Governor General of New France and chief of squadron, and to M. de Silhouette, Maître de Requêtes and Chancellor to the Duke of Orléans,[17] who had in turn been appointed as the French commissaries.[18]

At the first meeting of the commissaries on August 25 it was agreed, doubtless for the purpose of adding a touch of friendly intimacy to the proceedings, that all subsequent deliberations should be in the private apartments of the four, each acting in turn as the host.[19] After this fashion they were " to examine and adjust " the points in dispute between the two nations in America — but not in India — as well as those relating to prizes and prisoners of war taken at sea.[20] The importance of this international commission should not be obscured by its failure to accomplish any of its objectives; to the end it remained the symbol that peaceful solution of vexed questions was the civilized way for peoples involved in dispute.

The commissaries at their first formal meeting on September 1 had to face an initial difficulty when in the exchange of their full powers it was discovered that the French commissaries were again called upon, as were those of 1749, to bring up the question of all captures made at sea from 1738 to the present while the British were limited to act only " agreeable to the convention concluded at Aix la Chapelle." [21] When, however, the latter made clear that the question of prizes was under consideration by the ministers of the two crowns, the French agreed to put this aside and to enter immediately upon other points. The British thereupon urged the necessity of discussing the question of the limits of Acadia or Nova Scotia " as being the most important point to be Determin'd for settling the same Tranquility

---

[17] De Silhouette was not a French nonentity. He was charged with the affairs of one of the greatest of French families. Louis, Duke of Orléans, who died in 1752, was the son of the Regent Philip, who, passing away in 1723, left him the title but not the great power he himself had enjoyed. Louis was the grandfather of Philippe Égalité, father of King Louis Philippe.

[18] Many intimate details are presented in Mildmay's sycophantic correspondence with the Earl of Fitzwalter; the Clements Library also possesses this.

[19] The Mildmay " Memorandum Book," Clements Library.

[20] The instructions of the British commissaries are to be found in *Diplomatic Instructions*, VII, France, pp. 307-13; the first set relates to prisoners and prizes, the second to Acadia and the Neutral Islands.

[21] C. O. 323: 12. O. 50. 1.

in America as had been so happily established in Europe "; to which the French agreed under condition that the right to St. Lucia should be the subject of discussion at alternate meetings. When, however, it was pointed out that no account had arrived as yet of the French evacuation of the island, as provided for in the preliminary articles of peace, the French representatives gave way again in face of the British argument that the French and British Crowns were both seeking the peaceful settlement of the boundaries of Acadia without delay " least [sic] it might be brought to a more disagreeable Tryal & hazard the breach of . . . Friendship." [22]

The urgency of this problem, if peace were to be maintained in North America, lay in what seemed to be a shift in position of the French court regarding the justification for the presence of French soldiers upon the Isthmus of Chignecto, connecting the Nova Scotian peninsula with the mainland. For when early in the summer Albemarle had represented to the Minister of Foreign Affairs, M. Puysieulx, that these troops had been ordered to Chignecto and Beaubassin by the Governor General, La Jonquière, Puysieulx had entirely disavowed these proceedings in acknowledging that the places named were within the peninsula and had agreed to see that satisfaction should be rendered. [23] By August, however, he had so far changed his opinion that, in order to justify the conduct of La Jonquière, he was now endeavouring to make it appear that Governor Cornwallis of Nova Scotia was the real aggressor and that the troops upon the isthmus were not to be ordered to depart. [24]

The French commissaries in support of the policy of their court therefore proposed at the meeting of September 1 that as a basis for the solution of this problem of the boundary of Acadia the principle be laid down that each side should agree as a preliminary to renounce any claim that would give too great a facility to either of the two Crowns to inconvenience or to invade the other even in time of war. To this the British replied that it was their duty to support the rights of their King. [25] The French proposal, in fact, seemed to open up many large questions over and beyond that of Nova Scotia. Questions involving, for example, the western boundaries between the French and the British in North America relative to which the Brit-

---

[22] Ibid.
[23] British Diplomatic Instructions, 1689–1789, VII, France, Part IV, p. 10.
[24] See Newcastle to Albemarle, August 4, 1750, ibid.
[25] C. O. 323: 12. O. 50. 1.

ish commissaries were without instructions, for those that they had received limited their activities — outside of the questions of prizes and prisoners — to problems involving the ancient Acadia boundary and the respective rights to the Neutral Islands.[26] In fact, it soon became apparent that the British-French joint commission would be expected, upon the basis of new instructions that the French commissaries now received, to weld into a single general agreement all points in dispute between the two countries that might be referred to their decision; that no one point, therefore, no matter how urgent agreement upon it seemed to be, could be dealt with definitively apart from all others. Significantly, these new instructions further made clear that the failure of one party or the other to evacuate the Neutral Islands, as had been agreed upon, could not be urged as an excuse for a refusal to enter upon negotiations relative to their final disposition; in fact, the French were called upon to break off all deliberations should the British refuse to accede to these propositions.[27]

Faced by this determined attitude on the part of the French, the British commissaries were led to make some concessions, especially relative to the receipt of evidence that the settled inhabitants of St. Lucia had been evacuated before agreeing to enter upon a discussion of the question as to the respective rights of the two Crowns to that island.[28] In view of this conciliatory attitude the French now agreed to waive their demand for alternate discussions on Acadia and St. Lucia.[29] However, this was not necessary. For the desire of the British to meet the French point of view in matters of procedure was further emphasized at a subsequent meeting early in October when they produced additional instructions from the Lords Justices permitting the desired alternate discussions. It seemed, in other words, that the initial difficulties encountered in carrying on the conference were being overcome by a conciliatory spirit on both sides.

But to turn now to the initial discussion that took place on September 21 over the boundary of French Acadia, surrendered to the English by the Treaty of Utrecht in 1713: The words of cession provided

---

[26] C. O. 323: 12. O. 53. 4.

[27] The French commissaries made clear that M. Bompart, the successor to M. Caylus at Martinique, had embarked at Brest and carried strictest orders for the evacuation of the islands of St. Lucia, Dominica, and St. Vincent (C. O. 323: 12. O. 51. 2).

[28] Shirley and Mildmay to Nevil Aldworth, September 23, 1750, Mildmay "Letter Book."

[29] C. O. 323: 12. O. 57. 4. This concession apparently came as a result of Albemarle's remonstrance with the French Minister relative to their abrupt declaration, referred to above.

THE ENGLISH CLAIM, 1755.[1]

[1] KEY OF THE ENGLISH MAP: Claim of the English under the treaty of Utrecht (1713), marked – – – – –

Grant to Sir William Alexander (1621), and divided by him into Alexandria and Caledonia, being all east of line marked ·–·–·–

According to Champlain (1603–1629), all, excepting Cape Breton, east of this line, ··········

Grants of Louis XIII. and XIV. (1632–1710), the same as the claim of the English for Nova Scotia or Acadia.

Nova Scotia, enlarged westward to the Kennebec, as granted to the Earl of Sterling (Alexander).

Acadia proper, as defined by Charlevoix in accordance with the tripartite division, *shaded perpendicularly.*

Charnesay's government (1638), ═══════

La Tour's government (1638), + + + + + +

Cromwell's grant to La Tour, Crown, and Temple, being the same ceded to France by the treaty of Breda (1667), ─────

Norembega, according to Montanus, Dapper, and Ogilby, is the country between the Kennebec and Penobscot.

The Etechemin region, as defined by Champlain and Denys, *shaded obliquely.*

(From Jefferys's *Remarks on the French Memorials* . . . , 1756.)

THE FRENCH CLAIM, 1755.[1]

[1]KEY OF THE FRENCH MAP: Limits proposed by English commissaries, Sept. 21, 1750, and Jan. 11, 1751 (exclusive of Cape Breton), – – – – –

By the treaty of Utrecht, + + + + + +

Port Royal district, by the same treaty, ————

Grant to Sir William Alexander, Sept. 10, 1621, ...

Cromwell's grant to La Tour, Crown, and Temple, Aug. 9, 1656, ══════════

What was restored to France by the treaty of Breda includes Cromwell's grant and the country from Mirlegash to Canseau.

Denys' government (1654), *shaded horizontally.*

Charnesay's government (1638), *shaded obliquely.*

La Tour's government (1638), *shaded perpendicularly.*

(From Jefferys's *Remarks on the French Memorials* . . . , 1756.)

that "all Nova Scotia or Acadia with its ancient boundaries; as also the City of Port Royal, now called Annapolis-Royal," were "to be possessed alone hereafter by British Subjects." Reference was also made in the treaty to exclusive fishing rights to be enjoyed by the English "in the Seas, Bays, and other Places on the Coasts of Nova Scotia; that is to say, on those that lie toward the East, within 30 Leagues, beginning from the Island Commonly called Sable inclusively and thence stretching along toward the South-West." [30] What did this mean and imply as a basis for laying down a boundary for "all Nova Scotia or Acadia"? The memorial handed by the British commissaries to the French, but actually prepared by the Board of Trade,[31] asserted that this meant the relinquishment on the part of the French of all the lands from the mouth of the Penobscot River north to the St. Lawrence and then east along its southern bank to Cape Rosiers at its mouth, and then southeast along the coast to Cape Breton, then southward and southwestward by Cape Sable and the Bay of Fundy to the Penobscot, reserving to His Most Christian Majesty only those islands situated in the Gulf of St. Lawrence, including Cape Breton (Isle Royale); further, it emphasized the fact that all lands situated between the Penobscot and the Kennebec at the time of the treaty were a part of New England.[32] In contrast to this the French in their *mémoire*, much to the surprise of the British, while denying that even the whole of the peninsula had been relinquished to Great Britain by the treaty, did not point out what part had been, but limited themselves to making a distinction between Acadia that was ceded and the remainder of New France that was not ceded outside the cession of the city of Port Royal. When the French commissaries were pressed to be more explicit as to what they deemed were the boundaries of Acadia or Canada, they replied rather weakly that it was for the British to make out their right, and that whatever they could not prove to belong to them would therefore belong to the French, "they being in possession." [33]

Early in October the French consented to an oral discussion of the

[30] See George Chalmers, Collection of Treaties, I, 340–86.

[31] This is so stated in All the Memorials of the Courts of Great Britain and France since the Peace of Aix-la-Chapelle Relative to the Limits of the Territory of Both Crowns in North America; and the Right to Neutral Islands in the West Indies (The Hague, 1756).

[32] Ibid. See also Mémoires des Commissaires du Roi et ceux de Sa Majesté Britannique (Paris, 1756), I, 1–6.

[33] Shirley and Mildmay to the Board of Trade, September 23, 1750, C. O. 323: 12 O. 54. 7. The French mémoire is to be found in ibid., 323: 12. O. 55. 8.

limits of Acadia, which gave the English an opportunity to develop
their case informally. In this discussion the latter made clear that
years before 1621 the country of Acadia had been an established fact
and that in that year, as the result of letters patent issued by James I,
Nova Scotia came into existence with very definite limits laid down;
that in the course of the seventeenth century, although each of these
territories had distinct limits, Nova Scotia communicated its name to
the whole country of Acadia, so that at the Treaty of Utrecht, when
it was decided to award the region to Great Britain, Louis XIV in
agreeing to this used the following expression to describe its extent:
"*La Nouvelle Ecosse autrement dité Acadie en son entier confor-
ment à ses anciennes Limites*"—an expression that ruled out any
narrowing of the limits of Nova Scotia merely to the St. Croix River
on the mainland but extended them to include likewise the *ancient*
limits of Acadia. When the French in reply said that if Great Britain
claimed Nova Scotia she must drop Acadia on account of the use of
the Latin word "*sive*" in the treaty in the expression "*Novam Sco-
tiam quoque sivi Acadiam totam limitatibus suis antiquis compre-
hensam ut et portus regii urbem, nunc Annapolim regiam dictam,*"
the British replied that the attempt to make this distinction was on
the level of the attempt made in the French *mémoire* to prove that
Annapolis Royal was not in Acadia by criticizing the phrase "*ut et
portus regii urbem*"; that by such a line of reasoning it would be
possible to prove that Canada was not in New France.[34]

The impression seems to have prevailed among scholars and others that the French commissaries were too skilful and adroit for the
British, but the verbal encounter just related shows the opposite to
have been the case. Not only were the latter, it would appear, better
informed, but they presented their case much more effectively — so
effectively, in fact, that the French took refuge in the proposition that
the claims should be reduced to writing "so that the Reasons & Evidences being stated on both sides Our respective Courts might be
better enabled to come to a determination of these disputes." Writing to the Duke of Bedford after their conference, Shirley and Mildmay further declared:

> "What Justice ye French Comm[ries.] may do to ye Observations We
> offer'd We cannot presume to know, but we assure your Grace we
> have done no injustice to theirs, And if they cannot maintain their

pretensions in Writing in a better manner than they have hitherto done in their Discourse, the World will see that they have nothing but quibble & chicanery to oppose to reason & argum^t· supported by authentick proofs & Evidences of Facts." [35]

Able as was the defence of the British rights by the two commissaries, they did not escape a rebuke from the Lords Commissioners for Trade and Plantations, who felt that they had compromised their case — by making a distinction between the Nova Scotia of the Patent of 1621 and the Nova Scotia that Louis XIV and Queen Anne had in mind in 1713 — in violation of their instructions.[36] In justifying their conduct to the Secretary of State for the Southern Department, however, they made clear that it would have been impossible to have given proof of the King's right to the entire province of Nova Scotia or to Acadia but " by entering upon our proof of each part in that due order & method which must be followed. . . ."[37] Nevertheless, it was now agreed that in the future all communications with the French commissaries would first of all be submitted to the Board of Trade for approval. This brings us to the first evidence of a growing rift between the two British representatives. Mildmay had by this time persuaded himself that he was " joined with a slow mule that understands neither french or english and yet as obstinate in his way." In expressing these sentiments to the Earl of Fitzwalter he went on to say with reference to Shirley, his senior:

" But the worst part of his character is His secret & reserved manner of sending private accounts to the ministers upon points relating to our joint commission. This has been observed by other great personages here with proper indignity." [38]

It should be pointed out that early in September Shirley and Mildmay decided upon a division of labour in connection with which the former was to prepare a memorial defending the King's right to Acadia, the latter his right to St. Lucia. According to Mildmay, Shirley was so slow in preparing his memorial that after some two months it was not finished at the time they had agreed to present it. He further complained that

---

[35] Shirley and Mildmay to the Duke of Bedford, October 7, 1750, Mildmay " Letter Book."

[36] For the reply to the complaints of the Board of Trade see C. O. 323: 12. O. 62. 20.

[37] Shirley and Mildmay to the Duke of Bedford, November 14, 1750, Mildmay " Letter Book."

[38] Mildmay to Fitzwalter, October 20, 1750, Mildmay " Private Correspondence."

" when the foul Draught was produced, I found it dressed in so mean a stile, in so confused an Order & with so many improper observations, that I was forced immediately to take pen in hand & draw up one in a different form, which I finished in 5 Days & presented to my Ld. Albemarle & Mr. Yorke who were pleased to honour it with their approbation; but my colleague not abiding by their Judgement, We were obliged to send them Both over to His Grace the Duke of Bedford, in order to determine which ought to be presented or to prepare a Third more proper to this purpose. They are at present referred to the Board of Trade. . . ." [39]

Soon after the dispatch of the rival memorials on November 14 to London, a meeting of the joint commission was held at which the French commissaries again returned to the questions of prizes taken before the war without getting any satisfaction; they themselves in turn were criticized for delaying the discussion of the rival claims in the West Indies and in North America. When again called upon to be more specific as to their conception of the limits of Acadia, they soon after the conference sent to the British representatives a *mémoire* in which it was affirmed that " ancient Acadia " was but the southeastern portion of the peninsula and that its limits extended westward from the Atlantic only to the southern extremity of Baye Françoise [Bay of Fundy] to either Cape St. Mary or Forked Cape and from there northeastward through the peninsula to Cape Canso.[40] Writing to the Duke of Bedford, the British commissaries declared:

" Your Grace will note in what a loose manner these limits are set forth, which we imagine it will be impossible for them to Justify by the Terms of any Treaties whereby this Country has been yielded and restored, & under which it was particularly Ceded to the Crown of Great Britain." [41]

When at a subsequent meeting the French commissaries were asked to present, as agreed, their memorial concerning their right to St. Lucia, upon which, as has been stated, the British were prepared to engage in alternate discussion, the latter were given to understand that before they were ready to do so they must previously receive a documented memorial setting forth the British pretensions respect-

---

[39] Mildmay to Fitzwalter, December 2, 1750, *ibid.* The two drafts were sent over with a joint letter dated November 14 (Mildmay " Letter Book ").
[40] C. O. 323: 12. O. 65. 23.
[41] Shirley and Mildmay to Bedford, November 18, 1750, Mildmay " Letter Book."

ing Acadia.[42] This the Board of Trade was prepared to send by messenger about the middle of December together with a second memorial setting forth claims to the disputed island of Canso. However, the British commissaries felt impelled to translate them into French before delivering them. During this delay they also received an attested extract of the allotment to the Earl of Sterling of all the lands between the St. Croix and the Pemaquid Rivers, the latter lying between the Penobscot and the Kennebec, and two supporting charts. Upon delivery of all these papers to the French commissaries in January, the latter were called upon to set forth as explicitly with supporting documents their own claims.[43] Further, they were requested to present without further delay their promised memorial on St. Lucia. The latter, however, admitted that this had not as yet even been drawn up and were therefore unable to indicate when it would be ready. "This declaration," reported the British commissaries, "was made with an Air, which now plainly demonstrates an affected delay on their part, after a fair, regular method of proceeding on Ours." [44]

---

[42] On November 26 Bedford notified the Board of Trade that the French court had begun to complain "with Reason, of the Delays occasioned by Us . . . on the Affairs of Nova Scotia. The King has therefore thought proper to order me for the third time to send you the most pressing Orders to consider & report your Opinion . . . upon the two Draughts prepared by Messers. Shirley and Mildmay" (C. O. 323. 13. O. 80).

[43] Shirley and Mildmay to Bedford, November 25, December 2, 9, and 29, 1750, and January 13, 1751; the same to the Board of Trade, January 6, 1751, C. O. 323. 13. O. 80.

On December 30 Mildmay wrote a revealing letter of considerable urgency to the Earl of Fitzwalter indicating that he and Shirley had joined in a letter to the Hon. Mr. P. [Pitt] setting forth that a year would have passed without receiving any salary except that for a quarter paid in advance. Out of this advance Mildmay declared it had been necessary for him to lay out £160 for fees in passing the commissions for himself and his secretary; that he had now been eight months in lodgings in Paris that cost him eight guineas a month; that his coach and horses required another fifteen guineas a month and that he had been obliged to place his coachman and footman in liveries; that he was compelled to pay the latter seven shillings a week board wages and at the rate of seven pounds a year and his valet de chambre near twice that amount; that his secretary drew five shillings a day in pay and received thirty shillings a month in lodgings; that he was compelled to buy for himself two summer suits of silk and two winter suits — one of plain cloth and the other " of a plain crimson velvet "; besides which he had given " frequent Entertainments, in which according to the spirit of rivalship the Cooks & Confectioners . . . employed gained great reputation. Let me add to this," he made clear, " the expence of Linnen & Ruffles, Comedies & Operas, Books, firing & Cards — at which I have lost near 20 pds tho I never play, but I have gone halves with Ladies, & never watch'd them." With all these expenses, it may be added, Mildmay nevertheless, was hoping to be able to save almost half of his salary, "amounting to more than 1200 pds a year . . ." (Mildmay " Private Letters ").

[44] Letter to Bedford of January 13, 1751, C. O. 323. 13. O. 80.

The rift between Shirley and Mildmay, previously referred to, was re-emphasized when in communicating with Bedford the latter part of January they each enclosed a memorial relating to the British claims to St. Lucia, begging His Grace's directions as to which should be employed and also as to whether they should under the circumstances present to the French any statement until they had received one from the latter relative to the contested island.[45] Shortly after forwarding this letter, the French memorial on the West Indies covering seventy-six folio sheets was presented to the British commissaries with a promise that the " proofs " would also be furnished. But there was delay in providing the latter, which were not presented until some two months later in a rather formidable folio volume of 886 pages under title " *Les Preuves des droits du Roy sur l'Isle de Ste. Lucie.*" As it seemed to be impracticable to copy so extensive a document because of the time involved, it was forwarded to the Secretary of State for the Southern Department together with a comment by the British commissaries. The latter, with reference to the French proofs, pointed out that these were produced to show the reality of facts the consequences of which they, the British commissaries, denied. They cited, as examples, two documents presented by the French to make clear their own point of view: first, an extract from Père du Tertre's *Histoire générale des Antilles,* an important work published between 1667 and 1671 by the chief seventeenth-century authority on the West Indies, which, referring to the massacre of the English on St. Lucia in 1640, the subsequent appearance of the French on the island, and the dispossession of the latter by the English in 1664, argued that the pretensions of the latter to the island would have been well founded had they not themselves on a like occasion seized upon Surinam in 1643, then in the possession of the French; secondly, the instructions by the French court to Sieur Barrillon issued in 1687 — in connection with the appointment of an Anglo-French commission to settle the question, among others, of St. Lucia — which cited the driving out of the French again in 1686 by the English and which, while demanding that the island should be placed in the same situation it was left in by the Treaty of Breda of 1667, at the same time authorized an agreement whereby the English should continue to visit it for wood and water and to carry on

[45] Letter of January 27, 1751, C. O. 323. 13. O. 80. These drafts of memorials were based exclusively upon data furnished by the Board of Trade.

their former commerce with the natives settled there. In commenting upon these proofs Shirley and Mildmay declared that

> " all which . . . is establishing what we contend for: 1st that the French never made the least pretensions of right to the Island before the massacre and expulsion of the English in 1640; 2dly that the Island ought to be put into the same state, that it was left in by the Treaty of Breda; 3dly that the English were actually in possession of it at the time of the making of the Convention in 1687."

They further pointed out that the French willingness in 1687 to permit the English to continue their commerce with the island seemed to have been in a great measure an acknowledgment of England's right to do it, " which if the French had the sole right to the Island, the English could not, according to the rule of commerce settled & practic'd between the French and English colonies in the West Indies, have any right to do." [46]

Meanwhile, the British authorities in the West Indies and in London were becoming deeply concerned with what seemed to them a lack of good faith on the part of the French. It had been agreed between the two Crowns that the subjects of both dwelling upon not only St. Lucia but also Tobago, Dominica, and St. Vincent, should evacuate these islands until their ownership could be determined; it was likewise agreed that all British subjects should depart from St. Martin, the French portion of which had been invaded in the course of the late war. Although the orders not only were issued but were carried out by command of King George providing for the evacuations,[47] it had become evident to both Governor Grenville of Barbados and Commodore Holbourne, who had been commissioned to supervise the reciprocal evacuations, that the French were not abiding by their pledged word. M. de Caylus, the French Governor of Martinique, at first insisted that he was not authorized to affix the proclamation for evacuation in the most public places upon the islands in question; later this was read, apparently in a perfunctory manner, at certain places within these islands, but still de Caylus refused to co-operate with Holbourne in seeing that it was carried out. When the latter protested at this attitude, de Caylus declared that he could not, in case the French on these islands refused obedience, " hunt them out like wild boars." To this Holbourne replied: " Then

---

[46] Letter to Bedford, April 13, 1751, C. O. 323. 13. O. 80.

[47] Bedford to Albemarle, April 21, 1751, *Diplomatic Instructions, 1745–1789*, Vol. VII, France, pp. 14–16.

I must, for I can only look upon them at present as so many banditti or outlaws and by no means as subjects of His Most Christian Majesty." [48]

Happily, the issue was not carried to such display of force as was above suggested, but referred to London by the British representatives of the Crown. As a result the Duke of Bedford proceeded to place the matter before the British Ambassador in Paris, who, it was felt, could make clear the necessity of the French King sending the most positive orders to see that the French inhabitants were evacuated under threat that were this not done His Majesty would be under the necessity of commanding his officers in the West Indies " to look upon all English and French settlers in these islands as banditti, and to treat them accordingly. . . ." [49] While promises were freely given to the British Ambassador, these proved to be worthless. In fact, by January in 1753 the Earl of Holderness, who took Bedford's place, was impelled to make clear to Albemarle that the entire conduct of the court of France in the West Indies had been such since the signing of the peace as to convince the King that it had no

> " real and fair intention of bringing these matters to an amicable and just conclusion. The Neutral Islands still remain unevacuated, and notwithstanding Mo^r· de St. Contest's assertion I will venture to assure Your Lordship that many unjustifiable proceedings are carrying on in many parts of North America in direct opposition to the Treaty of Aix la Chapelle. . . ." [50]

Returning again to the work of the joint commission, from early May to August in 1751 it was almost exclusively concerned with the

---

[48] Ibid.

[49] Ibid.

[50] Letter of January 4, 1753, ibid., pp. 34–6. On August 24, 1753 Holderness felt under necessity to write to Albemarle that information had arrived in London, sent by Captain Pye from Barbados, that nothwithstanding " the solemn promise made to Your Excellency by His Most Christian Majesty himself, the island of Dominico (one of the disputed Neutral Islands) so far from being evacuated according to the agreement and the repeated orders . . . is actually inhabited by four thousand people and has a militia commanded by an officer who avows that he acts under orders of Mo^r· Bompar [successor of de Caylus], Governor of Martinico . . ." (ibid., p. 39). In spite of the subsequent denial by Rouillé, " in so positive and peremptory a manner," of Captain Pye's charges, it nevertheless seems to be true that the island was actually being colonized by the French. However, Holderness made clear in communicating with the British Ambassador in September that Bompar's " conduct has appeared so very shuffling with Governor Grenville that it is not impossible but he may likewise have attempted to deceive his own Court . . ." (ibid., p. 40).

question of prizes.[51] Shirley and Mildmay remained at odds,[52] while Holderness, ominously for the former, took over the Southern Department in June. In August Mildmay secured permission to go to England and did not return to take up his duties until November 12. Meanwhile, the French commissaries anxiously sought to get back their volume of documents relating to St. Lucia, which they declared was needed to draw up a state of their claims to Tobago, and pressed much for its return; it apparently was finally brought to Paris by Mildmay. However, it appears that in October they transmitted their formal reply to the British memorial on Acadia to Shirley, who thereupon proceeded to make a copy of it before sending it to England in November. About the middle of the latter month the French commissaries also received a reply to their St. Lucia memorial as approved by the Board of Trade.

Although the issue of the prizes was further considered by the joint commission, there was no further discussion of the rival claims in the West Indies or in North America until well along in March of the following year. It is of interest to note, however, that Shirley was being undermined during this period by his colleague. On December 15 Mildmay wrote to his relative, a close friend of Holderness's, in bitter complaint of the conduct of Shirley, who " still continues keeping both the french memorial & his reply a secret from me." He went on to say:

> " I shall be ready to add my Endeavours in support of his Majesty's Right, by either correcting what my collegue [sic] offers or offering One myself for his Correction, but working separately can no ways be compatible to the benefit of his Majesty's Service. I c$^{d.}$ offer some proposals on this head which Mr. De Cosne & myself if jointly commissioned might perhaps be able to bring into execution, but I can do nothing with One who will neither propose nor attend to proposals." [53]

On the 22nd of the same month he warned Fitzwalter that if " a certain Person " had written to one of His Lordship's acquaintances

---

[51] See letters to Bedford of May 5, 26, and 29, of June 9; and to Bedford's successor in the office of Secretary of State for the Southern Department, the Earl of Holderness, of July 7 and August 1, 1751, Mildmay " Letter Book."

[52] Mildmay was apparently very anxious to prevent certain letters that he was receiving from falling into Shirley's hands. Writing to Fitzwalter on July 10, he requested such letters should be sent under cover and directed to M. Lambert, Paris banker, with simply his (Mildmay's) initials on the inner cover (" Private Correspondence ").

[53] Ibid.

(Holderness), it should be made known that it was entirely without his knowledge, and then on January 5 he wrote:

> "I am afraid I must by the next messenger trouble my most Honble. Patron with an account of some additional Circumstances, omitted thrô haste on my part, which may be necessary for his knowledge not so much with regard to myself as the Publick." [54]

For five months, according to Mildmay, Shirley worked upon a rejoinder to the French reply to the British memorial on Nova Scotia — ignoring his colleague until he had completed it, when he handed it to him. Mildmay was suspicious that he had sent a copy of it likewise to Lord Halifax of the Board of Trade, passing over the latter's superior, Holderness — at least so he intimated in his letter of April 5.[55]

About the middle of March a meeting of the joint commission was held at which the French commissaries in commenting upon the British reply to their memorial on St. Lucia took deep exception to certain words and expressions that seemed too harsh and to reflect on the integrity of the French government,[56] with the result that the British agreed to change these, without, however, agreeing to weaken their own contentions or to prejudice His Britannic Majesty's right to the island. This was the last conference in which Shirley participated. In line with Mildmay's desires he was recalled and Lord Albemarle's secretary, Ruvigny de Cosné, was commissioned in his place.[57]

---

[54] *Ibid.* Mildmay was apparently apprehensive of making a copy of the letter in which he deals with the " additional circumstances," since it is not to be found in his letter book of " Private Correspondence."

[55] To Fitzwalter, " Private Correspondence."

[56] Such expressions, for example as *glissé, tronquée, furtivement, plus intéressé qu'honorable, faussement cité* (C. O. 323: 13. 106).

[57] When Albemarle transmitted to Shirley and Mildmay His Majesty's orders the middle of April, the former " received his Demission," according to Mildmay, " without making any Remarks, any farther than that he was not conscious He had done any thing that might give offense; I answered that if He had not, then possibly the reason of this change might be to save the Governm^t the expence of maintaining two Commissaries (for M^r De Cosne is to have no Salary) where nothing was likely to be done in the present train & that the reason of Recalling Him in particular probably was because as He had another Commission of being Governour of One of His Majesty's Colonies, His presence might be more necessary in that part of the world than this " (letter to Fitzwalter, April 19, 1752, " Private Correspondence "). This explanation doubtless did not entirely reassure Shirley, by reason of the fact that the Earl of Albemarle was Governor of Virginia as well as Ambassador to the court of Louis XV. He apparently could only rely in England upon the active friendship of the Earl of Halifax; as an appointee of the Duke of Bedford he was perhaps isolated upon the retirement of the latter from the Southern Department of State by reason of the strong hostility of the Pelhams toward the Bedford Whigs. Never-

The question may be raised as to the justification for continuing a commission which had done nothing to further the hope that it might show the way to a happy compromise of the many differences existing between Great Britain and France. The answer doubtless lay in the conviction then held by many in authority in Great Britain that, in spite of its lack of success, its sudden termination, in the words of Mildmay,

> "might have been construed into a declaration that the differences in question cannot be accommodated in an amicable manner, which might induce the Subjects on both sides to vindicate their pretensions by such Acts of Hostilities as might create a war between the two Crowns." [58]

Further, Mildmay was still convinced that real progress could be made by the joint commission, once his uncompromising colleague had been eliminated— thereupon making possible a new approach. This he outlined in his letter of May 3 to Holderness in pointing out the impossibility of determining rights already "too long disputed & which at last cannot be decided upon the argum^t & reasons so differently urged & so peremptorily insisted upon by both sides." He therefore recommended that each side ignore whatever had been advanced in justification of its particular claims and that all be settled in an amicable convention in terms that would protect each from further encroachments upon its "undisputed settlements already established." He thereupon proposed the following territorial settlement:

> "1. That His Majesty the King of Great Britain will not molest the Subjects of His Most Christian Majesty from settling on such coasts of Nova Scotia or Acadia as are towards the River or Gulf of St. Lawrence. In consideration of which His Most Christian Majesty shall not molest the subjects of the King of Great Britain from settling on any of the other Coasts of Nova Scotia or Acadia toward the Bay of Fundy & the Atlantic Ocean. The Inland parts comprised within the above described Coasts to be settled by Neither.
>
> "2$^{nd.}$ That the King of Great Britain will not molest the Subjects of His Most Christian Majesty from settling upon the Island of St. Lucia. In consideration of which his Most Christian Majesty shall not molest the Subjects of the King of Great Britain from settling

---

theless, it must not be forgotten that he had procured the governorship of Massachusetts Bay through Newcastle's support and still looked upon him as his patron (see Shirley to Newcastle, November 23, 1752, Correspondence of William Shirley, II, 1–4).

[58] Mildmay to Holderness, May 3, 1752, Mildmay "Letter Book."

upon the Island of Tobago. The two other Islands of St. Vincent & Dominica to be settled by neither.

"3rd. That it is to be understood at the same time that the Liberty granted to the Subjects of one crown to settle at the respective places above-mentioned, is to be deemed an Exclusion to the Subjects of the other from settling at the same place.

"4th. That these stipulations shall be without prejudice to the Rights set up either by the one Crown or the other." [59]

In view of the very close relations maintained by Mildmay with Albemarle, at whose home the former apparently spent much of his time,[60] it cannot be doubted that the above proposals had met with the Ambassador's approval before being forwarded to Secretary of State for the Southern Department. Further, it would seem that Mildmay had some reason for optimism that these would eventually become the basis for a firm international settlement since he was able to write to his kinsman some six weeks after communicating them to England:

"It is some satisfaction & indeed does me no little honour to find that the very scheme I proposed for an amicable determination of this entangled affair is equally approved by both Courts." [61]

However, he now anticipated that the major part of the negotiations along these lines would be advantageously carried forward in Paris by Albemarle and the Duc de Mirepoix, the French Ambassador to London, who was in France on one of his periodic leaves of absence — with the joint commission playing its part by "clearing up such points as might want explanation in order to bring the disputes to an amicable decision." [62]

By the summer of 1752 the disputes between the two Crowns, instead of tapering off, as it were, by reason of the endeavours of the diplomats, were unhappily becoming intensified and broadened. Now activities in the valley of the Ohio, the existence of the French fort on the Niagara River and another on Lake Champlain, and the control of the Iroquoian Confederation had become additional issues that led to direct and sharp representations by the British Ambassa-

---

[59] Ibid.

[60] "But my chief time is taken up in my Lord Albemarle's family whose House & Table are always open to me," confided Mildmay to Fitzwalter, writing on June 7 about his social activities (Mildmay "Private Correspondence").

[61] Mildmay to Fitzwalter, June 21, 1752, Mildmay "Private Correspondence."

[62] Mildmay and De Cosné to Newcastle, June 29, 1752, Mildmay "Letter Book."

dor at Paris.[63] In August the British commissaries were to be found engaging in direct discussion with the Marquis de St. Contest, Puysieulx's successor at the Foreign Office, but only over the vexed question of sea prizes which from time to time during the past four years had been *sur tapis*, without yielding any results.[64] In fact the French were now actually making preparations to appeal to the other countries of Europe as to the justice of their cause — at least in so far as it related to Acadia. In preparation for this they had by the latter part of August actually printed the British memorial together with the French answer, and, not content with this, had annotated the former with their observations, none of which had been submitted to their opponents for comment.[65] However, the Earl of Holderness, having been apprized of this very irregular step, had made such forthright representations as to the peril of such a move to the peace that publication was suspended.

Meanwhile the French reply to the English memorial on Acadia was being given the most deliberate and detailed consideration by the Board of Trade; likewise the British reply to the French *mémoire* on St. Lucia was receiving the same attention in Paris.[66] There was at the time a feeling that one or the other of the two courts was deliberately holding up negotiations. While there is doubtless some basis for this, it may at the same time be pointed out that since the appeal on each side continued to be founded upon rights derived not from what might be called purely equitable grounds, such as Mildmay had so ably advocated, but from historical precedents, great care and effort were necessarily involved in the preparation of each case or each reply. Such an approach, of course, meant delay and,

---

[63] See Memorial of Albemarle to Rouillé, March 7, 1752, Pease, *Anglo-French Boundary Disputes in the West, 1749–1763*, pp. 28–35; Newcastle to Albemarle, June 4, 1752, *Diplomatic Instructions, 1745–1789*, Vol. VII, France, p. 28.

[64] Mildmay and De Cosné to Holderness, August 2, 1752, Mildmay "Letter Book."

[65] Mildmay and De Cosné to Holderness, August 30, 1752, Mildmay "Letter Book."

[66] For example, on August 17 the British commissaries wrote to Holderness that the French commissaries had "lately required an explanation of some proofs referred to in our answer to their Mem¹· concerning the right of St. Lucia and seem to be preparing a reply to that answer." Mildmay and De Cosné in the same communication raised the question as to whether they in turn should not be prepared with a reply to the French answer to the British memorial respecting Acadia and made clear that should the Board of Trade have any observations to communicate upon this point they would be careful to make the proper use of them (Mildmay "Letter Book"). Soon after sending this letter they received information that the Board of Trade was "preparing instructions by way of reply to the French commissaries' answer to the British memorial concerning Nova Scotia" (the same to the same, August 30, 1752, *ibid.*).

also, increased the hazards to the peace. It is certain, for example, that the Board of Trade — apparently aided by Shirley, who was in London — was busily engaged during the summer and fall of 1752 on the answer to the reply of the French to the British memorial on Acadia.[67] This elaborate rebuttal was completed and transmitted late in December to Mildmay and De Cosné, together with specific instructions.[68] All the happy anticipations of Mildmay that, with Shirley eliminated from the picture, a settlement of difficulties would be attained were, however, by this time quite dissipated. In November we find him making reference "to the usual Chicanery of the French Commissaries who had proposed unreasonable terms of proceeding"; in January of the new year, referring again to the French "Chicanery," he despondently

> "hopes His Majesty will put an end to all wranglings & disputes by a happier method of accommodation, or more persuasive arguments than what are delivered in written Memorials." [69]

Mildmay's disillusionment with respect to the further usefulness of the joint commission was also reflected in the attitude of the British ministry. Nevertheless, in view of the very earnest desire of de St. Contest that "the Commissaries should still remain assembled at Paris while the negotiation is carrying on between the respective ministers of each Crown," it was decided to fall in line with this desire; but Albemarle was warned by Holderness in a letter dated January 4, 1753 that "the Court of France will be very much deceived if they imagine that . . . complaisance will be carried to such a degree as to diminish the King's attention to, and resolution to preserve the just rights of his subjects." [70] The joint commission, therefore, met the latter part of the month, at which gathering the British presented

---

[67] Mildmay "Letter Book." On November 22 in a letter to Fitzwalter, Mildmay states that he had received intimation from Shirley, his former colleague, that the Board of Trade would shortly transmit to the British commissaries "a long memorial concerning the limits of Acadia, which would perhaps occasion some further Disputes with the French Commissaries" (Mildmay "Private Correspondence"). This statement indicates that while Shirley may have been unfitted for the fine work of diplomacy, his solid knowledge of North American conditions was apparently relied upon by the Board in preparing its case, especially relative to Acadia. It is not without significance that he was permitted to stay away from his government over a year after he had been recalled from Paris.

[68] Mildmay and De Cosné to Holderness, January 3, 1753, Mildmay "Letter Book."

[69] See letters of Fitzwalter, November 29, 1752 and January 24, 1753, Mildmay "Private Correspondence."

[70] Diplomatic Instructions, 1745–1789, Vol. VII, France, p. 36.

to the French a copy in English of their answer to the French reply to the British claims to Acadia.[71] On this occasion the French commissaries requested the English original of the British reply to the French claims to St. Lucia which had been delivered in French and, as has already been made clear, was not acceptable by reason of certain expressions that seemed to reflect on French integrity.[72]

This conference might not be worthy of mention were it not that a serious misunderstanding arose out of it. For, in spite of the French request for the English original of the British St. Lucia memorial, Galissonière at a subsequent meeting of the joint commission in February refused to accept it and, in fact, intimated that he was expecting to receive orders from his court to return the last British memorial relating to Acadia, which was in English and not in French, as was the first memorial. The British commissaries, however, pointed out that this had been delivered over a month before and had been at the time accepted without protest and would therefore not be received, unless by direct orders of His Britannic Majesty, if an attempt were made to return it.[73] In March Galissonière at a meeting of the joint commission sought to persuade the British to agree to do so, but without success. Thus the issue was fairly joined involving the question: Was the French language the only proper medium of diplomatic intercourse? The British ministers upon appeal fully and very properly upheld the commissaries. As a result, at a meeting in April the latter made clear that if the French refused to accept British memorials in English, the British would refuse to accept French memorials in the original language.[74] However, they declared their willingness to employ a " neutral language," if this were agreeable to the French, and suggested Latin, the older language of international

---

[71] This memorial, bearing the date January 23, 1753 — that is, the date of the meeting of the joint commission — was, unlike the other British memorials coming from the Board of Trade, credited solely to Charles Townshend. It is an exceedingly able exposition of the British claims as these related to " ancient Acadia " and was described by the British commissaries as " a series of solid arguments & incontestable proofs drawn up with such clearness and exactness as evidently to establish his Majesty's right . . ." (Mildmay and De Cosné to the Board of Trade, January 24, 1753, Mildmay " Letter Book "). Shirley's contribution to this memorial was doubtless very important, although he was acting only in the capacity of Governor of Massachusetts Bay on leave while in attendance upon the Board of Trade during his stay in London.

[72] Mildmay and De Cosné to Holderness, January 24, 1753, Mildmay " Letter Book."

[73] Mildmay and De Cosné to Holderness, February 28, 1753, Mildmay " Letter Book."

[74] Mildmay and De Cosné to Holderness, April 18, 1753, Mildmay " Letter Book."

intercourse. At the same time it was insisted that in international law each nation had the right to use its own language should it see fit to do so. Not until in October 1754 — almost a year and a half later — were the French prepared to waive " their pretended right to treat in French alone." [75] Then it was that the British commissaries accepted a very long memorial in French in reply to the British answer to the French memorial on St. Lucia; they also agreed to look over and to correct the French translation of the last British memorial on Acadia.

Meanwhile the British Cabinet Council had determined in August 1753 not only to make the strongest representations respecting the non-fulfilment of the French promise to evacuate the Neutral Islands, but to issue general orders to the governors in North America to do their utmost to prevent by force, if need be, the French settlement of the Ohio Valley.[76] By the beginning of the new year the differences between the two Crowns were becoming still wider as the political situation in India was added to the issues in North America and the West Indies, not to speak of the problem of the prizes taken before and after the recent war. Early in January Holderness informed Albemarle [77] of the efforts to bring about an accommodation between the British and French East India companies respecting the control of Arcot, in the Carnatic; likewise of the proposals of the Secret Committee of the English United East India Company that all acquisitions or conquests on either side should be given up by either company and that all things be placed " upon the foot they were or ought to have been at the conclusion of the Treaty of Aix la Chapelle." He also made clear that he had urged the French Ambassador, the Duc de Mirepoix, as the basis for negotiating all differences in India, that the two companies should for the future remain " *des compagnies commerçantes* " and therefore no longer " *compagnies belligérantes ou conquérantes* " and in this connection affirmed that the United Company would not insist on the exclusive possession of the town of Masulipatam on the Bay of Bengal or of the Island of Divi in that same region. In harmony with these suggestions, he declared that at a meeting at his home a project of a treaty was presented to Mirepoix and the French Compagnie des Indes representatives appointed to

---

[75] Mildmay and De Cosné to Sir Thomas Robinson, October 5, 1754, Mildmay " Letter Book."

[76] Minute of the Cabinet Council, August 21, 1753, B.M., Add. Mss., 32, 995: 261.

[77] Letter of January 24, 1754, *Diplomatic Instructions, 1745–1789*, Vol. VII, France, pp. 41–5.

negotiate with the representatives of the English company and that after each article had been examined the French had agreed to advise their court to accept them. However, he admitted that he was greatly disturbed by reports that while the negotiation over India was being thus actively carried on, any ships, contrary to all expectations, should be sent by France into those parts with military forces. His letter ended with the significant statement that if the dissensions between the two companies could not be adjusted "upon the fair and equitable terms proposed from hence," the King would not fail to give that support to his subjects they were entitled to receive.

As for the joint commission concerned particularly with the settlement of American issues between the two Crowns, by March 1754 the British commissaries had become utterly disillusioned. In particular, Mildmay had a very low opinion of French diplomacy. In a letter to the Earl of Fitzwalter dated the 6th he wrote:

> "When I reflect on the manner in which this nation [France] treats, of which I have experienced a good deal, I am far from agreeing to [sic] the vulgar opinion that they are capable of outwitting us. . . . Low cunning can never impose upon solid Judgement, Chicanery must yield to Reason and Argument, and a Nation naturally brave is not to be bullied by Arrogance and Presumption; . . . by either one or other of these means . . . they have attempted to outwit us, till they have outwitted themselves." [78]

It was in this month that Henry Pelham died; as a result, his brother, the Duke of Newcastle, succeeded to the post he had occupied of First Lord of the Treasury; [79] Holderness was thereupon shifted to the Northern Department and Sir Thomas Robinson entered the administration as Secretary of State for the Southern Department. Irrespective of whatever reputation Newcastle had acquired at the hands of the London wits, he was known among his colleagues in the government as one given to "exactness and punctuality in business"; [80] he also was inclined, in spite of a certain natural timidity, toward a firm policy in regard to France. In July changes also took place within the administration of that country; the Minister of Foreign Affairs, de St. Contest, having passed away on the 24th, this post was now filled by Antoine-Louis Rouillé, the Comte de Jouy, who since 1749 had

---

[78] Mildmay " Private Correspondence."

[79] Pelham had also held the post of Chancellor of the Exchequer. This was now given to the Honourable Henry Bilson Legge.

[80] Mildmay " Private Correspondence."

been Minister of the Department of the Marine and was therefore most fully informed on American affairs, which had been under his constant supervision. Rouillé appeared to be much less aggressive than de St. Contest. Albemarle at the first interview with him in his new position reported that the French Minister had affirmed that he would be very happy " to see everything rooted up that might here- after occasion any uneasiness " between the two nations.[81] He indi- cated his goodwill by reversing the untenable policy of his predeces- sor with reference to the exclusive use of the French language in the memorials,[82] to which reference has been made. But harmony was not to prevail.

Soon after the friendly interview just mentioned, Machault, the new Minister of the Marine, sent a complaint to Rouillé received from Governor General Duquesne over what he called the " treach- erous manner " in which one of the French officers, Jumonville, had been killed by Washington's forces near the Ohio. When this was brought to Albemarle's attention the latter could only plead igno- rance of the facts. He suggested, however, that it must have been done by savages in the British service whose sense of honour could not always be depended upon and made clear that there had been a similar occurrence when complaint had been made some time before of the killing of a British officer " in a most barbarous manner " when engaged in carrying pacific propositions to the French.[83] As Robin- son had received accounts of the Washington affair near New Mead- ows which shed a very different light upon it, the British stood firmly upon the position that hostilities in the Ohio Valley had come as the result of hostile movements on the part of the French.[84] Therefore, while paying tribute to the personal character and good intentions of Rouillé, Sir Thomas was led to make clear to the British Ambassador in a letter dated September 12 that the conduct of the French court in America since the establishment of the peace was " the Effect of a settled, premeditated Plan to distress the English Trade in those Parts & to commit the most glaring Encroachments and Usurpations

---

[81] Albemarle to Robinson, August 14, 1754, Shelburne Papers, 36: 22, Clements Library.
[82] Ibid.
[83] Albemarle to Robinson, August 21, 1754, Shelburne Papers, 36: 25. The incident referred to above had to do with the assassination of Captain Edward How, who was sent from Fort Lawrence to the Missaguash under a flag of truce to meet a French officer who in turn had been sent out by Le Corne, commandant at Fort Beauséjour.
[84] Robinson to Albemarle, September 2, 1754, Shelburne Papers, 36: 35.

upon His Majesty's just Rights & Possessions." [85] Should this conduct alter, any fair offer of reciprocal confidence, he affirmed, might be embraced. But nothing could be a greater proof of a change of attitude than for the French to agree to the following line of action:

"1º· By executing the Treaty of Aix la Chapelle and fulfilling the subsequent Promises . . . as to the entire Evacuation of the Neutral Islands.

"2º· By relinquishing the Forts, which have been unjustly built, and the Possessions They have taken of so many Posts in Acadie or Nova Scotia; Notwithstanding the positive Agreement between the Two Courts, that no innovation should be made there, during the Negotiation of the Commissaries. And —

"3tio· By withdrawing their Forces from the Ohio, and the Countries adjacent thereto; so that every thing may be . . . put, in those Parts, upon the Footing it was at the signing of the said Treaty of Aix la Chapelle." [86]

Having thus outlined the necessary conditions for the restoration of an atmosphere in which negotiations could be effectively carried on, Robinson warned Albemarle that His Majesty would not suffer himself to be "amused" by referring to commissaries pretensions that had no foundation, while at the same time permitting the French to remain in possession of countries belonging to the Crown of Great Britain and to act in a hostile manner in North America.

Affairs across the Atlantic, in fact, were moving rapidly toward a crisis. In an interview between the British Ambassador and the French Minister of Foreign Affairs on September 12, Albemarle emphasized the gravity of the situation in light of the news just received of the French attack on Washington's troops at Fort Necessity and the capitulation of the latter. Rouillé, however, sought to reassure him that the whole incident would be found to have been much exaggerated; that the court of France had no intention of making in North America any "Invasions or Usurpations" contrary to the rights of His Britannic Majesty; and that as to the West Indies, he assured the Ambassador the Neutral Islands had been "strictly evacuated . . ." [87] — an incomprehensible statement in light of the feverish colonizing activities of the French on both Dominica and St. Vincent at this juncture.

---

[85] Shelburne Papers, 36: 48.

[86] Ibid.

[87] Albemarle to Robinson, September 18, 1754, Shelburne Papers, 36: 50.

With the British ministers now fully convinced of the untrustworthiness of any and all assurances on the part of the court of France, it is not surprising that under these circumstances they agreed to answer the appeals of Virginia for aid by sending to America two regiments and a commanding officer.[88] The news of this did not fail to impress the Minister of His Most Christian Majesty. Albemarle on October 23, upon being questioned by Rouillé, admitted that these troops were being sent to Virginia " to prevent the progress of the French Arms, in that part of the world." In this connection he stressed the fact that the British were at last imitating the example of the French, "who had been for many years sending Ships, Men, Arms and Ammunition to Their American Settlements." Rouillé agreed that this was true and even went so far as to admit that had his advice been followed even more would have been sent and that the court would now probably order a stronger force to go " as being (said he) the most effectual way to prevent a war in those parts (a Phrase he did not choose to explain)." When Albemarle referred to the "hostile unjustifiable Proceedings" of the French on the Ohio, the French Minister replied, according to the former:

> " that they only retook Possession of their own, and endeavoured to confine Us to Our Limits, since We had encroached upon Their's, so far as the above mentioned River, which could never be looked upon as the Boundary of the British Possessions. . . . "

This statement gave the British Ambassador an opportunity to ask

> " in virtue of what Principle They took upon Them to prescribe Our Limits to Us, when I understood that both Crowns had named Commissaries to settle those Points, and that during Their Negotiations, nothing was to be attempted on either Side " —

a reproach that so stung Rouillé that he abruptly changed the conversation.[89]

Late in November another important but brief interview took place between the British Ambassador and the French Minister. By this time the air was filled with rumours of plans for the sending of armed forces to the New World and for the movement of fleets across the Atlantic as well as into the Indian Ocean. Rouillé appeared to be deeply apprehensive and asked if there were no peaceful means of

---

[88] Albemarle was warned of this step in Robinson's letter of October 3. See *Diplomatic Instructions, 1745–1789*, Vol. VII, France, pp. 48–9.

[89] Albemarle to Robinson, October 23, 1754, Shelburne Papers, 36: 69.

accommodating things; to this the British Ambassador replied by proposing, though he admitted that he was uninstructed, that as a preliminary step his Most Christian Majesty

> " sho^d order his Troops who had made such rapid Encroachm^ts to return behind the Ohio, leave everything on the English side of that River in the State it was in before, after wch if France had any Compl^ts to make or proposals to offer they wo^d be rece^d wth the just Attention that wo^d be due them." [90]

The Minister in answer declared that he thought it impossible for the French to consent to this " as it wo^d be shewing too much Weakness on their part to recede from Measures that were founded on their un-doubted Right to the Territory they had enter'd. . . ." [91] On December 18, four days before the unexpected death of Albemarle, Rouillé confided to him that he wished that " things co^d be put in the State they were in, before & at the End of the War, conformable to the Trea-ties of Utrecht & Aix La Chapelle, as a means of preventing, any un-friendly Actions between the two Nations," a sentiment that the Am-bassador encouraged " as a Justice to be done Us on their part. . . ." After the two had reviewed the situation both in North America and in India the Minister — receiving assurances that the British land and sea forces destined for these parts were determined to avoid hostili-ties unless the French proceedings obliged them to act — thereupon optimistically declared that he was sure " that if these Matters were referr'd to two p^sons only, such as the E. of Holderness & the Duc de Mirepoix, they might finish the whole Affair, *d'un seul Coup de Plume* "; to which Albemarle replied that he hoped that Mirepoix's instructions would be framed agreeable to this way of thinking. [92]

   With the death of Albemarle [93] the centre of Anglo-French negoti-

---

[90] Albemarle to Robinson, November 27, 1754, Brit. Mus., Add. Mss., 33, 027: 283; this document is printed in part by Pease in *Anglo-French Boundary Disputes in the West, 1749–1763*, pp. 56–8.

[91] *Ibid.*

[92] B.M., Add. Mss., 33, 027: 287; Pease, *op. cit.*, pp. 58–9.

[93] Albemarle in maintaining the dignity of his post had incurred a debt estimated at £6,000. Mildmay thought that his " Plate, Horses, Equippages & furniture may per-haps sell for five, and the remainder no doubt will be satisfyed in some other manner for the credit of His Majesty's Embassy " (Mildmay to Fitzwalter, December 25, 1754, Mildmay " Private Correspondence "). Later he came to realize that Albemarle, who had lived without economy, had left a much larger debt than had been supposed, so that " the Sale of his Effects will scarcely half satisfy what is owing at this place " (Mildmay to Fitzwalter, January 22, 1755, *ibid.*). As a result, he was obliged to report that the re-mains of the late Ambassador were taken from Paris " in a common Voiture to be shipped

ation passes from Paris to London. The joint commission by this time had lost all significance, with the French commissaries fully occupied with other duties, with Mildmay on repeated leaves of absence flitting back and forth between Paris and London, and with De Cosné, the Secretary of the British Embassy, now serving as *chargé d'affaires*. As a result Mirepoix, who had been for some months recovering his health in France, was ordered to return to his post in London and was at the same time provided with new instructions.[94] These made it incumbent upon him to represent to the British ministers the surprise of His Most Christian Majesty at the military preparations now taking place both in England and in the English colonies and to request an explanation for these, which conformed so little " to the principles of the pacification of Aix-la-Chapelle." As to the region in the direction of the Ohio River, he was to make clear that if the governors of the English colonies " had thought they must lay claim to a part of the territory," the court of England should have ordered them to leave things as they were before the war until the claim could have been adjudicated in the manner prescribed by the late treaty. He was, nevertheless, to state that his Most Christian Majesty was so desirous of preserving the peace that he had agreed to join His Britannic Majesty in ordering their respective governors to put the affairs relating to the Ohio in the situation they were or should have been in before the war.

To guide Mirepoix in his important diplomatic assignment at this critical juncture he was furnished soon after his arrival in London with a confidential *mémoire* which restated in some detail the general position taken by France respecting developments particularly about the Ohio.[95] He was therein warned that the preparation of armaments in England and in the colonies then proceeding was for the specific purpose of breaking the French communication between Canada and Louisiana; by this means the British expected the more easily to wrest from France a grant of land toward the Ohio procured by Virginia merchants, land which the English governors had recently sought to invade. For preventing this new invasion, he had

---

at Rouen on board a merchant vessel " — much to the horror of Lady Sandwich, who " exclaimed much that one of the King's Yatchts was not sent to transport the Body of a Peer of the Realm and Ambassador to His Majesty " (Mildmay to Fitzwalter, January 15, 1755, *ibid.*).

[94] These instructions, dated December 23, 1754, are printed by Pease, *op. cit.*, pp. 60–5.

[95] This is dated December 31, 1754, and is also printed by Pease (*ibid.*, pp. 65–83).

been ordered, it was pointed out, to appear before His Britannic Majesty to renew the French complaints of such acts against French territory and also of such inexcusable violence as the assassination of Jumonville. In connection with giving utterance to these he was to stress the fact that since the year 1679, when the Ohio had been discovered by the Sieur de La Salle, it had been frequented by the French without hindrance in communicating between Canada and Louisiana and that only at the end of the late war had the English governors tried to cut this line of communication. He was to recall to the King his promise that disagreements between the two crowns were to be settled amicably by the joint commission and to point out that as early as March 1752 the British ministry had promised to state its position "with the most sincere openness of heart as to the arrangement of all the differences of the two nations in all parts of the world" — provided that the French would do the same — which promise had not yet been fulfilled though often solicited by the ministry of France.

It would appear that the French Ambassador early in January fulfilled the terms of the above instructions.[96] This led to interviews with both Newcastle and Robinson; the latter he found particularly well informed and in a position to brush aside much of the haze enveloping the issue over the Ohio Valley region. To Mirepoix's manifest surprise — so poorly was he informed [97] — Robinson was able to prove by maps, even by d'Anville's, that the activities of the British had in no way threatened Canada's communication with Louisiana, as the three routes employed since the days of La Salle [98] lay far to the west of the lands in dispute; he also insisted that the lands of the upper Ohio had been, before the Treaty of Utrecht, not in the possession of the French but of the Five Nations, who had destroyed the other Indians dwelling upon them and had subsequently sold them to the English; that therefore the sending of a thousand Frenchmen against some thirty people who had been ordered by the Ohio Company to prepare the way for a settlement in these parts was an act of aggression which in turn led the governors of the English colonies to assemble their militia to ward it off.

Mirepoix in reply could only plead lack of authority to go into

---

[96] Reference to this is made in a minute of the Cabinet Council meeting of January 16, 1755 (B.M., Add. Mss., 32, 996: 5–6; Pease, op. cit., pp. 85–6).

[97] Mirepoix to Rouillé, January 16, 1755, ibid., pp. 86–95.

[98] Robinson was in no position to dispute the statement, now considered to be without basis, that La Salle was on the upper Ohio in 1679.

these matters, and thereupon presented certain proposals which he had been ordered to make. These were to the effect that all the governors in America should be forbidden to engage in new enterprises and acts of violence directed against their neighbours; that things be restored without delay to the pre-war situation; and that the present disputes be referred to the joint commission for amicable settlement. However, writing to Rouillé subsequent to the conference, he warned the Minister that the British were not likely to grant an armistice unless the fort on the Ohio were razed and unless the French " evacuate all the settlements we have lately made on the river Ohio." He further intimated that upon the due performance of all this on the part of France, the British might then agree that the territory in this region be forbidden to either nation but would most certainly not consent to have the dispute referred to the joint commission as he had registered.[99]

This anticipates Robinson's formal reply of the 22nd in which His Britannic Majesty in turn proposed that all possessions in North America " be restored to the same state in which they were at the time of the conclusion of the said Treaty of Utrecht and in accord with the cessions and stipulations of that treaty." [100] Mirepoix forwarded this to Rouillé, who in turn, while agreeing to negotiation directly between the courts, again called for the submission of the British claims to the joint commission and for the foundation upon which these were based. In communicating his position to Mirepoix, he made clear that His Most Christian Majesty considered the territory about the Ohio River belonged incontestably to him and that the Treaty of Utrecht could give His Britannic Majesty no claim to it since it was not even mentioned in that document.[101]

The British Cabinet Council now proposed on February 7 that Robinson, in consequence of Mirepoix's full powers, should enter into negotiation with him upon the basis of the evacuation by both parties of all the region of the Ohio " from the Back of His Majesty's Colonies to the Lakes, and as far as the River Oubash [Wabash]. . . ." [102] On the 9th the Cabinet further agreed that they were willing to grant a mutual suspension of arms for a period to be agreed upon after the signing in London of preliminaries and that during this sus-

---

[99] *Ibid.*, pp. 97–8.
[100] *Ibid.*, pp. 99–101.
[101] Letter of February 3, 1755, *ibid.*, pp. 102–8.
[102] B.M., Add. Mss., 32, 996: 25; Pease, *op. cit.*, p. 109.

Map Showing the Iroquoian Control of the Region Between the Cuyahoga and Sandusky Bay.

(From *Amérique Septentrionale, par Mitchel, Paris: par Le Rouge, 1777; Corrigée en 1776 par M. Hawkins.* Reproduced from Winsor's *The Mississippi Basin.*)

The British Proposal of February 20, 1755 for a Neutral Zone
between the Cuyahoga and the Wabash.

(Reproduced from Pease's *Anglo-French Boundary Disputes in the West.*)

pension neither party should send either ships of war or troops to America.[103] On the 10th more definite proposals made by Robinson were taken into consideration by that body and entered as a minute.[104] These provided, first of all, for the mutual evacuation of all lands lying between the Allegheny Mountains, Lake Ontario, the Niagara River, Lake Erie, and the Wabash, with the demolition of all forts and other establishments indicating exclusive possession, with liberty for the subjects of both crowns, except " Corps of Armed Men," to pass through this region and to engage in trade, which liberty also should be extended to the waters of Lakes Ontario and Erie and those of the Niagara. Secondly, provision was made for a division of the territory lying south of the lower St. Lawrence which the British held to be contained within the boundaries of ancient Acadia; the lower portion of this, extending " one way toward New England, And the Other to the Gulph of St. Lawrence," including the lands on the west side of the Bay of Fundy — in depth an unspecified number of leagues — should appertain in full sovereignty to the King of Great Britain, and all forts and other establishments erected upon them by the French since the Treaty of Utrecht should be turned over to the British; the other portion bounded by the Gulf, the St. Lawrence, and a line dropped perpendicularly from that river down to a point opposite the mouth of the Penobscot to remain uninhabited by both the French and the British.

When these proposals were submitted to the astute Earl of Halifax, President of the Board of Trade, for comment, he asserted that the proposed line of the Alleghenies would be yielding a large portion of Pennsylvania, including townships and other settlements and also a considerable part of New York; further, that it meant the exclusion of the Six Nations from British protection.[105] This defect in the scheme Robinson was led to acknowledge, with the result that he now decided to describe the proposed boundaries by lines rather than natural features.

Meanwhile the Secretary of State had communicated to Mirepoix the less specific proposal considered by the Cabinet Council on the 7th, which the French Ambassador apparently sent without delay to Rouillé. The latter replied on the 19th to the effect that were the principle followed that all things be restored to the footing they were

---

[103] B.M., Add. Mss., 32, 996: 27–8; Pease, op. cit., pp. 109–10.
[104] B.M., Add. Mss., 32, 996: 29–30; Pease, op. cit., pp. 110–11.
[105] B.M., Add. Mss., 33, 029: 167–71; Pease, op cit., pp. 111–14.

on before the last war, it would be necessary for the English to retire behind the Alleghenies, "which are their true and ancient bounds"; as to the region between these mountains and the Ohio, he stressed the fact that were His Most Christian Majesty to consent to require its evacuation by his subjects, he would be making a real sacrifice; nevertheless, the King might agree to this, but his "complaisance" would not extend to the evacuation of the Wabash, where the French had had settlements long before the present controversy; further, in provisionally meeting the British demand for the destruction of the French forts within the Ohio territory, "which patently belongs to us," he would expect them in turn to demolish such forts as Oswego on Lake Ontario and Chignecto, Beaubassin, and Minas on the borders of the Nova Scotian Peninsula built on lands "the property of which is and always has been disputed to them." [106] Finally, as to Article XV of the Treaty of Utrecht, relating to "the dominion of Great Britain" over the Five Nations, Rouillé made clear to Mirepoix that the King considered this inapplicable in light of the fact that these Indians were in reality independent tribes and their abodes uncertain and shifting, as was true of all other tribes.[107]

Manifestly the French positions, avoiding the realities of the case, fell short of the British minimum demands for an armistice in what was yet an undeclared war that had now begun in America. The realities were not, first of all, the vague but emphatically supported claims based upon English colonial charters or even the supposed discovery of the Ohio by La Salle in 1679, which, had it occurred, would have by itself given the French no more substantial claim to the upper Ohio Valley than the Spaniards acquired in the Mississippi Valley through its penetration in 1541 by De Soto. The French had indeed acquired a recognized position in the latter valley and in the upper Great Lakes region by continued and generally unhindered exploitation of the resources of the two regions — limited as this was in most parts to the activities of fur traders. It is likewise clear that for over a generation before the beginning of the trans-Appalachian crisis the region of the upper Ohio, dominated by the Iroquoian Confederation, had been the scene of a similar exploitation on the part of the British; this exploitation, in which hundreds of traders participated, ultimately involved likewise all the region bordering the

---

[106] The Minas Fort was well within the peninsula.

[107] *Ibid.*, pp. 116–25. For the French project for a preliminary convention, see also *ibid.*, pp. 126–30.

southern shore of Lake Erie as far west by 1747 as Sandusky Bay — a region continuously under the domination of the Five Nations ever since their destruction of the powerful Erie tribe.[108] It should be emphasized that this exploitation had come about, not through the driving out of the French traders, who, as a matter of fact, had not — outside of a very few renegades, such as Seguin — ever ventured to enter this vast territory to the east of the lands of the Miami that lay about the Maumee and the Wabash, but by invitation of the Iroquois and their dependants.

Nor were the realities respecting the cession of Acadia with its ancient bounds the equally vague distinctions that the French sought to set up — in terms of the description by Champlain in his *Les Voyages* of the districts of Etchemins, Almouchiquois, and that of "*la grande rivière de Saint-Lâurent*" lying south of the lower St. Lawrence — whereby they sought to limit the extent of the Acadia ceded to the English to the eastern portion of the Nova Scotian Peninsula. This quite ignored the fact that the most ancient lands officially assigned as " La Cadie " were the regions between the fortieth and forty-sixth parallels of north latitude as embodied in the royal patent of 1603 granted to the Sieur de Monts; [109] that the earliest Acadian settlement was on an island close to the western shore of the Bay of Fundy, that the next earliest settlement within the limits of de Monts's " La Cadie " was Port Royal, also quite removed from the eastern part of the peninsula; that the French at the time of the Treaty of Breda of 1667 insisted that the " countries of Acadia " included not only all the lands of the peninsula but those on the mainland extending as far west as the Pentagoet — that is, the Penobscot — which interpretation was accepted in good faith by Charles II in surrendering the Pentagoet fort; [110] that in the preliminary discussions preceding the Treaty of Utrecht — after the words " Acadia with its ancient limits " had been inserted in the draft treaty at the insistence of the English — the French diplomats sought to persuade Her Britannic Majesty to restore this possession to France with the understanding that Acadia's western limits should thereafter be the St. George River, somewhat to the east of the Kennebec, rather than

---

[108] For the development of this British interest, see Chapter VI, " The Valley of the Ohio to 1749," of Volume IV of the present series.

[109] De Monts was commissioned lieutenant general " pour representer notre personne au pays, territoires, côtes & confines de La Cadie " (*Mémoires des Commissaires du Roi et de Ceux de sa Majesté Britannique* (Paris, 1755), II, 442).

[110] *Ibid.*, II, 581–91, 601–10.

the latter river; [111] that the court of France by implication acknowledged in the same preliminaries that the lands along the Gulf of St.
Lawrence up to the river of that name were a part of " ancient "
Acadia in desiring to preserve and fortify Cape Breton since otherwise, it was argued, the St. Lawrence " would be absolutely shut to
the ships of his Majesty, if the English masters of Acadie and Newfoundland still possessed the Isle of Cape-Breton . . .".; that this
court in reserving the right of fortifying their possessions likewise by
implication made the same acknowledgment when it indicated that
it would be necessary to proceed to construct such fortifications for
the protection of Canada " in the isles of the Gulph and in the Mouth
of the St. Lawrence, as well as in the Isle of Cape-Breton . . . as his
Majesty shall judge necessary " [112] — without the slightest indication
of a right to fortify the long coastline north of the peninsula and extending to the mouth of the St. Lawrence. Where indeed in this region extending west and north from the peninsula to the Kennebec
and to the St. Lawrence between the years 1713 and 1744, the year
King George's War began, had there been a single military post over
which was flown the fleur-de-lis as a sign of possession? Had not
France as a fundamental in her policy of North American expansion
since the days of Frontenac adopted this policy of locating such
posts upon all lands claimed to be within the reaches of New France?
Why did Intendant Bigot even as late as 1749 make clear that the
Acadians who might desire to leave the peninsula could not with confidence be placed in any part of the region between " Gaspé and Boston " by reason of the fact that the limits of Canada in these parts had
not been established? [113]

It is hard to escape the conclusion that in light of the record of bad

---

[111] *Ibid.*, II, 679.

[112] *Ibid.*, II, 670.

[113] Bigot to Puysieulx, October 13, 1749, Mémoires et Documents (Min. des Affaires Étrangères), Amérique, 9: 1, 146–53. In this connection, reference may be made
to the assertion of the French commissaries, Galissonière and Silhouette, in their *mémoire*
of 1751 respecting Acadia, that the Acadians settled about the St. John River had always
recognized the authority of the Governor General of New France and were controlled by
judges and notaries provided by Vaudreuil, their *seigneur* (*Mémoires des Commissaires
du Roi et de Ceux de sa Majesté Britannique*, IV, 37), which could be contrasted with
the statement by one of them, Galissonière, in writing to the Minister of the Marine on
July 25, 1749, while still in New France, that the St. John inhabitants were in truth
demi-sauvages who knew no other Frenchmen than those of the Peninsula of Acadia and
who, having obeyed the French Governor at Port Royal before the Treaty of Utrecht, had
been led to understand by the English Governor subsequently installed there that they
were to obey him in the same manner (*Canadian Archives, Report*, 1905, II, 304).

faith of the French in other matters, especially in insisting repeatedly in the course of the negotiations that the evacuation of the two " neutral " islands of St. Vincent and Dominica had taken place when at the same time they were using every effort to consolidate their position within them by colonization, the British ministry arrived at the conviction that French diplomacy was all in all too devious to deserve the slightest confidence, acting as it did in utter disregard of principles that France had herself previously demanded and still demanded should be applied in her favour whenever these would prove advantageous. Nevertheless, on February 20 the Cabinet Council laid down the basis for a solution of the major problems involved in the dispute over North America that might have given the continent a long period of peace had it been accepted in good faith by both sides.

This proposal very properly conceded the interest of France in the region to the west of the Maumee and the Wabash within the Miami country and just as properly conceded the interest of Great Britain in the region to the east of Cuyahoga Bay, into which flows the river of that name, then known among the French as *la Rivière Blanche*, upon which the Iroquois had long been settled in strength and where British traders had for many years been accustomed to gather.[114] The intervening region to the south of Lake Erie between these points and down to the thirty-seventh degree of north latitude was, according to the plan, to remain unsettled by either party.[115] But at the same time it was to remain open to both for peaceful trade and travel, which, incidentally, would have permitted the re-establishment of British trade at Pickawillany on the upper Great Miami and about Sandusky Bay, from which places it had been driven between 1749 and 1752. Further, it was provided that Fort Niagara, lying within the country of the Seneca Indians, should be dismantled, as well as Fort St. Frédéric upon Lake Champlain in the country long claimed, whether rightly or not, by the Mohawks — both of them constructed

---

[114] For the development of this point see Volume IV of this series, pp. 168–171.

[115] The western extremity of the zone was to be the mouth of the Maumee and then a line to the first spring of the Wabash and down this stream to its juncture with the Ohio and then due south to the 37th degree; the eastern extremity was to be a line running due south from Cuyahoga Bay to the 40th degree, and then southwest to the 37th degree — a trend perhaps suggested by the southwest trend of the Appalachians or perhaps designed to protect the interests of the Ohio Company upon the upper Ohio and the settlements already established by 1754 on the Greenbrier and the New Rivers (*ibid.*, IV, 227, 311).

in violation, it was contended, of the Treaty of Utrecht upon lands of the Five Nations — so that Lakes Erie, Ontario, and Champlain would thereby be open to the subjects of either crown without impediment, who could thereupon, as specified in that treaty, feel free to carry on peaceful trade with the Indians that were allied with, or subject to the dominion of, either Crown.

The failure of the Cabinet Council to include in its proposal the dismantling of Fort Oswego upon Lake Ontario may have been due to the fact that the British probably felt that since this post was clearly located upon lands of the Iroquois, over whom the British Crown enjoyed dominion, its retention could be amply justified, especially in light of the fact that France was to retain Forts Frontenac, Rouillé, and Detroit on the northern side of Lakes Ontario and Erie.

Finally, it was proposed that Acadia with its "ancient bounds" should be divided into two spheres; that the southern sphere — extending west to the Penobscot and to be separated from the northern by a straight line to start at an unspecified number of leagues up the east bank of that river from its mouth and to terminate at some point to the north of Cape Tormentine — should "belong, of absolute Right, to the Crown of Great Britain," while the northern sphere, bordering on the Gulf and the River St. Lawrence, "should be left unsettled and unpossessed, by the Subjects of Either Crown, and not to be used or resorted to, but for Purposes of Traffick and Commerce, with the Indians." [116] By this last proposal the French approaches to Canada by way of the St. Lawrence were to be protected; just as by the first of these proposals their customary approaches to Louisiana from the northern province were equally to be protected — in each case by a wide band of neutralized, demilitarized territory.

Had France been fortunate enough at this juncture to have been guided in her international relations by men possessing even a fair degree of statesmanship, she would have grasped at this plan for accommodating the North American disputes, a plan which had much to commend it, holding out the promise as it did of peaceful, steady development in Canada and in the Illinois country as against the risk of losing all that His Most Christian Majesty had in North America

---

[116] B.M., Add. Mss., 32, 996: 34–7; Pease, op. cit., pp. 135–8. The suggested line of separation of the two spheres was subsequently made more definite in the proposal that this start at a point twenty leagues up the Penobscot from its mouth and then run across the continent to a point on the gulf twenty leagues distant from Cape Tormentine (B.M., Add. Mss., 33,029: 291–2).

by an effort to rewrite, as it were, those embarrassing clauses of the Treaty of Utrecht in terms that had at best the most shadowy historical justification. Yet, in agreeing to these proposals, Louis would have been obliged to renounce once for all his most insistent of all demands: an outlet for New France via the St. John, the Bay of Fundy, and the isthmus. For the final British position upon this last point was as follows:

> "Whatever desire France may have to keep the isthmus and Beaubassin as the only communication during a considerable part of the year between Quebec and Isle Royale, Great Britain cannot consent to it without giving up the most essential security of the rest of the peninsula. The whole might as well be abandoned. The same difficulty is presented with regard to the proposal for leaving in the peninsula a certain extent of country which shall not be inhabited lying along the coast facing the Gulf of St. Lawrence, since the thickness of the woods and the defiles would be most convenient to cover the designs one nation might form against the other. Therefore, Great Britain must insist upon retaining and possessing a certain *lisière* along the coast of the Bay of Fundy which shall extend as far as the Gulf of St. Lawrence, without which, the possession of the peninsula and the Bay of Fundy would be precarious." [117]

The British proposals of February 20 marked the culminating-point in Anglo-French diplomacy. In all subsequent negotiations these are substantially maintained, with only certain slight modifications, as the only basis upon which a settlement of North American affairs could rest.[118] On the other hand the French continued to hold

---

[117] B.M., Add. Mss., 33,029: 296–8.

[118] On March 26, 1755 Sir Thomas Robinson presented to the Cabinet Council his "Three Points of Accommodation," which provided that the line from Cuyahoga Bay on Lake Erie should now be run so as to touch the "Mountains of Virginia" at the 39th degree of north latitude — to the east of which the British were to have control and to the west of which, to the east bank of the Wabash, the country should be neutral; the French by this were to remain in control of the Wabash and that part of the Ohio from the juncture of the two rivers. As to the Great Lakes region, Lakes Erie and Ontario were to be placed "upon the Foot of the Treaty of Utrecht," as were the Five Nations, who were to be no more molested on these two lakes and on the Niagara, with the destruction of the French forts on this river. Lastly, a line was to be run "from the Bay of Newbur [?] strait to Fort Chamblé or the bottom of Lake Champlain, and from thence in a strait line to the western source of the River St. Jean: and from thence to Bay —— upon the Gulph of St. Lawrence — the French side to belong to Them, in full sovereignty: the other side, to the Crown of Great Britain. If not in full Sovereignty on Both Sides; in that Case, what is left, to be Neuter . . ." (Pease, *op. cit.,* p. 148). But this proposal went beyond what the other ministers were prepared to concede, as is evident by the character of the British reply of June 7 to a *mémoire* submit-

tenaciously to their previously expressed claims not only to all the trans-Appalachian lands as well as all those on the mainland lying south of the St. Lawrence River and east of the Kennebec but likewise to an exclusive control and use of the Great Lakes region and the Lake Champlain approach to the St. Lawrence.[119]

Although the Duc de Mirepoix continued in London until the middle of July and seemed to be disposed to give sympathetic consideration to the British viewpoints, Rouillé had become reconciled by March 17 to the view that "*la guerre peut seule terminer nos discussions.*"[120] Yet neither side welcomed an open break, and more or less perfunctory suggestions for a solution of the grave problem of disputed territorial claims continued to be made until the news arrived of open hostilities that had occurred on June 10 when Admiral Boscawen sought to intercept, off the Banks of Newfoundland, the French fleet which was carrying reinforcements to Canada.[121] In fact, it may be affirmed that from the moment the British ministry in the fall of 1754 determined to send General Braddock with two regiments to North America to retrieve the situation on the western frontiers that arose with the surrender of Washington's forces at Fort Necessity, the chances for the success of peaceful means of meeting the international crisis had dimmed and by the summer of 1755, with the dispatch of Macnémara's fleet from Brest to Louisbourg and Quebec, had faded away.

---

ted by Mirepoix on May 14, in which the court was unwilling to admit that France had "the faintest title to the Ohio River and the territory in question" to the east of the Wabash, nor to an exclusive navigation of the waters of Lakes Erie and Ontario and of the Niagara River, nor the region between the north side of the Bay of Fundy and the south bank of the St. Lawrence which, however, might remain neutral, possessed by neither nation (Affaires Étrangères, Correspondance Politique: Angleterre, 439: 172–9).

[119] See Mirepoix to Rouillé, February 28, 1755, Aff. Étrang., Corr. Pol.: Ang., 438: 232–8; Rouillé to Mirepoix, March 5, 1755, *ibid.*, 438: 247–8; the British proposals delivered March 7, 1755, *ibid.*, 438: 253–8; and Rouillé's observations on the latter proposals, out of place in the series and incorrectly dated February 13, 1755, *ibid.*, 438: 139–47. Those portions of these documents bearing upon the Ohio River and the Great Lakes regions have been printed together with translations by Pease (*op. cit.*, pp. 138–54, 168–77, 234–43).

[120] Letter to Mirepoix, March 17, 1755, *ibid.*, p. 161.

[121] These negotiations have been treated in great detail by Max Savelle in his *The Diplomatic History of the Canadian Boundary, 1749–1763.* While his conclusions (pp. 77–8), based upon a most careful examination of the sources, are in some respects different from those here arrived at, I can only pay tribute to his fine sense of discrimination and spirit of detachment.

CHAPTER XI

Summarization

WE HAVE NOW, in traversing the bounds of the old British Empire, in this and the preceding volume, surveyed the chief zones of international friction, and in particular those that affected the relations between the British and French in the eighteenth century. We have noted that the contest between the two nations, carried on in many areas widely separated from one another, involved, as a rule, strategic objectives — objectives that combined both economic and military prospective, if not immediate, advantages. Some of these areas within which serious friction at one time or another had existed were, by the middle of the century, relatively quiet and indicated the establishment of some sort of equilibrium. Such was the case, for example, in the region lying east of the lower Mississippi, following the sharp but brief contest for control of the Choctaw Confederation that ended in 1747; such was also the case with respect to the so-called " neutral " islands of the Caribbeans, after the earlier struggles, particularly for Tobago and St. Lucia. Other areas — especially those embraced by the Ohio Valley, the Great Lakes, and lands lying about the Bay of Fundy, in North America, and the Carnatic in India — witnessed sharp clashes between the years 1748 and 1754, and the setting forth on the part of the two powers of pretensions that were mutually irreconcilable. In this conflict — ultimately involving the future not only of North America but of the lesser islands of the West Indies, and the subcontinent of India — certain patterns of statecraft characteristic of the two great rivals become apparent.

British expansion in both the seventeenth and the eighteenth centuries took place largely as the result of private rather than state initiative — supplemented in the case of the New World by involuntary white indentured and Negro slave immigration. The lure of life under better conditions urged countless thousands to seek the English possessions where they were welcome. As a result, Englishmen, Welshmen, Scots, Ulster Presbyterians, Germans, Swiss, and French Huguenots poured into the colonies during the first half of the latter century. The pattern of this expansion is indicated by a concentration of strength in the seaboard areas. Populous seaports, such as Charleston, Philadelphia, New York, Newport, Boston, and Halifax, were centres from which radiated energies that were directed toward new fields of exploitation; from these towns and their outposts, and from the old, settled tidewater, pressed self-reliant, hardy men and women, many of them newcomers. The better lands along the lower courses of navigable rivers having been appropriated, they spread into the interior regions. Each generation played its part in the conquest of the wilderness and, as a rule, that portion of the wilderness lying just beyond the line of settlement. It was a haphazard, unplanned, and voluntary movement westward — each family, as a rule, assuming its own risks, and government at best generally giving but passive encouragement and at worst seeking to restrain, particularly in the case of settlements along the frontiers of Pennsylvania. In the same unplanned fashion Indian traders penetrated the trans-Appalachian interior; in an eager search for peltry they journeyed for hundreds of miles, seeking out distant and friendly Indian tribes; Virginia planters as eagerly sought out lands in the same interior that they might patent and exploit.

Further, an unregulated commercial expansion led Englishmen into the logwood regions of the Mosquito Coast to defy the Spaniards, led them also to break through the trade monopoly of the South Sea Company in seeking out the Spanish Main, and of that of the Royal African Company in Africa to reap the rewards of the slave trade. Brushing aside formal regulation and restriction, they drove toward their objectives. Rugged individualism it has been called in our own day. To the Far East this commercial expansion, while much more under the control of the state, was at the same time carried out by the efforts of those who were prepared to rely upon their own financial resources, and who, as members of a private corporation once having become endowed with extensive and exclusive powers, sought to be free of government interference and in the main succeeded in doing so.

It is indeed remarkable that, in the building of the old British Empire, direct Crown participation plays so small a part — outside of the granting of letters patent to those who sought to assume leadership in the work. Only north of the Florida frontier, in the face of Spanish territorial pretensions to much of what is now South Carolina, and likewise south of the lower St. Lawrence in the face of French pretensions to most of the region between Maine and the Gulf of St. Lawrence, did the British government itself, in time of peace, assume direct responsibility before 1755 for protecting British claims in North America and the lawful opportunities of British subjects. Elsewhere, in so far as protection was afforded, it came through the local governments, governments to a great extent controlled by the colonials themselves and, therefore, usually fully sympathetic with the aspirations of those whose personal fortunes were directly and deeply involved. As a result, this meant, in practice — by reason of the wide measure of local autonomy permitted by the Crown even in the royal colonies — that only too frequently there were clashes in policy as there were in interest between colony and colony with respect to such important matters as Indian relations. In other words, there was absent the all-pervading presence of the central authority, there was absent that uniformity of control and direction, such as, for example, was to be found within the great Spanish Empire.

In truth, the eighteenth-century British Empire was a business man's world — a world of cockets, of ledgers, of bills of sale — in which only too frequently private interest, if not held to be superior to, at least crowded out, public interest; a world that reacted unfavourably to governmental regulation, even in the face of the elaboration of formal trade and navigation and industrial restrictions; a world in which men, while aggressive, were at the same time opposed to the intruding into their communities of regular military establishments as instruments of public policy. Within that world, which after all was also a world of abundance, a world that thought not of scarcity but in terms of a surplus of the material things of life and of the profitable disposal of these, with steadily advancing standards of living, a world, moreover, of literate people, of newspapers and pamphlets, of freedom of the press — after the Zenger trial — of freedom of discussion, a world of dissenters, of varied religious faiths, of contrasting social attitudes, of growing tolerance toward those not like-minded — within such a world, men had come to be increasingly confident of their capacity as individuals to shape environment to their own ends and, consequently, not only increasingly distrustful of the ability of a distant government to do this for them but increasingly resentful when the effort was so made.

On the other hand, the French Empire presents a far different pattern. As in the case of the Spanish Empire there was uniformity of design with not only the concentration of authority in the Crown but continuous exercise of that authority. From the days of the Company of One Hundred Associates, in the formation of which Cardinal Richelieu played a leading role, the Crown interested itself directly in Canada and the shaping of this province to its own ends and ideals. The same was true of Louisiana — even during the period of control of the Compagnie des Indes, behind the façade of which can be detected the constant exertion of the authority of the state. The colonization of both of these immense and all but empty provinces in the eighteenth century was largely, if not exclusively, a state enterprise and a matter calling for the government's deep solicitude in view of the fact that Frenchmen were not attracted to either the St. Lawrence or the Mississippi, and prospective colonizers of other nations were, as a rule, not desired. Therefore the seventeenth-century device of bringing regular troops to the New World and then giving inducements to the soldiers to remain and establish homes was continued into the eighteenth; in the case of Louisiana efforts were also made, but without much success, to promote the emigration of Frenchmen by subsidization.

Moreover, French empire-building in the eighteenth century was characterized by the old spirit of monopoly of the seventeenth, which stood squarely opposed to the spirit of free enterprise. Further, the seventeenth-century paternalistic policy of attempting to canalize the endeavours of the settlers along avenues that seemed desirable to the Crown remained that of the eighteenth. If it, therefore, may be fairly charged that the activities of British colonials, along certain lines at least, were under-regulated, it may be as fairly charged that those of French colonials along as many lines were over-regulated, depriving them of individual incentive and initiative. In this connection, it is not without significance that within the bounds of New France there was no escaping, for long, at least, the presence of the King's soldiers; they were quartered in every town of importance, they were to be found at every trading post of any consequence. Not only were these troops designed to defend the territorial rights of the Crown along the frontiers in times of war but they were the chief agency for maintaining its authority over the inhabitants in times of peace — in spite of the police powers of the Intendant in Canada and those of the Ordonnateur in Louisiana.

While travellers were impressed with the graciousness of the French court etiquette and the display of wealth at Quebec and at New Orleans, while they found in both Canada and Louisiana, with the exclusion of non-Catholics, a certain harmonious rhythm of life with all doubt removed from matters of faith such as in no wise existed in the rather inchoate social structure of British North America, while most of the inhabitants of both of these provinces were ordinarily, as the result of their exertions, able to live in rude comfort, there was, nevertheless, after their immediate needs had been met, little tangible surplus — outside of fish, furs, and skins — that could be exported to France in exchange for the multitude of articles desired and necessary to make life bearable. Sometimes even food was lacking and officials from time to time warned of famine conditions. Not that Canada and Louisiana taken together with their vast resources could not produce unlimited wealth, but that conditions were not favourable for the exploitation of these resources. For the world of New France was not a world of industry and commerce but really a world of officials, of *décrets,* of *ordonnances,* of King's soldiers, a world in which religious monopoly and trade monopoly were incompatibly linked together, a world without newspapers, without a press, without open discussion of public issues, a world of suppression of thought in which governmental policy affecting the most vital interests of the people was carried out without their consent expressed either directly or indirectly. In view of these facts, is it, therefore, surprising that, while the French West Indies were considered highly profitable, both Canada and Louisiana as colonies were in a sense held to be enormous parasites clinging to, and nourished by, the royal treasury? Is it surprising that they continued throughout their history as French overseas provinces to be the objects of continuous and heavy subsidization on the part of the nation at home? For neither in its economic weakness could begin to sustain the financial burdens that the pattern of control and administration involved. The heavy charges of this might conceivably have been met in the case of Canada — in spite of the corrupt conduct of colonial officials — had the French been left free to exploit without competition the apparently unlimited supply of pelts and skins that the great interior of North America afforded. But this was impossible in face of the irresistible inducements offered to the natives and even to Frenchmen themselves by British traders and merchants. Therefore none of the elaborate mechanisms set up by the ministers of His Most Christian Majesty for guaranteeing an efficient system of trade that would lead to the steady flow of the peltries into the warehouses of the Compagnie des Indes and of its predecessors in possession of the monopoly of beaver skins were effective in the face of offers of unlimited supplies of goods of superior quality and at lower prices at Oswego, Albany, and elsewhere — as against French scarcity of trading goods, inferior in quality, and exorbitantly priced. Thus the greatest single source of wealth that the French could look to within the bounds of North America was — in spite of the lavish annual distribution of Indian presents — diverted to such an extent as to leave even Canada, always much stronger than Louisiana, a financial liability of such proportions that more than once in the middle of the eighteenth century the French Minister felt impelled, in view of the near paralysis of the royal treasury, to threaten to leave the province to its fate. What a contrast to the vast increase of wealth that in the course of the first half of that century poured in varied form out of British North America! — wealth that served to buttress the already strong position of the British treasury.

The strategy of French expansion in the New World is also indicated by its peculiar pattern. Instead of a concentration of settlement along the seacoast and in areas contiguous to it, islands of Frenchmen appeared here and there within the vast ocean of a continental wilderness. Only along the upper and lower reaches of the Mississippi and the middle reaches of the St. Lawrence was there anything approaching the type of fairly contiguous settlement that characterized that of the British in the middle of the eighteenth century. In other words, there was nothing in New France that corresponded to the British "frontier line" — broken as that line was in actuality by the existence of topographical barriers of one kind or another. To illustrate: In the Gulf of St. Lawrence there was Louisbourg on Isle Royale (Cape Breton) and in addition a few other insignificant settlements on that island and on Isle St. Jean (Prince Edward). To reach the next centre of population in New France a traveller was obliged to enter the St. Lawrence and to mount it a distance of three hundred miles to Quebec — passing on the way, it is true, now and again, little, isolated hamlets. From there for a hundred and eightly miles, still up the river to Montreal, he would find himself in the midst of a fairly continuous settlement, but a settlement that clung tightly to the banks of that river or of the Richelieu. Passing beyond Montreal — after some weeks of arduous effort spent in mounting the river, in passing through Lake Ontario, by Fort Niagara, and over the Niagara portage, and the length of Lake Erie — he would at length arrive at Detroit, where once again he would find a considerable number of Frenchmen, other than regular soldiers, living either at the post or upon farms located along the Detroit River. The next settled region might be approached by various routes. The one our traveller would most likely use would require him to paddle across Lake Erie to the mouth of the Maumee, then up the river to the decayed Fort Miami; then, crossing the portage to the upper Wabash, float down that river — passing on the way Fort Ouiatenon and the little village of Vincennes — and into the Ohio and down it to its mouth; then breasting the Mississippi, in due season he would reach the Illinois country. But after all this effort he would be disappointed were he to expect to find in this great region of fertile plains and forest any settlement of importance. Kaskasia (Kaskaskia), the largest, could boast of no more than fifty-eight adult male inhabitants in 1752! Then pointing his *canot* southward, he would be obliged to descend the majestic Mississippi for a thousand lonely and also frequently dangerous miles — encountering on the way but a small military post at the mouth of the Arkansas and another at Natchez — before reaching once more a populated region, in the midst of which was New Orleans. Here as elsewhere the farms of the inhabitants clung to the water's edge. Finally — without bothering to mount the Red River to Natchitoches village — by leaving the mouth of the Mississippi and moving eastward through the Gulf of Mexico to Mobile Bay he would encounter at Mobile the last French settlement worthy of the name within the vast extent of New France.

But let it not be thought that with a scattered population of but one-twentieth of that of British North America New France did not enjoy certain advantages in this contest to have and to hold regions in dispute in the middle of the eighteenth century. The fact that disciplined regular soldiers were distributed about the interior of the continent and at strategically located posts as well as at forts provided with cannon; the fact that every Frenchman in the New World was expected to be exercised in the use of arms and subject at any moment to the King's call; the fact that this total force without regard to provincial boundaries could be concentrated rapidly against whatever objectives seemed most imperative; the fact that there were no popular assemblies to refuse to grant needed funds, to dispute, and to air to the world projected measures of defence and to delay the execution of these; the fact that there was a uniform Indian policy conceived with an understanding of the red man's heart and mind and, all in all, implemented with skill; the fact that those having the welfare of New France in their keeping were, as a rule, leaders who not only knew how to plan for future military contingencies but had done so and were skilled in improvising methods when needed for checking the pressure of the British colonial expansion into disputed areas in whatever quarter it might appear — these facts in combination, making up the pattern of French New World statecraft, could not but present an ominous challenge to the British. For among the latter, counsels were divided even in the greatest emergencies. Some of their popular assemblies were recalcitrant, unwilling to make any grant of money for defence; their military preparations where they existed were hopelessly inadequate; their so-called forts, outside of the defences of Halifax, were unworthy of the name; their management of Indian relations was chaotic and at cross-purposes; their Indian allies, such as could be counted on to give really effective assistance when called upon, were non-existent — for even the Six Confederated Nations no longer stood as a buffer to French designs. Further, the continued absorption of most of them in personal affairs, the determined pacifism of thousands of them, particularly a large proportion of those living within the borders of Pennsylvania with its critically important western frontier, the unwillingness of all but a few to agree to any plan to provide voluntarily leadership that could plan in terms of the protection of the interests of the colonies as a unit and could mobilize available resources and act in these terms — all taken together might in the face of this challenge have proved catastrophic in the developing crisis, in spite of their overwhelming preponderance of numbers, their vastly superior wealth and capacity to produce in America itself much of the means of defence.

However, in the face of the disappearance of the harassed and despoiled Pennsylvania traders from the interior, by reason of the aggressive movements of the French and their Indian allies about the Ohio and its tributaries; in face of the collapse of trans-Appalachian

plans of colonization on the part of Virginia planters; in the face of
the growing vulnerability from a military point of view of New York
in the region of the Great Lakes and that of Lake Champlain; in the
face, also, of the concentration of French troops on the isthmus of
Chignecto with the building of forts, the easy-going, lethargic British government at last began to stir. Yet at first the ministry thought
that its activity and also responsibility might be strictly limited by
giving encouragement to the colonial governments to take united
measures to ward off the impending dangers. It was reasoned that
the colonials themselves with their great potential strength voluntarily and properly applied could keep the French in place; it was
felt that they had so much to lose by failure to act that they would do
so; in this connection it was not forgotten what had been accomplished by a voluntary union of New England colonies in the late war
in the conquest of Cape Breton. Therefore a call to the colonies most
affected to attend a general conference with the Iroquoian Confederation and to concert measures for mutual protection was sent out
by the Board of Trade. All this was in harmony with the best tradi-
tions of liberal, semi-autonomous colonial government such as had
developed within the British Empire.

That the work of the Albany Congress so summoned did not con-
stitute a milestone of the greatest significance in the history of intercolonial co-operation cannot fairly be laid at the door of the British
government itself. This seems to be quite clear upon the basis of contemporary evidence. The Congress, made up of colonials of the highest competence, in its deliberations responded resolutely to the challenge of the French not only in a great but futile effort to revitalize
the Iroquoian alliance but with two state papers which testify to the
high level of British-American statesmanship. Its " Representation of
the State of the Colonies " surveyed with steady view the problem of
immediate importance facing the Empire in North America and in
general terms offered solutions for the more pressing; its " Plan of
Union " sought to make clear how within the constitutional frame-
work of the Empire the desired colonial concert with minor ad-
justments could be created and made the effective instrument for
preserving the integrity of British North America. In committing
themselves to these tasks the commissioners frankly went beyond the
powers granted to most of them — something that likewise was true
of those who later gathered in 1787 to frame the present Constitution of the United States. However, unlike the latter, they saw all

their efforts finally confounded under a torrent of criticism and even scorn let loose by the respective governments that had deputized them. Nor was the rather halting Board of Trade plan for a defensive colonial concert — adhering even more closely to the principles of freedom of action on the part of the individual colonies than did the Albany Plan — more successful in providing a solution of the problem of colonial co-operation. In the midst of this confusion of counsels, with some of the colonial governments dominated by particularistic sentiments that made voluntary support of any plan impossible, the ministry was impelled to admit that the only practicable solution to the problem of American colonial defence was to imitate the example of the French, at least to the extent of sending to the western frontiers a small army of British regulars, who, with the support of the colonial line of those colonies that could be induced to act, might relieve the great pressure the French forces were exerting upon the hinterland of Virginia and Pennsylvania.

In contrast to the high tension developed in North America between the British and the French, within the Caribbean Sea there was comparative quiet, in spite of the maintenance of the pretensions of each to St. Lucia, Tobago, Dominica, and St. Vincent. For these four islands were in the middle of the eighteenth century neutralized, at least temporarily, and therefore were, in theory at least, beyond the protection and sphere of influence of either power. In the case of the two last named, where the Caribs — once the possessors of all the Lesser Antilles — were still living in some strength and all in all conducting themselves inoffensively enough, it had been solemnly agreed that neither power should settle upon them. In actuality, however, the French were as busy quietly colonizing them as was the Minister of His Most Christian Majesty in emphatically denying charges that such a breach of faith was taking place. French Caribbean policy must therefore be charged with serious indirection in view of these developments. It also may be pointed out that the proof of this indirection was an important factor in determining the British government no longer to place further reliance on peaceful means of adjusting the outstanding issues that had arisen in the course of Anglo-French rivalry. Yet during the period under consideration the questions revolving about the ownership of the disputed islands were left for diplomacy to answer and to determine and did not therefore involve direct state action and open conflict. This is doubtless to be explained by the fact that there were at stake between the rivals matters of much greater importance.

In India the patterns of statecraft of the two powers had at least some things in common with those exhibited in North America. For example, during the period under consideration in each of these widely separated areas the British sought to place their chief reliance upon their superiority in trade contacts with the natives, the French upon their superiority in those of a political nature. The British concentrated their strength upon seacoast regions; the French, particularly within the interior of the Carnatic and the Deccan; the British were interested primarily in immediate objectives; the French in future developments and prospects; the British found themselves placed upon the defensive; the French enjoyed the advantage of taking the initiative; the British, in seeking means to protect their private interests, could by no means presuppose that the government at home would grant approval of policies and whatever military and financial support of these was required; the French, acting in harmony with preconceived plans that looked to public interests and that had the endorsement of the King's Minister, were able to assume this support. The degree of success that the British enjoyed in carrying out their policies in India between the years 1749 and 1754 largely depended upon the soundness of the financal structure of the United East India Company and upon the reserves in its treasury; while the French could forward their policies without regard to the solvency of the Compagnie des Indes and the profits derived from its commerce. In reality, therefore, it was a contest between a British private corporation and a French public corporation, with each enjoying certain advantages. It may further be stated that if the former acted on occasion with too much caution in view of the very real peril to its interests, the latter as frequently acted with too little, in view of the hazardous security of its own. As illustrative of this point, the British might well have gone further in the support of the Subahdar, Jasir Jang, in spite of his instability; while the French might well have hesitated to make the great sacrifices in men and *matériel* in their futile, repeated efforts to capture Trichinopoly, in spite of its theoretical value.

In following the course of developments in India between the years 1749 and 1754, it is of interest to note that in 1749 the directors of the United East India Company rebuked their local representatives upon the Coromandel Coast for interfering with the native princes, while those of the Compagnie des Indes applauded theirs upon the same coast for engaging in a like policy of interference; whereas in 1754 the British corporation gave its strong approval to the work of its agents, while the French corporation visited upon those locally responsible for policy, and in particular upon Dupleix, its sharp censure, overturning his work and recalling him to France. Curiously enough, the failure of the French in India is to be ascribed to some extent, at least, to their efforts to accommodate themselves to a policy in harmony with that which the British had previously approved — as indicated by the agreement entered into by Godeheu in 1754 — and the success of the British in India to their efforts, especially after 1757, to accommodate themselves to a policy approaching, if not in harmony with, that which the French had previously repudiated, with Clive at length assuming the role of Dupleix as the political reorganizer of India.

In thinking in terms of international rivalry on a grand scale such as one encounters in Anglo-French relations during the period under review, the question comes home with great insistence: Are wars the inevitable consequence of such situations? Are there no mechanisms of social control and stabilization, short of an appeal to arms, that can be applied successfully to liquidate international tensions of a serious nature? In other words, were all the efforts, sincere or otherwise, to arrive at a friendly solution of issues put forth between 1749 and 1755 on the part of Great Britain and France foredoomed to failure? There can be no question that the two nations in 1749 were desirous of maintaining peace, but to each it was to be peace with honour, peace that would permit the realization of old dreams of expansion. To each there had come the sense of a historic mission; in the case of North America, a mission to reach out to possess and to hold in trust for future generations the heart of a great continent.

How can a nation's high sense of mission be subject to ordinary processes of adjudication, particularly if this has become one of great urgency and can at the same time be fulfilled, it is felt, only by moving athwart a corresponding sense of mission held with equal intensity by a rival? For, while the concept of national mission may be in the first instance a pure rationalization and therefore subject to modification and adjustment by rational processes, there may come a time when, captured by popular sentiment and thereupon arrayed in emotional garb, it no longer is subject to control by logic; for it no longer dwells in that realm in which the laws of logic operate — it is now perhaps an irrational expression of national aspiration, an article of national faith of peculiar sanctity. Men die for their faith, seldom for their logic.

From the days of the Sieur de Champlain there had been present his vision of a great French empire ultimately embracing the limits of North America, an empire with one faith, one language, one civilization; an empire aristocratic in form, Franco-Indian in composition, French in spirit. Low as flickered the flame of that vision in days of trial and misfortune, always it remained alive and in the days of such men as Talon and Frontenac in the seventeenth century and of such as Iberville, Bienville, Galissonière, and Duquesne in the eighteenth, it glowed. It was glowing between 1749 and 1754. Correspondingly, from the days that Captain Argal destroyed the village of the " intruding " French at Port Royal on the Bay of Fundy and insisted that the Dutch, likewise " intruders " on Manhattan, recognize the superior rights of England to the soil of the North Atlantic seaboard, there had been embedded in the consciousness of Englishmen of the New World a sense of destiny that involved the idea of the planting and expansion of English civilization ever westward, ever following the retreat of the sun beyond countless horizons. So they moved, these men of destiny, pressing back the wilderness, generation after generation; so they could repeat as a warm article of faith, as well as a cold assumption, that Virginia, as it was charted in 1609 to stretch to the Pacific, was still in 1750, in the words of President Lee of the Virginia Council: " Bounded by the Great Atlantic to the East, by North Carolina to the South, by Maryland and Pennsylvania to the North, and by the South Sea to the West including California."

The appointment of the Anglo-French joint commission that met in Paris in 1750 and continued to deliberate off and on for the next four years was a token of the desire to liquidate all outstanding causes of friction between two great nations sharing in common so much of the rich heritage of earlier European achievement in thought and action and freely acknowledging the interdependence of their cultural life. That failure blasted the efforts of the joint commission and, after its demise, dogged those of the ambassadors and ministers between 1754 and 1756 does not alter the significance of the attempt to confront emotional nationalistic drives with rational and just principles of nationalistic restraints. For the present-day student of international politics can see in some of the compromise proposals — involving not only North America, but the disputed West India islands and the Carnatic in India — the possibility of a meeting of minds and the peaceful, even if temporary solution of the more pressing and, all in all, the more menacing issues. If, in this connection, French sea-power had been as formidable as British, and British defence of the British North American frontiers between 1749 and 1754 had been as effective as was the French defence of those of New France during those years, neither side might have seen fit to run the risks of another war; with the result that a reasoned international compromise might have won the day, instead of an unreasoned appeal to national prestige and honour — and to force. But the chief responsibility for this appeal, it would appear, must lie at the door of the French ministry, through its inability to understand, or at least its unwillingness to acknowledge, the plain implications flowing out of previous international covenants solemnly entered into by the French Crown.

Index

Abenaki [Abnaki; French, Abénaquis] Indians, at Becancourt and at St. Francis, christianized, 21; relations of the Acadians with, 169; de la Galissonière opposes the claims of the commander of Annapolis Royal to receive the submission of, 180; join the Micmac against the English, 192

Aboiteaux, employment of, by the Acadians, 168

Abraham, Indian convert, labours of, at Conajohary, 121

Acadia, description of, 167–8; spread of population in, 168–70; cession of, to England, 171; efforts of the French to win back, during King George's War, 177; within the diocese of the Bishop of Quebec, 178; French policy of redeeming, 178; a grave crisis in the affairs of, 190; the Anglo-French Commission, 1750–1754, and the question of the ancient bounds of, 304–20; proposal of the French commissaries of a principle for determining the limits of, 305–6; the English interpretation of the Treaty of Utrecht and, 307–8; the first British memorial and the first French mémoire on, 1750, 307; sharp differences respecting the interpretation of the Treaty of Utrecht and, 308–10; the second French mémoire on, 1750, 310; the French interpretation of the Treaty of Utrecht and, 308, 310; the second British memorial on, 1750, 311; the third French mémoire on, 1751, 315; Mildmay's proposals respecting, 317; the French plan an appeal to the world over, but stopped by British protest, 319; the third British memorial on, 320–1; Robinson asks as a test of French good faith that they relinquish the forts built in, in violation of a mutual agreement, 325; Robinson's proposal of February 10, 1755 to the British cabinet for a division of the territory of ancient, 331; the royal patent of 1603 to de Monts for, 333; early settlements in, 333; the meaning of the "countries of," in 1667; meaning attached to, before the Treaty of Utrecht, 333–4; the division of, according to the British proposal of February 20, 1755, 336; see also Nova Scotia

Acadians, spread of settlements of, in the seventeenth and eighteenth centuries, 168; manner of living of, 168; increase in numbers of, 168–9; characteristics of, 169; relations of, with the Indians, 169; relations of, with British authorities, 169–70; freedom of public responsibilities of, 169; great privileges enjoyed by, 170; distribution of, about Baye Françoise, 170–1; fate of the, under Article XIV of the Treaty of Utrecht, 171; efforts of many, to leave, 171–2; special privileges asked for, referred to the Crown, 171–2; the great body of, remain after 1714, 172; desire of, to depart weakens, 172; oaths taken by many, at the accession of George II, 173; exemptions accorded to, by Ensign Wroth, 173; unconditional oaths said to have been given by, under Governor Philipps, 173; influence of French priests upon, 174; desire of, for more land, and British policy, 174; shifting of, outside the peninsula, 174; growing recalcitrance of, 174; impossibility of enforcing orders upon, by Mascarene, 174; attitude of, during King George's War, 176–7; failure of, to warn the Annapolis garrison of impending attacks, 177; support given to Canadian troops by, 177; influence of the French clergy over, 178; agitation in favour of the removal of, during King George's War, 178; assurances given to, by Shirley, 178–9; removal of, delayed for a decade, 179; brought in 1749 within the scope of the protection of the French King, 180; of Merligueuche Bay, welcome the English settlers, 182; Cornwallis instructed to require oaths of allegiance from all, 183; not to be allowed to do damage to their homes before leaving the Province, 183; unwillingness of, to take the oaths, 184; fear of Indians by, 184; guarantees given, in case of loyal conduct, 184; refusal of, to take the oath, 184–5; willingness of, to leave their settlements, 185; reminded by Cornwallis that they are subjects of the English king, 185; support given by, to the garrison at Louisburg, 186; forbidden by Cornwallis to export provisions out of the Province, 186; appeal of, to the King of France and to the Governor General of New France, 190; seek a retreat in New France, 191; inveterate hostility of, for the English, 191; of Beaubassin, join de la Corne, 193; of other villages refuse to plant crops, 194; oppose the English on the Missaquash, 194; desire of, to return to deserted homes, 195; the French will not permit neutrality among, 195; the Governor General issues an *ordonnance* against, refusing to take up arms, 195; embodiment of, in the Canadian militia, 196; settlement of, on Isle St. Jean, 196; destruction of live stock of the refugee, by the Canadian Indians, 196; opposition of Le Loutre and the French government to providing priests for, still in Nova Scotia, 199; grounds for refusal of requests of, 199; difficulties facing refugee, 201; petition Col. Lawrence to be permitted to return to homes, 201–2; assurances desired, 202; refugee, refuse alterations in the oath, 202; resistance of, resumed on arrival of Le Loutre from France, 202; terrorized by Le Loutre's Indians, 203, 204; guarantees demanded by, refused, 203; show hostility against Le Loutre at Beauséjour, 204; of Annapolis Royal, Minas and Piziquid go to Beauséjour, to build dikes, 204; ordered to return to homes, 204; carry provisions to the French and Indians, 204; hostile conduct of, at Piziquid, 204–5; Governor Lawrence gives up hope to make loyal subjects of, 205; the problem of the disposal of, 205; the ground laid for the scattering of, 205; owed allegiance to the English king under the rule of *jus solis*, 206

Addaties, fabric of India exported, 252

Aden, English trading activities at, opposed by the Turks, 236

Adoption, policy of, and the Iroquoian Confederation, 71

Afghans, invasions of India by the, 232

Africa, the exclusive rights to trade to, reserved to the Compagnie des Indes, 264

Agra, India, an English factory established

at, in 1616, 237; the English factory at, in 1750, 260

Ahmad Shah, Grand Mogul, gives commission to Firuz Jang as Subahdar of the Deccan, 294; troubles faced by, at Delhi, 294; deposed in 1754, 294

Ahmad Shah Afdali, invasion of northern India by, in 1752, 294

Aix-la-Chapelle, activities at, in 1748, contrasted to those at Münster and Osnabrück in 1648, 300–1; secret articles signed at, by Great Britain, France, and Holland, 300–1; see also Peace of Aix-la-Chapelle; Treaty of Aix-la-Chapelle

Akbar, founder of the Mogul Empire, 233; address sent to, by Queen Elizabeth, 235

Albany, price of beaver skin at, 44; M. Callières-Bonnevue advises the seizure of, 45; arms furnished to Indians of Five Nations by merchants of, 74; importance of Sault St. Louis in the Montreal contraband trade with, 76; neutrality of the people of, in war, 76; report that merchants of, were planning a post at Niagara, 82; fundamental change in trading policy of, in 1716, 84; traders sent from, to the Five Nations, 84–5; great fortunes of merchants of, in contraband trade, 86; the neutrality agreement between Canada and, 92; Dutch Indian traders of, hostile to Anglican missionaries among the Iroquois, 97–8; charges of great activities of, in the contraband trade in 1754, 120

Albany Congress, the, efforts at, to grapple with the problem of the Iroquoian Confederation, 3; instructions of the delegates of Massachusetts Bay to, regarding the selling of provisions to the French, 34; 1754, the chief objective of, from the viewpoint of the Board of Trade, 111; Virginia refuses to send commissioners to, 112; colonies represented at, 113; type of commissioners sent to, 114; varied powers vested in the commissioners to, 114; peculiar position of the government of New York at, 116; delegates to, address the Six Nations, 119; reply of the Six Nations, 119; the Six Nations reconciled to the English by, 122; a committee on a plan of union appointed by, 124; various plans of union submitted to, 126–131; nature of the proceedings of, 138–9; no resolution of, authorizing the sending of the Plan of Union to England, 140; Gov. Shirley on the attitude of the commissioners at, 142, 160; work of, to be used in England for a union of the colonies, 160; observations of Shirley upon the work of, 165-6; statesmanlike achievements at, 347; cause of the failure of the efforts of, 347-8

Albany Indian Commissioners, the, and the maintenance of the New York-Canada neutrality policy during King George's War, 93-4; restoration of the power of, in 1750, 99; recommendations of, for reviving English influence among the Six Nations, 109; lack of influence of, among the Indians, 111

Albany Plan of Union, the, a fusion of the "Short Hints" and the "Plan of a Proposed Union," 133; not to include Nova Scotia and Georgia, 134; the Lower Counties on the Delaware ignored by, 134; to be created by an Act of Parliament, 134; analysis of, 135-9; the power of the Crown and, 138; degree of support of, by the colonial commissioners, 139; limited purposes of, 140; sent to the colonial assemblies, 140; forwarded by de Lancey to the Board of Trade, 141; hostile attitude of the Pennsylvania Assembly toward the, 144-5; Governor Dinwiddie's treatment of, 145-6; the ignoring of, by the governments of Maryland and South Carolina, 146; sympathetic attitude of Governor Arthur Dobbs toward, 146; hostile attitude of the New Jersey Assembly toward, 146-7; favourable attitude of the New Jersey Council toward, 147; James Alexander's criticism of, 147; the favourable attitude of the government of New York toward, 147; the struggle in Rhode Island for approval of, 147-8; ultimate rejection of, by the government of Rhode Island, 148; objections of the Connecticut Assembly to, 148-50; prolonged deliberations of the Assembly of Massachusetts Bay over, 150-4; final rejection of, by Massachusetts Bay and reasons, 154-6; suggested changes in, advocated by Governor Shirley, 158; treatment of, in England, 165; Shirley's further observations upon, 165-6

Albemarle, William Anne Keppel, Earl of, Governor of Virginia, becomes British Ambassador in France, 303; transmits to Shirley orders for recall, 316; very close relations between Mildmay and, 318; Mildmay's proposals approved by, 318; gives approval to Mildmay's proposals to end the Anglo-French disputes, 317-8; interview of, with Rouillé over the death of Jumonville, 324; brings to the attention of Rouillé the attack on Fort Necessity, 325; reproaches Rouillé with attempts on the part of France to lay down by force British territorial limits, 326; suggests that France might have peace by withdrawing behind the Ohio, 327; death of, and deep financial involvement of, 327-8

Aldees, the gift of eighty, by Chanda Sahib and Muzaffar Jang to the Compagnie des Indes, 277; surrender of eighty, by the Rajah of Tanjore to the French, 280

Alexander, James, a member of the New York Council, criticizes Franklin's plan of union, 125-7; preference of, for a legislature of three branches in a plan of colonial union, 147

Algonkin, King's Ship, carries Abbé Piquet to France, 107

Algonquian Indians, early trade contracts of, with the French, 38; aid in driving the Five Nations southward, 38-9

All the Memorials of the Courts of Great Britain and France since the Peace of Aix-la-Chapelle Relative to the Limits of the Territory of Both Crowns in North America and the Right to the Neutral Islands in the West Indies (The Hague, 1756), 307

Allamhana, India, the gift of, to d'Auteuil by Chanda Sahib, 277

Allegheny Mountains, the Albany Congress favours the contraction of the western bounds of the colonies to the, 133; Robinson's proposal of February 10, 1755 to the British cabinet for mutual evacuation between the Wabash and, 331; Mirepoix insists that the true western boundary of the British are the, 332

Allejars, fabric of India exported, 252

Allen, Mr., on the committee on colonial union of the Massachusetts Bay House of Representatives, 151

Allibannies, fabric of India exported, 252

Allibatties, fabric of India exported, 252

Allix, Mr., British commissioner respecting prizes, 303

Allouez, Father Claude, establishment of Great Lakes missions by, 142

Almouchiquois, the ancient district of, in Acadia, 333

Amadabat, India, English factory at, in 1750, 260

Amboyna, execution of English traders on, by the Dutch, 237

American colonial navy, provision for, in the Albany Plan of Union, 137

American colonies, views of Shirley and

Franklin on the relations between Great Britain and, 158-60

Amherst, Nova Scotia, built near site of Fort Lawrence, 194

Amikwa [Amicoué] Indians, Algonquian family, efforts by the French to prevent, trading with the Iroquois, 82

" An Account of the Charters Granted to the East India Company" by John Dunning, 236-7

Ananda Ranga Pillat, "Private Diary" of, 275; in the service of the French, 277; on Dupleix's recognition of the rule of Nasir Jang, 277

Ancient Bear, early Iroquoian clan, 71

Ancient Name Bearer, early Iroquoian clan, 71

Andres, Reverend William, description of the Mohawk villages by, 66

Anglo-Dutch Treaty of 1619 for a " Council of Defence " in the Far East, 237

Anglo-French joint commission, the, of 1687, respecting St. Lucia and Hudson Bay, 227; of 1750-1754, the Treaty of Aix-la-Chapelle and the appointment of, 302; duties of, 302-3; the activities of, 303-23; initial difficulties faced by, 304-6; the French instructions for, embracing all matters in dispute, 306; agreement of, in procedure, 306; the first English memorial on Acadia, 1750, and, 307; the first French mémoire on Acadia, 1750, and, 307; sharp difference faced by, respecting the interpretation of the Treaty of Utrecht, 308-10; developing friction between Shirley and Mildmay and, 309-10; the second French mémoire respecting Acadia, 1750, and, 310; the second British memorial respecting Acadia, 1750, and the memorial respecting the island of Canso, presented to, 311; the first French mémoire on St. Lucia presented to, 312; growing rift between Shirley and Mildmay and, 312; the first French mémoire on St. Lucia, presented to, 312; activities of, during 1751, 314; the third French mémoire on Acadia presented, 1751, to, 315; the English memorial on St. Lucia presented, 1751, to, 315; the undermining of Shirley and his dismissal from, 1752, 315-6; De Cosné takes Shirley's place on, 316; the justification for the continuance of, 317; Mildmay offers a basis of settlement of the differences faced by, 317-8; Mildmay's disillusionment respecting, 320; the third British memorial on Acadia presented to, 1753, 320-1;

the issue over the exclusive use of the French language by, 321-2; work of, taken over by the ambassadors, 1754, 323; attempt of the French to revive the activities of, 330

Anglo-French negotiations, 1750-1754, see Anglo-French joint commission

Anglo-French negotiations, 1755, Rouillé's protest over the death of Jumonville and, 324; British protest over the attack on Fort Necessity and, 325; French assurances of good intentions and of the evacuation of the Neutral Islands, 326; London in 1755 becomes the center of, 328; instructions given to Mirepoix for, 328-9; interview of Mirepoix with Robinson and, 329-30; Rouillé warned that the British would only grant an armistice if the French evacuate the late settlements on the Ohio, 330; Robinson's proposals of January 22, 330; Rouillé calls for the revival of the work of the joint commission and denies British rights in the Ohio country, 330; the British cabinet proposal of February 7, for mutual evacuation and the proposal of February 9 for a suspension of arms, 330-1; Robinson's proposals of February 10 before the Cabinet, 331; criticism of these proposals by the Earl of Halifax, 331; Rouillé suggests that the French might retire to the Ohio if the British retire behind the Alleghenies, 331-2; other demands by Rouillé, 332; the realities of the situation in North America considered with respect to, 332-4; influence of the evidence of bad faith displayed by the French on the course of, 334-5; the British proposals of February 20, 335-6; failure of French statesmanship, 336-7; the final British position upon the question of an overland route between Canada and Cape Breton, 337; Rouillé becomes reconciled to war, 338; the open break in, with the news of the activities of Boscawen off Newfoundland, 338

Anglo-French relations, terms of a temporary treaty signed at Madras in 1754, 296

Anglo-French rivalry, the Iroquoian Confederation and, 3; significance of the year 1749 in relation to, 275; of 1749-1754, active and quiet areas of, 339; characteristics of, in North America, 346-8; in the Caribbean, 348-9; in India, 349-50; the question of the inevitability of war in 1755 in connection with, 350-2

Anjengo, India, proposal of the East India Company to secure a supply of pepper from the ruler of, 256

Annapolis Royal, early capital of Nova Scotia, 169–70; a small garrison stationed at, 170; weakness of the garrison of, 174; Le Loutre's efforts to capture, in 1744, 177; appeal of Acadians of, to the Governor General of New France, 190

Anne, Queen of England, arms of, set up in the castles of the Five Nations, 78–9; agrees to permit the Acadians to dispose of their property, 172; the tripartite agreement respecting the East Indies signed by, 243; establishment of the United Company of Merchants of England trading to the East Indies by, 244

Antigua, West Indies, Carib attacks against, 210; a force sent from, against the Winward Caribs, 210

Anwar-ud-din [French, Anaverdikan], named Nabob of Arcot by the Subahdar of the Deccan, 272; Dupleix seeks aid of, in 1744, 272; forbids European naval hostilities in waters of India, 272; agreement of, with Dupleix over Madras, 272; army of, goes to take possession of Madras, but defeated by the French, 274; Dupleix supports Chanda Sahib in his project to overthrow, 276–7; vain reliance of, upon Dupleix, 277; death of, leading his troops, 277

Appalachian Mountains; see Allegheny Mountains

Arabs, commercial relations of, with India, 234

Arcot, rivalry for the nabobship of, in 1743, 272; Anwar-ud-din made Nabob of, 272; Muzaffar Jang at, 279; capital of Chanda Sahib, 286; left unprotected by Chanda who goes to Trichinopoly, 286; capture of, by Clive in 1751, 288; defense of, by Clive, 288; the Anglo-French issue over the control of, dealt with in London, 322

Armagon, India, an English factory established at, in 1626, 237; given up in 1640, 237

Armstrong, Major Lawrence, Lieut. Gov. of Nova Scotia, forbids the Acadians to make a road from Annapolis to Minas, 172

Aroüagues, of South America, drive the Caribs from Tobago, 218

Arpent, French measurement, length of, in the eighteenth century, 6

Arrack, East India, put up for auction, 257

Articles of Confederation of 1781, the Albany Plan of Union goes beyond the, 138

A Short Reply to Mr. Stephen Hopkins's Vindication, and False Reflections against the Governor and Council of the Colony of Rhode-Island, 1755, by "Philolethes," 148

Assiniboin (Siouan family) Indians, location of, 40; estimates of strength of, 40; the Crees allies of, 40

Atkinson, Theodore, Chief Justice of New Hampshire, an Albany Congress commissioner, 114; appointed on the committee on colonial union at the Albany Congress, 124

A True Representation of the Plan formed in Albany, 1755, by Stephen Hopkins, on the conduct and powers of the commissioners, 141

Aubert, Louis François, and Company, agreement of, with the Canada Company in 1706, 57

Aubert, M., Governor of Guadeloupe, treaty of friendship with the Caribs made by, 209

Auctions, of East India commodities by the East India Company, 257–8

Aurangabad, India, capital of the Deccan, Muzaffar Jang's plan to go to, 284; activities of Bussy at, 284

Aurangzeb, Mogul Emperor, failure of, to conquer the Deccan, 233; seizure of the English factory at Surat by, 241

Austrian Netherlands, France forced to surrender the, 33

"Authorized Names," the Iroquoian Confederation and, 70; the number of, 71; examples of, 71

Baber [Babar, Babour], invasion of India by, 233

Bahur, India, presented to the United East India Company by Muhammad Ali, 280; the French ejected from, 280

Baie St. Paul, settlement of, on the Lower St. Lawrence, 18; the production of naval stores at, 23

Baker, Capt., East India goods of, put up for auction, 257

Balance of power, as an English principle, 301

Balance of trade, amount of adverse, for Canada, 25; a consistent favourable, for India, 235

Balasore [Ballalore], India, an English factory at, in 1750, 260

Ball, early Iroquoian clan, 71

Ballasores, fabric of India exported, 252
Banalités, in Canada, 9
Bandannoes [bandannas], fabric of India exported, 252
Bank of England, the South Sea Company and, 245
Bank of France, connection of, with the Compagnie des Indes, 264
Bantam, Java, importance of the English factory at, 237; loss of factory at, by the London East India Company, 241
Banyan, chief native employee of the East India Company, activities of the, 252
Bar iron, production of, in Canada, 24
Barbados, easy approach to St. Lucia via, 208; trial of Philip Warner at, 210; Puritans of, seek to colonize Tobago, 218; desire of sugar planters of, to colonize St. Lucia, 226; the Governor of, sends Captain Temple in 1686 to drive the French from St. Lucia, 227; the Governor of, in 1700 demands the French evacuation of St. Lucia, 228–9; the Governor of, also commissioned Governor of St. Lucia, 230
Barbary, funds of the Compagnie des Indes tied up in, 268
Barclay, the Rev. Henry, son of the Rev. Thomas Barclay, missionary to the Mohawks, 98; becomes pastor of Trinity Church, 98
Barclay, the Rev. Thomas, minister of the Albany church, limited success of, in preaching to the Iroquois, 97–8
Barley, grown in Canada, 13
Barnes, Major Abraham, a Maryland commissioner at the Albany Congress, 114
Barnett [Barnet], Commodore Curtis, sent to the Far East, 273; in 1745 in the Indian Ocean, 273; death of, 273
Bartram, John, interest of, in natural history, 15; description of an Onondaga long house by, 66
Baskets, the making of, by the Indians, 36
Bassora [Basra], Persia, English factory at, in 1750, 260
Bastoes, fabric of India exported, 252
Bateaux, Canadian communication by means of, 6
Bay of Fundy, Acadian settlements on, 168–9; the British refuse to provide an outlet to New France via, 337
Bay of Newbur(?), a proposed boundary for New France to run through, 337
Baye Françoise, see Bay of Fundy
Bayonne Company, monopoly of, in the St. Lawrence whale fisheries, 27

Bayonne, France, interest of, in whaling in the St. Lawrence, 24; number of ships from, to Canada in 1754, 25
Beans, raising of, by the Indians, 36
Bear, Six Nations clan, 70
Bear skins, value of, in Canada, 55–6; importance of, as an export from Canada, 56
Bears, Great Lakes region haunted by, 36
Beaubassin, Acadians of, desire to leave after the cession of Acadia, 171; the priest of, ordered from, with the outbreak of King George's War, 176; inhabitants of, brought in 1749 under the protection of the French King, 180; Major Lawrence ordered to, 193; the burning of, 193; inhabitants of, desire to return to, 195; disavowal of the French proceedings at, by Puysieulx, 305; see also Chignecto
Beauharnois, Charles, Marquis de, Governor General of New France, plan of, to control Lake Ontario and the Niagara River, 88; sends a summons to the commander of Fort Oswego, 89; writes protest to Governor Burnet, 89; decides not to attempt to dislodge the English at Oswego, 89; directs an attack against the Fox Indians, 89; recommends the building of a fort at Cayuga Bay, 89–90; informed by van Rensselaer of the neutrality between Canada and New York, 92; permitted by the French minister to continue the neutrality, 92–3; orders received by, to destroy Oswego, 93; reasons why Oswego was not attacked by, 93
Beaujeu, Sieur de, commandant at Fort Niagara, reports on the difficulty faced by French traders at Niagara, 101
Beauséjour, ridge of, in Nova Scotia, description of the region about, 167–8; becomes the headquarters of Le Loutre, 199; a chapel constructed at, by Le Loutre, 204; the building of dikes at, 204; see also Fort Beauséjour
Beaver, Six Nations clan, 70
Beaver, the Great Lakes region haunted by, 36; eager search for, by the Indians, 38; extermination of, in the more accessible places, 38; and in the region of the Five Nations, 74
Beaver hats, flourishing condition of the manufacture of, in France, 60; the manufacture of, and the price of beaver skins, 60; plan to recover the European markets for French, 60; best Hudson Bay beaver secured for French, 60; establishment of the manufacture of, in France

in 1701, 60; manufacture of, in England depressed, 60

Beaver skins, value of, exported from Canada in 1748, 23; monopoly of export of, by the Compagnie des Indes, 27; a share in the monopoly of, enjoyed by the Governor General, 28; prices paid for, in 1689 at Montreal and at Albany compared, 45; prices paid for, in 1749 and 1754 in Canada, 55-6; value of, in relation to other skins exported from Canada in 1755, 56; history of the monopoly for the export of, from Canada, 56-63; price of, fixed in 1677, 57; price of, fixed in 1722, 58; lowering of the price of, in 1730 and 1733, 58; stabilization of the price of, in 1737, 58; advance in price of, in 1744, 58; lowering of the price of, in 1749, 58; further lowering of the price of, in 1750, 58; quantity of, exported from Canada in 1741, 59; transactions in, for 1746-7, 59; total value of, from Canada in 1741, 59; cost of the shipment of, to France, 59; total receipts for the sale of, in 1741 and 1746, 59; profits from, 59; demand for an advance in the sale price of, in Europe, 60; supply of best quality of, from Hudson Bay secured by the French hat-manufacturers, 60; exportation of, from England encouraged, 61; number of, exported to France from England, 61; difference in prices paid in 1745 by the English and the Compagnie des Indes for, 62; prices paid for, at Oswego and at Montreal in 1749, 101; funds of the Compagnie des Indes devoted to trade in, in 1752, 267; returns from, to the Compagnie, 269

Becancourt, Canada, christianized Abenaki at, 21

Bedford, John, 4th Duke of, Secretary of State for the Southern Department, on the British delay in completing the memorial on Acadia, 311

Beef, no export of, from Canada in 1754, 24

Belcher, Gov. Jonathan, of New Jersey, rebukes the assembly for refusing to send commissioners to Albany, 113

Belcher, Jonathan, Jr., Chief Justice of Nova Scotia, charges of, against the Acadians, 177

Bellevue, Sieur Martil de, a manager of the St. Maurice iron works, 28

Bencoolen, Sumatra, an English factory at, in 1702, 244; cost of supporting the factory of, 1729-33 and 1750-55, 258

Bengal, India, English factories within, in 1702, 244; English trading activities in, 247; interference with English trade in, 247; decision of the London Company to withdraw from, 247; concessions made by the Nabob of, 247; development of English interest in, 247; cost of freight to, in 1748, 254; number of ships sent to, in 1748, 254; see also Calcutta; Fort William

Benjar [Benjermasin, Bandjarmasin], Borneo, English commerce to, in 1748, 254; an English factory at, in 1750, 260

Bettellees, fabric of India exported, 252

Beucren, Hubert de, Governor of Tobago, 219

Biard, Father Peter, S.J., work of, among the Micmac, 41

Bigot, François, manner of living of, 16; Commissaire Ordonnateur of Isle Royale, commissioned Intendant of New France in 1748, 21; instructions to, 21-3; the cupidity of, 27; accused of great frauds, 28; the wife of Péan secured by, 28; favours of, to Péan, 28; on the dangerous food shortage of Canada, 30; people of Quebec succoured by, 30; profit secured by, from La Baye post, 55; approves conditionally of the military project of Abbé Piquet, 107; agreement of, with Le Loutre to break the peace, 187-8; sends military supplies secretly to Shediac for war against the English, 190; gave credit to Le Loutre for breaking the peace, 192; to provide funds to Le Loutre for payment of scalps, 203; uncertainty of, in 1749 respecting French claims to the region south of the St. Lawrence, 334

Bills of exchange, importance of, drawn in Canada against the French treasury, 25-6; postponement of payment of Canadian, 26; prompt payment of, drawn by the Ordonnateur of Isle Royale, 26

Bishop of Quebec, the, interest of, in lands, 8; amount of Canadian land controlled by, 11; the sale of brandy and, 91; the policy of, respecting the Acadians, 177-8; refuses the petition of the Acadians of Minas for priests, 200

Blankets, imported in Canada from Rouen, 25; value of, in the Indian trade at Albany and at Montreal, in 1689, 45; at Albany and Niagara in 1720, 84

Blewbek [Blawbeck], pro-English Seneca sachem, degraded through the influence of Joncaire, 84

Blockade, of France and Spain during the War of the Austrian succession, 298

Blomberg [Bloomberg, Blumberg], Baron, representative of the Duke of Courland in England, seeks to secure the encouragement of James II to colonize Tobago, 221

Blome, R., author of The Present State of His Majesty's Isles and Territories in America (London, 1687), 208; on the cannibalism of the Caribs, 212; on the Carib's respect for old age, 214; on the Carib virtues, 214–5

Board of Trade, the, request of, in 1753 that the colonial governments confer with the Six Nations, 111; Governor Fletcher's plan for a colonial concert for defence modified by, 123; asked by His Majesty to draw up a plan of colonial union, 161; the "Project" of, for a colonial union, 162–4; plan of, contrasted with the "Short Hints" and Shirley's suggestions, 162; criticism of plan of, by the ministry, 163–4; attitude of, toward a voluntary union of the colonies, 165; steps taken by, to colonize the eastern part of the Nova Scotian peninsula, 181–3; a rebuke administered to the British commissioners in Paris by, in 1750, 309; sends to the British commissioners its memorials on Acadia and Canso, 310–11; approves the memorial on St. Lucia, 315; careful consideration of, given to the French mémoire on Acadia, 319; the answer of, to the French mémoire, 320; the final memorial on Acadia prepared by Charles Townshend, a member of, 321; Shirley's contribution to the work of, 321; criticism of Secretary Robinson's proposals by Halifax, President of, 331

Boishebert, Charles Deschamps, Sieur de, commandant of Detroit, disposition of fur trade by, 46

Bollan, William, London agent of Massachusetts Bay, disturbing letter from, on the projected union of the colonies, 151–2; called upon to oppose the Albany Plan of Union, 155

Bombay, India, acquisition of, in 1668 by the London East India Company, 239; earlier acquisition of, by Charles II, 239–40; rights of Englishmen in, 240; suppression of mutiny at, 240; conditions under which, was held by the London East India Company, 240; right of coinage at, granted to the Company, in 1676, 240; a place of refuge after 1707, 247; the Portuguese in, made little progress, 248; great changes in, after its acquisition by the English, 248; incorporation of, in 1726, 249; local government within the presidency of, 249–50; cost of freight to, in 1748, 254; number of ships sent to, in 1748, 254

Bombay Presidency, creation of, after the death of Aurangzeb, 247; cost of supporting, in 1729–33 and 1750–55, 258

Bompar [Bompart], M., Governor of Martinique, orders carried by, for the evacuation of the neutralized islands, 306; shuffling conduct of, regarding the French evacuation of the neutralized islands, 314; forms a French militia in Dominica, 315

Bonaventure, M., commandant on Isle St. Jean, sends food supplies to Le Loutre, 190

Bonnard, M., Governor of St. Lucia, 226; surrenders St. Lucia to the English in 1664, 226

Bonne, Sieur de, concession of Sault Ste. Marie shared by, 54

Books, disturbing types of, not permitted in Canada, 12

Bordeaux, France, number of ships from, to Canada in 1754, 25; the amount of wine of, imported into Canada, 25

Borneo, Dutch factories on, 260; an English factory on, 260

Boscawen, Edward, vice-Admiral, arrival of, at Fort St. David, 274; assists in the attack upon Pondicherry, 274; supports the English expeditions against Tanjore, 275; aids in the peace treaty with the Rajah of Tanjore, 276; departure of, for England, 279; attempt of, to capture the French fleet in 1755, 338

Boston, Massachusetts Bay, size of, contrasted with Quebec, 15; opposition of, to a union of the colonies, 157; Capt. Cobb seeks aid in, for an expedition against Chignecto, 192; as a centre of British expansion, 340

Bouganville, Louis Antoine, an aide-de-camp of Montcalm, mémoire of, on the trading posts, 52–3

Boundary, vagueness of, between Canada and the Hudson's Bay Company lands, 4; vagueness of between Canada and New York, 5; dispute over, between Canada and Acadia, 187, 193, 306–10; 333–4; and between New France and the middle colonies, 327–38

Bowdoin, James, on the Massachusetts Bay committee of the House of Representatives on colonial union, favours a general union, 154

Brandy, use of, in Canada, 7; quantity of, imported into Canada, in 1754, 25; great premiums for, paid by Indian traders, 28; price of, in 1689, in the Indian trade contrasted with rum, 45; effect of restrictions on sale of, in the French Indian trade, 91; low price of, set at Niagara in 1750 to attract the Indian trade, 101

Brant, Molly, common-law wife of William Johnson, 95

Brattle, Col. William, on the committee on colonial union of the Massachusetts Bay House of Representatives, 151; favours a union of northern colonies, 154

Bread, great quantities of, sent to Cape Breton from the English colonies, 33

Bréard, Sieur, a monopoly of all Canadian charterings enjoyed by, 27

Brest, France, shipment of Canadian iron to, 24

Breton, Father le, French missionary on St. Vincent, 216

Bridges, Sir Tobias, leads the Barbadians against the Dutch on Tobago, 220

British colonies, in North America, lack of unity among, 110; the Board of Trade seeks to unite, on Indian policy, 111; meeting of representatives of, in Albany, 113–40; failure of, to agree upon a plan of union, 143–57

British Crown, see Crown, the British

British Empire, the, comment of Hutchinson on view of, held by Franklin in 1754, 160; characteristics of, 341–2; disadvantages of, in North America in face of French pressure, 345–6

British expansion in North America characterized, 340–1; small part played by the Crown in, 341; the local colonial governments and, 341

British manufactures, demand for, by the Canadian merchants, 62, 76, 78, 100; low prices of, in the Indian trade, in 1689, 45; and in 1749, 101; effect upon, of the New York law forbidding sale of trading goods to the French, 86

British navy, activities of, in the Indian Ocean in 1745–1756, 273–4; effects of superiority of, in King George's War, 298–9; the beginning of general Anglo-French hostilities and the, 338

British North America, British policy and the defence of, 1749–1754, 346–7; failure of the colonies to agree upon a plan to preserve, 347–8; the vision of, the future of, in the seventeenth and eighteenth centuries, 351

Broadcloth, value of English, sent to India in 1730, 255

Broglie, Duc de, French Ambassador in London, assurances given to, over Tobago, 222

Brosseau, Michil, contract of, as voyageur, 53

Budgrook, Malabar Coast coin, value of, 255–6

Bullion, prevailing movement of, from the west to the east, 235; export of, from England to India, 254

Burnet, William, Governor of New York, protests to Vaudreuil over the building of a post at Niagara, 83; encourages the movement of English traders to the Iroquois, 85; plan of, for a joint-stock Indian trading company, 85; secures a law against sale of trading goods to the French, 85; report of, on favourable effects of the law against sale of trading goods to the French, 86; requests permission of the Six Nations to erect a post at the mouth of the Onondaga, 86; writes that the English had traded for years at Oswego, 87; reply of, to the protest of Beauharnois over Fort Oswego, 89

Bussy-Castelnau, Charles-Joseph Patissier, Marquis de, sent to the Deccan to accompany Muzaffar Jang, 284; elevates Salabat Jang to the subahdarship of the Deccan, 284; chief adviser to Salabat in the Deccan, 284; profits by his position in the Deccan, 284; effect of absence of troops of, from the Carnatic, 284; advises Dupleix to act with decision in Indian affairs, 285

Butler, Thomas, at Oswego, does not fear a French attack, 94

Cabbages, cultivation of, in Canada, 13

Cabinet Council, British, proposal by, of February 7, 1755, for a mutual evacuation of the upper Ohio country, 330; proposal by, of February 9 for a mutual suspension of arms in North America, 330; convinced of the bad faith of France, 334–5; proposals of February 20 by, 335–6

Cabitibi [Abitibbi], Canada, trading post, number of bundles of furs drawn from, 54

Cadillac, Antoine de la Mothe, Sieur de, commandant of Detroit, extolls the Great Lakes region, 35; privileges enjoyed by, 46; comment of, on the criticism of the Indian trade by the French missionaries, 51; charges by, against the Jesuit mission of Michilimakinac, 51; hostility of, to the beaver monopoly of the Canada Company, 57

Cadiz, the purchase of silver at, for the East India Company, 255

Cahiers, of France, grievances of the peasantry and, 9

Caille, Laurend, contract of, as voyageur, 53

Calcutta, a place of refuge after 1707, 247; Job Charnock and the beginnings of, 247; the building of Fort William at, in 1696, 247; population of, in 1710 and in 1752, 247; incorporation of, in 1726, 249; local government within the presidency of, 249–50

Calcutta Presidency, the, organization of, after the death of Aurangzeb in 1707, 247; cost of supporting, 1729–33 and 1750–55, 258

Calicut, India, English factory at, 244, 260

Callières-Bonnevue, Louis Hector de, Governor of Montreal, advises in 1689 the seizing of Albany and New York, 45

Calot, Sieur, a monopoly of all slaughterhouse products for the King's troops at Quebec enjoyed by, 27

Camlets, imported by Canada, 25

Canada, the limits of, 4; colonization of, 5; the growth of the population of, 5; the habitants of, 6–8; the farms of, 8; churches in, 8; parishes of, 8; feudalism in, 8–10; isolation of, in the eighteenth century, 12; restriction on ideas in, 12; the development of a distinct civilization in, 13–4; the treatment of arable land in, 13; the life of women in, 13–4; military strength of, 19; the defence of, 19–20; fortified places in, 20; French Indian allies in, 20; government in, 21–3; value of furs exported from, 24; other exports from, in 1749, 24; total value of exports from, 24; manufacturing in, 24; shipbuilding in, 24; participation of, in the cod fisheries, 24; imports of, value of, 24–5; and description of, 25; ships required to bring imports to, 25; classification of ships arriving in, 25; amount of adverse balance against, 25; problem of providing cargoes for outgoing ships from, 25; shipping of, contrasted to that of Massachusetts Bay, 25; credit devices in, 26; a great financial liability, 26; royal expenditures for, 26; total revenues drawn from, 26; increasing cost of main-

taining, 26; danger of repudiating the debts of, 26; threat by the Crown to give up, 27; a public loan in France to save the credit of, 27; ruinous public economy in, 27; favouritism shown in the public affairs of, 27; monopolies for the supply of the King's troops in, 27; great frauds perpetrated by officials in, 27–8; the habitants of, long for independence, 29; control of people of, only by troops, 29; government of, faced by sedition, 29; wheat shortages in, 29; wheat imported into, from France, 30; impossibility of, competing on equal terms with British colonies, 32; a strong barrier to English ambitions, 32; the giving up of, considered, 31–2; life in the woods of, 32; the coureurs de bois a military asset of, 33; the progressive strengthening of, by France, 33; importation of wheat into, from the English colonies, 33; the dependencies of, 35; absolute dependence of, upon the fur trade, 42; the furs of, 55; the history of the beaver-skin monopoly in, 56–9; total value of furs exported from, in 1754, 61; total value of furs of, in 1754, 61; neutrality and the contraband trade between New York and, during and after the War of the Spanish Succession, 78; efforts directed against New England by, 78; Englishmen in, 90; foreigners in, forbidden to trade or to remain unless settled on the land, 90; merchants of, purchase wholesale from Oswego, 100; opposition of Massachusetts Bay to the English colonial provision trade with, 115; all kinds of supplies from the English colonies flow into, 115; Acadia and, during King George's War, 176–8; relations of, with Acadia after 1748, 179–205; French approaches to, to be protected by the British proposals of February 20, 1755, 336

Canada Company, organized in 1701, 57; acquires a monopoly of the export of beaver skins, 57; hostility of Cadillac to, 57; agreement of, with Aubert and Company in 1707, 57

Canassatego, Iroquoian chief, friendly to the English, death of, 107

Cannon, production of, in Canada, 24

Canots, Canadian communication by means of, 6

Canso, Isle of, British soldiers on, to protect the New England fisheries, 175; garrison of, overpowered in 1744, 176

Canso, Strait of, development of fisheries off, by New Englanders, 175

Cape Blomidon, Nova Scotia, 168

Cape Breton Island, great importation of food supplies from the English colonies into, 33; relation of, to the French fisheries, 80; the concert of New England colonies directed against, 123; see also Isle Royale

Cape Tormentine, the division of Acadia and, 336

Caps, the wearing of, in Canada, 7

Carassakaua, Indian convert at La Présentation, offers to get the Flat Heads to drive out the English, 106

Carénage (later Castries), St. Lucia, 224

Carew, Col., repossesses St. Lucia for the English, 226

Carheil, Father Etienne de, indictment of the French trading posts by, 51

Caribou, woodland, the Great Lakes region haunted by, 36

Caribs, chief centres of, in the Caribbeans, 208; basis of hostility of, on Dominica to the English, 209; treaty entered into with the French in 1640 by, 209; with the same in 1660, 209; the question of the original habitat of, 211; methods of conquest by, 212; cannibalism among, considered, 212-3; manner of waging war by, 213; no tribal government among, 213; the blood feud and, 213; military expeditions of, 213-4; enslavement of, 214; attempts at the christianization of, 214; the virtues of, 214-5; growing dependence of, upon the Europeans, 215; dying out of, on Dominica, 216; the relations of escaped Negroes and, of St. Vincent, 216; distinction between the red and black, of St. Vincent, 217; numbers of, on St. Vincent in 1763, 217; disappearance of, from Tobago, 218; expeditions of, against the Aroüagues, from St. Vincent, 218; drive Captain St. John from St. Lucia, 224

Carillon, Canada, number of bundles of furs drawn from, 54

Carlisle, John Hay, Earl of, grant to, by Charles I, 209, 224; failure of, and his heir to colonize St. Lucia, 225; lease of West India interests of, to Lord Willoughby, 225; surrender to the Crown of the patent to, 225

Carnatic, India, geographical limits of, 275; struggle for the control of, 276-96

Carts, the use of, at Niagara Falls in the handling of goods, 82

Carwar, India, best quality of pepper secured from, 256

Castor gras, the price of, fixed in 1677, 57; agreement of 1706 regarding surplus stock of, by Aubert and Company, 57; price of, fixed in 1722, 58; price of, in 1730, 58; and in 1746, 59

Castor gras d'hiver, finest of, drawn from de la Mer d'Ouest, 55

Castor sec, value of, in Canada, 56; the price of, fixed in 1677, 57; price of, in 1730, 58; price of, in 1746, 59

Catamount skins, value of, in Canada, 55-6

Catawba Indians, offer of Carassakaua of La Présentation to get the, to drive out the English, 106-7

Cathcard, Charles, 9th Baron, goes to Paris as a hostage in 1748, 301

Catherine, of Portugal, wife of Charles II, brings Bombay as part of her dowry, 239-40

Catholic Church, the, in Canada, as a landholder, 9; popularity of, 9; extent of its landholding, 11; freed of most obligations for holding seigneuries, 11; education by, 12; attitude of, toward the Indian trade, 51, 91

Cat-lynx, value of furs of, in Canada, 56

Cattle, the raising of, in Canada, 13

Caughnawaga Indians [Christian Indians, Praying Indians, French Mohawks], converted Iroquois, settled at Sault St. Louis, 76; great role of, in the Albany-Montreal contraband trade, 76; renounced by the Iroquoian Confederation, 76; efforts of the Six Nations to persuade the, to return home from Sault St. Louis, 96

Caulfeild, Deputy Governor of Nova Scotia, refuses passports to the Acadians, 171

Caylus, Marquis de, Governor of Martinique, proclamation of, respecting rights to Tobago, 223

Cayuga Bay, Beauharnois seeks to build a fort at, 90

Cayuga Indians, fighting strength of, 65; location of, 65; number of clans among, 70; number of phratries among, 70; number of ohwachira among, 71; position of, within the Confederation, 72; sachems of, express fear in 1720 of the French, 83; pro-French leanings of, after Aix-la-Chapelle, 98

Cazembazar, India, employees of the East India Company at, buy up the silk of Pultan, 256; English factory at, in 1750, 260

Cens et rentes, payment of, in Canada, 8-9

Censitaires, of Canada, relations of, to the seigneuries, 8

Ceylon, attempt of the French East India Company to capture, in 1673, 262

Chalet, Sieur François, representative in Canada of the Compagnie des Indes, posts of Niagara and Frontenac leased by, 47; willingness of, to cancel leases, 47

Chambers, John, a member of the New York Council, attends the Albany Congress, 114

Chambly, Montreal-Albany contraband trade by, 76; number of bundles of fur going to Albany via, 87

Champlain Fault and the St. Lawrence lowlands, 6

Champlain, Samuel de, seigneurial grants made by, 10; the vision of, for Canada lacks reality in the eighteenth century, 42, 351; Acadia and, 168

Chanda Sahib [French Sandesaeb], son-in-law of Dost Ali and rival for the nabobship of Arcot, 272; made captive by the Mahrattas in 1741, 272; release of, through the intervention of Dupleix, 276; agreement of, with Dupleix, 276; victory of, over Anwar-ud-din, 277; becomes Nabob of the Carnatic, 277; gifts showered upon the Compagnie des Indes and its agents by, 277; desires aid of Dupleix in the capture of Gingy, 279; expedition of, against Tanjore and Trichinopoly, 279–80; terms exacted from the Rajah of Tanjore by, 280; begins the siege of Trichinopoly, 281; goes to meet Nasir Jang, 281; continued support of, by Dupleix, 282; possession of Trichinopoly by, before 1741, 286; determination of, to repossess Trichinopoly, 286; sends forces against Clive at Arcot, 288; forced to defend himself at Seringham, 289; surrenders self to Monacjee, 289; death of, 289

Chandernagore, India, the French factory at, made subordinate to Pondicherry in 1699, 203

Chandler, Col. John, Judge of the Worcester County Court, a commissioner from Massachusetts Bay at the Albany Congress, 114

Chaplains, requirement for, on East India ships, 265

Charles I, King of England, grant of West India islands to Carlisle by, 209, 224; grant of a licence to trade in the Far East to the Courteen Associates by, 238–9

Charles II, King of England, agreement of, with Duke of Courland, 219–20; grant of a new charter to the London East

India Company by, 239; grant of Bombay by, 239

Charleston, South Carolina, as a centre of British expansion, 340

Charlevoix, Father, testimony of, as to the loyalty of the Acadians, 191

Charnisay, de, see D'Aunay

Charnock, Job, activities of, in Bengal, 247

Charters, alterations in the Rhode Island and Connecticut, recommended by Shirley, 161; account of, received by the East India companies, 235–42

Château of St. Louis, Quebec, fealty and homage by Canadian seigneurs made at, 11

Chauvreux, Father, priest at Piziquid, appeals for additional priests for Nova Scotia, 198; opposed by Le Loutre, 198–9; Abbé d'Isle-Dieu's opinion of, 199

Cheeves, Ezekiel, on the committee on colonial union of the Massachusetts Bay Council, 151

Chequamegon Bay, Indian mission, established at, 42; Indian trade at, granted to Sieur la Ronde, 47; decision of the French minister to continue leasing the post at, 48; number of bundles of fur drawn from, 54; post at, leased after 1733, 54; value of the lease for, 55

Cherokee nation, events among, 3; plan of Abbé Piquet to make war upon, 106; Iroquois at La Présentation encouraged to attack, 106

Chibouctou Bay, Halifax established on, 181; the Indians determine to destroy the settlement at, 189; see also Halifax

Chickens, raising of, in Canada, 13

Chignecto, Isthmus of, description of the region of, 167; Acadian settlements about, 168; church communicants within the parish of, 170–1; intractable attitude of the people living upon the, 175; Shirley desires a fortress erected on the, 180; supplies from, support the Louisbourg garrison, 186; hostile Indians gathered at, under Le Loutre, 192; Cornwallis plans for an expedition against, postponed, 192; disavowal of the French proceedings upon, by Puysieulx, 305; Rouillé points out the necessity for the destruction of the English fort on, 332

Child, Sir Josiah [Josia], Governor of the London East India Company, interest of, in territorial acquisitions, 250

Chilloes, fabric of India exported, 252

China, the freight charge from, in 1748, 254; exports from, to England in 1748, 254; number of ships leased for trade to, by the East India Company in 1748, 254; the trade of the Compagnie des Indes to, 266

Chinese, early commercial relations of, with India, 234

Chinsura, India, a Dutch factory at, in the eighteenth century, 260

Chintz, fabric of India, exported, 252; the production of, in England, 258; preferred to that of India, 258

Chippewa [Saulteurs], Indians, location of, 40; estimates of strength of, 40, 41; the Five Nations turned back by, 74; number of, trading at Oswego in 1749, 101

Choate, Col. John, on the committee on colonial union of the Massachusetts Bay House of Representatives, 151; favours a union of the northern colonies, 154

Choctaw nation, 3; civil war among, 72; projects of Abbé Piquet to use the, to drive the English traders from the Ohio, 106

Chowtars, fabric of India, exported, 252

Christian Indians, from the Lake of the Two Mountains, number of, trading at Oswego in 1749, 101; see also Caughnawaga Indians

Chuckloes, fabric of India, exported, 252

Church of St. Anne, the appearance of, on the St. Lawrence a good omen for mariners, 14

Church of the Assumption, Minas Bay, Nova Scotia, church communicants within the parish of, 170

Church of the Holy Trinity, Minas Bay, Nova Scotia, church communicants within the parish of, 170

Churches, in Canada, 8; in Acadia, 170

Clans, Iroquoian, numbers of, within the tribes, 70; names of, 70; marriage and, 70; activities of, 71; the preservation of, 71

Clarke, Lieut. Gov. George, of New York, importance of Oswego according to, 91; on the defenceless condition of Oswego, 93; plan of, to defend Lake Ontario, 131

Claus [Claasse], Lawrence, Indian interpreter for the New York Indian Commissioners, goes to Niagara to protest the building of the French post, 83; reply of, to Joncaire, 84

Claverie, Sieur, a monopoly of all supplies for the King's warehouse at Quebec enjoyed by, 27

Clinton, George, Governor of New York, orders the strengthening of Oswego in 1743, 90; plan of, in 1747 for an attack on Niagara and Crown Point, 44; puts aside plan fearing the Albany assembly-

men, 94; desires to lay hands upon young Joncaire, 96; complains to the Governor General in 1750 over French activities, 99; called the Albany Indian conference of 1750, 99; desires a colonial concert during King George's War, 123

Clinton, Sir Henry, British general, on the treatment of women prisoners by the Iroquoian Indians, 73

Clive, Robert, early activities of, in India, 287; permitted to lead a force against Arcot, 287-8; defence of Arcot by, 288; capture of d'Auteuil and troops by, 289

Cloth, types of, imported by Canada, 25; preference of Indians for English, 62; inability of the French to manufacture suitable, for the Indian trade, 62; high price of India, in 1754, 257; of East India, restrictions on the sale of, in Great Britain, 258; the reconditioning of, in Great Britain permitted, 258

Cloves, the importation of, into England from the Far East, 236

Cobb, Captain, places responsibility for Indian uprisings upon Le Loutre, 192; goes to Boston to recruit men for an expedition against Chignecto, 192

Cobequid Bay, Acadian settlement about, 168; church communicants of the parish of, 170; desire of Acadians of, to submit to the English, 197

Cochin, India, a Dutch fort at, in the eighteenth century, 260

Cod, dried, amount of export of, from Canada in 1754, 24

Cod fisheries, Canadian participation in, 24; number of French vessels engaged in, 24

Cognatic descent, Iroquois Indians and, 70

Coinage, the right of, granted to the London East India Company in 1676, 240; privileges of, enjoyed by Dupleix, 283

Colbert, Jean-Baptiste, Marquis de Seignelay, contrôleur général of France, organizes the Compagnie des Indes Orientales in 1664, 261

Colden, Cadwallader, Surveyor General of New York, interest of, in natural history, 15; on the treatment of women prisoners by the Iroquoian Indians, 73; on the advantages enjoyed in the fur trade by the English, 87; criticises Franklin's "Short Hints," 127

Coleroon River, India, English military operations on, in 1749, 276

College of the Jesuits, Quebec, description of the building belonging to, 16

Colonial concert, desire for, in 1754, 123; plans for, under Leisler, 123; suggestions for, during King William's War presented by Governor Fletcher, 123; revived during Queen Anne's War, 123; of New England colonies during King George's War, 123; *see also* English colonial union

Colonial revenues, plan of Halifax to support frontier forts by means of, 162

Colonial trade, with Cape Breton, 33; Massachusetts Bay opposes, with Louisbourg and Canada, 115; *see also* contraband trade, fur trade

Colonials, English, attitude of, toward nature, 6; lack of appreciation by, of the red man's culture, 108, insatiable desire of, for good land, 108; offer to the Indians greater material rewards, 108; particularistic attitude of, 144, 165–6; individualism among, 340–1; toleration among, 341; French, *see habitants*

Colonization, within the British Empire, 340; within the French Empire, 342

Commander-in-Chief, in America, the appointment of, urged by the Board of Trade, 163

Commerce, of New France, 24–5, 33, 268; of India, 234–5, 247–8, 252–7, 267–9, 349–50

Commissaries, Anglo-French, activities of, 304–27; royal, of the Compagnie des Indes, activities of, 270–1

Commissary General for Indian affairs, appointment of a, urged by the Board of Trade, 163

Commissaire Ordonnateur, of Isle Royale, criticism of the work of Bigot as, 21; of Louisiana, activities of, compared with those of the Intendant of New France, 22–3

Compagnie des Indes Occidentales, the grant of Canada to, in 1664, 10; failure of, to make seigneurial grants, 10; a monopoly of the beaver-skin trade enjoyed by, 56

Compagnie d'Occident, monopoly of the export of all beaver skins acquired by, in 1717, 58; organized by John Law, 58; merging of, into the Compagnie des Indes in 1719, 58

Compagnie des Indes Orientales, organization of, in 1664 by Colbert, 261; privileges of, 261; activities of, to 1719, 261–3; indictment of, in 1719, 263; poor management displayed by, 263; absorption of, into the Compagnie Perpetuelle des Indes, 263–4

Compagnie François des Isles de l'Amerique, 1642, 218

Company of One Hundred Associates, 1627, Canadian seigneurial grants made by, 10; a monopoly of the beaver trade enjoyed by, 56

Compagnie Perpetuelle des Indes, warehouses of, in Montreal, 17; bills of exchange against, written in Canada, 25; beaver-skin monopoly of, 27; the Governor General of New France shares in the beaver monopoly enjoyed by, 27; organization of, in 1719, 58; collapse of, in 1720, 58, 264; reorganization of, in 1722, 58, 264; monopoly of the export of beaver skins retained by, 58, 264; attempts of, to stabilize the price paid for beaver skins, 1722–1750, 58–9; losses sustained by, in sale of beaver skins in Europe, 58–9; the amount of beaver skins secured by, 59; criticism of the report of, by the Canadian merchants, 59–60; the proportion of the fixed capital of, invested in the beaver monopoly, 59, 267; most of the Canadian furs do not reach the warehouses of, 61–2; difference in prices paid for beaver by the English and by the, 62; deductions in the prices paid by, for beaver skins, 62; inability of, to supply the needs of the Indians, 62; great commitments of, 264; privileges retained, 264; capitalization of, increased, 264; monopoly of the African trade reserved to, 264; the *ferme* of tobacco enjoyed by, 264; also, the commerce of the East Indies and of Santo Domingo and the proprietorship of Louisiana reserved to, 264–5; retrocession of Louisiana by, in 1731, 265; involvement of, in debt, 265; expansion of harbour facilities of Port L'Orient by, 265; improvement of affairs of, in the Far East after 1726, 265; ships of, in the Far East in 1734, 265; commodities imported by, from the Far East, 265; value of imports sold at L'Orient in 1742 by, 266; shipping possessed by, in 1754, 266; disposition of the ships of, in 1754, 266–7; financial condition of, in 1752 analysed, 267–9; disposition of the funds of, 267–8; in reality an extension of government into business, 269–70; organization of activities of, under the decree of 1748, 270; the control of, in the directorate, 270–1; ships of, captured in the Indian Ocean in 1745, 273; warm approval by, of Dupleix's active support of Chanda Sahib, 278; gifts of *aldees* made to, by Chanda, 278; *aldees* secured from the Rajah of Tanjore for, 279–80; great gifts to, by Mazaffar Jang, 283; large revenues anticipated by, from new India acquisitions, 283; gifts previously received by, from Chanda Sahib and Muzaffar Jang ratified by Salabat Jang, 284; failure of revenues from the new possessions of, 285; the stifling of the commerce of, in India, 285; loss of troops of, in India, 289; optimistic report from Dupleix received by, 289–90; true state of affairs in India sent by the *Conseil Supérieur* to, in 1753, 290–1; the *directeurs* of, turn upon Dupleix, 292; a representative of, sent to London to work out an accommodation, 294; basis for an alliance suggested by, 294; attitude of the United Company toward the proposals of, 294; the plan of, for peace, 294; the repudiation of Dupleix by, 295; Godeheu sent to India by, 295; precarious condition of the affairs of, in India in 1754, 295–6; terms of the temporary treaty signed between the United East India Company and, in 1754, 296; why the treaty was advantageous to, 296–7

Conajohary [Conojoharie, Connojahary], Upper Mohawk Castle, a church with a bell requested for, 121; the mission of Jacob Eblig at, 121; scene of the Christian labours of the Indian Abraham, 121

Conajohary Indians, *see* Mohawks

Conduct of the Government with Regard to Peace and War (Dublin, 1748) 301

Conestoga Indians, Iroquoian family, crushing of, by the Five Nations, 69

Congés, see licences.

Congress of Aix-la-Chapelle, *see* Aix-la-Chapelle

Congress of Westphalia, contrast of, with that at Aix-la-Chapelle, 300

Connecticut, commissioners of, attend the Albany Indian conference of 1750, 99; not included by the Board of Trade in the call for an Indian conference in 1754, 113; commissioners sent to Albany to represent, 114; powers granted by, to its commissioners, 115; purchase of lands claimed by, from the Six Nations by the Susquehanna Company, 122; charter claims of western lands by, 122; quota of men assigned to, in King William's War, 123; representation of, under the " Plan of a Proposed Union," 130; under the Pownall proposal, to help defend Lake Ontario, 131; representation of, under the Albany Plan of

Union, 135; opposition of the commissioners of, to the Albany Plan, 139; objections of the Assembly of, to the Albany Plan of Union, 148–50; loyalty of, to the system of government established by England, 149; influence of the Susquehana Company over the proceedings of, 149–50; recommendation of, for the planting of western settlements, 150; later support of the Federal Constitution by, 150; Shirley advocates alterations in the charter government of, 161

Conseil Supérieur, of Pondicherry, the establishment of, in 1699, 262; jurisdiction of, 262–3; support of Dupleix's demands respecting Madras in 1746 by, 273; a true state of affairs in India sent to the Compagnie des Indes. by, 290–1; *see also* Superior Council of Canada

Considerations on the Definitive Treaty signed at Aix-la-Chapelle October 7 [18], 1748 (London, 1748), 301

Contraband trade, significance of Sault St. Louis in, between Albany and Montreal, 76; the French king's revenues affected by, 76; the Albany trade regulations and, 76; New York law of 1720 to do away with, between Albany and Montreal, 85; Peter Wraxall on, 86; law against, referred to the Board of Trade, 86; effect of restrictions placed upon, 86; London merchants petition against forbidding, 86; activity in, via Chambly, 87; connection of Lydius with, 90; renewed activity in, after the Peace of Aix-la-Chapelle, 99; charges by Chief Hendrick of great activity in, at Albany, 120; between Acadia and Cape Breton, 186, 190

Convents, of Canada, elderly nuns in, 14

Cooke, Robert, Governor of St. Lucia, disavows the restitution of St. Lucia to the French, 227

Coopies, fabric of India, exported, 252

Cope, Jean Baptiste, a leader of the Micmacs, makes peace with the English, 197

Copper, efforts of the French to discover, in the Lake Superior region, 47

Corne, Captain de la, victory of, at Grand Pré, 179; sent into the region of the Acadian peninsula, 187; commander of the French troops on the Isthmus of Chignecto, forces Major Lawrence to retire, 193; threatens the Acadians with a massacre, 194; Acadians petition, to return to their homes, 195

Cornwallis, Col. Edward, plan of ministry to send to America, as Lord Commissioner, 166; commissioned Captain General and Governor of Nova Scotia, 181–2; early favourable report of, on conditions in Nova Scotia, 182; poor opinion of, of the first English settlers in Nova Scotia, 182–3; instructions received by, respecting the oaths of allegiance to be taken by all Acadians, 183; decision of, to send soldiers to Minas, 184; guarantees given to loyal Acadians by, 184; sets date for an oath of fidelity, 184; protests the presence of Le Loutre in Nova Scotia, 188; complains of the hostile attitude of the French, 190; admits that the English have inveterate enemies in the Acadians, 191; orders companies of soldiers from Newfoundland to Nova Scotia, 193; sends a force to the Missaquash, 194; enters into a treaty with Cope's Micmacs, 197; agrees to secure a priest for the Acadians of Rivière aux Canards, 197; succeeded at Halifax by Hopson, 197; during the administration of, little progress in the spread of settlements in Nova Scotia, 200; accused of committing aggressions, 305

Coromandel Coast, cost of freight to, in 1748, 254; number of ships sent to, in 1748, 254; Dupleix becomes Mensebdar of, 283; *see also* Madras, Pondicherry, Fort St. David, St. Thomé

Corva and Associates, monopoly of, in the St. Lawrence salmon fisheries, 27

Corvée, the Canadian seigneuries and, 10

Cosné, Ruvigny de, see De Cosné, Ruvigny

Cossaes, fabric of India, exported, 252

Cotton, amount of, imported into England in 1701 and 1751, 258

Cotton cloth, of India, varieties of, exported, 252; of England, protected by law, 258; of Siam, imported into Canada, 25

Cotton yarn, amount of, imported from India in 1730, 256

Couagne, M. de, Montreal merchant, on the prices of furs, 55

Coulon, Captain, recommended by the Bishop of Quebec for his victory at Grand Pré, 178

"Council of Defence," agreement to a joint, by the Dutch and the English East India companies, in 1619, 237

Courcelles, Daniel de Remy de, Governor General of New France, on the extermination of beaver in the Iroquoian country, 74

Coureurs de bois, a great asset to New France in time of war, 33; activities of,

43; numbers of, 43; efforts to control, 44; excesses of, 45; find a market for their furs among the English, 61; resort to Oswego, 91

Courland, Jacobus, Duke of, plants a settlement on the Island of Tobago, 218; agreement of, with the Lampsins, 219; capture of, by the Swedes, 219; agreement of, with Charles II of England, 219–20; inability of, to re-establish himself on Tobago, 220–1; death of, 221; efforts of the successor of, to colonize Tobago, 221–2

Courteen, Sir William and Associates, given a licence to trade in the Far East, in 1637, 238–9; the London East India Company absorbs, 239

Coutis, Sieur de, Governor of St. Lucia, 226

Covelong, India, the gift of, by Chanda Sahib to Dupleix, 277

Cree [Christinaux] Indians, location of, 40; estimates of strength of, 40

Creek Nation, events relating to, 3

Cromwell, Oliver, the Charter of 1657 granted to the London East India Company by, 236

Cross fox skins, value of, in Canada, 56

Crown, the British, the Five Nations dependent on, 79; western lands of Iroquois deeded to, 83; attitude of the Albany Congress toward the powers of, 138; the prerogatives of, and the Albany Plan of Union, 160–1; prerogatives of, and the House of Commons, 242

Crown, the French, relation of, with the Compagnie des Indes, 270; concentration of all authority within the French Empire in, 342

Crown Point, production of naval stores at, 23; Mohawk raiding parties operate in the region of, during King George's War, 96; *see also* Fort St. Frédéric

Cuddalore, India, the location of Fort St. David on the outskirts of, 291

Cugnet, Sieur, manager of the St. Maurice iron works, a fortune acquired by, 28

Cullannies, fabric of India, exported, 252

Cumberland Basin, Nova Scotia, 167

Cumberland, George Clifford, 3rd Earl of, rediscovers St. Lucia, 224

Curatorship, the Canadian seigneuries and, 10

Curés, position of, in Canada, 8; the Canadian seigneurs and the, 11

Cushtoes, fabric of India, exported, 252

Cutcheries, headquarters in India for the gomastahes, 252

Cuyahoga Bay, the region between, and the Maumee proposed as neutral territory, 335

Cuyahoga River, see Rivière Blanche

Dabul, India, English factory at, in 1750, 260

d'Aigremont, Sieur, Governor of St. Lucia, 226

d'Amblimont, Marquis, Governor General of the French West Indies, English protest to, over French activities on St. Lucia, 227–8

Dartmouth, Nova Scotia, establishment of, 201

Daudin, Father, sent to Nova Scotia, 200; instructed by Le Loutre, 200; develops resistance among his parishioners against the English, 200; threatened with expulsion, 200; ordered to leave Nova Scotia, 205; permitted to remain when parishioners of Piziquid promise good conduct, 205

D'Aunay Charnisay, Charles, Seigneur, Acadia and, 168

d'Auteuil [Auteil, de], French officer in India, sent against Anwar-ud-din, 277; gift of Allamhana to, 277; French force under, aids in the investment of Trichinopoly, 288; the capture of the forces led by, by Capt. Clive, 289

Decca, India, an English factory at, in 1750, 260

De Cosné, Ruvigny, Secretary of the British Embassy in France, recommended to membership on the Anglo-French joint commission by Mildmay, 315; appointment of, in 1752, 316; becomes chargé d'affaires in Paris upon the death of Albemarle, 328

Deer, Six Nations clan, 70–1

Deer skins, importance of, as an export from Canada, 56

d'Heu, Father Jacques, S.J., activities of, at Onondaga during Queen Anne's War, 81

Dekanawida, culture hero of the Iroquois, the Great Binding Law and, 69

De la Mer d'Ouest, post of, and the search for the Western Sea, 51; number of bundles of furs drawn from, 54; value of the lease of, in 1750, 55; character of the furs secured from, 55

de Lancey, Lieutenant Governor of New York, takes over the duties of Governor, 111; presides at the Albany Congress, 114; determination of, to control the proceedings of the Congress, 116–7; answers the charges of the Indians respecting the Albany trade, 120; opposition of, to the Albany Plan of Union, 139; testifies to the strong support given by the commissioners to the Plan, 139; forwards to the Board of Trade the Plan, 146; presents to the New York Assembly the Plan, 147

Delaware Indians, dependence of, upon the Iroquoian Confederation, 66; invite the Pennsylvania traders to the Ohio, 120

De Léry, Gaspard Chassegros, military engineer, the fortification of Quebec planned by, 17; changes the site for Fort Niagara, 88

Denmark, the sale of French beaver hats in, 61

Denonville [Des Noville], Jacques Réné de Brisay, Marquis de, Governor General of New France, invasion of the Seneca country by, in 1687, 75; agreement of, to withdraw the French garrison from the Niagara, 75

Deseuslaves, Father, priest of Port Royal parish, appeals for additional priests for Nova Scotia, 198; opposed by Le Loutre, 198–9; Abbé d'Isle-Dieu's opinion of, 99

Desherbiers, M., commandant of Louisbourg, protest of Cornwallis to, over the activities of Le Loutre, 188

d'Esnambuc, Pierre, Sieur, grant to, by Richelieu, 209; nature of colonizing commission given by Richelieu to de Rossey and, 225

d'Estrées, Count, French Admiral, ejects the Dutch from Tobago in 1677, 200

d'Estrées, Marshal, grant of St. Lucia to, in 1719, 228; attempted colonization of St. Lucia by, in 1720, 228

De Soto, Hernando, the discovery of the Mississippi by, and Spanish claims, 332

Detroit, monopolies for the supply of the King's troops at, 27; methods of carrying on the fur trade at, 46; appearance of, in 1750, 50; value of the trade of, 46; the most important French trading post, 53; number of traders at, 53; number of bundles of fur obtained from, 53; cost of transporting fur between, and Montreal, 53; The Canada Company beaver monopoly adversely affects, 57; establishment of, in 1701, at the Iroquoian Tieugsachrondio, 45, 77; the uneasiness of the Iroquois with the founding of, 77–8; inferior to Oswego as a fur-trading center, 92; the retention of, by France provided for in the British proposals of February 20, 1755, 336

Devi-Cotah [Devicota], English capture of, in 1749, 276; ceded to the English, 276; the East India Company directors rebuke the Madras council for the taking of, 278; the retention of, authorized by the Company, 278; British soldiers from, go to the relief of Trichinopoly, 280; Anglo-French agreement over, 296

Diking, the practice of, in Acadia, 168

Dinwiddie, Gov. Robert, of Virginia, plans of, for an Indian conference at Winchester, 112; considers the Southern Indians more important than the Six Nations, 112; invitation of, to the Iroquoian Confederation for a treaty conference ignored, 120; unfavorable attitude of, toward the Albany Plan of Union, 145–6

Directeurs, of the Compagnie des Indes, appointment of, and powers of, 270–1

d'Isle-Dieu, Abbé, Vicar General of the French colonies, on the Micmac treaty with the English, 197; opposes sending additional priests to Nova Scotia, 199; suggests the ostensible grounds for refusal, 199; favours sending additional priests to Le Loutre, 199

Divi, Island of, India, given to the Compagnie des Indes, 283; temporary Anglo-French treaty neutralizes, 296; the United East India Company not inclined to insist on an exclusive control of, 322

Dobbs, Gov. Arthur, of North Carolina, praise of the government of Great Britain by, 146

Dolbeau, Father John, Recollet, work of, among the Montagnais, 41

Dominica, West Indies, neutralization of, 207, 211, 215; description of, 207; importance of, 207–8; early history of European contacts with, 208–9; hostility of natives of, toward the English, 204; guaranteed to the Caribs in 1660, 209; effort of English to build a fort on, 211; free of European inhabitants in 1700, 211; colonization of, from Guadeloupe and Martinique, 215; sugar plantations on, 215; failure of the French to evacuate, 215; situation of the French in, in 1763, 216; Mildmay's suggestion respecting the settlement of the problem of, 318

Dongan, Col. Thomas, Governor of New York, interest of, in the Niagara River, 75; policies of, respecting the Five Nations clash with those of Denonville, 77

Don Philip, the Treaty of Aix-la-Chapelle and, 301

Dooreos, fabric of India, exported, 252

Dost Ali, Nabob of Arcot, rivalry over the vacancy left by the death of, 272

Dravidians, invasion of India by, 232

Droit de chasse, the Canadian seigneuries and, 10

Droit de justice, Canadian seigneuries and, 9

Droit de pêche, the Canadian seigneuries and, 10

Drugs, East India, East India Company auction of, 257

Duchesneau, Jacques, Intendant of New France, report of, regarding the violation of royal orders, 44

Dumas, M., Governor of Pondicherry, 265

Dunkirk, the fortifications of, to be destroyed by the Treaty of Aix-la-Chapelle, 301; previously fortified contrary to treaty, 302

Dunning, John, author of " An Account of the Charters Granted to the East India Company," 236–7

Dupleix, Joseph François, superintendent of the Chandernagore factory, successful activities of, 266; appointed Governor of Pondicherry and placed in charge of all French factories in India in 1742, 266; Pondicherry aided by, with the private funds of, 271; becomes deeply involved in political activities in India, 271–93; proposes neutrality in India on outbreak of King George's War, 273; summons La Bourdonnais from Mauritius, 273; wins the neutrality of the Nabob of Arcot by the promise of Madras, 273; friction over Madras between La Bourdonnais and, 274; forces of, defeat the army of the Nabob of Arcot, 274; attack on Fort St. David by, 274; plans of, for Madras, 274–5; brings about the release of Chanda Sahib, 276; agreement of, with Chanda Sahib and Muzaffar Jang, in 1749, 276–7; forces of, aid in the overthrow of Anwar-ud-din, 277; receives the gift of Covelong, 277; sends an expedition to Tanjore, 279–80; grounds for hostility of, against the Rajah, 280; hard terms granted to the Rajah by, 280; negotiations of, with Nasir Jang, 282; a treaty agreed to between the Nasir and, 282; great favours shown to, by Muzaffar Jang, 283; becomes Mensebdar of the Coromandel Coast, 283; supplies Muzaffar with a French force, 284; upon death of Muzaffar agrees to elevate Salabat Jang to the Subahdarship of the Deccan, 284; the mastery of India and, in 1751, 285; implications of the system of, 285; sends troops from Pondicherry to recapture Arcot, 288; sends a force to aid Chanda Sahib before Trichinopoly, 288–9; dangerous situation of, in 1752, 289; optimistic report of, to the Compagnie in 1752, 289–90; refuses to compromise with Muhammed Ali, 290; provides a great display at Pondicherry, 290; wins over the *Dalaway* of Mysore, 290; sends a new force against Trichinopoly, 290; desires an attack on Fort St. David, 291; rebuked by the *directeurs* of the Compagnie, 292; seeks to clear his record at Pondicherry, 292; the Compagnie determines to repudiate the system of, 292–3; efforts of, to reach an accommodation with Madras in 1754, 293; replaced by Godeheu and ordered to return to France, 295; last days of, 295

Dupleix, Madame, receives the gift of Porto Novo, 277

Dupuy, M., Intendant of New France, desires to build additional forts on Lake Ontario and on the Niagara, 88; fears the presence of the English at Montreal, 90; recommends that Englishmen be removed to Quebec, 90

Duquesne, Ange de Menneville, Marquis de, Governor General of New France, seizure of Canadian wheat by, 31; finds famine in Canada, 31

Durel, Mr., military engineer, the site selected by, for the English settlement in Nova Scotia changed, 182

Dutch, appearance of, in the Far East, 235; the Portuguese driven from the Spice Islands by the, 235

Dutch nation, during the War of the Austrian Succession, 298

Dutch United East India Company, 1602, rivalry between the London East India Company and, 235–7; dividends paid by, 259; establishments of, in 1750, 260; defends Ceylon from the French in 1673, 262; recovers St. Thomé from the French, 262; capture Pondicherry from the French in 1693 but return it, 262

Du Vivier, attempt of, to attack Annapolis Royal, 177

East India Company, see Dutch United East India Company, 1602; Governor and Company of Merchants of London trading into the East Indies, 1600; English Company trading to the East Indies, 1698; United Company of Merchants of England trading to the East Indies, 1702; Compagnie de Indes Orientales, 1664; and Compagnie Perpetuelle des Indes, 1719

East India House, London, 251

East Indiamen, of the eighteenth century, tonnage of, 253–4; prices for lease of, paid by the East India Company, 254; owners of, members of the Company as a rule, 254; destination of, 254; privileges enjoyed by the captains of, 258

East Indies, the, activities of the Portuguese in, 235; of the Dutch in, 235, 237, 260; of the English in, 235–60, 273–96, 349–50; of the French in, 261–96, 349–50

East New Jersey, quota of men assigned to, in King William's War, 123

Eblig, Jacob, the mission of, at Conajohary, 121

Eboe Negroes, characteristics of, 68

Écarlatines, the manufacture of, in England for the Indian trade, 62; the purchase of, by the French, 62

Écu, French coin, value of, in Canada, 8

Education, in Canada, 12

Eel, a Six Nations clan, 70–1

Elizabeth, Queen, charters the London East India Company, 285; sends an address to Akbar, 235

Elk, the extermination of, in the region of the Five Nations, 74

Elk skins, value of, in Canada, 55–6

Emmerties, fabric of India, exported, 252

En arrière fief, some land in Canada held, 8

En censive, land in Canada held, 8

England, the naval power of, could never be equalled by France, 33; the beaver hat industry of, 60–1; Iroquoian mission to, 78

Englishmen, the sending of underground Belts to Indian nations by, 89; the removal from Montreal to Quebec of, ordered, 90; colonization of Nova Scotia by, 181–2; in the West Indies, 207–230; in the Far East, 235–60, 272–96, 349–50

English colonials, see Colonials, English

English colonial union, anxiety of Governor Shirley, for, in 1754, 113; strong support of, by the Massachusetts Bay assembly, 114; early efforts toward, 123; plans for, at Albany, 124–40; hostile attitude of colonials toward, in 1754, 143–57; plans developed in Massachusetts

Bay for, 152–5; Shirley's proposals for, 158; the Board of Trade's plan for, 161–2; final attainment of, in 1775, 166

English colonies, the, dangers to French and Spanish possessions in America from, 32; the Albany congress favours the contracting of the western bounds of, to the Appalachian Mountains, 133; the separation of, from the mother country and the failure of the Albany Plan of Union, 140

English Company trading to the East Indies, the, chartering of, in 1698, 243; activities of, 243–5; consolidation of, with the London East India Company, 245

English traders, among the Six Nations, 84–5; at Fort Oswego, 88, 91, 100; project of Abbé Piquet to drive from the Ohio all, 106

En roture, Canadian lands held, 9

Erie Indians, Iroquoian family, the crushing of, by the Five Nations, 69, 74

Escheats, the Canadian seigneuries and, 9

Estébe, Sieur, a manager of the St. Maurice iron works, 28

Etchemins, the ancient district of, in Acadia, 333

Europeans, disadvantages of, in commercial relations with India, 234–5

Evans, Lewis, Pennsylvania surveyor and map-maker, description of Oswego in 1743 by, 92

Fabrics, list of, exported from India in 1750, 252

Families, of Canada, the size of, 13

Family, the, in Canada, 7; meaning of, among the Iroquois, 20

Farms, in Canada, 6, 8

Far West Indians, the Iroquois and, 74; resort to Oswego, 91

Fealty and homage, Canadian seigneurial grants and, 11

Feuguieres [Fouguieres], Chevalier de, Governor General of the French Caribbee Islands, project of, against the Negroes of St. Vincent, 216–7; orders the retirement of the English from St. Lucia, 228

Firearms of Saint-Étienne, imported into Canada, 25

Firuz Jang, receives a commission as Subahdar of the Deccan, 293; Salabat Jang attacked by, 293–4; deposes the ruling Mogul, 294

Fish, the production of, in Canada, for the West Indies, 23

Fisher, the Great Lakes region haunted by, 36

Fisheries, participation of Canada in the cod, 24; of the Isle of Canso, growth of New England interest in, 175; French interest in, 175

Fish oil, amount of, exported from Canada in 1754, 24

Fitzwalter, Earl of, a Lord Commissioner of the Treasury, 303; Mildmay in Paris corresponds with, 304

Five Nations, origin of the expression of, 72; see also Iroquoian Confederation

"Flags of Truce," the use of English, in the War of the Austrian Succession, 299

Flanders, the War of the Austrian Succession and, 298

Flannel, imported into Canada, 25

Flat Head Indians, see Catawba

Flax, the application of the principles of mercantilism in Canada and the production of, 23

Fletcher, Gov. Benjamin, of New York, plan of colonial concert suggested by, 123

Florida, the northern frontier of, 3

Flour, lack of export of, from Canada in 1754, 24; seizure of, in Canada by Duquesne, 31; great quantities of, sent to Cape Breton from the English colonies, 33

Floyer, Charles, President of the Madras Council, responsibility of, for the taking of Devi-Cotah, 276; rebuked by the East India Company, 278; succeeded by Thomas Saunders, 279

Folles Avoines, see Menominee Indians

Food, supplies of, for the French forces in America secured from the English colonies, 34; shortage of, in Canada, compel the forces at Beauséjour to scatter, 196; abundance of, in the English colonies, 341; see also beef, bread, fish flour, pork, rye, vegetables, wheat

Fordyce, the Rev. Francis, complaint of, against Clive, 287

Forests, of the Great Lakes region, enormous size of trees of, 35

Fort Beauharnois, outpost for La Baye, established for discovery of the Western Sea, 51

Fort Beauséjour, building of, north of the Missaquash, 194; the French forces at, scatter due to food shortage, 196

Fort Chamblé, a proposed boundary for New France to run by, 337

Fort de Coque [Coc], St. Lucia, surrendered to the English, 226

Fort Detroit [de Tret], a strong garrison at, 20; *see also* Detroit

Fort Edward, establishment of, at Minas, 191; Acadians of Piziquid show hostility against the garrison of, 204-5

Fort Frontenac, need of repair of, 20; number of bundles of furs drawn from, 54; increase in trade at, in 1728, 90; factors involved in the decline of trade at, after 1728, 90-1; number of packs of fur received at, 91; the retention of, by France provided for in the British proposals of February 20, 1755, 336

Fort Hunter, New York, a chapel for the Mohawks built at, in 1741, 98

Fort Lawrence, construction of, at Beaubassin, in 1750, 194; efforts to dislodge the English at, 196; Major Scott, commander at, authorized to receive oaths of the refugee Acadians, 202

Fort Marlborough, Sumatra, English post in 1750, 260

Fort Miami on the Maumee, a symbol of French possession, 5; *see also* Miami

Fort Niagara, a symbol of French possession in 1754, 5; need of repairs of, 20; commandant of, sells brandy freely to the Indians, 52; the building of, in 1725, 87-88; cost of construction of, 88; ruinous condition of, in 1744, 93; defences of, described, 93; not threatened in King George's War, 93; Captain de Raymond's pessimistic report on, in 1748, 94; Abbe Piquet's description of the condition of, in 1751, 104; John Patten's description of, 104; the dismantling of, by the British proposals of February 20, 1755, 335; on lands of the Five Nations, 336; *see also* Niagara River

Fort Nicholson, at the great carrying-place, and the southern Canadian boundary, 5

Fort Oswego, not to be dismantled by the British proposals of February 20, 1755, 336; reasons for the maintenance of, 336; *see also* Oswego

Fort Ouiatenon on the Wabash, a symbol of French possession, 5; *see also* Ouiatenon

Fort Rouillé, the retention of, by France provided for in the British proposals of February 20, 1755, 336; *see also* Toronto

Fort St. David, India, English factory at, 244; within the jurisdiction of the Madras presidency, 249; unsuccessful attack upon, by the French, 274; trade of, falls off, 285; plan of Dupleix to attack, in 1753, not supported by his officers, 291

Fort St. Frédéric at Crown Point, a symbol of French possession, 5; built upon English territory, 5; description of, 20; Massachusetts Bay favours the erection of a fortress to dominate, 115; the dismantling of, by the British proposals of February 20, 1755, 335; on lands of the Five Nations, 336

Fort St. Jean, and English territorial claims, 5

Fort William, Calcutta, English factory, 244; *see also* Calcutta

Forts, the erection of, in the Iroquoian country favoured by Massachusetts Bay, 114-5; English colonial frontier, a series of, advocated by Halifax in 1754, 161; problem of financing the construction of, 161-2; Robinson's proposal of February 10 to the British Cabinet for a mutual demolition of all, in the region of the Ohio and Lakes Erie and Ontario, 331; strategic location of French, in North America, 345; British lack of strong, in North America outside of Halifax, 346

Fox [Outagamis] Indians, weakness of, in the eighteenth century, 39; furs of, traded to the Ottawas, 43; French expedition against, 90

Fox, the Great Lakes region haunted by, 36

Fox skins, value of, in 1749 and 1754, 55-6

France, burdens of the peasants of, contrasted with those of the Canadian *habitants*, 9; inability of, to furnish wheat to Canada, 31; importation into, of English grain, 31; why the loss of the colonies of, would greatly weaken, 32; organization of the Company of One Hundred Associates in, in 1727, 56; establishment of the Compagnie des Indes Occidentales in, in 1664, 56; the establishment of the Compagnie d'Occident in, in 1717, 58; the creation of the Compagnie Perpetuelle des Indes in, in 1719, 58; the exhaustion of, at the signing of the Treaty of Utrecht, 80; decline of the prestige of, in North America in 1714, 80; the recuperation of, 80; new aggressive spirit of, 80; government of, repents the decision made at Utrecht, 172; government of, determines to repossess Acadia and the Acadians, 185-6; interest of, in the West Indies, 208-30; late interest of, in trade with the Far East, 261; organization of the Compagnie des Indes Orientales in, in 1664, 261; the blockade of, during the War of the

Austrian Succession, 298; capture of the ships of, during the War, 298-9; apprehensions in, in 1747, 299; signing of the secret articles by the representatives of, at Aix-la-Chapelle, 300-1; concessions made by, in the Treaty of Aix-la-Chapelle, 301; the fleet of, unwilling to put to sea to fight, 302; the people of, rejoice at the coming of peace, 302

Franciscans, the College of, at Montreal, 18

Franklin, Benjamin, interest of, in natural history, 15; a Pennsylvania commissioner at the Albany Congress, 114; appointed on the committee on colonial union at Albany, 124; outline of a plan of union in 1751 by, 124; strongly committed to colonial union in 1754, 125; plan of, criticised by New York friends, 125-6; work of, at the Albany Congress later misjudged, 133-4; feels that Parliament must establish an American colonial union, 134-5; defends the right of the Crown to pass upon laws made by a colonial Grand Council, 138; support of the prerogatives of the Crown by, 138; later attitude of, respecting the Albany Plan of Union, 138; on the degree of support given to the Albany Plan by the commissioners, 139; shabby treatment of, by the Pennsylvania Assembly, 145; on the taxation of the colonies by Parliament, 158-9; opposes alterations of the Plan of Union as suggested by Shirley, 159; on colonial representation in Parliament, 159-60; comment of Hutchinson on the views held by, in 1754, 160

Franquet, M., of Isle Royale, on the English attitude toward the Micmac attacks, 197

Frederick II, King of Prussia, and the War of the Austrian Succession, 299; Walpole urges the support of, 300; the Treaty of Aix-la-Chapelle and, 301

French colonial policy, unity in, 110

French Crown, see Crown, French

French Empire, characteristics of, 342-4; advantages of, in North America in the face of British pressure, 345-6; the vision of, in North America maintained from the days of Champlain, 351

French expansion in North America, the strategy of, 344-5

French Minister, the, finances of New France and, 26-7; threat by, to give up Canada, 27; decision of, in 1749 in favour of the licensing system for the fur trade, 48; opposition of, to the military

project of Abbé Piquet, 107; opposes the use of Indians in any Ohio Valley expedition, 107

French Mohawks, see Caughnawaga Indians

French navy, the War of the Austrian Succession and, 273, 298-9

French traders, the Great Lakes region and, 42-5, 49-51; fear of the Bishop of Quebec by, and the sale of brandy, 91; see also coureurs de bois, voyageurs

French West Indies, near economic collapse of, during the War of the Austrian Succession, 299; held to be profitable, 343; see also Grenada, Guadeloupe, Martinique, St. Domingue

Frontenac, Louis de Buade, Comte de, Governor General of New France, on the importance of developing the Iroquoian trade, 75

Furs, application of the principles of mercantilism in Canada to, 23; value of, exported from Canada in 1748, 23; and in 1754, 61; total value of, produced in Canada in 1748, 23; and in 1754, 61; cost of transporting, between Detroit and Montreal, 53; weight of bundles of, 53; types of, secured in Canada, with prices paid, 55-6; most of, secured in Canada go to the English, 61; effect upon the export of, from New York, of the law against sale of trading goods to the French, 86; number of bundles of, brought to Albany in 1725, 87; packs of, brought to Oswego in 1749, 101

Fur trade, importance of, for Canada, 42; early dependence upon, in Canada, 42; Indian middlemen and, 43; Frenchmen take the place of Indians in, 43; changed methods of, 43; regulation of, in 1681, 44; system of licences established for, 44; all licences for, suppressed in 1686, 44; carried on by commandants of posts, 44; French in Canada fear the total loss of, 44-5; advantages offered by Albany in, 44-5; restoration of licences for, in 1716, 45; at Detroit, 45-6; policy of leasing posts for, 47; French adopt both leasing and licensing policies for, after 1744, 47; Indians prefer Oswego to Niagara or Frontenac for, 47; a black picture of, in 1745, 47-8; deficits incurred by the French in carrying on, 48; comparative importance of, at the French posts, 53-6; carts used by the French at Niagara Falls in the course of, 82; importance of, at Oswego in 1725, 87; advantages enjoyed in, by the English according to

Colden, 87; why the French were not ruined in, 87; great importance of Oswego in, 91; why the cost of administering Canada could not be carried by, 343–4; *see also* contraband trade

Fustians, production of, in England, 258

Galissonière, Comte de la, Michael Rolland Barin, Admiral and Governor General of New France, a cultural leader, 15; attitude of the Indians toward, 15; report of 1748 on the exports and imports of Canada by, 23–4; *mémoire* of, in favour of keeping New France, 32; report of, on great deficits incurred at the trading posts, 48; in favour of the licensing system for the fur trade, 48; desired to capture Oswego, 94; fears a war with the Six Nations, 95; receives at Quebec representatives of four of the Six Nations, 97; assists Piquet to establish the mission of La Présentation, 102; views of, respecting the protection of the French King enjoyed by the Acadians, 180; design of, to repossess Acadia, 185–6; a member of the Anglo-French joint commission, 1749–1754, 304; seeks to persuade the British commissioners to accept the return of the British memorial on Acadia, 321; on the relations of the Acadians to the government of Nova Scotia, 334

Galleon trade, Spanish, funds of the Compagnie des Indes devoted to, 267

Ganjam, India, an English factory at, in 1750, 260

Garden, Alexander, interest of, in natural history, 15

Gauthier, Jean François, royal physician at Quebec, cultural interests of, 15

General Society for English merchants trading to the East Indies, establishment of, by Parliament in 1698, 243; loan made by, to the government, 243; existence of rival companies within, 243–4

General Treasurer of the American colonies, provision for a, in the Albany Plan of Union, 138

Gentes, see clans

George I, of England, makes gift of St. Lucia and St. Vincent in 1722 to Montagu, 228

George II, of England, many Acadians take qualified oaths of loyalty to, 173

Georgia, the sea-to-sea territorial claims of, ignored by the Albany Congress, 132; not comprehended in the Albany Plan

of Union, 134; possibility of the absorption of, by South Carolina, 134

Gérard, Abbé, priest at Cobequid, informs La Jonquière that his people desire to submit to the English, 197; oath of fidelity to the English King given by, 197; ordered to Isle St. Jean, 197

Germain, Abbé, missionary to the St. John River Indians, warns the English of Indian hostilities, 189; earlier work as curé at Annapolis, 189; finally encourages the Indians to attack the English, 189; urges resistance to the English at Beaubassin, 194

German immigrants, in Nova Scotia, poor quality of, 200–1; Catholics among, desert to Isle St. Jean, 201; most of, settled at Merliqueche, 201; riotous conduct of, at Lunenburg, 201

German mercenaries, the employment of, by the Compagnie des Indes, 295

Germany, the sale of French beaver hats in, 61

Giasson, Jacque, partner of Rigaud in the trade of La Baye, 49

Gingham, fabric of India, exported, 252

Gingy [Gingi, Jingi], India, Chanda Sahib desires aid of Dupleix to capture, 279; Nasir Jang retreats to, 282; the French storm, after the departure of Nasir Jang, 282; gift of, to the Compagnie des Indes, 283

Ginseng roots, amount of export of, from Canada in 1754, 24; value of, 24

Glatz, the County of, and the Treaty of Aix-la-Chapelle, 301

Goa, India, the decline of, contrasted to the development of Bombay, 248

Godeheu, M., a *directeur* of the Compagnie des Indes, sent to India to displace Dupleix, 295; reaches a temporary accord with President Saunders, 296; terms of treaty signed by, in 1754, 296; advantages secured by, 296–7

Godolphin, Sidney Godolphin, 1st Earl of, Lord High Treasurer, award of, in 1708 respecting the two English East India companies, 244

Gold, rated too high in England in 1717, 255; supplies of, from India and China, 255; always valued in terms of silver, 255

Gomastahes, Indian brokers, the activities of, 252

Gomroon, Persian Gulf, English factory at, in 1750, 260

Gou, M. le, Governor of Pondicherry, 266

Governor and Company of Merchants of London trading to the East Indies, charter granted to, in 1600, 235; activities of, 235–9; growing powers of, 239–42; termination of activities of, 243

Governor General of New France, manner of living on the part of, 16; instructions of and powers of, in 1749, 19–22; see also Beauharnois, Courcelles, Denonville, Duquesne, Frontenac, Galissonière, La Jonquiere

Governor General, the English colonies to be provided with, under the plan " Short Hints," 126

Grammar, the study of, at Quebec, 12

Grand Council, for the American colonies, provision for, in the " Short Hints," 126; in the " Plan of a Proposed Union," 130; in the Albany Plan of Union, 135; apportionment of representation in, 135; Shirley's criticism of the dangerous powers assigned to, under the Albany Plan, 160

Grand Monarque, see Louis XIV

Grand Pré, Nova Scotia, church communicants within the parish of, 170; New England troops camped at, captured or destroyed, in 1747, 177; the Acadians summoned to, by the Micmac, 192

Granville, John Cartaret, 2nd Earl of, policy of, criticised by Westmorland in 1748, 302

Gravier, Father Jacques, calls the Ohio River region "the country of the Iroquois," 66

Gray Wolf, Tuscarora Indian clan, 70

Great Bear, early Iroquoian clan, 71

" Great Binding Law," basis of the Iroquoian Confederation, 69

Great Britain, the people of, loaded with debts, 162; attitude of the people of, during the War the Austrian Succession, 298–300; payment of subsidies to allies in the War by, 300; signing of the secret articles by the representatives of, at Aix-la-Chapelle, 300–1; advantages gained by, through the Peace of Aix-la-Chapelle, 301; concessions made by, in the Treaty, 301; criticisms of the Treaty in, 302; the people of, welcome the coming of peace, 302

" Great Immutable Law," see " Great Binding Law "

Great Lakes region, the, activities in, 3; a dependency of Canada, 35; description of, 35–6; Cadillac's estimate of, 35; most of the furs of Canada drawn from, 42; number of French trading posts within,

52–3; types of furs secured in, 55; see also Chapter III

Great Name Bearer, early Iroquoian clan, 71

Great Turtle, Tuscarora Indian clan, 70

Greeks, invasion of India by, 232

Green Bay, see La Baye

Grenada, West Indies, the French exterminate the Caribs of, 208

Grey Friars, see Recollets

Grey, Gov. Ralph, of Barbados, protest of, on the activities of the French on St. Lucia, 227–8; failure of, to secure the support of the Crown, 228

Grist-mills, the use of, in Canada and the banalités, 9

Guadeloupe, number of ships from, to Canada in 1754, 25; Dominica a life line between Martinique and, 208; early relations of the government of, with the Carbis, 209; colonization of Dominica from, 215

Guigues, Louis, acquires the monopoly of the export of beaver skins in 1697, 57

Guillot, M., French commissaire respecting prizes in 1749, 303

Guineas, the value of English, reduced in 1717 on the advice of Sir Isaac Newton, 255

Gulf of Cambay, English factories established along the, in 1612, 237

Gulf of St. Lawrence, the Anglo-French dispute over the region of the, 317, 331, 334, 336, 337

Guns, dependence of Indians upon the use of, 41; the French carry, to the tribes, 43; value of, in the Indian trade at Albany and at Montreal, 45; possession of, secured from Albany permit the Five Nations to crush the Erie, 75

Gurrahs, fabric of India, exported, 252

Habitants, of Canada, dwelt mostly in the country, 5; love of nature of, 6; attachment of, to the St. Lawrence, 6; means of communication of, 6; homes of, 6; characteristics of, 7; dress of women, 7; places of origin of, 7; method of landholding among, 8; light public burdens of, 9; seigneurs stand between the Crown and, 11; canalizing of learning among, 12; isolation of lives of, 12; ancestral homes of, in France fade from tradition, 12; had become by 1750 a distinct people, 12; the lure of the West to, 13; size of families of, 13; the application of the principles of mercantilism in Canada and, 23; desire of, for Montauban cloth,

25; longed for independence, by reason of corruption in government, 29; the use of troops required to control, 29; grievances of, 29; seditious conduct of, 29; reap but small wheat harvests, 29; faced by famine, 31

Hair, care of, among the French *habitants*, 7

Haiti, see St. Domingue

Haldane, Captain, East India goods of, put up for auction, 257

Halifax, George Montagu Dunk, 2nd Earl of, President of the Board of Trade, proposal of, for a series of frontier forts, 161; the "Project of a General Concert" of the English colonies and, 162–3; work of, and other members of the Board in colonizing eastern Nova Scotia, 181; the Anglo-French joint commission and, 309–20; criticism of Robinson's proposals of February 10, 1755 by, 331

Halifax, Nova Scotia, the founding of, 182–3; development of the defences of, 191; as a centre of British expansion, 340

Hall, Col. Robert, on the committee on colonial union of the Massachusetts Bay House of Representatives, 151; favours a general union, 154

Hamilton, Gov. James, recommends the Albany Plan of Union to the Pennsylvania Assembly, 144

Handsome Lake, Iroquoian hereditary title, 71

Haquet, M., Governor of St. Lucia, 226

Hardware, imported into Canada, 25

Hardwicke, Philip Yorke, 1st Earl of, Lord High Chancellor, observations of, on the Board of Trade "Project" for a colonial union, 164

Harfleur, France, number of ships from, to Canada in 1754, 25

Harvests, poor nature of, in Canada 1749–1752, 29–31

Hats, use of, among the French *habitants*, 7

Havre, see Le Havre

Hawk, Six Nations clan, 70

Heath, Captain, failure of, to bring naval aid to the English traders in Bengal, 247

Heckewelder, John, Moravian missionary, explains origin of the term Iroquoian "nations," 72

Heinsius, Grand Pensionary of Holland, reassures the French respecting Tobago, 221

Hemp, the application of the principles of mercantilism in New France and the production of, 23

Hendrick, Mohawk sachem, connection of, with William Johnson, 95; charges English neglect at the Albany Congress, 119; the French supplied with English arms according to, 120

Henry, Patrick, the Albany Plan of Union and the later attitude of, respecting the royal disallowance of colonial legislation, 138

Hereditary titles, examples of, within the Iroquoian Confederation, 71

Hiawatha, culture hero of the Iroquois, 69

Hinde, Mr., British commissioner respecting prizes in 1749, 303

Hinduism, the stability of, 233–4

Hindus, trade advantages enjoyed by, 234–5

Histoire Générale des Antilles habitées par les Français (Paris, 1667–71), by J. B. du Tertre, 209

Hocquart, Giles, Intendant of New France, report of, on the decline of the trade at Niagara and at Frontenac, 91

Hoffman, a ringleader among the mutinous Lunenburg Germans, 201

Holderness, Robert D'Arcy, 4th Earl of, Secretary of State for the Southern Department, prevents the publication of the French case respecting Acadia, 319; Albemarle warned by, that the British would uphold their rights, 320; urges that the English and French East India companies become again *compagnies commerçantes*, 322; disturbed by reports of the movement of French soldiers to India, 323

Holland, weakness of, during the War of the Austrian Succession, 300; desire of, for peace, 300; signing of secret articles by the representatives of, at Aix-la-Chapelle, 300–1; see also Dutch

Hopkins, Stephen, Chief Justice of Rhode Island, a commissioner at the Albany Congress, 114; appointed on the committee on colonial union at the Congress, 124; author of A True Representation of the Plan formed in Albany, 1755, 141; denies that the commissioners ordered the Albany Plan to be sent to England, 141; view of, regarding the powers of the commissioners, 142; halting defence of the Albany Plan of Union by, in the Rhode Island Assembly, 147–8; temporary favourable report on the Plan of Union secured by, in the Assembly, 148

Hopson, Gov. Peregrine Thomas, succeeds Cornwallis at Halifax, 197; favourable report of, in 1752, on the Acadians, 197;

complaint of, over the poor quality of German settlers, 201

Horses, the raising of, in Canada, 13; export of, from Canada, 23

Hôtel Dieu, Quebec lands of the, 11

Houel, Sieur, Governor of Guadeloupe, treaty with the Caribs entered into by, in 1660, 209

House of Commons, British, hostility of, to the London East India Company, 241-2; declaration of, as to the supremacy of acts of Parliament over royal patents, 242

Houses, of the *habitants* of Canada, 6-7; of the Iroquois, 66, 70; of the Acadians, 168

How, Capt. Edward, the treacherous killing of, at the Missaquash, 196; the assassination of, compared by Albemarle to that of Jumonville, 324

Howard, Martin, Jr., a commissioner from Rhode Island to the Albany Congress, 114

Hubert, Ignace, partner of Rigaud in the trade of La Baye, 49

Hudson Bay, beaver skins from, sold to French hat-makers, 60

Hudson's Bay Company, territorial claims of, and Canada, 4; temporary acquisition of posts of, by the French, 57

Hugli River, India, English trading activities along the, 247; *see also* Calcutta

Huns, invasion of India by, 232

Huron [Wyandot, Aragaritka] Indians, of Lorette christianized, 20-1; semi-agricultural, brought in contact with the French, 38; help in driving the Five Nations south of the St. Lawrence, 38-9; trade competitors of the Five Nations, 39; collapse of, as a power, 39; weakness of, in the eighteenth century, 39; efforts of the Recollets to christianize, 41; the power of, broken by Five Nations in 1649, 42; missions for, 42; some of the, christianized and domiciled at Lake St. Clair, 42; a *nation perfide*, 42; early chief middlemen in the French fur trade, 42-3; give way to the Ottawa Indians, 43; crushing of, by the Five Nations, 69; beaver lands of, taken by the Five Nations, 78

Hutchins, Capt. Thomas, enumeration of Indian tribes by, 40

Hutchinson, Thomas, a member of the Council of Massachusetts Bay, a commissioner at the Albany Congress, 114; appointed on the committee on colonial union at the Albany Congress, 124;

"Plan of a Proposed Union of the Several Colonies . . .", apparently prepared by, 128-9; author of the "Representation on the Present State of the Colonies," 1754, 132; position of, at the Albany Congress misjudged, 133-4; comment of, on the limitation of the western bounds of the colonies in the Albany Plan of Union, 137; on the degree of support given by the commissioners to the Albany Plan of Union, 139; placed on the Massachusetts Bay Council committee on colonial union, 152; in favour of a northern colonial union, 154; comment of, upon views held by Franklin in 1754, 160

Hydrography, the study of, at Quebec, 12

Île Dauphine [Madagascar], activities of the French East Company on, 261

Île de France [Paris], immigration into Canada from, 7; Canadian *habitants* and the ancestral homes in, 12

Illinois country, developments in, 3

Illinois Indians, furs of, traded to the Ottawa, 43; sad condition of, in 1750, 52

Immigration, into Canada, groups from France, 7; ceases in the eighteenth century, 12; into Nova Scotia, 182; into the English colonies, 340

Import duties, provision for American colonial, in the Albany Plan of Union, 137

Imports, into Canada, 24, 33; into France from Canada, 23; and from India, 265; into Great Britain from India, 256-7

Inch of Candle, all sales by the London East Company at open auction to be by, 242

India, control of, and Anglo-French rivalry, 3; natural defences of, 231-2; vulnerability of, to invasion, 232; political instability of, 232-3; the Mogul Empire of, 233; the stability of the social structure of, 233-4; ancient commerce of, 234; prevailing favourable balance of trade of, 235; the Portuguese and, 235-7; growing anarchy in, after 1707, 247; the growth of new commercial centres in, 247-8; the English presidencies and English local government in, 249-50; the activities of the United East India Company within, 251-60; fabrics secured from, 252; number of English ships sailing to, 253; the question of the exploitation of the native artisans of, by the East India Company, 253; the "country trade" of, 253; cost of freight to and from, 253-4; value of English exports to India in 1729, 1730, 1749, and 1753, 254-5; value of bullion sent to, by the East India Company, 254-5; English commodities sent to, in 1730, 255; value of exports to, in 1730, 1749, and 1753, 255; exports from, to England in 1730, 256; high prices of goods charged by the natives of, 256-7; late interest of France in the trade of, 261; efforts of the French East India Company to secure a footing in, 262; unsuccessful activities of the French East India Company in, before 1719, 262-3; growing importance of French interest in, after 1726, 265-9; determination of Dupleix to establish French territorial power in, 271; lack of interest of the English in the first half of the eighteenth century in territorial expansion in, 271-2; developing anarchy in, 272; political significance in, of the defeat of the army of the Nabob of Arcot by the French, 274; fear of the military prowess of the French by the natives of, 279; great concessions in, made to the French by the Nabob of the Carnatic and by the Subahdar of the Deccan, 285; war between rivals in the Carnatic, the Deccan, and the Punjab in, 293-4; temporary Anglo-French treaty signed respecting affairs in, 296; the Anglo-French crisis in, considered in England, 322-3; characteristics of British activity with that of the French in, contrasted, 349-50

Indian Commissioners, the appointment of two, for America advocated by Halifax, 161; see also Albany Indian Commissioners

Indian conferences, at Montreal held by the Governor General, 20; financial burden of presents for, 27; at Montreal in 1701, 77; and in 1710, 78; and in 1748, 97; at Albany in 1750, 99; and in 1754, 118-22; at Winchester in 1754, 112

Indian missions, lack of results of early, 42; the location of trading posts and, 49; see also Lorette, Becancourt, Lake of the Two Mountains, La Présentation, St. Francis, St. John, and Sault St. Louis

Indian presents, the Governor General and annual, 20; extravagance of the French government in making, 27; the French posts and the distribution of, 50; the sending of, to the Six Nations by the King, 111; the Albany Congress and, 122

Indian superintendencies, the establishment

of, and the "Representation on the Present State of the Union," 1754, 133

Indian trade, Montreal and, 17; the burden of presents in connection with, 27; great premiums paid in Canada for brandy to carry on, 28; characteristic of early inter-tribal relations, 36; Hurons and Ottawa as middlemen in, 42-3; the coureurs de bois and, 43; the congés and, 44; price levels and, 45; permanent posts and, 45-6, 49; value of, in 1741, 46; the leasing systems and, 46-7; abuses of, in the Great Lakes region, 51; relative importance of the posts in, 52-4; Albany and, 78; Oswego and, 91, 100; the Acadians and, 170

Indian tribes, the French carry arms to, 43; French trading posts and the control of, 50; sad effect upon, of the brandy trade, 51-2; preference of, for English products, 62-3; see also Indians

Indians, intermarriage between Frenchmen and, 14, 169; of Canada, attitude of, toward Galissonière, 15; as a defence, 20; desire of, for Montauban cloth, 25; for Rouen white blankets, 25; of North America, seek to keep the power of the French and the English equal, 33; the lodges of, 35; early presence of, in the Great Lakes region, 36; agricultural interests of, about the Great Lakes, 36; wide-spread practice of barter among, 36; generally peaceful relations of, 37; factors leading to wars among, 37; the white race creates new bases of conflict for, 37; the fruits of European technology sought by, 37; advantages enjoyed by groups of, in contact with the whites, 37; articles most eagerly sought from, 37; extermination of beaver by, 38; turn middlemen, 38; Great Lakes tribes of, difficulty of determining the strength of, 39-40; lack of unity among, 41; lack of mastery of the new techniques by, 41; dependence of, upon firearms, 41; devotion of, to tribal customs and primitive beliefs, 41; efforts of French missionaries to convert, 41-2, 102-4, 169; long houses among, 66; tribal, phratry, clan, and family organization among, 70-1; the contraband Albany-Montreal trade and, 76, 78, 85; efforts of English missionaries among, 97; the Albany Congress and, 118-22; see also Abenaki [Abnaki, Abénaquis], Assiniboin, Catawba, Caughnawaga, Cayuga, Cherokee, Chippewa [Saulteur], Cree, Creek, Delaware, Erie, Huron,

Iroquoian Confederation, Mascouten, Menominee, Miami, Micmac, Mingo, Missisauga, Mohawk, Montagnais, Neutral, Nipissing, Oneida, Onondaga, Ottawa [Waganhaea], Ouiatenon, Petun, Piankashaw, Potawatomi, Puant, Seneca, Shawnee, Sioux of the Prairies, Sioux of the Woods, Susquehanna [Conestoga], Tionontati [Petun, Tobacco], Tuscarora, Vermillion

Indigo, importation of, into England from the Far East, 235

Individualism, the British Empire and, 341–2; the French Empire and, 343

Indo-Aryans, invasions of India by, 232–3

Instructions, royal, of the Governor General and Intendant of New France in 1750, 19–22; compared with those of the Governor and Commissaire Ordonnateur of Louisiana, 22–3; of Godeheu, in 1754, 295; of Mirepoix, in 1754, 328

Intendant, of New France, home of, 16; joint instructions for the Governor General and, 21–43; as President of the Superior Council, 22; the public finances of Canada and, 26; see also Bigot, Duchesneau, Dupuy, Hocquart, Talon

Iron, the production of, in Canada, favoured by the French government, 23; of Canada exported to France, 24; corrupt practices in the production of, in Canada, 28; value of, sent to India in 1730, 255

Iron stoves, use of, among the habitants of Canada, 6–7; manufacture of, in Canada, 24

Irondequoit Bay, desire of Longueuil to build a post at, 82; Joncaire trades at, 82; licences given to English traders by the Albany Commissioners for, 84; French traders at, 85

Iroquoian castles, description of, 65–6

Iroquoian Confederation, delicate situation of, 3; the limits of Canada and, 4; brought in contact with the Dutch, 39; members of, become middlemen, 39; competition of, with Hurons and Ottawa, 39; sought the "Far West" Indians, 39; advantages enjoyed by, 39; failure of, to get control of Great Lakes furs, 39; increase in strength of, 39; holds the key to the fate of the Ohio Valley, 64; unwillingness of, to block the French, 64; sweeping territorial claims of, 64; number of souls embodied in, 65; number of warriors of, 65; ability of, to destroy all Canadian Indians, 65; estimated number of villages of, 65; location of principal

settlements of, 65; types of villages of, 65–6; the long house among, 66; unimpressive appearance of settlements of, 66; agricultural pursuits of, 66; vast extent of hunting grounds of, 66; the Mingo, Delawares, and Shawnee recognize the Onondaga council of, 66; Shawnee villages destroyed by, 66; claims of, to the northern third of Pennsylvania, 67; the Susquehannah Indians conquered by, 67; treatment of the Delawares and Shawnee in Pennsylvania by, 67; claims of, recognized by the Pennsylvania proprietors, 67; the question of an empire controlled by, 67; a unique force in eighteenth-century America, 67–8; strategic position of, 68; importance of the culture of, 68; significance of, in the history of the Five Nations, 68–9; symbolism of, 69; universal peace and, 69; Tuscarora welcomed by, 69; other Iroquoian tribes broken by, 69; policy of, 70–3; cognatic descent of families of, 70; clans of, 70–1; phratries of, 70; the ohwachira and, 70–1; the sachemships and hereditary titles and, 71; war decisions and the women of, 71; prisoners of war and adoption into, 71; possibility of dissolution of, each five years, 72; no peaceful secession from, 72; friction within, 72; no nation of, tries to secede, 72; no civil war within, 72; limitations on the effectiveness of, 72–3; distinctions within, between civil and military authority, 73; war lords and, 73; principle of equality within, 73; absence of slaves among members of, 73; treatment of prisoners by, 73; attitude of members of, toward stealing, 74; virtues of Indians of, 74; members of, go in search for furs, 74; contact of, with the Far West Indians, 74; the French bring about a rupture of friendly relations between the western Indians and, 74; destruction of Eries by, 74; armed by the Dutch at Albany, 74; attitude of, toward La Salle's Niagara post, 75; trade relations with the French desired by, 75; some Indians of, settle at Sault St. Louis, 75–6; converts to Roman Catholicism among, 76; the Praying Indians renounced by, 76; activity of the Jesuits within, 76; peace between the French and their allies and the, 77; the cession to the King of England of all the beaver grounds of, in 1701, 77; beaver grounds of, conquered from the Hurons, 78; a delegation from, sent to England, 78; neutrality policy of, in 1708, 78; the

Treaty of Utrecht and, 79; the pro-French faction within, prevails in 1710, 81; plans of, for an expedition against Canada in 1712, 81; council of three nations of, in 1720, to consider the English protest over the French Niagara post, 83; desire of, to live in peace with both English and French, 84; protest to, by the New York Indian commissioners over the French posts at Niagara and Detroit, 83; attitude of, in 1720, toward French movements, 83; plan of French to dominate the trade of, 84; the French occupy four places upon lands of, 85; English traders sent to, to watch the French, 85; Tuscarora received by, in 1723, as a sixth nation, 86; permit the English to build at Oswego, 86; continued support of the English at Oswego by, 89; hold the French from attacking Oswego in King George's War, 93; complain to Governor Clinton of the high price of trading goods at Oswego, 93-4; division of sentiment within, during King George's War, 96; Johnson meets the sachems of, at Onondaga, in 1748, 96; promises of, not to resort to Canada broken, 97; repudiates the overlordship of the King of England, 97; asked to be instructed in Christianity, 97; efforts of the Anglicans to make converts within, 98; pro-French leanings of, after Aix-la-Chapelle, 98; testimony of Conrad Weiser respecting, after visiting Onondaga, 98; the conference of 1750 at Albany of commissioners from Massachusetts Bay, Connecticut, and South Carolina with, 99; meaningless promises made by, 99; Piquet hopes to draw to La Présentation, 103; the number of Indians from, at La Présentation, in 1751, 105; project of Abbé Piquet to drive the English traders from the Ohio by using, 106; loss of English influence within, 107; the English the greater menace to, 108; policy of, one of "balance" between English and French, 108; appropriation of the Ohio Valley lands of, by the French, 109; fear of French by, 109; recommendations of the Albany Indian Commissioners to revive the loyalty of, 109; degeneration of the warriors of, according to Conrad Weiser, 109; explanation for the loss of respect for the English by, 110; Board of Trade in 1753, requests that a colonial conference be held with, 111; the English and French hem in, 111;

small number of representatives of the, at Albany, 118; coldness of the Indians of, toward the English, 118; grievances of, respecting the fur trade and the sale of Indian land, 118; protest of, against the encroachments of the French, the Pennsylvanians, and the Virginians, 120; did not respond to Dinwiddie's invitation to a treaty conference, 120; change of attitude of, toward the English, 121; asks that the English act without delay, 121; requests that no rum be sold in the castles of, 121; asks for a church with a bell, 121; sells land to the Pennsylvania Proprietors in 1754, 121-2; sells to the Susquehanna Company lands on the Upper Susquehanna in 1754, 122; friendship of, with the English recemented, 122; representatives of, return home from Albany with a great present, 122; the territorial rights of, stated by the Albany Congress, 132; lands of the upper Ohio in the hands of, before the Treaty of Utrecht, 329; Rouillé denies that Article XV of the Treaty of Utrecht is applicable to, 332; domination of the region to the south of Lake Erie by, 333

Iroquoian family, see Cayuga, Cherokee, Erie, Huron, Mohawk, Neutral, Susquehannah [Conestoga], Tionontati [Petun, Tobacco], and Tuscarora
Iroquoian Matriarchate, 70–1
Iroquois Indians, at Sault St. Louis and at the Lake of the Two Mountains, christianized, 21
Isle Royale, within the governor generalship of New France, 4; Bigot Commissaire Ordonnateur of, 21; efforts to remove the Acadians to, 171–2; the building of the fortress of Louisbourg on, 117; Acadians resort to, to trade, 174; interest of, in the Canso fisheries, 175; capture of the island of Canso in 1744 by troops from, 176; dependence of, upon the Acadians, 186; see also Cape Breton
Isle St. Jean [Prince Edward Island] Acadians resort to, to trade, 174; food supplies from, sent to Le Loutre, 190; Acadian refugees settle on, 198
Italy, the sale of French beaver hats in, 61

Jacobite Pretender, the repudiation of the, by France in the Peace of Aix-la-Chapelle, 301
Jamaica, privateers from, eject the Zeelanders from Tobago, 220

James I, grant of privileges in perpetuity to the London East India Company by, 236; grants licence to Mickelborne to trade to the Far East, 238

James II, of England, the government of, adverse to the claims of the Duke of Courland to the right to colonize Tobago, 221; grant to the London East India Company of right to exercise martial law by, 241

Java, early English trading activities in, 236; loss of trading station in, 241; Dutch by 1750 in control of western and northeastern portion of, 260

Jesuit College, at Quebec, a centre of learning, 12

Jesuits, amount of Canadian land controlled by, 11; chief propagators of Christianity among the Indians, 21; early efforts of, among the Micmac, 41; Indian mission of Michilimakinac established by, accused of grave abuses, 51; activity of, among the Six Nations, 76-7

Johnson, William, fighting strength of the Six Nations, according to, 65; significance of the Iroquoian League in the eyes of, 69; report of, that the Tionontati and the Ottawa would help destroy Niagara, 94; settles on the Mohawk, 95; relations of, with the Indians, 95; received into the Mohawk nations and named Warraghiyagee, 95; great interest of, in the fur trade, 95; accepts a contract in 1746 to supply the Oswego garrison, 95-6; appointed by Governor Clinton colonel of the warriors of the Six Nations, 96; sends out raiding parties, 96; unable to secure the person of Joncaire among the Seneca, 96; leads raid against the French at Crown Point, 96; lack of success of, in war efforts in 1747, 96; becomes colonel of the New York militia in 1748, 96; effort of, at Onondaga to keep the Six Nations from resorting to the French, 96; encourages Anglican missionaries among the Mohawks, 98; the effective influence of, among the Six Nations limited to the Mohawks, 98-9; resigns the New York Iroquoian superintendency, 99; admitted to the New York Council in 1750, 99; interest of, in New York lands, 99; sent by the New York authorities to Onondaga in 1753, 111; the Six Nations rebuked by, 111; at the Albany Congress, 114; the Six Nations declare its love for, 119; retains the "large Belt" sent by Pennsylvania to the Six

Nations, 121; proposals offered by, for defence of the Iroquoian country, 131

"Join or Die," device employed by Franklin in the Pennsylvania Gazette in 1754, 124-5

Joncaire, Sieur Chabert de, the Elder, helps to construct a house at Onondaga, 79; adopted by the Seneca, 81; employed to keep the Five Nations neutral in Queen Anne's War, 81; assists Baron de Longueuil in the Iroquoian country, 81; trades at Irondequoit Bay, 82; takes his son Philip Thomas to the Seneca, 82; establishes by order of the government a picketed post on the Niagara, 82; Seneca voice dissatisfaction to, over the Niagara post, 83; continued influence of, among the Seneca, 84

Joncaire, Philip Thomas Chabert de (Ontachsina, Jean Cour), taken to the Seneca as a child, 82; dwells among the Seneca during King George's War, 96; great influence of, over the Indians, 96; Clinton anxious to lay hands on, 96; retires from the Seneca country, 96; activities of, on the Ohio, 99; promise of, to bring Indians to La Présentation, 105; extent of the actual influence of, over the Six Nations problematical, 107

Joncaire de Clauzonne (Clazonne, Clozonne), takes the place of his brother, Philip Thomas, among the Seneca, 96; at Little Niagara, 99; difficulties, faced by, in 1751, 104

Jumonville, Sieur de, the death of, reported to Rouillé, 324; Mirepoix ordered to protest the "assassination" of, 329

Juniata River, lands along, Pennsylvania desires to purchase from the Six Nations, 121

Justice, in New France, 22-3; in India, 239, 241, 249-50

Kalikata, the purchase of the village of, by the London East India Company, 247; out of, and other nearby villages arises Calcutta, 247

Kalm, Peter, journey of, along the St. Lawrence, 6; on the unequality of the rentes in Canada, 7, 9; statement of, regarding the inmates of Canadian convents, 14; tribute of, to the people of Quebec, 15; on the construction of warships in Canada, 24; on abuses at the St. Maurice iron works in Canada, 28

Kamenistigouia [Kaministiquia], trading post, location of, 154; lease of, in 1743,

54; number of bundles of furs drawn from, 54

Karikal, the Rajah of Tanjore cedes, to the French in 1739, 276

Karnul, India, the Nabob of, kills Nasir Jang, 283

Karwar [Carwar], India, English factory at, in 1750, 260

Kayarondiargh Creek, lands in Pennsylvania as far north as, sold by the Six Nations to the Pennsylvania proprietors, 122

Kennedy, Archibald, Receiver General of New York, author of *Importance of Gaining and Preserving the Friendship of the Indians*, 125; consulted by Franklin on his plan of colonial union, 125

Kent, Captain, East India goods of, put up for auction, 257

Kernsoret, M. de, on the great debts owed by the planters of Louisiana, 268

Kettles, production of, in Canada, 24; Indians prefer English, 63

Kilpatrick, Captain, brings reinforcements to Clive at Arcot, 288

King George's War, effect of, upon the French fur-trading methods, 47; the neutrality of New York in, 93–5; the concert of New England colonies during, 123; Acadia and, 176–7; India and, 272–5; *see also* War of the Austrian Succession

King William's War, a colonial concert for defence during, 123

Koromantyn Negroes, characteristics of, 68

Kyrie Eleison, the singing of, by Canadians, 8

Labat [Labbat], Father, author of *Nouveau Voyage aux Isles de l'Amérique*, 211; comments of, on Dominica in 1700, 212; views of, respecting the origin of the Caribs, 211–2; on the blood feud among the Caribs, 213; on the impossibility of christianizing the Caribs, 214; comments of, on St. Vincent, in 1700, 216; on St. Lucia in 1700, 227

La Baye [Green Bay], establishment of an Indian mission at, by Father Allouez, 42; the trading post at, lucrative, 48; history of the leasing of, 49; exploitation of, enjoyed by Rigaud de Vaudreuil, 49; cost of the lease of, 49; trade of, carried on by a partnership, 49; number of bundles of fur secured from, 54; value of the lease of, 55; convenient location of, for fur trade, 55; great profits drawn from, 55

La Bourdonnais, *see* Mahé de la Bourdonnais

La Breton, M., Governor of St. Lucia, 226

La Cadie, *see* Acadia

La Caron, Father Joseph, Recollet, efforts of, to christianize the Hurons, 41; work of, at Thunder Bay, 41

La Chine, Canada, 18

Lacquered ware of East India, put up for auction, 257

La Fleur, French fur-trader at Niagara, forced to leave by the Seneca, 75

Lahore, India, English factory at, in 1750, 260

La Jonquière, Pierre Jacques de Taffanel, Marquis de, Governor General of New France, arrival of, at Quebec, 19; description of, 19; the royal instructions brought by, analysed, 19–23; corrupt practices of, in Canada, 28; profits secured in the beaver trade by, 28; profits from the brandy trade enjoyed by, 28; on the lack of grain in Canada, 29; death of, in 1752, 30; profit secured by, from La Baye post, 55; reply of, to Governor Clinton's protest, 99–100; sends soldiers to guard La Présentation, 104; commissions Abbé Piquet to go to Lake Erie to find sites for trading posts, 104; approves conditionally of the military project of Abbé Piquet, 107; refuses to support hostile acts of the Indians against Halifax, 189–90; appeal of Acadians to, 190; orders the French to resist the English on the Missaquash, 195; offers rewards for English prisoners and scalps, 195

Lake Champlain, and the limits of Canada, 4; proposal of Pownall for the defence of, 131; the Albany Congress claims, as Iroquoian, 132; and desires warships to patrol, 133

Lake Erie, proposal of Pownall for the defence of, 131; the Albany Congress claims, as Iroquoian, 132; Robinson's proposal of February 10, 1755 to the British Cabinet for a mutual evacuation of, 331; to be placed by Robinson's proposals of March 26, 1755 on the footing of the Treaty of Utrecht, 337; the British Cabinet denies that the French have the exclusive navigation of, 338

Lake George, *see* Lake St. Sacrement

Lake of the Two Mountains, christianized Iroquois at, 21; a trading post at, 54; number of bundles of fur drawn from, 54

Lake Ontario, proposal of Pownall for the defence of, 131; earlier proposal of Governor Clarke for defence of, 131; the

Albany Congress claims, as Iroquoian, 132; the Congress desires warships to patrol, 133; Robinson's proposal of February 10, 1755 to the British Cabinet for a mutual evacuation of forts on, 331; to be placed by Robinson's proposals of March 26, 1755 on the footing of the Treaty of Utrecht, 337; the British Cabinet denies that the French have an exclusive navigation of, 338

Lake St. Sacrement [George], the limits of Canada and, 4

Lalande, M., Governor of St. Lucia, 226

L'Algonkin, King's ship built in Canada, poor quality of, 24

Lamberville, Father Jean de, S.J., activity of, among the Six Nations, 76-7; a French-Seneca war avoided in 1684 by, 76; presence of, embarrassing to Governor Dongan, 77; supports policy of Denonville, 77; withdrawal of, from Onondaga in 1687, 77

Lampsins, Adrien, a director of the Dutch West India Company, efforts of, to plant Tobago, 219

Lampsins, Corneille, Burgomaster of Flushing, efforts of, and his brother to plant Tobago, 219; agreement of, with the Duke of Courland, 219; Zeelanders sent by, to Tobago, 219; created Baron of Tobago by Louis XIV, 219

Land, nature of grants of, to the *habitants* of Canada, 8; obligations for holding en censive, 8-10; large revenues from, secured by the Church in Canada, 9; seigneurial grants of, in Canada, number of, made between 1674 and 1755, 10; and average size of, 10; total area of, in Canada held under seigneurial grants in 1755, 10-11; the amount of, held by the Church in 1755, 11; conditions attached to such grants of, 11; treatment of, in Canada, 13; grants of, by the Governor General and the Intendant in Canada and by the Governor and Commissaire Ordonnateur in Louisiana, 23; grant of, of Sault Ste. Marie to de Miselle, 28; utilization of, by the Iroquois, 66; extent of, claimed by the Iroquoian Confederation, 66-7; cession of, by the Five Nations to the English Crown in 1701, 77; Indian, the Iroquoian Confederation and the New York policy regarding, 118; treatment of, by the Acadians, 168; obligations of the Acadians for the holding of, 169; the Acadians faced by the problem of obtaining additional,

174; Shirley recommends that all Acadians hold, by knight service, 179-80; Shirley arranges for a survey of vacant, in Nova Scotia, 180; recommends that a division of pasturage, in Nova Scotia be made, 180-1; appeal of Acadians to the French Crown for a grant of, on the borders of Acadia, 190; promise of, to the refugee Acadians by La Jonquière, 195; settlement of Acadians on, upon Isle St. Jean and elsewhere, 196; grants of, to Germans at Lunenburg, Nova Scotia, 201; large grant of, east of the Bay of Fundy by the British Crown, 201; conditions under which Acadians might retain peaceable possession of, 202; the largest and best tracts of, in Nova Scotia possessed by the Acadians, 205; grant of, of Dominica by the French Crown in 1626 and by the English Crown in 1627, 209; sale of, of St. Lucia in 1663 and of Dominica in 1668 by Warner, 210, 226; exploitation by the French of, of Dominica, 215-6; and of St. Vincent, 217-8; grant of, of Tobago by the English Crown to the Duke of Courland, 219-20; Dutch utilization of, in Tobago, 220; large grant of, by the young Duke of Courland in 1698, 221; grant of, of St. Lucia to Carlisle, 224; utilization of, of St. Lucia by the French before 1664, 225-6; lease of, of Madraspatam to the London East India Company, 1640, 237; acquisition of, of Bombay Island by the Company in 1668, 239-401; annual rental paid for, about Madras, 240; acquisition of, of St. Helena by the Company, 240; the purchase of, about Sutanati and Kalikata by the Company in 1698, 247; purchase of, about Pondicherry by the Dutch East India Company, 262

Languedoc, effort of the Compagnie des Indes to manufacture *écarlatines* in, 62

La Pointe du St. Esprit, mission of, established by Father Allouez, 42

La Présentation, Indian mission of, established by Abbé Piquet, 102; descriptions of, 103, 105; prospects of, in 1748, 103; the defence of, 103; attack upon, in 1748 by the Mohawks, 103; soldiers sent to guard, 104; Indian recruits for, secured at Niagara, 105; Christian converts at, go to Montreal, 106; Praying Indians assert the presence of spies at, 108

Larce, a Malabar Coast coin; value of, 256

Large Mouth, Iroquoian hereditary title, 71

Large Plover, early Iroquoian clan, 71

La Rivière, Sieur, Governor of St. Lucia, 226

La Rochelle, France, immigration into Canada from, 7; number of ships from, to Canada in 1754, 25

La Salle, René-Robert Cavalier, Sieur de, a trading at Niagara erected by, in 1676, 75; French claim to the Ohio based upon the discovery by, in 1679, 329; untenable basis of claim of the French based upon the discovery of, 332

Lambert, M., Paris banker, the confidential correspondence to Mildmay entrusted to, 315

Lascelles, Captain, East India goods of, put up for auction, 257

La Tour, Charles de, Acadia and, 168

Laurentian Plateau and Canada, 6

La Vérendrye, Pierre Gaultier de Varennes, Sieur de, search of, for the Western Sea, 51

Law, Jacques-François, in charge of French troops sent against Trichinopoly, 289; compelled to take up a defensive position at Seringham, 289; surrender of, to Major Lawrence in 1752, 289

Law, John, organizes the Mississippi Company, 263; consolidates various French trading companies into the Compagnie Perpetuelle des Indes, 264

Lawrence, Major Charles, sent to Beaubassin with troops, 193; faced by a superior force, is obliged to retire, 193; return of, to the Missaquash River with a large body of troops, 194; the building of a fort by, 194; becomes Colonel, and Governor of Nova Scotia, 202; petition to, by the refugee Acadians, 202; gives up hope that the Acadians will be good subjects, 205; problem of the disposal of the Acadians stated by, 205

Lawrence, Major Stringer, in charge of the expedition against Tanjore in 1749, 278; rebuked by the East India Company directors, 278; aid brought by, to Muhammad Ali, 288; efforts of, to save Chanda Sahib, 289; forces Law to surrender, 289; plan of, to capture Pondicherry and Dupleix, laid aside on orders of President Saunders, 289; forces way into Trichinopoly in 1753 with a great convoy, 291

Lawrencetown, Nova Scotia, grants of lands upon site of, 201

Lawyers, in New France, opposition to, 22

Lead, value of, in Indian trade at Albany and at Montreal, 45; value of, sent to India in 1730, 255

Leadenhall Street, home of the London East India Company, 243

Le Caribou, King's ship built in Canada, poor quality of, 24

Leeks, cultivation of, in Canada, 13

Le Havre, France, number of ships from, to Canada in 1754, 25; manufacture of tobacco by the Compagnie des Indes at, 267

Leigh [Leagh] Sir Oliph, activities of followers of, on St. Lucia, 224

Leisler, Jacob, New York leader, a northern colonial concert for defence fostered by, in 1690, 123

Le Long Sault, Canada, number of bundles of furs drawn from, 54

Le Loutre, Jean Louis, Abbé, effort of, with his Indians to capture Annapolis Royal in 1744, 176-7; missionary to the Micmac in Nova Scotia, 187; enjoys a pension from the French King, 187; establishes a mission at Shubenacadie in 1738, 187; influence of, over the Micmac, 187; goes to France to seek support in the reconquest of Acadia, 187; arrival of, at Louisbourg, 187; agreement of, with Bigot in 1749 to break the peace, 187-8; incites the Micmac to make war on the English, 188; acts under the orders of the Governor General of New France, 188; secures food supplies from Bonaventure, 190; gathers his hostile Indians at Chignecto, 192; given credit by Bigot for breaking the peace, 192; Indians under leadership of, destroy Beaubassin and oppose Major Lawrence, 193; threatens the Acadians with a massacre, 194; rewards Indians for English prisoners and scalps, 195; goes to Quebec to make clear the difficulties of the Acadians, 196; opposes the sending of priests to Nova Scotia, 198; views of, supported by Abbé d'Isle-Dieu and the French minister, 199; asks additional priests for the refugee Acadians, 199; establishes headquarters at Beauséjour, 199; instructs Father Daudin in his duties, 200; return of, from France in 1753 stiffens resistance of the Acadians, 202; again sends his Indians against the English, 203; payments made by, for English scalps, 203; refugee Acadians show hostility against, 204

Lemaire, Father, permitted to serve in

Nova Scotia without taking the required oath, 199–200

Lescarbot, Marc, Acadia and, 168

Le St. Lawrent, King's ship built in Canada, poor quality of, 24

Libraries, in Canada, 12

Licences, the granting of, to engage in the Canadian fur trade in 1681, 44; method of distributing, 44; number of, granted, 44; suppression of, in 1686, 44; value of, at Detroit, 46; granted to English traders in 1716 by the Albany Commissioners, 84; the securing of, by the East India Company for the export of silver from England, 251; granted by the East India Company to those engaged in the country trade, 253; granted by the Compagnie des Indes Orientales to individual merchants to trade to the East Indies, 263; granted by the Compagnie Perpetuelle des Indes to those engaged in the slave trade, 267

Lindsay, John, Commissary at Oswego, report of, in 1749 on the fur trade, 91

Linen thread, importation of, into Canada, 25

Little Niagara, trading post constructed by Clauzonne de Joncaire, 99; description of, in 1751, 104

Little Plover, early Iroquoian clan, 71

Little Turtle, Tuscarora Indian clan, 70

Livingston, Philip, accused of appropriating the land of one of the Mohawk villages, 118

Livingston, William, supposed author of A Review of Military Operations in North America, 131

Livre tournois, value of, in terms of English money, 23

Loans, made by the "General Society" to the government, 243, 244–5

Lodges, Indian, appearance of, in the Great Lakes region, 36; peculiarities of, built by the Algonquians, 36

Lodi dynasty, overthrow of, by Baber in India, 233

London, merchants of, favour the Albany-Montreal contraband trade, 86; merchants of, secure a charter from Elizabeth to trade to the East Indies, 235; opposition of stockholders of, to Clive's attempt to control the East India Company, 250

London, supplies from Bigot to Le Loutre on the ship, 188

London East India Company, see Governor and Company of Merchants of London trading into the East Indies

Long House, Iroquoian, description of, 66; symbolism of, in Iroquoian tradition, 69

Longueuil, Charles le Moyne, 1st Baron de, a house at Onondaga built by, in 1711, 78; seeks the construction of a post at Irondequoit Bay, 82

Longueuil, Charles le Moyne, 2nd Baron de, acting Governor General of New France, 1752, seeks in vain to secure food for his proposed expeditionary force, 30–1; advises Abbé Gérard not to feel bound by his oath, 198; desire of, to send priests to the Acadians, 198

Lord Commissioner, plan of the ministry to send to America a, 166

Lords Commissioners for Trade and Plantations, see Board of Trade

Lords Justices, permit the British commissioners at Paris to deal with Acadia and St. Lucia in alternate discussions, 306

Lords of the Confederation, Iroquoian, the Tree of Peace and, 69; number of, 70; distribution of, among the Five Nations, 71; hereditary titles and, 71; meetings of, and "the Great Binding Law," 72; title not recognized in military operations, 73; poverty of, 73

L'Orient, Brittany, establishment of, by the French East India Company, 262; value of East India commodities sold at, in 1742, 266

Lottery, Walpole suggests a, in England to raise funds for colonial defence, 162

Louis XIV, of France, attitude of, toward the coureurs de bois, 43–4; regulation of the fur trade by, in 1681, 44; the cession of Acadia by, 171; concessions for the Acadians secured by, 171

Louis XV, Acadians appeal to, in 1749, 190

Louisbourg, Isle Royale, plans for the strengthening of, 20; inability of Canada to supply wheat for the garrison at, 29–30; establishment of, in 1717, a part of the New French imperialistic program, 80, 182; opposition of Massachusetts Bay to the English colonial provision trade with, 115; ships from, to Acadia, sent to bring back the Acadians, 172; successful attack upon, by the New Englanders, 176, 298; the return of, to the French by the Treaty of Aix-la-Chapelle, 179; dependence of, upon supplies furnished by the Acadians, 186

Louisiana, Province of, developments in, 3; within the governor-generalship of New France, 4; the vulnerability of, in case of attack, 31; no compensating revenues from the possession of, 32; debts owed by the planters of, to the Compagnie des Indes, 268; small returns to France made by, 268; the French inland approaches to, to be protected by the British proposals of February 20, 1755, 336

Lower Counties on the Delaware, not comprehended specifically in the Albany Plan of Union, 134

Lucknow, India, English factory at, 244

Lunenburg, Nova Scotia, establishment of, 201; early turbulence of Germans at, 201; progress at, 201

Lydius, John Henry, activities of, in Canada, 90; sent as a prisoner to Rochefort, France, 90; subsequent activities of, in New York, 90; aids the Susquehanna Company to purchase the Wyoming lands, 122

Lynde, Benjamin, placed on the Massachusetts Bay Council committee on colonial union, 152

Lynx, the Great Lakes region haunted by, 36; value of skins of, in Canada, 55

Lyon, France, the establishment of a beaver-hat manufactory at, in 1702, 60

Macarty-Martique [Macarthey-Mactaig], Major Commandant of the Illinois country, attention of, concentrated on sale of brandy to Indians, 52

Mace, the importations of, into England from the Far East, 236

Machault d'Arnonville, Jean Baptiste de, Minister of the Marine, sends report of the death of Jumonville in the Ohio country, 324

Macnémara, Admiral, Boscawan's attempt to capture the fleet under, in 1755, 338

Madras [Madraspatam], India, the lease of, to the English in 1640, 237; the building of Fort St. George at, 238; becomes the headquarters of the eastern Presidency, 238; drawbacks of, and advantages of, 238; a place of refuge after 1707, 247; early slow growth of, 248; remarkable development of, after 1685, 248; population of, in 1750, 248; incorporation of, in 1726, 249; local government within the Presidency of, 249–50; investment of, by the French in 1746, 273; the promise of, to the Nabob of Arcot by Dupleix, 273; the surrender of, 273, 298; the ransom treaty involving, 273–4; quarrel between La Bourdonnais and Dupleix over, 274; Dupleix's plans respecting, 274–5; returned to the Brit-

ish by the Treaty of Aix-la-Chapelle, 275; native merchants of, refuse to transfer interests to Pondicherry, 274–5; trade of, falls off, 285; military supplies and troops sent to, 285–6; the inclusion of, in the Treaty of Aix-la-Chapelle only by inference, 301

Madras Presidency, the, cost of supporting, 1729–33 and 1750–55, 258; lack of interest of, in the politics of India before 1745, 271–2; agrees not to engage in land hostilities, 273; the ransom treaty signed by, in 1746, 273–4; expeditions against Tanjore sent by, 275–6; rebuked by the East India Company directors, 278; support of Muhammad Ali by, 280; receives for the United Company Bahur and St. Thomé, 280; support of Nazir Jang with men and money by, 281; preparations of, to resist Dupleix's system, 286; basis of peace with French suggested by, 286; support of Muhammad Ali and the rulers of Tanjore and of Mysore by, 286; continued aid sent to Muhammad Ali at Trichinopoly by, 292; refusal of, to recognize the authority of Dupleix as protector of the Coromandel Coast, and the superior authority of Salabat Jang, 293

Maestricht, psychological effect of the appearance of Marshall Saxe before, in 1747, 300

Mahé de la Bourdonnais, Bertrand-François, French naval officer, summoned to India from Mauritius by Dupleix, 273; indecisive naval engagement between Peyton and, 273; investment of Madras by, 273; ransom treaty signed by, 273–4; serious friction between Dupleix and, 274; departure of, from the Coromandel Coast, 274

Mahrattas, rise of the power of, in the Western Ghats, 233; support Clive at Arcot, 288; raid the region about Pondicherry in 1752, 290

Maillard, Father, enters Nova Scotia to win back the pro-English Micmac, 203; makes plans with Le Loutre to send the Indians again against the English, 203

Maize, raising of, by the Indians, 36, 66

Man Frightened, Iroquoian hereditary title, 71

Maria Theresa, Empress and Queen, the War of the Austrian Succession and, 299

Marin, Pierre Paul, Sieur, commandant at La Baye, the quest of the Western Sea by, 51; great profit drawn by, from La Baye, 55

Marine, French Minister of the Department of, responsibility of, for the government of New France, 21–2; see also Maurepas, Rouillé, Machault

Market days in Canada, 13

Marquette, Father Jacques, S.J., missionary activities of, 42; account of early Shawnee villages on the Ohio by, 66

Marriage, in Canada, 14

Marseille, France, number of ships from, to Canada in 1754, 25

Marshes, treatment of, in Acadia, 168

Martel, Sieur, a monopoly of all supplies for the King's troops at Montreal enjoyed by, 27

Marten, the Great Lakes region haunted by, 36; skins of, drawn from de la Mer d'Ouest, 55; value of, in Canada, 55–6; importance of skins of, as an export from Canada, 56

Martial law, right to exercise in the Far East accorded to the London East India Company, 247

Martin, François, Governor of Pondicherry, the fortification of the factory by, in 1687, 262; the second period of the governorship of Pondicherry by, of great importance, 262

Martin, M., sent to Canada to study trade needs, 62

Martinique, West Indies, number of ships from, to Canada in 1754, 25; Dominica a life line between Guadeloupe and, 208; the Governor of, prevents the building of an English fort on Dominica, 211; the French colonization of Dominica from, 215; expedition of the French from, against the Negroes of St. Vincent, 216–7; the Governor of, asserts French rights to Tobago, 223; claims to, purchased by du Parquet in 1650, 225; the settlers of St. Lucia surrender the island to the Governor of, 227; debts owed by the planters of, to the Compagnie des Indes, 268

Maryland, Province of, invited to be represented at the Six Nations conference, 111; commissioners sent to Albany to represent, 114; powers granted by, to its commissioners, 116; the quota of men assigned to, in King William's War, 123; under the Pownall proposal, to help defend Lake Erie, 131; representation of, under the Albany Plan of Union, 135; government of, ignores the Albany Plan of Union, 146; recommendation by Walpole that the defence of Virginia be aided by, 162

Mascarene [Mascareene, Mascarin], John Paul, Governor of Annapolis, on the light financial burdens of the Acadians, 169; on the rapid growth of the population of Nova Scotia, 174; on the influence of French priests upon the Acadians, 174; disobedient attitude of the Acadians according to, 174–5; warns the Board of Trade that the Acadians were a potential danger, 177; asks that French Protestant and non-French Catholic priests be sent to the Acadians, 177; discourages the Bishop of Quebec who plans to enter Nova Scotia, 178; difficulty of removing the Acadians presented by, 178; recommends the planting of British families on the eastern shore of Nova Scotia, 181

Mascouten [Mas-Koutin] Indians, location of, 41; strength of, 41; furs of, traded to the Ottawa, 43

Massachusetts Bay, Province of, shipping of, contrasted to that of Canada, 25; opposition of the government of, to the selling of food-supplies at Cape Breton, 34; commissioners of, attend the Albany Indian conference of 1750, 94; the government of, invited to be represented at the Six Nations conference of 1754, 111; commissioners sent to Albany to represent, 114; powers granted by, to the Albany commissioners, 114–5; favours the erection of forts in the Iroquoian country, 114–5; the commissioners of, resent the conduct of de Lancey at Albany, 117; quota of men assigned to, in King William's War, 123; commissioners of, to the Albany Congress favour a northern colonial union, 129; representation of, under the " Plan of a Proposed Union," 130; under the Pownall proposal to help defend Lake Champlain, 131; representation of, under the Albany Plan, 135; aim of the commissioners of, to secure the office of President General, 139; commissioners of, alone possessed adequate power to form a union, 143; the prolonged deliberation of the government of, over plans for an American colonial union, 150–8; a new plan of union formulated by the general committee of, on a union, 152; vote of the Assembly of, in favour of a general union of the colonies, 154; rejection of the Albany Plan of Union by, 154–5; refusal of, to approve the new plan of union, 156; the London Agent of, called upon to oppose the Albany Plan, 155;

reasons for opposition to the Albany Plan of Union by, 155; alone of the colonial governments, sought earnestly to provide a satisfactory basis for union, 157–8; great interest in the Canso fisheries developed by the people of, 175–6

Masse, Father Enomond, S.J., work of, among the Micmac, 41

Masulipatam, India, an English factory established at, in 1614, 237; gives way to Madras as a commercial centre, 248; French factory at, made subordinate to Pondicherry in 1699, 262–3; the gift of, to the Compagnie des Indes by Chanda Sahib, 277; Dupleix rebuked by the Compagnie in 1753 for antagonizing the English and Dutch at, 292; the Compagnie des Indes willing to surrender its privileged position at, 294; temporary Anglo-French treaty neutralizes, 296; the United East India Company unwilling to insist on the exclusive control of, 322

Matron mother, importance of, among the Iroquois, 70

Mats, the making of, by the Indians, 36

Maumee River, lands of the Miami Indians lying about, 333; the region west of, conceded to the French by the British, 335

Maurepas, Jean Frederick Phelippeaux, Comte de, Minister of the Marine, permits the Governor of New France to continue the Canada-New York neutrality, 92–3

Mauritius, La Bourdonnais, outfits a French fleet at, 273

Melons, cultivation of, in Canada, 13

Mémoires des Commissaires du Roi et ceux de La Majeste Britannique (Paris, 1756), 307

Memramcook, settlement of, by Acadians, 174

Menard, Father, mission to the Ottawa by, 42; martyrdom of, 42

Menominee [Folles Avoines, Oumoominiees] Indians, location of, 40; enumeration of, 40; furs of, traded to the Ottawa, 43; number of, trading at Oswego in 1749, 101

Mercantilism, application of the principles of, in New France, 23

Merchants, of Albany and the fur trade, 76, 78, 82, 85–6, 120; of England, and the East Indies, 235–60; of France, and Canada, 10, 17, 25, 27, 56, 58; and the East Indies, 261–70, 278, 292, 294; of Holland and the East Indies, 235–7, 259–60; of Montreal and the fur trade,

17, 56, 58; and the contraband trade, 62, 76, 78, 85; and Oswego, 89, 91; of Quebec, manner of living of, 16

Merligueche Bay, Acadians of, welcome the English, 182

Miami [Twightwee] Indians, location of, 40; strength of, 40; mission to, established by Father Allouez, 42; furs of, traded to the Ottawa, 43; number of, trading at Oswego in 1749, 101; project of Abbé Piquet to fall upon the revolting, 106–7

Miami, trading post on the Maumee, the trade of, leased to St. Ange, 47; terms of trading lease of, 47; number of bundles of fur drawn from, 54; see also Fort Miami

Michilimakinac, establishment of a mission at, by Father Allouez, 42; the mission at, accused of serious abuses in the Indian trade, 51; importance of, as a trading post, 53–5; number of bundles of fur secured from, 54; number of Indians of, trading at Oswego in 1749, 101

Michipicton [Michipictou], trading post, location of, 54; lease of, in 1743, 54; number of bundles of furs drawn from, 54

Mickelborne, Sir Charles, receives a licence from James I to trade to the Far East, 238

Micmac Indians, early efforts of the Jesuits among, 41; relations of the Acadians with, 169; friendly behaviour of, upon the arrival of the English settlers in Nova Scotia, 182; declaration of war of, against the English, 189; war belt of, sent to the St. John River Indians, 189; deadly forays of, 192; under Le Loutre destroy Beaubassin, 193; threaten to massacre the Acadians, 194; receive rewards from Le Loutre for English prisoners and scalps, 195; a band of, led to St. Michel by Le Loutre, 196; a band of, under Cope makes peace with the English, 197; again go on the warpath against the English, 203; do not want to receive paper money as payment for scalps, 203; terrorize the Acadians, 203–4

Mildmay, William, on the low price of English wheat in France, 31; a member of the Anglo-French joint commission of 1750–4, 303; expresses a low opinion of French diplomacy, 308–9; Shirley and, rebuked by the Board of Trade, justifies conduct to the Secretary of State, 309; agrees to prepare a memorial on St. Lucia, 309; criticism of Shirley's work on the memorial respecting Acadia by, 309–10; prepares a separate memorial on Acadia, which is sent to England, 310; manner of life of, in Paris, 311; joint statement of Shirley and, on the French mémoire on St. Lucia, 312–3; temporary return of, to England, 1751, 315; the undermining of Shirley by, 315–6; proposes De Cosné as a colleague, 315; ignored by Shirley in framing the English reply to the French mémoire on Acadia, 316; explanation offered to Shirley of his recall offered by, 316; proposals of, to end the Anglo-French disputes, 317–8; disillusionment of, 320; account of Albemarle's deep financial involvement by, 327–8

Milet, Father Pierre, S.J., mission to the Oneida established by, 77; great authority enjoyed by, while a prisoner among the Oneida, 77

Militarism, the French Empire and the spirit of, 342–3

Military law, right to exercise, in India accorded to the London East India Company, 240

Military service, implied obligation of, for Canadian seigneurs, 11; demand of Acadians of exemption from, 184

Militia, strength of, in Canada, 19

Milliquet, Mr., agent for the Crown to send to New York the King's present, 123

Minas, Nova Scotia, Acadians of, desire to leave after the cession of Acadia, 171; intractable attitude of the people of, 174–5; soldiers sent to, to construct barracks, 184; establishment of Fort Edward at, 191; Acadians of, threatened with death by the Micmac, 192; the priest at, permitted to serve without taking required oaths, 200; inhabitants of, petition the Bishop of Quebec for priests, 200; Rouillé points out the necessity for the destruction of the English fort at, 332

Minas Basin, Nova Scotia, Acadian settlements about, 168; parishes in the region of, 170; supplies from, support the Louisbourg garrison, 186

Mines, reserve of, by the French Crown found on Canadian seigneuries, 11

Mingo Indians, dependence of, upon the Iroquoian Confederation, 66

Mink, the Great Lakes region haunted by, 36; value of skins of, in Canada, 55

Mirepoix, Charles Pierre Gaston François de Levis, Duc de, French Ambassador in London, agrees to recommend that the court of France accept the British proposals relative to disputes in India, 322–3; a confidential mémoire to guide, in London negotiations, 328–9; interview of, with Robinson over the Ohio Valley, 329; shows lack of knowledge of the Ohio country, 329; proposes that all disputes be preferred to the joint commission, 330; counter proposals of Robinson to, of January 22, 1755, 330; accorded full powers of negotiation, 330; instructions to, of February 19, 331–2; continuance of, in London until July, 1755, 338

Miselle, Captain de Bonne de, nephew of La Jonquière, shares in the exclusive trade of Sault Ste. Marie, 28; receives a land patent, 28

Missaquash River, Nova Scotia, description of the region of, 167; de la Corne entrenches himself on the north bank of, 193; Major Lawrence builds a fort on the south bank of, 194; the building of a French fort on the north bank of, 194

Missisauga [Mississagué] Indians, a branch of the Chippewa, efforts by the French to prevent the, from trading with the Iroquois, 82; number of, trading at Oswego in 1749, 101

Mississippi Company, establishment of, by John Law, 263; absorbs the Compagnie des Indes Orientales, 263; absorbed into the Compagnie Perpetuelle des Indes, 264

Mocha, English trading activities at, opposed by the Turks, 236

Moguls [Mongols], invasions of India by the, 232

Mohammedanism, inability of, to uproot Hinduism in India, 234

Mohammedans, destruction of the Hindu Empire of Vijayanagar by, in 1565, 232

Mohawk Indians, location of the principal village of, 65; number of clans among, 70; number of phratries among, 70; number of ohwachira among, 71; position of, in the Confederation, 72; converts among, settle at La Prairie in 1668, 76; efforts of the Society for the Propagation of the Gospel to christianize, 97–8; determination of, to drive encroaching Englishmen away from their lands, 108; treatment of Oswego traders by, 108; the Board of Trade requests New York to take steps to win back the friendship of, 111; grievances of, against Philip Livingston and others for appropriating their lands, 118; conferences of, with the New York Council, 119; de Lancey promises justice to, 119; request a church with a bell, 121; proposal of William Johnson to send teachers to, 131; *see also* Caughnawaga

Monacjee, commander of the Tanjore troops, carries out the Rajah's command to put Chanda Sahib to death, 289

Money, in Canada, credit devices used as, 26; in India, 255–6; in England, 255

Monopoly, the spirit of, in New France, 27–8; and the Canadian fur trade, 44; and the export of beaver skins from Canada, 56–9; and the English East India trade, 235–60; and the Dutch East India trade, 235–7, 260; and the French East India trade, 261–98; the breakdown of British, within the Atlantic areas, 340; the spirit of the French Empire and, 342–3

Monsoon, destructive nature of the, in India, 238

Montagnais Indians, early trade contacts of, with French, 38; aid in driving the Five Nations southward, 38–9; efforts of the Recollets to christianize, 41

Montagu, John, 2nd Duke of, grant of St. Lucia and St. Vincent to, in 1722, 222, 228; unsuccessful application of, for Tobago, 222; sends Uring to settle St. Lucia, 228; failure of, to retain possession of St. Lucia, 228

Montague, Captain, of the *Mermaid*, ordered to protect the shipment of specie from Lisbon to Cadiz, 255

Montauban, France, cloth of, exported to Canada, 25

Montgomery, Philip Herbert, Earl of, grant of West India islands to, 218

Montreal, Canada, the Order of St. Sulpice and, 9, 17; population of, compared with that of Connecticut towns, 17; a great fur-trading centre, 17; leading structures in, 17; winter home of the Governor General, 17; appearance of, 17; social life at, 18; military defences of, 20; monopolies for the supply of the King's troops at, 27; price of beaver skin at, 44; contracts of *voyageurs* among the notarial records of 50, 53; fur-trading activities at, 56; the merchants of, find a market for furs among the English, 61; importance of Sault St. Louis in the contraband trade between Albany and, 76; high price of strouds at, 86; meeting of the estates of, to consider Canadian policy regarding Oswego, 89; the large

number of English at, 90; merchants of, buy goods wholesale from Oswego, 100; furs sent to Oswego by merchants of, 101

Monts, Pierre du Guast, Sieur de, Acadia and, 168

Moore, the Rev. Thoroughgood, sent to the Iroquois by the Society for the Propagation of the Gospel, 97; discouraging situation faced by, 97

Moose, the Great Lakes region haunted by, 36

Mootas Ali, supported by Dupleix as Nabob of the Carnatic, 290

Morris, Captain Charles, desire of, to bring about intermarriage between the Acadians and loyal Protestants, 179; survey of lands about the Bay of Fundy by, 179

Morris, Gov. Robert Hunter, of Pennsylvania, failure of, to support the Albany Plan of Union, 144–5

Mortars, production of, in Canada, 24

Mosquito Coast, British commercial expansion to, 340

Mount Johnson, on the Mohawk, home of William Johnson, 95

Muhammad [Mohammad] Ali, son of Anwar-ud-din, secures a refuge in Trichinopoly after his father's death, 280; claims to be Nabob of the Carnatic, 280; presents the United East India Company with Bahur and St. Thomé, 280; receives the support of the English at Trichinopoly, 280; support of Nazir Jang by, 281; repudiation of claims of, by Muzaffar Jang, 285; offer of, to surrender Trichinopoly for a stronghold in Golconda, 285; agrees not to turn over Trichinopoly to Chanda Sahib, 286; guaranteed aid by the English, 286; attack against, by Chanda Sahib in 1751, 286; an English force sent to aid, 286; secures as allies the rulers of Mysore and Tanjore, 288; approves the putting to death of Chanda Sahib, 289; promise of Trichinopoly to the King of Mysore by, 290; loses the support of the *Dalaway* of Mysore, 290; refusal of the French in 1754 to recognize the authority of, in the Carnatic, 293

Münster, Westphalia, activities at, in 1648 contrasted with those at Aix-la-Chapelle in 1748, 300–1

Murray, James, British general and Governor of Canada, on the limits of Canada, 4; on the French *arpent*, 6; report on *rentes* in Canada, 9; value of furs exported from Canada according to, 23

Murray, Joseph, a member of the New York Council, attends the Albany Congress, 114; influence of de Lancey at the Congress over, 139; Attorney General Smith's criticism of, 139

Muskrat, the Great Lakes region haunted by, 36; value of the skins of, in Canada, 56

Musquodoboit Valley, Nova Scotia, English plans to plant, 201

Muzaffar Jang [Muzaffar-ed-din, Musaffar-ed-din, French, Mousafirsingue], claimant of the subahdarship of the Deccan, basis of claims of, 276; agreement of, with Dupleix and Chanda Sahib, 276-7; aids in the overthrow of Anwar-ud-din, 276; at Arcot, 279; falls into the hands of Nasir Jang, 281; life of, saved by the death of Nasir Jang, 282; recognized by Nasir Jang's army as Subahdar of the Deccan, 283; goes to Pondicherry, 283; favours granted by, 283; a body of French troops accompanies, 284; revolt against, and death of, 284

Mysore, support of the Rajah of, by the English as against the French in 1751, 286; alliance of, with Muhammad Ali, 288; the Dalaway of, turns against Muhammad in favour of Dupleix, 290; the Rajah of, dissatisfied with the French alliance in 1754, 296

Nadir Shah, of Persia, invasion of India in 1739 by, 233

Nasir Jang, son of the Nizam, takes over the subahdarship of the Deccan, 275; Dupleix supports Muzaffar Jang in movement against, 276; previous recognition of the rights of, by Dupleix, 277; invasion of the Carnatic by, 281; description of the army of, 281; joined by English troops, 281; the French after an indecisive engagement retreat before, 281; capture of Muzaffar Jang by, 281; fruitless negotiations of, with Dupleix, 282; lack of discipline in the army of, 282; night attack against, 282; retreat of, to Jingi, 282; Pondicherry again threatened by, 282; difficulties faced by the army of, 282; the Pathan conspiracy against, 282; agrees to a treaty with Dupleix, 282; army of, attacked by the French, 282; the death of, 283

Nation du Chien, see Cherokee

Naval stores, the production of, in Canada favoured by the French government, 23; the manufacture of, at Crown Point and at Baie St. Paul, 23

Navy Board, the, France, disappointment of, over the poor quality of Canadian ships, 24

Negroes, the transportation of, and the Compagnie des Indes, 267

Nerbudda River, northern limit of the Vijayanagar empire, 232

Neutral Indians, Iroquoian family, crushing of, by the Five Nations, 69

Neutrality, policy of, adopted by Albany and Canada, 76, 78, 92; suggested agreement of, respecting Tobago, 221; between the French and the English proposed by Dupleix in King George's War, 273

Neutralized West India islands, the problem of, 3, 207; failure of the French to evacuate, according to treaty, 215-6, 217, 229; Robinson asks that the French evacuate, as a test of desire to fulfill the terms of the Treaty of Aix-la-Chapelle, 325; assurance by Rouillé in 1754 of the complete evacuation of, 325; see also Dominica, St. Lucia, St. Vincent, Tobago

Newcastle, Thomas Pelham-Holles, 1st Duke of, Secretary of State for the Northern Department, seeks funds for supporting resistance to the French, 161; succeeds his brother as Minister and First Lord of the Treasury, 1754, 323; conduct of public business by, 323

New England, the payment of quit-rents in, 8; hostility of the people of, toward the Albany neutrality policy, 76; development of the Canso fisheries by the people of, 175; troops of, destroyed at Grand Pré, 177; the capture of Louisbourg by troops from, 176, 298

New England Confederation of 1643, an English colonial union in 1754 and the, 123

New France, territorial limits of the governor-generalship of, 4; the government of, 19-23; a great financial liability, 31-2; difficulty of providing a proper administration for, 31; weakness of, in time of war, 31; need for great military supplies for, 31-2; arguments in favour of France giving up, 31-2; Galissonière's arguments for retaining, 32-3; resources of, 32; authorities of, take steps to arouse the resistance of the Acadians, 187; internal order within, provided for by the soldiers, 342-3; uniformity of pattern within, 343; scarcity within, 343; a world of officials, 343; a financial parasite, 343-4; settlements within, 344-5; advantages enjoyed by the government of, in face of British expansion, 345-6; see also Canada, Louisiana, and Cape Breton

New Hampshire, Province of, the payment of quit-rents in, 9; the government of, invited to be represented at the Six Nations conference, 111; commissioners sent to Albany to represent, 114; powers granted by, to the commissioners, 114-5; quota of troops assigned to, in King William's War, 123; representation of, under the "Plan of a Proposed Union," 130; under the Pownall proposal, to help defend Lake Champlain, 131; under the Albany Plan of Union, 135

New Jersey, Province of, invited to be represented at the Six Nations conference, 111; the Assembly of, refuses to send commissioners to Albany, 113; representation of, under the "Plan of a Proposed Union," 130; under the Pownall proposal to help defend Lake Ontario, 131; under the Albany Plan of Union, 135; hostility of the Assembly of, to the Albany Plan, 146-7; the Council of, asks that the Plan of Union be presented to the British ministers, 147

New Orleans, the City of, establishment of, a part of the New French imperialistic program, 80

Newport, Rhode Island, as a centre of British commercial expansion, 340

Newton, Sir Isaac, the value of English guineas reduced in 1717 on the advice of, 255

New York, the City of, size of, contrasted with Quebec, 15; as a centre of British commercial expansion, 340

New York, Province of, M. Callières-Bonnevue advises the seizure of, 45; neutrality between Canada and, during Queen Anne's War, 78; law passed by, in 1720 forbidding sale of Indian goods to the French, 86; the report of the Council of, on the effect of the law forbidding the sale of trading goods to the French, 86; the Assembly of, provides funds for a fort at Oswego, 88; the neutrality agreement between Canada and, continued, 92; Johnson becomes colonel of the militia of, 96; representatives of, at the Albany Congress not commissioned, 114; peculiar position of, with respect to the Congress, 116-7; grievances of the Six Nations against the people of, 118-9; quota of men assigned to, in King William's War, 123; the Assembly of, desires a colonial concert

during King George's War, 123; representation of, on the Grand Council under the "Plan of a Proposed Union," 130; under the Pownall proposal to help defend Lake Ontario, 131; under the Albany Plan of Union, 135; favourable attitude of, toward the idea of a colonial union, 147

New York Indian Commissioners, agents sent by, in 1720 to the Iroquois to protest against the French post at Niagara, 83; report of, on the fur trade of New York in 1725, 87; loss of influence with the Indians, 96, 99

Niagara River, number of bundles of furs drawn from, the trading post on the, 54; strategic importance of, 75; La Salle builds a trading house on, in 1676, 75; a temporary post on, constructed in 1687, 75; failure of early efforts of the French at, 75; the French rebuilt their post on, after the Treaty of Utrecht, 80; advantages enjoyed by the French in reoccupying, 80; a road constructed at the falls of, 82; Joncaire builds a trading post below the falls of, 83; the New York Indian Commissioners and the Indians express dissatisfaction over the French post at, 83-4; extravagant prices charged by the French at, 84; the French post at, in a ruinous condition in 1725, 87; new site selected for a fort on, 87-8; cost of constructing the French fort on, 88; Beauharnois and Dupuy desire the rebuilding of the trading house on, 88; increase in trade at, in 1728, 90; factors involved in the decline in trade at, after 1728, 90-1; number of packs of furs secured at, 91; the building of a French trading post above the falls of, 99; failure of the French at, to secure the Indian trade, 101, 104; low ratio of furs secured at the post on, by the French, 101; Robinson's proposal of February 10, 1755 to the British Cabinet for a mutual evacuation of, 331; the dismantling of the fort on, proposed by the British Cabinet on February 20, 335

Nicholson, Gov. Francis, of Nova Scotia, permits arrangements to be made for the departure of the Acadians, 171; refers to the Crown the requests of the Acadians, 172

Nieu Walcheren, see Tobago

Nipigon, trading post, lease of, in 1744, 54; number of bundles of fur drawn from, 54

Nipissing Indians, establishment of a mission for, by the Grey Friars, 42

Nizam-ul-Mulk, Subahdar of the Deccan, makes Anwar-ud-din Nabob of Arcot, 272; death of the, in 1748, 275

Noir, M. le, Governor of Pondicherry, improvement of the Far Eastern affairs of the Compagnie des Indes through the enterprise of, 265

Normandy, immigration into Canada from, 7, 12; the *habitants* of Canada retain the spirit of, 7; Canadian *habitants* and their ancestral homes in, 12

Normanville, Sieur de, enjoys a licence to trade at the Ouiatenon post, 47; terms of agreement of, with Montreal merchants, 47

Norris, Isaac, Speaker of the Pennsylvania Assembly, a commissioner at the Albany Congress, 114; failure of, to support the Albany Plan of Union in the Assembly, 145

North America, English claims in, according to the Albany Congress, 132; as set forth by the government in 1755, 335–8; French claims in, as set forth in 1755, 310, 337–8; sense of destiny of the French in, 351; and of the English in, 351

North Carolina, Province of, under the Pownall proposal, might help defend Lake Erie, 131; the sea-to-sea territorial claims of, ignored by the Albany Congress, 132; representation of, under the Albany Plan of Union, 135; the failure of the government of, to act on the Albany Plan of Union, 146

Northern Circars, India, French claim to, in 1754, 294; temporary Anglo-French treaty accords equality of privileges within, 296

Northern fox, drawn from de la Mer d'Ouest, 55

Northwest Ordinance of 1787, the " Representation on the Present State of the Union " of 1754 and the, 133

Nouveau Voyage aux Isles de l'Amérique (Paris, 1722), by Labat, 211

Nova Scotia, complexities presented by, 3; not comprehended in the Albany Plan of Union, 134; description of, 167–8; early settlers of, 168–75; humane government of the French Acadians of, 176; invasion of, by the French during King George's War, 177; desire of the Bishop of Quebec to enter, at the end of the war, discouraged, 178; determination of the British ministry to break up the

homogeneity of, through immigration, 179; the issue of the boundaries of, made acute in 1749, 180; survey of vacant lands in, secured by Shirley, 180; views of Shirley and Mascarene respecting the colonization of, 181; work of the colonization of, in the hands of the Board of Trade, 181; survey of steps taken to colonize, 181–3; provision for Protestant clergy and teachers in, 181–2; friendly attitude of the Acadians and Indians of, toward the newly arrived English settlers, 182; analysis of groups sent to colonize, 182; expense involved in establishing the English settlement in, 182; poor quality of the first English settlers of, 182–3; fortifications built in, 191; a military road constructed through the peninsula of, 191; determination of the French government not to send further priests to, 198–200; great expense of the English colonization of, 200; poor quality of Germans sent to, 200–1; establishment of other settlements than Halifax in, 201; *see also* Acadia

Noyan, Pierre Jacques Payen de, report of, on the Indian trade at Detroit, 46; becomes commandant of the Detroit post, 46; estimate of, as to the cost of transporting furs from Detroit to Montreal, 53

Nuns, elderly women of Canada become, 14

Oaths of loyalty, the Acadians and the issue of, 173–4; the refugee Acadians demand, taken in 1728, 202; Col. Lawrence stipulates new, 202

Oats, growing of, in Canada, 13

Occupatio, Roman law principle of, and the French claims in the New World, 50

Ogdensburg, New York, the mission of La Présentation on the site of, 103

Ogilvie, the Rev. John, missionary to the Mohawks, 98; encouragement of, by William Johnson, 98

O'Haguerty, Pierre André, author of *Essai sur les Intérêts du Commerce* (1754), 60; recommendations of, regarding the price of beaver skins, 60

Ohio Company, the sending of a French force against the agents of, an act of aggression, 329

Ohio River, the British Cabinet denies the French claim to, 338

Ohio Valley, developments in, 3; the sending of great food supplies to, secured by the French from the English colonies, 34; large amount of furs to be drawn from, 55; upper portion of, a vast Iroquoian hunting preserve, 55; project of Abbé Piquet to drive the English from, 107; the British prepared to use force against the French in, 322; Robinson suggests that the French, as a proof of peaceful intentions, withdraw from, 325; lands of, before the Treaty of Utrecht in the possession of the Five Nations, 329; sale of lands of the upper, to the English, 329; contention of Rouillé that no English claims to, could be based on the Treaty of Utrecht, and that France possessed the, 330; the British proposal of February 7, 1755 for a mutual evacuation of the upper, 330

Ohwachira, Iroquoian chosen brood family, ideas embodied in, 70; number of, distributed among the Five Nations, 71

Old Pretender, influence of the activities of, upon Anglo-French relations, 172

Olive oil, imported into Canada, 25

" One-fifth," payment of the, by Canadian seigneur upon alienating land, 11

Oliver, Andrew, on the committee on colonial union of the Massachusetts Bay Council, 151

Oneida Indians, fighting strength of, 65; location of, 65; number of clans among, 70; number of phratries among, 70; number of ohwachira among, 71; position of, within the Confederation, 72; converts among, settle at La Prairie in 1668, 76; work of Milet among, 77; sachems of, express fear in 1720 of the French, 83; pro-French leanings of, after Aix-la-Chapelle, 98; the Oswego traders forced to employ, at the portages, 109

Onondaga, the Tree of the Great Peace planted at, 69; council center for the Six Nations, 69, 72; work of Lamberville at, 76; William Johnson rebukes the Six Nations at, 111; plan to have the Indian conference of 1754 at, changed, 112; proposal of William Johnson for a fort at, 131

Onondaga Council, significance of, considered, 68-9; efforts of Johnson at the, to keep the Six Nations from resorting to the French, 96-7

Onondaga Indians, fighting strength of, 65; location of, 65; description of the long house of, 66; cosmology of, 69; number of clans among, 70; phratries among, 70; number of ohwachira among, 71; posi-

tion of, in the Confederation, 72; give Longueuil, an adopted son, permission to build at Niagara, 87; pro-French leanings of, after Aix-la-Chapelle, 98; sent from La Présentation to Montreal, 106; question of the sincerity of the conversion of, to Roman Catholicism, 106; proposal of William Johnson to send teachers to, 131

Onondaga River, New York traders permitted to erect a trading post at the mouth of, 86; see also Oswego

Opposite-Side-of-the-Hand, early Iroquoian clan, 71

Order of St. Sulpice, the great church of, at Montreal, 17; seigneur of the Island of Montreal, 18

Orléans, Philip, Duke of, 304

Orry, Philibert, French Comptroller General of Finance, interest of, in the Compagnie des Indes, 265

Orry de Fulvy, a royal commissary of the Compagnie des Indes, 205

Osborne [Osborn], Sir Danvers, Governor of New York, requested by the Board of Trade to call an English colonial-Six Nations' conference, 111; death of, 111

Osnabrück, Westphalia, activities at, in 1648 contrasted to those at Aix-la-Chapelle in 1748, 300-1

Oswegatchie River, the location of La Présentation mission on, 103

Oswego [Choueguen], English build a post at, 86; threats of the French to prevent the English trading at, 87; plan of Indians to sell land of, to the French, 87; number of English traders at, in 1726, 88; construction of a fort at, by vote of the New York Assembly, 88; description of, by Governor Burnet, 88; defences of, 88-9; Beauharnois sends a summons to the English governor of, 89; Burnet prepared to defend, from the French, 89; the French give up plans to destroy, 89; effect on the French trade of the abundance of rum at, 91; likened to a " trap " and " a Silver Mine " by the Indians, 91; number of packs of furs secured at, in 1749, 91; description of, by Lewis Evans, 92; the Six Nations a barrier to the destruction of, by the French, 92; brought within the scope of the New York-Canada neutrality, 92; ruinous and defenceless condition of, in 1744, 93; not seriously threatened in King George's War, 93; relations of William Johnson to the trade of, 95; garrison of, supplied by Johnson, 95; trade of, after the Peace of

Aix-la-Chapelle takes two forms, 100; fierce competition among the Indian traders at, 100; demand for a trading monopoly at, 100–1; enumeration of Indian groups at, in 1749, 101; price paid for beaver skins at, in 1749, 101; military weakness of, according to Abbé Piquet, 105; traders of, mistreated by the Mohawks, 108; the debauching of the Indians at, 118; proposal of William Johnson for a stronger fort at, 131; Rouillé points out the necessity for the destruction of the English fort at, 332; see also Fort Oswego

Otis, Col. James, on the committee on colonial union of the Massachusetts Bay House of Representatives, 151; favours a general union of the colonies, 154

Ottawa [Outawa, Utaüois, Waganhaes] Indians, become middlemen in the French fur trade, 39, 43; retreat of, in the face of opposition of the Five Nations, 39; scope of trading activities of, 43; cowed by the Iroquoian blows, 43; missionaries complain of the brandy trade among, 51; the establishment of Detroit to prevent inconveniences by, 77; offer to aid the English destroy Niagara in 1747, 94

Otter skins, value of, in Canada, 55–6

Oudiette, Nicholas, farmer of the royal revenues of Canada, enjoys a monopoly of the export of beaver skins, 57; price paid by, for the monopoly, 57; enjoys the royal fourth part of all skins, 57; bankruptcy of, in 1685, 57

Ouiatenon, trading post of, method of carrying on trade at, 47; a leased post after 1743, 47; number of bundles of furs drawn from, 54; value of the lease of, 55–6; see also Fort Ouiatenon

Ouiatenon Indians, location of, 40; enumeration of, 40

Ouvernard, Madame, a Carib woman, mother of Thomas Warner, early friendship of, for the English and later hostility toward them, 210

Oxen, the use of, in Canada, 13

Pacifism, within the British Empire, 346

Pagoda, India coin, value of a, 256; the, minted by Dupleix to circulate in the Deccan, 283

Painted Turtle, early Iroquoian clan, 71

Parishes, of Canada, 8; and the seigneuries, 10; of Acadia, enumeration of, 170; the providing priests for, 170, 198–9

Parliament, the authority of, recognized in the Albany Plan of Union, 134–5; taxation of the colonies by, advocated by Shirley, 158; conditional support by Franklin of colonial taxation by, 158–9; colonial representation in, suggested by Shirley, 159; Franklin's conditional support of colonial representation in, 159–60; the final authority in respect to the constitution of the British Empire, 166; the House of Commons declaration of the supremacy of acts of, over royal patents, 242; the creation of the "General Society" for trade to the East Indies by, in 1698, 243

Parma, Dutchy of, and the Treaty of Aix-la-Chapelle, 301

Parquet, Sieur du, Governor of Martinique, charges by the English against the conduct of, on St. Lucia, 225; defence of, by the French commissaries, 225; grant of St. Lucia to Sieur Rousselan by, 225; earlier purchase of claims to St. Lucia, Martinique, and Granada, from the Compagnie des Isles by, 225; death of, 226

Parson's Cause, the issues involved in, and the Albany Plan of Union, 138

Parthians, invasion of India by, 232

Partridge, Col. Oliver, a commissioner for Massachusetts Bay at the Albany Congress, 114

Parvana, given by Chanda Sahib to the Compagnie des Indes for forty-two aldees, 277

Paseund, Sieur, a monopoly of walrus and seal fishing on the Magdalen Islands enjoyed by, 27

Paternalism, in New France, 23

Pathans, of northwest India, conspiracy of, in Nasir Jang's army, 282; death of Nasir Jang at the hands of, 283; support the claims of Muzaffar Jang, 283; revolt of, against Muzaffar, 284

Patna, India, English factory at, in 1719, 244; and in 1750, 260; activities of Charnock at, 247

Patten [Pattin], John, English trader, description of Detroit by, 50; number of French traders resorting to Detroit according to, 53

Pays d'Aunis, France, immigration into Canada from, 7

Peace of Aix-la-Chapelle, Anglo-French relations after the, and the Six Nations, 98; and Acadia, 179–205; and the West Indies, 222, 229; and India, 275–296; and the Paris joint commission, 302–22; and direct diplomacy, 322–38; and the

Ohio Valley, 318, 324–5; *see also* Treaty of Aix-la-Chapelle

Peace of Nijmegen, the Dutch concede Tobago to the French in the, 220

Péan [Bearn], Major Michel Jean Hugues, contracts for flour and vegetables for Canadian troops enjoyed by, 27; wife of, appropriated by Bigot, 28; fraudulent practices of Bigot and, 28; compelled to pay a great fine, 28

Peas, cultivation of, in Canada, 13

Penn, John, son of Richard Penn joint-Proprietor of Pennsylvania, commissioned to attend the Albany Congress, 114; proposed purchase of Pennsylvania land from the Iroquois announced at the Albany Congress by, 121

Pennsylvania, Province of, invited to be represented at the Six Nations conference, 111; commissioners sent to Albany to represent, 114; powers granted by, to its commissioners, 115; the traders of, accused of making unauthorized paths upon Iroquoian lands, 120; lands along the Susquehanna River purchased of the Six Nations by the Proprietors of, in 1754, 122; quota of men assigned to, in King William's War, 123; under the Pownall proposal, to help defend Lake Erie, 131; representation of, under the Albany Plan of Union, 135; the Albany Plan of Union recommended by Governor Hamilton to the Assembly of, 144; shabby treatment of Franklin by, 145; rejection of the Plan of Union by, 145; recommendation by Walpole that the defence of Virginia be aided by, 162

Penobscot River, in 1667 the French insist that Acadia extends westward to, 333; the division of Acadia and, 336

Pentagoet River, see Penobscot River

Pepper, quantity of, imported from India in 1730, 256; high prices demanded by natives for, in 1750, 256; arrangements for a supply of, to be furnished by the ruler of Anjengo, India, 256; efforts of the East India Company to secure from Sumatra supplies of, 256

Pepperell [Pepperrell], Sir William, leader of the New England troops against Louisbourg, 298

Perpetuana, English woolen fabric, value of, sent to India in 1730, 255

Persia, English factories in, in 1702, 244; in 1750, 260

Persians, invasions of India by, 232

Peters, Richard, Secretary of Pennsylvania, on the loss of influence among the Six

Nations of the English, 107; a commissioner at the Albany Congress, 114; probable author of "A Plan for a General Union," 127

Petitcodiac, the settlement of, by Acadians, 174

Petite Rivière, Canadian village of, 18

Petun [Tionontati] Indians, Iroquoian family, the crushing of, by the Five Nations, 69

Peyton, Commodore Edward, takes the place of Barnett in command of the fleet in East Indies, 273; indecisive engagement between La Bourdonnais and, in 1756, 273; takes fleet to Calcutta, 273

Philadelphia, size of, contrasted with Quebec, 15; to be the temporary capital of the colonies under the Plan of Union, 136; as a centre of British expansion, 340

Philipps, Colonel Richard, Governor of Nova Scotia, said to have secured from the Acadians in 1729 unconditional oaths of loyalty, 173

"Philolethes," author of *A Short Reply to Mr. Hopkins' Vindication*, 1755, 141; on the limited powers of the Albany commissioners, 141; on the desire of the commissioners to secure adoption of the Plan of Union by Parliament, 142

Philosophy, the study of, at Quebec, 12

Phratries, a grouping of clans, the Six Nations and, 70

Physics, the study of, at Quebec, 12

Piacenza, the City of, and the Treaty of Aix-la-Chapelle, 301

Piankashaw Indians, location of, 40; enumeration of, 40

Pice, a Malabar Coast coin, the value of, 256

Pichon, Thomas, commissaire at Fort Beauséjour, becomes British agent and supplies information, 201

Pickawillany, inability of Longueuil to secure food for his proposed expedition against, 31; the prospect of the restoration of British trade at, 335

Piece goods, quantity of, imported from India in 1730, 256

Pigeon Hawk, early Iroquoian clan, 71

Pike, Lieut. Z. M., enumeration of Indians by, 41

Pipe-smoking in Canada, 7

Piquet [Picquet], Abbé François, of the Order of St. Sulpice, in charge of the Indian mission of the Lake of the Two Mountains, 95; influence of, combatted by William Johnson, 95; establishes the mission of La Présentation, 102; assistance received by, from the Canadian government, 103; commissioned by La Jonquière to go to Lake Erie, 104; description of trip of, to Lake Erie in 1751, 104; report of, on the progress of La Présentation, 105; bold project of, to drive the English traders from the Ohio Valley, 106; the French minister opposes the military expedition of, 107; visits France, 107; rewarded by the King, 107; extent of real influence of, with the Six Nations problematical, 107

Pirogues, Canadian communication by means of, 6

Pitkin, Deputy Gov. William, a Connecticut commissioner at the Albany Congress, 114; appointed on the committee on colonial union at the Albany Congress, 124; on the committee that drew up "The Reasons Considered . . . by the Assembly of Connecticut . . .", 148

Piziquid, Nova Scotia, parishes of, and communicants of, 170; inhabitants of, threatened by death, 192; hostile conduct of Acadians at, 204; influence of Daudin at, 204; inhabitants of, agree to mend their ways, 205

"Plan for a General Union of the British Colonies in North America," 127; Richard Peters probable author of, 127

"Plan of a General Concert" of the North American colonies, drawn up by the Board of Trade, 161–4

"Plan of a Proposed Union of the Several Colonies . . .", 1754, apparently framed by Thomas Hutchinson, 128–9; hostility of de Lancey to, 129; the union of colonies under the Dominion of New England and, 129–30; representation of the colonies in the Grand Council provided for, 130; the extent to which the Albany Plan of Union follows the, 133–8

Plough, type of, used in Canada, 13

Pointz, Capt. John, and Company, agreement of, in 1681, with the Duke of Courland, to colonize Tobago, 221; revival of the claims of, in 1699

Poitou, France, immigration into Canada from, 7; Canadian habitants and the ancestral homes in, 12

Polk, the Rev. Robert, appointed chaplain at Madras, 287

Pondicherry, the acquisition of, in 1674 by the French East India Company, 262; description of, 262; temporary loss of, to the Dutch, in 1693, 262; return of, at Ryswick, 262; increased importance of, after 1699, 262; the Conseil Supérieur established by, 262; great improvement in the affairs of the Compaigne des Indes at, after 1726, 265; M. le Noir, governor of, 265; M. Dumas succeeds le Noir at, in 1735, 265; financial difficulties of, in 1742, relieved by Dupleix, 271; the Conseil Supérieur of, supports Dupleix's Madras policy, 274; determination of, to eliminate the British from the Coromandle Coast, 274; attack against, by the English, 274; threatened by Nasir Jang, 282–3; exposed position of, after the surrender of Law and d'Auteuil in 1752, 289; reenforcements received at, from France in 1754, 295; danger to, in the War of the Austrian Succession, 299

Popow Negroes, characteristics of, 68

Population, of Canada, increase in, 1666–1754, 5; of the various Great Lakes Indian tribes, 39–40; of the Iroquoian Confederation, 65; of Acadia, 1658–1750, 168–9

Pork, no export of, from Canada in 1754, 24

Port Louis, Brittany, gift of, to the French East India Company, 262; erection of the new port, L'Orient near, 262

Port Royal, Nova Scotia, church communicants of the parish of, 170; Acadians of, desire to leave after the cession of Acadia, 171; see also Annapolis Royal

Porto Nova, India, the gift of, from Chanda Sahib to Madame Dupleix, 277

Portugal, the sale of French beaver hats in, 61; a beaver hat manufactory in, 61

Portuguese, the significance of the activities of, in India, 234; difficulties faced by, 235; give way to the English and Dutch, 235; opposition of, to the English in India, 236

Potawatomi [Poutouatomis] Indians, location of, 40; enumeration of, 40; furs of, traded to the Ottawa, 43; number of, trading at Oswego in 1749, 101

Poutrincourt, Sieur de, Acadia and, 168

Powder, value of, in Indian trade, at Albany and at Montreal, 45

Pownall, Thomas, secretary to Governor Osborne, consulted by Franklin on his plan of union, 125; plan presented by, for the defence of the colonial frontiers, 130–1; attack against, apparently by William Livingston, 131; defence of, by the Massachusetts Bay commissioners, 131; thanks voted to, by the Albany Congress for defence proposals, 131

Pragmatic Sanction, the renewal of, in the Treaty of Aix-la-Chapelle, with exceptions, 301

Prairie de la Madeleine, see Prairie de la Magdelene

Prairie de la Magdelene [Madeleine], and the New York boundary, 5; Canadian stockaded village, 18

Praying Indians, see Caughnawaga Indians

Première navigation, of the Compagnie des Indes, explanation of term, 266; significance of, 266–7

President General of the English colonies, provided for in the Albany Plan of Union, 136; powers of, 136–9

Prévost, M., Commissaire Ordonnateur of Isle Royale, on the Micmac peace with the English, 197; reports on Indian hostilities against the English, 203

Prince, Richard, member of Madras Council, rebuked for his connection with the Tanjore expedition, 278

Prince Edward Island, see Isle St. Jean

Printing, not permitted in Canada, 12; freedom of, in the English colonies, 341

Prisoners of war, treatment of, by the Iroquois, 71

Privy Council, the, Albany Congress favours the disallowance of laws by, passed by the Grand Council, 137

Proclamation Line of 1763, the " Representation on the Present State of the Union," 1754, and the, 133

Prizes, the question of, taken before and after the War of the Austrian Succession, 302–4

Puant Indians, furs of, traded to the Ottawa, 43

Puckle, Thomas, and Company, offer of lands in Tobago by the Duke of Courland to, 221; efforts of, to enlist the support of the English government, 222

Pultan, India, silk produced at, bought up by East India Company employees, 256

Puma, the Great Lakes region haunted by, 36

Pumpkins, cultivation of, in Canada, 13; by the Indians, 36

Purches His Pilgrimmes (London, 1625), 236

Puysieulx [Puyzieulx, Puisieux], Louis Philogène Brulart de Sillery, Marquis de, French minister of Foreign Affairs, disavows the French aggressions in Acadia, 305; change of attitude of, 305

Pye, Captain, testimony of, on the colonization of Dominica by the French, 215, 314

Pyrlaeus, the Rev. J. Christopher, Moravian missionary, on the distinctions observed among the members of the Six Nations, 72

Quebec, the Church as a landholder and, 9; the Jesuit College at, a centre of learning, 12; as a centre of culture and fashion in the New World, 15–16; size of, in comparison with New York, Philadelphia, and Boston, 15; Peter Kalm's estimate of, 15; divisions of, 16; public buildings of, 16–7; early fortifications of, 17; the new fortification of, in 1750, 20; shipbuilding at, 24; monopolies for the supply of the King's troops in, 27; disorders in, by reason of food shortages, 30; people of, frequently aided by Bigot, 30; early Grey Friars mission at, 41

Queen Anne; see Anne, Queen of England

Queen Anne's War, a plan for a colonial concert during, 123; see also War of the Spanish Succession

Quit-rents, comparison of, in the English colonies and rentes in Canada, 9

Quotas, a plan for the English colonies to furnish troops according to, during King William's War, 123; plan for, revived during Queen Anne's War, 123; nature of, recommended to Sir Danvers Osborne, 123

Raccoons, the Great Lakes region haunted by, 36; value of skins of, in Canada, 55–6

Rajah Sahib, son of Chanda Sahib, sent against Clive at Arcot, 288

Ram Raja, grants permission to the French East India Company to erect a factory at Pondicherry, 262

Ramasay [Ramazay], Jean Baptiste Nicolas Roch de, recommended by the Bishop of Quebec for his victory at Grand Pré, 178

Rattans, of East India, put up for auction, 257

Raymond, Captain de, commandant at Fort Niagara, pessimistic report of, in 1748, regarding the uselessness of Niagara as an effective defence, 94

Raymond, Comte de, Governor of Isle Royale, sends Indians to Nova Scotia to break the peace, 197; agrees to secure a priest for the Acadians of Rivière aux Canards, 197

Re, a Malabar Coast coin, value of, 256

" Reasons Considered and Offered, by the Assembly of the Colony of Connecticut,

Concerning the Plan of Union," 1754, on the attitude of the Connecticut commissioners toward the Albany Plan of Union, 139; on the Albany Plan, 148–9

Recollets [Recollects, Observant Franciscans] interest of, in Quebec lands, 11; home of, in the upper town of Quebec, 16; efforts of, to christianize the Canadian Indians, 41; missions established by, 41–2

Red deer, the Great Lakes region haunted by, 36

Red fox skins, value of, in Canada, 55–6

Redwood, amount of, imported from India in 1730, 256

Regular soldiers, number of companies of French, in Canada, 19; at Annapolis Royal, 170; the Canso fisheries protected by, 175; at Halifax, 183; at Minas, 184; French, on the borders of the Nova Scotia peninsula, 191, 193; sent from Newfoundland to Halifax, 193; French, in St. Lucia during King George's War, 229; French, sent to India, 1754, 323; English, ordered to America, 326; constant movement of French, to America, 326

Relation de l'Isle de Tobago (1666), by Sieur de Rochefort, 218

Relation of the Late Intended Settlement of St. Lucia and St. Vincent in the Right of the Duke of Montague (London, 1725), 228

Relief, payment of, when Canadian seigneurs alienate land, 10

Religious freedom, the British Empire and, 341–2; the French Empire and, 343

Remy, Sieur, Governor of Tobago, 218

Repentigny, Jean Baptiste François Xavier, Chevalier de, concession of Sault Ste. Marie to, 54

"Representation on the Present State of the Union," 1751, drawn up by Thomas Hutchinson, 131; adopted by the Albany Congress, 131; analysis of, 131–3; sent to the Board of Trade, 133

Review of Military Operations in North America, 1757, apparently written by William Livingston, 131; Pownall is taunted in, 131; on the attitude of the commissioners toward the Albany Plan of Union, 139

Revolt, threatened by the Canadians, 29; of the Acadians, 194–5, 203; of the Zeelanders on Tobago, 219

Rhetoric, the study of, at Quebec, 12

Rhode Island, Colony of, the population of, compared with that of Canada in 1666 and in 1754, 5; not included by the Board of Trade in the call for an Indian conference, 113; commissioners sent to Albany to represent, 114; powers granted by, to its commissioners, 115; quota of men assigned to, in King William's War, 123; representation of, under the "Plan of a Proposed Union," 130; under the Pownall proposal, to help defend Lake Champlain, 131; under the Albany Plan of Union, 135; struggle within the Assembly of, over the Albany Plan of Union, 147–8; ultimate rejection of the Plan by, 148; Shirley advocates alterations in the charter government of, 161

Richelieu, Armand-Jean du Plessis, Cardinal, Duke of, grant by, to d'Esnambuc and de Roissey, 209

Richelieu River, within the limits of Canada, 4; settlements of Canadian habitants about, 14

Rigaud de Vandreuil, Pierre François, Sieur de, profit secured by, from La Baye, 55

Rivière aux Canards, Nova Scotia, church communicants within the parish of, 170; Acadians of, ask for a priest, 197

Rivière Blanche, Indian trade of, leased to St. Ange, 47; see also Cuyahoga River

Rivière Piziquid, see Pizaquid

Robinson, Sir Thomas, becomes Secretary of State for the Southern Department, 1754, 323; critical attitude of, toward French colonial policy, 324–5; suggests to Albemarle a test of the French desire for peace, 324; in interview with Mirepoix shows superior knowledge of the Ohio Valley, 329; proposals by, of January 22, 1755, 330; proposals by, of February 10, to the Cabinet, 331; sharp criticism of the proposals of, respecting North America, by the Earl of Halifax, 331; the proposals by, of March 26, submitted to the British Cabinet, 337–8

Rochefort, César de, author of Tableau de l'Isle de Tobago (Leyden, 1665) and of Relation de l'Isle de Tobago ou de la Nouvelle Oualcre (Paris, 1666), 219; description of Tobago in 1666 by, 220

Rochefort, France, shipment of Canadian iron to, 24

Rodney, George Brydges, 1st Baron, drives the French from St. Lucia, in 1762, 230; affords protection to specie carried from Lisbon to Cadiz, 255

Roe, Sir Thomas, Ambassador to the Court of the Great Mogul, opposition of, to English political activity in India, 237;

advice of, ignored in the fortification of Madras, 238

Roebucks, value of skins of, in Canada, 55–6

Roissey [Rossey] Urban de, grant to, by Richelieu, 209; nature of the colonizing commission given by Richelieu to d'Esnambuc and, 225

Ronde, Louis Denys, Sieur de, granting of post at Chiquamegon Bay to, 47; agrees to discover and operate copper mines, 47; interest of family of, in the Bay, 55

Rouen, France, white blankets of, imported by Canada, 25

Rouillé, Antoine-Louis, Comte de Jouy, becomes French Minister of Foreign Affairs, 323–4; desire of, to restore friendly relations with England, 324; presents the French protest to Albemarle over the death of Jumonville, 324; Albemarle brings to, the British protest over the French attack on Fort Necessity, 325; assurances given by, over French intentions in North America and of the complete evacuation of the neutral islands, 325; questions Albemarle on the sending of British regiments to America, 326; shows a compromising attitude in interviews with Albemarle, 327–8; comment of, upon the British Cabinet proposals of February 7, 1775, 331–2; reconciled to war, 338

Rousselan, Sieur, granted St. Lucia by du Parquet, 226; popularity of, with the Caribs, 226; death of, 226

Royal African Company, British private enterprise and the monopoly of the, 340

Royal fourth of all beaver skins exported, claim of Oudiette to, 57; the right to, waived by Aubert and Company, 58

Royaneh, lordly families of the Iroquois, 70

Rum, value of, in Indian trade at Albany, 45; tax upon, for the Indian trade, 118

Rupee, coin of India, silver, value of, 255, 256; gold, value of, 256; the minting of the, in India, by the East India Company, 255

Russell, Judge Chambers, on the committee on colonial union of the Massachusetts Bay House of Representatives, 151; favours a general union of the colonies, 154

Russia, army of, in western Europe in the War of the Austrian Succession, 299

"Russian" beaver, meaning of term, 44

Rye, summer, the growing of, in Canada, 13

Sachems, Iroquoian, see Lords of the Congregation

Sadras, India, Dutch factory at, 293; meeting of representatives of the English and French companies at, 293

Sail-cloth, importation of, into Canada, 25

St. Alonzie, St. Lucia, French settlement of, surrendered to the English, 226

St. Contest, François Dominique Barberie, Marquis de, French Minister of Foreign Affairs, discusses with the British commissioners the question of prizes, 319; the death of, 323; the aggressiveness of, 324

St. Domingue [Haiti], West Indies, number of ships from, to Canada, 1754, 25; debts owed by the planters of, to the Compagnie des Indes, 267

Saint Esprit, seminary of, France, priests from, sent to Le Loutre, at Beauséjour, 199

Saint-Étienne, firearms made at, imported into Canada, 25

St. Francis, Canada, christianized Abenaki at, 21

St. George River, Maine, the French willing in 1712 to limit western extent of Acadia to, 333–4

St. Helena, right to fortify, given to the London East India Company in 1661, 239; acquired by the Company in 1673, 240; previous temporary capture of, by the Dutch, 240; suppression of mutiny at, 240; cost of maintaining in 1729–33 and in 1750–55, 258–9

St. Jean, Canada, description of, 20

St. Jean River, see St. John River

St. John, Capt. Nicholas, contemplates the settlement of St. Lucia, 224

St. John River, Acadians settled about, cared for by the missionary to the Abenaki, 171; inhabitants of the region of, brought in 1749 under the protection of the French King, 180; Indians of, receive a Micmac war belt, 189; friendly attitude of Indians of, toward the English, 189; Abbé Germain missionary on, warns the English, 189; the question of the political control of the Acadians settled on, 334; the British refuse to provide an outlet to New France via, 337; a proposed boundary for New France to run to the western source of, 337

St. Joseph, trading post, location of, 54; leased after 1745, 54; number of bundles of furs drawn from, 54

St. Lawrence River, the Canadian *habit-*

ants and, 6; navigation of, 6; cultivation of lands about, 6; spring navigation of, 14; whaling in, 24

St. Lucia, West Indies, neutralization of, 207; early great importance of, 223; description of, 223-4; Napoleon's plans for, 224; discovered by Columbus, 224; and by the Earl of Cumberland, 224; attempt of Leigh to colonize, 224; granted to the Earl of Carlisle, 224; failure of the Carlisle family to colonize, 225; basis of French claims to, 225; beginnings of French settlement of, before 1664, 226; early French governors of, and their fate, 226; included within the jurisdiction of the Governor of Barbados, 226; the so-called sale of, by the Caribs to the English, 226; conquest of, by the English in 1664, 226; the restoration of French control of, in 1666, 226-7; the Treaty of Breda and, 227; Captain Temple's expedition to, in 1686, 227; the neutralization of, in 1687, 227; no permanent settlers on, in 1700, 227; continued French activities on, 227-8; gift of, to d'Estrées, in 1718, 228; temporary French resettlement of, 228; gift of, to Montagu in 1722, 228; English attempt to occupy, 228; Anglo-French agreement of 1723 that neither should occupy, 228; reaffirmation of the neutralization of, in 1730, 228-9; a French garrison in, during King George's War, 229; agreement for mutual evacuation of, in the Treaty of Aix-la-Chapelle, 229; failure of the French to evacuate, 229; comparison of British and French claims to, 229-30; offer of the British commissaries respecting, 230; French in control of, during the Seven Years' War, 230; French rights to, recognized in 1763, 230; subsequent history of, 230; interest of the French commissaires in the question of, in 1750, 305-6; both Mildmay and Shirley send memorials on, to England, 312; the French mémoire on, criticized by the English commissioners, 312-3; attitude of de Caylus respecting the evacuation of, 313-4; Holbourne's threat to the French dwelling on, 313-4; Mildmay's suggestion respecting, 316-7

Saint-Malo, France, number of ships from, to Canada in 1754, 25; failure of the Anglo-French conference at, in 1749, 303

St. Martin, West Indies, occupied by both the French and the Dutch, 229; English drive the French from, 229; the French settlers return to, 229

St. Martin's Day, and the payment of cens et rentes in Canada on, 8

St. Maurice, Canada, at Trois Rivières, the royal iron-works of, 18; corrupt practices at, 28; favourable factors enjoyed by, 28; deficits in the iron operations at, 28; description of, 28

St. Ours, commander at Beauséjour, order by La Jonquière to resist the English, 195

St. Sauveur, Sieur de, monopoly of brandy for the Indian trade possessed by, 28

St. Thomé, India, attempt of the French East India Company to secure, 262; occupied by the Dutch, 262; the gift of, to the Padre de la Purification by Chanda Sahib, 277; given to the English by Muhammad Ali, 280; the French ejected from, 280

St. Vincent, West Indies, neutralization of, 207; description of, 208; large concentration of Caribs on, 216; a place of refuge for escaped Negroes, 216; the division of, between the two peoples, 216; project of de Feuguieres against the Negroes of, 216-7; numbers of Caribs on, in 1763, 217; colonization of, by the French, 217-8; slavery on, 218; gift of, to Montagu in 1722, 228; Mildmay's suggestion respecting the settlement of the problem of, 318

Salabat Jang, son of the Nizam, with army of Muzaffar Jang, 284; becomes Subahdar of the Deccan upon the death of Muzaffar, 284; supported by Bussy, 284; confirms the gifts made by Muzaffar to the French, 284; attack against, by Firuz Jang, 293-4

Salmon, amount of, exported from Canada in 1754, 24

Salmon fishery, monopoly of, in the St. Lawrence, 27

Salt, the production of, in Canada, for the West Indies, 23; importation of, into Canada, 25

Saltpetre, quantity of, imported into England from India in 1730, 256; imports of, by the East India Company for the government, 257

Sandusky Bay, the Iroquoian control of the Lake Erie region as far west as, 333; the prospect of the restoration of British trade at, 335

Sandwich, Lady, on the treatment accorded to the body of the late Earl of Albemarle, 328

Santo Domingo, *see* St. Domingue

Sardenia, the conduct of the King of, during the War of the Austrian Succession, 298

Sauk [Sac, Sakis] Indians, furs of, traded to the Ottawa, 43

Sault St. Louis, Canada, christianized Iroquois at, 21; mission of, for the Five Nations, 75-6; the entrepôt for the contraband trade, 76

Sault Ste. Marie, exclusive trade of, shared by Captain de Bonne de Miselle, 28; mission of, established by Father Allouez, 42; post of, leased to Chevalier de Repentigny, 54; number of bundles of furs drawn from, 54; chief purpose of, 54

Saulteur Indians, *see* Chippewa Indians

Saunders, Thomas, takes the place of Floyer as President of the Madras Presidency, 279; limitations upon the actions of, 279; supports Muhammad at Trichinopoly, 289; forbids an attack on Pondicherry by Major Lawrence, 289; efforts of Dupleix to reach an accommodation with, in 1754, 293; friendly attitude of, toward the French in 1754, 295; terms of treaty with Godeheu signed by, 296

Saxe, Maurice, Comte de, Marshal of France, psychological effect of the army of, before Maestricht in 1747, 300

Scalps, payments made by Le Loutre for English, 203

Scarouady [Schaioady], Iroquoian chief friendly to the English, death of, 107

Schickalamy, Iroquoian chief friendly to the English, death of, 107

Schuyler, Colonel Peter, activities of, among the Five Nations, 78; persuades the Iroquois in 1712 to make an expedition against Canada, 81

Scott, Captain, commander at Fort Lawrence, to receive the oath of the refugee Acadians, 202; refugee Acadians ask guarantees of, 203

Scythians, invasions of India by, 232

Seal fishery, monopoly of, on the Magdalen Islands, 27

Sechelles, Madame Herault de, *mémoire* on the French trading posts sent to, 53

Seconde navigation, of the Compagnie des Indes, explanation of term, 266-7; discontinuance of, by the Compagnie, 267

Seguin, renegade French trader in the Iroquoian hunting grounds, 333

Seigneuries, in Canada, *cens et rentes* and, 8; *banalités* and, 9; *droit de justice* and, 9; escheats of lands and, 9; the *corvée* and, 10; wardship and curatorship and, 10; treasure-trove and, 10; *droit de chasse* and, 10; *droit de pêche* and, 10; the parish and, 10; humble position of many holders of, 10; history of grants of, 10-11; size of, 10; conditions attached to securing, 11; the *habitants* of, and the seigneurs, 11; the parish curé and, 11

Séminaire, home of the lay clergy in Quebec, 16

Seneca Indians, fighting strength of, 65; location of, 65; number of clans among, 70; number of phratries among, 70; number of *ohwachira* among, 71; position of, within the Confederation, 72; contacts of, with Far West Indians, 74; claim of, to the Niagara River region, 75; ultimate cession of Niagara lands by, 75; hostility of, to La Salle's trading house at Niagara, 75; French make war against, in 1687, 75; villages of, destroyed by de Denonville, 75; war against the French by, 77; influence of Joncaire, the Elder, among, 81; refusal of, to join the expedition against Canada, 81; a delegation of, goes to Montreal, 81-2; employed by the French at Niagara, and help to build a picketed post at Niagara, 82; the sachems of, express fear of the French, 83; request the New York Governor to see that the French Niagara post is destroyed, 84; the question of the sincerity of, 84; existence of pro-French and pro-British factions among, 84; continued influence of Joncaire among, 84; grant to the English the privilege of a post at Irondequoit, 85; leading sachems of, go to Canada to live, 85; the French flag hoisted at a castle of, 85; protect young Joncaire during King George's War, 96; pro-French leanings of, after Aix-la-Chapelle, 98; a group of, leave Niagara to live at La Présentation, 105; support of the rebellious Hurons by, 108; proposal of William Johnson to send teachers to, 131

Senegal, funds of the Compagnie des Indes tied up in, 268

Sepoys, the use of, by the English, 249

Seringham, an island on the Cauvery, near Trichinopoly, 289; Law attempts to defend himself at, 289

Sewall, Stephen, on the committee on colonial union of the Massachusetts Bay Council, 151

Shawnee Indians, location of, 40; enumeration of, 40; destruction of villages of, by the Iroquois, 66; dependence of, upon the Iroquoian Confederation, 66; invite the Pennsylvania traders into the Ohio country, 120

Shediac, Acadia, military supplies sent secretly to, for war against the English, 190

Shellac, amount of, imported from India in 1730, 256

Shepody, Acadia, the settlement of, 174

Sherburne, Henry, Jr., a New Hampshire commissioner to the Albany Congress, 114

Sherlock, Thomas, Bishop of Salisbury (Sarum), later Bishop of London, on the War of the Austrian Succession, 298

Shipbuilding, in Canada, encouraged, 23; discontinued, 24

Shippen, Edward, Lancaster, Pa., merchant, on the weight of bundles of skins, 53

Shipping, of Canada, contrasted with that of Massachusetts Bay, 25; of the United East India Company, 253; of the Compagnie des Indes, 266–7

Ships, inferior quality of, constructed in Canada, 24; specifications for, in the English East India trade, 253

Shirley, William, Governor of Massachusetts Bay, report of, on the strength of the Six Nations, 65; criticizes in 1754 suggested quotas of colonial troops, 123; sees the urgency of a colonial union, 124; on the attitude of the Albany commissioners toward a union, 142; recommends that Governor Morris support the Albany Plan, 144; calls upon the Massachusetts Assembly to speed consideration of the Plan, 150–1; opposition of, to features of the Plan, 158; on a voluntary union of the colonies, 158; favours the taxation of the colonies by Parliament, 158; suggests colonial representation in Parliament, 159; high opinion of the Albany Congress delegates by, 160; favours the creation of a colonial union in England, 160; the Grand Council under the Albany Plan vested with dangerous powers according to, 160–1; advocates alterations in the charter governments of Connecticut and Rhode Island, 160–1; on the unwillingness of the colonies to establish voluntarily a union, 165–6; the support of New England enlisted by, for an attack upon Louisbourg, 176; assurances given to the Acadians by, respecting deporta-

tion, 178–9; favours the planting of loyal Protestants among the Acadians, 179; favours requirement of knight service for tenure of land by the Acadians, 179; recommends the building of two Nova Scotian fortresses, 180; secures a survey of vacant lands about the Bay of Fundy, 180; recommends a rigid examination of Acadian land titles, 181; a member of the Anglo-French joint commission, 1750–52, 303; expresses a low opinion of French diplomacy, 308–9; Mildmay and, rebuked by the Board of Trade, 309; justifies conduct to the Secretary of State, 309; agrees to prepare a memorial on Acadia, 309; Mildmay's criticism of the work of, 309–10; memorial of, sent to England for study, 310; rift between Mildmay and, 312; sends to England a memorial on St. Lucia, 312; joint statement of Mildmay and, on the French mémoire on St. Lucia, 312–3; Mildmay ignored by, in framing the reply to the French mémoire on Acadia, 316; the recall of, from the joint commission, 1752, 316; work of, in London, 320–1

Shirts, value of, in the Indian trade, at Albany and at Montreal, 45

Short Hints toward a Scheme for Uniting the Northern Colonies, 1754, by Benjamin Franklin, 126–7; vote of the Albany Congress in favour of, as the basis for colonial union, 131; extent to which the Albany Plan of union follows, 133–8

"Short Reply to Mr. Hopkins," 1755, by "Philolethes," on the limited powers of the Albany commissioners, 141

Shubenacadie, Nova Scotia, Le Loutre establishes his Micmac mission at, in 1738, 187; a road between Halifax and, 204; plans for a military post at, 204

Silesia, the War of the Austrian Succession and, 299; Walpole urges the support of Frederick's claim to, 301; and the Treaty of Aix-la-Chapelle, 301

Silhouette, M. de, Maître de Requêtes and Chancellor to Philip, Duke of Orléans, a member of the Anglo-French joint commission, 1749–1754, 304

Silk, importation of, from India, 252; amount of, brought to England in 1730, 256

Silk cloth, English, protected by law, 258; raw, quantity of, imported from India in 1730, 256; extravagant price of, in India in 1750, 256; speculators in India control supply of, in 1750, 256; East

India Company servants buy up the, of Pultan, 256

Silver, value of, exported to India before 1726, 235; value of, exported to India by the East India Company in 1729, 1730, 1749, and 1753, 254–5; methods of securing, used by the East India Company, 255; drainage of, from England, 255; methods employed in England to keep, 255; the fixed standard of value in England, 255; the minting of, in India, 255

Silver fox skins, value of, in Canada, 55–6

Silvestro, Jean, testimony of, with reference to the grievances of the Canadians, 29

Sioux of the Prairies Indians, enumeration of, 40

Sioux of the Woods and the Lakes Indians, location of, 40; enumeration of, 40

Sisters of the Congregation, activities of, in Canada, 14

Six Nations, enumeration of warriors of the, 40; see also Iroquoian Confederation

Skinner's Hall, home of the English Company trading to the East Indies, 243

Skunks, the Great Lakes region haunted by, 36

Slave trade, penalties for Frenchmen for encroaching upon the Compagnie des Indes' monopoly of, 267

Smith, Mr., of Cape Cod, on the seditious conduct of the Canadians, 29

Smith, William, Attorney General of New York and a member of the Council, attends the Albany Congress, 114; appointed on the committee on colonial union at the Albany Congress, 124; description of the proceedings of the Congress by, 138–9; the degree of support given by the commissioners to the Albany Plan of Union, according to, 139

Snipe, Six Nations clan, and, 70

Soap, importation of, into Canada, 25

Society for the Propagation of the Gospel in Foreign Parts, interest of, in the christianization of the Iroquoian Confederation, 97–8; provision made by, for preachers and teachers in Nova Scotia, 181–2

Sœurs Grises, interest of, in Quebec lands, 11

Sol, value of, in Canada, 8

South Carolina, Province of, commissioners of, attend the Albany Indian conference of 1750, 99; under the Pownall proposal, might help defend Lake Erie,

131; the sea-to-sea territorial claims of, ignored by the Albany Congress, 132; representation of, under the Albany Plan of Union, 135; government of, ignores the Plan of Union, 146

South Sea Company, relations of, with the Bank of England and the United East India Company, 245–6; British private enterprise and the monopoly of, 340

Southern fox skins, value of, in Canada, 55–6

Southern Indians, large numbers of, according to Dinwiddie, 112

Spain, the sale of French beaver hats in, 60; the blockade of, during the War of the Austrian Succession, 298; capture of the ships of, during the War, 298–9; the adherence of, to the Treaty of Aix-la-Chapelle, 301; the fleet of, unwilling to put to sea during the War, 302; the principle of visit and search and the treaty of peace with, 302

Spanish Empire, a member of the Bourbon Family becomes ruler of, 171

Spices, importation of, into Canada, 25; export of, from India, 234, 236; the lure of, and early English East India commerce, 236; the Dutch monopoly of the finer, 259

Stag skins, value of, in Canada, 55–6

Stick-lac, amount of, imported from India in 1730, 256

Standing Rock, early Iroquoian clan, 71

Sterling, William Alexander, Earl of, grant of land to, between the St. Croix and the Pemaquid rivers, 311

Stockholders, of the United East India Company, privileges and activities of, 250; number of active, 250; of the Compagnie des Indes, 270

Stockings, value of, in the Indian trade at Albany and at Montreal, 45

Stoddard, Capt. Benjamin, observations of, upon the Canadian settlement, 6; estimate of the size of Quebec in 1750 by, 15; commander at Schenectady, 100; becomes commander at Oswego, 100; sale of goods by, to Montreal merchants, 100; demands a trade monopoly at Oswego, 100

Stoves, use of, in Canada, 7

Stroud blankets, price asked for, by the French at Niagara, 84

Strouds, value of, in Albany and in Montreal, 86

Subinfeudation in Canada, see en arrière fief

Sulpicians [Sulpitians], Montreal lands of,

liv

liv

INDEX

11; control of the christianized Indians near Montreal by, 21

Sumatra, English trading activities in, 236; English factories in, in 1702, 244; the English factories in, within the jurisdiction of the Madras Presidency, 249; efforts of the East India Company to secure supplies of pepper from, 256

Superior Council of Canada, the Intendant as President of, 22; of Louisiana, the Commissaire Ordonnateur as President of, 22; limitations of the powers of, 22; composition of, 22; of India, 261, 262

Surat, a London East India Company factory at, in 1612, 237; attempt of the Dutch to drive the English from, 237; comparison of, with Bombay in 1661, 248; an English factory at, in 1750, 260; the French East India Company centres its activities at, in 1669, 261–2

Suspension of arms, Anglo-French, in India in 1754 for three months, 296; British proposal of February 7, 1755 for a mutual, in North America, 330–1

Susquehanna [Susquehannah] Company, purchase of lands from the Six Nations in 1754 by, 122; opposition of, to the Albany Plan of Union, 149–50

Susquehanna River, lands along, purchased from the Six Nations in 1754, 122

Sussex, George Augustus Yelverton, Earl of, goes to Paris as a hostage in 1748, 301

Sutanati, India, English trading activities at, 247; purchase of, in 1698, 247

Sutton's Air Pipes, provision made for, on the Nova Scotia emigrant ships, 181

Swallowing Himself, Iroquoian hereditary title, 71

Sweden, the sale of French beaver hats in, 61

Swegatsy, see Oswegatchie

Syndics, the election of, to the directorate of the Compagnie des Indes, limited choice of, by the stockholders, 270

Tadousac [Tadoussac], early Grey Friar Indian mission at, 41

Taffanel, Abbé de Cabanac de, nephew of La Jonquière, secures the Deanery of Quebec, 28

Tallard, Comte de, French Ambassador in London, complaint of, in 1699, over English efforts to colonize Tobago, 222

Talon, Jean Baptiste, Intendant of New France, increase of the population of Canada by, 5

Tanjore, India, disputed succession in, 275;

English expeditions against, in 1749, 275–6; agreement between the English and the Rajah of, 276; the United East India Company rebuked its servants for the movement against, 278; joint French-Indian expedition against, 279–80; the country of, ravaged, 280; terms of peace exacted from the Rajah of, 280; Rajah of, supported by the English against the French in 1751, 286; alliance of, with Muhammad Ali, 288

Tantramar marsh, Nova Scotia, 167

Tasker, Benjamin, Jr., President of the Maryland Provincial Council, a commissioner at the Albany Congress, 114; appointed on the committee on colonial union, 124

Tasker, John, a member of the Massachusetts Bay Assembly committee on a union of the American colonies, favours a general union, 154

Taxation, in Canada, 26; of the English colonies, by Franklin's "Short Hints," 126; by the "Plan for a General Union," 128; by the "Plan of a Proposed Union," 130; by the Albany Plan of Union, 137; by the Connecticut proposals, 149; by the Massachusetts Bay "Project of Union," 152; by the Massachusetts Bay new plan for a general union, 156; Parliamentary, of the colonies advocated by Shirley, 158; conditional support of, by Franklin, 158–9

Tea, amount of, imported from China to England in 1730, 256; the regulation of the sale price of, at the East India Company auctions, 257–8; amounts of, sold in 1729, 1730, 1731, and 1734, 257; opposition of buyers to the sale of small lots of, 257–8; inland duty on, re-exported to Ireland and America abolished in 1748, 258

Tellicherry, India, English factory at in 1702, 244; and in 1750, 260

Temple, Captain, sent to St. Lucia in 1686 to drive out the French, 227

Terre d'Eboulemente, on the lower St. Lawrence, 18

Tertre, J. B. du, author of Histoire Générale des Antilles habitées par les François (Paris, 1667–71), 209; also author of Histoire Générale des Isles de S. Christophe, de la Guadeloupe . . . et Autres dans l'Amérique (Paris, 1654), 212; on the origin of the Caribs, 212; on the cannibalistic practices of the Caribs, 212; on the virtues of the Caribs, 214

The Boston, Captain Wheeler, ordered by the French from Tobago, 222

The Importance of Gaining and Preserving the Friendship of the Indians to the British Interest Considered (1751), by Archibald Kennedy, 125

The Present State of His Majesty's Isles and Territories in America (London, 1687), by R. Blome, 208

Theology, the study of, at Quebec, 12

Thirty Years' War, termination of, contrasted with that of the War of the Austrian Succession, 300–1

Tiengsachrondio, Fort Detroit constructed at, 77

Timber, reserve of, by French Crown on Canadian seigneuries, 11

Timis Kamingue [Temiscomingue], Canada, post of, location of, 54; number of bundles of furs drawns from, 54

Timur [Timour, Tamerlane], conquest of Delhi by, 233

Tin, the value of, exported to India in 1711, 255

Tionontati [Chanundadies] Indians, Hurons, offer to aid the English to destroy Niagara, in 1747, 94

Tobacco, the cultivation of, in Canada, 13; by the Indians, 36, 66; the *ferme* of the supply of, for France given to the Compagnie des Indes, 264; separate funds of the Compagnie des Indes devoted to the *ferme* of, in 1752, 267; annual profits to the Compagnie from the *ferme* of, 269

Tobacco Indians, see Tionontati Indians

Tobago [Toboga, Nouvelle Oualere, Nieu Walcheren], the neutralization of, 207; importance of, 208; geographical features of, 218; great rivalry for the control of, 218; attempt to colonize, from Barbados, 218; granted to the Earl of Montgomery, 218; attempted settlement of Zeelanders on, 218; the Duke of Courland colonizes, 218; included in the grant to the Compagnie des Indes de l'Amérique, 218; second group of Zeelanders come to, 219; ejected from, by the English, 220; description of, by de Rochefort, 220; subsequent efforts of the Dutch to colonize, 220; final disappearance of the Dutch from, in 1677, 220; conceded to the French by the Dutch in 1678, 220; the island deserted, 220; efforts of the new Duke of Courland to colonize, 221–2; Englishmen forbidden to attempt to settle, 222; efforts of the Duke of Montagu to secure, in 1729,

222; the situation of, after 1748, 222–3; Mildmay's suggestion for the settlement of the problem of, 317–8

Toganunty, Iroquoian chief friendly to the English, the death of, 107

Tonti [Tonty], Jr., commandant of Detroit post, disposition of the fur trade of Detroit by, 46

Toronto, Canada, the founding of, in 1750, 54; number of bundles of furs drawn from, 54; Fort Rouillé built at, in a vain effort to attract the Indian trade, 101

Touche, de la, French officer in India, attacks Nasir Jang's army, 282

Townshend, Charles, a Lord of the Admiralty, objections of, in 1754 to the Board of Trade "Project" for a colonial union, 164; offers to prepare a plan for providing an American defence fund, 164; as a member of the Board of Trade prepares in 1752 the third British memorial on Acadia, 321

Townshend, Chauncey, London merchant, contracts to arrange for the passage of prospective settlers to Nova Scotia, 181

Traders, see English traders, French traders

Trading goods, prices of, at Albany and Montreal contrasted, 45; superior quality of English, 62; prices of, at Niagara and Albany contrasted, 84; law of New York against sale of, to the French, 86

Trading posts, the policy of leasing, 46; deficits incurred in maintaining in New France, 48; new policy for, announced in 1749, 48; location of, at strategic points, 49; first appearance of, 50; soldiers posted at, 50; chief purposes of, 50–1; indictment of, by the missionaries, 51–2; number of, dependent upon the government of Canada, 52; number of, in the Great Lakes Region, 52–3; comparative importance of, 53

Train oil, the production of, in Canada and the mercantilistic system, 23; quantity of, exported from Canada, 24

Treasure-trove, the Canadian seigneuries and, 10

Treaty of Aix-la-Chapelle, 1748, diplomatic negotiations after, 4; the return of Louisbourg to the French and the, 179; secret articles of the preliminaries to, 300; hurried negotiations resulting in, 300–1; criticism of, in Great Britain, 302; provision for an Anglo-French commission and, 302–3; the evacuation of the "neutral" West Indies and, 303;

Robinson asks that the French fulfill the terms of, respecting the neutral islands, and put all things in North America upon the footing that they were at the signing of, 325

Treaty of Ryswick (1697), Pondicherry restored to the French by the Dutch in the, 262

Treaty of Union and League, 1660, for joint Anglo-French policy toward the Caribs, 209

Treaty of Utrecht, the restoration of the Hudson's Bay Company posts and, 60; the Five Nations and, 79–80; exhaustion of France at the time of, 80; the building of Forts Niagara and Oswego after, 89; Acadia at the time of, 169; the meaning of, as to the limits of Acadia or Nova Scotia, and the Anglo-French commission, 1750–1754, 307–9; proposal of Robinson of January 22, 1755 that possessions in North America be placed in the same state they were at the time of, 330; contention of Rouillé that no English claims to the Ohio could be based on, 330; Rouillé denies that Article XV of, is applicable to the Five Nations, 332; the limits of Acadia, according to the French, before the signing of, 333–4; Robinson proposes that the Ohio country and the Great Lakes region be placed on the footing of, 337

"Tree of the Great Long Leaves," symbolism of, in Iroquoian tradition, 69; the location of, 69; for all peoples, 69

"Tree of the Great Peace," see "Tree of the Great Long Leaves"

Trees, varieties of, in the Great Lakes region, 35; of Nova Scotia, 167; of the West Indies, 207

Trevor, Bishop of St. David's, later Bishop of Durham, on the War of the Austrian Succession, 298

Trichinopoly, Kingdom of, and City of, India, plans of Chanda Sahib to capture, 279–80; Muhammad Ali given a refuge in, 280; English send aid to, 280; Chanda and the French besiege, 281; siege of, lifted, 281; offer of Muhammad Ali to exchange, for a stronghold in Golconda, 285; attack against, by Chanda in 1751, 286; support given to, by the English, 286; the offer of, to the ruler of Mysore not honoured by Muhammad Ali, 290; Lawrence forces way into, with supplies, 291; repeated attacks against, in 1753, 291–2; importance of, in relation to the Carnatic, 292

Trinity Church, New York, the Rev. Henry Barclay becomes rector of, 98

Trois Rivières, Canada, the Church as a landholder and, 9; population of, compared with that of New England towns, 18; principal public structures of, 18; lack of importance of, in 1750, 18; early Grey Friar Indian mission at, 41

Tryon, William, Governor of New York, report of, on the fighting strength of the Six Nations, 65

Tughlaks, massacre of, at Delhi, 233

Turtle, Six Nations clan, 70, 71

Tuscarora Indians, fighting strength of, 65; location of, in 1750, 65; number of clans among, 70; number of phratries among, 70; position of, within the Confederation, 72; removal of, from North Carolina to New York, 86; received by the Iroquoian Confederation in 1723 as a sixth nation, 69, 86

Union of the English colonies, see English colonial union and also Albany Plan of Union.

United Company of Merchants of England trading to the East Indies, establishment of, in 1708, 243–5; possessions of, in the Far East, 244; financial arrangement of, with the government, 244–5; the question of the permanence of, 245; the South Sea Company and, 245–6; opposition to, in 1730, 246; reduction of interest on loans of, to the government, 246; activities of, as an agency of the government, 246–50; number of stockholders of, participating in the Proprietors' Court, 250; efforts of Clive to secure control of, 250; powers and activities of the directors of, 250–1; the committees of, 250–1; responsibilities of the servants of, in India, 251–2; classification of the servants of, 252; India fabrics desired by, 252; relations of, with the native industrial hierarchy, 252–3; the "country trade" of India and, 253; numbers of ships sent out by, 253; policy of leasing ships by, 253–4; exports sent from England by, in 1730, 254–5; total value of exports sent by, in 1730, 1749, and 1753, 255; goods secured in India in 1730 by, 256; commodities imported by, from Bengal and the Coromandel Coast in 1730, 256; imports secured in 1730 from India by, 256; high prices for commodities in India demanded of the agents of, 256; the sale in England of East India commodities by, 257–8; restrictions on sale of East India cloth by, 258; cost of supporting forts and factories in India by, for the years 1729–33 and 1750–55, 258–9; value of stock of, in 1711 and in 1749, 259; dividends paid by, from 1708 to 1756, 259; dividends of the Dutch East India Company compared with those of, 259; value of goods exported compared with value of goods imported by, in 1749–50, 259; establishments of, in 1750, 260; establishments of, contrasted with those of the Dutch East India Company, 260; ransom treaty between La Bourdonnais and the agents of, 273–4; rebukes the Madras Presidency for the expedition against Tanjore, 278; authorizes the retention of Devi-Cotah, 278; receives from Muhammad Ali Bahur and St. Thomé, 280; the servants of, support Muhammad, 280; situation of the affairs of, in India in 1753, 293–4; attitude toward the peace proposals of the Compagnie des Indes in 1754, 294–5; confidence of, in its superior trading ability, 295; terms of the temporary treaty signed by the agents of the Compagnie des Indes and those of, 296–7; proposals of, for settling differences with the French in India, 322

Uring, Capt. Nathaniel, sent by Montagu to capture St. Lucia, 228; failure of, to hold the island, 228

Ursulines, Quebec and Trois Rivières lands controlled by, 11

Vallière, Sieur de la, author of " Journal de ce qui s'est passé à Chienetou," 194; the events on Chignecto in 1749–50; given by, 194, 196

Van Rensselaer [Renselaer, Renzelaer, Rineslar], Colonel Jeremiah, of Rensselaerswyck, New York, informs Beauharnois of the old neutrality agreement between New York and Canada, 92; accused of not furnishing the French with information, 93

Varin, Jean Victor, a commissary of the marine and intendant at Montreal, involved in the monopoly of supplies for the King's troops at Detroit, 27

Vaudreuil, Philippe de Rigaud, Marquis de, Governor General of Canada, orders the building of Louisbourg, 80; Governor Burnet sends a protest to, over the post at Niagara, 83; reply of, to Burnet, 83; a secret correspondence between Albany and, during Queen Anne's War, 92; assertion that the Acadians on the St. John were governed by, as seigneur, 334

Vegetables, grown in Canada, 13

Vegia, Jean Baptiste [La Bonté Garçon], contract of, at Montreal as a voyageur, 53

Vermillion Indians, location of, 41; strength of, 41

Vern, Father de, designated for a parish in Nova Scotia, 200

Véry, M., in command of troops sent by Dupleix against Clive at Arcot, 288

Vice-admiralty, the right to exercise, jurisdiction conferred on the London East India Company, 24

Vijayanagar, Hindu Empire of, extent of, and destruction of, 232–3

Villenore, India, gift of aldees in the region of, to the Compagnie des Indes, 277

Vindhya Mountains, a barrier to the Deccan, 232; northern limit of the Vijayanagar Empire, 232

Vinegar, importation of, into Canada, 25

Virginia, Province of, invited to be represented at the Six Nations conference, 111; declines to send commissioners to Albany, 112; plans of, for a Winchester Indian conference, 112; the traders of, accused of making unauthorized paths upon Iroquoian lands, 120; quota of men assigned to, in King William's War, 123; under the Pownall proposal, to help defend Lake Erie, 131; the interests of, struck at by the " Representation on the Present State of the Union," 1754, 133; representation of, under the Albany Plan of Union, 135; hostility of the government of, toward the Albany Plan, 145–6; recommendation by Walpole that for frontier defence a fund be secured by, through paper money, 162

Visit and Search, the principle of, and the War of the Austrian Succession, 302

Vivier, Father, report of, regarding the sad condition of the Illinois Indians in 1750, 52

Vizagapatam, India, an English fort at, 244, 250; the English factory at, within the jurisdiction of the Madras Presidency, 249; high price for cloth demanded by natives of, in 1745, 257

Voyageurs, the fur trade to be carried on by licensed, 44; contracts made with, 53; find a market for their furs among the English, 61

Vueüil, Sieur de, Governor of Tobago, 218

Wabash [Ouabache] River, the British Cabinet proposal of February 7, 1755 for a mutual evacuation of the Ohio country as far west as, 330; Robinson's proposals of February 10 to the Cabinet involving mutual evacuation up to, 331; the region west of, conceded to the French by the British, 335, 337

Waganhaes Indians, see Ottawa Indians

Waller, Sir Thomas, offered lands on Tobago by the Duke of Courland, 221

Walpole, Horace [Horatio], Auditor General for the British Plantations, on the taxation of the British to support colonial enterprises, 162; suggests a lottery in England and the issue of paper money in Virginia for securing a frontier defence fund, 162; plan of, for establishing peace in Europe, 300

Walrus fishing, monopoly of, on the Magdalen Islands, 27

War, the question of the inevitability of, in international relations considered, 350–1

War of the Austrian Succession, attitude of Englishmen toward, 298; effect of English sea superiority upon, 298–9; the House of Commons and, 299; Walpole's plan for ending, 300; the termination of, 300–1; the question of prizes and prisoners taken in connection with, 302–4

War of the Spanish Succession, the Iroquoian Confederation and, 78; a policy of neutrality between Canada and New York and their Indian allies in the course of, 78; New England suffers during, 78; Albany flourishes during, 78; capture of Port Royal, Acadia in the course of, 171; the cession of Acadia at the end of, 171; and the "General Society" for trading to the East Indies, 244–5; East India Company shipping during, 254

Wardship, the Canadian seigneuries and, 10

Warner, Capt. Philip, son of Sir Thomas, leads force against the Windward Caribs, 210; puts to death Thomas Warner, 210; trial of, 210–1; on the population of St. Vincent, 216

Warner, Thomas, reputed son of Sir Thomas Warner, activities of, on Dominica, 210; sale of Dominica and St. Lucia to the English by, 210; death of, 210; aids the English to repossess St. Lucia in 1664, 226

Warraghiyagee, Mohawk name of William Johnson, 95

Warren, Sir Peter, Admiral, the capture of Louisbourg and, 298

Washington, George, the death of Jumonville by the forces of, reported to Rouillé, 324

Watson, Admiral Charles, orders to, to avoid the monsoon at Madras, 238; fleet under, appears in the Indian Ocean, 296

Watts, Samuel, on the committee on colonial union of the Massachusetts Bay Council, 151

Weare, Meshech, Speaker of the New Hampshire Assembly, a commissioner at the Albany Congress, 114

Weiser, Conrad, Pennsylvania Indian interpreter, significance of the Iroquoian League in the eyes of, 69; on the distinctions observed between the tribes of the Six Nations, 72; finds that the Six Nations have pro-French leanings, 98; observations of, on the conversion of Onondaga Indians to Roman Catholicism, 106; low opinion of the Six Nations by, in 1754, 109; attends the Albany Congress, 120; reply of, to the charges of the Six Nations, 120; requested by the Pennsylvania authorities early in 1754 to go to Onondaga, but refuses, 121; feels that the Iroquoian Indians can be reached with money, 121

Welles, Samuel, a Massachusetts Bay commissioner at the Albany Congress, 114

West Indies, see Antigua, Barbados, Dominica, Granada, Guadeloupe, Jamaica, Martinique, St. Domingue, St. Lucia, St. Vincent, Tobago; see also neutralized West India islands

Westmorland, John Fane, 7th or 13th Earl of, comment of, on the War of the Austrian Succession, 302

West New Jersey, quota of men assigned to, in King William's War, 123

Western land policy, the "Representation of the Present State of the Colonies" of 1754 and, 133; the Albany Plan of Union and, 137

Western Sea, the French search for the, and the establishment of trading posts, 51

Whale fisheries, monopoly, of the Bayonne Company in the St. Lawrence, 27

Whaling, in the St. Lawrence, 24

Wheat, of Scandinavia, grown in Canada, 13; the application of the principles of mercantilism in Canada and the production of, 23; corrupt practices in Canada in the purchase of, for the King's use, 28; unsatisfactory harvests of, in Canada, 29; price of, fixed in Canada, 29; appropriation of, by public authority, in Canada, 30; Longueuil's inability to secure a supply of, 30-1; the seizure of, in Canada by order of Duquesne, 31; importation of, into France from England, 31; price of, imported into France from England less than in England, 31; great supplies of, imported into Canada from the English colonies, 33

Wheeler, Captain, of the *Boston*, ordered away from Tobago, 222

Wibird, Richard, a New Hampshire commissioner to the Albany Congress, 114

Wife, position of the, in the home of the French *habitant*, 7

Wildcats, the Great Lakes region haunted by, 36; importance of the skins of, as an export from Canada, 56

Wild Potatoes, early Iroquoian clan, 71

William and Mary, of England, the London East India Company during the reign of, 241-3

William, Col. Elisha, a commissioner from Connecticut to the Albany Congress, 114

Willoughby, Lord, plan of ministry to send, to America as Lord Commissioner in 1755, 166

Willoughby of Parham, Francis, 5th Baron, commission granted by, to Thomas Warner, 210; lease of the Carlisle West India interests by, 225; a regiment of troops sent from Barbados to St. Lucia by, 226

Willoughby, William, Lord, recommissions Thomas Warner, 210; Dominica conveyed to, 210

Wilson, Captain, East India goods of, put up for auction, 257

Winchester, Virginia, plans of the Virginia government to hold an Indian conference at, in 1753, 112; slight importance of the gathering at, 112

Wine, quantity of, imported by Canada from Bordeaux, 25

Wolcott, Roger, Jr., a justice of the Connecticut Superior Court, acted as a commissioner at the Albany Congress, 114

Wolf, a Six Nations clan, 70

Wolverine, the Great Lakes region haunted by, 36; value of the skins of, in Canada, 55-6

Wolves, the Great Lakes region haunted

by, 36; value of skins of, in Canada, 55-6

Wolf-lynx [*loup cervier*], value of skins of, in Canada, 55-6

Women, position of, among the Canadian *habitants*, 7; and in the towns of Canada, 7, 16, 18; activities of, among the Indians, 36; place of, among the Iroquois, 70-1; high value placed on life of, by the Iroquois, 71

Woodbridge, Rev. Timothy, Indian missionary, aids the Susquehanna Company in the purchase of lands from the Six Nations, 122

Wood rat skins, value of, in Canada, 56

Worthington, John, a Massachusetts Bay commissioner at the Albany Congress, 114

Wraxall, Peter, author of *Indian Records*, secretary for the Albany Congress, on the fortunes of contraband Albany traders, 86; forwards the Plan of Union to Governor Dinwiddie, 146

Wroth, Ensign Robert, Acadians take an oath of loyalty with concessions permitted by, 173

Wyoming Valley, Pennsylvania, interest of the people of New England in, 121

Xeraphim, a Malabar Coast coin, value of, 256

Yellow Wolf, a Tuscarora Indian clan, 70

York Fort, Bencoolen, Sumatra, English factory of, 244

Yorke, Col. Joseph, secretary of the British embassy in France, author of *Mémoire au sujet de Tobage*, 219; as chargé d'Affaires in 1749, 303

Zeeland, the War of the Austrian Succession and, 298

Zeelanders, attempt of, in 1632 to colonize Tobago, 218; second attempt of, in 1654, 219; overthrow of the government of the Duke of Courland on Tobago by, 219; second colony of, ejected from Tobago by the English, 220

Zemindar courts, establishment of, within the presidencies of the United East India Company, 249

Zenger, Peter, defended by James Alexander and William Smith, 125; influence of the trial of, on the freedom of the press, 341

A NOTE ABOUT THE AUTHOR

Lawrence Henry Gipson is Research Professor of History, Emeritus, at Lehigh University. Born in Greeley, Colorado, he went at an early age to live in Idaho. After graduating from the University of Idaho, he entered Oxford as the first Rhodes Scholar from that state. Later he brought into existence the departments of history and government at the College of Idaho, Wabash College, and Lehigh University. He received his doctorate at Yale, and his thesis, Jared Ingersoll: A Study in American Loyalism in Relation to British Colonial Government, *was awarded the Justin Winsor prize by the American Historical Association on publication. Since that time he has written and published many other books and articles on aspects of colonial American history (including the ten volumes of his* magnum opus), *and his efforts have earned him world-wide acclaim. Recently Professor Gipson has devoted himself to the encouragement of younger scholars in his chosen field and to the completion of the final volumes of the series. His project continues to be supported by a Rockefeller Foundation grant and the generous aid of Lehigh University.*

On the occasion of his eightieth birthday, on December 8, 1960, tributes from all over the English-speaking world were paid to "our most eminent living historical scholar," as he was called in a salute by Allan Nevins in the press.

A NOTE ON THE TYPE

This book is set in Linotype Caledonia. Caledonia belongs to the family of printing types called " modern face" by printers — a term used to mark the change in style of type-letters that occurred about 1800. Caledonia is in the general neighborhood of Scotch Modern in design, but is more freely drawn than that letter.

The book was designed by W. A. Dwiggins, and composed, printed, and bound by The Plimpton Press, Norwood, Massachusetts.